CASTELLO BRANCO
The Making of a Brazilian President

By

JOHN W. F. DULLES

Foreword by

ROBERTO DE OLIVEIRA CAMPOS

Texas A&M University Press

COLLEGE STATION AND LONDON

Library of Congress Cataloging in Publication Data

Dulles, John W. F.
   Castello Branco: the making of a Brazilian
president.

   Bibliography: p.
   Includes index.
   1. Castello Branco, Humberto de Alencar.
2. Brazil—Presidents—Biography. 3. Brazil—
History—1954-   4. Brazil—History—1930-1954.
F2538.22.C37D84   981'.06'0924 [B]   77-99279
ISBN 0-89096-043-7

Manufactured in the United States of America
FIRST EDITION

CASTELLO BRANCO

Contents

Illustrations

MAPS

Foreword

JOHN W. F. DULLES has produced a careful study, based on painstaking research, of the life of Castello Branco, encompassing the latter's young years and subsequent military career, from which he never departed until being called upon to exercise the presidency. It is therefore an essay on the formation of a statesman, not a critique of governance. Let us hope that Dulles will pursue his study in Brazilian historiography—which already includes works on Getulio Vargas and on communist activities—to cover the cycle of revolutionary governments that was initiated in 1964.

The picture of Castello Branco that emerges from this book is an impressive one: a diligent student of modest means, following the military career partly by family tradition, partly because alternative educational opportunities were less accessible; a dedicated family man, whose devotion to his beautiful wife was in itself a moving love story; a thorough military professional, who maintained the purity of his career, repeatedly refusing the economic attraction of civilian administration or the lure of regional politics; a warrior of great stamina, deft in careful planning and ready to assume responsibilities for tough decisions; an intellectual, who constantly sought to enlarge his reading and learning interests into sociology and literature, beyond the mere arts of violence.

In many ways Castello Branco was a pleasant surprise in a history fairly abundant in unpleasant surprises. His formation, as described in this book, equipped him adequately to become an outstanding military leader. But when elected to the presidency in April, 1964, he revealed sterling qualities as a civilian administrator. And he quickly revealed a liking and ability for political maneuvering and negotiation. In such arts he had not been trained. Though it might be said that his specialization in logistics and military planning was an excellent preparation for civilian administration, the principles involved are basically different: military logistics operates largely on *requisition* of resources, while civilian administration is in constant *competition* for resources. Political acumen and statesmanship, on the other hand, appear to be innate arts. They can be polished and perfected, but not created by study. Throughout the ages the philosopher king has been on the whole no more successful than the haranguer of multitudes, the manipulator of precincts, the commandant of armies.

History is likely to pass the verdict that the Revolution of 1964 was fortunate in having Castello Branco as its first leader. For the movement was born as a *negative* instead of a *positive* ideology. It was against the corruption and economic chaos of the Goulart regime and against communist infiltration. But there was no clear alternative reform program. Some of the other military commanders that vied for leadership might have overemphasized the repressive aspect of the system. Some of the civilian leaders wanted power and urged change, but it is doubtful that they would have been prepared to face the political consequences of the drastic surgery that had to be performed. Castello Branco, not without considerable opposition from sectors of the armed forces who called him "soft," skillfully managed to blend the disciplinary and the transformational elements—repression and reform. From the outset, the Revolution of 1964 was as much, if not more, a rebellion of the urban middle class as a movement of the barracks. Castello Branco made sure that it became an exercise in institutional modernization and not a conventional South American military "putsch."

The roots of Castello Branco's behavior can be detected in several passages of Dulles' book. Castello Branco had the constant preoccupation of defining the appropriate role of the military in a democratic society. In 1933, writing under the pseudonym of "Colonel Y" for the short-lived *Gazeta do Rio*, he defended the strict professionalization of the armed forces, drawing a distinction between the "regular" army, which should remain above politics, and the "police armies" subordinated to governors and politicians. As noted by Dulles: "The feeling, for example, that military men should not become involved in politics, nor interrupt their careers by assuming civilian positions, continued to be almost an obsession with him."

It behooves us to note that despite the enthusiasm of many of his friends, civilian and military, for the Ação Integralista Brasileira, Castello's deep democratic convictions led him to reject and even to ridicule the Integralistas, largely because they sought a single political party for Brazil.

A second and much more overt protest of Castello against the "politicization of the military" occurred during the episode of popular political mobilization in favor of presenting General Lott with a golden sword in November, 1956. Castello, then acting commander of the Escola Superior de Guerra, rejected openly, in a letter subsequently published in *O Globo*, the invitation of the Auxiliary Committee of the Federal District of the Frente de Novembro to participate in the homage to Lott. He inveighed against the regimentation of the military as a class "aligned in a politically suspect manner," and he castigated the proposals of "militarization of the national economy," which, in his view, "would achieve neither economic nor military efficiency." It is also significant that when he became a candidate (subsequently defeated) for election to the presidency of the Military Club in May, 1958—an election which was bitterly divisive within the military—he insisted in naming his party the Democratic Crusade in protest against his opponents, who attributed to themselves a monopoly of nationalism and termed their adversaries *entreguistas*. This dissension was subsequently to grow wider and more bitter as Goulart and Brizola sought to divide further the armed forces by distinguishing between the *generais do povo*, supposedly *progressistas*, and the "gorillas," supposedly reactionaries.

An important part of the process of Castello Branco's maturation for leadership was, of course, his fighting experience as head of the Third Section (operations) of the Brazilian Expeditionary Force in the Italian campaign during World War II. There his qualities for meticulous planning, his capacity for making difficult decisions, and his willingness to assume responsibilities were put to a hard test and were not found wanting either in defeat or in victory. Dulles' detailed account of the experience of defeat at Monte Castello in December, 1944, and of subsequent victories at Castelnuovo and Collecchio make vivid reading and indicate a considerable research effort to present a balanced view between often dissenting Brazilian evaluations on the one side and the assessment of the American command of the Fourth Army on the other.

What are then the main characteristics of the man as he emerges from this story? Three appear to deserve special mention: his devotion to legality, his balanced view of nationalism, and his deep sense of justice.

Castello Branco's *legalismo* was legendary in the army. Despite his intellectual solidarity and affinity of political views with the young lieutenants who rose in 1922 and in 1924 in protest against political fraud and the humiliation of the army, he refrained from transforming his political feelings into rebellion against the established authority. He also opposed the Revolution of 1930, and despite his profound aversion to Getulio Vargas' political customs and administrative practices, he remained a *legalista* during the Revolution of 1932. He took great interest in the reconstitutionalization of the country within a more liberal framework in 1934.

The only exception to this unblemished loyalist record was his decision, after great reluctance, to sign on August, 1954, the Manifesto of the Generals calling on Vargas to resign. By then Castello, who earlier had disapproved of the Manifesto of the Colonels as representing a breach of hierarchy and discipline and another instance of politicization of the armed forces, had become convinced that Vargas' permanence would lead to a chaotic situation and perhaps to civil war.

It is precisely Castello's moral authority as a long-time defender of constitutional principles that proved a decisive factor in eliciting the support of substantial sectors of the armed forces for the Revolution of 1964 which overthrew the Goulart regime. Coming from the most *legalista* of the generals, the chief of staff of the army, the famous circular of March 20, 1964, could not but cause an enormous impact. The choice at that time, in Castello's view, was no longer between the preservation of democracy and revolutionary upheaval. Democracy was being destroyed by "superversion" (subversion from the top), since the executive power, manipulating the illegal (political) power of the trade unions, fomenting the breakdown of the hierarchy within the armed forces, allowing communist infiltration in the administration, and proposing the closure of the existing Congress (to be replaced by a dubious Constitutional Assembly), was readying itself to embark on a totalitarian adventure.

In defending the "need to act offensively on behalf of legality," Castello asserted the doctrine that the armed forces should not be used (1) to serve the privileges of the rich, (2) to support the fascist or communist trade union dictatorships, or (3) to enforce specific government programs or serve government propaganda. He established the principle that the constitutional loyalty of the armed forces should be to uphold the constituted government, and not necessarily one of the powers of the government if it was bent on destroying the institutional setup.

This overriding preoccupation with constitutional order led Castello Branco, after taking over the presidency in 1964, to two decisions that met with considerable opposition from those who considered him soft and lacking in revolutionary fervor. The first decision was to maintain in operation the formal democratic structures of Congress and the judiciary, which the radicals wanted to dissolve as hopelessly corrupt and inadequate, to be replaced by a new, undefined "revolutionary legality." The second decision was his insistence on the restoration of constitutional normalcy and extinction of the "state of exception." This goal was achieved, albeit temporarily, through the enactment, by Congress, of the Constitution of 1967 in the final days of his administration. But lest the pendulum should swing from the radical Left to the unreformed Right, Castello warned from his very inaugural speech that "the remedy for evil deeds by the extreme Left will not be the birth of a reactionary Right, but the reforms that have become necessary."

Another remarkable example of the consistency of Castello's views, as illustrated in this book, relates to his position on nationalism, and particularly economic nationalism. Castello had little use or respect for the manichean manipulators of nationalism ("*nacionalistas de fancaria*"), who seemed to monopolize the virtue of patriotism and accused all dissenters of being *entreguistas* even though, more often than not, the divergences were methodological instead of doctrinal. When running for president of the Military Club on the slate of the Democratic Crusade, he had himself experienced the venom of slanderous accusations by self-appointed *nacionalistas*, in many of whom he identified the foreign inspiration and the scent of intolerance shown in Marxist or Communist doctrines.

His views on nationalism were balanced, and on foreign investments, realistic. In "Nationalism in Underdeveloped Nations," a speech given in São Paulo in 1962, he warned against those that saw in nationalism a panacea to cure the ills of underdevelopment. That idea might impede a realistic view of means and possibilities and could easily be perverted into a national and international instrument of communism. Mindful also of the experiences of fascism and nazism, which he had witnessed and fought at first hand, he feared the manipulation of nationalist feelings to foster the power dreams of dictators and would-be dictators.

In the atmosphere of the early sixties, in which it was popular to excoriate foreign investments, he defended their useful contribution while recommending the practice of an authentic nationalism by establishing conditions to cause foreign investors to observe national goals and restrain profit remittances within reasonable bounds. Again, bucking the tide, he warned against the propensity of developing countries to indulge in "obstinate" industrial protectionism at the cost of severe misallocation of resources. Furthermore, as noted by Dulles: "He urged periodic corrections to tariffs lest excessive protection result in unreasonable prices and lack of honesty in national manufacture."

Later on, during his governance, Castello had plenty of opportunity to put into practice his distinction between "authentic economic nationalism" and "sham nationalism" (*nacionalismo de fancaria*). He had to make courageous decisions in foreign investment policy by attenuating some punitive provisions of the law on profit remittances, by converting into a "negotiated nationalization" the confiscatory expropriation of American public utilities, and by formulating rational mineral exploration and export policies, a field strewn with irrational emotions. Without those measures the investment boom of the late sixties, which was the basis for the "Brazilian miracle," would certainly not have taken place.

A profoundly ethical man, Castello Branco was imbued with a sense of justice. This explains his willingness, or even insistence, as a leader to assume responsibility for decisions. For in his view it would be unethical to profit selectively from success without accepting the pain and frustration of defeat. No more vivid experience can I recall of this sense of justice than the episode of the enactment of Institutional Act No. 2 in October, 1965, which Castello signed with a heavy heart as the price to pay for preserving the unity of the armed forces and assuring the inauguration of two popularly elected opposition governors. Against the advice of Costa e Silva, Luís Viana Filho, Daniel Krieger, and Cordeiro de Farias, who felt that this self-imposed political mutilation was unnecessary, he insisted on adding, with his own handwriting, a provision rendering himself ineligible. As minister for planning I had remained in Rio de Janeiro, together with Professor Octavio Bulhões, then minister of finance, for both of us feared a banking crisis as a result of rumors of a rebellion of military hard-liners in the Vila Militar. Advised by Luís Viana Filho of Castello Branco's intention, I phoned Brasília to urge him, regardless of his decision to refuse any further prorogation of power, not to disqualify himself openly, thus forsaking bargaining power for influencing a suitable succession. I argued that both the fight against inflation and the revival of investment, foreign and national, were slow and painful processes requiring all of the psychological confidence that could be mustered for the stability of the rules of the game. Both would be, I feared, negatively affected by this premature and unnecessary decision.

Castello Branco remained unmoved. His first preoccupation was ethical. In the process of purge, through deprivation of political rights of colleagues and citizens, he feared that injustices might have been committed. He owed it to his conscience and to the nation that it be known that whatever he had done was done in order to save the institutions and not in the pursuit of personal power. The second reason was political. "*Continuismo* [holding on to power]," he said, "has been since the Vargas example the cancer of the Brazilian fledgling democracy. We ought to try for continuity of ideas without the continuation of persons." And he repeated with wry wit the famous words of Rivarol: "The cemeteries are full of the bones of irreplaceable persons."

Both of us were right. The fight against inflation and the recovery of investment took longer than expected, and undoubtedly Castello's renunciation added to the psychological uncertainty. But in the long view of history he was probably right.

His example was so compelling that all his successors adhered strictly to their legal mandates. The rotation of leadership was maintained. This is not a sufficient but is certainly a necessary condition for democracy to prevail.

The whole of Castello's story, from the early days in Messejana to the trials and tribulation of World War II and finally to the presidency, was one of firmness, unswerving purpose, and moving compassion. "It is impossible," he wrote while in the Italian campaign, "that a hecatomb such as we have seen will not bring a great revolution of ideas, from which will spring a more humane, more Christian, social evolution, less hard on the poor and limiting as much as possible the exploitation of man by man."

He did not yield to fear, fad, or prejudice. In this sense he reached that kind of glory which Charles de Gaulle once described as "la plus grande gloire du monde: celle des hommes qui n'out pas cédé."

London, December, 1977   ROBERTO DE OLIVEIRA CAMPOS

Preface

EVEN if Humberto de Alencar Castello Branco had not become president of Brazil in 1964, his life before that event seems well worth reviewing. The study of any career of forty-six years of uninterrupted service in the Brazilian army can perhaps throw light on the functioning of that important institution and on the behavior of at least a few officers of note who were closely connected with that career. But a look at the professional life of Castello Branco offers a somewhat unusual opportunity, for he was an officer whose deeds and words were to make him the most influential in molding the thinking of younger army officers.

Furthermore, the life of Castello Branco, both personal and professional, is interesting in itself. Starting with his years as a schoolboy who shared with classmates the ideals of political reform, Castello Branco was deeply concerned with the events that formed a part of the story of his country. His years as a lieutenant coincided with the uprisings carried out in Brazil in the 1920's by former fellow cadets of the military academy at Realengo. While Castello Branco attended the Ecole Supérieure de Guerre in France as a captain in the 1930's, he witnessed the gathering of storm clouds in Europe, and after his return to Brazil he did much to prepare officers for the participation of the Brazilian Expeditionary Force in the fighting in Italy during World War II. Lieutenant Colonel Castello Branco's own key role in the Brazilian battles in Italy has no doubt been insufficiently appreciated, and a purpose of this account of his life is to set that record straight.

After the war, Castello Branco reorganized advanced Brazilian army instruction and then began his career as a general by filling a command post in his birthplace in the north of Brazil. He was back in Rio de Janeiro, participating in national events, during the crises that led to the suicide of President Getúlio Vargas (1954) and that followed the coup of General Henrique Lott (1955). During the early 1960's, when international attention was directed to the "unrest" in Brazil's impoverished northeast, Castello Branco headed the Fourth Army, with headquarters in that area. As army chief of staff in Rio de Janeiro during the most agitated days of the presidency of João Goulart, Castello Branco was the leader who organized a large part of the army for a movement designed to save Brazil from a coup by the far Left. The narrative of his participation in that movement, like the story of much of his pre-presidential life, has information to offer to those who are interested in Brazil's fairly recent past.

As things turned out, Castello Branco was chosen to take over the presidency on April 15, 1964. This fact may give additional value to the story of his life before that date, because one of his foremost contributions was the imprint of his personality on the administration and the nation during his three years in the presidency. Those familiar with incidents in his earlier life could hardly have been astonished at the stories that were to pour out of Brasília, starting with the small matter of a few cruzeiros paid for some liver pills that the new president felt he needed on his first evening in Alvorada Palace. ("Buy the pills with my money," Castello sternly ordered a surprised attendant.)

Soon it became known that Castello Branco, no populist, would never appear in public in informal attire and was determined to bring dignity to his high position. At Planalto Palace, the presidential administrative office, Castello Branco instituted at once a new ritual that at first seemed strange to reporters and some of the executive personnel. Unlike his predecessors, he did not enter the building by way of the downstairs garage. In full sight of the curious, he walked up the Planalto ramp, with an air that was serious and confident, while members of the Presidential Guard stood at attention and while the presidential bugle call was played. At the top of the ramp on the second floor he was customarily received by the head of the presidential military staff and the chief of protocol.

Gradually the most fundamental characteristics of the new presidency became known. Castello Branco refused to shirk any responsibility, however unpleasant, and was resolved to make the hard decisions and to stick to them. He insisted on teamwork.

Much has been written about the administration of Castello Branco, and much more will doubtless be written, for it was a supremely important period for Brazil. It is to be hoped that this story of Castello

Branco's life before April 15, 1964, might contribute to an understanding of the thinking and conduct of the man in the presidency, thus
furnishing to the pages that follow an additional reason beyond those
mentioned earlier in this preface.

J.W.F.D.

Austin, Texas, May 31, 1977

Finding a Career and Winning a Bride (1897-1922)

I devoted myself to studies with an unshakable determination to succeed, spending silent hours at my desk during winter nights, always cold and always yearning for my family and for my Ceará.

1. The Parents of Humberto

On the morning of September 20, 1897, a passenger ship of the Lloyd Brasileiro lines reached the northern Brazilian city of Fortaleza, capital of the sunny state of Ceará, and anchored off the city's long beach. Among the passengers who went ashore in small boats was a family that had embarked in Recife, in the northeast:[1] thirty-seven-year-old Army Lieutenant Cândido Borges Castello Branco, his very pregnant twenty-six-year-old wife Antonietta, their four-year-old son Cândido (known as Candinho), and their one-year-old daughter Maria de Lourdes (known as Lourdinha).

A life of constant transfers and inadequate income had become familiar to the pious Antonietta ever since her marriage to the awkward but conscientious Cândido in 1891, when he had been an aide-de-camp of the first republican governor of Ceará. Antonietta had come to know the far south of Brazil and Rio de Janeiro, the federal capital. Of all the transfers, the most recent one was the most welcome, for it brought her back to the state of Ceará, home of her family, the Alencars.

Antonietta's return to Ceará occurred just in time for her expected baby to be a Cearense, a native of Ceará. On the very evening after the vessel docked, he was born in a typical Fortaleza home that had been rented by her husband: a small, one-story, high-ceilinged house on Solon Pinheiro Street.[2] The newborn boy was named Humberto de Alencar Castello Branco.

[1] Edgard Antunes de Alencar interviews, Fortaleza, Ceará, December 27, 28, 1975.
[2] Ibid.

After a few weeks in Fortaleza, a city of forty-five thousand, the Castello Brancos moved fifteen kilometers to the south to the outskirts of the little town of Messejana, where Antonietta had been born.[3] There they lived at a *sítio*, or country place, that belonged to Antonietta's seventy-two-year-old grandfather, Tristão Antunes de Alencar. Tristão, a former state legislator who was known as "the colonel" because of his service in the National Guard, was a relatively prosperous man in a land of poverty. He owned several *sítios* which produced cattle, sugar, and manioc.[4]

Colonel Tristão de Alencar's influence on Antonietta and her younger sister and brothers had been considerable because their father, Augusto Gurgel do Amaral, had deserted them and their mother. Colonel Tristão barred the use of the name of his errant son-in-law, and thus Antonietta and her sister and brothers had been known as Alencars. And for this reason the colonel's new great-grandson was not named Humberto Gurgel do Amaral Castello Branco.[5]

Alencar, the middle name chosen for the infant, was one that he would one day be proud of. It had been brought to Ceará from Portugal by Tristão's great-great-grandfather, whose descendants had played notable roles in Ceará's history. Early in the nineteenth century progressive-minded Alencars had won renown, and harsh reprisals from the first Brazilian empire, during a stubborn and unsuccessful struggle to establish a republic in the north of Brazil. In the second Brazilian empire Alencars were to be found in the national legislature. Certainly the most famous of these was José de Alencar (1829–1877), not because he served as minister of justice and later as an opposition politician, but because his great novels, based on life in the north and northeast, gained him the reputation of being "the creator of a genuinely Brazilian literature."[6]

Colonel Tristão's *sítio*, just outside of Messejana, was not far from

[3] "Castelo Nasceu em Fortaleza . . . ," *Gazeta de Notícias*, Fortaleza, June 21, 1964.

[4] Alencar interviews, December 27, 28, 1975.

[5] Ana (Nina) Castello Branco Santos Dias and Beatriz Castello Branco Gonçalves, "Depoimento sôbre o irmão Humberto de Alencar Castello Branco," 1973, File B, Castello Branco Collection, Centro de Pesquisa de Documentação de História Contemporânea do Brasil, Instituto de Direito Público e Ciência Política, Fundação Getúlio Vargas, Rio de Janeiro (hereafter cited as CPDOC).

[6] Academia Cearense de Letras, *A Antologia Cearense*, p. xxiii.

the novelist's birthplace. It was set on a flat area studded with tall palms
—wax-bearing carnaubas, spindly coconuts, and stately imperials—as
well as banana and cashew trees, with the usual assortment of oxen,
horses, mules, and cattle grazing or lying in the shade. A special attraction was placid Lake Tristeza de Iracema, surrounded by white sand and
mango trees.[7]

Map 1

[7] HACB to his uncle, Edgard Antunes de Alencar, Rio de Janeiro, January 28,
1956, File B, p. 6, CPDOC.

The stay of the Castello Brancos at the rustic *sítio*, where the croaking of frogs and the chirping of crickets helped to remind Antonietta of her youth, lasted for several months. During that time Humberto was baptized in the seventeenth-century Jesuit-built Messejana Church, whose white steeple was the only part of the village that tall trees did not hide from the *sítio*.[8]

Late in 1897 Lieutenant Cândido, attached to the Thirty-fifth Infantry Battalion in Fortaleza, moved his family to another rented house in the state capital, this time on Sena Madureira Street, near the governor's palace, the Palácio da Luz.[9] But Antonietta had only six months to become acquainted with this new address, for in the middle of 1898 Cândido was transferred to the Fortieth Infantry Battalion in Recife, whose population of 110,000 made it the largest city in the north and northeast.

In Recife in 1899 a promotion to captain was awarded to Cândido, whose zeal for the army, indefatigable work, and good sense of organization counted for more than his unfortunate stammer, illness at ease, and frequent demonstrations of nervousness. Upon his promotion Cândido moved with his family to Rio de Janeiro, and there, in 1903, he received his silver medal for having served the army well for over twenty years.

Cândido's military career had begun in December, 1876, when at the age of sixteen, he had applied for a place in the infantry in his native province of Piauí in the north. Accepted with the rank of *segundo cadete*, the youth had explained to the *juiz de orfãos* (judge of orphans) that he was selling forty-five head of cattle, bringing in 405,000 réis, in order to "dress appropriately" for his new career and because his father, practicing law in Campo Maior, Piauí, was "in poverty."[10]

Despite his father's unrewarding fling at the law (in an area where everything was financially unrewarding), and despite the interest shown in cattle raising by some of Cândido's Piauí forefathers, the Castello Branco name had long been associated with notable feats of arms. Following a fourteenth-century battle in Portugal near a white castle built by the Romans, the name Castello Branco was assumed by a hero of the

[8] Luiz Gonzaga Bertelle, *Castello Branco, o 1º Presidente da Revolução*, File HP8, CPDOC.

[9] Alencar interview, December 27, 1975.

[10] Cândido Borges Castello Branco, resumé of career, File B, Part 2, CPDOC.

battle, and descendants of this first Castello Branco brought further military prestige to the family in the fifteenth century.[11]

The Castello Branco name was taken from Portugal to Brazil in 1693 by Francisco da Cunha Castello Branco, who had orders from his sovereign to strengthen the Portuguese garrison in the captaincy of Pernambuco, in the Brazilian northeast. Receiving new orders after he disembarked in Recife, capital of Pernambuco, Francisco set forth with his family for Maranhão to help defend that northern captaincy against incursions by the Dutch and French. Along with his three daughters he survived a shipwreck during that trip, but he lost his wife and his possessions. After reaching Maranhão, Francisco went to what is now the state of Piauí to try to recoup some of his losses by farming and cattle raising, an endeavor that required beating back bands of thieves.[12] One of his three daughters was the originator of the branch of the family to which Cândido belonged.

Cândido's undistinguished military career cannot be compared with those of some of the fourteenth- and fifteenth-century Castello Brancos of Portugal, but as a dedicated army officer he was regularly promoted. In the southern state of Rio Grande do Sul in 1912 he was named major, and after commanding battalions there and in Recife, he became a lieutenant colonel in 1916. As archivist of the Army Staff in Rio he was promoted in 1918 to full colonel, and he was retired in the same year with the rank of brigadier general, receiving a commendation for his zeal and competence.[13]

Cândido's agitated manner was made worse by sclerosis, which first afflicted him in middle age. In his later years he invariably shouted when it was unnecessary to do so—a habit not appreciated by those who found themselves close to him.[14]

"In the awkward figure of father," Humberto wrote later, "I see a man with a sense of order in a routine life, with a methodical preoccupation about paying off his debts, and, above all, with the generous interest in educating us children and in always desiring conditions for us that would be better than his own." [15]

[11] "Família Castello Branco," File A, Part 1, CPDOC.
[12] Lena Ferreira Costa, "Uma Família na História," File A, Part 3, CPDOC.
[13] Cândido Borges Castello Branco, resumé of career, File B, Part 2, CPDOC.
[14] Santos Dias and Gonçalves, "Depoimento," File B, CPDOC.
[15] HACB to his sister Beatriz, Belém, June 30, 1959, File B, CPDOC.

Photographs of Cândido and Antonietta invariably portray the couple in a serious mood. The heavyset military man with a mustache favored a pose in which he appeared firm—even fierce. Antonietta, much thinner, was inclined to be solemn-looking. Resignation often showed itself on the face of this patient and devoted wife and mother. But one can occasionally see a bit of determination in her expression. As her daughters wrote later, "although she was gentle, she could be firm and positive when it was necessary." Humberto was to recall that she was "not afraid of obstacles, facing them with a serene spirit of sacrifice, and always turning to God and seeking to help her family." [16]

The spirit of sacrifice had to be great, because by the time Cândido received his twenty-year silver medal in 1903, the number of surviving children had become six. Younger than Humberto were Ana (known as Nina), born in 1899; Beatriz, born in 1901; and Lauro, born in 1903. Old Colonel Tristão de Alencar helped out occasionally, especially with fares that would bring the family to Ceará during holidays.[17]

2. Formative Years in the North (1904–1911)

Antonietta, firm and positive when she gave her children their earliest lessons, was not averse to using an occasional slap to get them to study their ABC's.[1] For Humberto this introduction to learning was followed by formal education first received at the age of six at a private school run by two sisters in Recife. His teacher glumly warned his parents that because of Humberto's "limited capacity," the task of educating him could not be guaranteed to be a great success, and in the classroom the teacher lost no opportunity to let the boy know of his "intellectual deficiencies."[2]

In 1905 another transfer brought the family back to Fortaleza, and this turned out to be a four-year stay. During that time, Humberto, between the ages of seven and eleven, received lasting influences.

The foremost influence came from the teaching that he received as

[16] Ibid.
[17] Santos Dias and Gonçalves, "Depoimento," File B, CPDOC.
[1] "Castelo Nasceu em Fortaleza . . . ," *Gazeta de Notícias*, Fortaleza, June 21, 1964.
[2] Santos Dias and Gonçalves, "Depoimento," File B, CPDOC; Luís Viana Filho to Paulo V. Castello Branco, Bahia, April 12, 1976.

a day student at the Colégio São Rafael, a part of the Colégio da Imaculada Conceição, housed in an extensive two-story structure in the middle of Fortaleza. The director of Humberto's studies in 1907 and 1908 was Sister Inês. This nun, dressed in the habit of São Vicente de Paula, gave him encouragement and such a fondness for studies that the boy, who had theretofore been in the habit of asserting that he wanted to be an army captain when he grew up, now expressed his wish to become a teacher.[3] Humberto, a child who enjoyed life, remained a bit of a prankster, but his family noted a new veneration for books and learning; he no longer sacrificed his studies for his play.[4]

Speaking of Sister Inês when he was older, Humberto Castello Branco said: "She caused us to live with the best of sentiments. Forgiveness was always in the look and the words of Sister Inês. She was dominated by intelligence and wisdom."[5] When Humberto Castello Branco was president of Brazil, he would sometimes contrast the teaching received from her with the humiliations that he received at the school in Recife. Luís Viana Filho, with whom President Castello Branco sometimes reminisced about his past, concludes that when Antonietta placed young Castello Branco in the school run by the Catholic order in Fortaleza, she took a step that turned out to be decisive in the formation of his personality: "Helped and stimulated by Sister Inês, he changed completely; he acquired confidence in himself, and this fact cannot fail to have been essential for the future conduct of the President."[6]

Sister Inês was present at the chapel of the Colégio da Imaculada Conceição on November 1, 1907, when Humberto received his first communion. Photographed on the occasion, he appeared serious but not unhappy. Far from handsome, he was small for his age, short and thin. In other words, he was a true Cearense.

Second in importance to the influence of Sister Inês were the childhood impressions of the surroundings and the people—impressions that became so cherished with separation that they constituted an important part of the personality of Humberto. Particularly vivid were the memo-

[3] Bertelle, *Castello Branco*; Santos Dias and Gonçalves, "Depoimento," File B, CPDOC.

[4] "Castelo Nasceu em Fortaleza. . . ," *Gazeta de Notícias*, Fortaleza, June 21, 1964, quoting HACB's cousin Eduardo Alencar.

[5] HACB quoted in *Grandes Acontecimentos da História*, November, 1973, pp. 34–41, in File HP7, p. 18, CPDOC.

[6] Viana Filho to Paulo V. Castello Branco, Bahia, April 12, 1976.

ries of vacations and infrequent weekends spent at the *sítio* near Messe-jana before and after the death of Colonel Tristão in May, 1907. It was there in the country that Humberto and his brothers and sisters bathed in the dam of the sugar mill and found delicious flavors in the coconuts, *maracujás*, mangos, and *cajus*. ("What fruits!" Humberto would one day write to his sister Lourdinha.)[7]

At the *sítio* the ten-year-old boy, befriended by the mason of the Alencars, liked to fill buckets with sand and help mix the mortar. Hum-berto never lost track of Ignácio, the mason, and he never ceased to praise the poor, good people of Ceará—men described by Rachel de Queiroz (another descendant of the Alencars) as "lean, toasted, asce-tic."[8]

These people, commonly short, were descended from Portuguese, Negroes, and Indians.[9] Some Jews had found a haven there from the Inquisition and were said to have been a source of the sarcasm or irony sometimes practiced in Ceará.[10] Whatever its source, the use of irony was a characteristic of the Alencars, and it was inherited in full measure by Humberto, along with no little obstinacy and a tendency not to forget quickly any act that he considered disloyal.[11]

The influence of Sister Inês and the influence of the land and its people turned Humberto into a devotee of the literature about Ceará. Before he left the state at the age of eleven, Humberto had memorized passages from the books of José de Alencar.[12]

Starting in 1909, Humberto attended three schools in three years: the Colégio Aires Gama in Recife, the Liceu do Piauí in Teresina, and the Liceu do Maranhão in São Luís. At the Liceu do Piauí, Humberto is remembered for not having joined in with students who made it a practice to boo and jeer at vendors trying to sell goods in the neighbor-

[7] Bertelle, *Castello Branco*; HACB, "Sugestões para a Lourdinha (sugestões dadas a sua irmã que ia ao Ceará visitar o filho)," File B, CPDOC.

[8] "Castelo Nasceu em Fortaleza . . . ," *Gazeta de Notícias*, Fortaleza, June 21, 1964; Rachel de Queiroz, "Terra," in "Última Página," *O Cruzeiro*, unidentified issue, underlined by HACB, File B, CPDOC.

[9] See Billy Jaynes Chandler, "The Role of Negroes in the Ethnic Formation of Ceará: The Need for a Reappraisal," *Revista de Ciências Sociais*, 4, no. 1 (1st semes-ter, 1973), 31–43.

[10] José Jerônimo Moscardo de Souza interview, Brasília, October 23, 1975.

[11] Santos Dias and Gonçalves, "Depoimento," File B, CPDOC.

[12] "Castelo Nasceu em Fortaleza. . . ," *Gazeta de Notícias*, Fortaleza, June 21, 1964.

hood of the school.[13] Besides helping Candinho put out a small news-paper at the Liceu do Piauí, Humberto rewarded Inês for her faith and patience; at the end of the term, in December, 1910, he was the only member of his class of seven to receive a passing grade, for which achievement he was booed by his classmates all during his walk from school to his parents' home in the commercial center of Teresina.[14]

Humberto was attending the Liceu do Maranhão early in 1912 when his life in the north came to an abrupt end; his father's transfer this time was to Rio Pardo in the southern state of Rio Grande do Sul.

3. At the Colégio Militar de Porto Alegre (1912–1917)

Faced with more changes in schools for his children, Captain Cân-dido considered the future of his two older sons. Candinho, the first-born, was enrolled in the Escola Naval (Naval Academy) in Rio.

Cândido had once suggested that Humberto consider the study of law, although how such a study could have been financed must have been difficult to see. Anyway, Humberto insisted that he preferred the career of his father. This meant turning to a *colégio militar*, of which there were three in Brazil. One was in Rio de Janeiro, and a second was in Barbacena, Minas Gerais. The third was just about to be opened in Porto Alegre, capital of Rio Grande do Sul. With Captain Cândido being transferred to Rio Grande do Sul, the new school there, with its ex-cellent facilities, was selected.

The matter of showing that the fourteen-year-old Humberto was less than twelve when admitted—necessary for receiving the education without charge—was easily handled; it was simply stated that the year of his birth was 1900 instead of 1897, a date-changing practice com-monly employed under the circumstances. And so, on April 17, 1912, after taking the required examinations, Humberto was placed in the second year of the three-year preliminary course (*curso de adaptação*), which was to be followed by a four-year general course.[1]

Of the 275 boys who attended the first classes given at the Colégio

[13] Letter to Moysés Castello Branco, Teresina, October 1, 1973, File B, CPDOC.

[14] Santos Dias and Gonçalves, "Depoimento," File B, CPDOC.

[1] Décio Palmeiro de Escobar memorandum, Rio de Janeiro, January 15, 1974, File G1, CPDOC.

Militar de Porto Alegre in April, 1912, Humberto alone was from Ceará, and he quickly gained the nickname of "Cearense" (along with some less flattering ones).[2] Almost all of his schoolmates, such as the Etchegoyen brothers (Nelson and Alcides), the Kruel brothers (Riograndino and Amauri), Artur da Costa e Silva, and Napoleão de Alencastro Guimarães, were natives of Rio Grande do Sul. It seemed to them that Humberto, who had practically no neck and who was small, thin, and not at all handsome, looked like a northeasterner.

In an unfamiliar setting in which most of the boys were more robust and prosperous than he, Humberto gained respect for the grades that he received.[3] His application to his work brought him results that were especially outstanding in the preliminary course. After he was given the maximum grade of 10 in the examinations at the end of 1913, the director of the school wrote to Major Cândido Castello Branco, who had once again been transferred to Recife, to tell of the boy's "brilliant" performance—"perhaps the most distinguished in this institution."[4]

In April, 1914, Humberto was advanced to the general course, where he was outstanding in Portuguese, English, and mathematics. He did rather well in all subjects except physics, for which he was apt to receive a grade of 5 or 6.

If Humberto's character was formed in the north of Brazil, most of his lasting attachments developed while he was at school in Porto Alegre. To his devotion to his work, now woven in his mind to his career, must be added the strong feelings for family and Ceará, to which painful separation contributed. During most of his schooling in Porto Alegre, Humberto missed his family, which moved to Recife one year after coming to Rio Grande do Sul and then moved to Rio de Janeiro. Humberto developed into a good letter writer, sending his family his news and expressions of affection. The occupation of filling pages with a distinctive and usually clear handwriting, which eventually became rather easy

[2] Heitor Lopes Caminha and Jurandir Palma Cabral, "Humberto de Alencar Castello Branco, O Cearense: Colégio Militar de Porto Alegre, Periódo de 1912–1917," File G1, CPDOC; Amauri Kruel interview, Rio de Janeiro, December 11, 1975.

[3] Paulo V. Castello Branco, "Um Liberal, um Revolucionário, e um Democrata," *Jornal da Tarde*, July 13, 1972.

[4] Brazil, Ministry of the Army, Department of Instruction and Research, Colégio Militar de Porto Alegre, memorandum, September 13, 1973, File G2, Part 1; letter, Colégio Militar de Porto Alegre, January 22, 1914, File G1, CPDOC.

for him and which would one day require much of his time, had its start with these letters.

The sentimental young student in Porto Alegre was stirred by the memories of the markets of Fortaleza, the green sea off Ceará, and the sun "gladdening" the lake at Messejana.[5] Called on to read some appropriate lines at a gathering of students considering the literature of the Brazilian backlands, Humberto recited with emotion a passage of José de Alencar that he had memorized.[6]

During Humberto's five years in the south he also discovered attachments that were unrelated to his past and that persisted throughout his life. His family learned of the pleasure that he found in attending the theater in Porto Alegre—often with his best friends, the Kruels. He mentioned the performances of the *teatro lírico* group, on tour from Rio.

Although Humberto enjoyed good health, he participated in physical exercise only to the extent that it was required. He did not spend leisure time developing his muscles on the parallel bars in the school's patio, and he did not engage in fencing, a popular pastime at which the Kruel brothers excelled. Nor did he play *futebol* (soccer) or even follow the fortunes of any favorite *futebol* team.[7] For Humberto leisure time was time for reading literature and the political columns of the press.

It is therefore not surprising that the extracurricular activities that most absorbed him were those connected with the Sociedade Cívica e Literária, an organization founded by *colégio militar* students who were concerned with political matters, oratory, and literature. The approximately forty members were chosen for their speaking ability and interest in events.[8] Humberto, who turned out to be the kind of participant who made his presence felt while fostering teamwork, became as well known to the student body for his contributions to the Sociedade Cívica as for his intelligence. In 1916 he was elected orator of the *sociedade*. Among the other officers were Gabriel Mena Barreto, president; Riograndino Kruel, vice president; and Amauri Kruel, treasurer. First Secretary Mil-

[5] HACB, "Sugestões para a Lourdinha," File B, CPDOC.

[6] Costa, "Uma Família na História," File A, Part 3, CPDOC.

[7] João Batista Barreto Leite Filho interview, Rio de Janeiro, November 25, 1975; Décio Palmeiro de Escobar memorandum, Rio de Janeiro, January 15, 1974, File G1, CPDOC.

[8] Riograndino Kruel interview, Rio de Janeiro, September 21, 1975; Amauri Kruel interview, December 11, 1975.

ton Cezimbra became one of Humberto's close friends. Second Secretary Décio Palmeiro de Escobar, a class behind the other officers, was building up a grade record at the school that seemed unlikely ever to be equaled.[9] According to a partisan of this directorship, its members were "inspired by noble sentiments of civic pride and patriotism and fought the unbridled cliques and pernicious and unsociable germs that corrupted and perverted the Sociedade."[10]

At the literary sessions Humberto quoted from Machado de Assis, Eça de Queiroz, and Alexandre Herculano as well as José de Alencar.[11] At the political sessions he cited oppositionist orators Irineu Machado, Alexandre José Barbosa Lima, and Rui Barbosa—particularly the last, whose speeches he read and reread with admiration. "Just imagine," one of Humberto's schoolmates has written, "as a student he took out a subscription to the *Diário Oficial* in order to read the speeches given by Rui Barbosa in the Senate and, I believe, the speeches given by Barbosa Lima in the Chamber of Deputies."[12]

The Sociedade Cívica leaders assumed a "liberal" position. In 1916 ten of them, including Humberto, the two Kruels, and Gabriel and Celso Mena Barreto, organized a new student organization, the República Liberal (so named by Humberto), to support the opponents of the dominant regime in Brazil.[13] In Rio Grande do Sul politics the República Liberal backed the local opposition party, the Partido Federalista, and it denounced the repeated reelections of Governor Borges de Medeiros, ruler of the Partido Republicano Riograndense. Humberto and the Kruel brothers would go to the state legislature and join those in the galleries whose fiery support for the speeches of oppositionist Alves Valença violated the rules about conduct in the galleries.[14]

---

[9] Barreto Leite Filho interview, November 25, 1975.

[10] Notes on the back of a photograph of officers of the Sociedade Cívica e Literária, Porto Alegre, November, 1916, File G1, CPDOC. This directorship was long remembered. For many years in the future, orators of the Sociedade Cívica opened their speeches with the words, "In this tribune, where Castello Branco and Mena Barreto once spoke."

[11] Escobar memorandum, January 15, 1974, File G1, CPDOC.

[12] João de Machado Linhares to Paulo V. Castello Branco, Porto Alegre, April 5, 1976. Riograndino Kruel (interview, September 21, 1975) mentioned the interest that HACB showed in the speeches of Rui Barbosa and Irineu Machado.

[13] See Caminha and Cabral, "Humberto de Alencar Castello Branco, O Cearense."

[14] Riograndino Kruel interview, September 21, 1975. Sometimes the Colégio Mili-

By the time Humberto reached his last year at the school, his grade average and conduct brought him the post of captain of the student body. Among his classmates, only Artur da Costa e Silva—almost as well known for flute playing as the Kruels were for fencing—received a grade record superior to that of Humberto. As the first in his class, Costa e Silva was awarded the rank of commander of the student body.[15]

Students with outstanding grades were rewarded, during their last year, by the assignment of a special room in which to do their homework. Although these leaders were therefore seldom in the general study hall, some of the younger students—including even *bichos* (animals), as the new students were called—found opportunities to be in their company. Humberto, they noted, was not one of those who liked to boast about amorous exploits. In conversation he was regarded as one who expressed himself well and held to firm convictions.[16] He was ever ready with a quip or sarcastic observation, as when the discussion turned to the food at the school. His cutting irony, although intended for fun rather than the humiliation of anyone, was not always appreciated, and references were made to the "sardonic twist" of his mind.

Some of the lasting attachments developed by Humberto in Porto Alegre were mentioned in a letter that he wrote several years after completing his studies there:

At the Colégio Militar . . . , far from my parents, I began . . . the course of six years, during which I saw my youth pass without those happy chants of the young who do not find thorns in the "rising slope of life." I witnessed, nevertheless, within myself, the birth of an ardor for ideas, for causes that were of interest to my country, protecting and nourishing, with love and affection, dreams, projects, ambitions. . . . I devoted myself to studies with an unshakable determination to succeed, spending silent hours at my desk

---

tar students participated in oppositionist demonstrations that were crushed with severity. Amauri Kruel still bears the scar of a bullet wound received in his leg when the mounted state military brigade fired on demonstrators, killing a medical student and another person who were standing close to him (Amauri Kruel interview, Rio de Janeiro, July 22, 1977).

[15] Nelson Dimas Filho, *Costa e Silva: O Homem e o Líder*, p. 20. For final grades, see Colégio Militar de Porto Alegre, *Boletim 365*, December 31, 1917, File G2, CPDOC. Earlier *boletins* (also in File G2, CPDOC) show honor rolls (*quadros de honra*).

[16] Escobar memorandum, January 15, 1974, File G1, CPDOC.

during winter nights, always cold and always yearning for my family and for my Ceará.[17]

4. Realengo (1918–1921)

Humberto, twenty, joined his family in Rio in January, 1918, and three months later became a cadet at the three-year course of the Escola Militar (Military Academy) at Realengo. As Realengo was only about twenty-four kilometers from Rio, Humberto's visits to his family were no longer limited to the summer vacations that occurred in the early months of each year.

In Rio, Humberto found that his older brother, Candinho, was away at sea, for he had joined the merchant marine after doing poorly in the naval academy.[1] Lourdinha had married Lieutenant João Hipólito da Costa in Recife; for a while she lived with her husband and two babies at the modest home of the Castello Brancos in the north zone of Rio, but late in 1918 a new military assignment took the young family to Belo Horizonte, the recently built capital of Minas Gerais.[2] Humberto's younger brother, Lauro, attended the Colégio Militar of Rio until he was transferred, on account of his asthma, to the Colégio Militar of Fortaleza, which opened in 1919.

To his younger sisters, Nina and Beatriz, Humberto was gallantly attentive, and he took them to the theater when he could. They found that Humberto's deportment had become rigidly military. But if he seemed more formal than the boy they had known in Ceará, in conversation his playful sarcasm had become a more persistent trait.[3]

Nina and Beatriz concluded that Humberto, who had no girl friends, was something of an introvert. He liked to stay at home, and there he spent much time reading books and newspapers. He devoured the political news and continued to admire Rui Barbosa, who once again became the opposition candidate for president. But when Humberto's father, a retired general as of late 1918, offered to arrange for Humberto

[17] HACB to Argentina Vianna, Rio de Janeiro, January 18, 1921 (shown as 1920), Files C and G1, CPDOC.

[1] Santos Dias and Gonçalves, "Depoimento," File B, CPDOC.

[2] Maria de Lourdes Vianna, "Humberto e Argentina" (typewritten), Belo Horizonte, September 14, 1974, p. 1.

[3] Santos Dias and Gonçalves, "Depoimento," File B, CPDOC.

to meet Rui Barbosa, Humberto declined. He said that he did not want a personal contact to do anything to harm a great admiration.[4]

At Realengo, Humberto was not, as he had been in Porto Alegre, the only Cearense. Sixteen cadets, including tall Juarez Távora, were from Ceará. Nor was Realengo the sea of entirely new faces that the school in Porto Alegre had once been for Humberto. More than half of the cadets at the Escola Militar were from Rio Grande do Sul, and they included almost all of Humberto's Porto Alegre classmates. Those who had organized the República Liberal at the Colégio Militar of Porto Alegre remained united at Realengo, where they rented an inexpensive old house that they used on weekends.[5]

The classmates whom Humberto invited occasionally to share meals with his family included Gaúchos who were far from home; among them was Amauri Kruel, who had become Humberto's best friend but whom Nina and Beatriz found "rather conceited."[6] Some of his new friends were Mineiros: Antônio José Coelho dos Reis ("Toné"), with whom Humberto attended light opera performances in Rio, and José de Melo Alvarenga.[7]

In 1919, when it became necessary for Humberto and his more than two hundred classmates to select their specialties, Humberto chose the infantry, the most popular branch. Unlike the Kruels, who chose the cavalry, Humberto disliked horseback riding and only did it, according to one of his contemporaries, "when forced to."[8]

Discipline-minded Lieutenant Henrique Batista Duffles Teixeira Lott, a young instructor, taught the cadets trench-building and other forms of fortification as well as how to judge distances by observation. But the Escola Militar training, Humberto found, put him at a disadvantage by stressing physical education to a greater degree than had been done in Porto Alegre.[9] Long remembered by Humberto were his experiences on a steeply inclined ramp with fences, holes, and other

---

[4] Ibid.

[5] Caminha and Cabral, "Humberto de Alencar Castello Branco, O Cearense."

[6] Santos Dias and Gonçalves, "Depoimento," File B, CPDOC. People from Rio Grande do Sul are called Gaúchos.

[7] Mineiros are people from Minas Gerais. Other new friends made by Humberto at Realengo were Ademar Vilela dos Santos and Waldemar Alves.

[8] João Punaro Bley note, File G2, p. 27B, CPDOC.

[9] Henrique Batista Duffles Teixeira Lott interview, Rio de Janeiro, October 13, 1975; Emygdio da Costa Miranda interview, Rio de Janeiro, December 1, 1975.

obstacles. Known as the "ramp of death," it was used to grade the courage of the gym-suited cadets taking physical education: top grades went to those who hurdled all the obstacles. On one occasion an instructor decided to test the "moral qualities" of the cadets by ordering them to run the obstacles in full military uniform and bearing a rifle. Surprisingly, Humberto succeeded, but at the cost of a bruised leg that required him to be hospitalized.[10]

5. Vacation in Belo Horizonte (January–March, 1919)

In Belo Horizonte, a city of fifty-four thousand, Humberto's older sister Lourdinha and her husband, Captain João Hipólito da Costa, were befriended by the socially prominent family of one of the captain's former classmates, Arthur Vianna, a pioneer in business in the growing new city. Nevertheless, the warmhearted Lourdinha missed her own family and was ever pleading that its members visit her. It was Humberto's turn during his holidays early in 1919, and he made the trip despite his brother Lauro's report that Belo Horizonte had a delightful climate but was otherwise a grim place. The Mineiros, Lauro had concluded, lived in isolation and had no interest in amusing themselves.[1]

One evening soon after Humberto's arrival, Lourdinha received a visit from two of the Vianna daughters and two of their girl friends. These teenage girls were curious to see Humberto, who had already been described to them by Lourdinha as short, dark, and ugly but a very intelligent and splendid person. Having been led to expect the worst in the case of Humberto's appearance, the girls decided that Lourdinha had been unfair in her description.[2] In the course of the evening the eighteen-year-old Argentina, eldest of the ten Vianna children, took Lourdinha aside and said with firmness and spirit, "I don't think he's so ugly, and he's most attractive."[3]

Argentina had already been described to Humberto in glowing terms that Humberto came to find were altogether true. She was one of the

[10] Ademar Vilela dos Santos, "Depoimento: Humberto de Alencar Castello Branco no 12º RI," Rio de Janeiro, March, 1974, File G1, CPDOC.

[1] Vianna, "Humberto e Argentina," p. 1.

[2] Ibid.

[3] Santos Dias and Gonçalves, "Depoimento," File B, CPDOC.

prettiest girls in Belo Horizonte (and had recently placed third in a newspaper-sponsored beauty contest in which the readers were asked to send in votes). Educated at the Dominican Sisters' Colégio Santa Maria and later at the Colégio Izabela Hendrix, a Protestant institution, she spoke English and French extremely well. Reflective study had given her a deep knowledge of the Bible, and in 1916 she had been admitted to the Pia União das Filhas de Maria (Charitable Union of the Daughters of Mary). According to one admirer, her religious training, together with her classical education, made her company a "spiritual delight."[4]

For Humberto, Belo Horizonte was hardly what Lauro had described. Several parties were given to acquaint Humberto with the younger set. The first was at the home of the Viannas, who were then living, like Lourdinha, in the Floresta district. Humberto appeared in his cadet's uniform and participated much in the dancing, which was done to the accompaniment of piano music and lasted until 11:00 P.M.[5] Humberto danced well.[6]

Among those whom Humberto met at the Viannas' party was eighteen-year-old Francisco Negrão de Lima, whose family, as large as that of the Viannas, also lived in the Floresta district. The company of Francisco, who was completing secondary school and planning to go into law, gave Humberto a welcome opportunity to converse about books and politics. Borrowing two volumes at a time from Francisco, Humberto read sixteen volumes of the sermons that had been delivered in colonial times by Father Antônio Vieira.[7]

Many a night at 10:00 P.M. Humberto and Francisco went to the Central do Brasil Railroad Station, for it was at that hour that the morning newspapers arrived from Rio. So excited was Humberto about the speeches of presidential candidate Rui Barbosa that he would read them aloud before leaving the newsstand at the station.[8]

The friendly Argentina Vianna was the chief reason for Humberto's

[4] Francisco Negrão de Lima interview, Rio de Janeiro, December 10, 1975; "Diploma de Admissão: Argentina Vianna foi admittida na Pia União das Filhas da Maria canonicamente 8 de dez., 1916, na Igreja Matriz de S. José, Bello Horizonte," File D, Part 4, CPDOC; speech given by Eurípides Cardoso de Menezes on Rádio Nacional, Rio de Janeiro, December 16, 1965," File D, Part 3, CPDOC.

[5] Negrão de Lima interview, December 10, 1975.

[6] Vianna, "Humberto e Argentina," p. 2.

[7] Negrão de Lima interview, December 10, 1975.

[8] Ibid.

happiness in Belo Horizonte. But his opportunities to speak alone with
the well-chaperoned girl were largely limited to the dances he had with
her, such as the Tea Dance held at the Clube Belo Horizonte in March,
1919, shortly before his return to Rio. An orchestra played the popular
tangos, fox-trots, sambas, maxixes, one-steps, and two-steps, many of
them imported from abroad: "Tipperary," "Grizzly Bear," and "Oh
Johnny, Oh." With Maria Vianna, Humberto tangoed ("Tristeza de
Caboclo" and "Chão Parado"). With Argentina Vianna he danced to
the music of "Over There" (ragtime) and "Mumblin' Moss" (one-
step).[9]

Argentina seemed pleased with the attention that Humberto showed
her, but Humberto could not be sure that the well-brought-up girl was
being more than polite. He returned to Realengo uncertain of whether
she had serious feelings about him.

As for his own feelings, Humberto spoke to no one. Nor did Lourdinha say anything, although she must have had a good idea because at
Realengo Humberto's souvenirs included not only the Belo Horizonte
Club Tea Dance program but also a photograph of Argentina that he
had taken from Lourdinha's album.[10]

6. The Cadet Corresponds with Argentina (September, 1920)

Humberto's Realengo classmate Toné Coelho dos Reis was from Belo
Horizonte and made trips back home whenever he could, especially after
falling in love with Maria Amália Drumond (who had placed second
in the local newspaper's "beauty contest").[1] From Realengo, Toné engaged in a heavy correspondence with Maria Amália. Humberto's correspondence was hardly comparable: it was with Francisco Negrão de
Lima.

Finally, in July, 1920, more than fifteen months after the vacation
with Lourdinha in Belo Horizonte, Humberto persuaded Toné to explain to Argentina Vianna that he was serious about her. Toné returned
from Belo Horizonte with the report that Argentina welcomed this

---

[9] Program of Chá Dansante, Clube Bello Horizonte, March 8, 1919 ("em bene-
fício das vítimas das enchentes de Januária e São Francisco"), File C, CPDOC.
[10] Santos Dias and Gonçalves, "Depoimento," File B, CPDOC.
[1] Negrão de Lima interview, December 10, 1975.

news. Then, at Humberto's request, Toné wrote Maria Amália asking
her to find out whether Argentina would be agreeable to exchanging
letters with Humberto. In September, 1920, Maria Amália wrote Toné
to say that Argentina had no objection.

Humberto was in a good mood when he sat down on September 28,
1920, to construct, in an extremely careful handwriting, his first letter
to Argentina:

The life of a man has days of real happiness. They are the unforgettable
moments in which sentiments, the value of one's word, and the sincerity of
one's aspirations are set forth.

I find myself in one of those days. To be writing this letter to you confirms that I am in a happy moment in which I realize an intention long
cherished and today fully satisfied.

One week has passed since Toné received the agreeable message from Maria
Amália that you do not oppose a correspondence between the two of us. Only
today, however, after "protocol" no longer requires my presence in the ceremonial parades for King Albert, am I able, with relative calm, to send you
this first letter, which will doubtless mark a new phase in our relationship.[2]

Humberto explained that in the year and several months after leaving Belo Horizonte he had lacked the certainty of Argentina's "good
disposition" toward him, having received, when he was there, no words
to confirm a "reciprocation" of feelings. "I believe that the same thing
happened with you." He went on to tell Argentina that in view of the
happy news brought to him by Toné, he felt that letter writing would
be important so that they could "advance and adjust" their aspirations.
He said that he considered her acceptance of his letter-writing proposal
to be a proof "of full confidence, for which an expression of gratitude
can only be a clear affirmation of my esteem and of the persistence of
my intention."

I consider unnecessary a "declaration." "Declarations" have come to have
no merits to recommend them. Today they constitute the ineffable phrases of
some young men at dances and parties, where they express to their "god-
desses," always with the same words, their impassioned admiration for the
eyes that captured them and for the smile that dominated them. Therefore a
"declaration" does not belong in this letter. What should be recorded here is

[2] HACB to Argentina, Realengo, September 28, 1920, File C, p. 4, CPDOC.

the sincere expression of friendship and the assurance that I must find in you the same affection. Write to me, then, so that a complete understanding may exist between the two of us.[3]

Humberto asked Argentina to find some conveyer of letters other than Maria Amália, "who already has her hands full receiving what Toné writes to her." Could not Argentina suggest some relative or friend to whom he could address his letters? Expressing the hope of receiving an early answer, Humberto said that he would then initiate his "conversations," writing, without restraint, about his projects and receiving her advice; his future letters, he promised, would not be like this first "protocol" letter. In conclusion, Humberto asked Argentina to "accept as sincere what is written above by (if you permit me) your Humberto."

Humberto added a postscript to give his address (general delivery, Realengo), and he enclosed a little piece of printed verse that began: "If I should ever forget you, darling, I would be forgetting myself."[4]

The letter-writing between the two idealists did not get off to a hasty start. Not until October 25, almost one month after Humberto wrote, did Argentina reply: "Although you sought my opinion about whether we should maintain a correspondence, I do not know whether what we are doing is right. This doubt is not due to any lack of trust; but what would my mother say, what would yours say, about this? As for me, I can see the excuse in the distance that separates us; but will everyone think that way?" Nevertheless, Argentina gave, for Humberto's use, the address of an intimate relative in Belo Horizonte, and she asked that on the envelopes he show her name simply as A. Vianna. In closing, she wrote: "To a 'protocolish' letter, an equally 'protocolish' reply, isn't that so? Argentina."[5]

Humberto's answer to this was returned to him by the postal authorities because he forgot to put the street and house number on the envelope! Writing again on December 6, 1920, Humberto told of his oversight and explained that his apparent silence was caused by no illness or change in his feeling. He cited the increase in schoolwork occasioned by the end of the year and the extended stay in Brazil of King

---

[3] Ibid.
[4] "Se eu te esquecesse, querida,/A mim próprio esqueceria. . . ." (File C, CPDOC).
[5] Argentina to HACB, Belo Horizonte, October 25, 1920, File C, CPDOC.

Albert of the Belgians. He described the final exams as "an epoch in which intranquility predominates in the student." He also wrote of the daily visits he made to see Antonietta, his sick mother.[6] Early in the new year he received a brief reply that asked about Antonietta's health and told of Argentina's prayers that 1921 would be a happy year for Humberto and his family.[7]

The letters were rather formal, and no "dear" was used before the name. It was simply Argentina and Humberto. As Argentina did not destroy the letters that reached her, and as they were discovered in a drawer in her bedroom by her mother early in 1921, Argentina received the answer to the question she had raised about her mother's reaction: "Argentina, how could you have been so bold as to receive and answer letters from a boy? This is an absurdity!" Argentina's parents were also upset at the relative whose house address was being used by Humberto.[8]

The discovery of the letters occurred just as Humberto was about to end any need for secrecy by seeking an engagement. This is clear from Humberto's reply on January 18, 1921, to Argentina's year-end good wishes. Humberto opened with the news that he had passed his examinations and just been classified as an officer-candidate (*aspirante a oficial*). He turned then to Argentina's note "in which, with kind phrases, you wish me a happy new year. They are wishes of happiness which bring me the gentle tone of words that are sincere and that therefore go deeply to my heart. May 1921 be a good year for both of us. May it bring with its days the realization of our hopes, bringing us happiness and joining us under the blessing of God."[9]

It was in this long letter that Humberto spoke of his studies in Porto Alegre during cold nights and of his professional dreams. He went on to say that in the daily work at Realengo his desire for an army career had become strengthened. "There I witnessed the evolution of my knowledge and ideas. There also I guarded the love I have for you."

Having finally obtained, after "so much work, patience, hope, and faith in the future," his new classification, the ambition of his life, he now reached for a new goal: to be stationed in Belo Horizonte. If he

[6] HACB to Argentina, Realengo, December 6, 1920, File C, CPDOC.

[7] Argentina to HACB, December 30, 1920, File C, CPDOC.

[8] Vianna, "Humberto e Argentina," p. 2.

[9] HACB to Argentina, January 18, 1921 (shown as 1920), Files C, G1, CPDOC.

did not get the requested assignment, he wanted to make a visit there in February "so that we can attend to all the arrangements necessary for my presentation to your parents." Humberto implored Argentina to reply quickly about this matter. He wanted to learn whether she noted any aversion by her parents to their marriage plans; he wanted her suggestions of what to do if some obstacle arose. "With urgency I await your news and advice."

The reply was agreeable but not exactly complete: "If you should make a trip to Belo Horizonte, it is not necessary for me to tell you how happy that would make me."[10]

Humberto, whose Escola Militar grades put him in thirty-third place among ninety-eight infantry officer-candidates,[11] learned that he was to be stationed, as he had requested, in the Twelfth Infantry Regiment (12th RI) in Belo Horizonte. He rushed a letter to advise that he would not be making the visit there. He would, he added happily, be coming there to live![12] As the Belo Horizonte press had mentioned only Mineiros (Humberto's friends Toné and José de Melo Alvarenga) when it listed new officer-candidates who would be stationed in the city, Argentina was pleasantly surprised.

"Here in Belo Horizonte, far from Rio," she wrote, "I, too, was happy with the ceremony of the blessing of the swords, and when I read in a newspaper the news of that ceremony, I thought of the pleasure that I would have had if I had heard the class orator."[13]

7. Engagement (1921–1922)

The *Boletim* of the 12th RI reported on February 28, 1921, that three of the regiment's six new officer-candidates, Humberto de Alencar Castello Branco, Antônio José Coelho dos Reis, and Olímpio Mourão Filho, would present themselves that day at the Second, Seventh, and Fifth companies, respectively.[1] Castello Branco, presenting himself, was filled with curiosity about the activities he would be carrying out and

10 Argentina to HACB, January 21, 1921, File C, CPDOC.
11 Note in File G1, p. 27B, CPDOC.
12 HACB to Argentina, January 31, 1921, File C, CPDOC.
13 Argentina to HACB, February 12, 1921, File C, CPDOC.
1 Brazil, Army, Twelfth Infantry Regiment, "Boletim do 12 RI," February 28, 1921, File G1, CPDOC.

with the conviction, implanted at Realengo, that he would be serving Brazil well. "On February 28, 1921," he said many years later, "I felt the fascination of the profession which I embraced."[2]

The officer-candidate lost no time in calling at the Viannas' spacious new home, in a new district, and there he found that the number of children had grown from ten to twelve. That Argentina was in love with Humberto was clear and soon became the subject of comments by her cousins, uncles, and aunts: "Argentina in love with a soldier! And one so small! So ugly! She who is so pretty!" But as an old friend of the Viannas replied, "And why shouldn't Argentina be in love? Is she supposed to sit around waiting for a prince charming to come along?"[3]

In a typed letter to his parents dated May 4, 1921, Humberto expressed his desire to ask for the hand of Argentina Vianna right after receiving his promotion from officer-candidate to second lieutenant, expected that month. Seeking his parents' consent, Humberto said that while resolutions of good men were the product of much meditation, the resolutions of good military men represented, in addition, "the moral integrity of the feelings and aspirations of the soul of the soldier." Argentina, he wrote, was very well educated and "is the living expression of Christian virtues, which have made her a model of exemplary conduct and given her a loving heart, full of affection, and an understanding of her duties within a family. I think that I have found the companion of my life, to the happiness of which she will bring this treasury of precious value."[4]

Castello Branco's marriage hopes were not a secret in Belo Horizonte. He discussed them with his one civilian friend, law student Francisco Negrão de Lima, who predicted that conservative Arthur Vianna would be slow in reaching a decision about his daughter's future. At the officers' casino of the regiment, skepticism was expressed about the chances of Castello Branco marrying into the wealthy and socially prominent family.[5]

As Negrão de Lima had expected, the parents of the officer-candidate agreed with the idea more quickly than did Arthur Vianna. Ar-

[2] HACB longhand notes (on presidential stationery) for speech, 1966, File G1, CPDOC.

[3] Vianna, "Humberto e Argentina."

[4] HACB to his parents, Belo Horizonte, May 4, 1921, File C, CPDOC.

[5] Negrão de Lima interview, December 10, 1975; Virgílio Távora interview, Brasília, October 22, 1975.

gentina's father, reflecting on some observations made by his brother-in-law, a physician, about the young man's physique, called on Humberto to undergo a medical examination. Humberto's response to this demand was to prepare a farewell letter to Argentina. But it was never sent because he first consulted his father, who wired him to go ahead and submit to the examination.[6]

Finally, all parents having given their approval, and Humberto having been commissioned a second lieutenant on May 16, 1921, announcements were sent out on May 19 to advise that Argentina and Humberto were engaged to be married. Humberto gave his fiancée a gold brooch in the form of a small sword. From her he received a chocolate cake that she had baked and for which he showed appreciation despite his aversion to chocolate.[7]

During the eight-and-one-half-month engagement, Argentina made herself a trousseau and saw something of Humberto. The Viannas allowed him to visit their home on Tuesday, Thursday, and Sunday evenings until 9:00 P.M. sharp. Occasionally on Sundays the couple could attend a symphony concert. Humberto complained to Argentina that he found Saturdays dreadful.[8]

Returning to the barracks after one evening at the Vianna home, Humberto could not sleep. On the back of a card bearing the words TU SÓ TU (you only you), Humberto wrote to Argentina:

Today I left your house with the idea that the day before yesterday I offended the delicacy of your sentiments and of your affection for me because of a word that contains an indelicate meaning. It was an involuntary act without the slightest intention of hurting you. Because of it I feel the indispensable need to send you (not in a jesting tone, but with the sincerity and seriousness of my happy passion) a "declaration" which is a general affirmation and which, instead of containing trivialities, brings in its three words the vital substance of my love. Only in that way shall I now be able to enjoy the sleep of the "just." Your betrothed who loves you deeply, Humberto.[9]

[6] Vianna, "Humberto e Argentina."

[7] Announcement, May 19, 1921, File C, CPDOC; Paulo V. Castello Branco conversation, Rio de Janeiro, December 21, 1974.

[8] Vianna, "Humberto e Argentina." As a bachelor in Belo Horizonte, Castello Branco spent some of his time acting as secretary of the São José parish of the União dos Môços Católicos (Union of Catholic Young Men). See Ivan Martins Vianna, "O Estadista Castello Branco," Forum Econômico, No. 87 (1977).

[9] HACB note on card, November 11, 1921, File C, CPDOC.

A few days later flowers arrived for Argentina accompanied by Humberto's calling card, on which was written: "These flowers go before me. They will bring, in their simplicity, the news that I shall be there at 5 P.M. Divide their perfume among your vases, reminding yourself of the great happiness possessed today by your betrothed, Humberto."[10]

Captivated by a picture of Argentina as a young girl which had been reproduced on some cards, Humberto covered a few of the cards with his reactions. On one card he wrote: "Contained in your simplicity and naturalness are the remembrances of infancy and the symbol of beauty and grace. . . . You lived amidst the majesty of the mountains of Belo Horizonte and the natural bonanza of Minas; I in the native sands, under the scorching blaze of the sun, of Ceará."[11]

8. Marriage (February 6, 1922)

The time that Argentina and Humberto had with each other was limited not only by the strict rules governing the engagement, but also by army assignments that took Humberto from Belo Horizonte. Frequently he had to be in Juiz de Fora. These trips gave him the opportunity to see his sister Lourdinha, whose husband had been transferred there; besides, its proximity to Rio de Janeiro made it possible for Humberto to visit his parents.

Humberto's mother, Antonietta, continued to be ill. However, when Humberto wrote to Argentina from Juiz de Fora to tell her of a trip made to Rio late in May, 1921, he said that his mother's condition was not serious and that they should not be dispirited.[1] Antonietta, writing Argentina in September to thank her for remembering her birthday, mentioned the pain she was in and added that she was praying to God that He grant her the happiness of some day embracing Argentina.[2]

With the approach of the wedding date, February 6, 1922, it became clear that Antonietta could not travel to Belo Horizonte. General Cândido Castello Branco made the trip alone. Reaching the Vianna resi-

10 HACB note on card, November 16, 1921, File C, CPDOC.
11 "Declaração de HACB sôbre o retrato" on four cards, File C, CPDOC.
1 HACB to Argentina, Juiz de Fora, May 23, 1921, File C, CPDOC.
2 Antonietta to Argentina, September 20, 1921, File C, CPDOC.

dence at ten o'clock on the evening of the fifth, he was introduced to Argentina and the other Viannas by Humberto. Humberto observed that this was the first time that he had broken the nine o'clock curfew. "But," he added laughingly, "I promise that it will be the last."[3]

Both the civil and religious ceremonies were carried out in the home of the bride's parents on the evening of February 6. The occasion brought a throng of relatives of the bride to rooms that were decorated with flowers and to a table that was heaped with Minas sweets prepared by Argentina's mother. Humberto, dressed in his gala blue and red uniform, carried his plumed army hat in one hand. For Argentina, in a white bridal gown with a long silk train, he brought a gold ring with one diamond and one pearl.[4]

At the religious ceremony, held before an altar in the parlor, the *padrinhos* (sponsors) were the young couple's parents, Antonietta being represented by a sister of Argentina. Viannas were the *padrinhos* at the civil ceremony, with a single exception: Second Lieutenant Amauri Kruel was one of Humberto's two *padrinhos*, but, as he was serving in Rio Grande do Sul, he was represented by Second Lieutenant Ademar Vilela dos Santos, of the 12th RI.[5]

The bridal couple, seated at the head of the sweets-laden table, heard Francisco Negrão de Lima give the toast.[6] Then, after the traditional drinking of champagne, Humberto and Argentina left. First they went to their new home—a small house, inexpensive to rent, that had been suggested by Negrão de Lima and that was in the Floresta district, far from the main part of Belo Horizonte.[7] Then they completed the week of leave granted by the army by taking the Central do Brasil Railroad to Juiz de Fora and to Rio de Janeiro.[8] The ailing Antonietta at last had the pleasure of embracing Argentina.

After this brief honeymoon, Argentina and Humberto entered happily into their new life. Toné had already married Maria Amália Drumond and was living with her in the Floresta district, and José de Melo Alvarenga quickly followed the example of Toné and Humberto.

[3] Vianna, "Humberto e Argentina."
[4] Ibid.
[5] Letter to Paulo V. Castello Branco, April 3, 1972, File C, CPDOC. See also Vianna, "Humberto e Argentina."
[6] Negrão de Lima interview, December 10, 1975.
[7] Vianna, "Humberto e Argentina." See also Vilela dos Santos, "Depoimento."
[8] "Caderneta de Oficial," File G2, CPDOC, entry for February 7, 1922.

The couples were frequently together, discussing the regiment and how to live on the equivalent of one hundred dollars a month[9]—with Humberto explaining that his father felt that one-quarter of one's pay should go for rent and another quarter for food.[10] The young officers hoped to be promoted to first lieutenants by the time their first children were born.

Argentina accompanied her little second lieutenant, who weighed only fifty kilograms,[11] into the fields during maneuvers of the regiment. A photograph shows her in a long dress, seated in a camp chair beside her uniformed husband, who stands in front of a small tent, sword in hand. This event was before she was far along in the pregnancy that preceded the birth, on November 7, 1922, of the couple's first child, a girl they named Antonietta ("Nieta").

Humberto's mother, after whom the baby was named, had died on September 9, 1922. She was being nursed by Nina and Beatriz at the family house in Rio de Janeiro when Humberto had last seen her on June 29, 1922. It had been so hard to leave that three or four times Humberto had returned from the front door to embrace her again and again.[12]

Humberto particularly remembered 1922 for the sorrow caused by the loss of his mother and for the joy provided by his marriage, by his parenthood, and by the hundredth year of Brazil's independence.[13]

And how did he feel about the unsuccessful uprising of July 5, 1922, by lieutenants who hated Brazil's fraudulent political ways and the insults that they felt the army was suffering at the hands of President Epitácio Pessoa, President-elect Artur Bernardes, and the civilian war minister? It was a brief uprising, a prelude to more serious ones, made by idealistic young officers who could see no peaceful way of bringing "Representation and Justice" to Brazil. Officers at Realengo, including Assistant Instructor Juarez Távora, persuaded cadets to revolt. In the most dramatic episode, First Lieutenants Antônio de Siqueira Campos and Eduardo Gomes, close friends who had completed their artillery

[9] According to Ademar Vilela dos Santos ("Depoimento"), the pay of a second lieutenant was 450 mil-réis a month. This was approximately equal to one hundred U.S. dollars of the 1922 variety.
[10] Vianna, "Humberto e Argentina."
[11] Paulo V. Castello Branco interview, Rio de Janeiro, August 11, 1974. Fifty kilograms is the equivalent of 110 pounds.
[12] Santos Dias and Gonçalves, "Depoimento," File B, CPDOC.
[13] Ibid.

training at Realengo in 1919, led a handful of revolutionaries from Rio's Fort Copacabana. On the sands of Copacabana Beach on July 6, 1922, government forces smashed the "Eighteen of the Fort," severely wounding the two friends and killing, among others, two second lieutenants.

We find Castello Branco being praised by the antirevolutionaries in August, 1922, for his conduct in July. According to the commander of the 12th RI, who could not have found better words to describe Castello's convictions, the young lieutenant "placed above his political sentiments the exact fulfillment of his military duty, refraining from making pronouncements and remaining faithful to order and to the law."[14] The regiment commander was authorized to quote the commander of the Fourth Military Region, General Setembrino de Carvalho, as saying that he could find no words to express the extent of his gratitude.

Despite a reprimand that in mid-July, 1922, had been placed on Castello's record ("complaining about his superior without justification"),[15] Castello was advanced to first lieutenant on November 8, 1922—one day after he became a father.

[14] "Caderneta de Oficial," File G2, Part 2, entry for August, 1922, CPDOC.

[15] "Castigo. 15/VII/1922: foi repreendido como incurso na última parte da n-26 do Art. 421 do RISG (queixou-se de seu superior sem fundamento)." See "Caderneta de Oficial," File G2, Part 2, CPDOC.

Building a Reputation
(1922-1943)

I am happy that our first meeting is here, in the field of instruction. The task of small infantry units is not learned in the lecture room. . . . It is here that we shall work, and work hard, intensely, day after day.

1. A Legalist during Rebellious Times (1924–1925)

AFTER three years of drilling and teaching conscripts in Belo Horizonte,[1] Humberto Castello Branco achieved the first rung for young officers on the long ladder of an army career; he was assigned to take the course at the Escola de Aperfeiçoamento de Oficiais (School for Advanced Training of Officers) at Vila Militar, near Realengo. Therefore, late in February, 1924, he moved to Rio with Argentina, Nieta, and one of Argentina's sisters, who wanted to get to know the *cidade maravilhosa*. They filled the home of General Cândido, who was living with Nina and Beatriz. For Humberto the new routine in Rio began at 4:00 A.M. each day when he arose in order to make the twenty-four-kilometer streetcar and train trip that would bring him to the school before 6:00 A.M.[2]

Suddenly, in July, 1924, this routine and the *aperfeiçoamento* course —and also the normal functioning of the government—were interrupted by the startling news that military rebels of 1922, with new adherents, had gained control of the city of São Paulo. The authorities in Rio made wholesale arrests of the many suspected of sympathizing with

[1] Praise for HACB's work at this time is given in "Caderneta de Oficial," File G2, Part 2, items for June 19, 28, 1923, CPDOC. Ademar Vilela do Santos in his "Depoimento: Humberto de Alencar Castello Branco no 12º RI," Rio de Janeiro, March, 1974 (File G1, CPDOC), mentions the enthusiasm brought by the junior officers to a regiment that already had a high esprit de corps.

[2] Maria de Lourdes Vianna, "Humberto e Argentina" (typewritten), Belo Horizonte, September 14, 1974.

the new revolt. A state of siege was enacted, and the Rio jails were filled with military men, politicians, writers, labor leaders, and workers.

Castello Branco, founder of the República Liberal, understood the discontent with fraudulent political practices that induced some of his Realengo schoolmates, such as Juarez Távora and Riograndino Kruel, to rebel. But he placed discipline and allegiance to the Constitution at the very peak of military merits and argued that no circumstances could justify a revolt by military men. His conduct during the brief 1922 uprising represented a basic principle and a personal philosophy that he was stubbornly determined to follow as long as he was in the army. As a result, rebels of the 1920's said that he was both a legalist and a reactionary, and they pictured him as desiring to curry favor with those who headed the army hierarchy.[3]

Castello Branco's conduct in 1922 was ignored by an administration desperate to defend itself. On orders of the war minister, Castello reported on July 20, 1924, to the command of the First Military Region,[4] which put him under arrest for his political views. Argentina, pregnant again, sent him affectionate letters that could hardly have interested the censors who read her prim handwriting. Her letter of September 18, addressed to the prisoner when he was aboard the naval vessel *Cuyabá*, contained birthday wishes for the twentieth, but the censorship prevented it from reaching her husband on time.[5]

Castello was placed in liberty on September 22, long after the rebels had fled from São Paulo and gone westward to the Paraná River. Thus he was able to resume his course and graduate in his class of about fifty infantry officers in December, 1924. With an overall grade of 8.074 (and with an "aptitude for commanding" set at 9.5), Castello was second in his class, only being excelled by Lieutenant Henrique Batista Duffles Teixeira Lott, who had instructed him at Realengo. The examiners recommended that Castello, "modest and very hardworking," be granted the teaching assignment he wanted at Realengo and be admitted to the Escola de Estado Maior (Army Staff School) as soon as his age would allow.[6]

[3] Emygdio da Costa Miranda interview, Rio de Janeiro, December 1, 1975.

[4] "Caderneta de Oficial," File G2, Part 2, items for July–September, 1924, CPDOC.

[5] Argentina to HACB, September 18, 1924, File C, CPDOC.

[6] Henrique Batista Duffles Teixeira Lott interview, Rio de Janeiro, October 13, 1975. Castello's grade is given in "Caderneta de Oficial," File G2, Part 2, entry for December 16, 1924, CPDOC. According to Joffre Gomes da Costa, *Marechal Henrique*

Argentina had gone to her parents' country house in Belo Horizonte for the birth of her second child, Paulo Vianna Castello Branco. Humberto, joining his enlarged family when his course ended before Christmas, was so delighted at being a father again—this time of a boy—that he was restrained in his remarks about the short hair that he found Argentina wearing.[7]

The Christmas reunion was brief. With the federal administration sending all the troops it could muster against the two thousand rebels in the west of Paraná state, Castello was packed off by train late in December, 1924, to join the 12th RI, which was in campaign near the Paraná River.

In the course of several months, Castello commanded a company, a battalion, and, for a while, the entire regiment while the 12th RI executed its mission of blocking the rebels' path to the north. After that, the campaign became one of movement, because about eight hundred Paulista rebels, joined by an equal number from Rio Grande do Sul under former Army Captain Luís Carlos Prestes, marched through Paraguay and reemerged in the woods and prairies of Mato Grosso.[8] The dramatic Long March of the so-called Prestes Column of revolutionaries through the Brazilian interior had begun. Until the column turned to the north of Brazil late in 1925, the 12th RI participated in the unsuccessful army action against it.

Castello received a taste of reconnaissance work in Mato Grosso before it was reported, in August, 1925, that the elusive Prestes Column was in the São Francisco Valley in Minas or Bahia. Placed in charge of a heavy machine gun company, he took the Central do Brasil Railroad to its most northerly station and then accompanied his men on a river steamship trip into Bahia.[9] Seeking first to cut off a deeper penetration of the enemy into Bahia and then to reinforce a town that was felt to be threatened, Castello helped lead a battalion of the 12th RI on marches

---

Lott, p. 121, twenty-nine final grades were given, with Lott (in first place) receiving a grade of 8.587 and Castello Branco (in second place) 8.179; the lowest grade was 5.272.

[7] Vianna, "Humberto e Argentina." Paulo Vianna Castello Branco was born in Belo Horizonte on December 16, 1924.

[8] "Caderneta de Oficial," File G2, Part 2, items for January–March, 1925, CPDOC; Neill Macaulay, *The Prestes Column: Revolution in Brazil*, p. 95.

[9] "Caderneta de Oficial," File G2, Part 2, items for August–November, 1925, CPDOC.

that lasted for thirty days. The marching was usually done between 5:00 A.M. and 9:15 A.M. and covered between three and five leagues a day.

In November, 1925, when reports made it clear that the Prestes Column was approaching the north of Brazil and was far from Bahia, the battalion of the 12th RI was ordered to return to Belo Horizonte by boat and rail. Castello's official record was embellished by a notation of seven months of campaigning and by praise for his conduct that mentioned the "difficult march."[10]

One of the stories that has been told of Castello's participation in the campaign against the Prestes Column concerns an evening of festivities by soldiers, the observation of a historical date, in a town in the interior. A government general ordered the orchestra to stop playing and made an announcement. "We have," he said, "danced a great deal, and so now let us turn to culture. Lieutenant Castello Branco, who is good at reciting literature, will open the session." Castello, according to the story, took a place in the center of the group and recited two poems of Olavo Bilac, for which he received much applause. Others familiar with verse followed his example.[11]

Another incident involving Castello in the campaign against the Prestes Column occurred in Santa Maria da Vitória, Bahia. Having received orders to take his men, together with a battalion of the Bahia State Police, to the town of Barreira, Castello had his force ready to march at 5:00 A.M. But some members of the state troop did not want it to participate in the operation, and so Castello received word that he should go with his army men to the square by the church, where the soldiers of the police had congregated. After Castello and his unit arrived there, the commander of the Bahia police battalion told him that the presence of the federals was necessary to help deal with the lack of discipline. Then the police commander asked the leader of the revolt to identify himself. A large police sergeant, the chief instigator of the rebellion in the force, stepped forward and was seconded by another man. The state battalion commander shot them both dead and in this way restored discipline to his troop. (In recalling the incident, Castello Branco explained that it was the only time that he ever witnessed the use of such an extreme measure for the purpose of upholding discipline

---

10 Ibid.

11 Joaquim Gilberto, "Duas Épocas," *Jornal de Luziânia* [Goiás], May 30, 1977.

in a troop. "Discipline," he added, "is maintained by education in the barracks. Authority is not something to be imposed, but is something that we earn by our example of fulfilling our duty.")[12]

2. Assistant Instructor at Realengo (1927–1929)

Professionally, the little lieutenant found himself in his element as never before in March, 1927, when he became an assistant infantry instructor at the Escola Militar in Realengo. Soon he was something of a legend in army circles.

At the outset, fifty third-year cadets heard their newly arrived assistant instructor, in a voice that was self-assured but not overbearing, order them into full battle gear. They were shocked, for it had become a tradition to restrict to the first- and second-year cadets the more disagreeable training with rucksacks and heavy equipment. Resentfully the members of Castello Branco's platoon brought out the mules and loaded them and themselves with light and heavy machine guns, munition chests, and sacks—all according to the manual. Throughout this operation each cadet felt the scrutinizing eye of the assistant instructor. Then Castello ordered a march, and when it got under way the cadets were sweating under the weight of the equipment and were "fuming with rage." Nor was this just an opening-day exercise. Time and again throughout the school year these men who were soon to be officers found themselves carrying equipment on their backs and loading and unloading the mules just as though they were soldiers in a real military campaign.[1]

Castello's appearance as well as his toughness inspired comments. To such descriptions as "ugly and twisted" and "the lieutenant without any neck," infantry cadet Agildo Barata, recalling the hunchback of Notre Dame, added a nickname that caught on pretty well: "Quasimodo."[2]

Cadets like João Adyl de Oliveira counted themselves fortunate not to be in Castello's platoon. But those who had fumed with rage—among them Sizeno Sarmento, Luís Tavares da Cunha Melo, and Luís Mendes

[12] HACB quoted in congressional speech by Theódulo de Albuquerque (typewritten manuscript), undated (probably 1967), p. 3.

[1] Luís Mendes da Silva, "Testemunho" (typewritten), Part 1, "Castello Branco, Tenente Instructor."

[2] João Adyl de Oliveira interview, Rio de Janeiro, October 18, 1975.

da Silva—came at least to respect the firm traits of the assistant instructor. He was a hard worker himself, determined to implant a solid foundation of infantry training. As they had learned all too well, he had no compunction about breaking with tradition if by so doing he felt that he could be effective in eliminating soft spots in the routine at the school. Above all, he was eager to develop the maximum potential of each cadet.

The cadets may not have had much fondness for him, but they gave him their support when, in the middle of his first year, he found himself in a clash with a new Escola Militar commander whose bellicose ways with cadets seemed to Castello to be unnecessary and unproductive. The new assistant instructor, in the opinion of one of his cadets, was successful in the case of his dispute "although he did not use extreme measures. . . . He did not lead the cadets in an uprising. He never criticized the Command. But neither did he join up with it." [3]

Castello had moved with his family from Belo Horizonte in March, 1927, into Vila Militar barracks near the Escola Militar. Later in the year he rented a small house in the Andaraí district, in the far north section of Rio, beyond Tijuca, and this change of residence meant a return to beginning his days long before sunrise in order to reach Realengo by 6:00 A.M. Despite the modest district, Argentina wrote happily to her younger brother Hélio to say that with the change "our status has risen." [4]

In another letter to Hélio, Argentina wrote that her husband devoted his leisure hours to reading the Viscount of Taunay, Rui Barbosa, Chateaubriand, Joaquim Nabuco, "and other serious and classic writers." [5] This was no surprise to Hélio Vianna; while in Belo Horizonte the unusual lieutenant had spent much time stimulating the boy's interest in literature, and he had loaned him books by Rui Barbosa and the poet Olavo Bilac as well as many tomes by Taunay. [6] At the end of 1927, when Hélio Vianna came to live in Rio to study law and gain some commercial experience, Humberto continued to discuss literature with him.

[3] Mendes da Silva, "Testemunho," Part 1, "Castello Branco, Tenente Instructor."
[4] Argentina to Hélio Vianna, November 8, 1927, File D, CPDOC.
[5] Argentina to Hélio, September 7, 1927, File D, CPDOC.
[6] Hélio Vianna, "Humberto," *Jornal do Commercio*, July 18, 1968 (in File HP4, CPDOC).

Early in 1929, after Castello Branco had been promoted to captain, he was accepted at the Escola de Estado Maior (Army Staff School). The commander of the Escola Militar recorded the intelligence, drive, and high professional competence of the departing assistant instructor and predicted that he would be "a superb captain and superior officer."[7]

3. Attending the Escola de Estado Maior (1929–1931)

So large was the Vianna tract of land outside of Belo Horizonte that Arthur Vianna gave a parcel of it to each of his twelve children. On the lot that went to Argentina, Humberto, with help from his father-in-law, built a cottage, and there, during the heat in Rio's Andaraí district in the first months of each year, Argentina and her two children spent summer vacations. Humberto, his daughter Nieta recalls, "would arrive later when his work permitted."[1]

Captain Castello Branco's work for three years consisted of studies at the Escola de Estado Maior (EEM). This was serious business; if Castello's outstanding grades at the Escola de Aperfeiçoamento had gained him admittance to the EEM course at this relatively early age, now his showing at the EEM itself, the most advanced school for army officers in Brazil, would hold the key to his future. The teaching, supervised by a French colonel, was carried out by officers of the French Military Mission, assisted by Brazilian officers.

An early assignment required the officer-students to train in military pursuits unfamiliar to them. Therefore in 1929 Castello attended the Escola de Aviação Militar (School of Military Aviation), where the instruction was directed by a French air force officer and where the training planes were so worn out that students marveled at their own survival.[2]

Following a vacation in Belo Horizonte in 1930, Castello went to attend lectures at the EEM, a vast white building of two stories on Barão

7 "Caderneta de Oficial," File G2, Part 2, entry for February 14, 1929, CPDOC.

1 Maria de Lourdes Vianna, "Humberto e Argentina"; Antonietta Castello Branco Diniz quoted in "Castello Branco, Meu Pai," *Manchete*, March, 1973, pp. 44, 46. See File HP7, p. 8, CPDOC.

2 João de Deus Pessoa Leal, "Minhas Recordações de Humberto de Alencar Castello Branco," Rio de Janeiro, July 13, 1974, File G1, CPDOC.

de Mesquita Street.[3] To work on the written assignments, the students formed small groups that generally included officers whose specialties differed, this being helpful for the study of general tactics. Castello was the sole infantary officer in his group of six, the others being artillery and cavalry officers.

Meeting regularly at the home of one or another member of the group during two years, the group members and their families became close friends.[4] Humberto's group voluntarily took to turning out lecture notes that were typed by a sergeant, checked by the professors, and then mimeographed for the benefit of the whole class. Argentina, becoming well known for her devotion to her husband, would help cut up paper for maps (with the five-year-old Paulo using the discarded paper to make kites).

During October, 1930, it became necessary to suspend classes and assign the officer-students to active army units when a revolution broke out against the presidential administration of Washington Luís Pereira de Souza. It was a carefully planned revolution in which young army officers who had rebelled in the 1920's were allied with important political forces. The 1930 revolutionaries favored the Aliança Liberal, whose candidate for president, Rio Grande do Sul Governor Getúlio Vargas, had been officially declared the loser in the recent elections. They enjoyed the considerable popular support that was given to the liberal program of the Aliança Liberal, and they were no doubt assisted by the general discontent caused by the economic depression.

In Vargas' home state, where the Aliança Liberal conspirators had placed Major Pedro Aurélio de Góis Monteiro in charge of the military uprising, the revolution was quickly victorious. In the north and northeast it was led by Juarez Távora, and there its success, following some tough fighting in Recife, was as spectacular as in the south. In Minas, where the overthrow of Washington Luís was favored by many politicians, the 12th RI in Belo Horizonte sought to defend the federal administration, but after a four-day struggle the regiment had to surrender to units of civilians and the state police.

[3] Today the building is used by the Batalhão de Polícia do Exército. See Leal, "Minhas Recordações."

[4] João Punaro Bley, "Depoimento do companheiro Gral. João Punaro Bley," Rio de Janeiro, July 25, 1974, File G1, p. 27B, CPDOC. See also Leal, "Minhas Recordações."

While Aliança Liberal revolutionaries moved toward the federal capital from the south and northeast, the administration of Washington Luís issued unfounded announcements about federal victories. However, the steps that it took, such as calling all civilian reservists to serve in the army, bespoke of trouble.

Castello Branco, who opposed the 1930 revolution, was assigned on October 13 to help train reservists in the federal capital, but few reservists heeded the government's call. On October 17 Castello was transferred to Juiz de Fora to serve with the 10th RI.[5]

The fall of Washington Luís on October 24 occurred before Castello saw any military action with the 10th RI. Getúlio Vargas entered Rio de Janeiro amidst a frenzied acclaim. Early in November the Constitution of 1891 was set aside, the Congress was closed, and Vargas became chief of the Provisional Government of Brazil, with legislative as well as executive powers.

At the EEM classes were resumed, but it was decided that the month of intranquility warranted suspension of the customary year-end examinations. Castello, who had prepared himself well, was not agreeable to the waiving of the examinations in his case, and he succeeded in having them given to him.[6]

Back in Rio in March, 1931, after another holiday in Belo Horizonte, Castello started his third year at the EEM. As in the previous year, the students made a field trip for the study of maneuvers. The trip in 1931 was to an area outside of Belo Horizonte. There, on iron-rich soil, the young officers and their professors, a group of about thirty-five, might be seen studying papers and maps.

When the final examinations were held in December, 1931, Castello achieved first place—the only one whose performance was classified as *très bien*. Argentina, present without the children at the graduation exercises at which the results were announced, looked especially radiant. Cândido Castello Branco, also present, embarrassed Humberto; the seventy-one-year-old retired general shouted in excitement: "Someday my son will be another Góis Monteiro; someday my son will be the minister of war."[7]

[5] "Caderneta de Oficial," File G2, Part 2, and "Folhas de Alterações," File G2, Part 3, items for October, 1930, CPDOC.

[6] Leal, "Minhas Recordações."

[7] Antonietta Castello Branco Diniz and Paulo V. Castello Branco interview, Rio

The correctness of Cândido's prophecy about the War Ministry post would depend somewhat on politics, which Humberto felt had no place in the military.[8] But whether or not the prophecy would be fulfilled, Humberto had secured with the *très bien* a place for himself among the elite of the Brazilian army.

4. "Colonel Y" (late 1933)

Early in 1932 Humberto Castello Branco became assistant to the director of military studies at the Escola Militar in Realengo. He added to his reputation of being tough on cadets and himself and was respected for "exceptional intelligence"—for his *crânio*, as it was put in the army.[1]

He was handling his Realengo assignment in July, 1932, when a rebellion broke out in São Paulo, this one against President Getúlio Vargas. Although Castello Branco was no Vargas admirer, he remained faithful, during the unsuccessful three-month uprising, to his contention that military uprisings were never to be supported. The commander of the Escola Militar praised the captain "for the example he gave . . . of subordination to the legal authorities, strengthening the conviction that his decisive backing could be counted on at the opportune moment, if that were necessary."[2]

Castello, who detested dictatorships, welcomed the liberal atmosphere that prevailed in Brazil following the collapse of the São Paulo revolt in September, 1932. New political parties sprang up to participate in the May, 1933, elections for a constitutional assembly, and discussions were widely held, before and after the elections, about what the new, reconstitutionalized Brazil should be like.

Humberto and Argentina heard much about this subject when they

de Janeiro, December 13, 1975; Ana (Nina) Castello Branco Santos Dias and Beatriz Castello Branco Gonçalves, "Depoimento sôbre o irmão Humberto de Alencar Castello Branco," 1973, File B, CPDOC.

[8] See biographical notes about HACB reviewed and revised by HACB, File G1, p. 47, CPDOC.

[1] Renato Moniz de Aragão interview, Rio de Janeiro, November 22, 1975; Carlos de Meira Mattos interview, Washington, D.C., January 5, 1976.

[2] "Caderneta de Oficial," File G2, Part 2, and "Folhas de Alterações," File G2, Part 3, item for November 30, 1932, CPDOC.

dropped in at the Rio home of Hélio Vianna. Hélio, who had turned to newspaper work, frequently entertained intellectuals, and with them Humberto liked to discuss political matters, literature, and European affairs.[3] He found that Hélio and some of his friends—among them Francisco San Tiago Dantas, Thiers Martins Moreira, and Américo Lacombe —were attracted to the ideas of Paulista writer Plínio Salgado, founder in 1932 of Ação Integralista Brasiliera, a nationalistic political party that denounced Communism and preached devotion to "God, Country, and Family."

Castello, proud of being a democrat, disputed the ideas of the Integralistas, who sought a single political party for Brazil—their own. And he poked fun at their behavior: they paraded in green shirts and made use of trappings and salutes akin to those of the European fascist movements. But Castello was devoted to his intellectual brother-in-law, and he supplied some of his deep-rooted ideas about the military for the articles that Hélio wrote for *A Nação* in 1933.[4]

Feeling that these ideas were vital to the army and national defense, Castello himself presented them to the public in articles that he published in a short-lived daily, the *Gazeta do Rio*, after the constitutional assembly began meeting late in 1933. Signing the articles "Coronel Y," Castello explained to his readers that it was up to the army to help the constitutional assemblymen study military matters and national defense. In one of his ten articles, Colonel Y criticized prestigious General Góis Monteiro for lacking the courage to speak out on these matters in a Clube Militar speech in December, 1933.[5]

Colonel Y was especially disappointed in the positions taken by the dozen-odd military officers who had been elected to the Constitutional Assembly. He found them discussing "agrarian battalions" and "battalions of engineers and workers" and introducing amendments to allow "political regimentation" of the military and to assure military promotions for officers whose political duties allowed them no time for taking advanced military courses. Colonel Y pointed out that such ideas revealed ignorance of the army and national defense: "From all of this it is to be concluded that the military man absolutely does not, in politics, rep-

[3] Américo Lacombe interview, Rio de Janeiro, November 3, 1975.

[4] Ibid.; Hélio Vianna, "Humberto."

[5] HACB ["Coronel Y"], "Os Politicos e o Exército," *Gazeta do Rio*, November 24, 1933, and "O Almoço do Dia 12," *Gazeta do Rio*, December 17, 1933.

resent the armed classes. Experience has demonstrated that, as a rule, the officer who dedicates himself to other activities is a mediocre professional, little devoted to military duty and forgetting almost always the vital problems of his class." [6]

Colonel Y argued that promotions in the army for time spent in political activities were prejudicial to those who dedicated themselves to instruction and discipline—to those who "remain working in the Army and for the Army." The army promotion policy advocated by the military assembly members was, in Colonel Y's opinion, "almost destitution for the true professional, disparagement of his honesty, and discouragement for those who are dedicated to the anonymous work of the troop, the schools, and the staffs." [7]

This "anonymous work" was praised in an article in which Colonel Y cited the recent year-end field maneuvers by students at military schools. The anonymous officer was pictured as working stoically for the army's permanent existence above politics, despite being sometimes forgotten by leaders and despite the threat of the "many police armies." [8]

These "police armies" of the states, subordinated to the governors, seemed to be the pets of politicians, some of whom, Colonel Y found, would put them on a par with the regular army. At the same time, Colonel Y found that an army captain, elected to the Constitutional Assembly from Pernambuco, was proposing that the regular army carry out police work in the backlands—"a negation of the principal objective of the army." [9]

The views enunciated by Colonel Y were strongly held by Castello Branco, and he did not deviate from them during his lifetime. The feeling, for example, that military men should not become involved in politics, nor interrupt their careers by assuming civilian positions, continued to be almost an obsession with him.[10] But it was a practice common in the 1930's. Many of Castello Branco's colleagues spent a large part of

[6] HACB ["Coronel Y"], "A Defesa Nacional e as 'Novidades,'" *Gazeta do Rio*, December 13, 1933, and "A Defesa Nacional na Constituinte," *Gazeta do Rio*, December 8, 1933.

[7] HACB ["Coronel Y"], "O Militar Político," *Gazeta do Rio*, November 28, 1933.

[8] HACB ["Coronel Y"], "O Trabalho Anonymo do Exército," *Gazeta do Rio*, December 1, 1933.

[9] HACB ["Coronel Y"], "A Defesa Nacional e as 'Novidades.'"

[10] Paulo V. Castello Branco memorandum, July, 1976.

their careers from the 1930's to the 1960's in civilian clothes, enjoying the prestige and better pay that went with the nonmilitary positions.

5. Curitiba (1935–1936)

Castello Branco, who had praised in one of his articles the recent renewal of Brazil's contract with the French Military Mission,[1] became an adviser to a French colonel concerned with Brazilian military education. He served in this Army Staff post from March, 1934, until March, 1935. Thus he was in Rio when his father, General Cândido, died there on April 25, 1934, at the age of seventy-four.

In March, 1935, an entirely new chapter began in Castello's life. He was named subcomandante of the Fifteenth Batalhão de Caçadores (15th BC) in Curitiba, Paraná. As the battalion commander left his work up to Captain Castello Branco and was sometimes absent (giving the captain the title of acting commander), the battalion was Castello's to revitalize. And if the effect of Castello's personality on the Escola Militar cadets had been considerable, the effect on the Curitiba battalion was extreme.

Captain Luís Mendes da Silva, who had been one of Castello's 1927 cadets, was already in Curitiba. So depressed had he become by the inertia, apathy, "irregular discipline," and inadequate physical installations which he had found there that he had become morose and withdrawn. He had aspired to something vastly different, and he considered that he had been duped by the army.[2]

Upon learning that Castello was coming to give commands, Mendes da Silva expected some improvement. So did other young officers who were familiar with Castello's reputation and who were awaiting leadership. But what they witnessed was no mere improvement; rather, it was a complete transformation beyond their expectations, carried out according to an overall plan that their senior captain developed soon after reaching Curitiba.

According to João Adyl de Oliveira (who was in the army air force

[1] HACB ["Coronel Y"], "Missão Militar Franceza," *Gazeta do Rio*, December 6, 1933.

[2] Mendes da Silva, "Testemunho," Part 2, "Capitão Humberto de Alencar Castello Branco, na Tropa."

regiment in Curitiba), "people never saw such action. Castello Branco moved lots of people around; he even moved the kitchen!"[3] Luís Mendes da Silva reports that the use of the installations was drastically rearranged, and the areas for instruction were enlarged; the instruction itself, formerly lackadaisical, became dynamic. Castello, determined to develop the full capacity of every officer of the 15th BC, and of the battalion as whole, spent hours each day with the company commanders and lieutenants while they were with their troops in the field. Some officers were pleased, but most of them were not.[4]

In November, 1935, when Castello received information about the Communist uprisings in Natal, Recife, and Rio de Janeiro, he called in two 15th BC officers known to favor Communism. "In Rio de Janeiro," he told them, "an officer with Communist ideas killed a sleeping colleague who did not share his ideas. I am advising you that here you people will not be the first ones to do the shooting." One of his listeners declared vehemently that he was not a Communist; the other asked to be transferred from Curitiba.[5]

Curitiba was regarded as "an army garrison town," and it made the army officers and their families welcome.[6] With the Imbassahys, Humberto de Melos, and Adyl de Oliveiras, the Castello Brancos lived in a boarding house owned by a Belgian woman, and there Castello helped João Adyl prepare for an examination for admittance to the Escola de Estado Maior.

Argentina, writing to Hélio Vianna soon after she and her family had become settled, said that "we are pleased with Curitiba." The boarding house, she wrote, was considered the best in the town, and while it was nothing fancy, it had a more pleasant atmosphere than was to be found in the typical Rio boarding house. She went on: "I am taking the opportunity of practicing my French with a woman who lives in this house and who understands no Portuguese."[7]

Argentina congratulated Hélio on the sale of his book, *Formação Brasileira.* And she dwelt on a matter of deep concern to her and Humberto, that of securing the best possible education for their children:

[3] Adyl de Oliveira interview, October 18, 1975.
[4] Mendes da Silva, "Testemunho," Part 2, "Capitão Humberto de Alencar Castello Branco, na Tropa."
[5] Hélio Vianna, "Humberto."
[6] Adyl de Oliveira interview, October 18, 1975.
[7] Argentina to Hélio Vianna, May 28, 1935, File D, CPDOC.

"Antonietta obtained an average of 92 in the examination for admittance to the Colégio Cajurú, run by French nuns. Paulo is taking his course in the School of the Marista Brotherhood."

When Humberto wrote to Hélio Vianna he commented on the Integralista movement that had already attracted Hélio and some of his friends in Rio. "Integralismo in Curitiba," Humberto told his brother-in-law, "is, without doubt, a widely spread idea and is partially victorious. The adherents put on the green shirt without 'human respect.'" Humberto explained that Gustavo Barroso, one of the Integralista leaders, had been in Curitiba. "He enjoyed much success, and it can be said that for almost a week this subject had priority in all conversations here. I attended his three lectures." [8]

At the end of the one year that the family spent in Curitiba, Captain Castello Branco supervised maneuvers of the battalion that reflected months of careful preparation. "The battalion," Mendes da Silva has written, "regained the brilliance that it had had in years past and became one of the elite units of the army." [9]

6. Discovering Paris (1936–1938)

In March, 1936, Humberto was transferred to Rio to teach at the Escola de Estado Maior (EEM). Argentina wrote to Hélio that their new house was like the one they had rented before going to Curitiba: "The only difference is that the rent was formerly 400$000 and now it is 530$000. The worst is that in one year everything has increased in the same proportion." [1]

Again she touched on the education of the children. As she and Humberto had established a budget priority that would allow them to send Nieta and Paulo to schools that were among the best and most expensive in Rio, she wrote her brother that "the children have been studying since March 16, Antonietta in the second year of the Instituto Jacobina and Paulo in the first year at Santo Ignacio. Both are enthusiastic

[8] HACB to Hélio Vianna, Curitiba, October 6, 1935.

[9] Mendes da Silva, "Testemunho," Part 2, "Capitão Humberto de Alencar Castello Branco, na Tropa."

[1] Argentina to Hélio Vianna, Rio de Janeiro, March 19, 1936, File D, CPDOC. The Castello Branco's new home was in Botafogo, a better part of Rio than the section where they had lived before going to Curitiba.

with their new schools." (The budget, however, would not stretch far enough to allow Nieta and Paulo to have bicycles, as their colleagues did.)

Humberto hoped that this new stay in Rio would be a short one. Since it had been the army's custom to offer study abroad to those who had graduated in first place with *très bien* at the EEM, Humberto applied for an assignment that would allow him to study for two years at the Ecole Supérieure de Guerre in Paris.

The application was supported by a memorandum from Major Floriano de Lima Brayner, of the war minister's office. Major Brayner argued for the need of a continuing relationship with French military teaching. "It is," he wrote, "ridiculous to consider a few hundred thousand réis such a palpitating problem when the civilian ministries furnish pompous and innocuous commissions to . . . pseudocongresses at which the name of Brazil is not even mentioned. Men and women, some even using the *Graf Zeppelin*, have recently been sent as representatives to Turkey, Czechoslovakia, Poland, Geneva, etc. . . . The training ship *Almirante Saldanha* leaves for a long cruise of instruction in Europe, taking more than one hundred navy officers." [2]

The War Ministry approved Major Brayner's conclusion, and in Paris the Ecole Supérieure de Guerre found a place for the Brazilian captain. Therefore in October, 1936, the Castello Brancos embarked on their new adventure aboard the English liner *Arlanza*. Traveling by first class, Humberto, Argentina, thirteen-year-old Nieta, and eleven-year-old Paulo were accompanied by Tomázia, the maid. (It sometimes amused the Castello Brancos to see the ugly, young, and small colored girl being served aboard ship by a handsome, blond British waiter.)

The ocean trip was pleasant, the chief drawback being that the stops at ports almost always occurred at night.[3] In Salvador, Bahia, the Castello Brancos were taken on an automobile ride between 2:00 A.M. and 4:30 A.M. by the secretary of Army Captain Juraci Magalhães, who had been elected governor of Bahia.

During the ocean crossing, which followed a stop of only forty-five

[2] Floriano de Lima Brayner, Documento Interno, Gabinete do Ministro da Guerra, Rio de Janeiro, approved May 15, 1936, File G1, CPDOC.

[3] The ocean voyage is described in Argentina to Hélio Vianna, Paris, November 7, 1936. Reminiscences of the voyage are mentioned in Paulo V. Castello Branco memoranda to JWFD, 1975 and July, 1976.

minutes in Recife, the *Arlanza* was passed one night by the *Graf Zeppelin*, making its regular flight to Brazil. Long would the Castello Branco children remember the effects of the bright searchlights of the airship, turned on the *Arlanza*. Nor would they forget the night of November 3, 1936, when the family reached its destination, moving into an apartment at 55, avenue de Suffren.

The building in which the Castello Brancos settled was one commonly used by Brazilian army officers and their families. In 1934 its apartments had served as the residences of members of a Brazilian Army Equipment Purchasing Commission: Major Canrobert Pereira da Costa and Captains Ademar de Queiroz and Frederico Buiz. Late in 1935 Artillery Captain Hugo Panasco Alvim had moved in to take the Ecole Supérieure de Guerre course, and he was still there, about to enter his second year, when the Castello Brancos arrived. Artillery Major Nestor Penha Brasil, starting his first year at the school, took up residence with his family in the building at the same time as the Castello Brancos.

In Paris, Humberto and Argentina were enchanted with bookstores, Humberto becoming well acquainted with every important one in the city. They got to know the historic churches by attending service in a different one each Sunday.

Sundays were also for visits to the museums, with the children protesting that they would prefer to go to the movies. Before the family visited the museums outside of Paris, Argentina received briefings from a tutor she engaged to improve her already good French. Then at the palaces of Versailles and Fontainebleau, Humberto proudly let Argentina serve as his guide.[4] "Last Sunday," Humberto wrote to Hélio Vianna, "I went to Fontainebleau. What emotion! I saw things I knew intimately through books. How beautiful is the 'Cour des Adieus'—the patio in which Napoleon said farewell to the guard." In the same letter Humberto wrote: "Argentina already knows Paris. She gets around as though she were in Rio. Subway and bus. The children have not yet been able to take advantage of much, because so far their studies have not allowed them to visit many places."[5]

In Paris, as in Brazil, Argentina helped her children with their

---

[4] Reminiscences about Paris were kindly provided by Antonietta Castello Branco Diniz (Diniz and Castello Branco interview, December 13, 1975) and by Paulo V. Castello Branco (interviews, Rio de Janeiro, 1974 and 1975).

[5] HACB to Hélio Vianna, Paris, undated, File E, CPDOC.

homework, and she and Humberto followed closely the grades they received at school. For the children, discipline and a certain amount of formality (especially where Argentina was concerned) had become part of a family life that was unusually close. Nieta and Paulo were proud of their mother's beauty. And their father, Nieta felt, had nice, wavy, black hair, eyes that could speak, and attractive, big hands that gave a message.[6]

For each parent the other parent came first in life, and, on evenings when he could, Humberto delighted in taking Argentina out. They were still in their thirties, Argentina was at the peak of her beauty,[7] and Humberto, for the first time in his life, received a more than adequate income from the army: the pay to Brazilian officers attending schools abroad was several times the pay they received in Brazil.

Humberto took Argentina to restaurants, and there they partook moderately of wine, which was not then expensive in France.[8] Particularly, Humberto enjoyed the theater and all types of music—light and classical music and choral singing. He and Argentina liked to go to the opera and the serious theater at the Comédie Française.

Sometimes the couple went dancing, and not infrequently Humberto and Argentina attended the Casino de Paris to hear Maurice Chevalier, who on one occasion expressed from the stage a delicate compliment on Argentina's beauty. At the Folies Bergère they saw Josephine Baker appear dramatically on stage in the nude. They hummed the sentiment, expressed in a popular song: "I have two loves, my country and Paris."

In drinking up so much culture and *l'esprit français* the couple gained an experience unusual for a Brazilian troop commander and his wife. Argentina wrote happy letters to the Viannas about her life in Paris, and in turn she was kept posted on happenings at home.

Letters told of Hélio Vianna and his wife, Edith, becoming parents, and of some opposition among Argentina's brothers and sisters to the plans of their father, Arthur, now a widower, to remarry. He should, one of his sons suggested to him, undergo a physical examination.[9]

Castello Branco followed with keen interest the political events that were occurring in Europe and in his own country. News about Brazil he

[6] Diniz, in Diniz and Castello Branco interview, December 13, 1975.
[7] Ibid.
[8] Castello Branco memorandum, July, 1976.
[9] Hélio Vianna to Argentina, Rio de Janeiro, December 3, 1936, File D, CPDOC.

collected at the Brazilian embassy in Paris and from the newspapers and magazines that reached him from Rio. Also helpful in keeping him posted on Brazil's agitated situation were the letters from friends in Brazil. In one of these, dated January 5, 1937, Toné wrote from Rio:

> Everything is politics: *política paulista, política mineira ou gaúcha*, politics of coffee, of sports, of the army. Integralista politics. Governor Armando de Sales resigned with the declaration that he was doing so in order that Brazil might continue! Flores da Cunha, *caudilho* of the XXI Century, prepares his *provisórios*. . . . Gêgê [Getúlio Vargas] undefined, provisorily. . . . Big changes in the War Ministry: João Gomes left and in came Dutra—that quiet one. The rumor is that Gomes left because he is not political. But then why did Dutra come in? Well, that is clear: because he is not political! Politics is that way, Gêgê concludes smiling. . . .[10]

Toné added: "Your absence is felt, believe me, principally in the daily confabs where we miss the acute wit of your shrewd remarks and the mirth of your ironic touch. Pity the devil if he wants to be your enemy!"

7. Discovering Europe (1937)

It was summer in Paris, 1937—the year of the World Exposition there. All was going well for Castello Branco. He had just completed his first year at the Ecole Supérieure de Guerre and had received a high rating. In the opinion of the command of the school, the Brazilian captain was very serious and intelligent and had a solid knowledge of military matters, including tactics. "In the discussions he revealed a firm personality without departing from the most perfect behavior. He is certainly a valuable officer."[1]

Having the income to make a tour of Europe—an opportunity that few Brazilians could then afford—Castello bought a small four-door

[10] Antônio José Coelho dos Reis to HACB, Rio de Janeiro, January 1, 1937, File E, CPDOC. *Provisórios* were men of a "provisional" fighting force being maintained by José Antônio Flores da Cunha, governor of Rio Grande do Sul.

[1] The school's *conceito* (1937), signed by Colonel Toussaint, second in command, is in File G1, CPDOC. It reads as follows: "Officier très sérieux, très cultivé, ayant une intelligence très fine, beaucoup de méthode de jugement. S'est très bien adapté à l'enseignement de l'Ecole. Ayant de solides connaissances militaires et un sens tactique très sûr, il a obtenu d'excellents résultats se classant au niveau des bons officiers de sa

Fiat and took some driving lessons in Paris. As his family soon found out, he was a better student of military tactics than of handling automobiles. But luck was on the side of the Castello Brancos. Even when the Fiat rolled off a road and turned over in the vicinity of Orléans, no one was hurt; field workers put the car back on the road, and the minor damage was repaired in the next town.[2]

During the tour of Europe, a pilgrimage to many places that the Castello Brancos had read about, Humberto showed more interest in history, theater, and opera than in paintings. As he and his family made their way through France, Holland, Belgium, Italy, Switzerland, Czechoslovakia, Austria, and Germany, postcards flowed to Brazil, particularly from Italy (the Vatican, Vesuvius, the Roman Forum, Venice, and Lake Como).[3] Perhaps because Brazilians were few in Europe at that time, the captain and his family were invited for lunch or dinner at the Brazilian embassies in the European capitals.

After the return to Paris on October 12, 1937, Argentina wrote to Hélio Vianna about the steamer trip down the left bank of the Rhine, the castles she seen there, and the cities where the steamer had stopped. She described Bonn as "a large and beautiful garden, worthy birthplace of Beethoven. As it was summer, there were green leaves on all the trees, and some of the streets reminded me of many there in Rio."[4] Argentina concluded that Germany had more beautiful large cities than France. Of the French cities, she liked Nice, Cannes, and Reims.

Humberto, writing to his brother-in-law, said that the long trip had not been tiring. In Florence, he said, he and Argentina had thought of Hélio because of the world of art that they saw. Humberto described Paris as an orgy of light due to the World Exposition—"a gigantic complex, bizarre because of the multiplicity of styles, and bringing here an incessant multitude." However, he added, "we shall be returning to the

---

promotion. Très bien élevé, ayant une personnalité accusée dont il fiat preuve dans les discussions sans se départir de la plus parfaite correction, c'est certainement un officier de valeur."

[2] Lott interview, October 13, 1975; Paulo V. Castello Branco interviews, Rio de Janeiro, November, 1974. A photograph of the Fiat is in File E, CPDOC.

[3] Diniz in Diniz and Castello Branco interview, December 13, 1975; snapshots and postcards, File E, CPDOC. See also interviews with Paulo V. Castello Branco and Antonietta Castello Branco Diniz in "Castello Branco: Meu Pai," *Manchete*, March, 1973 (in File HP7, CPDOC).

[4] Argentina to Hélio Vianna, Paris, November 6, 1937, File D, CPDOC.

aspect of the city that we began to know on November 3, 1936, a Paris that is cold, spotted, and shadowy. Without my wanting it, my letter has fallen into the commonplace of literature of the letters of Brazilians: Paris—dark, dirty, cold, and expensive."[5]

8. Farewell to Europe (1938)

The field trips taken during the second year at the Ecole Supérieure de Guerre brought postcards from Castello Branco to his wife and children in Paris (such as one for Paulo showing "la Bértha abandonée par les Allemands"). On a trip to the battlefield of Waterloo, Castello was photographed with two other Brazilians who were studying at the *école*: Major Nestor Penha Brasil and Captain Hugo Panasco Alvim.[1]

The second-year curriculum was more difficult than that of the first. In March, 1938, Humberto wrote to Hélio Vianna: "The work at the school is intense, and I am almost exhausted from the series of tests that go on until April 10. Gétulio has reduced the payments. The trips are over with. My coming to Europe has hurt my promotion, already held back. Now I very much need to limit my expenses."[2]

As the Nazi troops took over Austria, Humberto advised Hélio Vianna that "France has come to a halt. The Jew Blum now declares that he is going to organize a government of 'national union' in order to save the peace and prevent fascism from taking over Europe. I do not believe in a European conflagration. Germany is not totally ready for a *grande guerra*, and France has no aviation. The German and French generals do not feel that they have sufficient equipment for total war. Besides, there is the horror as to what would result from the use of the new engines of war. But politics could precipitate the war, which Marshal Blomberg would rather see delayed until the spring of 1940."[3]

At the *école* Castello was elevated to the rank of commander of the Fourth Group. Attending a dinner given in observance of this honor, he spoke in French, expressing joy and regret. The joy was occasioned by

---

[5] HACB to Hélio Vianna, Paris, October 25, 1937, File E, CPDOC.

[1] Postcards and photographs, File E, CPDOC.

[2] HACB to Hélio Vianna, Paris, October 25, 1937, and March 12, 1938, File E, CPDOC.

[3] HACB to Hélio Vianna, Paris, March 12, 1938, File E, CPDOC.

his advancement "during a stay in France that represents an exceptional phase in my military life. The regret is at having to say goodbye." Castello pointed out that although the three other foreigners who were in the Fourth Group were Europeans who no doubt would frequently return to France, "I am certain that I shall not be able to return to Europe." Bidding farewell, he spoke of the opportunities received in the study hall of *la traditionnelle maison du Champ de Mars* and in the field trips.[4]

Upon the conclusion of the two-year course, the command of the school issued its final evaluation of Castello Branco. It found his character pleasing and commented highly on his judgment, methods, knowledge of tactics, and performance on field trips.[5] At about the same time, Castello learned from Brazil of his promotion, after almost nine and one-half years, to the rank of major.

The Castello Brancos did not return at once to Brazil, because Humberto was assigned to spend several weeks visiting French army units. During one of these visits, which allowed for some sightseeing, the Castello Brancos were joined by Major Henrique Batista Duffles Teixeira Lott and his family. Lott, who had enrolled in the Ecole Supérieure course one year later than Castello and was also residing at 55, avenue de Suffren, had been appalled by Castello's poor driving and unfamiliarity with the workings of an automobile. Now, on a scenic cable car ride with his daughters and the Castello Brancos, he received another poor impression. He saw Castello become visibly furious (inwardly violent, Lott felt) when one of the passengers, a stranger, referred to Castello as a "hunchback." Lott concluded that a psychological problem existed.[6]

The Castello Brancos' maid, Tomázia, homesick for Brazil, had al-

[4] HACB, "Promoção e Despedida," speech to the Ecole Supérieure de Guerre, File G1, pp. 33–34, CPDOC.

[5] France, Army, Ecole Supérieure de Guerre, evaluation in "Folhas de Alterações," Sec. Geral do Ministério da Guerra, File G2, Part 3, for the period October 14, 1936, to October 11, 1938, CPDOC. Also in File G1, CPDOC. The *conceito*, signed by Colonel Mer, reads as follows: "Officier intelligent très sérieux, esprit fin et compréhensif. Du jugement, de la méthode et de la distinction. A travaillé sérieusement, suivant avec fruit l'enseignement de l'Ecole, acquérant de bonnes connaissances tactiques et donnant très bonne impression sur le terrain. Capable de faire un très bon officier d'Etat-Major: s'est élevé au niveau des bons officiers français de sa promotion. Caractère des plus sympathiques. Officier de valeur."

[6] Lott interview, October 13, 1975.

ready left Europe on a Lloyd Brasileiro ship that departed from Antwerp. As Humberto would tell it, he and Argentina, having seen her off, were relaxing in an Antwerp café when a stranger came up to Humberto and said that he must be from Ceará, Brazil. After Humberto asked how the stranger knew that, he received the inevitable answer that all Cearenses could be recognized by their flat heads. Embroidering the story with a comment on the poverty in Ceará, Humberto would add: "And why do all Cearenses have flat heads? From the tapping on their heads by their fathers, who keep tapping them and saying: 'Go south, my child, go south.' "[7]

The Castello Brancos returned to Rio on the Brazilian *Siqueira Campos*, a much more modest vessel than the English *Arlanza*. With them they brought a 1938 American Ford that Castello had recently purchased and used in Paris. They brought also furnishings for a house that they hoped their savings would help them acquire: three Persian rugs, one tapestry, a landscape painting, a carved wooden cabinet, a marble statue, a bust of Napoleon, and a plate decorated with a Napoleonic battle scene.

The first Brazilian stop of the *Siqueira Campos* was at Recife. Argentina, having just seen so many European cities, was struck by the great evidence of poverty around the Recife docks.[8]

9. Brazil's Most Respected Infantry Instructor

To Castello Branco's regret, the Brazil to which he returned in October, 1938, was not the democracy he had left behind. Getúlio Vargas, with support from some important governors and from army leaders such as War Minister Eurico Gaspar Dutra and Army Chief of Staff Góis Monteiro, had set up a dictatorship late in 1937. The presidential election that was to have determined Vargas' successor had been canceled. Congress had been closed, political parties outlawed, and censorship imposed. Vargas, Castello remarked years later, "loved power too much and was unwilling to turn it over to a successor."[1]

Castello Branco, who would one day have an opportunity to set ex-

[7] Vernon Walters interview, McLean, Virginia, June 12, 1975.
[8] Castello Branco interviews, November, 1974.
[1] Luís Viana Filho, *O Governo Castelo Branco*, p. 175.

amples in favor of press freedom and against *continuísmo* in the presidency, had turned forty-one in September, 1938. With rich finishing touches in Paris, he had completed twenty years of army officer formation. During that time he had engaged in military campaigning against the Prestes Column and, in one year at Curitiba, had revealed that he could, when in command of troops, revitalize an apathetic unit. But the characteristics that attracted the greatest attention were his mental powers and broad knowledge. Based on reports from France received by civilians and officers in Uruguay, the Brazilian military attaché in Montevideo wrote that "Castello Branco is reputed to have a military and general knowledge that is among the most brilliant and complete of all officers, including those in France and other foreign countries."[2] These traits of knowledge and intelligence, together with Castello's record as a hardworking instructor, made it seem likely that in the years ahead the army would seek its return on its investment in his career largely in the use of his teaching abilities.

And so it was between his forty-first and forty-sixth birthdays; Castello spent two years teaching at the Escola de Estado Maior (EEM), one year in the War Ministry, and then two years directing infantry instruction at Realengo.

Named assistant instructor of the EEM in January, 1939, Castello reformed the first-year general tactics course, drawing up all of the teaching material from scratch. But what brought him the greatest renown were his lectures to advanced classes on military history and the War of the Triple Alliance with Paraguay. The lectures on the war with Paraguay aroused the enthusiasm of the chief of the French Military Mission, General Chadebec de Lavallade, who pronounced them "very vivid and very meaningful." In 1940 they were published as a brochure.[3]

Students excited by the lectures on military history included Captain Ademar de Queiroz, an artillery officer who had been a Realengo classmate of Castello without knowing him well.[4] In 1940 Ademar de Queiroz was promoted to major and appointed instructor at the EEM. Castel-

[2] Brazil Army, Military Attaché, Montevideo, Oficial No. 96, February 3, 1941, File G1, CPDOC.

[3] *Boletim Escolar*, January 8, 1940, quoted in "Folhas de Alterações," File G2, Part 3, CPDOC; HACB, *O Alto Comando Aliado na Guerra entre a Tríplice Aliança e o Paraguai.*

[4] Ademar de Queiroz interview, Rio de Janeiro, October 13, 1975.

lo, who built up lasting friendships with those with whom he could work congenially, became particularly close to the admiring and handsome Ademar de Queiroz, whose intelligence and gaiety made him a warm companion.

When Castello was transferred to the War Ministry in September, 1940, the commander of the EEM, in his official commendation, reminded the departing instructor of his agreement "to continue his course on military history with his accustomed brilliance and proficiency." [5] In the ministry Castello spent a year as an aide in the office of War Minister Dutra. While there, he received his silver twenty-year medal.

One day in September, 1941, which was late in the Realengo school year, about fifty third-year cadets, being drilled by Captain Luís Mendes da Silva at the edge of the Gericinó training field near Vila Militar, awaited the arrival of their new chief infantry instructor and battalion commander. They had become fed up with their past chief instructor's habit of pouring out a vast sea of mimeographed papers about theoretical concepts on the army division level.[6] Reading about the German armed advances, and expecting that Brazil would become involved in the war, the cadets found the concepts of their former chief instructor to be obsolete, besides being of no practical value at the battalion level.

Castello Branco, in uniform and wearing a helmet, approached on horse and dismounted. The cadets, standing at attention, saw an ugly figure, apparently with no neck, and when he identified himself his voice revealed a northeasterner, a typical Cearense. Calling his orderly for his small packet, he pulled out some papers and had two sheets distributed to each cadet: the first sheet explained the relation of the battalion to the higher echelons, and the second dealt, simply and concisely, with the function of the battalion and its supporting units. "You have," Castello said, "five minutes to read the two sheets, after which I shall make some observations and question you to see if they are well understood. They will serve as the basis for all of our work from now on. I do not plan to distribute any more documents. I am happy that our first meeting is here, in the field of instruction. The task of small infantry

[5] "Folhas de Alterações," File G2, Part 3, item for Escola de Estado Maior, second semester, 1940, CPDOC.

[6] Murilo Gomes Ferreira, "O General Castello Que Conheci" (transcript of tape prepared for interview), Rio de Janeiro, November 12, 1975, "Contato Inicial," pp. 1–3.

units is not learned in the lecture room. . . . It is here that we shall work, and work hard, intensely, day after day." [7]

Castello, warning the men that he did not want vague and theoretical replies, said that his mission would be to see and hear the cadets in the field, facing their problems, learning how and where to place their arms and their men. He would, he said, be at their side to examine the most minute details, to hear their decisions, and to criticize and counsel. He would call for maneuvers to be repeated as often as he felt it necessary to get them carried out correctly and in accordance with the problems presented: "Don't be afraid to explain frankly your ideas and decisions, however absurd they may appear. Combat is not a rigid scheme and does not obey formulas for solutions. Each case is a separate problem and requires good sense, rapidity of decision, and capacity for leadership." [8]

During the repeated maneuvers, hypothetical ranks were assigned to different cadets. Unexpected changes were introduced into the situation being studied. Lieutenant Carlos de Meira Mattos, one of the instructing lieutenants, noted that Castello also sought to inculcate initiative and leadership by stressing the verbs in the expressions of missions: *go* to Point 205; *protect* the southern flank. The cadet was always to make sure that he was not emphasizing secondary matters. In the fulfillment of missions, he was to ask himself: What is the objective? [9]

The cadets received in an arduous form the practical training they had lacked before Castello's arrival. In giving one of the examinations, Castello took the cadets into the field and distributed to each a piece of paper with a question. One cadet, whose question was to tell where the machine gun should be placed, pointed to a location and answered, "there." Castello, furious, explained that such an imprecise answer might be given in the classroom but never in the field. He added that the cadet was expected to lie down on the exact spot, just as Castello himself had sometimes done next to cadets while training them to be precise about positions. [10]

Major Castello Branco, a stickler for exactitude, had a reputation

[7] Ibid.

[8] Ibid.

[9] Mário da Cunha interview, Tucson, Arizona, April 14, 1976; Meira Mattos interview, January 5, 1976 (notes revised by Meira Mattos, January 20 1976).

[10] Ismael da Rocha Teixeira interview, São Paulo, November 6, 1975.

for being tough, but there were instructor captains who were at least as tough as he was. What principally made Humberto outstanding in the minds of cadets and fellow-instructors was his brilliance and his memory: he surprised them by his precise knowledge, unexpected in a major, of every little detail that should have been in the minds of sergeants as well as commissioned officers. Carlos de Meira Mattos simply confirms the admiration expressed by others when he declares that "without doubt Castello Branco was the most highly respected at the military academy."[11]

10. Life at 394 Nascimento Silva Street

For Humberto and Argentina a crowning event of the post-Paris years was the building of their own house on a ten-meter by twenty-meter property that they bought in a new section of the Ipanema district for 50 *contos* (equivalent to about U.S. $3,500). With the help of savings from the European trip and financing by the War Ministry's Caixa de Construções de Casas (Housing Construction Bank for officers), contracts for the construction, costing 130 *contos* (about U.S. $9,100), were signed in June, 1940.[1] And therefore, early in 1941, the Castello Brancos were able to move from their rented house in the fashionable Copacabana district to their attractive two-story home at Rua Nascimento Silva 394.

There the customs of the past were carefully observed. Although a maid was usually present, the children always made their own beds, and they never sat down at a meal before their parents sat. Despite the ages of Nieta and Paulo, on Christmas eve they continued with the tradition of putting their shoes under their beds to be filled with presents during the night.[2]

Paulo was preparing to enter the naval academy, and the Castello

11 Ibid.; Cunha interview, April 14, 1976; Meira Mattos interview, January 5, 1976. See Ferreira, "O General Castello Que Conheci," p. 3.

1 Paulo V. Castello Branco interview, Rio de Janeiro, December 7, 1975; Paulo V. Castello Branco, in Diniz and Castello Branco interview, Rio de Janeiro, December 13, 1975; contracts between HACB, Custódio Tinoco & Cia. Ltda., and Caixa de Construções de Casas (Ministério da Guerra), June 1, 20, 1940, copies in possession of JWFD. One *conto* was equal to one thousand *mil-réis*.

2 Diniz and Castello Branco interview, December 13, 1975.

Brancos therefore sold Argentina's Belo Horizonte property, the gift of her father, in order to pay for naval uniforms. The navy, unlike the army, did not pay for the expensive uniforms required of entering cadets, and this condition caused many a would-be naval officer to turn, instead, to a career in the army.

Humberto was putting on a little weight for the first time in his life.[3] As always, he was excessively attentive to Argentina. He was the one who washed the dishes in the pantry if the maid was out, and in the mornings he shaved in a small bathroom off the pantry so that the large upstairs bathroom would be available to his wife. For her use he would leave in the garage, at the back of the house, the 1940 Chevrolet that had replaced the 1938 Ford; he would make use of buses—probably a good thing for the Chevrolet and perhaps also for Rio's pedestrians. If Argentina, less sturdy than Humberto, needed medicine before dinner, Humberto would take it to her on the front veranda, and at the meal he would never touch his fruit until Argentina had begun to eat hers.[4]

Seldom did Humberto go to the beach. He preferred to read, either in his first-floor front study off the veranda, or else in a comfortable sofa in the entrance hall, to which the main doorway opened, at the side of the house.

More than Argentina, Humberto liked to entertain at home in the evenings. The dinners were either for army friends and their wives, for civilian friends, or for relatives (innumerable birthdays being observed), and the three categories were never mixed. Although not a drinker, Humberto enjoyed preparing the alexanders and other cocktails that were fashionable. Wanting everything to go off flawlessly, he was excited during the few hours preceding a party at home, and sometimes he became so nervous that he lost his temper.[5] As in the case of Humberto's own parents, the wife was the calmer of the two. Discreet and more self-contained than Humberto, Argentina was less apt to reveal the excitement that she felt.

On a religious retreat in Belo Horizonte (the Retreat of Christian Mothers), Argentina had written in January, 1934: "The triumph of

---

[3] Paulo V. Castello Branco interview, Rio de Janeiro, August 11, 1974.
[4] Diniz and Castello Branco interview, December 13, 1975.
[5] Ibid.

the wife over the husband is to yield."[6] But Argentina's success lay in more than yielding, and the triumphing was done by the pair. She was always attractive and neatly dressed; she enjoyed reading, was an intelligent helper of her husband, and was devoted to his career. "We made, she and I," Humberto wrote years later, "an alliance in which everything that is human and real entered. . . . But what dominated was affection, the understanding about a single path, and a reciprocity of purpose, in renunciations for adjusting equally. There was thus a conjugal association rising from the search for a result that would bring us unity."[7]

Humberto, conservative in dress, was also conservative about personal finances. If he and Argentina went out to the costly gambling casinos of Urca and Atlântico, where good food and good shows were featured, it was only as the guests of Argentina's brother Niso, who had become a wealthy São Paulo businessman.[8]

Humberto, his Realengo classmates found, was more than a faithful attendant of their annual reunion dinners. So great was his spirit of comradeship in the army that he became a principal organizer of those gatherings to recall January 18, 1921.[9] Soon after such a reunion he would customarily join his family, already in Belo Horizonte for the annual vacation.

[6] Argentina Castello Branco, notes written at Retiro das Mães Cristãs, Belo Horizonte, January, 1934. See File D, CPDOC.
[7] HACB to his children, Recife, May 5, 1963, File C, CPDOC.
[8] Paulo V. Castello Branco memorandum, 1975.
[9] Vilela dos Santos, "Depoimento."

Setbacks in Italy
(1944)

My section is the "nerve center" of the division; everything goes out from here, to those below or to those above.

1. Organizing the FEB (1943-1944)

CASTELLO BRANCO, turning out infantry lieutenants at Realengo, was promoted to lieutenant colonel on April 15, 1943. By this time Brazil was in the war against Germany and Italy, and instruction at Realengo had been speeded up by the elimination of vacations.[1] War Minister Dutra was working on plans to implement President Vargas' surprise suggestion of December 31, 1942, that Brazil furnish troops—not just a "simple expedition of symbolic contingents"—for combat overseas against the enemy. Dutra's plans, which envisioned sending one hundred thousand Brazilian soldiers abroad, were modified and remodified during lengthy discussions with United States officials. And in the meantime, Brazilian army officers were sent to courses in the United States, many of them going for three months to the Command and General Staff School at Fort Leavenworth, Kansas.

Castello Branco left Rio in July, 1943, as a member of the first group of Brazilian army officers to train at Fort Leavenworth. Together with three colonels, including Henrique Batista Duffles Teixeira Lott and Floriano de Lima Brayner, and eight other lieutenant colonels, including Amauri Kruel, Castello learned about replacing French fighting methods with United States methods. Instead of heavy reliance on trench warfare oriented toward massive defense, speedy and audacious movement was to be featured. It was to be highly motorized, with less marching on foot and a greatly reduced role for horses.[2] Compared with the French

[1] Mário da Cunha interview, Tucson, Arizona, April 14, 1976.
[2] Luís Tavares da Cunha Melo interview, Rio de Janeiro, November 17, 1975;

and Brazilians, the Americans appeared to have an infinite amount of mechanized equipment available. And they proposed to standardize on 105-mm and 155-mm arms such as Brazil did not possess.

The Brazilian colonels and lieutenant colonels in the first Fort Leavenworth group could expect to serve in the staff posts of the three divisions (about twenty-five thousand men each) of the Força Expedicionária Brasileira (FEB) that Brazil then planned to send overseas. By the time these officers returned to Brazil in October, 1943, General João Batista Mascarenhas de Morais, chosen to head the First Infantry Division of the FEB, was picking the senior men for his staff. Following the suggestions of Major Aguinaldo José Senna Campos, who had worked closely with Mascarenhas in the northeast and in São Paulo, the general decided to have Castello Branco head the staff's Third Section (operations) and Amauri Kruel head the Second Section (intelligence).[3] The warm friendship between the two lieutenant colonels was considered important. Mascarenhas felt that Senna Campos himself should head the Fourth Section (logistics), despite his being only a major and not having gone to Fort Leavenworth.[4]

For chief of staff, Mascarenhas ruled out senior Colonel Lott, with whom he had had a serious altercation in Pernambuco. The post went to Colonel Brayner, whom Mascarenhas hardly knew but who had the advantage of being favored by Dutra. Brayner, Senna Campos told Mascarenhas, had been a good tactics instructor at the EEM.[5]

Brayner had supported Castello Branco's 1936 petition to study in Paris, but relations between these two officers had been cool when they were both concerned with instruction at Realengo in 1941.[6] On October 12, 1943, when Mascarenhas and Brayner discussed staff positions,

---

Renato Moniz de Aragão interview, Rio de Janeiro, November 22, 1975; Emygdio da Costa Miranda interview, Rio de Janeiro, December 1, 1975; Carlos de Meira Mattos interview, Washington, D.C., January 5, 1976.

[3] Aguinaldo José Senna Campos interview, Rio de Janeiro, November 26, 1975; Aguinaldo José Senna Campos, *Com a FEB na Itália: Páginas do Meu Diário*, p. 23.

[4] Cunha Melo interview, November 17, 1975.

[5] Miranda interview, December 1, 1975 (see also Floriano de Lima Brayner, *Luzes sôbre Memórias*, p. 64); João Batista Barreto Leito Filho interview, Rio de Janeiro, November 25, 1975 (see also Brayner, *Luzes sôbre Memórias*, p. 22); Senna Campos, *Com a FEB na Itália*, p. 23.

[6] Floriano de Lima Brayner, *Recordando os Bravos*; *Eu Convivi com Eles*; *Campanha da Itália*, p. 281.

Castello was not Brayner's choice to head the Third Section. Mascarenhas, however, had already made up his mind about the top members of Brayner's staff, and therefore the only suggestion that he accepted from the colonel was that Kruel head the Second Section. The general revealed that Senna Campos would direct the Fourth Section, and he rejected Brayner's candidates for the First Section (personnel) and the Third Section, assigning these posts instead to Thales Ribeiro da Costa and Castello Branco. Mascarenhas pointed out that Castello Branco, whom he did not know, had been highly recommended by Ademar de Queiroz.[7]

"Shoulder to the wheel, Mendes," Castello Branco would say good-humoredly to Major Luís Mendes da Silva, whom he had called to help with the Third Section's work of training the division.[8] It was no easy task. For one thing, the infantrymen lacked new weapons which the United States proposed to furnish them when they reached their overseas destination (the Brazilians had some relics from World War I). An even greater obstacle was the location, over much of the Brazilian map, of the units to be trained; they were subject to the commands of the local military regions, not of the FEB.[9] For a while the FEB hardly seemed to exist—except at the São Francisco Xavier Street office in Rio, where the massive paperwork included translating United States military regulations and setting an impossible target date for "Americanizing" the fighting force.

Castello Branco thrived on trying to get his job done even if it meant, as it often did, irritating people—superiors as well as subordinates. With the authorization of Chief of Staff Brayner, he did much of the work that belonged to the First Section as well as his own, and thus handled organization and instruction simultaneously. Making the first

[7] Ibid., pp. 282–283. Brayner suggested Lieutenant Colonel José Theophilo de Arruda to head the First Section and Lieutenant Colonel Augusto da Cunha Maggessi Pereira to head the Third Section.

[8] Luís Mendes da Silva, "Testemunho," Part 3, "Tenente Coronel Humberto de Alencar Castello Branco na Guerra, 1944–45."

[9] Floriano de Lima Brayner, A Verdade sôbre a FEB: Memórias de um Chefe de Estado-Maior na Companha da Itália, 1943–1945, p. 28; João Baptista Mascarenhas de Moraes, A F.E.B. pelo Seu Comandante, p. 25; João Baptista Mascarenhas de Moraes, Memórias, I, 136. In the footnotes and list of sources, authors' names are spelled as they appeared on the actual works cited although they sometimes differ from the commonly used reformed spelling. Thus spellings of proper names in the notes may differ from those in the text.

trips to the dispersed units, he insisted on setting up programs of daily exercises and frequent marches.[10] At Gericinó, near Rio, he installed training areas with obstacles, pits, and land mines.

Some of the lack of harmony within the budding FEB has been attributed to discord between artillery officers and infantry officers. Bearing this in mind, if we turn to the highest ranks, we find that First Division commander Mascarenhas de Morais, a sixty-year-old, artillery-trained *general de divisão*, was closer to Brigadier General Osvaldo Cordeiro de Farias, director of the division's artillery, than he was to Brigadier General Euclides Zenóbio da Costa, selected by Dutra to head the division's infantry.[11] It seems probable, however, that the strains that sometimes developed between Mascarenhas and Zenóbio were due more to the striking contrast in their characters than to the differences in their training. The austere Mascarenhas, a short, grandfatherly figure, was better known for his quiet and methodical devotion to duty than for his brilliance or imagination. Zenóbio, always ready to display boldness, was far less reserved; he was inclined to be exuberant, sometimes impetuous. He had a great interest in sports and, during his rise up the ladder in the army, had gotten some of the best athletes into his units, which had become well known for their victories on the fields of sports.

For Mascarenhas the most serious problems were those created outside the FEB instead of within it. Men who opposed the whole idea of the FEB, some of them in the Brazilian government, tried to obstruct the work of Mascarenhas and his team.[12] Nor could Mascarenhas expect any help from Army Chief of Staff Góis Monteiro. The redoubtable Góis was forever criticizing Mascarenhas and everything about the FEB.

Within the FEB, pessimism was considerable during December, 1943, while Mascarenhas was away conferring with Allied leaders in Africa and Italy. But with his return and with the resignation of Góis, an improvement occurred. Belatedly, steps were taken to bring most of the FEB's First Division units to Vila Militar and to other barracks in

[10] Murilo Gomes Ferreira, "O General Castello Que Conheci," transcription of tape prepared for interview, Rio de Janeiro, November 12, 1975, p. 3; Brayner, *Recordando os Bravos*, p. 285; Meira Mattos interview, January 5, 1976.

[11] Mendes da Silva, "Testemunho," Part 3, "Tenente Coronel Humberto de Alencar Castello Branco"; Brayner, *A Verdade sôbre a FEB*, pp. 42, 106. Brayner writes (pp. 43, 312) that Mascarenhas was not consulted in the selection of Zenóbio da Costa, and that "perfect harmony" did not exist between the two.

[12] Mascarenhas de Moraes, *Memórias*, I, 129.

the vicinity. The moves, which required the reassignment of some facilities and the construction of others, were not made simultaneously, and
it was not until late in March, 1944, after the 11th RI from São João
del Rei, Minas Gerais, and the 6th RI from Caçapava, São Paulo, had
joined the 1st RI in the Rio area that the First Division resembled a
unified body.[13] If departure was to take place in mid-1944, as rumored,
little time was left for training in Brazil. But, some thought, perhaps
supplemental training would be provided in Africa.

In May, 1944, Vargas and other notables looked on proudly while
the First Division's infantry marched in downtown Rio and while the
artillery demonstrated its prowess at the Gericinó training grounds.
These exercises were widely acclaimed. But Mascarenhas de Morais
called on Castello Branco to write up the commentaries of the command
about the artillery demonstration, and the resulting critique had a fault
to find. What had been witnessed, it said, was an exhibition appropriate
for peacetime. Where were the factors, unexpected by the artillerymen,
that would have brought their exercises closer to the realities of war?[14]

Castello easily survived unfavorable reactions to his criticism, for he
was making an excellent impression on Mascarenhas, who found him
"an alert collaborator, conscientious and exacting in the technical preparation of the troops." He was, the commanding general decided, "bril-
liantly intelligent" and "endowed with a capacity for highly effective
work."[15]

With the rest of Mascarenhas' staff, Castello now concentrated on
preparations for the forthcoming embarkation. A huge wooden imitation of the side of a ship was set up at Vila Militar.[16] Embarkation re-
hearsals were supervised, and detailed instructions issued.

Changes in the embarkation procedure had to be introduced after
the United States military attaché in Rio secretly advised Mascarenhas

[13] Ibid., p. 40. The 1st RI (Sampaio Regiment) was commanded by Colonel
Aguinaldo Caiado de Castro. The 6th RI (Ipiranga Regiment) was commanded by
João de Segadas Viana. The 11th RI (Tiradentes Regiment) was commanded by Del-
miro Pereira de Andrade.

[14] Mendes da Silva, "Testemunho," Part 3, "Tenente Coronel Humberto de Alencar Castello Branco."

[15] "Folhas de Alterações," File G2, Part 3, 1ª Divisão da Infantaria Expedicionária,
Quartel General, January 1 to June 30, 1944, CPDOC. Also in "Campanha da Itália,"
collection of documents in File G1, CPDOC.

[16] Manoel Thomaz Castello Branco, O Brasil na II Grande Guerra, p. 149; Brayner, A Verdade sôbre a FEB, pp. 72–73.

and some of his staff, including Castello, that the transportation overseas, threatened by the Germans, would not be made by the Brazilian
merchant marine but by formidable and speedy United States vessels,
each capable of carrying six thousand men. To prepare for the embarkation of the first contingent, a temporary Estado Maior Especial was set
up, with the United States military attaché as coordinator. The other
members were Brayner, Castello, Kruel, and two officers of the United
States military mission.[17]

2. The First Days in Italy (July 16–31, 1944)

Early on June 30, 1944, Castello Branco was at the Rio docks. There,
one of the FEB tactics groups, secretly selected to be the first detachment
to go abroad, was arriving from Vila Militar in a train with boarded-up
windows.[1] About five thousand surprised men, who had been advised
only that they would be moving from their recent training place, received orders to march aboard the veritable sea fortress that they faced,
the *General W. A. Mann*. Many had not bid farewell to their families.

Most of the men belonged to the 6th RI, of Caçapava, São Paulo,
known as the Ipiranga Regiment. Although on the ocean voyage they
were to be under the command of General Zenóbio da Costa, who had
his own small staff, General Mascarenhas insisted on going along, together with the top staff officers of his division.[2]

During the afternoon Humberto went to the naval academy to say
goodbye to his son Paulo. He found Paulo "affectionate and virile," full
of encouraging words. After father and son embraced and kissed, Humberto sped to Nascimento Silva Street for a last evening meal with Argentina and Nieta. He was so filled with emotion that he could not
speak of his parting visit with Paulo.[3]

At 8:45 P.M., when a car came for Humberto and his luggage, the

---

[17] Brayner, *A Verdade sôbre a FEB*, p. 52.

[1] Ismael da Rocha Teixeira, in Ariel Pacca da Fonseca, Antônio Ferreira Marques,
and Teixeira interview, São Paulo, November 6, 1975.

[2] Brayner, *Luzes sôbre Memórias*, pp. 64–65.

[3] HACB to Argentina July 15, 1944, File H1, Castello Branco papers in the possession of Paulo V. Castello Branco (hereafter cited as PVCB). Files H1, H2, and H3
have not been copied and are not included in the Castello Branco Collection at the
CPDOC.

final embraces were given in the front living room lest a parting in the street alert neighbors about embarkation plans. Humberto's chin trembled, as it always did when he was close to tears, and all three wept.[4]

Castello Branco was on the *General W. A. Mann* at midnight when President Vargas came aboard to tell the men that the nation would follow their activities "with the most fervent prayers to God." Then, many hours before the ship put to sea, Humberto wrote to Argentina. He was, he said, tired, nostalgic, and full of emotion. Sending his wife an ardent kiss and many embraces, he told her that it was important for her and Nieta to recover their spirits. "In the depths of my heart I guard your affection for me and the sweetness of Nieta." He told her of his emotional visit with Paulo.[5]

Two weeks later, when the *General W. A. Mann* was close to Naples, Humberto wrote a second letter to Argentina. His family was much on his mind: "Time passes, and, as it does, my longing increases for you, Nieta, and Paulo. In the midst of the sadness that enveloped us on the evening of June 30, I had the compensation of the testimony of your love and the affection of my children."

Humberto said that the ocean trip, which had begun on July 2, had had its moments of monotony, of apprehension, and of amusement: "Much conviviality with comrades, together with reading during a large part of the day, and movies on some nights (instructive films, or, for the soldiers, films that always have a great deal of music). I am in the Mediterranean in the quiet of the sea that you know." Advising that he would go ashore the next day, Humberto said that during the ocean voyage Amauri Kruel had been his closest traveling companion. He added that he knew quite a few other officers aboard, principally two dozen who had been his former students, and that his orderly, José Edésio Oliveira, had washed his clothes and had been so solicitous that he had been envied by the other officers.[6]

The landing at what remained of Naples took place under a warm sun in a harbor full of ships, with blimps overhead and with Mount Vesuvius smoking in the background. The Brazilian soldiers, mistaken for German prisoners by some of the Italians because of their olive green

[4] Antonietta Castello Branco Diniz, in Diniz and Paulo V. Castello Branco interview, Rio de Janeiro, December 13, 1975.

[5] HACB to Argentina, July 1, 1944, File H1, p. 6, PVCB.

[6] HACB to Argentina, July 15, 1944, File H1, PVCB.

uniforms,[7] went by train and on foot to Agnano, twenty-five kilometers from Naples. Happy to be out of the holds of the *General W. A. Mann*, they were scheduled to encamp in tents in the wooded crater of an extinct volcano, but instead they spent their first night in Italy in the open because the Americans were late in furnishing most of the promised tents.[8]

All had been fixed up by July 20, when Humberto wrote to Argentina "beneath magnificent trees and in the delightful temperature of a European summer. . . . *Ah você, minha filha!* Be patient. When everything is over you will understand this absence better. Let us be faithful to our old affection so that we and our children will be happy."[9]

When Humberto had time off from training men at Agnano, he went with his tent-mate, Amauri Kruel, to Naples and the ruins of Pompeii. Visiting places and shops where he had been with his family in 1937, he could see Argentina as she had stood then, "fascinated by works of art two thousand years old."[10] Humberto bought corals and cameos for Argentina and Nieta.

Recollections of 1937 returned to Castello Branco later in July when he and other staff members sped 350 kilometers north in automobiles with General Zenóbio da Costa to look over a new campsite at Tarquinia, twenty kilometers from the badly bombed port of Civitavecchia. The officers spent two nights in Rome, one on their way north and the other on their return. But what changes since 1937! Italy, Humberto wrote Argentina, "is devastated and in misery."[11]

[7] Teixeira, in Pacca da Fonseca, Ferreira Marques, and Teixeira interview, November 6, 1975; U.S. Army, Historical Section, United States Army Forces South Atlantic (USAFSA), "History of the United States Army Forces South Atlantic" (typewritten), p. 327, Historical Manuscript File, Office of the Chief of Military History, Washington, D.C.

[8] Senna Campos, *Com a FEB na Itália*, p. 76. According to Historical Section, USAFSA, "History of the USAFSA," p. 325, "the difficulty resulted from the fact that originally the FEB was scheduled to disembark at Oran [Algeria] and train in North Africa."

[9] HACB to Argentina, July 20, 1944, File H1, PVCB.

[10] HACB to Argentina, July 30, 1944, File H1, PVCB. See also postcard, House of the Vetti Brothers, Pompeii, HACB to Argentina, September 7, 1944, File H1, p. 23, PVCB.

[11] "Folhas de Alterações," File G2, Part 3, second semester, 1944, CPDOC; HACB to Argentina, July 30, 1944, File H1, PVCB.

During their second evening in Rome the Brazilian ambassador to the Vatican advised Zenóbio that Pope Pius XII would receive him and his group at noon the next day. Zenóbio's reaction to the news of the appointment, the result of a misunderstanding about the general's wishes, was an explosion. He exclaimed that he had no time for visits. "I must continue my journey at dawn and cannot lose half a day's march when I have a mission to fulfill."[12] Only when it was pointed out to him that a cancellation of the appointment would embarrass the ambassador did the general accede.

Although Zenóbio, calling himself a spiritualist, said that he would not kneel, he was the first to do so when the Pope Pius XII received the Brazilian officers in their green uniforms and the ambassador in his full-dress tails. Speaking in good Portuguese, His Holiness told the officers that "divine mercy is infinite and will know how to protect you and return you to your homes in our beloved Brazil."[13] He gave each a medallion and a picture of himself.

Like the others (including Zenóbio), Humberto was deeply moved by the brief ceremony. Receiving the Pope's blessing after kissing his hand, Humberto thought of Argentina and the children. He had with him a silver medallion that he had bought that morning and that he wanted Argentina to have during their separation. A few days later he sent it to her, together with a letter, via a *portador*.[14]

The *portadores*, or officers who happened to be making trips by plane between Italy and Brazil, offered Humberto the opportunity to send letters that did not go through the censorship. In these, and there were to be many of them, he could tell where he was and speak in considerable detail about his work. But the dominating theme of these letters, like the others, was love. "Today it is one month since I left you, embracing you repeatedly. What has been happening at home during this time? God grant that the days have passed without mishaps. When the automobile took me from home, I saw, between the leaves of the hedge, your hand and Nieta's waving goodbye. And today I feel as though they beckon to me with friendship and caress me."[15]

12 Brayner, *A Verdade sôbre a FEB*, p. 125.
13 Ibid., pp. 127–128.
14 HACB to Argentina, July 20, 1944, File H1, PVCB.
15 Ibid.

3. Instruction in Italy (August–September, 1944)

Early on the morning of July 31, 1944, a sunburned Castello Branco set forth from Agnano to take the first of the Brazilians by truck on the 350-kilometer trip north to Tarquinia.[1] The route was in an area that had been occupied two months earlier by the Germans, who were now defending themselves in Florence and at other points along the valley of the Arno River.

Following the departure of the trucks on the thirty-first, the rest of the Brazilians were transported by rail to Tarquinia.[2] There on August 5 all of Zenóbio's force of five thousand was incorporated into the American Fifth Army, which had been moving successfully up the southwest coast of Italy. Mascarenhas then flew to the American headquarters at Cecina, forty kilometers south of the Arno River, to confer with Mark Clark, the tall and efficient commander of the Fifth Army. It was known that the British Eighth Army had just dislodged the Germans from Florence, but it was also known that the Allied forces in Italy were to be weakened by large-scale transfers for the invasion of the south of France. Allies remaining in Italy had the task of keeping the pressure on the Germans in order to limit the number of units that the Germans could transfer to France.[3] In this strategy the Brazilians could play a useful role, but before deciding when this should be, Clark resolved to dispatch American officers to inspect the Brazilians.

During this inspection in Tarquinia on August 12, Castello and other Brazilian officers explained, through interpreters, their training plans. The Americans, satisfied with what they saw and heard, decided that the new, rigorous training should be carried out in appropriately hilly terrain nearer the fighting front, and they borrowed Castello to work with them while they chose a new site.[4] Following the selection of the coastal town of Vada, south of Pisa and close to the Fifth Army

---

[1] Senna Campos, Com a FEB na Itália, p. 79.

[2] Historical Section, USAFSA, "History of the USAFSA," p. 327.

[3] Mascarenhas de Moraes, Memórias, I, 168. Mark Clark discusses the Fifth Army's troop shortages in Calculated Risk, pp. 396–397.

[4] Brayner, A Verdade sôbre a FEB, pp. 134–135; "Folhas de Alterações," File G2, Part 3, CPDOC: "On August 15 he was assigned to the general barracks of the Fifth Army as assistant to the chief of the detachment that was locating bases in order to look over the new site to be chosen by the General Headquarters of the Fifth Army."

headquarters at Cecina, the Brazilians' nocturnal move two hundred kilometers from Tarquinia was carried out in five hundred vehicles.

The transfer to Vada had almost been completed when Winston Churchill visited Cecina, and there his guard of honor included a Brazilian company. After the British Prime Minister had spoken appreciatively of Brazil's participation in the Italian campaign, Castello wrote to Argentina, describing Churchill as "calm, happy, and enormously sure of himself." "You can imagine," Humberto added, "the emotion I felt, principally when he referred to the Brazilian force."[5]

For the most part, Humberto's letters showed a burning desire to hear something from his family. But when, on August 18, he finally received Argentina's letter of July 25—not the first to have been sent by her—he was disappointed. It brought the news that she had received none of his letters, and it was much too short to suit Humberto. "I reached the last line and felt disappointed. . . . Doesn't Nieta write? And Paulo? Amauri has had the pleasure of receiving four letters. I beg of you not to wait for my letters, but to keep writing to me. I feel very isolated, very much enclosed within myself. And then I keep conjecturing about my family and this I do almost always with apprehension."[6]

During the period of rigorous training at Vada, undertaken with equipment furnished there and earlier at Tarquinia, the Brazilians received instruction from about 270 United States commissioned and noncommissioned officers.[7] Castello Branco had daily contacts with Major Vernon Walters, Mark Clark's linguistically proficient liaison officer and personal representative to the Brazilians. Walters found Castello firm in demanding the equipment to which he felt the Brazilians were entitled, but he always found him fair, in complete grasp of what he was handling, and inclined to introduce a note of humor or wit when a discussion with the Americans appeared to be sliding into acrimony. The lanky American major was impressed by Castello's "quick analytic mind, his ability to overlook the trivial and get to the heart of what was essential."[8] Walters also observed that the little Brazilian lieutenant colonel

[5] Mascarenhas de Moraes, *A F.E.B. pelo Seu Comandante*, p. 50; HACB to Argentina, Italy, August 22, 1944, File H1, PVCB.

[6] HACB to Argentina, Italy, August 18, 1944, File H1, PVCB.

[7] Historical Section, USAFSA, "History of the USAFSA," p. 330.

[8] Vernon Walters, "Humberto de Alencar Castello Branco" (typewritten), Part 1, "The Years of War."

was never ill at ease, neither arrogant nor subservient, and never afraid to express his opinion. Walters, a deeply religious man, admired Castello's integrity, and he noted that Castello was impatient with incompetence and little disposed to tolerate weakness or untruthfulness.

As Walters learned at Vada, August 25 is the Brazilian "Day of the Soldier." Consequently, on that day Mark Clark and other American officers came to Vada to review the proud, martial parading of the Brazilians and to hear them sing the Brazilian national anthem and "God Bless America." It should have been a good day for Castello. Chadebec de Lavallade, the French general who had so much enjoyed Castello's lectures in Rio on the war with Paraguay, was present, having come all the way from Toulon, France, for the ceremonies. Besides, General Clark had a warm greeting for Castello.[9]

But for Humberto the day was disappointing. A major arrived from Rio—so close a friend that Humberto felt that surely he must have something from Argentina. "What a let-down," Humberto wrote. "He told me that he had not had time to phone our house."[10]

Castello was very busy, for he and an American colonel were in charge of organizing the last stage of intensive training of the five thousand Brazilians. It lasted until September 10, when the Brazilians were assigned a two-day "regimental combat team problem" under the scrutiny of the 270 United States instructors. General Mark Clark, present for the second day of the testing, found the Brazilian combat team "looking pretty good" and "enthusiastic about getting into action."[11] He declared it ready for battle. With Zenóbio da Costa in command of the combat team, it was incorporated into the Fifth Army's Fourth Corps, headed by General Willis D. Crittenberger.

Castello, the Brazilian most concerned with the infantry instruction, can only have been delighted with the outcome of the tests. And while they were being conducted he had another joy. Colonel José Bina Machado, of Dutra's staff, brought him a letter from Argentina. The letter, dated August 15, was long and newsy and filled with thanks for the

[9] Mascarenhas de Moraes, A F.E.B. pelo Seu Comandante, p. 51; HACB to Argentina, Italy, August 25, 1944, File H1, PVCB: "General Clarck [sic] also visited us, and he spoke to me in a respectful and charming manner."

[10] HACB to Argentina, August 25, 1944, File H1, PVCB.

[11] HACB to Argentina, Quiesa, October 2, 1944, File H1, PVCB; Historical Section, USAFSA, "History of the USAFSA," p. 331; Mascarenhas de Moraes, A F.E.B. pelo Seu Comandante, p. 53; Clark, Calculated Risk, p. 392.

cameos and the corals. "For me," Humberto hastened to reply, "the best moment of this absence is to have news from you." Humberto had hardly sealed his letter when he received a package from Argentina containing a confection made of bananas.[12]

4. With Zenóbio's Victorious Combat Team (September, 1944)

The Brazilians, the only Latin Americans fighting on European soil, were about to play a part in the attacks being made by the Allied Fifteenth Group of Armies, commanded by General Sir Harold Alexander, against German troops, commanded by Field Marshal Albert Kesselring, that were defending themselves along northern Italy's Gothic Line, running roughly from La Spezia on the Ligurian Sea to Rimini on the Adriatic Sea. The Allied Fifteenth Group of Armies was made up of the British Eighth Army in the eastern half and the American Fifth Army, commanded by Mark Clark, in the western half. Clark's Fifth Army, which had recently lost seven divisions to make the landings in southern France,[1] consisted of two army corps: the Second and the Fourth. The Second Corps operated just to the left of the British Eighth Army, that is, north of Florence; with its concentration of strength and reduced front it hoped to dislodge the Germans from Bologna. Crittenberger's Fourth Corps, defending a long front running ninety kilometers westward from the Second Corps to the Ligurian Sea, faced the most rugged part of the Apennines.

The Fourth Corps had the task of opening fissures in the Gothic Line, and it hoped "to convince the enemy that the main attack was being mounted in its area." But, according to *The Final Campaign across Northwest Italy*, the role of the Fourth Corps, as originally conceived, was not a particularly aggressive one: the Fourth Corps "was to hold the shoulder, maintain contact on its right with the troops engaged in the main attack and defend the rest of the Army front all the way to the [western Italian] coast. It was to prevent any hostile penetration to the south and at the same time follow up, as it could, any enemy withdrawal. Nothing spectacular was expected from IV Corps; its long,

[12] HACB to Argentina, September 11, 14, 1944, File H1, pp. 25, 28, PVCB.
[1] Mark Clark quoted in Historical Section, USAFSA, "History of the USAFSA," p. 357.

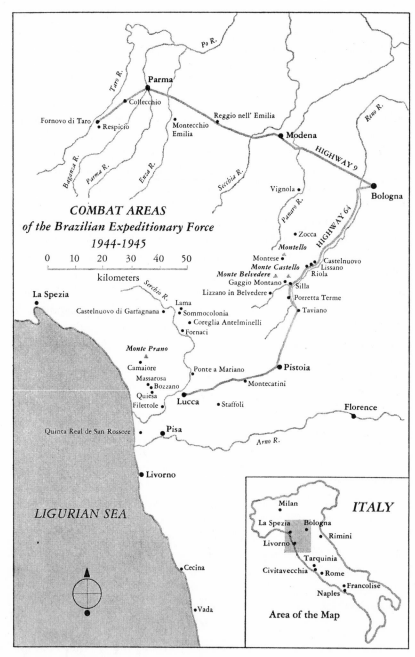

Map 2

tenuous front was thinly held, much of it by units which had not had extensive combat experience." Serving in the Fourth Corps were the American First Armored Division, the South African Sixth Armored Division, the British Forty-seventh Light Antiaircraft Regiment, the Japanese-American Infantry Battalion, and Task Force Forty-five, which described itself as "a polyglot task force of American and British anti-aircraft gunners acting as infantry, with Italian Partisans, Brazilians, and colored American troops."[2]

The job to be done by Zenóbio's five-thousand-man combat team was discussed at a meeting at the headquarters of the American Fourth Corps. "That meeting," Humberto wrote Argentina, "was the most important held up to now with the Brazilian command. The entrance of the FEB into combat was studied: how, when, and in what place? I was the one who wrote up the agreed-upon plan and the ideas that were presented for discussion. I have a happy memory of that moment. General Crittenberger became my friend."[3]

Humberto, who had been writing Argentina that the Germans would probably surrender before Christmas, now predicted that the end would come in the next month, October.[4] The hearty Zenóbio and his men, while perhaps not that hopeful, were full of optimism as they set forth from Vada on September 14.

The early part of the march took them through Pisa, which had been partially destroyed in the recent fighting. "The tower, the baptistry, and the church are still standing," Humberto wrote Argentina. He added: "I thought a lot about you, the children, and our trip."[5]

On September 15, at Vecchiano, north of Pisa, Zenóbio's combat team replaced Americans who were being withdrawn from the Fourth Corps, and it was joined by three American tank companies.[6] Still

---

[2] Ulysses Lee, *The Employment of Negro Troops*, pp. 537, 539; U.S. Army, Fourth Corps, *The Final Campaign across Northwest Italy, 14 April–2 May 1945*, p. 2.

[3] HACB to Argentina, Ponte a Moriano, October 8, 1944, File H1, p. 43, PVCB.

[4] HACB to Argentina, Italy, August 10, 1944, September 2, 4, 1944, File H1, PVCB. In the letter of September 4, HACB added: "In spite of the modesty of my commentaries, I see, with each step, the fulfillment of my prognostications about the progress of the war."

[5] HACB to Argentina, Quiesa, October 4, 1944, File H1, p. 40, PVCB.

[6] Peter S. Wondolowski, "History of the IV Corps, 1941–1945" (typewritten), p. 354, Historical Manuscript File, Office of the Chief of Military History, Washington, D.C.; U.S. Army, Fourth Corps, "The North Apennines Campaign, 10 September 1944 to 4 April 1945" (typewritten), p. 63, Historical Manuscript File, Office of the Chief

further north, the Brazilians met little resistance when they wrested from the Germans the control of three towns: Massarosa, Bozzano, and Quiesa. The liberation of Massarosa, the first Italian town to fall to the Brazilians, occurred on September 16 and prompted Clark to send a congratulatory telegram to Mascarenhas. Crittenberger congratulated Zenóbio.

Brayner has written: "We were in Massarosa, Quiesa, and Bozzano, spurring on and stimulating the attack."[7] While it is true that Mascarenhas and top members of the division staff made visits to the fighting front, all of these officers, except for Castello Branco, spent most of their time at the Fifth Army headquarters in Florence, or else near Pisa, setting up the FEB's First Division headquarters at the Quinta Real de San Rossore, a former hunting estate of the Italian royal family. There training facilities were prepared for the FEB's Second and Third detachments, due soon to sail from Brazil.

"The staff of the division," Humberto wrote Argentina, "remained behind, awaiting the rest of our troops. But I was chosen to be the representative of the command of the FEB, its observer, and its liaison with Zenóbio's command. And so I marched with the Brazilians to the front and saw them, calm and uncomplaining, enter into action." In his new work, Humberto wrote another time, he had the advantage of having observed the battle of the Arno River and the successful fighting of the Americans there.[8]

Zenóbio, after setting up headquarters at Quiesa, was asked by the American command to attack German positions in Camaiore, an important communications center to the northwest, and to try to gain con-

---

of Military History, Washington, D.C. Zenóbio's combat team consisted of the 6th RI (the Ipiranga Regiment from Caçapava, São Paulo, commanded by Colonel João de Segadas Viana), whose three battalions were commanded by Major João Carlos Gross (the First Battalion), Major Abílio Pontes (the Second Battalion), and Major Silvino Nóbrega (the Third Battalion). It also included the First Company of Engineers (commanded by Captain Floriano Moller), which, while working on an Arno River bridge earlier in September, had been the first Brazilian unit to carry out a combat mission in Italy. The combat team also included one artillery battalion and one medical company. Zenóbio's staff was directed by Lieutenant Colonel João de Almeida Freitas; its Third Section head (S-3) was Major Álvaro Alves da Silva Braga, who, Brayner writes (*Recordando os Bravos*, p. 410), worked very well with Castello Branco.

[7] Brayner, *A Verdade sôbre a FEB*, p. 164.
[8] HACB to Argentina, Quiesa, October 2, 4, 1944, in File H1, pp. 39, 40, PVCB.

trol of 1,220-meter-high Monte Prano, which overlooks Camaiore. Zenóbio, pleased, lost no time in penetrating further into what Castello Branco called "the interminable unfolding of hills, today so agitated," and the "steep mountains," with their "old hamlets" that "make one recall the history of this land."[9]

In a movement in which dozens of cobblestoned villages and towns were "liberated" by Zenóbio's force, Camaiore itself fell to Brazilians without much difficulty on September 18. Steep Monte Prano was more difficult, but the Germans left it on September 26 after four Brazilians had been killed (the first to lose their lives in action) and seven wounded. Twenty-three German prisoners were taken.

The capture by the Brazilians on September 20 of their first German prisoners, four deserters, had caused a great stir. What were the demonic superwarriors like? Castello was asked by his jeep driver. "No different from any of us," Castello answered, and showed the driver one of the prisoners.[10]

Castello, besides being the representative of the division, had the respect of Zenóbio. He worked with the officers of Zenóbio's staff and went repeatedly with them to the front line.[11] Happy to be busy,[12] he shared the euphoria then felt by the Brazilian soldiers. "Everything is going very well," Humberto told Argentina:

Here I am in the command post of General Zenóbio. The other comrades of the Mascarenhas headquarters did not have the same mission, and I am the only one here. I was present at all the principal actions, including the taking of Quiesa, Massarosa, Camaiore, and the famous combat of Monte Prano. . . . I have seen how our soldiers march to combat, quiet and confident, how they behave in the face of bombardments, laughing and fun-making, and how they stand resigned before our wounded and dead. . . . The British and the Americans do not like the American Black, but, on the other hand, they accept the Brazilian Black. The latter is nimble, smart, and fatalistic, whereas the former

[9] HACB to Argentina, Italy, August 28, 1944, File H1, p. 17, PVCB.
[10] Mascarenhas de Moraes, *A F.E.B. pelo Seu Comandante*, p. 79 n. 34; João Carlos Gross, in Gross and Oswaldo Gudolle Aranha interview, Rio de Janeiro, October 2, 1975.
[11] Meira Mattos interview, January 5, 1976; HACB to Argentina, Ponte a Moriano, October 16, 1944, File H1, p. 51, PVCB; "Folhas de Alterações," File G2, Part 3, CPDOC; statement of Euclides Zenóbio da Costa about HACB, October 12, 1944, in "Campanha da Itália," File G1, CPDOC.
[12] Barreto Leite Filho interview, November 25, 1975.

is almost a coward. Most of the Americans do not tire of praising the conduct of the Brazilians in the battle of the Apennines.[13]

"What has been unpleasant for our soldiers," he wrote two days later, "is the terrain. For military campaigning, the Apennines are terrible." Besides, with the unending rain of autumn, mud had become one of the soldiers' most telling enemies.[14]

"The Italian people," Humberto told his wife, "see the Brazilian as a liberator." Each town taken by the Brazilians "becomes tumultuous in its expression of relief. The Germans submit the Italians to a horrible captivity, forcing them blindly to work, killing without restraint, robbing everything, including children's clothes. When they withdraw, they take with them almost all the able-bodied men."

The *jéca* (rustic Brazilian) was described by Humberto as feeding the famished natives from his rations. "The people think that the *jéca* is better than the Englishman or American. He is more sentimental and enjoys chatting with the Italians."[15]

5. The Move to the Serchio Valley (October, 1944)

The Brazilian combat activities attracted foreign newspaper correspondents. "You cannot imagine," Humberto wrote Argentina, "how many war correspondents are behind the lines." Some did not seem to Humberto to be doing much work. "They speak with the soldiers, eat with them, and leave at the end of the day without sending out any reports."[1]

But others, Castello felt, were to be admired. Among them was *O Jornal*'s João Batista Barreto Leite Filho, who had been at the Colégio Militar de Porto Alegre with Castello and who was the first Brazilian

[13] HACB to Argentina, Quiesa, October 2, 1944, File H1, p. 39, PVCB. Problems caused at this time by "crumbling units" of American black troops are mentioned in Lee, *Employment of Negro Troops*, pp. 547–553. That author quotes a company commander (a black officer) discussing his men: "They will not stay in their positions unless constantly watched and give as their reason for leaving the fact that the men next to them will leave anyway so there is no reason for them to stay. . . . Morale is bad and I dread to make a night move, because so many of the men can slip away" (p. 550).

[14] HACB to Argentina, Quiesa, October 4, 1944, File H1, p. 40, PVCB.

[15] Ibid.

[1] HACB to Argentina, Ponte a Moriano, October 16, 1944, File H1, p. 51, PVCB.

reporter sent overseas in World War II. Having sent reports from North Africa and France, he had come to report on the FEB and spent three days with Castello at the front. Barreto Leite found his old schoolmate a perceptive officer of vast vision who enjoyed every minute of his work and was able to discuss overall strategy and tactical details with great clarity.[2]

To Barreto Leite and other reporters, including a French journalist and several American war correspondents, Castello Branco explained his wish that the news coverage not be of a personal nature. Nevertheless a story by Barreto Leite in *O Jornal* on September 26, 1944, was almost entirely about Castello Branco, who was quoted as saying that the Brazilians now had proofs about German atrocities. With the appearance of such articles mentioning Castello Branco's name, Argentina was kept busy—"the entire day," she wrote to Humberto—answering phone calls from relatives and friends.[3]

Later the American correspondents congratulated Castello Branco on articles that appeared under his name in a New York newspaper. Readers, they told him, believed him to be a leading correspondent and commentator on the FEB.[4]

The Brazilian advances had occurred while the Germans, avoiding decisive combat and destroying bridges behind them, retreated in orderly form to stronger positions.[5] The Germans who withdrew from Monte Prano, which had little tactical value, reached a particularly mountainous area that the Fourth Corps felt would be extremely difficult to penetrate at that moment. Therefore on September 28 the Zenóbio combat team was ordered to move eastward into the valley of the Serchio River and to follow the valley northward, thus approaching the German stronghold at Castelnuovo di Garfagnana.

The move brought Castello Branco from Quiesa to Ponte a Moriano, an ancient town on the Serchio River surrounded by walls over one thousand years old. "I am," he wrote Argentina, "sleeping in a castle already robbed of all of its furniture and dishes. During this campaign

[2] Barreto Leite Filho interview, November 25, 1975.

[3] João Batista Barreto Leite Filho, "Atrocidades Alemãs," *O Jornal*, September 26, 1944. Argentina to HACB, Rio de Janeiro, October 12, 1944, File H3, Part 1, PVCB.

[4] HACB to Argentina, Ponte a Moriano, October 12, 1944, File H1, p. 49, PVCB.

[5] Newton C. de Andrade Mello interview, Rio de Janeiro, November 1, 1975; Newton C. de Andrade Mello, *O Brasil na II Grande Guerra*, p. 17.

I have been installed in peasants' homes as well as castles of counts and barons."[6]

At the outset of their new operation, the Brazilians were handicapped by heavy rainfall. But they were on the move again on October 4, and on October 6 they entered the towns of Fornaci and Coreglia Antelminelli.

Then the Fourth Corps, in need of help along the west coast, borrowed Major João Carlos Gross's First Battalion and a part of the combat team's artillery battalion. Zenóbio's remaining men, unhappy with this development, had to limit themselves largely to reconnaissance work and the repair of roads and bridges until the units were returned to Zenóbio on October 14.[7]

6. A Pause in the Action (October, 1944)

During the pause in the drive of Zenóbio's combat team, Humberto wrote long letters to Argentina to be taken to Rio by officers who had recently come to Italy with War Minister Dutra and who would soon be returning to Brazil with him.

Telling Argentina about Allied orders to occupy "houses and more houses," Humberto said that they were issued to reduce the exposure of the soldiers to the cold weather:

The Allies don't rob, but the invasion of properties is almost merciless. The Italian, however, is already used to this: his home has lodged Italian and German soldiers, and now comes an enormous wave of Americans, British, Brazilians, Indians, Poles, New Zealanders, and South Africans, not to mention the French, who have marched victoriously through Italy. A nation defeated is the greatest collective and individual punishment for a people. How horrible! And the Italian population is without men between 20 and 30; hundreds of thousands are prisoners of the Allies, millions are working in Germany, many are fugitives, an enormous number are dead, and, besides, the German, when he retreats, shoots and burns men and women, and takes much with him. This is a gigantic struggle. One has to put the wholesale carnage out of one's mind and understand that humanity is struggling for a better so-

[6] HACB to Argentina, Ponte a Moriano, October 8, 1944, File H1, p. 43, PVCB.
[7] Mascarenhas de Moraes, *A F.E.B. pelo Seu Comandante*, pp. 86–90; Mascarenhas de Moraes, *Memórias*, I, 180.

cial and political order. You cannot imagine the horror that the Allied Forces have of Nazism. The Englishman is foremost in his hostility to it. The American says: what I want is to live and not be forced into conformity by having to belong to a herd. The Allies do not practice barbarity; they mistreat no one, neither Italians nor Germans.[1]

Also during the pause in the action Humberto made a four-hour visit to Florence to buy gifts to send home via the *portadores*. The possibilities of finding many worthwhile gifts, Humberto told Argentina, were reduced thanks to German theft and the enormous purchases already made by the Americans and British, and, he added, they were further reduced by his own insufficient funds—less than those of Amauri Kruel, who made this trip to Florence with him. Nevertheless Humberto sent home three large packages containing hats, purses, gloves, blouses, bracelets, perfume, pewter objects, paintings, miniatures, medallions, cameos, and a silk handmade suit for Argentina. And although Humberto, when he made these trips to Florence, always seemed to be in a hurry to get back to his work, he was careful in his selections. Delighting in giving presents—and in being thanked for them—he wrote many pages to Argentina describing each gift in detail.[2]

Amauri Kruel, who temporarily headed the Fourth Section of the division staff while Major Senna Campos prepared for the disembarkation of the Second and Third FEB detachments in Livorno, told Castello Branco about the mail being brought with the new FEB contingents. Soon, therefore, Castello was driven in his jeep from Ponte a Moriano to Pisa, and there he received a mountain of letters (including one written by Argentina, Nieta, and Paulo as far back as July 8); he received also messages and presents from his family brought by newly arrived friends, among them Major Luís Mendes da Silva and Lieutenant Colonel Ademar de Queiroz. Colonel Henrique Batista Duffles Teixeira Lott, a new arrival hoping for an assignment in Italy, disappointed Humberto, for he had not bothered to phone the Castello Branco home before leaving Brazil.[3]

[1] HACB to Argentina, October 8, 1944, File H1, p. 43, PVCB.

[2] HACB to Argentina, October 10, 1944, File H1, PVCB; Barreto Leite Filho interview, November 25, 1975.

[3] HACB to Argentina, Ponte a Moriano, October 15, 1944, File H1, p. 50, PVCB; Senna Campos interview, November 26, 1975.

Lott, a rigidly correct military man without much sparkle of humor, was not in a good mood. Of the sixty small amphibious boats (LCI's) that arrived in Livorno from Naples with the ten thousand Brazilians who had crossed the ocean on the *General W. A. Mann* and *General Meigs*, Lott's little boat provided the most miserable trip and was the last to reach shore. Colonel Lott therefore arrived in Livorno one day later than artillery General Cordeiro de Farias, who had graduated from Realengo six years after Lott and whom Lott had known as a little boy in knee breeches.[4]

Once in Italy, Lott sought a jeep for himself, but with his every request he was asked by some officer of inferior rank, "What is your function?" and was referred to someone else.[5] After being referred to Major Senna Campos (who asked his function), he was told to see Colonel Brayner, who had been picked by Mascarenhas ahead of Lott although he had graduated from Realengo four years later. Brayner sent Lott to Mascarenhas, with whom Lott had squabbled in Pernambuco.

Lott already had a matter for Mascarenhas, a weapons list that he felt he needed. When he reached Mascarenhas' trailer he found the division commander in no hurry to finish having coffee with Cordeiro. Granted admittance after a long wait, Lott had an unsatisfactory conversation. "What are you here for?" Mascarenhas asked. "I was sent here," Lott replied correctly. "All right, go back," Mascarenhas is said to have told him.[6]

Later, Lott advised Dutra that he did not like what he saw of the situation of the FEB in Italy, and he predicted trouble.[7] Dutra thanked him for his opinion and invited him to accompany him on his flight back to Brazil.

Castello Branco, after his disappointment from Lott in Pisa, returned to Zenóbio's combat post in Ponte a Moriano. There he hastened to write more long letters to be carried by the Dutra party after it made a brief visit to the fighting front. Much moved by Argentina's affectionate words, he wrote: "Your good pile of letters, presents, and news! What

[4] Henrique Batista Duffles Teixeira Lott interview, Rio de Janeiro, October 13, 1975.

[5] Senna Campos interview, November 26, 1975.

[6] Lott interview, October 13, 1975; Miranda interview, December 1, 1975.

[7] Lott interview, October 13, 1975.

an immense pleasure for me." The presents were sweets, socks, pajamas, and a sweater. They added to his wardrobe, which included a cap, brought from Brazil by Dutra, socks and pajamas given him by Crittenberger, as well as galoshes, a blanket, and a heavy coat that had come with the compliments of the American army.[8]

In a last letter for the Dutra party to carry, Humberto told Argentina: "Your sacrifice is great and mine no less: besides the hard life of the campaign, I feel, and feel very deeply, the separation. How good is our home!" Humberto had praise for the Brazilian troop and wrote that it continued to be successful.

The soldiers are well adapted. It is a shame that the cold has anticipated itself, as the Italians say. If Brazil would send three divisions, what an enormous prestige for the nation. You can't calculate what international advantage this would bring us after the war. The Americans, now lacking reserves, admire our performance. The Germans did not imagine that we could do what we are doing. . . . I continue at the front, and, in the *estado-maior* of the front, I await the entrance into the line of the rest of the Division.[9]

During Dutra's visit with Mascarenhas to the front on October 17, all agreed that the Brazilian soldiers, like the Americans, should wear distinctive insignia on their uniforms. The idea, which had been suggested earlier by Clark at a lunch attended by Dutra, resulted in a design by Senna Campos. With modifications it became *a cobra está fumando*, the pipe-smoking snake proudly worn by the Brazilians.[10]

[8] HACB to Argentina, October 10 and 15, 1944, File H1, PVCB.

[9] HACB to Argentina, Ponte a Moriano, October 16, 1944, File H1, p. 51, PVCB.

[10] Senna Campos, *Com a FEB na Itália*, pp. 95–98; About *a cobra está fumando* (the snake is smoking), Elber de Mello Henriques (*A FEB Doze Anos Depois*, pp. 194–195, reproduced in Raul Mattos A. Simões, *A Presença do Brasil na 2ª Guerra Mundial: Uma Antologia*, pp. 67–68) writes: "Many times I was told the following: one of the corps of troops of Rio de Janeiro had a commander with a changeable temperament. If he arrived at the barracks smoking a cigar it was one of the signs that he was in bad humor. The soldiers would say *a cobra está fumando!* And everyone would be warned. Captain Antorildo Silveira gives another version: In maneuvers in the Paraiba Valley the soldiers compared a long railroad train, its locomotive pouring out smoke in the front, with the winding image of a smoking snake. When they faced Vesuvius they had that recollection of struggles and hard work, and the expression stuck." Joel Silveira (interview, Rio de Janeiro, December 25, 1975) said that the expression *a cobra está fumando* was used in Minas Gerais by the 11th RI to say that

7. A Defeat for Zenóbio's Combat Team (October 31, 1944)

The Brazilian combat team, back to its full strength of five thousand on October 14, prepared to push on to further victories.

So great was the prestige of Zenóbio da Costa that some of his admirers presented to War Minister Dutra, during the minister's stay in Italy, a proposal for making the division command available to Zenóbio; Mascarenhas would be pushed upstairs to carry out glorified administrative work and promoted to some new superior rank of generalship not yet in existence. Mascarenhas, learning about the proposal from Clark after Dutra left Italy, objected to the "diabolical plan" in a conversation with Clark and in a letter to Dutra.[1]

While Mascarenhas awaited a reply from Dutra, Zenóbio eyed Castelnuovo di Garfagnana, the communications center far up the Serchio River that the Germans decided they must hold. It was in a section of particularly rugged mountains, where the Germans had constructed concrete-reinforced pillboxes and where the Allies relied on scarce pack mules for carrying supplies from base installations.[2]

Undeterred by recent reconnaissance reports that made it clear that the Germans were bringing reinforcements to Castelnuovo di Garfagnana, Zenóbio appealed to Crittenberger for permission to attack the stronghold, where a victory for his combat team would be the crowning glory of its campaign in the Serchio Valley. Mascarenhas, consulted by Crittenberger, did not oppose the idea, so Zenóbio's combat team prepared to improve its position by taking small towns in the area along a front of about twenty kilometers.[3] To reinforce the Brazilian effort, the Fourth Corps moved two field artillery battalions from the coastal area to the Serchio Valley; one of them could only establish its positions

---

things were difficult. For further discussions, see Maria de Lourdes Ferreira Lins, *A Força Expedicionária Brasileira: Uma Tentativa de Interpretação*, pp. 243–244, and Gentil Palhares, *De São João del Rei ao Vale do Pó (Ou a Epopéia do 11º R.I. na 2ª Guerra Mundial): Documentário Histórico do 11º, 6º e 1º R.I.*, pp. 163–164.

[1] Mascarenhas de Moraes, *Memórias*, I, 193–197.

[2] Ibid., p. 186; Mascarenhas de Moraes, *A F.E.B. pelo Seu Comandante*, p. 92; Andrade Mello, *O Brasil na II Grande Guerra*, p. 18; Wondolowski, "History of the IV Corps," pp. 371, 393.

[3] Mascarenhas de Moraes, *Memórias*, I, 186; Andrade Mello, *O Brasil na II Grande Guerra*, p. 18.

"after literally dragging and carrying its guns over the muddy trail."[4]

"Starting yesterday," Castello wrote home on October 22, "my work has doubled, and it is greatly absorbing me. It is a new phase that I have begun and brings me greater responsibilities."[5]

Sommocolonia fell to the Brazilians on October 24, and two more towns on the twenty-fifth. On October 30, despite rain and a steep and slippery terrain, the first part of the operation was completed: the over-optimistic Brazilians, seizing Lama di Sotto and Monte San Quirico, found themselves within four kilometers of Castelnuovo di Garfagnana.

Before dawn on October 31, the Germans, in the midst of a rain-storm, counterattacked fiercely. The Brazilians, who had underestimated the enemy, were taken by surprise. They retreated to some of the re-cently taken positions, such as Sommocolonia.[6]

This ended the campaign of Zenóbio's combat team, because with the incorporation of the Second and Third detachments into Brazil's fighting force, Masarenhas assumed, early in November, 1944, the com-mand of the First Division, Zenóbio becoming commander of the divi-sion's infantry.[7]

Furthermore, at a meeting of the Allied High Command it had been decided that the Brazilian First Division should operate in the valley of the Reno River, 120 kilometers northeast of the Serchio Valley. The narrow, winding Serchio Valley, the Americans concluded, was at best an uncertain route to the north, easily defended and costly to seize, and they took note that the continual attention to offensive action was threat-ening to bring an early exhaustion of ammunition, priority for which had gone to General Eisenhower's forces on the western front.

The American leaders in Italy believed that the area of the Belve-dere hill mass, a ridge of modest height to the north of the Reno River, presented an approach to the north more feasible than the Serchio Val-ley, and they considered that the possession of the Belvedere hill mass would assure protection of Second Corps' left flank and facilitate the ad-vance on Bologna. Also, it was the decision of Crittenberger that the mission of the Fourth Corps to detain the maximum of enemy troops in

---

4 Wondolowski, "History of the IV Corps," pp. 385–386.

5 HACB to Argentina, Italy, October 22, 1944, File H1, PVCB.

6 Mascarenhas de Moraes, *Memórias*, I, 184–185.

7 Ibid., pp. 202, 220.

northwest Italy could "best be accomplished by a series of blows, scattered across the IV Corps front," rather than by concentration in one area.[8]

The Zenóbio combat team, now extinct, had in one and one-half months advanced forty kilometers and taken 208 prisoners. Thirteen Brazilians had been killed, 87 wounded, 183 hurt in accidents, and fewer than 10 taken prisoner.[9]

In Brazil the war minister, greatly influenced by the Castelnuovo di Garfagnana setback, rejected the plan to kick Mascarenhas upstairs.[10] Brayner writes that as a result of the Castelnuovo di Garfagnana failure, Zenóbio's earlier brilliant accomplishments went unrecognized, and that "his wings" were broken. But, he asserts, a part of the responsibility for the final failure rests with Castello Branco, as "the immediate adviser" of Zenóbio.[11]

Brayner, who developed the custom of finding Castello responsible only for failures in combat and never for successes, was having trouble with his Third Section head. He was unhappy that Castello occasionally spoke alone with Mascarenhas. The division commander, after one such conversation, summoned Brayner to tell him, in the presence of Castello, that it would be best to find a new head of the First Section. Brayner, who felt that information about such a matter should reach the general only from the chief of staff, replied that the First Section head had been selected by Mascarenhas, despite his lack of training at Fort Leavenworth, and that his work would improve with experience. For Castello's benefit, Brayner added, "Among us there are no stars or geniuses." But Mascarenhas felt it best to make a change. First Section head Thales Ribeiro da Costa was transferred to the inspectorship of the division. Lieutenant Colonel João da Costa Braga, an artillery officer who had received training at Fort Sill, was named to replace him.[12]

[8] Fourth Corps, "The North Apennines Campaign," p. 144. The comment about ammunition is taken from Wondolowski, "History of the IV Corps," p. 396.

[9] Mascarenhas de Moraes, Memórias, I, 185. Newton C. de Andrade Mello (O Brasil na II Grande Guerra, p. 19) says that the combat team took possession of a great area, "hundreds of hamlets, and some cities, advanced forty kilometers, and captured 208 prisoners" while giving up 290 casualties, including the dead, wounded, hurt in accidents, and those who disappeared.

[10] Mascarenhas de Moraes, Memórias, I, 197.

[11] Brayner, A Verdade sôbre a FEB, pp. 186–188.

[12] Brayner, Recordando os Bravos, p. 293–294.

8. Porretta Terme (November, 1944)

Early in November, 1944, ten thousand men of the recently arrived Second and Third detachments were at Filettole, near Pisa, awaiting weapons and receiving training without them under the supervision of Generals Zenóbio da Costa and Cordeiro de Farias. Meanwhile, the 6th RI, commanded by Colonel João de Segadas Viana, was ordered to go from the Serchio Valley to the Reno Valley to take over a sector at the front from other Allied units.

On the Reno River at Porretta Terme, once a small, attractive hot springs resort, Mascarenhas set up his division advance headquarters, which grew to have sixty officers and seventy other men. For the location of the headquarters, he and his staff chose one of the hotels, equipped in the basement with facilities that in happier days had provided visitors with natural springwater baths; they also occupied an adjoining house.[1]

Castello Branco and American liaison Major Vernon Walters took bedrooms on the top floor of the old hotel. There Castello found protection from the cutting cold of the nights in an eiderdown sleeping bag that he bought at the American officers' supply post; he usually referred to it as his "envelope."[2]

In offices next to each other in the adjoining house,[3] Amauri Kruel and Castello organized their staffs, the Second and Third sections, with the help of recently arrived majors. Major Hugo de Mattos Moura, good at languages, and Major Emygdio da Costa Miranda, famed for the bravery he displayed as a participant in the Prestes Column in the 1920's, were among those who worked with Kruel. Castello built up a group that included majors who had been cadets at Realengo when he had taught there in the late 1920's: Luís Mendes da Silva, Luís Tavares de Cunha Melo, Antônio Henrique Almeida Morais, and José Pinheiro de Ulhoa Cintra (son of Dutra's wife by a previous marriage).[4] Elsewhere

[1] Mascarenhas de Moraes, *Memórias*, I, 217. See File H2, p. 74, PVCB, for an incomplete letter from HACB telling of the hotel and the adjoining house.

[2] Vernon Walters interview, McLean, Virginia, June 12, 1975; HACB to Argentina, November 11, 1944, File H1, PVCB.

[3] Miranda interview, Rio de Janeiro, December 1, 1975; incomplete letter from HACB, File H2, p. 74, PVCB.

[4] All of these, except for Almeida Morais (who became an *aspirante* in January, 1927) were at Realengo when Castello Branco taught there. Ulhoa Cintra became a lieutenant colonel on December 25, 1944 (*Almanaque do Exército*, 1948).

in Porretta Terme, General Cordeiro de Farias found a house in which to organize his artillery staff, whose operations section (S-3) was headed by Lieutenant Colonel Nestor Penha Brasil and included Lieutenant Colonel Ademar de Queiroz.[5]

From Porretta Terme, Highway 64 led to Bologna, fifty kilometers to the northeast. The Allies, with the forthcoming Reno Valley operations in mind, were inspiring themselves with the slogan "Bologna before Christmas," but it was a difficult assignment for the weakened American Fifth Army and British Eighth Army. The highway was at the mercy of artillery fire from the German troops dominating the mountains that faced Porretta Terme from the northwest to the northeast: Monte Belvedere, Monte Gorgolesco, Mazzancana, Monte della Torraccia, Monte Castello, Monte della Croce, Torre de Nerone, and (not as high as the others) Castelnuovo.[6]

Almost as soon as Mascarenhas set up his headquarters, the Germans began to shell Porretta Terme heavily with both medium and heavy (170-mm) artillery. The bridges and rail installations were struck, as were the headquarters of the Brazilian division. So bad did the shelling become that Mascarenhas transferred to a more southerly area two sections of his staff, the First (Personnel) and the Fourth (Logistics).[7]

On several occasions when the shelling at night was heavy, Walters phoned Castello Branco, the only other person who slept on the top floor, to ask whether he felt that they should go down to the shelter in the basement. Castello would usually answer that he was a Brazilian and did not like the cold. He was snug in his "envelope" and had no intention of getting out of it, shelling or no shelling. Walters, although inclined to take to shelter, did not do so lest he lose face.[8]

On one night a shell exploded right outside Walters' window, and

[5] Ademar de Queiroz interview, Rio de Janeiro, October 13, 1975. Ademar de Queiroz had worked in the office of War Minister Dutra before accepting Cordeiro de Farias' invitation to join the staff of the artillery in Italy. In June, 1945, Penha Brasil was promoted to colonel and left the headship of S-3, being replaced by Queiroz.

[6] Not to be confused with Castelnuovo di Garfagnana, sixty-five kilometers to the west of Castelnuovo.

[7] Walters, "Humberto de Alencar Castello Branco," Part 1, "The War Years," p. 3. Porretta Terme and its destruction are described in Gilberto Peixoto, *A Campanha da Itália*, pp. 63–67. Mascarenhas de Moraes, *Memórias*, I, 215–216.

[8] Walters, "Humberto de Alencar Castello Branco," Part 1 "The War Years," pp. 3–4.

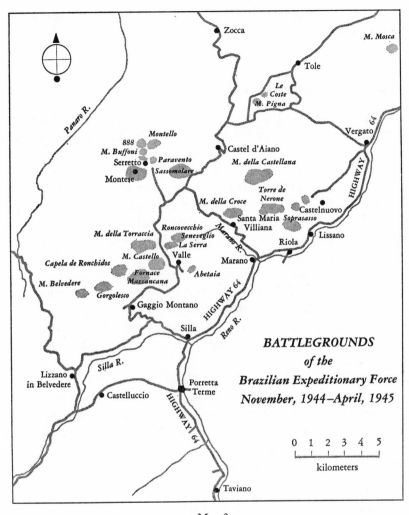

BATTLEGROUNDS

of the

Brazilian Expeditionary Force
November, 1944–April, 1945

0 1 2 3 4 5

kilometers

Map 3

several fragments embedded themselves in the wooden shutters (the windows had long since been smashed); the force of the explosion almost threw the American major off the camp cot on which he had spread his sleeping bag. Castello, commenting on the explosion at breakfast the next morning, said that it must have been quite loud on Walters' side of the building. Walters said that indeed it had, and he brought up the possibility of their moving to another building in Porretta Terme. Castello laughed and said that sometimes in trying to move away from trouble one moves into it.[9]

9. The Role of the Third Section (November, 1944)

Castello Branco's Third Section, constantly studying the military situation and drawing up operational plans based on information supplied by other sections and services, became the focal point at the Porretta Terme headquarters. It received a stream of visitors, such as Cordeiro and his artillerymen.[1] Crittenberger, who seldom let a day go by without visiting the Brazilians, was frequently there. (The Fourth Corps commander had a pointed cap and a flat-topped hat, and the Brazilians came to feel that when he wore his pointed cap he could be expected to be in a critical mood.)[2]

Humberto, writing to Argentina, described himself seated in an "exquisite Louis XIV chair" behind a "First Empire desk." "Ademar is at my side in a large armchair of fine and beautiful tapestry. Mendes, further on, is in an artistic chair of Gobelin tapestry of gold fabric. Nobody knows who owns it. We are all seated, the Americans with their feet on the chairs."[3]

Mascarenhas worked closely with Castello Branco. This type of association between generals and the heads of their third sections (G-3), Mascarenhas notes, was common in the Allied armies. But it represented a transformation from his earlier relationship with his staff. Chief of Staff Brayner, who did not like the change, attributed it to an "improper hypertrophy" on Castello's part.[4] But the officers were coming to find

[9] Ibid. See also Luís Viana Filho, *O Governo Castelo Branco*, p. 35.

[1] Ademar de Queiroz interview, Rio de Janeiro, October 13, 1975.

[2] Walters interview, June 12, 1975.

[3] Incomplete letter from HACB, File H2, p. 74, PVCB.

[4] Mascarenhas de Moraes, *Memórias*, I, 216–217. Frank D. McCann, Jr. (*The Brazilian-American Alliance, 1937–1945*, p. 499) explains, "When the FEB was formed, its staff was organized in the French style with a chief of staff coordinating its efforts and responsible only to the commander. In Italy Mascarenhas, without changing the staff structure, shifted to the American procedure of the commander dealing directly with his operations staff officer (G-3), who was Lt. Colonel Humberto de A. Castello Branco. This left full-Colonel Lima Brayner with a substantially reduced operations role." Brayner, *A Verdade sôbre a FEB*, pp. 229, 243, 262.

that when they spoke with Brayner they could get no decisions, whereas Castello had no hesitancy in making them.[5]

After Major João Carlos Gross brought his First Battalion of the 6th RI from the Serchio Valley to a position south of Porretta Terme, he received his orders from Castello: he was to take his men through Porretta Terme to a more forward position and have them replace a South African unit. When they reached the more forward position, an enemy barrage of mortar and artillery fire struck, and Gross himself was lucky not to be killed.[6]

After that experience, Gross was asked by an irate Castello why he had not stopped in to see him while bringing his men through Porretta Terme. The major said he had received no order to do so. Castello said he had given the order. "I received no order," and, "I gave the order," were repeated over and over until the men were shouting at each other. This was an unusual occurrence, for subordinates did not dare shout at Castello; those who did not know him well were in fear of him.

Gross, before leaving the enraged Castello, asked him to check to see if his order had been given to Gross. When the major saw Castello about this matter later, Castello told him to see Brayner. Gross, who had no respect for Brayner and expected to find him practically asleep at his desk, burst out laughing disrespectfully—a reaction that put Gross further into Castello's disfavor.[7]

Whenever the Third Section completed a set of studies, and only then, was Mascarenhas in the habit of calling meetings, attended by himself, Generals Zenóbio da Costa and Cordeiro de Farias, Colonel Brayner, and Lieutenant Colonel Castello Branco. Castello Branco submitting a clear explanation, would propose what action he felt should be taken. Mascarenhas would listen to the comments of his generals and his chief of staff and then give the final decision.[8]

At Porretta Terme in mid-November Castello Branco could be found absorbed in the plans for the first phase of the Allied operations in the Reno Valley which bore the name "Aggressive Defense." The immedi-

[5] The officers, generals today, making this observation prefer not to be quoted. It agrees with remarks on p. 3 of HACB to Argentina, Alessandria, May 17, 1945, File H2, p. 48, PVCB.

[6] Gross, in Gross and Aranha interview, October 2, 1975.

[7] Ibid.

[8] Mascarenhas de Moraes, Memórias, I, 216.

ate plan, devised by the Fourth Corps' Task Force Forty-five, was for a surprise attack on the Belvedere hill mass. The plan called for the Task Force to use two American battalions to take Monte Belvedere and Monte della Torraccia while the 6th RI's Third Battalion, commanded by Major Silvino Nóbrega, was to seize the high ground in the vicinity of Monte Castello. Mascarenhas did not like the fragmentation of his First Division by such borrowings, but he agreed to the suggestion after Crittenberger spoke enthusiastically about the chances for a successful action.[9]

Castello Branco was studying the proposed attack when unexpectedly he received a batch of letters from home. Written months before, they were filled with comments about his visit to Pompeii and his audience with the Pope. "How different everything is today!" Humberto replied to Argentina. "Rain, mud, snow, cold winds, battles and more battles." It being clear by now that he would not be home for Christmas, he sent suggestions about how it should be observed: "On Christmas, my dear Argentina, don't forget to have supper with Paulo and Nieta, just as though I were at home. Flowers, radio music, and French toast. Live well on that night in our home. . . . Here I shall be thinking of the happy Christmas of our home."[10]

Late at night on November 19, with Task Force Forty-five's surprise attack scheduled to occur in four or five days, Mascarenhas found that Castello, wet and covered with mud, had just come in from outside in order to study plans.

"When," Mascarenhas asked, "will you finish this work?"

"At five o'clock in the morning."

"How would you like two days of rest in Florence?"[11]

Castello welcomed the idea and received the general's permission to have Amauri Kruel go with him. The two friends shared a room in an excellent hotel, luxuriated in warm baths, and enjoyed good restaurant meals accompanied by orchestra music. They attended the theater (as they had done in Porto Alegre thirty years earlier) and went shopping. Castello picked up a miniature that he had ordered on his previous visit

[9] Wondolowski, "History of the IV Corps," p. 407; Mascarenhas de Moraes, Memórias, I, 224.

[10] HACB to Argentina, Italy, November 19, 1944, File H1, PVCB.

[11] HACB to Argentina, Italy, November 21, 1944, File H1, PVCB.

to Florence, and he commissioned a painting by one of Italy's foremost artists. Kruel's considerable purchases included a cuckoo clock.[12]

10. The Setbacks at Monte Castello (November, 1944)

Humberto Castello Branco and Amauri Kruel were back at the front in time to witness the hard fighting of November 24, 25, and 26 in the Monte Belvedere–Monte Castello area, during which the American Task Force Forty-five failed to achieve its objectives. Mascarenhas, although without responsibility for these attacks, went with Castello to the field to observe them from an abandoned house standing next to a church that served as the command post of the 6th RI's weary Third Battalion. The general was impressed by the personal assistance that Castello gave to the battalion.[1] "Lieutenant Colonel Castello Branco," he wrote later, "provided dedicated help to our troop, hurling himself to the front in collaboration with the battalion commander in order to select a better location for the attacking men, and, despite the enemy fire, he remained at the side of the battalion commander in order to explain details of his mission."[2]

General Crittenberger (probably wearing his pointed cap) met with Mascarenhas, Brayner, and Castello Branco at Porretta Terme on November 26, after the Brazilian battalion had been forced back from its earlier advance on Monte Castello. While the fifty-five-year-old Crittenberger was known for the encouragement he frequently gave to the Brazilians, on this occasion differences developed between the Brazilian and American officers; the presence of Walters was a help, because when he felt it advisable he introduced diplomacy into translation.[3] In the end,

---

[12] Ibid; Amauri Kruel (interview, Rio de Janeiro, December 11, 1975) says that they also went to museums.

[1] Mascarenhas de Moraes, *Memórias*, II, 224. Both Mascarenhas (p. 222) and Brayner (*A Verdade sôbre a FEB*, p. 250) state that the Third Battalion of the 6th RI was in a state of exhaustion when it was used by Task Force Forty-five.

[2] Praise of HACB by Mascarenhas de Morais, published in Information Bulletin of the Brazilian forces, April 1, 1945, and given in "Folhas de Alterações," File G2, Part 3, and "Campanha da Itália," File G1, CPDOC. This reference is to November 24, 1944.

[3] Walters interview, June 12, 1975; Brayner, *A Verdade sôbre a FEB*, pp. 245–

the battalion of the 6th RI that had been borrowed by Task Force Forty five, was returned to Mascarenhas' command. Together with its return, the boundary between Task Force Forty-five and the FEB was shifted westward in order to place Monte Castello in the Brazilian zone.[4] Crittenberger, turning over to Mascarenhas the responsibility for the seizure of Monte Castello, said: "I pass the ball to you."[5]

Mascarenhas was to use fresh troops, and more of them than had earlier advanced on Monte Castello, and he was also to have the assistance of a platoon of tanks and a platoon of tank destroyers transferred from Task Force Forty-five. Nevertheless, the Brazilian division commander, whose defensive responsibility in Operation Aggressive Defense now covered a front of fifteen kilometers, was not keen on attacking Monte Castello immediately.[6] The training of the men who had reached Italy early in October had been less efficient than that of the First Detachment.[7] Furthermore, the Germans were aided by the fog and cold rains and held a commanding geographical position. Many of them had firing stations in crevices among very large rocks that were impervious to the Allied artillery,[8] and others fired from "permanently fixed concrete emplacements."[9] But the Fourth Corps, still in grim combat around Monte Belvedere, considered it essential for the Brazilians to act because of Monte Castello's importance and because the tie-up of Germans in the area would help prevent a setback of the Fifth Army in the Bologna area.

254; Cunha Melo interview, November 17, 1975. According to Aguinaldo José Senna Campos (interview, November 26, 1975), Lott, on one occasion when he was waiting to see Mascarenhas, heard Walters make what Lott felt was an inaccurate translation of Crittenberger's words, and therefore Lott, when he saw Mascarenhas, said that Walters had not translated correctly.

[4] Wondolowski, "History of the IV Corps," pp. 409–410; Operations Instructions No. 70, November 26, 1944, signed by Crittenberger, in Fourth Corps, "North Apennines Campaign."

[5] Brayner, A Verdade sôbre a FEB, p. 250.

[6] Wondolowski, "History of the IV Corps," pp. 409–410; Andrade Mello, O Brasil na II Grande Guerra, p. 22; Mascarenhas de Moraes, A F.E.B. pelo Seu Comandante, 119 n. 68; Mascarenhas de Moraes, Memórias, I, 225.

[7] Newton C. de Andrade Mello writes (O Brasil na II Grande Guerra, p. 21) that the instruction of the new contingent of 10,375 men "did not develop with the same efficiency revealed in the previous contingent."

[8] Renato Moniz de Aragão interview, November 22, 1975; Pacca da Fonseca, Ferreira Marques, and Teixeira interview, November 6, 1975.

[9] Wondolowski, "History of the IV Corps," p. 414.

To participate in the new attack, Mascarenhas brought in artillery and infantry who had been training near Pisa and who were being moved to the Reno Valley in trucks during the cold nights of late November.[10] The infantry attack, to be commanded by Zenóbio da Costa, was to be undertaken by the First Battalion of the 1st RI (Sampaio Regiment) and the Third Battalion of the 11th RI (Tiradentes Regiment). The former battalion, led by Major Olívio Gondim de Uzeda, had reached the Reno Valley on November 22, but the latter, which was commanded by Major Cândido Alves da Silva and was the only 11th RI battalion moved at that time from the training camp, did not arrive until November 28, just before it was to play its role.

The attack by these inexperienced troops began at 7:00 A.M. on November 29 under the protection of Cordeiro de Farias' artillery. As was his custom, Castello Branco took to the battlefield, and was much of the time close to the commanders of the attacking groups in order, as Mascarenhas put it, "to translate the thinking of the division commander in the course of all the action." [11]

Despite the fact that on the night of November 28 the Americans had been forced to retire from the vicinity of Monte Belvedere, leaving the Brazilians without support on their left, the Brazilians were advancing well by noon on November 29, and soon the battalion of the 11th RI was close to its objective. But later in the day heavy bombardments and counterattacks inflicted severe losses on the battalion of the 1st RI, and it retreated to its starting point. When darkness began to fall it was decided that it would be better to call off the attack than to send for reserves from the 6th RI (Ipiranga Regiment).[12]

The 1st RI reported 29 dead and 128 wounded, whereas the more fortunate 11th RI suffered 5 deaths and 25 wounded.[13] Captain Newton

[10] Senna Campos, *Com a FEB na Itália*, pp. 113–114; Mascarenhas de Moraes, *Memórias*, I, 207; Brayner, *A Verdade sôbre a FEB*, p. 256.

[11] Praise of HACB by Mascarenhas de Morais, published in Information Bulletin of the Brazilian forces, April 1, 1945, and given in "Folhas de Alterações," File G2, Part 3, and "Campanha da Itália," File G1, CPDOC. This reference is to November 29, 1944.

[12] Castello Branco, *O Brasil na II Grande Guerra*, p. 252; Peixoto, *A Campanha da Itália*, p. 82; Fourth Corps, "North Apennines Campaign," p. 90; Mascarenhas de Moraes, *A F.E.B. pelo Seu Comandante*, p. 118.

[13] Brayner, *A Verdade sôbre a FEB*, p. 258. Accounts of the participation by the 11th RI are given in Delmiro Pereira de Andrade, *O 11º R.I. na 2ª Guerra Mundial*, pp. 71–73, and Palhares, *De São João del Rei ao Vale do Pó*, pp. 235–238.

Correa de Andrade Mello, after participating with the 11th RI in the conflict, wrote in his diary that "the action of the American tanks, as on other occasions, left much to be desired." Chief of Staff Brayner has defended Zenóbio's role by pointing out that Zenóbio issued no orders, the whole operation being handled by Castello's Third Section.[14]

11. The Defeat at Monte Castello, December 12, 1944

Monte Castello stood defiantly—mockingly, some felt. As the scene of the setbacks suffered in six days late in November, it was becoming regarded as a sort of spook or taboo for the Brazilians, leaving according to one narrator, "deep marks in the spirit of the men."[1]

Characteristically, Castello Branco immediately set to work devising possible new attacks. "He moved about the battlefield," Walters says, "talking to officers, NCO's, and soldiers, trying to ascertain what had caused the failure, what weaknesses there had been in the training, what could be done to make success more certain in the next attack."[2]

In this work Castello was much assisted by Zenóbio, and he was encouraged by the Americans, who continued to want to have Germans drawn from the Bologna area, where the Fifth Army was having a hard time. "The commander of the Fifth Army," Mascarenhas writes, "still persisted with the idea of retaking the offensive before winter." Therefore, Mascarenhas adds, Crittenberger issued instructions on December 5, calling on the Brazilian Division to capture and hold the ridge extending all the way from Monte Belvedere to Monte della Torraccia.[3]

On December 6, Mascarenhas, accompanied by Zenóbio, Cordeiro, Brayner, and Castello Branco, looked over the terrain, after which Mascarenhas, with the support of his two generals, chose Monte Castello as

[14] Newton C. de Andrade Mello, *Meu Diário da Guerra na Itália: De 30-VI-1944 a 18-VII-1945*, p. 96; Brayner, *A Verdade sôbre a FEB*, p. 257.

[1] Castello Branco, *O Brasil na II Grande Guerra*, p. 252.

[2] Walters, "Humberto de Alencar Castello Branco," Part 1, "The War Years," pp. 5–6.

[3] Miranda interview, December 1, 1975; Osvaldo Cordeiro de Farias interview, Rio de Janeiro, December 16, 1974; Mascarenhas de Moraes, *Memórias*, I, 226; Mascarenhas de Moraes, *A F.E.B. pelo Seu Comandante*, p. 119; Operations Instructions No 72, December 5, 1944, signed by Crittenberger, in Fourth Corps, "North Apennines Campaign."

the objective again. Starting at once, the artillery of Cordeiro made some telling blows, including one that knocked out a German pillbox on Monte Castello.

Amauri Kruel, using the information supplied by the Second Section, drew up an evaluation of the enemy's strength and gave it to the Third Section to show that the attack, as it was being planned, could not succeed. According to reports from German prisoners and from *partigiani* (Italian antifascist guerrilla fighters), the Germans had fortified themselves with trenches and mines behind barbed-wide protection since the November attacks and had augmented their artillery positions in the Monte Belvedere sector. Kruel felt that it would be a mistake to try to send the Brazilian infantrymen all of the long distance up to the heights of Monte Castello; he had in mind other plans that he believed would be more likely to be effective.[4]

But Kruel found that Castello Branco, acting in what the intelligence officer considered a touchy, conceited manner, was quite unwilling to accept the evaluation of the Second Section. Therefore on December 8, at a morning meeting attended by Mascarenhas, his generals, and his top staff officers, Kruel argued his case, forecasting the failure of the plans of the Third Section. Mascarenhas, however, agreed with Castello. The Americans, too, believed that the Brazilian attack, "carefully planned by the Division staff," had "every chance of success."[5]

Heavy rains and badly sleeted roads so delayed the buildup of supplies that the attack was postponed from December 11 to December 12.[6] Following this postponement, Brayner spoke with Mascarenhas, at 9:00 P.M. on the eleventh, to complain that the operations instructions issued by his Third Section were too complicated.[7] He considered them to be a model of pure academicism, the sort of document that the Escola de Estado Maior might produce to give cadets a difficult time. But he found that the instructions had already been distributed to the troop commanders.

Unfortunately for the Brazilian attack, the miserable weather continued on December 12. Rain and dense fog hampered what the artillery

----

[4] Wondolowski, "History of the IV Corps," pp. 436–437; Amauri Kruel interview, Rio de Janeiro, December 11, 1975.

[5] Wondolowski, "History of the IV Corps," p. 438.

[6] Ibid., pp. 436–437.

[7] Brayner, *Recordando os Bravos*, pp. 117–118, 316.

could do to provide help to the two chief attacking units, the Second and Third Battalions of the 1st RI, and to the troops of the 11th RI that were to support those two battalions.[8] Climatic conditions ruled out promised air coverage by the Americans, and the vast areas of mud limited the mobility of the American tanks.[9]

The 1st RI's Third Battalion, commanded by Major Franklin Rodrigues de Morais, was off at 6:00 A.M., half an hour ahead of schedule, right after American artillery fire against Monte Belvedere prematurely broke the silence and alerted the enemy.[10] Making its way across a sea of mud, the battalion grappled with slopes and ledges after reaching the steep incline. A few men came close to the elusive crest, but they were shot down.

In the meantime the enemy had opened full fire from strongholds in front of Monte Castello: Mazzancana, Fornace, Viteline, Valle, and Abetaia ("the corridor of death"). Mortars poured into the starting point of the 1st RI's Second Battalion, commanded by Major Sizeno Sarmento. This battalion, getting under way at about 8:00 A.M., an hour and a half late, was unsuccessful in giving support to Major Franklin's Third Battalion.[11]

At about 9:30 A.M. a false report that Mazzancana, Valle, and Abetaia had been taken from the enemy led the Brazilian artillery to suspend shelling in the direction of those areas and resulted in orders for the First Battalion of the 11th RI to "clean up" the areas, a mission impos-

[8] Nelson Rodrigues de Carvalho, *Do Terço Velho ao Sampaio da F.E.B.*, p. 94; Pereira de Andrade, *O 11º R.I. na 2ª Guerra Mundial*, p. 77; Mascarenhas de Moraes, *A F.E.B. pelo Seu Comandante*, p. 122; Castello Branco, *O Brasil na II Grande Guerra*, pp. 261 ff.; Brayner, *A Verdade sôbre a FEB*, p. 290. Captain Carlos de Meira Mattos, who was Mascarenhas' liaison with the American Fourth Corps during most of the Italian campaign, served as commander of the Second Company of the First Battalion of the 11th RI at the time of the December 12 attack (see Pereira de Andrade, *O 11º R.I. na 2ª Guerra Mundial*, pp. 78, 84–85, and Brayner, *Recordando os Bravos*, p. 311). Major Jurandir de Bizarria Mamede served as the S-3 on the staff of the 11th RI (see Pereira de Andrade, *O 11º R.I. na 2ª Guerra Mundial*, pp. 75–76; Palhares, *De São João del Rei ao Vale do Pó*, p. 47).

[9] Floriano de Lima Brayner has stated that on account of the weather it would have been advisable to postpone the attack again but that Crittenberger did not want to do so (interview, Rio de Janeiro, October 6, 1975).

[10] Brayner, *A Verdade sôbre a FEB*, p. 281; Castello Branco, *O Brasil na II Grande Guerra*, p. 265.

[11] Palhares, *De São João del Rei ao Vale do Pó*, p. 268; HACB and Aguinaldo Caiado de Castro, quoted in Brayner, *Recordando os Bravos*, pp. 119–122.

sible to accomplish in the face of a "violent reaction by the enemy." Colonel Aguinaldo Caiado de Castro, commander of the 1st RI, called for assistance by the American tanks and was told that they were stuck in the mud.[12] The violent barrage by the Germans forced a general, if orderly retreat.

During this calamity, in which the 1st RI suffered 112 casualties and the 11th RI received 33,[13] Mascarenhas was at his Porretta Terme headquarters, for he had important visitors—Brazilian Air Minister Joaquim Salgado Filho and his party. Crittenberger was present. And so was Major Walters—a man, Brayner tells us, on whose work Mascarenhas relied too heavily.[14]

Castello Branco, covered with mud, broke into this distinguished gathering at 3:00 P.M. He had already persuaded Zenóbio that in order to prevent useless sacrifices, offensive efforts should be ended, and he wanted the approval of the top command. "I was looking for generals, including the American," he later wrote to Argentina, "in order to resolve the matter before nightfall."[15]

Soon Zenóbio himself entered the Porretta Terme headquarters and advised that the operation against Monte Castello had been terminated. Crittenberger, irritated, was critical of the decision to call it a day so soon, and he dwelt on the fact that the Brazilians had used only thirty-five hundred of the twelve thousand artillery and mortar shells made available to them.[16]

[12] Castello Branco, O Brasil na II Grande Guerra, p. 265; Carvalho, Do Terço Velho ao Sampaio da F.E.B., pp. 95, 96; Aguinaldo Caiado de Castro and Carvalho Lisboa, quoted in Brayner, Recordando os Bravos, pp. 122, 126.

[13] Castello Branco, O Brasil na II Grande Guerra, p. 268. Aguinaldo José Senna Campos, A Conquista de Monte Castelo pela FEB, p. 12, says that the Brazilian dead from the December 12 operation "remained unburied, some almost on the top of the hill, for two months, preserved by the snow that covered all the region on the night of December 23–24." Mascarenhas de Moraes, A F.E.B. pelo Seu Comandante, pp. 124 n. 76, 303, gives the following figures for Brazilian losses in late 1944: October, 8 killed in action, 53 wounded in action, 104 injured in accidents; November, 74 killed, 241 wounded, 84 injured; December, 84 killed, 267 wounded, 146 injured. Aguinaldo José Senna Campos (interview, November 26, 1975) estimates that 87 percent of the accidents were in vehicles.

[14] Brayner, A Verdade sôbre a FEB, p. 243.

[15] Ibid., p. 324; HACB to Argentina, Italy, December 13, 1944, File H1, p. 67, PVCB.

[16] Brayner, A Verdade sôbre a FEB, pp. 283–285; Floriano de Lima Brayner interview, Rio de Janeiro, November 25, 1975.

Air Minister Salgado Filho, finding himself in the midst of arguments, received some enlightenment from Colonel Brayner: "In war, Mr. Minister, things don't always go well." [17]

12. Consequences of the Monte Castello Setbacks

Beginning on the afternoon of December 12, 1944, the causes of Brazilian failure of that day were analyzed. Brazilians commented on the weather, the terrain, the absence of any element of surprise, and the lack of support by American planes and tanks. They argued that without visibility it was impossible to make effective use of the twelve thousand artillery and mortars shells, and some of them insisted that the plan of the infantry attack, being essentially no different from the previous unsuccessful ones, had failed to inspire the confidence necessary for the maximum exhibition of combativeness.[1]

To discuss the Brazilian performance, Crittenberger and other Americans met with Mascarenhas, Zenóbio, and Cordeiro at 5:00 P.M. on December 12 at the Fourth Corps headquarters at Taviano, south of Porretta Terme. A crestfallen Mascarenhas assumed the responsibility for the Brazilian reverse.[2]

The Brazilians made their points, but the Americans were critical of the behavior of the Brazilian troops, which, they kept repeating, had not been sufficiently trained. Upon hearing the suggestion of some Americans that the Brazilians should be retired from the front due to a "lack of offensive spirit," Cordeiro asserted that the Americans were mistaken in their judgment, and he cited the promised American assistance that had not been forthcoming.[3] In the end, the Brazilians were not retired from the front, but they were relieved, at least for the time being, of playing an aggressive role in Operation Aggressive Defense. They were to spend the oncoming winter months defending a fifteen-kilometer

---

[17] Brayner, *A Verdade sôbro a FEB*, p. 285.

[1] Castello Branco, *O Brasil na II Grande Guerra*, p. 269.

[2] Mascarenhas de Moraes, *Memórias*, I, 226.

[3] Brayner, *A Verdade sôbre a FEB*, p. 287. Peter S. Wondolowski writes ("History of the IV Corps," p. 438) that "enemy resistance had been too great for some of the green troops." Miranda interview, December 1, 1975.

front (facing the stretch between Monte Belvedere and Lissano) and noting any moves there by the enemy.[4]

At Porretta Terme on the night of December 12–13, Castello Branco could not sleep. He arose early to arrange, in a handsome hand-carved box, Christmas gifts from Florence to be taken to Brazil by a *portador*. Then he wrote a long and affectionate letter to Argentina describing the gifts and mentioning his state of exhaustion on the previous afternoon. He was, he said, "extremely concerned with the reverse that we suffered about 2:00 P.M.: a German counterattack that was a horrible, deadly struggle and that forced us to retreat a little!"[5]

To review the retreat carefully, Mascarenhas had scheduled a meeting at 7:30 A.M. on December 13, and Brayner therefore called Castello and Amauri Kruel to join him in a preparatory session earlier in the morning. At this session, Castello spoke of the failure of the two 1st RI battalions to begin the attack simultaneously at 6:30 A.M. But during most of the painful early half-hour session Castello listened to the chief of staff and Second Section head criticize his conduct and that of the Third Section on December 12. Brayner and Kruel maintained that during the combat the Third Section had issued incorrect reports, advising that Abetaia, Valle, and Mazzancana had been seized from the enemy, causing costly confusion around Abetaia and Valle and the suspension of artillery fire on Mazzancana. The issuance of such reports, as well as bulletins for Brazil, by the Third Section was upsetting to Brayner, because he claimed he had been kept in the dark, and it was upsetting to Kruel, who considered it an infringement on the area that was supposed to be under his control. Brayner, writing about this early-morning meeting, says that it "resulted in a complete disagreement and clash of ideas" between Castello and Kruel. "They almost came to blows," he adds.[6]

At the larger meeting conducted by Mascarenhas, commanders of regiments and other units were present, together with Zenóbio, Cordeiro, and staff members. A report by Colonel Caiado de Castro, 1st RI commander, told of the unexpected outburst of American artillery fire at

[4] Mascarenhas de Moraes, *A F.E.B. pelo Seu Comandante*, p. 126; Mascarenhas de Moraes, *Memórias*, I, 239.

[5] HACB to Argentina, Italy, December 13, 1944, File H1, p. 67, PVCB.

[6] Brayner, *A Verdade sôbre a FEB*, p. 289; Brayner, *Recordando os Bravos*, pp. 115–116, 313.

6:00 A.M. The colonel spoke also of misinformation about who held Mazzancana that he said had been brought to him by Major Almeida Morais of the Third Section. During the debate that followed, Castello asked for permission to leave the room. Receiving it, he walked out after recommending that his assistants remain.[7]

One thing Humberto long remembered about that meeting was the voice of Cordeiro de Farias in his defense. Years later, when Castello, president of Brazil, had occasion to pay tribute to Cordeiro de Farias, then his outgoing cabinet minister, Castello recalled the dark days of December, 1944: "During the attempts that were made to explain the defeat, the coverage that you gave me caused me to go ahead with more confidence in myself and in General Mascarenhas de Morais. I saw in you—more than a brother-in-arms—a friend." [8]

When Cordeiro, after bringing the Second FEB Detachment from Brazil, first came to Porretta Terme, he saw nothing in Castello to indicate that they would become friends. Castello's appearance, sometimes suggesting vanity, and his terribly efficient manner seemed to Cordeiro to be highly uncongenial. The two officers, courteous to each other, had a relationship that was strictly formal as they worked on possible artillery coverage for alternative infantry plans. But gradually Cordeiro's respect for Castello grew, particularly as it became clear to him that Castello was always willing to make decisions, even if the decisions were not easy to make, and was always willing to assume the responsibility for them. "The drama of Castello Branco," as Cordeiro came to see it in Italy, was that the lieutenant colonel was more respected than befriended.[9]

Cordeiro also had to deal with the "drama of Mascarenhas." So painful for the commander were the Brazilian defeats, and the bitter meeting of December 12 at the Fourth Corps headquarters, that Mascarenhas contemplated resigning. On December 14 he told Cordeiro of his plan to resign and heard the artilleryman plead that he not "abandon us to another commander. . . . You are able and respected by your subordinates, and without doubt will achieve the success you so desire."[10]

[7] Brayner, A Verdade sôbre a FEB, pp. 289–291; Brayner interview, October 6, 1975; Brayner, Recordando os Bravos, p. 123.

[8] HACB, "Discurso na Saída de Osvaldo Cordeiro de Farias," Brasília, June 15, 1966, File M, p. 52, CPDOC.

[9] Cordeiro de Farias interview, December 16, 1974.

[10] Mascarenhas de Moraes, Memórias, I, 227.

Mascarenhas not only decided to stay on, but he also resolved to alter his style of command, assuming complete charge of combat operations. He would do this by relying more than ever on Castello Branco, and at the same time he would encourage Castello Branco to have a close relationship with the head of the operations section, G-3, of the Fourth Corps' staff.[11]

Like Castello Branco, Mascarenhas gained confidence in himself from the words of Cordeiro. To his American allies he reiterated, now without apology, his conviction that missions that had been assigned to the Brazilian division were, as a rule, beyond the possibilities of a single division. Presently he learned that the Allies, who were fighting in northern Italy with twenty-four divisions against the enemy's thirty, had decided that the slogan "Bologna before Christmas" was impossible to achieve and was to be abandoned.[12]

The name of the new phase was "Stabilization."[13] Mascarenhas decided to use this new period to provide, with the help of the Fifth Army, efficient training for his men. He also sought to improve the morale of officers and soldiers by giving them time to relax in Florence and Rome.

While Mascarenhas thus prepared for the successes that Cordeiro had assured him would eventually be his, he was troubled by the rumors that followed the Brazilian defeat of December 12. Some of them had to do with his own replacement, while others pictured Castello Branco to be on his way out.[14] Mascarenhas came to the defense of the chief of the Third Section in a statement of praise that was unusually long and that said, in part: "Lieutenant Colonel Castello Branco constituted the perfect guarantee for the absolute success of the Third Section, which he headed with great brilliance. . . . He also stood out because of his vigilance, always being attentive, and intervening, with ability and perspicacity, in all decisive situations; he demonstrated great confidence and

[11] Ibid.

[12] Ibid., pp. 227, 239.

[13] According to Mascarenhas de Moraes (*Memórias*, I, 220, 230, and *A F.E.B. pelo Seu Comandante*, pp. 105, 125), Defensiva Agressiva lasted from November 5 to December 12, 1944, and Estabilização lasted from December 13, 1944, to February 18, 1945.

[14] Mendes da Silva, "Testemunho," Part 3, "Tenente Coronel Humberto de Alencar Castello Branco na Guerra, 1944–1945"; Ferreira, "O General Castello Que Conheci."

skill in directing operations, matching his unusual fearlessness under fire."[15]

13. Stabilization

Early in the Stabilization phase, which extended through heavy snowfalls, General Mark Clark succeeded General Sir Harold Alexander as commander of the Allied Fifteenth Group of Armies, and General Lucian K. Truscott, Jr., became Fifth Army commander. Truscott, addressing himself at once to aggressive German activity in and around the Serchio Valley, ordered Crittenberger "to protect the theater supply base in the Leghorn area at all costs and to prevent enemy interference with the vital Leghorn-Lucca-Pistoia supply route."[1]

As recommended by Truscott, the Fourth Corps headquarters were moved late in December to Lucca, southwest of the former headquarters at Taviano. With this shift in emphasis to the west, the Fourth Corps lost the services of the Sixth South African Armored Division, but the Ninety-second Infantry Division was reincorporated into its ranks, and it received, as new attachments, the Eighty-fifth Infantry Division and most of the Eighth Indian Division. The Fourth Corps, its troop strength thus raised to eighty-nine thousand,[2] continued to include the FEB, which now found itself at the extreme east of Fourth Corps territory adjoining the South Africans, who had become incorporated into the Second Corps. Already in early December the FEB troops had been augmented by the arrival of the Fourth Detachment, forty-five hundred members of replacement battalions and companies. These new Brazilian soldiers, little instructed before embarkation, were given training first near Pisa and then, starting late in December, near Staffoli, east of Lucca.[3]

In the Porretta Terme area training was administered to Brazilians who had recently been fighting. The men found themselves required to devote hours to gymnastic exercises that they deeply resented and that

[15] Statement of Mascarenhas de Moraes, January 14, 1945, in "Campanha da Itália," File G1, CPDOC.

[1] Lucian K. Truscott, Jr., to Willis Crittenberger, in Fourth Corps, "North Apennines Campaign," p. 97. Leghorn is another name for Livorno.

[2] Fourth Corps, "North Apennines Campaign," p. 101.

[3] Historical Section, USAFSA, "History of the USAFSA," pp. 341–342.

Brayner felt were designed to humiliate them.[4] Some of the men were given lessons in skiing with the thought that this might help them in their patrol work.

Altogether, the patrol work of the Brazilians along their fifteen-kilometer front was active and successful. The men formed small groups that were usually led by sergeants and were often accompanied by Italian antifascist *partigiani*. These patrol groups, ordered to maintain "aggressive contact" with the enemy, exchanged fire with enemy groups. Germans and Brazilians were frequently killed and wounded.[5] The Brazilian patrols picked up information about what the enemy was doing and brought in a total of twenty-three prisoners, who were interrogated by Major Hugo de Mattos Moura and another Second Section officer and sometimes by Vernon Walters.

"Our troop," Humberto wrote home in January, 1945, "has improved its positions. The men are bellicose; they fight well. . . . But the whole Fifth Army is blocked by snow and ice."[6] What surprised the Americans was that the cases of trench foot, or frozen feet, among the Brazilians were fewer than expected. The Brazilians tended not to wear the uncomfortable combat boots under their snow boots. Together with more than one pair of socks, they used a lot of paper around their feet—issues of *Stars and Stripes* or *Cruzeiro do Sul*—which allowed good blood circulation.[7]

During Stabilization heavy artillery fire was exchanged. The Brazilian advance installations at Porretta Terme were hit in this period by about 250 heavy 170-mm shells, which caused destruction and wounded men. Crittenberger suggested that Mascarenhas move his base beyond the enemy artillery fire. But Castello Branco and Mascarenhas were agreed that the Brazilian headquarters should not withdraw an inch.[8]

[4] Brayner, *A Verdade sôbre a FEB*, pp. 332–333. See also Castello Branco, *O Brasil na II Grande Guerra*, pp. 296–300.

[5] Rubem Braga, *Com a F.E.B. na Itália: Crônicas*, pp. 63–64, 99; Joel Silveira, *Histórias de Pracinha*, pp. 50–51; Castello Branco, *O Brasil na II Grande Guerra*, pp. 284, 289; Mascarenhas de Moraes, *A F.E.B. pelo Seu Comandante*, p. 129 n. 85. See also Fourth Corps, "North Apennines Campaign," pp. 106–109.

[6] HACB to Argentina, January 20, 1945, File H1, p. 90, PVCB.

[7] Barreto Leite Filho interview, November 25, 1975; Senna Campos interview, November 26, 1975; Peixoto, *A Campanha da Itália*, pp. 114–115.

[8] Mascarenhas de Moraes, *A F.E.B. pelo Seu Comandante*, p. 127 n. 81; Mendes da Silva, "Testemunho," Part 3, "Tenente Coronel Humberto de Alencar Castello Branco na Guerra, 1944–1945"; Mascarenhas de Moraes, *Memórias*, I, 231.

"Let us always move forward," Humberto said in a letter to Argentina in which he described his duties as "difficult, arduous, and of great responsibility." "My section," he wrote in another letter, "is the 'nerve center' of the division; everything goes out from here, to those below or to those above. So you can imagine my responsibilities." After cautioning Argentina not to repeat these words about his work, he went on to say that the situation was more of expectation than of calm. "The German continues to resist obstinately, in spite of some sign of weakening. For example: in one place today he attacked us furiously before dawn, wounding men and officers; whereas, in another place, three German sergeants deserted and surrendered to our men."[9]

"My dear Didina," Humberto wrote another time, addressing Argentina by his nickname for her, "I read the piece in *Correio da Manhã.* What favorable publicity about me! Thank God, we asked for nothing of this sort. We must avoid being in the limelight."[10]

Castello's relations with Kruel during this first phase of Stabilization started off rather poorly, again on account of information issued by the Third Section. On December 15 Kruel found the Third Section sending a cable to Brazil that he considered misleading. Following a disagreeable altercation about the matter with Castello, he discussed it with Brayner.[11] The often-neglected chief of staff, reluctant ever to find a good word for Castello or Cordeiro, could be counted on to support Kruel; for that matter, he could be counted on to contribute to a worsening of the relationship between the two old friends.[12]

Zenóbio, continually praised and defended by Brayner, was sometimes described as a supporter of the views of Brayner and Kruel.[13] But Zenóbio made a serious effort to heal the breach developing between Castello and Kruel. He called them into his quarters in the barracks and pleaded with them, saying: "You have been friends for almost forty years." Kruel told him: "I have nothing against Castello Branco. . . .

[9] HACB to Argentina, Italy, December 13, 1944; January 2, 1945, File H1, pp. 67, 81A, PVCB.

[10] HACB to Argentina, Italy, December 15, 1944, File H1, p. 70, PVCB.

[11] Amauri Kruel interview, December 11, 1975.

[12] The general who supplied this information has written a letter to say that while it is true, he deems it inconvenient to have it reported; it is therefore to be assumed that he would rather not be quoted.

[13] Miranda interview, December 1, 1975.

Just what happened is this, . . ." and he went on to explain his position.[14]

The complete backing that Mascarenhas always gave to Castello, and the advantages that went with it, were not likely in the long run to work in favor of a reconciliation between Castello and Kruel because of the presence of jealousy.[15] But Castello evidently decided that the differences that arose in the first half of December were not insurmountable problems. He responded to Zenóbio's appeal. When he went to Florence in the first days of January, he spent three thousand cruzeiros (about U.S. $160) on a "beautiful tablecloth" to adorn Kruel's home in Rio. He gave it to Amauri with the explanation that the gift was made "in appreciation of our good comradeship here."[16]

14. Christmas and the New Year

Castello Branco's letters to his wife in December were full of Christmas thoughts: "I received the *doce de manga* for Christmas and shall eat it, thinking that I am at supper with you and the children. How difficult it will be to go through that day without you!" On December 19 Humberto sent Argentina four Christmas cards. "This year," one of his messages said, "I cannot be with you. But I send you the best that I am able: a very, very affectionate kiss."[1]

On Christmas Eve Castello Branco went out to inspect the snow-covered grounds around the Porretta Terme headquarters. Climbing a hill, he saw Brazilian soldiers on patrol, dressed for the first time in their white capes. He returned at 10:00 P.M. for the Third Section's Christmas Eve supper, which was attended by his orderly Edésio, sergeants, a chauffeur, some Americans, and the four majors then assisting him: Luís Mendes da Silva, Luís Tavares da Cunha Melo, Antônio Henrique de Almeida Morais, and José Pinheiro de Ulhoa Cintra.

[14] Amauri Kruel interview, December 11, 1975.

[15] Ibid. Kruel said that Mascarenhas "began to give *força* [power] to Castello." Miranda interview, December 1, 1975; HACB to Argentina, Alessandria, May 17, 1945, p. 3, File H2, p. 48, PVCB.

[16] HACB to Argentina, Porretta Terme, January 6, 1945, File H1, PVCB.

[1] HACB to Argentina, Italy, December 17, 1944, File H1, p. 72, PVCB; four Christmas cards, HACB to Argentina, Italy, December 19, 1944, File H1, p. 75, PVCB.

Castello Branco opened his remarks to his men by calling on them to remember, besides their loved ones at home, those who at that moment were fighting at their posts. As the supper began, presents were given to the sergeants, Edésio, and the chauffeur. Then came a surprise that warmly touched Castello. The four majors presented him with a Florentine leather briefcase, and a lieutenant gave him a desk calendar.[2]

Amauri Kruel and other officers who did not belong to the Third Section joined the supper, and then all of them went through heavy snowflakes to the division's chapel to attend midnight Mass. After Mass, Castello worked at his desk, and before going to sleep, he wrote to Argentina:

Just as it became time for supper, I had a very happy experience: I received your card with wishes for a good Christmas—gentle, so loving, that it brought tears to my eyes. . . . And, shortly before the Mass, I received the present from Nieta, the diary with the affectionate inscription that also made my eyes humid. War, when it does not brutalize man, gives him moments of high elevation. I am truly elevated by the emotions of this Christmas, unprecedented for me, and by the longing for you and my children. . . . Don't forget me; pray for me. . . . I can see our dining room, the setting, the table arrangements. You, pretty and discreet. Nieta irrepressible, and talking. Paulo trying to make the evening a cheerful one. And I have faith in God that you are all happy![3]

Again, on New Year's Eve Castello pictured how his family must be at home. This was at midnight during a deafening welcome to the new year that was given by the artillery all over the north of Italy. "Greetings even from our adversaries," Humberto wrote Argentina. After the shooting was over, the members of the Third Section met for a party: "Sweets, wine, embraces, reciprocal good wishes and renewals of sincere expressions of confidence in their old chief, moving me very much. They, that is my assistants and soldiers, are a great stimulation to me."[4]

"Oh!" Humberto wrote to Argentina few days later, "what a happy Section, with Morais, Cintra, Mendes, and Cunha Melo."[5]

On January 5 Castello was driven in his "valiant jeep" through an

[2] HACB to Argentina, December 25, 1944, File H1, p. 76, PVCB.
[3] Ibid.
[4] HACB to Argentina, January 1, 1945, File H1, p. 80, PVCB.
[5] HACB to Argentina, January 6, 1945, File H1, PVCB.

"incredibly cold snowstorm" to Florence, which he reached in two and one-half hours.[6] With his twenty-third wedding anniversary in mind, he purchased gifts to be taken home by Colonel Brayner, who was to spend a few weeks in Brazil, and by Major Almeida Morais, who was being transferred back to Brazil. Later Humberto sent Argentina a Fourth Corps helmet that had been inscribed to Colonel Castello Branco. ("They tell me that in the American army I already have this rank.")[7]

On the wedding anniversary date, February 6, Humberto wrote to Argentina:

Far from you, very, very far from our home, I turn as though it were 1922, to the greatest affection of all my life, greater even than the one I had for my mother. And it could not be otherwise, because in you I have the best that I possess, the reason for the existence of my happiness and the enchantment of the best days of my life. Besides, if I have lived well, if I have accomplished anything in my existence, I owe it to you, to your stimulation and help. You gave me our two children, in whom today I relive our childhood and youth. We four are happy because you are one of the four.[8]

[6] Ibid.
[7] HACB to Argentina, February 6, 1945, File H1, p. 96, PVCB.
[8] Ibid.

Victories in Italy
(1945)

Imagine my responsibility, deciding where and how to attack. And what if the result is a failure? But it is my duty not to vacillate, nor to pass the responsibility elsewhere.

1. The Discipline-minded Acting Chief of Staff (January, 1945)

ON January 7, 1945, Brayner left on his three-week trip to represent Mascarenhas in giving a first-hand account of the FEB's activities to President Vargas and War Minister Dutra. In Italy Castello Branco became acting chief of staff. Ademar de Queiroz, known as "Tico Tico" (Sparrow), assumed the headship of Castello's Third Section despite Brayner's feeling that the lieutenant colonel was an "artillery officer who knew little about the problems of the FEB." [1]

Two or three days after becoming acting chief of staff, Castello was informed that two men in Major João Carlos Gross's battalion had raped a girl and murdered her uncle. To his office he called Gross, an outstanding sportsman whose inclination to ask questions had gained him the nickname of João Pergunta. Locking the door after the major entered, Castello said, "Two men of your battalion killed a man in order to put themselves into the man's niece." Castello added that the crime was a disgrace for Brazil and that the two men should be shot. He gave Gross one hour in which to bring the men to him. [2]

Gross was surprised. His battalion, having replaced South Africans in November at the foot of Soprasasso Peak, twelve kilometers from Porretta Terme, had been relieved only on January 8; the men were very tired when they reached the headquarters area late on the ninth. It also surprised Gross to find Castello acting on his own as "judge and

---

[1] Floriano de Lima Brayner, *A Verdade sôbre a FEB*, pp. 312, 332.

[2] João Carlos Gross, in Gross and Osvaldo G. Aranha interview, Rio de Janeiro, October 2, 1975. *Pergunta* means "question."

executioner." But Gross, who had stood up very vocally to Castello in the face of an accusation made in November, was not surprised to find Castello apparently hostile to him. The major believed that Castello, due perhaps to his physique, was prejudiced against well-known athletes and was inclined to consider them stupid.

Gross told Castello that in his battalion of 1,032 men he had "saints, angels, and demons. . . . It is possible that two of my men did what you say, but I don't think so." He explained that he had had had bad men when his battalion had been trained in Brazil, and that he had worked personally to try to straighten them out. There were, Gross said, about twenty of them, but they were all Paulistas of Italian extraction and spoke such good Italian that they had no need to kill to get what they wanted.

After leaving Castello's office, Gross called his captains, giving them twenty minutes to bring him true information. He learned that all of the battalion's men had been sleeping and that because of their exhaustion, none had left camp.

With the assurances of the captains that no one in the battalion was responsible, Gross went with his report to Castello. Castello was furious and placed Gross directly under his orders (on the *reserva* of Castello) but with instructions to report to him three times a day instead of the usual once a day. Whenever Gross reported, the saluting was followed by Castello's asking Gross whether he had prepared a platoon to carry out the executions. This went on, day after day.

Gross, assigned to reconnaissance work, returned one day from a study of the German position to find his battalion in a happy frame of mind: police had found that the murderer was a member of the staff of the division! Continuing to report three times daily to Castello, Gross would always ask if Castello had a platoon ready to carry out the execution. Finally Castello wrote a memorandum that ordered Gross to report only once a day; later the military justice system (which Castello had all along intended to use) condemned the murderer to thirty years' imprisonment. Gross felt that he had scored a second time.[3]

Commenting years later on the FEB, Castello stated that the discipline of a wartime campaign had not been properly administered before the embarkations from Brazil. "Then there was a sort of shock, with the

[3] Ibid.

officers realizing that the former control had not been adequate. Sergeants were surprised by the unexpected change in treatment. Soldiers did not understand the discipline of a nation at war, and wanted to react subtly." [4]

Walters writes of Castello: "At time of danger he clearly felt fear as do all men, but the iron self-discipline he always maintained guaranteed his icy calm and demanded it of others." To illustrate this point, Walters tells of an incident that occurred after he was awakened at about 2:00 A.M. on a snowy night by Brazilian artillery fire, which, he noted, was falling not far from the command headquarters. Forcing himself to abandon his sleeping bag, Walters threw on his clothes and knocked at Castello's door. But Castello had gone down to the Third Section, and there Walters found him wrapping himself in heavy clothing, preparing to go out. He was going to Silla Bridge, three kilometers to the north, where, he said in reply to Walters' inquiry, something peculiar was going on. As the Fourth Corps would no doubt be calling Walters later about the matter, Castello asked the American if he wanted to go along. Although Walters felt that the evidence indicated that the Germans had penetrated south to Silla Bridge, he could hardly decline Castello's invitation, because it had been given in the presence of several Brazilian officers. "So," Walters writes, "trying to hide my 6′ 3″ behind his 5′ 6″, I climbed into the jeep behind him and we drove to Silla Bridge with shelling continuing." [5]

At the bridge, where Brazilian soldiers were milling around, Castello found the lieutenant in charge and asked him severely who he was and what he was doing there. The lieutenant came to attention and said that he and his platoon had gone into position at the front, north of the bridge, that night after coming up from the personnel replacement center. They had, the lieutenant said, relieved another Brazilian platoon and then at about 2:00 A.M. had been attacked by the Germans. The excited lieutenant told of how "thousands of huge, blond Germans had swarmed over his positions, shouting "Heil Hitler."

Castello eyed the lieutenant coldly and said that there were not thou-

[4] HACB, handwritten notes of speech delivered in Campos, R.J., in the collection at the Escola de Comando e Estado Maior do Exército (ECEME), Praia Vermelha, Rio de Janeiro, p. 13.

[5] Vernon Walters, "Humberto de Alencar Castello Branco" (typewritten), Part 1, "The Years of War," pp. 6, 7.

sands of Germans facing his positions and that no one had charged shouting "Heil Hitler" since Tunisia. The lieutenant replied that this was indeed what had happened. Then Castello asked if the lieutenant had orders to leave his position. When the younger officer answered that he did not, Castello sternly ordered him to go back at once. "Colonel," the lieutenant said, "I don't mind dying for Brazil, but I don't want my son to be an orphan in a hopeless cause." Castello looked sharply at him and, casually reaching down and loosening the cover of his holster, ordered: "Lieutenant, go back at once or your son really will be an orphan before morning." The lieutenant, Walters writes, "grasped the full portent" of the lieutenant colonel's meaning, and "obviously impressed by Castello's coolness," clicked his heels, saluted, and, followed by his men, moved silently into the night to resume his position.

Six weeks later, Walters adds, that same lieutenant was decorated for heroism. "Castello's icy calm had made the lieutenant and his men understand their duty as soldiers of Brazil." [6]

2. Still Snowbound (January, 1945)

Late in January, important visitors came to Porretta Terme. One of them, brought on January 24 by General Crittenberger, was General Lucian K. Truscott, Jr., the recently appointed commander of the Fifth Army. Assisted by Castello, Mascarenhas explained to Truscott the defensive work being carried out by the Brazilians.[1] Truscott, having been advised by the Americans that he might find a tendency on the part of the Brazilians never to admit a mistake but to blame something or other when things went wrong, told the top Brazilian officers about a serious error that he had once made. Exaggerating, for the sake of his purpose, he said that the error had cost "thousands of lives." Mascarenhas and the other Brazilians were deeply impressed by Truscott's "admission." During the following months they became fond of Truscott—almost as fond of him as they were of Crittenberger, who could be found somewhere in the Brazilian division sector almost every day.[2]

[6] Ibid., p. 8.

[1] João Baptista Mascarenhas de Moraes, *Memórias*, II, 375.

[2] Vernon Walters interview, McLean, Virginia, June 12, 1975; Vernon Walters to JWFD, Washington, D.C., July 11, 1975.

On the day after Truscott's first visit, a group of Brazilian diplomats, escorted from Rome by Amauri Kruel, reached Porretta Terme; among them were Maurício Nabuco, ambassador to the Vatican, and Vasco Leitão da Cunha, minister to the headquarters of the Allied forces.[3]

Castello, assigned by Mascarenhas the mission of briefing the diplomats on the military situation, gave what Barreto Leite has called an "amazing" performance—one which led the war correspondent to feel that Castello might regret "having only a division to fight with."[4] Revealing great vision and imagination, as well as a vast knowledge, Castello first covered the area of the entire Fifth Army and then, in a closeup, dwelt on the tactics of the Brazilian First Division.

A few days later Amauri Kruel fulfilled the mission assigned to him by taking the diplomats to Montecatini to meet with General Olímpio Falconière da Cunha, who had arrived from Brazil at the same time as Cordiero de Farias and was serving as coordinator of noncombat organs.[5]

In one of the long letters that Humberto wrote almost daily to Argentina late in January, he said that Maurício Nabuco and Leitão da Cunha had become his good friends. Paragraphs in this and other letters were devoted to new gifts that Humberto was sending, including hats for the wives of Ademar de Queiroz and Luís Mendes da Silva. Along with a package for Argentina containing a work of art that he had commissioned by "the best painter of Tuscany," Humberto sent a biography of the artist and instructions for unpacking, framing, and avoiding humidity. "We are building up one of the best collections of paintings in Brazil. . . . All that our art 'gallery' lacks is a landscape of Minas."[6]

Castello himself continued to receive presents from the American Fourth Corps. One was a radio that brought "the world" to his desk and that allowed him sometimes to work while listening to Maurice Chevalier sing *Ma Pomme* and other songs in Paris. But it was not so easy to work when the radio brought messages from Germany for the Brazilian troops. Messages asserting that the wives of the FEB officers made love to the Americans who had "taken over Brazil" were described by Hum-

---

[3] Mascarenhas de Moraes, *Memórias*, II, 376; Vasco Leitão da Cunha interview, Rio de Janeiro, November 23, 1974.

[4] João Batista Barreto Leite Filho interview, Rio de Janeiro, November 25, 1975.

[5] Mascarenhas de Moraes, *Memórias*, I, 208–209, describes the responsibilities of General Falconière.

[6] HACB to Argentina, January 27, 28, 1945, File H1, pp. 93, 95, PVCB.

berto as "filth." They were part of a campaign that included leaflets,
sent by special projectiles, with drawings of a one-legged Zé Carioca on
crutches or of Americans raising their flag over Brazil. One of them argued, "Why does Brazil produce so little petroleum? Because the Americans don't want Brazil to produce petroleum." [7]

3. Preparing for Operation Encore (February, 1945)

Also late in January Mascarenhas went from the front to Naples to
inspect service units and to learn recent Brazilian news from the returning Brayner. Brayner said that in Rio he had detected rumors that Mascarenhas was to be replaced and that he had discouraged the idea.[1]

Mascarenhas proposed to Brayner that Ademar de Queiroz remain
as head of the Third Section and that Castello Branco assume a new
post, that of assistant chief of staff, in charge of the Second and Third
sections. This plan, which would have left the chief of staff with direct
authority over the First and Fourth sections only, was rejected by Brayner.[2]

Mascarenhas and Brayner were still away from the front on February
8 when Fourth Corps commander Crittenberger held a meeting at Lucca
with Brazil's representatives, Zenóbio and Castello Branco.[3] The Brazilians, accompanied by Walters, learned that it was time to prepare Operation Encore, a general all-out offensive.

The Brazilian role, it was decided at the Lucca meeting, would be to
capture Monte Castello in close association with the recently arrived
American Tenth Mountain Division. The Brazilians were to move
against Monte Castello after the mountain division had overcome strong-

[7] HACB to Argentina, January 6, 1945, File H1, PVCB. Zé Carioca was a nickname for the Brazilian soldier (and was the title of a newspaper put out by the FEB).
For German propaganda, see Aguinaldo José Senna Campos, *Com a FEB na Itália*:
Páginas do Meu Diário, pp. 144–150; Maria de Lourdes Ferreira Lins, *A Força Expedicionária Brasileira*: *Uma Tentativa de Interpretação*, pp. 145–150; Peter S. Wondolowski, "History of the IV Corps, 1941–1945" (typewritten), Historical Manuscript
File, Office of the Chief of Military History, Washington, D.C., p. 486. Rubem Braga,
Com a F.E.B. na Itália: *Crônicas*, p. 79, writes that the Portuguese in the German
propaganda leaflets was faulty.
[1] Brayner, *A Verdade sôbre a FEB*, p. 325.
[2] Floriano de Lima Brayner, *Recordando os Bravos*, pp. 154–155.
[3] João Baptista Mascarenhas de Moraes, *A F.E.B. pelo Seu Comandante*, p. 133.

holds to its west (Monte Belvedere, Monte Gorgolesco, and Capela de Ronchidos) and had started to attack Monte della Torraccia, which lies north of Monte Castello. Following the hoped-for fall of Monte Castello, the FEB's assignment was to advance eastward, attacking Santa Maria Villiana (south of Monte della Croce), Torre de Nerone, and Castelnuovo.[4]

As a morale booster, every day in the interval before the scheduled offensive the FEB's soldiers received Brazilian *feijão* (beans) and rice. Brazilian food, which had been available in the past months from time to time depending on ship arrivals, was certainly greatly preferred to C ration (or K ration, consumed during combat) and was more welcome than the food usually provided by the Americans—due in part to the Brazilian cooks' lack of familiarity with what they generally received.[5]

"We are going to take the offensive," Humberto wrote Argentina on February 10. He explained that he would have to write her less frequently. "Oh! how much work, how many trips from one place to another, and what enomous anxiety! . . . Imagine my responsibility, deciding where and how to attack. And what if the result is a failure? But it is my duty not to vacillate, nor to pass the responsibility elsewhere."[6]

Already in January Major Alcyr d'Ávila Melo (of the Realengo class of January, 1929) had joined the Third Section, replacing Major Almeida Morais (described by Humberto as "the best assistant I have had here"). And on February 11, when Mascarenhas and Brayner returned to Porretta Terme, they brought with them Captain Newton Castello Branco Tavares, who joined the Third Section and delivered to Humberto from Argentina a letter and a green neckerchief ("the most beautiful in the whole Division," Humberto told her). Brayner also brought the Third Section head letters from home as well as "all sorts of news." "Brayner has a fertile imagination," Humberto wrote Argentina, adding, "This is a pity, for the news may be exaggerated."[7]

On February 11 Mascarenhas and his top officers called on Major General George Price Hays, commander of the Tenth Mountain Division, which was well prepared for the difficult weather and terrain. "I have," they heard Hays say, "a troop recruited and trained in the moun-

[4] Mascarenhas de Moraes, *Memórias*, I, 240.
[5] Aguinaldo José Senna Campos interview, Rio de Janeiro, November 26, 1975.
[6] HACB to Argentina, Porretta Terme, February 10, 1945, File H1, p. 99, PVCB.
[7] HACB to Argentina, February 11, 12, 1945, File H1, pp. 100, 105, PVCB.

tains; in spite of that, we have an immense respect for the mountains." Mascarenhas was delighted to receive confirmation of the news that, thanks to a decision made by Crittenberger in Mascarenhas' absence, Monte Castello had been assigned to the Brazilians,[8] for its capture had become a point of honor for the FEB.

Castello, asked by Mascarenhas on the afternoon of February 12 to draw up details for the Brazilian operation, presented at a meeting the next day his plan for a two-pronged attack. After hearing the comments of Zenóbio and Cordeiro, Mascarenhas approved the plan and told Zenóbio to choose the unit that would carry it out. Zenóbio named the 1st RI (Sampaio Regiment), commanded by Colonel Caiado de Castro.[9]

In a final meeting at Lucca on February 16, Mascarenhas and Castello went over the details with Hays, whose mountain division was at that time detached from Task Force Forty-five. The Mazzancana area, originally considered within the scope of the FEB, was added to the assignment of the Tenth Mountain Division.[10]

Following the meeting, Humberto wrote to Argentina to say that "we are going to enter into a very active period of operations, decisive for us, that is, for the prestige of the Division and the improvement of our tactical situation." After describing the assistance given him by a lieutenant on whom Argentina had commented, Humberto added:

I know men very well and now they hold no secrets from me. As for [the lieutenant] there is, in my favor, a large difference in our ages, which causes him even to be frightened of me, without my giving reason for fear in anyone. Respect, yes, that is very high. War is a very difficult and brutal undertaking. For this reason, we see men as they are and not as they want to be. We appear as in X-ray pictures. Men, then, reveal matchless sentiments, including unselfishness and the sacrifice of their lives. But others are truly in less attractive garb: they lower themselves, they become weak, they rush to ruin or become useless. Ah! men. How I know them. How much quality, how much weakness! All this in connection with [the lieutenant]. But he is a child in comparison with the men with whom I really deal and work.[11]

---

[8] Brayner, *A Verdade sôbre a FEB*, p. 337; Mascarenhas de Moraes, *Memórias*, I, 240.

[9] Mascarenhas de Moraes, *Memórias*, I, 242.

[10] Ibid.

[11] HACB to Argentina, February 16, 1945, File H1, p. 107, PVCB.

4. Victory at Monte Castello (February 21, 1945)

On the night of February 18 the Tenth Mountain Division surprised the enemy by taking points to the west of Monte Belvedere, some of them so steep that the mountaineers had to use ropes to haul themselves up. On the next night the mountain division commenced its grim assault on Monte Belvedere, without artillery coverage, while the Brazilians, far to the east, created diversion by machine-gun and small-arms fire. At daybreak on February 20, Monte Belvedere fell, and within hours Gorgolesco was also in American hands. When Hays's sturdy men next turned to Mazzancana, they met powerful resistance, but by this time they had the assistance of nearly 150 guns, including the Brazilian artillery, considered by many to be more accurate than the American.[1]

Mascarenhas, ready to take personal command of the new Brazilian offensive, moved on the morning of the twentieth to his observation post, a modest country house five kilometers south of Monte Castello. There he had telephones connecting him with the commands of the Fourth Corps, the Tenth Mountain Division, the Brazilian artillery, and the 1st RI. Among those at the commander's side were Zenóbio, Brayner and Walters.[2] The sunny, cloudless days were perfect for planes and artillery.

With the help of attacks by the Brazilian air force,[3] the American Tenth Mountain Division forced the Germans from the Mazzancana area at about 5:00 P.M. on February 20. Then at 5:30 the next morning the highly successful mountain division moved against Monte della Torraccia, north of Monte Castello.

This was the signal for the FEB, using two-thirds of its infantry and practically all of its artillery, to unleash against Monte Castello its most formidable attack. While Colonel Nelson de Melo, who had taken over

1 Wondolowski, "History of the IV Corps," p. 513; U.S. Army, Fourth Corps, "The North Apennines Campaign, 10 September 1944 to 4 April 1945" (typewritten), Historical Manuscript File, Office of the Chief of Military History, Washington, D.C.; Emygdio da Costa Miranda (interview, Rio de Janeiro, December 1, 1975) said that the Germans feared the Brazilian artillery the most because of its unusual accuracy. Renato Moniz de Aragão (interview, Rio de Janeiro, November 22, 1975) described the Tenth Mountain Division as "belíssimo!" ("magnificent!").

2 Mascarenhas de Moraes, Memórias, I, 245.

3 Ibid.; Nelson Freire Lavenère-Wanderley, A Aeronáutica Militar Brasileira, p. 30.

the command of the 6th RI, undertook diversionary action to the east, the primary assault was entrusted to the 1st RI's First and Third battalions, the latter being the Franklin battalion that had fought with distinction during the setback of December 12.[4] Castello Branco and artillery officer Ademar de Queiroz spent much of their time at the post of 1st RI commander Caiado de Castro.

As specified in Castello's plan for a two-pronged attack, the 1st RI's First Battalion, commanded by Olívio Gondim de Uzeda, approached Monte Castello from Mazzancana and the west while to its right the Franklin battalion made a frontal attack from the south. Orlando Ramagem's battalion (the Second Battalion of the 11th RI), moved against Abetaia and gave coverage to the Franklin battalion's right flank. Important supporting roles were also carried out by the battalions of Sizeno Sarmento (the Second Battalion of the 1st RI) and Cândido Alves da Silva (the Third Battalion of the 11th RI).

The Uzeda battalion made good progress from Mazzancana but was delayed when a Tenth Mountain Division company mistook some of its men for Germans and fired on them.[5] The Franklin battalion, undertaking the frontal attack, had the more difficult time, encountering heavy fire from German pillboxes. Thus the Brazilian advance was not making much progress at 4:00 P.M. when Mascarenhas, at his observation post, received a visit from an American group that included Clark, Truscott, and Crittenberger. Before the Americans left, Crittenberger commented on the rather late hour. To help speed things up, Mascarenhas phoned Uzeda and sent Zenóbio and Brayner to speak with Caiado de Castro.[6]

The Brazilian infantry, helped by a thunderous bombardment direct-

---

[4] Mascarenhas de Moraes, *Memórias*, I, 246.

[5] Ibid., p. 247. Nelson Rodrigues de Carvalho (*Do Terço Velho ao Sampaio da F.E.B.*, p. 107) writes that "Brazilians and men of the mountain division ran the risk of not recognizing each other, due to the similarity of our uniforms to those of the Germans (for many had taken off their field jackets)." Manoel Thomaz Castello Branco (*O Brasil na II Grande Guerra*, p. 367) reports that a Brazilian was killed by a company of the mountain division. Brayner (*A Verdade sôbre a FEB*, pp. 355–356) states that the Americans killed one Brazilian and wounded others and that Mascarenhas had to intervene energetically to prevent the major commanding the First Battalion of the 1st RI from carrying out a threat to "give a lesson" to the Americans.

[6] Brayner, *A Verdade sôbre a FEB*, p. 356; Mascarenhas de Moraes, *Memórias*, I, 247.

ed by Cordeiro, achieved its goal at about 6:30 P.M. in the light of the setting sun.[7] "We have the mountain," Zenóbio exclaimed jubilantly on the telephone to Mascarenhas' observation post. He announced that the Uzeda and Franklin battalions had scaled the top and captured some prisoners, although many had escaped. While the Tenth Mountain Division still struggled to gain control of Monte della Torraccia, the Brazilians prepared the defense of Monte Castello. Around some of the formidable-looking but battered old stone buildings Italians kissed their liberators.

Humberto could not wait to tell Argentina. Writing at 2:00 A.M. on February 22 from the command post of the 1st RI, he said:

The 21st has just passed and it was a great day. We have defeated the Prussians at Monte Castello. . . . The battle began at daybreak and, until 6:00 P.M., was a matter of hand-to-hand encounters. At this hour of the night, all that remain are isolated pockets of resistance, already surrounded. At this moment I know that only one German pillbox, completely surrounded, is resisting.

The battle of Monte Castello will remain in the Military History of Brazil as a great feat of arms by her soldiers. It fell to me to map out the maneuver, conceive it, and set up the conditions for its execution. But that represents nothing. What counts is the valor of those who expelled the Germans and took control of Monte Castello. . . . The ones who survived will continue the battle tomorrow on other mountains.

I am going to sleep a little. Edésio has just fixed a bed for me. I think of you, Nieta, and Paulo on this great day. God bless you.[8]

5. Moving Eastward at High Elevation (February–March, 1945)

As a result of the fighting around Monte Castello on February 21, forty-one wounded Brazilians were admitted to the medical treatment post (*posto de tratamento*), whereas in each of the defeats of November 29 and December 12 the number had exceeded one hundred. Following the victory, fourteen frozen bodies of Brazilians killed on December 12 were recovered; ropes to lower them down the mountainside

[7] Carvalho, *Do Terço Velho ao Sampaio da F.E.B.*, p. 112.

[8] HACB to Argentina, Italy, February 21, 1945, File H1, p. 109, PVCB.

were applied with care because the Germans had placed explosive "booby traps" next to the dead bodies.[1]

The Monte Castello victory, important in the context of the Allied strategy, was a turning point for the Brazilans, who thereafter went ahead with confidence and success. To help the Tenth Mountain Division, locked in battle at Monte della Torraccia, Major Sizeno Sarmento (one of Humberto's cadets in 1927) led the 1st RI's Second Battalion to victory at nearby La Serra on the night of February 23–24. Hours later Monte della Torraccia fell to the Americans.[2]

In the subsequent eastward movement by the FEB and the Tenth Mountain Division—over high, rough terrain that was sometimes covered with snow—the FEB captured Roncovecchio and Seneveglio on February 25 and 26. After that the FEB was split by the Fourth Corps into two groups to protect the flanks of the Tenth Mountain Division as it drove further eastward toward Monte della Croce. Mascarenhas assigned to offensive-minded Zenóbio the command of the "Western Group," which was mostly the 1st RI (Sampaio Regiment) and which had a defensive assignment, that of protecting the communications of the Americans. Mascarenhas himself assumed command of the "Eastern Group," which could look forward to more offensive action, especially as Castelnuovo was approached. Castello Branco was given the task of helping Mascarenhas plan and execute operations in coordination with the Americans.[3] In one of these operations, carried out to assist the Americans in their fight at Monte della Croce, the 6th RI, led by Nelson de Melo, took Santa Maria Villiana on March 3–4.

"The offensive continues, and we continue to advance," Humberto wrote to Argentina. "Today I saw the 'Fritz' of the great Reich, of the great Germany, invincible soldiers of Hitler, with his hands raised over his head, dropping his weapons and surrendering to the 'pracinhas,' to the Jéca from the other side of the Atlantic. Many resist until they realize that they might be killed, and then they surrender, saying 'kamarade'

---

[1] Gilberto Peixoto, *A Campanha da Itália*, pp. 84, 93, 120, 122; Senna Campos interview, November 26, 1975.

[2] Mascarenhas de Moraes, *Memórias*, I, 251–252.

[3] Referring to this arrangement, the Brazilians spoke of the FEB as forming the "corridor of the Tenth Mountain Division." Mascarenhas de Moraes, *Memórias*, I, 256–257; Brayner, *A Verdade sôbre a FEB*, p. 374.

in a choking voice. Others die at their combat posts, without surrendering. Others flee in time. This is the enemy that we face."[4]

A few days later Humberto wrote:

Who was it who said to Brayner that I would be going now to Rio? No one has spoken of this matter here, at least until now. He is a man given to imagination, even for these things. As for the rotation of officers, nothing has been resolved until now. I learned, from a personal inquiry, that Mascarenhas said that he would send me on the day of the armistice. . . . I have not taken the matter up. But I tell you that I shall return home with the satisfaction of having fulfilled my duty. . . .

One who has helped me a great deal here is Ademar. What good judgment, what a heart, what competence! He is here as my temporary assistant. The regular ones are: Alcyr, Cunha Melo, Mendes, Newton Castello Branco, and Cintra. A splendid team of elite offcers. Many want to serve with me, honoring me with this desire.[5]

Walters has written that Castello Branco's "small figure became legendary in the Division" as he was driven around in his jeep, catching a nap sometimes on these rides. According to a journalist, the soldiers on the battlefield had become familiar with the sight of the quiet, unsmiling officer, who, regardless of enemy artillery, would be close at hand, concerned with their problems. Often, the journalist reported, Castello Branco was alone except for his driver; always he could be counted on to indicate the paths that the soldiers should follow.[6]

Castello Branco was also a questioner. Appearing unexpectedly, accompanied occasionally by Major Luís Mendes da Silva, occasionally by Lieutenant Rubem Argollo (his efficient interpreter), and occasionally by his orderly, he would ask officers about their missions, the location of their principal weapons, and who was on their right and left. During the replacement of one detachment by another, which usually occurred at night, he was apt to be stationed at a certain point, observing and coordinating.[7]

[4] HACB to Argentina, February 26, 1945, File H1, PVCB.

[5] HACB to Argentina, March 1, 1945, File H1, p. 111, PVCB.

[6] Walters, "Humberto de Alencar Castello Branco," Part 1, "The Years of War," p. 8; "Nota elogiosa de jornal sôbre HACB na FEB," File G1, CPDOC.

[7] Murilo Gomes Ferreira, "O General Castello Que Conheci," (transcript of tape

Customarily Castello had a kind word for those who had been his cadets at Realengo. One of these, Lieutenant Ismael da Rocha Teixeira, was surprised when a jeep bearing Castello and his driver stopped at his side. "So," Castello said, "we see each other again. What are you doing here?" After Ismael reported that he was going to his position, Castello used his jeep to take him there.[8]

6. Victory at Castelnuovo (March 5, 1945)

The attack by the Eastern Group's 6th and 11th RI's (Ipiranga and Tiradentes regiments) against Castelnuovo, the last and most eastward of the German-held points above Highway 64, was planned by Humberto and his team and was subsequently approved by Mascarenhas at a meeting attended by Zenóbio, Cordeiro, and Brayner.[1] Scheduled for March 5, it was not to begin until the signal came from the Americans in order that it might be synchronized with the mountain division's operation, to the north and west, against Castel d'Aiano and Monte della Castellana. But this schedule did not prevent the Brazilians from moving to better their positions early on the morning of the fifth.

At Palazzina, a spot commanding an excellent view of the terrain where the Castelnuovo battle was to be fought, Brayner set up the division's observation post. There, starting at dawn on March 5, Brayner and Amauri Kruel awaited Mascarenhas; they were under the impression that Palazzina was the site of the "advanced command post" of the division. But they waited in vain because Mascarenhas, who wanted to exert his personal control over operations, decided to install his command post at Riola, adjoining the command post of the 11th RI. In Brayner's opinion, Riola's lack of view of the battlefield could not "inspire great decisions," and its concentration of commands—he described it as holding the decision-making posts of the Third Section, the First

---

prepared for interview), Rio de Janeiro, November 12, 1975, Part 3, "Campanha da Itália," pp. 4–5.

[8] Murilo Gomes Ferreira, in Ferreira and Paulo V. Castello Branco interview, November 12, 1975 (untaped portion); Ismael da Rocha Teixeira interview, São Paulo, November 6, 1975.

[1] Mascarenhas de Moraes, Memórias, I, 259.

Division, and the American Fourth Corps—"atrophied" the authority of the colonel commanding the 11th RI. But Mascarenhas remained at Riola, with Ademar de Queiroz at his side. He called on Castello Branco to be his representative at Palazzo, the command post of the 6th RI.[2]

As devised by the Third Section, the attack against Castelnuovo was to develop from an encirclement. The encirclement began early in the day before the Americans gave the Brazilians the signal to begin their attack. The 11th RI's First Battalion, commanded by Manoel Rodrigues de Carvalho Lisboa, gained control of Precaria, just southwest of Castelnuovo, while the 11th RI's Second Battalion, commanded by Orlando Ramagem, in a move that cost it twenty-two casualties, reached ground to the southeast of Castelnuovo.[3]

With the signal from the Americans, which came at noon, the 6th RI's First and Second battalions, commanded by Gross and Henrique Cordeiro Oeste, started on their first mission, which was to overcome the effective German firing position at Soprasasso, southwest of Castelnuovo. Around Precaria the 11th RI's First Battalion covered the flank of the 6th RI and at the same time supported the principal immediate attack on Castelnuovo, executed from the east by Ramagem's men.

Mined ground and heavy enemy fire held up the progress of the Ramagem battalion. Crittenberger, dropping in at Riola at 5:00 P.M. to complain about the time being taken by the Brazilians, phoned the 6th RI commander, Colonel Nelson de Melo, to stress the need of dominating Castelnuovo before nightfall.[4] The colonel then ordered the battalion of Major Gross to proceed to Castelnuovo without awaiting the capture of Soprasasso, and at 6:00 P.M. Castelnuovo fell to the FEB, with considerable help from the artillery. At the same time, Oeste's battalion gained control of Soprasasso. The relative ease of these 6th RI successes was due in part to the 11th RI action in the south and east. Ninety-eight Germans were captured. Of the approximately seventy Brazilian casual-

[2] Brayner, *A Verdade sôbre a FEB*, pp. 377–378. The commander of the 11th RI was Colonel Delmiro Pereira de Andrade. Mascarenhas de Moraes, *Memórias*, I, 259–260.

[3] Brayner, *A Verdade sôbre a FEB*, p. 379; Castello Branco, *O Brasil na II Grande Guerra*, p. 384; Delmiro Pereira de Andrade, *O 11º R.I. na 2ª Guerra Mundial*, pp. 104–105.

[4] Brayner, *A Verdade sôbre a FEB*, p. 379; Castello Branco, *O Brasil na II Grande Guerra*, p. 383; Pereira de Andrade, *O 11º R.I. na 2ª Guerra Mundial*, p. 108.

ties, about half were suffered by the 11th RI's Second Battalion (Ramagem), which ran into difficulties in the east early in the day.[5]

Crittenberger, as he had after the Monte Castello victory, delivered a congratulatory message to Mascarenhas, this time mentioning also valuable work of Zenóbio in protecting the mountain division's left flank. Mascarenhas praised the work of many, including the artillery groups of José de Souza Carvalho, Waldemar Levi Cardoso, and Hugo Panasco Alvim and the engineers of Colonel José Machado Lopes.[6]

The commander of the Brazilian division has declared the capture of Castelnuovo "notable for precise planning and faithful execution."[7] Newton C. de Andrade Mello, who served as a captain in the FEB and later wrote about its battles, also feels that the Castelnuovo victory was the result of superb planning, which led to the retirement of the enemy after relatively little bloodshed.[8]

Brayner, less impressed, writes that "there was much confusion, due to the preoccupation of the 'operations' sector of the staff to carry out only what suited the Fourth Corps and the Tenth Mountain Division." Mascarenhas' chief of staff speaks of the "orders and counterorders" issued by the Third Section during the night of March 4–5 which caused the Second Battalion of the 11th RI to "roam from place to place." The conqueror of Castelnuovo, he says, was the 6th RI, which was out of reach of "so many 'guides' and received direct orders from the Commander of the Fourth Corps." Brayner adds that if the operation had been commanded by Zenóbio da Costa, the 11th RI would have achieved a rapid victory, and he argues that the delay allowed many Germans to escape.[9]

[5] Castello Branco, *O Brasil na II Grande Guerra*, p. 384; Delmiro Pereira de Andrade quoted in Gentil Palhares, *De São João del Rei ao Vale do Pó (Ou a Epopéia do 11º R.I. na 2ª Guerra Mundial): Documentário Histórico do 11º, 6º, e 1º R.I.*, p. 321; Mascarenhas de Moraes, *Memórias*, I, 262. J. B. Mascarenhas de Moraes (*A F.E.B. pelo Seu Comandante*, p. 154 n. 105) reports that the Second Battalion of the 11th RI suffered thirty-three casualties and the 6th RI suffered thirty-five (three killed, twenty-one wounded, and eleven hurt in accidents). Peixoto, *A Campanha da Itália*, p. 135, sets the total losses at thirty-seven wounded and two hurt in accidents.

[6] Mascarenhas de Moraes, *Memórias*, I, 260, 263.

[7] Ibid., p. 262.

[8] Newton C. de Andrade Mello interview, Rio de Janeiro, November 1, 1975.

[9] Brayner, *A Verdade sôbre a FEB*, p. 376–380; Brayner, *Recordando os Bravos*, pp. 168, 240.

But Castello Branco had every reason to be pleased. When the Brazilians entered Castelnuovo, Mascarenhas, with tears in his eyes, embraced Castello Branco, thanking him for his plan of attack.[10]

Writing to Argentina at 10:00 P.M. on March 5, Humberto spoke of the "resounding, courageous victory" of the Brazilian troops and of the felicitous battle maneuver. "The prestige of our troops," he wrote, "is great among the Americans, English, and Italians."

"Monte Castello and Castelnuovo," he went on to say, "are two great accomplishments of the Brazilian troops—the two greatest. They will equal those of the Paraguay War, not in order to compete, but to show that we seek to honor the past. I have received congratulations from everyone, including the Commander of the Fourth Army Corps, for the work of my Section."

Humberto was adding lines to express his gratitude to Argentina ("You are always in my destiny, with your smile and the good luck that you give me") when he was interrupted by a call to be present at a "drink" to be offered to him by the Americans and the members of his section. At this occasion the Third Section head was toasted by Ademar de Queiroz and by an American colonel who spoke in the name of his comrades. "We drank cognac," the usually abstemious Humberto reported to Argentina—"and also coffee prepared by Edésio." [11]

7. A Trip to the Holy Land (March, 1945)

Humberto's letter of March 5 to Argentina advised that the Brazilians at Castelnuovo had accomplished the last part of the offensive of Operation Encore and were getting ready for the operation to be known as Spring Offensive. A week later he wrote that flowers were coming into bloom, the sun was brilliant, and the snow remained only in the highest peaks.[1]

To play a role in the spring offensive, the FEB moved its fighting force northwest of Castelnuovo to the eastern sector of the valley of the Panaro River, which flows northward to the Po River. And in the mean-

[10] HACB to Argentina, March 5, 1945, File H1, p. 114, PVCB.
[11] Ibid.
[1] HACB to Argentina, March 5, 13, 1945, File H1, PVCB.

time, back at the depot near Staffoli, the FEB's fifth and last detachment, about five thousand men brought from Brazil during February, received training in order to bring up to ten thousand the replacement troops for the fifteen thousand men that the FEB used at the front.

The lull that preceded the spring offensive allowed the recently active Allied troops, including the Brazilians, to enjoy some recreation in Rome, Montecatini, and Florence. And it allowed Brazilian officers, unsure of the nature of the FEB's future role in the Panaro Valley, to review the cost of the campaigning since Zenóbio da Costa had set forth from the Vada training grounds in September, 1944: 285 killed, 1,087 wounded in action, 728 injured in accidents, and 52 missing, mostly as prisoners.[2] More than six hundred German prisoners had been captured.

During the preparation for the spring offensive, Lieutenant Murilo Gomes Ferreira, who had been one of Castello Branco's cadets in 1941, was called in to the Third Section with a group of other lieutenants and some captains. Castello presented them to Major Júlio Óliver and told them that they now constituted the Óliver Detachment, which was to replace a unit of the Tenth Mountain Division. "When?" asked a captain. "Immediately," Castello replied, causing much surprise because it was late in the afternoon and no reconnaissance or other preparations had been made. "There will," he added, "be no prior reconnaissance; the guides who are ready for you here are American soldiers who speak Italian, and they will take you to your positions. Don't forget that the troop you are replacing has been attacking successfully at night and maintaining its positions for more than two weeks, suffering heavy losses. The men need to be replaced in order to prepare for the Spring Offensive." The substitution of troops was completed that night.[3]

The move of the Brazilians to the Panaro Valley had just about been completed in mid-March, when Castello, working with all of his assistants in the Third Section, found Mascarenhas at his side.

"Prepare," the general told him, "for a trip to Egypt and the Holy Land." This surprising news was followed by the explanation that General Mark Clark had decided to offer the one-week trip, as a prize, to some of the Fifth Army's most outstanding officers and that one member of the Brazilian division was to be rewarded in the same way. With

[2] Mascarenhas de Moraes, *A F.E.B. pelo Seu Comandante*, p. 158 n. 110.
[3] Ferreira, "O General Castello Que Conheci," Part 3, "Campanha da Itália," p. 5.

warm sincerity Castello's assistants congratulated him on his selection, which had been made by Mascarenhas.[4]

On March 15 Castello found that arrangements had been made for him to be accompanied by his interpreter, Lieutenant Rubem Argollo. The other passengers in the two-motor army plane were ten American men and two American women lieutenants who had been serving as nurses. All were well decorated.

As the plane flew from Florence, Castello could see below, along the Mediterranean coast, some of the places that he had come to know in his early months with the FEB in Italy: Vada, Cecina, Tarquinia, and Civitavecchia.

The plane's first stop in Africa was at a base near Benghazi, Libya. Benghazi, whose oriental cupolas fascinated Castello, had changed hands six times during the African campaign; the houses along the coast, Castello noted, had been destroyed by the British navy. Castello enjoyed an eleven-hour sleep at the Benghazi base before boarding the plane for the second day's flight over the blue Mediterranean and the yellow desert that was a vast "nothingness" except for "one oasis and then another."[5] At the El Alamein region in Egypt the plane flew low to allow the passengers a good view of the mass of overturned and broken combat vehicles that marked the famed battlefield where Field Marshal Montgomery had fought. More sights followed that Castello had never dreamed of seeing: the Nile Valley ("settlements and more settlements"), the houses of Cairo, the pyramids ("how impressive!").

Castello joined the pilot as the plane took in a view of the Suez Canal ("a thread of water through the desert; ports; large ships"). "Without Argollo, I am speaking English with the pilot," Castello recorded in his diary of the trip.

In Palestine the plane landed at the port of Haifa. It had been a whirlwind of continents for Castello: "Yesterday in two, Europe and Africa; today in Asia." The hotel in Haifa provided a "civilized bath, . . . I want to cry out: I am in a large, clean, warm, and inviting bathtub!" Later Castello took supper alone at a small table in a restaurant, and there he was surrounded by Jews, one of whom spoke Portuguese

[4] HACB to Argentina, March 15, 1945, File H1, p. 119, PVCB; Walters interview, June 12, 1975.

[5] HACB diary, "Viagem à Libya, Egito, e Palestina, Mês de Março," entry for March 16, 1945, File H2, PVCB.

and all of whom had relatives in Brazil. Going back to the hotel for another good night's sleep, Castello ran into the American nurses, who were returning in the company of three of the American officers. All of them, Castello observed, were intoxicated.

The nurses and some of the other Americans slept late on March 17, thus missing the main excursion, a bus ride to Jerusalem and Bethlehem. Castello, at the holy places, was filled with emotion, and constantly his thoughts turned to Argentina and the children.[6]

Tel Aviv, the clean Jewish city of less than thirty years, was on the schedule to be visited on March 18. There Castello made a discovery: "The three-story apartment houses in Ipanema, Leblon, and Copacabana are copies from Tel Aviv. I have not seen this in Europe or America. It was the Jew who brought to Brazil that horrible thing, without a tile roof, without art."[7]

On the morning of March 19 Castello, leaving his companions in Haifa, took a bus to Nazareth. He returned to Haifa for dinner in a restaurant that he had not tried before, and there he was hardly alone, for once again he was surrounded by Jews who asked him "a thousand questions." Following the meal, Castello and an English officer went to the home of one of the Jews and spent an evening that was not completely notable for international fraternity. The Englishman had a tendency to speak poorly of the Americans. And when the Jews declared that the Allies should avenge the massacre of six million Jews, Castello, not appreciating obstacles faced by the Jews, remarked that it would be good if the Jews would follow the example of Brazil and send a division from Palestine to the battlefields.[8]

Before returning to Italy, the travelers spent two nights in Cairo, where Castello was lodged in a private home notable for strong Arab servants, rich furnishings, and "a bathtub that looks like a swimming pool!"[9] On the morning of the twenty-first he went with three Americans to the Egyptian tombs and the pyramids "that had gazed upon the French and been gazed upon by Napoleon." As the Americans were "tired and disinterested" after lunch, Castello went sightseeing alone to

[6] Ibid., entry for March 17, 1945.
[7] Ibid., entry for March 18, 1945.
[8] Ibid., entry for March 19, 1945.
[9] Ibid., entry for March 20, 1945.

the mosque ("what richness!"), Fort Napoleon, and the museum containing remains from Tutankhamen's tomb.

The officers spent the night of March 22 in Benghazi, Libya. Then they flew over Sicily, Capri, the Arno Valley, Lucca, and Tuscany, reaching Florence early on the afternoon of the twenty-third.

In closing the diary of his trip, written for his family, Castello said that he had found a great deal of interest in Brazil, and, among English, American, and Greek officers, much praise for Brazil's offensive actions at Monte Castello and Castelnuovo. "All speak of Brazil as a great power. They also speak invariably of Carmen Miranda. If our international policy, backed by stable internal politics, does not take advantage of the efforts made on the battlefields, with the loss of Brazilian blood and lives, there will remain abroad only the effects of the samba of Ary Barroso and the famous wiggle of Carmen Miranda." [10]

8. Poor Relations with Brayner and Kruel

The military calm in northern Italy continued well beyond Castello's return (with a large Hindu vase) from the Middle East, and this calm allowed him to reply to many of the letters he found awaiting him. Sending his replies via Ulhoa Cintra, who had become a lieutenant colonel and was leaving the Third Section, Castello commented on family matters, Brazilian politics, and the Third Section.

He repeated inquiries, often made earlier, about whether Nieta was putting on needed weight and about how Paulo was doing in this, his final year at the naval academy. With Nieta visiting Belo Horizonte and Paulo home only on weekends, Humberto pictured Argentina as too much alone and suggested that she join Nieta.[1]

Brazilian politics were naturally of great interest to the members of the FEB. Not a few had wondered about fighting dictatorships abroad while the Vargas dictatorship existed in Brazil, and although Vargas was now proposing a presidential election in which he would not be a candidate, his record did not make this proposal an assurance that he would step aside. Brayner tells us that "conspirators" against the Vargas

---

[10] Ibid., entry for March 23, 1945.
[1] HACB to Argentina, Italy, March 23, 31, 1945, File H2, pp. 8, 18, PVCB.

regime came to Italy in the Second Detachment and held meetings in Montecatini, the "rear-guard" headquarters of General Falconière da Cunha, "intimate friend of Cordeiro." After mimeographed copies of a *Diário de Notícias* article, scathing in its attack against Vargas, were distributed in one of the regiments, Brayner warned troop commanders against this sort of "dangerous activity."[2]

Correspondent Barreto Leite, strongly opposed to Vargas, noted some anti-Vargas sentiment, but among FEB officers he limited his political discussions pretty much to those he had with his old friend and veteran revolutionary, Major Emygdio Miranda, who was equally anti-Vargas. Certainly Barreto Leite did not talk politics to Castello Branco, who was extremely careful in this regard. Correspondent Joel Silveira, who loaned Brazilian newspapers to Castello (and always got them back), found that Castello enjoyed discussing Anatole France and other literary figures but never touched on Brazilian politics.[3]

When Castello heard a rumor that the wife of an FEB officer was making political statements in Rio, he hastened to send some advice to Argentina. "I must tell you," he wrote, "that here I do not give opinions about politics. I know that there are two presidential candidates, Dutra and Eduardo Gomes, but I do not know their programs or who their backers are. I do know that Brazil cannot continue at the mercy of dictators and parasites. I also know that it would not be proper to offer political opinions here." Humberto urged Argentina to keep away from political groups and not to discuss political matters, even on the telephone. "I do not think that you should subject yourself to a 'dictatorship' by me, but I also think that influence of others should be avoided. . . . It is just that I want a good position for you . . . and not have you considered a *política*."[4]

As for the Third Section, Humberto wrote that it had become "an example. It is not I who say this, but others—Brazilians, Americans,

[2] Brayner, *Recordando os Bravos*, pp. 263, 275, 324.

[3] Barreto Leite Filho interview, November 25, 1975; Joel Silveira interview, Rio de Janeiro, December 25, 1975.

[4] HACB to Argentina, Lizzano in Belvedere, March 25, 1945, File H2, p. 10, PVCB. The Brazilian division's advanced headquarters had been moved from Porretta Terme six kilometers westward to Lizzano in Belvedere, a town south of Monte Belvedere and not to be confused with Lissano, which lay at the eastern end of the fifteen-kilometer front (starting from Monte Belvedere) that the Brazilians were directed on December 12 to defend during the winter months.

and Englishmen." Humberto particularly praised the dedication, and loyalty to himself, of Cunha Melo, "my former cadet at the Escola Militar," and of the departing Ulhoa Cintra. "All my assistants," he explained, "are my friends—with a friendship built upon work (and what work!)." [5]

General Mascarenhas de Morais, Humberto added, "places great trust in me—a declaration that I give you confidentially." However, this was hardly a confidential matter at the division headquarters, where Castello Branco was frequently the mealtime guest of Mascarenhas. And of course there was nothing confidential about the superlative statements that Mascarenhas issued on March 8 and March 27 to praise Castello Branco's "felicitous judgment" at Monte Castello and "tireless supervision" in the battles in and around Castelnuovo. [6]

Amauri Kruel, who was seldom a mealtime guest of Mascarenhas and who received less generous statements from the general, declared that the general's eulogies of Castello Branco were caused by Castello Branco's being a part of the "general's circle." [7] Castello Branco, while he revealed an almost filial concern and affection for Mascarenhas, stated that he was serving the army and the division, not the general or any person, and that the general was well aware of this. [8] Furthermore, it was not just Mascarenhas who turned to Humberto when military problems had to be settled. The other Brazilian generals, the troop commanders, and the Americans, finding Brayner indecisive, relied on Humberto.

Humberto later wrote Argentina:

I tried to prevent any embarrassment for Brayner. But the whole world came to the Third Section. I assure you that I never took the initiative in setting him aside. But, during the operations, the Americans, their generals included, showed an immense esteem for me. I dedicated my efforts to the division, and, above all, I accepted all the responsibility that was mine. I was where I ought to have been, and, whenever it was incumbent on me, I gave

[5] Ibid.

[6] Barreto Leite Filho interview, November 25, 1975; Mascarenhas de Moraes statement of March 8, 1945, in "Campanha da Itália," File G1, CPDOC; Mascarenhas de Moraes statement of March 27, 1945, Files G1 and G2, Part 3, CPDOC.

[7] Barreto Leite Filho interview, November 25, 1975; HACB to Argentina, Alessandria, Italy, May 17, 1945, File H2, p. 48, PVCB.

[8] Vernon Walters to JWFD, Washington, D.C., July 11, 1975; HACB to Argentina, Lizzano in Belvedere, March 25, 1945, File H2, p. 10, PVCB.

everyone my opinion. In the most difficult moments all turned to me. . . . But Brayner, inactive, indecisive, never giving a solution to anything, did not carry out his job.

Finding himself in a secondary position, he decided to carry on a war against my person. A quiet, ruthless war, seeking to annihilate me. He attributed all the failures to me and all the successes to others.[9]

In this campaign, Brayner had the support of Amauri Kruel—"and nobody else except Amauri, my old friend," Humberto told Argentina.

What a harsh and painful reality! Amauri, besides being consummately poisoned by Brayner, was devoured by spite and envy. I did all that I could to have him change his unfriendly attitude. . . . But it was all in vain. To everyone he spoke badly of everything that I did.

More than anything else, the trouble with Amauri was that, even before leaving Brazil, he thought that he was going to be the "man" of the Division. Miserable wretch! He thought that I would be a weak one and that he, helped along by Brayner, would lead the Division. Miserable wretch, once again! For accomplishing such a thing, he lacked a great deal.[10]

Kruel, described by Castello as "desperate once again" when Castello was rewarded with the trip to the Middle East, managed to find a passage for himself to Cairo on a service plane. "He insinuates himself into the favor of the Americans and Brazilians in order to acquire medals, all due to fear that I shall earn them and that he won't." But what was more important to Amauri than medals or a trip to Cairo was the matter of promotions. "He has," Humberto wrote Argentina, "a horror that I shall be promoted."[11]

Castello no longer invited Kruel to the little parties given at the Third Section. But he never failed to include Kruel's subordinate, Emygdio Miranda, who had displayed his customary bravery as well as excellent leadership at the front in dealing with soldiers in panic during one of the Monte Castello setbacks. Emygdio, meanwhile, was having no end of troubles in his relationship with Kruel. Perhaps in part his problems stemmed from his denunciation of the wording of a Second Section bulletin that stated that a German infantry unit was withdrawing tem-

[9] HACB to Argentina, Alessandria, May 17, 1945, p. 3, File H2, p. 48, PVCB.
[10] Ibid.
[11] Ibid.

porarily to get a "deserved rest"; perhaps in part it was due to Emygdio's siding with Castello in what Emygdio has called the "fray [*briga*] between Castello and Kruel"—a fray that he says was caused by jealousy and became progressively worse. Kruel called Emygdio in and said, in the presence of others, that he was dissatisfied with him and did not like his attitude. "Since when," Emygdio retorted, without thinking, "have you had the idea that I seek to please men?"[12]

Kruel and Brayner concluded that Emygdio was neurotic, afflicted by "war sickness," and should therefore be returned to Brazil. Cordeiro, learning of this decision, spoke to Mascarenhas. The division commander resolved that Emygdio should remain but should keep quiet and not cause trouble with discussions. As for Kruel, Mascarenhas is reported to have said that the Second Section head had "exceeded his limits" and would be sent back to Brazil as soon as the Fifth Army offensive ended.[13]

This reaction by the division commander is consistent with the description of his relationship with the Second Section head that is furnished by Brayner. Brayner puts it this way: "General Mascarenhas was so poisoned against Lieutenant Colonel Amauri that he almost charged Amauri with committing an act of insubordination. I had to act with extreme prudence to prevent this. I shielded Lieutenant Colonel Amauri against intrigue and jealousy."[14]

9. The Bloody Struggles around Montese, April 14, 1945

Early in April, 1945, the front battle line of the FEB, facing the northwest, extended for about ten kilometers from south of the Monte della Torraccia region (near Monte Castello) in a northeasterly direction to Sassomolare, a hill. Near Sassomolare the FEB was in contact with the American Tenth Mountain Division, the safety of whose left (southern) flank was the responsibility of the Brazilians.[1]

[12] Barreto Leite Filho interview, November 25, 1975; Miranda interview, December 1, 1975.

[13] Ibid.

[14] Floriano de Lima Brayner, letter published in *Jornal do Brasil*, January 25, 1976.

[1] Mascarenhas de Moraes, *Memórias*, I, 268.

With Operation Spring Offensive about to begin, on April 8 Crittenberger called his generals to the Fourth Corps headquarters at Castelluccio, well to the south of the disputed areas, in order to review assignments. There Mascarenhas, accompanied by Castello Branco and Vernon Walters, heard General George Hays of the Tenth Mountain Division express his preoccupation with the German strength on the hills around Montese, a small town west of Sassomolare. Mascarenhas suggested that the FEB's Spring Offensive assignment include an attack on that area, and the offer was accepted.[2]

This meeting of the generals was the second occasion that morning on which Castello had been with Crittenberger, for he and Walters had made a very early call on the Fourth Corps commander. Between the two calls, word was received at the Italian front that Crittenberger's eighteen-year-old son had been killed in the fighting in Germany. Crittenberger was the American general for whom Mascarenhas and Castello had the greatest warmth and affection, and the news left them desolate.[3]

It impressed Humberto to find Crittenberger, at the meeting to draw up Spring Offensive plans, handling the problems and the officers in his usual manner. Humberto was moved when Crittenberger, in his only show of emotion, concluded the meeting with the words: "This will probably be the last offensive. For those who are stricken down and can make no more blows, we must make this a good one."[4]

The advance headquarters of the FEB was moved to the town of Gaggio Montano (southwest of Monte Castello), while at Sassomolare Amauri Kruel's Second Section set up an observation post.[5] Looking west from the post, one could observe, running from left to right, some of the points in the string defended by the Germans: Montese, Monte Buffoni, Elevation 888, and Montello.

The Brazilians were scheduled to advance west from Sassomolare on April 12 against Montese and Serretto, while the Tenth Mountain Division moved against Monte Pigna, Le Coste, and Tole to the north and northeast. But fog and clouds on the Italian west coast, where the Americans had their air bases, persuaded Fifth Army commander Lucian

[2] Ibid., pp. 270–271; Brayner, *A Verdade sôbre a FEB*, p. 394.

[3] Walters interview, June 12, 1975; Vernon Walters to JWFD, Washington, D.C., July 11, 1975.

[4] Walters interview, June 12, 1975.

[5] Brayner, *A Verdade sôbre a FEB*, p. 398.

Truscott to postpone the attacks until the weather allowed better air support.[6]

Only on the morning of April 14, when it was learned that American fighter planes could get into the air, did Truscott inform Crittenberger that "the show is on." At 9:45 A.M., after waves of bombers flew over the mountains from the south, the Tenth Mountain Division led off with the first blows.[7]

Mascarenhas, sharing the Sassomolare observation post with Zenóbio, Brayner, Kruel, Walters, and others, prepared to direct the Brazilian attack when the signal came from Crittenberger. As in previous battles, Castello Branco served as Mascarenhas' representative at the command post of the regiment that had been assigned the chief role in the attack;[8] this time it was the 11th RI, commanded by Colonel Delmiro Pereira de Andrade.

At 12:15 P.M. on April 14 Crittenberger notified Mascarenhas that he could start his offensive whenever he liked.[9] At 1:30 P.M. the 11th RI's First and Third Battalions, with support on the right by the 1st RI's Second Battalion, advanced into the enemy fire. Each of the 11th RI battalions had the help of an American group of about half a dozen light or medium tanks and two tank destroyers.[10] As the area had been unusually well filled with explosive mines, Colonel José Machado Lopes' engineers worked hectically and heroically clearing mines and booby traps.[11]

Castello Branco dropped in at the Sassomolare observation post when the officers there, with an excellent view, watched the effects of the enemy's devastating artillery. They saw the Brazilian infantry and the American tank destroyers, close to the cemetery on the eastern edge of Montese, come to a halt. Mascarenhas said to Castello: "Get down there

[6] Mascarenhas de Moraes, Memórias, I, 277–279; U.S. Army, Fourth Corps, The Final Campaign across Northwest Italy, 14 April–2 May 1945, p. 14.

[7] Wondolowski, "History of the IV Corps," pp. 561–562.

[8] Mascarenhas de Moraes, Memórias, I, 280, 282; Brayner, A Verdade sôbre a FEB, p. 398.

[9] Wondolowski, "History of the IV Corps," p. 576.

[10] Pereira de Andrade, O 11º R.I. na 2ª Guerra Mundial, p. 135.

[11] Walters interview, June 12, 1975. The commander of the 11th RI, Delmiro Pereira de Andrade (O 11º R.I. na 2ª Guerra Mundial, p. 148), describes the "tireless" work by the Third Engineering Company of Floriano Moller and by the 11th RI Mines Platoon of Lieutenant Mário Silva O'Reilly de Souza, which was carried out under an intense barrage of enemy fire.

and get those soldiers and the tank destroyers moving." Castello saluted and beckoned to Walters, who followed him out of the observation post. The two men got into Castello's jeep, behind the crest of the hill, and drove down to a point about halfway to the cemetery, and there they dismounted, feeling that the jeep was too much of a target.[12]

On foot they moved forward cautiously past the mine clearing crew and ran from sheltered spot to sheltered spot until they reached the Montese cemetery. At that point they found confusion between the Brazilian battalion commander and the American tank destroyer commander. With Walters translating when necessary, Castello quickly explained to all the officers what they were to do: move into Montese at once, securing the town before dark, and then push on beyond, both west and north. Castello was tough in giving commands and, after answering questions, told the men to get going.[13]

Castello's action, which helped win for him the only Combat Cross, First Class, awarded to a member of the division's staff, was mentioned in a letter written to Argentina by his orderly, José Edésio Oliveira:

Twenty minutes after our artillery ceased pounding Montese, I and our colonel [Castello Branco] were the first to reach the bridges of Montese. At the place we reached, there was a platoon of American combat vehicles. The platoon commander had stopped there because he could not advance any further in the face of the barrage of fire from the German artillery.

Without losing any time, the colonel had a sergeant bring a telephone. And thus he was able to have some artillery platoons come up, and in this way we supported the combat vehicles, which then entered the city. Then the Germans fled to the crest of the hill from where they hit us with a great artillery bombardment. I myself cannot find words to tell you of the danger that I and the colonel were in. Late at night, when the Germans somewhat reduced their activity, we returned to camp. . . . The terrain appeared to be all mined.[14]

The first to enter Montese, in the face of great danger, was a platoon boldly led by Lieutenant Iporan Nunes de Oliveira. At once the lieu-

[12] Walters, "Humberto de Alencar Castello Branco," Part 1, "The Years of War," p. 9.
[13] Ibid.
[14] José Edésio Oliveira to Argentina, Alessandria, Italy, May 16, 1945, File D, CPDOC.

tenant sent a messenger to his company commander, with the result that the 11th RI commander, Delmiro Pereira de Andrade, brought a halt to the Brazilian artillery fire on Montese. Following this first penetration into the town, which occurred at 2:45 P.M., Iporan's platoon and another spent three hours gaining control of the battered houses from the Germans.[15]

While Montese thus fell to the 11th RI's First Battalion (commanded by Manoel Rodrigues de Carvalho Lisboa), the 11th RI's Third Battalion (commanded by Cândido Alves da Silva) carried out its assignments to the northeast of Montese. It occupied the hamlet of Serretto, on the way to German-held Monte Buffoni, and it reached Paravento Hill, to the northeast of Serretto.[16] Helpful to Cândido's battalion was the parallel advance made to the right of it by the 1st RI's Second Battalion (commanded by Sizeno Sarmento). Sarmento's men, also under constant fire, reached the heavily mined outskirts of the village of Cá di Bortolino, to the northeast of Paravento Hill.[17]

At the 11th RI command post Captain Carlos de Meira Mattos (Mascarenhas' liaison to the Fourth Corps) and newspaper correspondent Joel Silveira congratulated Delmiro Pereira de Andrade for his regiment's "glorious day."[18] On that day the 11th RI suffered 183 casualties and captured 107 German prisoners, including officers.[19] Although the Brazilians could make no further progress on April 14, and were left open to a formidable barrage from Monte Buffoni, Montello, and the high points identified as Elevations 888 and 927, the Brazilians had made much more progress than the Tenth Mountain Division, which suffered 553 casualties.[20]

The very progress made by the Brazilians attracted the greatest concentration of enemy fire. Captain Peter S. Wondolowski, historian of the Fourth Corps, writes that during the first twenty-four hours of the Fourth

---

[15] Pereira de Andrade, *O 11° R.I. na 2ª Guerra Mundial*, pp. 140–141.

[16] Delmiro Pereira de Andrade quoted in Palhares, *De São João del Rei ao Vale do Pó*, p. 334; Carvalho, *Do Terço Velho ao Sampaio da F.E.B.*, p. 140.

[17] Newton C. de Andrade Mello, *A Epopéia de Montese: Conferência Proferida no Dia 14 de Abril de 1954, por Ocasião das Comemorações do 9° Aniversário da Conquista de Montese Realizadas na "Casa do Expedicionário" de Curitiba*, p. 16.

[18] Pereira de Andrade, *O 11° R.I. na 2ª Guerra Mundial*, pp. 142–143.

[19] Mascarenhas de Moraes, *Memórias*, I, 283.

[20] Castello Branco, *O Brasil na II Grande Guerra*, p. 434; Wondolowski, "History of the IV Corps," p. 564.

Corps attack, the Brazilian area "received over 1,800 of the 2,800 rounds of enemy fire reported in the entire IV Corps zone."[21]

The Montese battles, still unfinished at the end of April 14, were the biggest ones in which the Brazilians participated in Italy. They called for the greatest display of courage.[22] "During the tough battles of Montese, Serretto, and Paravento," writes 11th RI commander Delmiro Pereira de Andrade, "our battalions were terribly punished by enemy fire." According to a bulletin issued by General Crittenberger, the Brazilian division was the only unit under his command to carry out its mission in full on April 14. The bulletin went on to say that the Brazilian division did not retreat on the night of April 14–15 from positions taken in Montese despite receiving at that time more enemy shells than were fired at all of the rest of the Fourth Corps.[23]

Brayner, nevertheless, had a few critical points to make. Viewing the difficulties encountered by the Brazilians during the latter part of April 14, he reached the startling conclusion that Mascarenhas was "a mere spectator, ignorant of what was happening." The chief of staff also concluded that "everyone was satisfied with the conquest of Montese, whereas the mission involved other objectives."[24] He decided that Castello Branco lacked the capacity to take the initiative of sending into the fray the 6th RI's Second Battalion, held in reserve, and he felt that greater use should be made of Zenóbio's talents.

10. The Montese Area (April 15–18, 1945)

For the attacks of April 15 Mascarenhas had in mind replacing Major Cândido Alves da Silva's much-hit Third Battalion of the 11th RI, whose objective was to advance from Paravento Hill to the German

[21] Wondolowski, "History of the IV Corps," p. 576.

[22] Walters interview, June 12, 1975. According to 11th RI commander Delmiro Pereira de Andrade, "Montese was the greatest operation of force carried out by a regiment in all of the action of the F.E.B." (see Palhares, De São João del Rei ao Vale do Pó, p. 336). Andrade Mello interview, November 1, 1975.

[23] Delmiro Pereira de Andrade quoted in Palhares, De São João del Rei ao Vale do Pó, p. 337. Willis D. Crittenberger quoted in Brayner, Recordando os Bravos, pp. 243, 321.

[24] Brayner, A Verdade sôbre a FEB, p. 401.

strongholds at Elevation 888 and Montello. But Colonel Delmiro Pereira de Andrade insisted that his men should remain, their morale continuing high. Considering this and the advantages of "economizing on time and resources," Mascarenhas left to Major Cândido's battalion the attack from Paravento Hill, whose occupation had been turned over to the 1st RI's Second Battalion.[1]

Enemy resistance on April 15 was even more formidable than it had been on the previous day. It brought to a halt a courageous advance undertaken from Paravento Hill by Captain Olegário de Abreu Memória and his Seventh Company, and it turned Montese into an inferno. Soon after Lieutenant Iporan Nunes de Oliveira's brave platoon made a hopeful move beyond that battered village to Elevation 726, the principal objective of Major Lisboa's battalion had to be limited to holding Montese "at all costs."[2]

In the meantime the Tenth Mountain Division, having more success than it had had on the fourteenth, secured control of Monte Pigna and Le Coste. This success, Walters explains, was because two-thirds of the German artillery fire against the Fourth Corps was directed against the Brazilian sector, where the Germans felt that the main attack was to be made.[3]

On the night of April 15 Mascarenhas ordered the Third Battalion of the 6th RI to replace Cândido's battalion. After this fresher unit, led by Major Silvino Nóbrega, made unsuccessful attempts on April 16 to advance on Montello, Mascarenhas took to the battlefield to discuss the situation with Major Nóbrega at the battalion command post, installed "over the ruins of Montese, under permanent bombardment by the German artillery."[4] Mascarenhas, whose division in three days had lost 426 men, including 34 dead (while capturing 453 prisoners),[5] felt that an interval was needed for the recuperation of the Brazilian troops. Nevertheless, as Monte Buffoni, Elevations 888 and 927, and Montello were still in German hands, he ordered the 6th RI's Second Battalion, under

[1] Mascarenhas de Moraes, Memórias, I, 283; Pereira de Andrade, O 11º R.I. na 2ª Guerra Mundial, p. 143.

[2] Pereira de Andrade, O 11º R.I. na 2ª Guerra Mundial, pp. 144–147.

[3] Castello Branco, O Brasil na II Grande Guerra, p. 423; Walters interview, June 12, 1975. See also Carvalho, Do Terço Velho ao Sampaio da F.E.B., p. 141.

[4] Mascarenhas de Moraes, Memórias, I, 284–285.

[5] Castello Branco, O Brasil na II Grande Guerra, p. 434.

Major Henrique Cordeiro Oeste, to replace Silvino Nóbrega's troops and carry out the attack on April 17.[6]

However, early on April 17, before any action was taken, Mascarenhas received orders from the Fourth Corps to suspend the attack because the situation of the Fourth Corps had changed on the afternoon of April 16 when the Tenth Mountain Division penetrated the German defense by capturing Tole and Monte Mosca.[7] An all-out effort would be made at this important breakthrough. To the right of the mountain division the U.S. Eighty-fifth Infantry Division, which had been held as a Fifth Army reserve, was thrown into the combat being waged by the Fourth Corps. To secure the left flank of the mountain division and make more of its troops available at the breakthrough area, the FEB was to replace mountain division units. Already on April 16 one FEB 1st RI battalion had replaced a mountain division battalion, and on April 17 another 1st RI battalion received a similar assignment, the boundary of the Brazilians being shifted to the right.[8]

According to Mascarenhas' recollections, Crittenberger, visiting Sassomolare on the morning of April 17, explained the new situation and confirmed the decision, made earlier by Truscott, to cancel the attack that the Brazilians had been undertaking for three days. But Brayner recalls hearing Crittenberger suggest a renewal of the Brazilian effort at daybreak on April 18 with American artillery, air, and tank support— all on the condition that Mascarenhas place the attack under the direction of General Zenóbio da Costa.[9] Brayner, delighted with this idea, tells of going with Mascarenhas in a jeep to the Brazilian division's Gaggio Montano headquarters and hearing Mascarenhas praise Zenóbio and resolve to send for him and appoint him to his new mission.

It is clear from Brayner's detailed narration that the chief of staff was not happy long. At Gaggio Montano, he says, Mascarenhas had to deal with Cordeiro and Castello Branco:

[6] Mascarenhas de Moraes, *Memórias*, I, 285.

[7] Ibid., p. 286; Carvalho, *Do Terço Velho ao Sampaio da F.E.B.*, p. 142; Mascarenhas de Moraes, *A F.E.B. pelo Seu Comandante*, p. 179. Brayner (*A Verdade sôbre a FEB*, p. 410) says that this reporting is inaccurate.

[8] Mascarenhas de Moraes, *Memórias*, I, 286, 287; Fourth Corps, *The Final Campaign across Northwest Italy*, pp. 27, 29.

[9] Brayner, *Recordando os Bravos*, pp. 172, 245, 322. See also Brayner, *A Verdade sôbre a FEB*, p. 406.

CORDEIRO: General, are you going to give the command of the operation tomorrow to Zenóbio?

MASCARENHAS: Yes, Cordeiro. The idea comes from Crittenberger himself and I am entirely in agreement. . . .

CORDEIRO: But don't you agree that that staff of Zenóbio is deficient?

MASCARENHAS: . . . That is a problem for Zenóbio. . . . Besides, the matter cannot be examined from that angle, because it is a decision agreed to by me and the commander of the Fourth Corps.

CORDEIRO: But don't you think that the command of Zenóbio is not up-to-date on details? It would be better to postpone the attack for 24 hours.

MASCARENHAS: I don't think so, Cordeiro. General Crittenberger is going to give full support to the operation and has already taken the necessary steps.

CASTELLO BRANCO (playing the decisive card): In addition to the reasons given by General Cordeiro, it is imperative to postpone the operation for 24 hours in order to arrange a better coordination.

MASCARENHAS (exasperated): How can I propose a 24-hour postponement of an attack that is to be started, with my approval, within two hours?[10]

But Brayner writes that Mascarenhas, "who had a paternal affection for Cordeiro," finally yielded and sent for Walters in order to receive the blessing of Crittenberger for the change in plans. Describing his own reaction, Brayner says that he listened, aghast, not understanding what Cordeiro and Castello really had in mind: "It was inconceivable that the commander of the Division would go back on a commitment practically imposed from above. I remained silent. For one reason because I had the impression that Cordeiro and, principally, Castello were convinced that I had been the originator of the idea, due to the insistence with which, on other occasions, I recommended making use of Zenóbio."[11]

Brayner adds that Walters, told by Mascarenhas of the postponement "in accordance with the suggestion of the Third Section," received a phone message in which Crittenberger left it up to the Brazilians to attack when they wanted.[12]

The cessation of the Brazilian attacks on Monte Buffoni and Montello occurred at the very moment when the Germans began a massive

[10] Brayner, *A Verdade sôbre a FEB*, p. 408.
[11] Ibid., p. 409.
[12] Ibid., p. 410.

retreat that took them from these strongholds. (According to Brayner, the Germans "broke contact without difficulty and without being molested" due to the Brazilians' "inertia beginning on the 17th.")[13]

An American assessment of the Brazilian activity in the Montese area is given in *The Final Campaign across Northwest Italy*, published by the Fourth Corps:

> The efforts of the 1st Infantry Division, FEB, during the first phase of the Spring drive had been effective, and the Brazilians had made their distinct contribution to that part of the IV Corps attack. Their aggressiveness had undoubtedly held in place both infantry and artillery which the German, had he dared to move them, could well have used elsewhere. The continued Brazilian activity in the Montese area had attracted no small amount of artillery and mortar fire which would otherwise have been directed at the flank of the 10th Mountain Division, and would have complicated its problems of supply and security. The help given also included the relief of the 10th Mountain elements, which not only took from the latter the responsibility for defense but also made these troops available to take part in the main attack. [P. 27]

11. The Victory at Collecchio (April 26–27, 1945)

Humberto's letters to Argentina, written before the Montese conflicts, were those of the sentimental family man who recalled with longing past vacations spent in the cottage in Belo Horizonte. Writing after Montese to express his pleasure at Paulo's having passed his exams, Humberto raised the burning question of when an end to the war would allow the family to reunite. In answer to his own question, all that he could say was that the Germans, although struck down all over Europe, still retained their ability to resist.[1]

In northern Italy, during the week that followed this comment, the Germans' ability to resist became more and more questionable. The Americans cut off Bologna's connection to the west, leading the Germans to abandon that strategic city. In the meantime the Brazilians, overcoming occasional pockets controlled by the Germans, moved north from the Montese area and then struck out to the west.

13 Ibid., p. 411.
1 HACB to Argentina, Italy, April 3, 5, 19, 1945, File H2, PVCB.

On the night of April 21, during this phase that followed the fighting in the Montese area, Mascarenhas came to Brayner's office to inquire whether or not Kruel had ordered the Reconnaissance Squadron, with its 140 men, to replace the 3,200-man 1st RI along the Panaro River. The rumor that Mascarenhas had heard about the conscientious Second Section head was indeed a strange one, and Brayner assured the commanding general that it was false. But, Brayner writes, the incident resulted in Kruel's resolution to leave the FEB. "At 3:00 A.M.," Brayner adds, "he had his jeep packed and was ready to go to Naples. I did not allow it."[2]

To keep up with the fleeing enemy and the American Fourth Corps, the FEB had to move rapidly. Mascarenhas, observing some of the Brazilian infantry plodding on foot because the Fourth Corps had taken twelve vehicles from his division, spoke to Castello: "After dinner I want to meet with Generals Zenóbio and Cordeiro. You and Colonel Brayner will be present. I am counting on your full support for the decision that I am going to make."[3]

Mascarenhas' decision was to use most of the artillery trucks to move men instead of heavy guns that had little to do under the new conditions. After Cordeiro expressed his desire to cooperate, the Brazilian division went into the final phase of the war with two artillery batteries instead of the normal twelve. It made the westward dash over hills and plains south of the Po River with a total of 676 trucks of various sizes and 606 jeeps.[4] At the FEB's right, also south of the Po, was the U.S. Thirty-fourth Infantry Division, which had participated in taking Bologna; the Tenth Mountain Division and the Eighty-fifth Infantry Division were starting to operate north of the Po.

Besides continuing to protect the left flank of the American Fourth Corps, the FEB kept on the alert to cut off a suspected move northward by the German 148th Division from the Liguria region on the Gulf of

[2] Brayner, *Recordando os Bravos*, pp. 173–174.

[3] Mascarenhas de Moraes, *Memórias*, I, 299–300.

[4] Andrade Mello interview, November 1, 1975. Already on April 21, Fifth Army commander Truscott had sent a directive to corps and division commanders calling for a maximum use of transportation and saying, in part, that artillery and tanks were to carry infantry as superloads (see Fourth Corps, *The Final Campaign across Northwest Italy*, p. 40). Senna Campos, *Com a FEB na Itália*, p. 155. Fourth Section head Senna Campos had been promoted to lieutenant colonel on December 25, 1944.

Genoa. Already some German divisions had crossed the Po and escaped to the north.[5]

The advance took the FEB across rivers flowing north toward the Po from the Apennines: the Panaro, Secchia, Enza, Parma, and Baganza. Entering town after town, soldiers of the Brazilian vanguard, the Reconnaissance Squadron led by Captain Plínio Pitaluga, heard the natives shout, "Long live our Liberators." They noted also that pro-Communist *partigiani* guerrilla groups and other long-suffering Italians were grimly setting out to get their revenge against hated local fascists.[6]

The FEB's Reconnaissance Squadron, generally one or two rivers ahead of the bulk of the Brazilians, reached the Taro River on April 26. There it reported a concentration of German troops at Collecchio, a village southwest of Parma. Mascarenhas therefore sought to rush troops westward to reinforce the Reconnaissance Squadron, and he personally sped to a town on the Enza River where the Second Battalion of the 11th RI was preparing to encamp for the night and was celebrating a false report about the war's end.

Mascarenhas overcame the arguments of Major Orlando Gomes Ramagem against moving his battalion at once. "The old general," Brayner writes, acted "with the enthusiasm of a lieutenant." Taking Ramagem in his jeep, Mascarenhas accompanied eight trucks that brought one company before sunset to the command post of Pitaluga's Reconnaissance Squadron, south of the Collecchio church.[7] While the trucks returned to the Enza River to bring more of the battalion, Major Ramagem was placed in charge of the attack to be made by his own men together with the Reconnaissance Squadron, two 6th RI companies, a unit of engineers, and an American tank company.

Mascarenhas was joined by Zenóbio, Cordeiro, and Castello, but he missed the battle because Castello recommended that he return to his headquarters, a schoolhouse at Montecchio Emilia, on the Enza River. "Several matters about the Division's advance to the northwest," Castello said, "depend on your decision. Allow me to suggest that you go to

[5] Brayner, *A Verdade sôbre a FEB*, p. 43.

[6] Mascarenhas de Moraes, *Memórias*, I, 297; Brayner, *A Verdade sôbre a FEB*, p. 431.

[7] Mascarenhas de Moraes, *Memórias*, I, 304, 306, 307; Brayner, *A Verdade sôbre a FEB*, p. 437; Pereira de Andrade, *O 11º R.I. na 2ª Guerra Mundial*, pp. 165–167.

Montecchio. General Zenóbio can remain here as long as he feels it necessary, considering that Major Ramagem is able to carry out the command of the action."[8]

Starting at 7:30 P.M., attacks were made on Collecchio, first from the southeast by a company of the 11th RI, which quickly seized the church, and then from the northeast by a company of the 6th RI.[9] The Brazilians had the use of some small artillery of the Reconnaissance Squadron, but neither they nor the Germans, who were limited to mortar and rifle fire, had any regular artillery.

The attack was suspended during the night when a torrent of rain fell. When the attack was renewed at 6:00 A.M. on April 27, the Brazilian force had been augmented by two more companies, one each of the 11th and 6th RI's. By the time of Mascarenhas' return to the scene at 8:00 A.M., most of Collecchio was in the hands of Major Ramagem. A few hours later, when the last pocket of resistance was overcome at a castle near the railroad station, the Brazilians emerged from a successful battle in which, Brayner notes, "we did not have any interference by Americans to disfigure the rhythm of the operations."[10]

According to a history of the Fourth Corps, the Brazilian action at Collecchio "eased considerably the dangerous situation on the left" of the corps. It resulted in the capture of about four hundred Germans along with much equipment belonging to the vanguard of the 148th Infantry Division. Its cost was sixteen Brazilians wounded and one killed.[11]

After the battle was over, the victors found in Collecchio the body of the German commanding colonel, apparently killed in combat. From its reclining position in an armchair, the uniformed body was taken and buried in the Collecchio cemetery on the orders of the Brazilian command.[12]

[8] Mascarenhas de Moraes, Memórias, I, 306.

[9] Castello Branco, O Brasil na II Grande Guerra, pp. 450–453.

[10] Mascarenhas de Moraes, Memórias, I, 307; Brayner, A Verdade sôbre a FEB, p. 437.

[11] Wondolowski, "History of the IV Corps," p. 642; Castello Branco, O Brasil na II Grande Guerra, p. 455.

[12] Brayner, A Verdade sôbre a FEB, p. 444.

12. Surrender of the 148th German Division (April 29, 1945)

The prisoners taken at Collecchio confirmed the news, already supplied by the *partigiani*, that the German 148th Division had come from the Gulf of Genoa and had reached an area around Fornovo di Taro, ten kilometers southwest of Collecchio.

This situation was made known to Truscott and Crittenberger on the morning of April 27, when in succession they visited the Brazilian advance headquarters at Montecchio. There they found Brayner. Brayner, who preferred the "diplomatic tact" of the "well-educated" Clark, received a poor impression of the two Americans, particularly of Truscott, who seemed curt and rude to him.[1]

The American generals insisted that the Germans at Fornovo were under no circumstances to be allowed to cross the Po and go on north. "The 148th Division shall not pass," Brayner calmly declared to Crittenberger. But, Brayner writes, this assurance did not satisfy the Americans, for after they left Montecchio, the Fourth Corps commander sent a radio message to Mascarenhas saying that he counted on him to prevent hostile elements, including the 148th Division, from crossing the Po. "This," Crittenberger advised Mascarenhas, "is a great opportunity to annihilate these hostile forces," and he added that the Brazilian commander should work in coordination with the commanding general of the American Thirty-fourth Division.[2]

Mascarenhas, in the Collecchio area, was arranging, with the assistance of Zenóbio and Castello Branco, to have the Brazilian division close in on Fornovo, defended by the 148th Division and remainders of the German Ninetieth Armored (Panzer) Division and the Italian Bersaglieri Division.[3] While to the northeast and northwest of Fornovo contingents of the 1st RI and 11th RI blocked possible exits of the enemy, Colonel Nelson de Melo's 6th RI prepared to attack Fornovo with the help of the two artillery batteries, the Reconnaissance Squadron, a company of engineers, and an American tank company.

On the morning of April 28 Zenóbio phoned Mascarenhas at Montecchio to propose that an additional battalion be thrown in to assist the 6th RI. Mascarenhas, relying on Castello Branco's assessment of the

---

[1] Brayner, *A Verdade sôbre a FEB*, pp. 438–439.
[2] Ibid., p. 441; Castello Branco, *O Brasil na II Grande Guerra*, p. 456.
[3] Mascarenhas de Moraes, *A F.E.B. pelo Seu Comandante*, p. 205.

situation, advised that an additional battalion would not be needed.[4] Therefore the encircling movement and attack was carried out by three battalions, as originally planned.

The principal offensive was undertaken by Major Gross's First Battalion, which advanced south from the Collecchio region. Moving to within six kilometers of Fornovo, it met and resisted violent counter-attacks at 9:00 P.M. on April 28 and at 1:00 A.M. on April 29. In the meantime at closer range Fornovo was attacked from the northwest by Major Silvino Nóbrega's Third Battalion and Captain Pitaluga's Reconnaissance Squadron and from the southeast by Major Cordeiro Oeste's Second Battalion. "The very determined Brazilians," Wondolowski writes, "were wreaking havoc" on every German attempt to break through. "It may be added," he continues, "that the Brazilians also found troops to send to Piacenza and to the pocket north of Cremona; they did not require all of their strength for this job of blocking Highway 62."[5]

On the afternoon of April 27, a day before the offensive against Fornovo, Major Cordeiro Oeste persuaded a village vicar to carry to the Germans a suggestion that they surrender. The vicar walked six kilometers to Respicio, close to Fornovo, and there he spoke with German officers; asked about the strength and location of the Brazilian troops, the vicar said that the Germans were surrounded and should surrender. One of the older Germans, whose Italian had been polished during a stint as ambassador to Rome, asked the vicar to obtain written surrender conditions and return with them. As a result, early on April 28, still before the 6th RI attacked, Nelson de Melo drew up an unconditional surrender ultimatum and, through Castello Branco, secured Mascarenhas' approval of it. The vicar took this to the Germans and returned early in the afternoon with a message signed by Major Kuhn, chief of staff of the 148th Division, saying that a reply would follow consultation with superiors.[6]

While the Germans procrastinated, the 6th RI proceeded according to plan. Then at 10:30 P.M., after Gross's men had repulsed strong

[4] Mascarenhas de Moraes, *Memórias*, I, 311.

[5] Wondolowski, "History of the IV Corps," p. 644. See also Fourth Corps, *The Final Campaign across Northwest Italy*, p. 80.

[6] Mascarenhas de Moraes, *Memórias*, I, 309–311. See also "Depoimento de D. Alessandro Cavalli," the vicar, in Mascarenhas de Moraes, *Memórias*, I, 320–323.

enemy resistance, Major Kuhn and two other German officers crossed the Brazilian lines to negotiate surrender details. Gross conducted them to the 6th RI's command post at Collecchio. Nelson de Melo, learning that the mission of the three Germans had been authorized by 148th Division commander Otto Fretter Pico, sped to Montecchio to see Mascarenhas.[7]

At Montecchio just before midnight Humberto was writing to Argentina: "While Milan is already celebrating . . . a peace soon to be announced," and "while radios shout about imminent peace, this afternoon we gave the order to attack; the combat continued with several dead and many wounded. . . . Some fall in order to liberate many, to redeem others, and to give peace to everyone, including the enemy."

Humberto had just finished a sentence about the German "arrogance and stupid mania to dominate the world" when he learned of the new development. "The German, entirely surrounded by us, wants to surrender," he added to his letter.[8]

Mascarenhas ordered Brayner and Castello Branco to deal with the German negotiators. Therefore in the rain the two officers were driven to Collecchio. There, "in a room of a country house," Humberto wrote later in a postscript to Argentina, "I was presented to three German staff officers of a division (a Prussian division surrenders to a Brazilian!). They asked for surrender conditions. We said that it could only be unconditional. They talked and they talked about military honor and humanitarian principles. And they accepted the surrender! It is a matter of several thousand men, two generals, etc."[9]

As a result of the terms imposed at the all-night meeting at Collecchio—modified only by Mascarenhas' subsequent insistence that the laying down of arms take place at once (on April 29 instead of April 30)—the first German division to surrender in Italy surrendered to the Brazilians. A total of 14,779 Germans and Italians became prisoners in two nearby camps that were set up by the Brazilians. German General Otto Fretter Pico and Italian General Mario Carloni were escorted to Florence by Generals Falconière and Zenóbio and turned over to the

[7] Mascarenhas de Moraes, Memórias, I, 315.

[8] HACB to Argentina, "in Montecchio, close to Parma, in the Valley of the Po," April 28, 1945, File H2, p. 24, PVCB.

[9] Ibid.

American Fifth Army, together with six million lira also taken by the Brazilians.[10]

In the fighting outside of Fornovo five Brazilians had been killed and about fifty wounded. What had been accomplished was remarkable in warfare: the surrender of one division not to two or more divisions, but to a single division.[11]

"You cannot imagine," Humberto wrote to Argentina on April 30, "How busy I have been. But from the newspapers you will learn that things are now advancing rapidly. I believe that before long I'll have more time for writing to you. Ah! Peace! I continue in very good health and spirits and keen on the work. But homesickness, already overflowing, becomes an avalanche. God grant before long my return to that garden where I last saw you and Nieta." [12]

13. The End of the War (May 8, 1945)

On April 30, while the handling of the surrender of the German 148th Division was still under way, the FEB was instructed by the American Fourth Corps to continue cutting off German movements from the south and to occupy, to the west of Fornovo, the area around Alessandria, where the German Seventy-fifth Corps was known to be.

To exchange ideas about this new offensive against the enemy, Castello Branco flew on May 2 to the command post of the Fourth Corps, recently set up in Milan. There, when he met in the evening with an American general, an English general, and two interpreters, startling new developments were discussed. The news of Hitler's death had been received on May 1, and already in Milan the bodies of Mussolini, his mistress, and a few of his last associates were hanging by their heels from a filling station girder.

As the officers turned to military tactics in northwest Italy, they received the news that German generals were coming to the headquarters

10 Brayner, *A Verdade sôbre a FEB*, p. 462. Brayner discusses the surrender in considerable detail in chapter 17 (pp. 451–490).

11 Andrade Mello interview, November 1, 1975; Miranda interview, December 1, 1975.

12 HACB to Argentina, Italy, April 30, 1945, File H2, p. 26, PVCB.

in Milan in order to surrender. The frowning faces of the tacticians became radiant. While work papers were set aside and mutual compliments were exchanged, a German general was escorted into the room. Politely he congratulated the victors.[1]

Castello was teeming with emotions and thoughts of returning to Rio as he made his way to his hotel at 1:00 A.M. through the unlit, vacant streets of badly battered Milan. Leaving the airport at 6:00 A.M. on May 3, he was flown to Alessandria, where Mascarenhas had just set up the new command post of the FEB. The general, Castello found, was working on a victory proclamation listing the FEB's successes and casualties. "You can," it told the troops, "be proud of your honorable fulfillment of your duty and of your brilliant contribution to our nation's having a place reserved for it in the reconstruction of the world."[2]

Castello, filling pages of news for Argentina, said that it would be impossible for her to imagine what was going on within him. Nor, he added, could he try to tell her, except in a "calmer letter."[3]

After going to church to thank God for peace, Humberto wrote again on May 5. "I have entered a period truly different from those that ended on the night of May 2. No more combats, no more operations orders! The relief is so great that I still cannot believe that I am awake."

"Here," Humberto continued, "I did what I could, giving what there was of my energy and what it was possible for me to draw from my modest intellectual capacity." Not yet having advised Argentina of the miserable time that Brayner and Kruel had given him, he added: "Sometime I want to tell you everything, so that you can understand what my lot was here and how much I suffered. But, let's leave it for later, or perhaps it would be better if I left everything behind."

Turning to a possible promotion, something that had been brought up in a letter from Argentina, Humberto told his wife not to think about the matter. He could not, he said, be promoted ahead of a large group that was especially well connected in Rio. "Above all, I have in Catete Palace a '*firme*' opposition."[4]

Castello was not aware that in April Mascarenhas had cabled Presi-

---

[1] HACB to Argentina, Italy, May 3, 1945, File H2, p. 28, PVCB.
[2] Mascarenhas de Moraes, *Memórias*, II, 333–335.
[3] HACB to Argentina, Italy, May 3, 1945, File H2, p. 28, PVCB.
[4] HACB to Argentina, Italy, May 5, 1945, File H2, p. 30, PVCB.

dent Vargas asking that Castello be promoted. Replying from Petrópolis on April 24, General Firmo Freire had cabled that the president had received "with much favor" the request on behalf of Castello Branco, "it being agreed that the Minister will take care of it at the next promotions." In May Mascarenhas followed up this cable with a radiogram to War Minister Dutra requesting, "as an exceptional case," the promotion of Castello Branco "because of his indispensable services to the military operations as head of the Third Section of the staff of the Division. Our successes depended, to a large extent, on the personal valor of this officer and his physical and moral force, bravery, professional capacity, and continuous effort." [5]

Castello, who was to remain in the dark for some time further about his promotion, heard rumors in Alessandria early in May that "within a few days" a group of Brazilian officers would leave for Rio to prepare for the arrival of the troops there. "Ah, *minha filha*," he wrote to Argentina on May 5, "now everything is over for me here and I only think of returning to Brazil."

But on the following day Mascarenhas told Castello that as he had further need of him in Italy, he would not be among the members of the Destacamento Precursor (Precursory Detachment) that was to fix up the installations and barracks in Brazil for receiving the troops from Italy.[6]

Mascarenhas had decided to send Brayner and Amauri Kruel back to Brazil with the Destacamento Precursor. He would name Brayner head of the detachment and elevate Castello to the post of acting chief of staff, putting him in Brayner's old position. Neither Humberto nor Brayner was particularly pleased with this decision. While Humberto appreciated the honor and expressions of confidence, the prospect of remaining for months in Italy with considerable bureaucratic responsibilities was not altogether attractive.[7] Writing to Argentina to explain his

[5] Cable, General Firmo Freire to Mascarenhas de Moraes, Petrópolis, April 24, 1945, in "Campanha da Itália," File G1, CPDOC; radiogram, Mascarenhas de Moraes to Eurico Gaspar Dutra, May 22, 1945, in "Campanha da Itália," File G1, CPDOC.

[6] HACB to Argentina, Alessandria, May 6, 1945, File H2, p. 33, PVCB; Brayner, *A Verdade sôbre a FEB*, p. 510.

[7] HACB to Argentina, Alessandria, May 6, 1945, File H2, p. 33, PVCB, Brayner writes (*Recordando os Bravos*, p. 181) that Kruel was quick to volunteer for the Destacamento Precursor because of the "animosity" of Mascarenhas and because "under no circumstances" did he wish to serve in Italy under Acting Chief of Staff Castello

delay in returning, Humberto said: "I did nothing to prolong my stay here. The situation created for me is such that I cannot ask, at least at this moment, to leave at once." He begged her not to be sad and to believe that "for me to return now would be a blessing from heaven." [8]

Mascarenhas thought that the appointment of Brayner to head the Destacamento Precursor would free the colonel somewhat from his inactivity. But Brayner, who felt that the staff of the Brazilian division was being "mutilated prematurely to satisfy the ambitions and maneuvers of insiders," argued that the Destacamento Precursor was entirely unnecessary: there had long existed an "internal" *estado maior* of the FEB in Brazil, and a few men from the First and Fourth sections in Italy could easily deliver the necessary documents to it. [9]

As head of the Destacamento Precursor, Brayner left Alessandria on May 8 and flew to Brazil twenty days later. His departure from his former duties, he has written, occurred "without euphoria, without happiness, and without any spiritual separation from my real work, which began on October 10, 1943, when I and General Mascarenhas organized the Estado Maior." [10]

May 8 was a happier day for others. "Today," Humberto wrote Argentina, "is the final day of the war in Europe. . . . Germany surrendered unconditionally, is completely crushed, hopelessly routed. And this is what it needed, and so did the world. Hitler, without doubt, was a primitive type and Mussolini a comedian. You cannot begin to have an idea of all the cruelties carried out by the Germans. They are incalculable and unimaginable. The things they did with prisoners of war amount to cold, bestial, unpardonable atrocities.

"But let us sing about the peace!" [11]

Branco. HACB to Argentina, Alessandria, May 23, 1945, File H2, PVCB, states that "bureaucratic work" absorbed most of his time.

[8] HACB to Argentina, Alessandria, May 9, 1945, File H2, p. 36, PVCB.

[9] HACB to Argentina, June 10, 1945, File H2, p. 79v, PVCB; Brayner, *A Verdade sôbre a FEB*, p. 511. Writing about the Destacamento Precursor, Brayner says, "I formally opposed its existence."

[10] Brayner, *A Verdade sôbre a FEB*, pp. 510–511.

[11] HACB to Argentina, Alessandria, May 9, 1945, File H2, p. 36, PVCB.

The Last Days in Italy
(1945)

It is impossible that a hecatomb such as we have seen will not bring a great revolution of ideas, from which will spring a more humane, more Christian, social evolution, less hard on the poor and limiting as much as possible the exploitation of man by man.

1. The Acting Chief of Staff Remains in Alessandria

CASTELLO BRANCO, noting the Allied victory ceremonies in Verona and Milan on May 4, 6, and 7, and Mascarenhas' preparations for a victory lunch in Alessandria on May 13, made a suggestion: it would be appropriate to remember those who had died in the FEB's campaign (and who numbered 451). This idea was accepted, and on May 11 at Alessandria's Madonna della Salve Cathedral a solemn Mass was held, followed by music by a "magnificent Italian choir and a moving sermon by the chaplain." Mascarenhas laid flowers on a symbolic sepulcher that, in accordance with Castello's ideas, was simple rather than "grandiose and luxurious." [1]

May, 1945, was a month of victory banquets, at which the FEB offered printed menus featuring such dishes as Monte Castello salad, filet à la Montese, and pastries à la Castelnuovo. [2] It was a month of parading and of awarding medals and citations.

When Generals Truscott and Crittenberger came to ceremonies held in Alessandria on May 19 to present decorations to Brazilians, Castello Branco received the United States Army's Bronze Star from Truscott. The award was given

for meritorious service in combat from February 19 to March 5, 1945, in the Reno Valley, Italy. As Chief of the G-3 Section of the Brazilian Infantry Division, Lieutenant Colonel Castello Branco displayed aggressive leadership,

[1] HACB to Argentina, Alessandria, May 11, File H2, PVCB. For details of the church service, see Manoel Thomaz Castello Branco, *O Brasil na II Grande Guerra*, pp. 481–482.

[2] Menus in File H2, PVCB.

sound tactical knowledge and foresight which enabled the Brazilian troops successfully to accomplish continuous and effective operations over difficult and mountainous terrain. He made frequent visits to the front line units and studied the terrain in preparation for the operations that culminated in the successful occupations by Brazilian troops of Mt. Castello and Castelnuovo. Showing a complete disregard for his personal safety while under enemy artillery and small arms fire, Lieutenant Colonel Castello Branco demonstrated outstanding efficiency in the execution of his duties and closely cooperated at all times with the G-3 Section of an American corps. His exemplary conduct and skillful planning are in keeping with the highest traditions of the Allied Armies. . . .[3]

May, 1945, was also a month of diversion for the Brazilian soldiers. Permissions were given for visits to cities in the south of France and to the lake region in the north of Italy. "Have you seen what it is like when goats are released after a long confinement?" Humberto wrote Argentina. "It is the same thing. Excursions, dances, and an infiltration into the Italian environment."[4] After the FEB formed soldiers' and officers' clubs for dances, movies, and games, Italians found that the Brazilians were enthusiastic samba teachers and skillful soccer players.

The inauguration of an officers' club in Alessandria was the occasion of a large reception and dance. Castello, deciding not to attend, resolved to avoid boredom in another manner: he would read a lot and work.

"My present work," Castello wrote home on May 6, "is to put in order a voluminous mass of documents, especially with regard to the last hurried and tumultuous part of the campaign. Besides, I am drawing up a report on the Third Section. My assistants are a great help to me and are always showing their respect and attention. They bring me good wines and fruits and their impressions about everything."[5]

The task of the acting chief of staff, the position to which Castello was advanced on May 17, was neither intense nor difficult. But, as Castello saw it, he had to remain most of the time in Alessandria in order to guide subordinates. "I like to do what is incumbent on me, and therefore I do not let anyone else do what I am supposed to do."[6]

[3] English version in "Campanha da Itália," File G1, CPDOC; Portuguese version in "Folhas de Alterações," File G2, Part 3, first semester of 1945, CPDOC.
[4] HACB to Argentina, Alessandria, May 6, 1945, File H2, p. 33, PVCB.
[5] Ibid.
[6] HACB to Argentina, Alessandria, May 26, 1945, File H2, PVCB.

Castello found three more reasons for sticking to his post. As he explained to Argentina, (1) having visited Egypt and Palestine, he did not want to deprive others of their vacations in Venice, Stresa, and Nice; (2) he had to finish a series of chief of staff reports; and (3) as Mascarenhas was making a round of trips, his own place was in Alessandria.[7] The work, Castello calculated, would keep him in Italy until the latter part of June, when he was, according to Mascarenhas' promise, scheduled to return to Brazil with Mascarenhas on the ship taking the first contingent of returning troops.[8]

As these plans would bring Castello to Rio later than Amauri Kruel, who was leaving Naples late in May with Brayner's Destacamento Precursor, it became necessary for Castello to alert Argentina about his relations with Kruel. This he did in a letter entrusted on May 17 to Ademar de Queiroz, who was about to fly to Rio not as a member of the Destacamento Precursor but as an emissary of Mascarenhas to War Minister Dutra. Ademar, Humberto confided to Argentina, "has been more than a friend; he has been a brother. To him I owe a very great deal."[9]

In the letter of May 17 taken by Ademar to Argentina, Humberto, in anguished sentences, told of how Brayner and Amauri had joined forces. He wrote that Amauri had spoken to everyone against him, joining Brayner's campaign of attributing "all failures" to Humberto and "all successes to others." Humberto explained that he had done everything possible to get Amauri to change from his "unfriendly attitude at Brayner's side. . . . It was in vain. He lost his head and his heart. This is one of the greatest disappointments of my life. It was as though it happened to a brother. . . . My wound is still open."[10]

Kruel had excluded Castello when inviting many officers to his birthday lunch on April 11, which may not have been surprising because Castello had ceased inviting Kruel to the Third Section's "little parties." However, Kruel in May did not act as though his relationship with Castello had reached the depths described by Humberto to Argentina. All smiles, he asked Castello what he could take to Rio for him, and Castello did decide to give him one letter for Argentina.[11]

[7] Ibid.
[8] HACB to Argentina, Alessandria, May 17, 1945, File H2, p. 48, PVCB.
[9] Ibid.
[10] Ibid., quoted in Luís Viana Filho, *O Governo Castelo Branco*, p. 37.
[11] HACB to Argentina, Alessandria, May 17, 1945, File H2, p. 48, PVCB; Amauri Kruel interview, Rio de Janeiro, December 11, 1975.

Ademar de Queiroz, after delivering Castello's May 17 letter to Argentina, worked in Dutra's office as he had before joining Cordeiro. Brayner writes that with the arrival of Ademar de Queiroz in the minister's office, "the administrative measures, sometimes harebrained and incomprehensible, were issued without any judgment." Ademar de Queiroz, Brayner points out, "did not belong to the Destacamento Precursor, but acted in accordance with his missions without giving any satisfaction to the Colonel Chief of Staff of FEB, alleging that he was doing so with the full assent of the general commanding the First Division, who was a personal friend of his." [12]

2. A Call for Social and Political Reforms (May, 1945)

Vernon Walters, out of action because of burns received in an accident following the Montese battles, used his left hand on May 3 to scrawl a note to Castello congratulating "the FEB and especially the Third Section for the glorious triumphs of the final days." Walters, whose translating work had been taken over by Lieutenant Rubem Argollo, told Castello of his sorrow to have missed the "end of the operations." Writing that "the rations in this Jailhouse are worse than ours were in Porretta Terme," the American major expressed the hope of returning soon to the Brazilans and their "good *cafezinhos*." [1]

On May 8 Walters rejoined the FEB in Alessandria, where, he states, he shared an apartment with Castello. For a while Mascarenhas shared the apartment with Castello, but the general was frequently away from Alessandria and, according to Walters, made considerable use of his trailer when he was not away. In any case, Castello had an enormous room of his own with a splendid "Italian bed." Many of the other men of the Brazilian Division resided in houses that had previously been occupied by Germans and that were scattered throughout the region, a rich agricultural and industrial zone that had not been much damaged by the war. [2]

---

[12] Floriano de Lima Brayner, *A Verdade sôbre a FEB: Memórias de um Chefe de Estado-Maior na Campanha da Itália, 1943–1945*, pp. 519–520.

[1] Walters to HACB, May 3, 1945, File H3, Part 2, p. 16, PVCB.

[2] Vernon Walters interview, McLean, Virignia, June 12, 1975; HACB to Argentina, Alessandria, May 5, 6, 23, 1945, File H2, PVCB.

Castello received an invitaton to dine with General Crittenberger, and therefore on May 10 he made a brief visit to Milan, where he noted the destruction of the hotel where he and his family had stayed in 1937. At Crittenberger's apartment, he wrote Argentina, "everyone stared at me, especially the British, curious about the prestige given to a *'tupiniquim.'* " [3]

Why, Crittenberger asked, were the Brazilians, including Castello, in such a hurry to return home? Castello replied that the only troops that should remain to occupy Italy were those of countries having representatives on the council for establishing an Allied government there. Brazil had no such representative and, in Castello's opinion, did not want one, having no political interest in Europe. Crittenberger said that he had become accustomed to Castello's frankness in tactical matters and appreciated his frankness on the occupation question. [4]

Brayner would have agreed with Castello that the FEB had accomplished its mission and had no reason to participate in the occupation of Italy or any other territory. A few days earlier, when General Clark had consulted General Mascarenhas about the possibility of the transfer of the FEB to Austria to serve as an occupation force there, Brayner had recommended rejecting the idea. [5]

Nevertheless, the Brazilians played a role in the occupation of Italy until their departure in June from the extensive area in which they had found themselves when hostilities ceased. [6] A difficult part of the work was to persuade the *partigiani* to exercise restraint in carrying out revenge against former fascists and their collaborators. Less delicate were the other tasks that the command of the FEB assigned to its men "to fill their days": the protection of public services and the reconstruction of bridges and highways to facilitate the eventual movement of the FEB to a port area. [7]

[3] HACB to Argentina Alessandria, May 11, 1945, File H2, PVCB. A *tupiniquim* is an Indian of an extinct tribe.

[4] Ibid.

[5] Brayner, *A Verdade sôbre a FEB*, p. 511; Floriano de Lima Brayner, *Recordando os Bravos; Eu Convivi com Eles; Campanha da Itália*, p. 180.

[6] João Baptista Mascarenhas de Moraes, *A F.E.B. pelo Seu Comandante*, p. 239. The FEB is described (p. 240) as developing its relations with the Italian people so successfully that it came close to being called on to remain in Italy as a part of the Allied occupational forces.

[7] Castello Branco, *O Brasil na II Grande Guerra*, pp. 477–479; HACB to Argentina, Alessandria, May 26, 1945, File H2, PVCB.

Humberto told Argentina that the mere presence of foreign troops in Italian cities practically eliminated disorder. The life of an officer of an occupational force seemed to him to be an indolent one, but he conceded that the work was necessary: "If Italy is abandoned by the Allies it will catch fire and, moreover, nazi-fascism will resurge a little from the ashes, slyly, secretly, undermining the victory won at such cost by the United Nations." However, another aspect of military occupation did not appeal to him; prominent Italians were calling for occupation in order to preserve what was theirs. "Good for them but horrible for me. *I am saturated* with all of this and it is high time to return."[8]

The protection of the property of the rich at the expense of the poor worried Castello. He had a great deal to say to Argentina about "the ideas felt by the soldiers of many nations. It is impossible that a hecatomb such as we have seen will not bring a great revolution of ideas, from which will spring a more humane, more Christian, social evolution, less hard on the poor and limiting as much as possible the exploitation of man by man."[9]

Brazil, he felt, was in great need of change. Looking at pictures of receptions, teas, and banquets in Brazilian magazines, he saw "the same old faces, the same lack of thoughtful people, and the same matrons, who, despite being elegant, have an appearance that lends them little respect." He had the impression that wealth was anchored to one stratum: a government group that carried out dishonest deals with the public treasury and another group, made up of important men of commerce and business, that exploited the poor consumers. "It is the farce at the top and the drama of those who are below. This war is going to take care of all of this."[10]

The Brazilian presidential contest between Dutra and Eduardo Gomes did not excite the admiration of Castello. Describing the propaganda on both sides as "discouraging," he said that he had not yet been able to catch a glimpse of any objective program demonstrating clear interest in the good of Brazil.[11] The Brazilian politician, Humberto wrote

[8] HACB to Argentina, May 23, 26, 1945, File H2, PVCB.

[9] HACB to Argentina, May 27, 1945, File H2, PVCB.

[10] Ibid.

[11] See p. 75 of File H2, PVCB (which contains a stray eighth page of a letter from HACB).

Argentina, had no "sense of the public good" but only dealt with matters related to himself, his family, and his backers. "That is the basis of all of our folly. . . . The Dutra candidacy is the child of so-called officialdom, and that of Eduardo attracts the discontented and the oppositionists of all complexions. One candidacy has a benedito valadares, and the other a bernardes, each the symbol of a type of political corruption." (Castello deliberately omitted capitals in mentioning Valadares and Bernardes.)[12]

This was not to say that Castello lacked a high opinion of the candidates. He had always regarded Dutra as an upright, conscientious, serious man, and he felt the same way about Eduardo Gomes. "One was my chief, and in him I never saw a dishonest gesture; the other was my student, who in school circles revealed an irreproachable conduct. But politics tempts men and tarnishes them, when it does not cover them with mud. How will Dutra be? How will Eduardo be?"[13]

As far as Dutra was concerned, Castello gave an answer to this question in a letter written later, when it seemed to him that Eduardo Gomes was losing ground. "Dutra will know how to lay his hand on the present gang that is making money dishonestly."[14]

3. Promotion to Colonel (June, 1945)

Late in May, Castello Branco was assigned the task of preparing and supervising the southward move of all of the soldiers of the FEB in Italy to a camp in the Francolise region, where they were to await embarkation from Naples, fifty kilometers further south. Humberto wrote Argentina that he expected to devote June to handling the move and the installation at Francolise, while a part of July would be spent preparing the departure of the first Brazilian troopship from Naples. As this em-

[12] HACB to Argentina, Alessandria, May 14, 1945, File H2, p. 43, PVCB. Benedito Valadares was governing Minas Gerais as intervenor on behalf of the Vargas government, having been appointed in 1933. Artur Bernardes, against whom the *tenentes* had rebelled in the mid-1920's, served as president of Brazil from 1922 to 1926 and supported Eduardo Gomes in 1945.

[13] Ibid.

[14] See p. 75 of File H2, PVCB (which contains a stray eighth page of a letter from HACB).

barkation was to await the evacuation of Americans who were wounded, sick, or recently freed from imprisonment, Castello now felt that he and Mascarenhas would reach Rio only in late July.[1]

On the night of May 30 Castello decided to use the radiophone of the division to speak with Argentina. Tense with excitement at the thought of hearing her voice for the first time in eleven months, he was keenly disappointed when Nieta told him that her mother was in Niterói. "What a letdown for me," he wrote, and then he went on to describe the worries that filled him at the thought of Argentina alone in Niterói at 7:30 P.M., later taking the ferry to Rio, and waiting there in "an endless line" at night for a bus to get home.[2] He could not sleep.

Trying the radiophone again on May 31, Humberto found the connection troubled by interference. But on June 2 he got through to Argentina. His inability to sleep that night was the result of emotion; the thrill of hearing her voice and of feeling her interest in his return were too much. He promised to call again on June 12 and begged her to keep sending letters, one after the other. "In this campaign," he wrote, "your letters have always been the greatest comfort for me; they brought me stimulation, and the fragrance of our old and constantly renewed affection."[3]

Letters from Argentina were pouring in. Of this new series, only the first letter, written soon after the final victory, disappointed him because it did not mention "the last achievements of the Division."[4] But all of the others overwhelmed the sentimental warrior. "You have such wonderful expressions for your husband that tears came to my eyes. You speak of my 'successful way of acting' and 'dedication,' and you close everything with compliments for your 'beloved husband' and with a 'friendly kiss.' What a magnificent recompense you give me, one that I know comes from a heart that is mine, that has lived for me for over twenty years."[5]

After using the radiophone on June 12, Humberto wrote: "I heard your voice clearly and it seemed to me that I could see you sitting in the

[1] HACB to Argentina, Alessandria, June 3, 1945, File H2, PVCB.

[2] HACB to Argentina, Alessandria, May 31, 1945, File H2, PVCB. (The Castello Brancos' Chevrolet had been sold to a relative when Humberto went to Italy.)

[3] HACB to Argentina, Alessandria, June 3, 1945, File H2, PVCB.

[4] HACB to Argentina, Alessandria, May 29, 1945, File H2, PVCB.

[5] See p. 77 of File H2, PVCB (the last part of a letter from HACB).

wickerwork chair, reclined, talking on the phone. If our connection wasn't better it was because in addition to so many people being around, there was much emotion." [6]

Sending Argentina a copy of Mascarenhas' lengthy praise of his "exceptional performance" in the last phase of the campaign, Humberto attributed his success to the stimulus that she and the children provided. Confessing that Mascarenhas did not exactly stimulate him, Humberto nevertheless described the general as a "man of courage" because "without vacillating he always says that the operational plans were made by me." Humberto also pointed out that the general's praise was based purely on professional matters ("I was the professor of tactics, making practical plans"), for Humberto did not, he wrote, spend any time obsequiously professing friendship for the general. [7]

"You must have been very sad," Humberto wrote a few days later, "with the letter in which I told of the impropriety of Amauri. Now that I am alone, I perceive even more the extent of his improper behavior—not to use a stronger expression. He abandoned me in difficult moments, and, more than that, he continued to oppose me, allying himself criminally with Brayner. The two spoke so badly of me!" [8]

Late in June Castello was in Francolise when his old friend Toné (Lieutenant Colonel Coelho dos Reis) and Lieutenant Colonel Ademar de Queiroz told him, on the radio from Rio, that his promotion to colonel had become effective. Castello spoke at once on the radio with Argentina and Nieta. "I received," he then wrote to his wife, "the best congratulations that it was possible to receive—yours." [9]

To no one, he told Argentina, did he owe the promotion more than to her. She had been the greatest and best participant in his life. Seeking to be worthy of her, he had gained strength. "In you, therefore, I have a permanent stimulation. This declaration is not a formality. It is the very sincere feeling that I have at this moment, when I attain the position of colonel." [10]

[6] HACB to Argentina, Alessandria, June 13, 1945, File H2, p. 83, PVCB.

[7] The text of this *elogio* of HACB by Mascarenhas de Moraes is given in the information bulletin of the Brazilian forces for May 30, 1945, and is reproduced in "Folhas de Alterações," File G2, Part 3, "Teatro de Operações no Mediterrâneo," first semester, 1945, CPDOC; HACB to Argentina, June 6, 1945, File H2, PVCB.

[8] HACB to Argentina, June 10, 1945, File H2, p. 79v, PVCB.

[9] HACB to Argentina, Francolise, June 26, 1945, File H2, p. 90, PVCB.

[10] Ibid.

4. Francolise (June–July, 1945)

The five-hundred-kilometer transfer of the Brazilian soldiers to Francolise, which occupied most of June, was carried out by trucks, by rail, and by coastal steamer. This large-scale move, Mascarenhas writes, was "facilitated above all by the proficient cooperation" of Castello Branco with Senna Campos' Fourth Section.[1] During its execution Humberto confided to Argentina that he was "sick of Italy" and a bit tired from "so much work." "While the others enjoy vacations," he wrote from Alessandria, "I am here, handling the work of everyone, including the general. He is going to Paris and Germany."[2]

Before leaving the north of Italy, Castello made two more brief visits to Milan to have meals with friends in the Fourth Corps, and there he followed the practice, popular with the FEB, of buying ladies' hats to be sent to Brazil. After a farewell lunch given in his honor by the Fourth Corps staff on June 14, Castello wrote: "the staff was so gracious to me that I shall never forget it."[3]

Three days later Castello left Alessandria for Francolise in his jeep, with his chauffeur and Edésio, who had been promoted to corporal. During the hot and dusty forty-eight-hour ride, the colonel took time off to show his two traveling companions some of the sights of the Vatican.[4]

Francolise, an agricultural region of wheat and olive plantations, lies on the Rome-Naples highway about fifteen kilometers inland from the coast. There, while Allied doctors and engineers fought to protect the men against malaria, German prisoners built sheds, and the Fourth Section supervised the crating of equipment.[5]

Castello, who lived in a tent under an olive tree, wrote to Argentina to say that "General Mascarenhas left for France and put me in charge of carrying out all of this. And, thanks to God, everything is being carried out."[6] Castello had more to do than arrange for the forthcoming

---

[1] Mascarenhas de Moraes, *A F.E.B. pelo Seu Comandante*, p. 241. The move is discussed in Aguinaldo José Senna Campos, *Com a FEB na Itália: Páginas do Meu Diário*, pp. 179–181.

[2] HACB to Argentina, Alessandria, June 8, 1945, File H2, p. 78, PVCB.

[3] HACB to Argentina, Italy, June 17, 1945, File H2, p. 85, PVCB.

[4] HACB to Argentina, Italy, June 21, 1945, File H2, p. 87, PVCB.

[5] Aguinaldo José Senna Campos interview, Rio de Janeiro, November 26, 1975; Gilberto Peixoto, *A Campanha da Itália*, pp. 197–199.

[6] HACB to Argentina, Italy, June 21, 1945, File H2, p. 87, PVCB.

embarkation of men and materials. He needed, as he put it, to "readjust the division" to its new life—a painful process. After the pleasant and sometimes lively times recently enjoyed by the troops, life under the scorching sun in the tents of the dusty Francolise camp seemed "insipid" and "uncomfortable." [7] (According to Brayner, the Brazilian soldiers in Francolise experienced "the first reaction of ingratitude, which they did not expect so soon.") [8]

Card playing at Francolise was a far cry from the sort of behavior that brought Cordeiro de Farias to Castello's tent to lament what he called the fame for dissipation in Italy that the FEB was said to have gained in Rio. Castello told Cordeiro that the "bad conduct" practiced by "a few" could not ruin "the reputation of many." But Cordeiro shook his head sadly and would not allow himeslf to be comforted on this score. [9]

Finally, on July 6 the first Brazilian returning contingent of 4,660 soldiers and 271 officers left Naples for Rio on the *General Meiggs* under the command of Zenóbio da Costa. Cordeiro de Farias became the top commander of the men remaining in Italy, for Mascarenhas, deciding that he might as well reach Brazil before the first contingent, left by plane, also on July 6, with his three aides (a major and two captains) and with Acting Chief of Staff Castello Branco.

A week before the departure, Humberto wrote Argentina a letter that he said would be his last from Italy. Again he recalled those unforgettable scenes of exactly one year earlier when he had been encouraged by Paulo's serenity and so touched by the sight, through the garden leaves, of the waving hands of Argentina and Nieta. "We could not imagine what would transpire. . . . We only knew one thing: that the two of us would maintain a mutual support and be indissoluble in our affection."

Humberto thanked Argentina for all that she had done for him in the year. "To you I owe everything, and everything that I did was based on our affection and on honoring our children." Turning to the future, he wrote: "Let us do everything possible to live it well, under the blessing of God. Let us both live happily, one for the other, and the two of

[7] Castello Branco, *O Brasil na II Grande Guerra*, p. 492. See also HACB to Argentina, June 21, 23, 1945, File H2, pp. 87, 88, PVCB.

[8] Brayner, *A Verdade sôbre a FEB*, p. 513.

[9] HACB to Argentina, Francolise, June 26, 1945, File H2, p. 90, PVCB.

us for the two children. I say to you again that we can only be happy with you and that you are the source of our happiness at home. Love me well, have patience with me, and know that I am the person who loves you the most in the world."[10]

5. Parades, Receptions, and Toasts (July, 1945)

Ahead of the returning officers lay countless occasions at which the achievements of the FEB would be honored. But never were the observances as strenuous and time-consuming as in the weeks that succeeded the arrival of Mascarenhas and Castello at the air base near Natal, Rio Grande do Norte, before dawn on July 8, 1945. The affairs, marked by eloquent oratory, were attended by civilian and military authorities, and when they were held in public they attracted enormous crowds. Pipe-smoking snakes glared from many a poster.

Following the first receptions in Natal, Mascarenhas and Castello spent two days attending ceremonies in Recife, where they were lodged in the Governor's Palace.[1] On July 11, two hours were dedicated to a welcome at the airport of Salvador, Bahia, before the general's plane continued on its way to Rio. At Rio's Santos Dumont Airport a huge throng that included Dutra and scores of other high officials was on hand to participate in the honors to be shown to the returning Brazilian commander.

Because of weather conditions on the afternoon of July 11, the general's plane landed not at Santos Dumont, but at the Santa Cruz base in a suburb of Rio. Brayner, writing about Mascarenhas' disappointing reception at the Santa Cruz airstrip, says that other planes were landing at Santos Dumont and that nothing prevented a landing there of the general's plane, as it was only threatening to rain. "The most disappointed of all," he adds, "was Lieutenant Colonel [sic] Humberto Castello Branco, who did everything possible to advise the General on that return and was unsuccessful."[2]

[10] HACB to Argentina, Italy, June 30, 1945, File H2, PVCB.

[1] João Baptista Mascarenhas de Moraes, *Memórias*, II, 420.

[2] Brayner, *A Verdade Sôbre a FEB*, p. 518. Brayner, mentioning the "declining" official prestige of the FEB, says that "bad luck and witches worked against it with the collusion of some who belonged to it and wanted to possess all of the floral pieces of

Dutra and other members of the reception committee, among them General Canrobert Pereira da Costa, General Firmo Freire, and Lieutenant Colonel Ademar de Queiroz, sped in cars in the direction of Santa Cruz. They met up with Mascarenhas and his party at Largo do Campinho.[3]

Argentina and Nieta, who had kept in touch with Ademar de Queiroz, were driven through the rain to the meeting. Argentina had bought a good selection of clothes and was prepared for any type of weather. Wearing gray, with a leather jacket and a gray hat, she shone with an air of expectation. Emotion filled her and Humberto when they embraced, but both were quiet.[4]

The house at Nascimento Silva Street was stocked with food and champagne as well as the ingredients used in alexander cocktails. For as Argentina had expected, the house was full of relatives when she, Nieta, and Humberto arrived there at about 6:00 P.M. Entering through the veranda on the Nascimento Silva Street side of the house, Humberto cried. Two hours later the throng was joined by Paulo, who had been given special permission by the Escola Naval to be absent for the rest of the day. He found his father tired but in splendid health and spirits, answering scores of questions.[5]

On the next morning Castello joined Mascarenhas and his three aides for the welcoming ceremonies at which the general was honored in the War Ministry.

The most spirited demonstrations of welcome were those to celebrate the arrival in Rio of Zenóbio da Costa and the first returning contingent on the *General Meiggs* on July 18. For these prolonged manifestations in Rio, Belo Horizonte, São Paulo, and Porto Alegre, American Generals Mark Clark, Willis Crittenberger, and Donald Brann (of the Fifth Army staff) were in Brazil, together with forty-two members of the famed Tenth Mountain Division. At the Rio cocktail receptions (where Ademar de Queiroz was an outstandingly handsome figure), orchestras

---

its glories." Aguinaldo José Senna Campos (*Com a FEB na Itália*, p. 196) writes that the arrival of Mascarenhas in Rio was "one of the deplorable absurdities carried out by men of the Government! . . . Alleging bad weather, they switched his plane to the Santa Cruz Base. . . ."

[3] Mascarenhas de Moraes, *Memórias*, II, 423.

[4] Antonietta Castello Branco Diniz, in Diniz and Paulo V. Castello Branco interview, Rio de Janeiro, December 13, 1975.

[5] Ibid.; Paulo V. Castello Branco interview, Rio de Janeiro, November 13, 1974.

played the "Canção do Expedicionário," "God Bless America," and "Begin the Beguine." Humberto and Argentina were happy.[6]

"Sometimes," Clark has written, "the crowds in the street were so thickly massed and so demonstrative that we were forced to move at a snail's pace from one official function to another, throwing the program far off schedule and keeping high officials waiting. Nobody seemed to mind. The returning soldiers could hardly push their way through the crowds when they attempted to parade through the capital." By the last week in July, General Clark and his wife and associates were close to exhaustion.[7]

Before the departure of Clark and the other Americans, Mascarenhas left for Lima to head the Brazilian delegation to the inauguration of the president of Peru, and he took Brayner with him.[8]

Colonel Castello Branco, chosen to represent the absent Mascarenhas at the celebrations in São Paulo for the FEB and the Americans, asked Lieutenant Colonel Amauri Kruel to go with him. Kruel replied: "With you I am not going anywhere. You have been full of ingratitude (*ingratidão*) toward me. I do not want to go anywhere with you." Thereupon the former friends ceased to be on speaking terms.[9]

6. Visiting Europe and the United States (September–November, 1945)

Clark, about to assume his new post of high commissioner for Austria, delivered an invitation of the United States government to Brazil to send a commission to visit the theater of recent military operations in Europe and to visit the United States. Mascarenhas, back from Peru on August 3, was named chief of the new commission. Among its ten other members, not all of whom had served in Italy, were General Zenóbio da Costa and Colonel Castello Branco, of the FEB's infantry, and Colo-

[6] Diniz, in Diniz and Castello Branco interview, December 13, 1975.

[7] Mark W. Clark, *Calculated Risk*, p. 450.

[8] Mascarenhas de Moraes, *Memórias*, II, 436–438; Brayner, *A Verdade sôbre a FEB*, p. 526. Aguinaldo José Senna Campos (*Com a FEB na Itália*, p. 196) writes that the Vargas government, which did not want Mascarenhas to appear as a national hero, sent the general to Peru.

[9] "Folhas de Alterações," File G2, Part 3, second semester, 1945, CPDOC; Amauri Kruel interview, December 11, 1975.

nel Nestor Penha Brasil, of the FEB's artillery.[1] Brigadeiro Ápel Neto and Lieutenant Colonel João Adil de Oliveira represented the air force. Major Vernon Walters was assigned to accompany Mascarenhas.

Before leaving Brazil on this new mission, Mascarenhas took from Brayner a task that Brayner felt should have been his: supervising the writing of the history of the FEB's operations in Italy. Brayner believed that Mascarenhas' step was probably due to "insinuation" by Mascarenhas' "Third Section head," who was about to "travel with him on the excursion."[2]

The "excursion" began with the departure of an American plane for North Africa on September 21, 1945, and it lasted until the Brazilians were flown early in November from Miami to Brazil. The Brazilian commission members were toasted at receptions and dinners in France, Germany, Hungary, and Austria (including a banquet given by Mark Clark). They were shocked by the destruction they saw in Europe.[3]

In Italy they went to Porretta Terme and other places where the FEB had been active. Castello was filled with emotion; Penha Brasil had much to say, recalling with enthusiasm and pride the achievements of the artillery.[4] At the cemetery in Pistoia, northwest of Florence, the commission paid tribute to the members of the FEB who had died in the Italian campaign. General Falconière, still in Italy, was arranging to have the bodies brought to Pistoia from various places in Italy.[5]

After visiting Portugal, the commission was flown from Lisbon, via the Azores, to the United States, where high officials, including President Truman, had warm praise for the FEB. Visits were made to Brazilian amputees in a United States hospital and to West Point, Fort Knox, Fort Leavenworth, Fort Sill, and Fort Benning.

While the members of the Brazilian commission traveled in the United States, electoral democracy made headway in their homeland, but not without difficulty. Supporters of President Vargas among the working classes, known as Queremistas, expressed their dissatisfaction with the candidacies of General Dutra and Brigadeiro Gomes and demonstrated repeatedly in Rio against holding the scheduled presidential

[1] Mascarenhas de Moraes, *Memórias*, II, 441. Nestor Penha Brasil, like Castello Branco, was promoted to colonel on June 25, 1945.

[2] Brayner, *A Verdade sôbre a FEB*, pp. 526–527.

[3] João Adyl de Oliveira interview, Rio de Janeiro, October 18, 1975.

[4] Ibid.

[5] Brayner, *Recordando os Bravos*, p. 274.

election. When Vargas, suspected of scheming to remain in office, aided the demonstrators by naming his brother, a pro-Queremista, to be Rio police chief, he alarmed the democrats who wanted the election. As these democrats now included the military leaders, Vargas was deposed, the result of a coup headed by War Minister Góis Monteiro. The former dictator, still popular with a large segment of the workers, returned to his home state of Rio Grande do Sul while the chief justice of the supreme court, placed temporarily at the head of the government, prepared to preside over the December election.

At Fort Benning late in October, 1945, Vernon Walters was the first man with the Brazilian commission to learn of the overthrow of Vargas. He asked Castello Branco, who had become his best friend, whether he should inform Mascarenhas of the news. Castello told him to go ahead.[6]

Mascarenhas, in daily contact with Castello Branco during the trip, found the colonel always "frank, friendly, helpful, and wise." The general praised his contribution to "the greatest harmony and cordiality between our representatives and those of the North American, British, French, Russian, and Portuguese armies. . . . Faultless in his military and civilian manners, he carried out with dedication all of the missions that were assigned to him."[7]

The trip home brought a stopover in Puerto Rico. There the Brazilians were met at the airport by General Willis Crittenberger, who now commanded the American troops in the Caribbean. At the dinner given by Crittenberger the toasts were particularly warm.[8] For the Brazilian infantry officers who had served in Italy, one of the most emotional occasions of the trip to Europe and the United States was to be again with this fifty-six-year-old American general who had commanded them and planned with them and who, in his daily contacts (wearing his pointed or flat-topped hat), had expressed concern, irritation, encouragement, and satisfaction.

By this time the burial of the FEB dead in the Pistoia cemetery was being handled by Colonel Brayner, who had been named military attaché in Italy shortly before the fall of Vargas.[9]

[6] Walters interview, June 12, 1975.

[7] "Folhas de Alterações," File G2, Part 3, November 9 to December 31, 1945, CPDOC.

[8] Mascarenhas de Moraes, *Memórias*, II, 450.

[9] Brayner, *Recordando os Bravos*, pp. 189, 274.

Back to the Challenges of Peacetime (1946-1954)

What Brazil needs is a President not geared to—not seeking—popularity.

1. Brazilian Doctrine for the Staff School (1945–1949)

EURICO GASPAR DUTRA won the election of December, 1945, and was therefore in the presidency in August, 1946, when Dwight D. Eisenhower, chief of staff of the United States Army, visited Brazil. The American general declared himself deeply impressed with the high quality of instruction attained by the Brazilian army's Escola de Estado Maior.[1]

Castello Branco, director of the EEM's instruction from November, 1945, until February, 1949, was less well impressed. He believed that the three-year course of instruction at the spacious building at Rio's Praia Vermelha, still based on old French doctrine, was in need of reform. For one thing, he was determined to use the experience gained on the battlefields of Italy to bring theory closer to reality, and for this reason he brought officers who had served in the war to speak to the students.[2]

From the start Castello Branco himself made extensive use of the Italian experience. In his address opening the 1946 school year he spoke of American and Brazilian officers who had remarked in Italy that the military plans and operations there bore little resemblance to the teachings received at Fort Leavenworth and Praia Vermelha. He pointed out that while teaching could not provide the conditions to be found in all

1 "Folhas de Alterações," File G2, Part 3, second semester, 1946, CPDOC.
2 Luís Mendes da Silva, "Testemunho," Part 4, "O Professor"; Raimundo Teles Pinheiro interview, Fortaleza, Ceará, December 28, 1975; Reynaldo de Melo Almeida interview, Rio de Janeiro, October 17, 1975.

of the battle zones of the world, it did seek to give the basic elements necessary for resolving the tactical problems in the "inevitable reality of the battlefield." Describing military dogmatism as disastrous, he quoted Crittenberger as saying: "I do not know whether I am waging an American, Brazilian, or French type of warfare; I know that I am now waging ing the war of the Apennines and I am certain that afterwards I shall wage the war of the Po Valley."

Castello devoted most of this address to a description of the Fourth Corps offensive of February, 1945. He called it "a model of modern tactics, exemplifying the essential aspects of the Doctrine of the Escola de Estado Maior," which he summarized as (1) defining the objective, (2) making the most economical use of force, and (3), in the attainment of the objective, applying three principles: concentration of force, liberty of action, and intellectual discipline.

Castello spoke of the "concentration of force" brought to bear against the German-held high points in February, 1945; the "liberty of action" by a diversionary expedition that seized some German positions on the eve of the Monte Belvedere–Gorgolesco attack, thus facilitating that major action; and the "discipline" of Mascarenhas, who, while the Tenth Mountain Division advanced, followed through against Monte Castello despite a lack of coverage of the FEB's western flank.[3]

The enormous pile of documents that had been used at the EEM for over twenty-five years—ever since the French military mission had come to Brazil—was revised by Castello; new EEM operations manuals were issued and, finally, a completely new *regulamento* (set of regulations) for all instruction at the school was drawn up. As far as the structure of instruction was concerned, the revisions called for greater centralization.[4] Lieutenant Colonel Antônio Carlos da Silva Murici, who worked at Castello's side for one year as general tactics instructor, found Castello a great *centralizador*, and this characteristic, he says, accounted for some of the difficulties that Castello had with many instructors—among them Lieutenant Colonel Orlando Geisel, a Realengo classmate of Murici.

The radical alteration of the contents of the instruction met with re-

[3] HACB, "A Doutrina de Guerra e a Guerra Moderna," speech at the EEM, 1946, File J, Part 3, p. 39v, CPDOC.
[4] "Folhas de Alterações," File G2, Part 3, second semester, 1947, CPDOC; Antônio Carlos da Silva Murici interview, Rio de Janeiro, November 18, 1975.

sistance, especially from those who had not served in the FEB.[5] Castello introduced new concepts about the work to be done by the estado maior (staff) at all levels of study. He made considerable use of United States tactical doctrine, but he modified it to make it appropriate for Brazilian conditions.[6] (There was, according to Virgílio Távora, one of Castello's better students at the EEM, a grain of truth to the Brazilian joke to describe United States doctrine: find out how many regiments the enemy has and send three times as many to oppose them.)

The introduction of the new tactical doctrine was a herculean work. In addition, Castello made certain that it was properly taught on the brigade level (studied by first-year students), division level (studied in the second year), and the army corps and army levels (studied in the third year). This he did by personally supervising the concluding session of every field maneuver or classroom exercise (forty-two by first-year students, twenty by those in their second year, and sixteen by those in their last year). On these occasions he pointed out what was correctly done and what was not.[7]

Castello, very demanding, did not make himself popular.[8] He was, Virgílio Távora recalls, "absolutely severe." But he had the support of the commanding generals of the EEM, first Francisco Gil Castello Branco and then Tristão de Alencar Araripe. This support, together with his own prestige and drive—and possibly his clear explanations—overcame most of the resistance.

In the end, Humberto Castello Branco came to be credited with providing, for the first time, a "Brazilian military doctrine."[9] As one army officer has put it, concepts were given a "feeling of reality" and were no longer simply taken from foreign manuals.[10]

[5] Carlos de Meira Mattos interview, Washington, D.C., January 5, 1976.

[6] Virgílio de Morais Fernandes Távora interview, Brasília, October 22, 1975. Raimundo Teles Pinheiro, a student at the Escola de Estado Maior when Castello was the director of instruction, said (interview December 28, 1975) that Castello instituted United States systems and implanted ideas brought from his Italian experience.

[7] Meira Mattos interview, January 5, 1976.

[8] Ferdinando de Carvalho interview, Rio de Janeiro, October 30, 1975.

[9] Melo Almeida interview, October 17, 1975; Meira Mattos interview, January 5, 1976; Távora interview, October 22, 1975; Mendes da Silva, "Testemunho," Part 4, "O Professor."

[10] Melo Almeida interview, October 17, 1975.

2. Accusation against Major Gross

Colonel Castello Branco, writing in 1949 about the Escola de Estado Maior, said that the institution was "ennobling" for those who were associated with it: "It assumes leadership through ideas and through men, and is on a plane which differs from that of the prosaic life—and sometimes poorly spent life—in a number of the nooks and crannies of our army."[1]

The EEM students included officers who had served in Italy, such as Captain Carlos de Meira Mattos and former 6th RI battalion commanders João Carlos Gross and Silvino Nóbrega, both majors. For Gross, new encounters with Castello Branco were in store. They began on April 10, 1946, when he was ordered to the office of the school commander, then occupied by Colonel Castello Branco, the acting commander. Gross found Castello in the company of Colonel Armando de Morais Âncora and Major Silvino Nóbrega, who had been chosen the leader (*chefe da turma*) of the class to which Gross belonged.[2]

Castello, a terrible expression on his face, told Gross: "I called you because of a denouncement by Chief of Staff Góis Monteiro, who said that you and another are Communists." Gross asked if the charge had been made by Góis himself. Learning that it had, Gross spoke in a loud voice, saying that Castello knew Góis better than he did and therefore knew that Góis was absolutely no good—and a fascist as well. Receiving no reaction to this from Castello, Gross observed that the charge against himself, if true, was very serious, and that an investigation should be made. He was ordered to report to Castello on the tenth of each month.

For the rest of the year Gross reported regularly, asking each time if he had been found to be a Communist and always learning from Castello, "I have not discovered." December was a month of vacation for the EEM, but as Castello kept right on working, Gross reported as usual on the tenth, only this time he brought a book by English labor leader Harold Laski, which he gave as a Christmas present after remarking that he particularly liked two chapters, one opposing the Nazis and the other opposing Communism. Gross then asked if any evidence had

[1] HACB to commander of Escola de Estado Maior, February 20, 1949, File G1, CPDOC.

[2] João Carlos Gross, in Gross and Osvaldo G. Aranha interview, Rio de Janeiro, October 2, 1975.

been found that he was a Communist. "Still none," said Castello, and he added that he had a Christmas present for Gross: "You are not a Communist."

Soon after this, Gross was honored by being chosen to talk at the school on how the Brazilians took Castelnuovo. Called to Castello's office after giving his talk, which had been well received, he heard no words of appreciation—no comments, even—about his talk. Instead, the tough director of instruction severely reprimanded Gross, a poor student, for neglecting to prepare his lessons. Gross had to admit that for once in his skirmishes with Castello, Castello was right.[3]

3. Associação dos Ex-Combatentes (1947–1949)

João Carlos Gross had more contacts with Colonel Castello Branco because the major was an active figure in the Associação dos Ex-Combatentes do Brasil (Association of Brazilian Combat Veterans). The association, founded in October, 1945,[1] was to lobby on behalf of a broad membership that included those who had played wartime roles in the three branches of the armed services in Brazil or abroad and in the merchant marine.

At a convention of the *associação* in Rio in November, 1946,[2] the presidency of the *conselho nacional* (national board) went to Osvaldo G. Aranha, who was son of the prominent statesman and who had joined the FEB as a private and been promoted to corporal in Italy. Communists, their movement strong and legal in Brazil immediately after the war, had helped elect young Aranha to the *conselho* presidency and had put several party members on the *conselho* with him. But Aranha, unwilling to serve as a puppet of the Communists, broke with them.[3]

During 1947, a Cold War year, army officers became dismayed at the Communist strength in the upper echelons of the *associação*; with support from the war minister they decided to form a new veterans' organization. For this purpose a meeting took place at the Military Club. Colonel Castello Branco, chosen to conduct the well-attended meeting,

[3] Ibid.

[1] *Ex-Combatente* 1, no. 11 (November, 1947), in File H3, Part 3, PVCB.

[2] Pedro Paulo Sampaio de Lacerda, "O Que Foi a 1ª Convenção Nacional," ibid.

[3] Osvaldo G. Aranha, in Gross and Aranha interview, October 2, 1975.

was surprised to find Aranha, a civilian, present; however, as a "special concession" he agreed that "Corporal Aranha" might later address the officers.[4]

Rigidly erect, Castello opened the session by announcing: "We are here to form a new association, because the only one in existence has been undermined by Communists." But he allowed the representatives of the existing association to be heard: Aranha, Gross, and Henrique Cordeiro Oeste, who had been a 6th RI battalion commander and was now a congressman elected on the ticket of the Brazilian Communist Party.[5] Cordeiro Oeste's remarks were poorly received at the Military Club, but Gross and Aranha were applauded. Aranha argued that if the non-Communists created a new organization, the original one would become definitely Communist, thus bringing to naught all of the conscientious work done for the association by men such as Gross, Sizeno Sarmento, Moziul Moreira Lima, Meira Mattos, and Pitaluga, and nurses such as Sílvia de Souza Barros and Olímpia de Araújo Camerino. Aranha added that assistance being sought by the association from government bodies, much of it for the most helpless former soldiers, would be lost.

Castello's constant references to "Corporal Aranha" seemed to put the young man in his place, and the colonel was somewhat repetitious in remarking that Aranha spoke only by "special concession." But Castello was quick to come to Aranha's aid when remarks, rude to Aranha and the *associação*, were made by another colonel who prided himself on his immense anti-Communism and on his resolve never to have anything to do with anyone who even associated with Communists. It did not matter to Castello that the colonel had more seniority than he had. Speaking forcefully, he said that he would not tolerate such rudeness to a person who, although opposed to the purpose of the meeting, had handled himself correctly. The colonel apologized.[6]

Castello arranged to have two ballot boxes set up, one to be used by those favoring a new organization and the other by the opponents. Hardly a secret vote, Aranha thought, but, rather, an arrangement, perhaps clever, that would achieve the purpose of the meeting. With Ara-

[4] Ibid.

[5] Osvaldo G. Aranha undated memorandum prepared for Luís Vianha Filho but not delivered to him.

[6] Ibid.

nha unable to vote because he was not an army officer, only two voted against forming a new veterans' organization: Gross and Cordeiro Oeste.

By the votes of the officers, high posts in the new organization were given to the FEB generals and to Mascarenhas,[7] who had recently been named marshal of the army by an act of the federal legislature. But despite the prestige of these military figures, nothing came of the new organization. And while it collapsed, Aranha, Gross, and Major Moziul Moreira Lima (an infantry captain during the Italian campaign) went ahead with their plan to prevent the Communists from dominating the old *associação*. In the latter part of 1947 they finally convinced Colonels Nelson de Melo and Castello Branco that the solution lay in a "single slate" of officers of the all-important Federal District section of the *associação*—a slate, acceptable to all parties, that would include Communists and non-Communists.[8] The Communists, experts at working with such compromise slates, expressed their agreement.

It took more time to persuade Castello Branco that he should be the candidate for the presidency of the Federal District section on a slate that would include Communists, principally Pedro Paulo Sampaio de Lacerda, who had lost a leg from infantile paralysis as a boy but had nevertheless served the FEB in Italy as a lieutenant colonel with the Bank of Brazil. Pedro Paulo, president of the Federal District section, would become candidate for first secretary on the "single slate." Seeking Castello's agreement to the scheme, Gross and Aranha argued with him at the Nascimento Silva Street house one night from 9:00 P.M. until 2:00 A.M. They pointed out that the term would be for only four months, as the election was to complete a regularly scheduled term. They heard some uncomplimentary remarks about their persistence, but they finally gained Castello's acceptance on condition that they help him.[9] Furthermore, Castello soon assured himself of additional help by persuading Lieutenant Colonel Ademar de Queiroz to accept the position of finance secretary in the list of posts being split between Communists and non-Communists.[10]

[7] Osvaldo G. Aranha interview, Rio de Janeiro, September 25, 1975.

[8] Gross and Aranha interview, October 2, 1975.

[9] Ibid.

[10] See list of positions in article, "A Associação dos Ex-Combatentes Estará Sempre Vitoriosa," *Ex-Combatente* 1, no. 11 (November, 1947), in File H3, Part 3, CPDOC.

Castello was away from Rio in October, 1947, when the election meeting, attended by more than three hundred association members, took place. The voting, expected by many to be a perfunctory matter, became tumultuous after Communists broke their "single slate" agreement. Jacob Gorender and Henrique Cordeiro Oeste pushed for a Communist slate, and even Pedro Paulo Sampaio de Lacerda was only lukewarm in supporting the "single slate" that included Castello and himself. Zenóbio da Costa, commander of the army's Eastern Military Zone, and Nelson de Melo were strenuously booed, and they retired from the meeting. It lasted until 3:30 A.M., when the "single slate" won by the slim margin of thirteen votes.[11]

Under these circumstances Castello found himself president of the Federal District section. Furious at Gross and Aranha for having placed him in a position far more difficult than the one originally pictured, he wagged his finger at them. It was all their fault, he declared, and he added that he did not know how to deal with "these people." Gross, who in the past had had the temerity to shout in anger at Castello, remained calm. "You are mad now," he said, "but you will thank me later. You will learn how to treat with the Communists."

Castello, accustomed to a setting in which orders were given, was indeed out of his element, and at first he seemed to lack the sort of flexibility that Gross had acquired through holding posts for many years in sports clubs. But before his term ended on February 23, 1948, Castello became accustomed to the bickering, the arguing, the sessions with people who were either essentially civilians or who were below him in the military hierarchy but who, in *associação* affairs, never hesitated to tell him, "You are wrong." Aranha describes him as "holding meetings, and presiding over assemblies, where the matters of the association were debated freely by men who professed ideologies that . . . conflicted with his conception of life." Meira Mattos speaks of the discussions that Castello had to carry out calmly with Communists and adds that this was the only occasion when he dealt directly with active Communists.[12]

Years later, when Castello Branco had to deal with civilians in the Escola Superior de Guerra, he said to Gross: "I have a greater facility for this work, thanks to that experience I had with the Associação dos

[11] Aranha undelivered memorandum; Gross and Aranha interview, October 2, 1975.

[12] Aranha undelivered memorandum; Meira Mattos interview, January 5, 1976.

Ex-Combatentes." He told Aranha: "That experience was one of the good things of my life."[13]

4. Disappointing Elections in 1950

As they had before the war, Humberto and Argentina spent occasional evenings at the home of the Hélio Viannas. Hélio, professor of history at the University of Brazil, was the author of numerous books, and at the Vianna home the Castello Brancos were apt to find intellectuals whose faces were new to them, as well as their old acquaintance, lawyer San Tiago Dantas.[1] At their own residence at Nascimento Silva 394 the list of dinner guests now often included Vernon Walters and his mother. Major Walters, assistant United States Army attaché in Brazil from 1945 until 1948, was living in Rio with his mother, and she became a close friend of Argentina.

"Where Castello was sometimes aloof and formal," Walters writes, "Argentina was warm and friendly." Between Humberto and Argentina, Walters noted "not just love and affection, but also a real camaraderie. Frequently they would come to my house or I would go to theirs. . . . We spoke often of the war, of France, of Brazil. Never at any time did I hear a word from Castello that would indicate an interest in taking part in political life."[2]

The friends of the Castello Brancos, along with their relatives, attended church services in 1947, when Humberto and Argentina observed their twenty-fifth wedding anniversary, and in 1948, when Nieta married Salvador Diniz, an economist. Among the Castello Brancos at these formal family gatherings were Humberto's two brothers. Candinho, the oldest brother, had married a cousin of Getúlio Vargas and was forging ahead well in the Bank of Brazil and making quite a few business trips to Ceará. Lauro, the youngest, had tried many jobs, all of short duration until he ended up as a Finance Ministry bureaucrat, thanks to the help of a brother-in-law.[3]

[13] Gross and Aranha interview, October 2, 1975; Aranha undelivered memorandum.

[1] Artur César Ferreira Reis interview, Rio de Janeiro, September 29, 1975; Renato Archer interview, Rio de Janeiro, September 30, 1975.

[2] Vernon Walters, "Humberto de Alencar Castello Branco" (typewritten), Part 2, "The Years of Peace," p. 1.

[3] Ana (Nina) Castello Branco Santos Dias and Beatriz Castello Branco Gonçalves,

Humberto, who became fifty-one in September, 1948, was enjoying his life and his work.[4] With his transfer from the Escola de Estado Maior to the headship of the Army Staff Operations Section early in 1949, he was at first "deeply homesick for everything and everyone" at the EEM, but soon he was absorbed in implanting "Brazilian military doctrine" in the Army Staff and attacking the bureaucracy there.[5]

As Walters reported, Castello Branco had no interest in running for political office. But Castello continued to show a keen interest in politics, and he hoped that Getúlio Vargas would not be returned to the presidency in the October, 1950, elections, this time as the successor to President Dutra. The sixty-seven-year-old former dictator, in retirement on his ranch in Rio Grande do Sul and smarting under attacks coming from the União Democrática Nacional (UDN) and the Dutra wing of the Partido Social Democrático (PSD), was eager to achieve a popular vindication that would bring him to the presidency "on the arms of the people." After the PSD and UDN, unable to agree on a joint ticket, put separate presidential candidates in the field, Vargas accepted the candidacy offered by the Partido Trabalhista Brasileiro (PTB).[6]

Presidential electioneering in 1950 gave a special meaning to the Military Club election of May, 1950, because Vargas, who had been deposed by the military in 1945, felt the need of a Military Club victory by the "nationalist" slate, regarded as favorable to him. This "nationalist" slate, considered to be leftist, was headed by General Newton Estillac Leal. Among its candidates for other Military Club offices were Captain Nelson Werneck Sodré, of Marxist inclinations, and Lieutenant Colonel Luís Tavares da Cunha Melo, who had worked closely with Castello Branco in the Third Section in Italy.

Castello, disappointed in Cunha Melo's decision, ran for a Military Club office on the opposing, "anti-Communist" slate, which was headed

---

"Depoimento sôbre o irmão Humberto de Alencar Castello Branco," 1973, File B, CPDOC.

[4] Antonietta Castello Branco Diniz in Diniz and Paulo V. Castello Branco interview, Rio de Janeiro, December 13, 1975.

[5] HACB to Colônia (friend), January 20, 1949, File G1, CPDOC; Melo Almeida interview, October 17, 1975; Meira Mattos interview, January 5, 1976.

[6] Of Brazil's numerous political parties, the PSD, UDN, and PTB, all founded in 1945, were the most important. Although in 1950 the PSD nominated Cristiano Machado to oppose Vargas (PTB) and Eduardo Gomes (UDN), Vargas had some support in the PSD, whose organizers had been influential during the Vargas dictatorship.

by General Osvaldo Cordeiro de Farias and which included General Emílio Rodrigues Ribas Júnior (an artillery colonel during the Italian campaign), General Nelson de Melo, Colonel Ademar de Queiroz, and Lieutenant Colonel Sizeno Sarmento. In the eyes of FEB veteran Emygdio Miranda, one of the organizers of the candidacy of Estillac Leal, Castello took a position "with the reactionaries." [7]

In May the "reactionary" or "anti-Communist" slate of Cordeiro was defeated by that of Estillac Leal, and in October Vargas was elected president of Brazil. Vargas named Estillac Leal to be his war minister.

Despite the apparent strength of the anti–United States "nationalism" that flourished in the recently elected slate of the Military Club and in some of the War Ministry circles, this was not the view that prevailed among the military officers selected to accompany Foreign Minister João Neves da Fontoura when he went to Washington in March, 1951, to attend the Fourth Meeting of Consultation of the Ministers of Foreign Affairs of the American Republics. The meeting had been called by the United States government, which feared that the Korean War might spread and wanted a manifestation of continental solidarity.

Castello Branco was appointed to go to Washington with the delegation's chief army adviser, General Paulo de Figueiredo. Flying with Argentina on the special plane that carried the large Brazilian delegation, Humberto noted that one of the air force advisers was Nelson Freire Lavanère-Wanderley, who had been an outstanding student of his at Realengo and the Escola de Estado Maior and had gone on to Italy, as a member of the air force staff, to help coordinate air force attacks and serve himself as pilot in thirteen offensive missions. Among the navy's representatives on the delegation to Washington were Sílvio Mota and the well-known anti-Communist Carlos Pena Boto.

Argentina, writing to Hélio Vianna from Washington, spoke of her pleasure of being present at the inaugural session of the conference, held in the Pan American Union Building. It was at this session that Congressman Osvaldo Trigueiro, representing the anti-Vargas UDN, sought help from São Paulo industrialist Paulo Nogueira Filho to identify members of the Brazilian delegation. "Who is that flat-headed fellow?"

[7] Ronald M. Schneider, *The Political System of Brazil*, pp. 56–57, 104; Thomas E. Skidmore, *Politics in Brazil*, p. 104; Emygdio da Costa Miranda interview, Rio de Janeiro, December 1, 1975.

Trigueiro asked. "That's Colonel Castello Branco, adviser of the general. He served in the FEB, and is one of the brains of the Army." [8]

Following the conference, which lasted one week, Humberto showed Argentina something of New York. On a night at the "Latin Quarter," spent with another army colonel and his wife, they were joined by Paulo Castello Branco, who had come to the United States because the Brazilian navy was receiving the cruiser *Barroso* (formerly the *Philadelphia*). Paulo was engaged to be married, and this pleased Humberto and Argentina; they had been wanting their twenty-six-year-old son to marry, and they liked the girl very much.

5. Happiness in Fortaleza (1952–1954)

On August 2, 1952, Castello Branco was promoted to brigadier general, and later in the year he was named commander of the army's Tenth Military Region, with headquarters in Fortaleza, Ceará. As commander of the Tenth Region, which included Piauí and Maranhão as well as Ceará, Castello reported to Osvaldo Cordeiro de Farias, who had been appointed commander of the North Military Zone, with headquarters in Recife, after becoming a *general de exército* on August 2, 1952.

Castello's good relations with Cordeiro were matched by the splendid ones that he developed with Raul Barbosa, the short, stocky PSD governor of Ceará, whose wife was an Alencar.[1] Everything, it seemed, combined to make the two and one-half years in Ceará, lasting from November, 1952, until May, 1954, the happiest period in the lives of Humberto and Argentina.[2]

The relatively young general, in his first post as region commander, at headquarters where his father had once commanded a battalion, could hardly wait to show Ceará to Argentina, and she loved being shown. Often Humberto took her to Messejana, and on one of the visits there he explained to her how fortunate he had been to have known a childhood so close to nature. He took her to the interior to spend days on the

[8] Osvaldo Trigueiro, "Humberto Castelo Branco" (typewritten), p. 1.

[1] Raul Barbosa interview, Washington, D.C., June 13, 1975; Waldetrudes and Justina Amarante interview, Rio de Janeiro, November 21, 1975.

[2] Paulo V. Castello Branco interview, Rio de Janeiro, November 21, 1975.

ranch of Plínio Câmara, which adjoined that of politician Armando Falcão in the municipality of Quixerámobim.[3] Argentina found that she, like her husband, was fond of the people of Ceará—all of them, no matter how simple.

With their children married and raising families of their own, Humberto and Argentina were closer than they ever had been.[4] Argentina's dedication to her husband was complete. And as a person of position— "second lady" in Ceará after the governor's wife—she was everything Humberto could be proud of. Well-educated and fond of reading, she was admired for her intelligence as well as her character, dignified behavior, and charm. In the words of Justina Amarante, the wife of one of Humberto's Tenth Region officers, "she had class."

In army circles, Humberto and Argentina saw much of Lieutenant Colonel and Sra. Murilo Borges Moreira, Lieutenant Colonel and Sra. Raimundo Teles Pinheiro, and Lieutenant Colonel and Sra. Waldetrudes Amarante. Justina Amarante, whom Argentina had previously met in Rio, was especially close to Argentina. "I understand your position," Argentina said in a reference to some formality resulting from Waldetrudes' post on Humberto's staff, "but when we are together it is different." As for the officers, they found Humberto a man of two parts: a rigorous *chefe*, but also an affectionate friend.[5]

"The healthy cordiality between the military and civilians" was a characteristic of the Tenth Military Region that was praised by Cordeiro de Farias after an inspection trip.[6] Humberto and Argentina set the example. "Because of their ability to enchant," historian Raimundo Girão wrote in 1954, "Fortaleza did not need to be coaxed to admire and pay homage to the pair. Both edified everyone with their courtesy and correct behavior. The families opened their drawing rooms to them and received them with affection."[7]

Some of the families belonged to the group of writers and intellectuals whom Castello came to know by regularly attending the meetings

[3] Ibid.; Armando Falcão interview, Rio de Janeiro, October 10, 1975.

[4] Walters, "Humberto de Alencar Castello Branco," Part 2, "The Years of Peace," p. 2; Castello Branco interview, November 21, 1975.

[5] Justina Amarante, in Amarante interview, November 21, 1975; Teles Pinheiro interview, December 28, 1975.

[6] "Folhas de Alterações," File G3, second semester, 1953, CPDOC.

[7] Raimundo Girão, "Cidadão da Farda," *Unitário*, May 22, 1954, reprinted in Raimundo Girão, *Palestina, uma Agulha e as Saudades*, pp. 261–262.

of the Instituto do Ceará.[8] Many, too, were leading politicians, both "ins" and "outs." As Tenth Region commander, Castello attended, with the governor, the state cabinet, and Fortaleza Mayor Paulo Cabral de Araújo, more official functions than he had ever attended before; the local newspapers carried photographs of the slightly pudgy general, usually with a smile on his chubby face. Argentina frequently graced the ceremonies, as when she and Humberto flew with local officials to join Vice-president João Café Filho and federal cabinet ministers Tancredo Neves and João Goulart in celebrating the one hundredth anniversary of the city of Crato.[9]

Castello, following politics as closely as ever, remarked to Governor Barbosa that what Brazil needed was a president who was "not geared to—not seeking—popularity."[10] So great was Castello's interest in politics that federal Congressman Virgílio Távora, then the state leader of the anti-Vargas UDN, speaks of it as politics with "a capital P." This interest contributed to the particularly warm friendship that Humberto and Argentina enjoyed with UDN federal Congressman Paulo Sarazate and with Sra. Sarazate, whose mother owned *O Povo*, a leading Fortaleza newspaper.[11] Humberto found Sarazate an intelligent and energetic extrovert, deeply devoted to the UDN. Journalist Sarazate, along with sociologist Parcival Barroso, engineer Virgílio Távora, and state Agriculture Secretary Plácido Aderaldo Castelo, were future Ceará governors whom Humberto and Argentina came to know well during their stay in Fortaleza.

Such was Castello Branco's prestige and popularity in Ceará that a movement grew to try to persuade him to follow the example of Cordeiro de Farias, who agreed to run for governor of Pernambuco in the elections of October, 1954. Antônio de Almeida Lustosa, archbishop of Fortaleza, told Castello that his candidacy would be acceptable to so many currents in Ceará that it would "solve, without discord, without

[8] Girão, *Palestina*, p. 261.
[9] Barbosa interview, June 13, 1975; Teles Pinheiro interview, December 28, 1975. The ceremonies took place on October 17, 1953, and featured a great parade that included *vaqueiros do nordeste* (cowboys of the northeast), *cambiteiros* (drivers of pack animals), and other colorful local groups.
[10] Barbosa interview, June 13, 1975.
[11] Sarazate's full name: Paulo Sarazate Ferreira Lopes.

struggle, the state's political problems, which appear so difficult." [12] But it was not as easy as the archbishop hoped to launch a "unity candidate." Besides, Castello was not interested in running for political office. [13]

6. Fish for the Commander's Wife

Starting in December, 1952, Castello made inspection trips almost monthly from Fortaleza to Teresina, Piauí, and to São Luís, Maranhão. On a more exotic trip, made in March, 1953, he assumed command of the garrison in Campo Maior, Piauí, where his father had been born, and led it in two days of maneuvers that were intended to reenact battles fought in the same region in colonial times. [1]

As commander of the Tenth Military Region, Castello kept everything in his own hands, and for this and for his severity he was disliked by some of the officers. But a majority considered him a "great chefe" and admired the innovations he introduced in instruction. General Cordeiro de Farias had praise for the Tenth Region's instruction as "the best possible notwithstanding the shortage of funds" and for the region's methods of recruitment, which provided "human material superior to that commonly incorporated." [2] (As elsewhere, the soldiers, recruited for nine months, learned how to present themselves well and received medical attention.)

Castello's concern about instruction was equaled by his determination to have his units carry out superlative maneuvers. The maneuvers that he supervised in Piauí, Maranhão, and the interior of Ceará were remembered by the men of the barracks for many years because other commanders had not required such extensive ones or so great an attention to details. [3]

[12] Archbishop Antônio de Almeida Lustosa to HACB, Fortaleza, April 29, 1954, File G1, CPDOC.

[13] Távora interview, October 22, 1975; Castello Branco interview, November 21, 1975.

[1] "Folhas de Alterações," File G3, second semester, 1952, first and second semesters, 1953, CPDOC. See also Lena Ferreira Costa, "Uma Família na História," File A, Part 3, CPDOC.

[2] Waldetrudes Amarante, in Amarante interview, November 21, 1975; "Folhas de Alterações," File G3, second semester, 1953, CPDOC.

[3] Waldetrudes Amarante, in Amarante interview, November 21, 1975.

Equally well known were General Castello Branco's rigid concepts of personal financial integrity. After he inspected a maneuver of the 24th BC, the battalion commander, at the farewell, gave him a dozen eggs that he said had come from a local poultry farm that was in economic difficulties. Castello made a quick calculation, took out his wallet, and paid cash for the eggs.[4]

But Castello's rigid concepts were more sensationally demonstrated in an episode long remembered by many, including a major who served as a supply corps officer for the Tenth Military Region. The major, son of a former Fortaleza mayor who liked Castello and had known his father, had a contract with a fisherman to supply fish—medium-class fish—to the barracks several days each week.

For dinners at her home, Argentina would phone the major when she wanted fish. She was very well treated. According to talk that developed in the local military circles, after each phone call by Argentina a truck would go on a six-kilometer trip to find her the finest fish, and it would be purchased at something like twenty cruzeiros a kilogram and then sold to her at around twelve cruzeiros, the contract price for the medium-class fish. "It is sold to your wife for twelve cruzeiros," a colonel told General Castello Branco one day.[5]

To investigate the matter, Castello Branco issued an order creating a commission that included Lieutenant Colonel Raimundo Teles Pinheiro, head of the First Section of the staff, and Lieutenant Colonel Waldetrudes Amarante, in charge of supply for the Tenth Region.[6] Waldetrudes listened to the major explain that the arrangement about the fish for the Castello Brancos had been considered a way of honoring, or showing respect for, the commander. Then Waldetrudes wrote his report and, after receiving confirmation of its contents from the major, submitted it to Castello.

Castello imposed on the major a fifteen-day imprisonment in the barracks of the Twenty-third Battalion and personally made a payment of about four hundred cruzeiros, the accumulated price difference. As a result of this episode, the only sad experience for Humberto and Argentina during their assignment in Fortaleza, the major's father, the old

---

[4] Castello Branco interview, November 21, 1975; Waldetrudes Amarante, in Amarante interview, November 21, 1975.

[5] Waldetrudes Amarante, in Amarante interview, November 21, 1975.

[6] Ibid.; Teles Pinheiro interview, December 28, 1975.

friend of Cândido Castello Branco, cut off relations with Humberto. But the major, despite his imprisonment, did not withhold his friendship for long.[7]

[7] Melo Almeida interview, October 17, 1975; Amarante interview, November 21, 1975; Teles Pinheiro interview, December 28, 1975.

The Sword of Gold
(1955-1960)

The regimentation of the military as a class and as a force, at the side of other classes, aligned in a politically suspect manner, is, above all, subversive.

The War Ministry has become a large political party center, an open organ of electoral propaganda, and a perfidious checker of who is against and who is in favor.

1. Generals Call on Vargas to Resign (August, 1954)

IN May, 1954, Castello Branco received an appeal from seventy-year-old Mascarenhas de Morais, chief of staff of the armed forces, to help him by assuming the post of assistant chief of staff of the armed forces for army matters. Therefore on May 21 Humberto and Argentina flew from Fortaleza to Rio.

By this time the army's anti-Communist "Democratic Crusade," which Castello warmly supported, was in a strong position. In March, 1952, antileftist sentiment had forced Estillac Leal out of the War Ministry post, and in May of that year the Democratic Crusade had elected its Military Club slate, headed by Alcides Etchegoyen and Nelson de Melo (Castello's Porto Alegre classmates). The Democratic Crusade was victorious again in May, 1954, electing Canrobert Pereira da Costa (Dutra's war minister) as Military Club president and Juarez Távora as vice-president.

The ideas of the Democratic Crusade flourished at the Escola Superior de Guerra (ESG, National War College), founded in 1949 by Cordeiro de Farias with help from Colonels Golberi do Couto e Silva and Jurandir de Bizarria Mamede as an "institute of higher learning for the development and consolidation of the knowledge necessary for the direction and planning of national security."[1] There civilians and military officers took nine-month courses given by civilians and members of all three branches of the armed forces.

[1] Law 785 of August 20, 1949, quoted in Ronald M. Schneider, *The Political System of Brazil*, p. 245 n. 6. Humberto de Melo and Geraldo Knaack de Souza interview,

Army officers giving instruction at the ESG felt that Brazil's national security was not helped by what they considered to be demagogic appeals of politicians to labor. In 1953, after Juarez Távora had succeeded Cordeiro as ESG commander, these instructors, known as the "Grupo da Sorbonne," became concerned about the close relations of Labor Minister João Goulart with Communist labor leaders and with Argentina's Juan Perón, who wanted Brazil to join Argentina and Chile in an anti–United States bloc. They feared that Perón would persuade Goulart to try to turn Brazil into what they called a *"república sindicalista"* (a nation run by labor unions). Nor were these officers at all happy about Goulart's proposed 100 percent increase in the minimum wage; it would bring this minimum for urban workers in the Federal District up to the scale being received by army second lieutenants.

Colonel Golberi do Couto e Silva, with some help from other army colonels instructing at the ESG, drew up a manifesto that complained of labor agitation, conditions in the army, and corruption in political life. Issued in February, 1954, it bore the signatures of eighty-two colonels and lieutenant colonels, among them Golberi, Mamede, Geraldo Menezes Cortes, Amauri Kruel, Ademar de Queiroz, Sizeno Sarmento, Antônio Carlos da Silva Murici, Orlando Ramagem, Adalberto Pereira dos Santos, and Alfredo Souto Malan. Like Golberi and Menezes Cortes, many of the younger signers had been cadets at Realengo when Castello Branco first taught there in 1927 and 1928.

As a result of the "manifesto of the colonels," Vargas appointed a new war minister (his third), this time FEB veteran Zenóbio da Costa. Vargas also accepted the resignation of Labor Minister Goulart, but the influence of Goulart in his administration was not much diminished, and on May 1, 1954, the 100 percent increase in the minimum wage was made effective.

The colonels, recognizing that most of the generals would oppose their manifesto as contrary to the hierarchical principles of the army, had not consulted Castello Branco or any general before releasing it. When the manifesto was released, the colonels of the "Sorbonne Group," responsible for it, felt certain that Castello was upset by their initiative and perhaps also hurt at not having been consulted.[2] A year and one-half

---

Rio de Janeiro, November 30, 1967; Júlio Sérgio Vidal Pessoa interview, Rio de Janeiro, December 16, 1975.

[2] Heitor A. Herrera interview, Rio de Janeiro, December 16, 1975.

later it seemed clear that they continued in his bad graces, for Castello, speaking at the ESG in September, 1955, delivered a speech in which he described the "manifesto of the colonels" as an example of the "aspects of a disciplinary and ethical nature that were harmful to Army unity." Castello said that the colonels had acted without "functional authority" and without consulting those of other ranks, subordinates and generals; their manifesto, he said, "injured the commands, over-threw a minister, and, despite the discretion of its signers, was un-fortunately used by political interests in an unscrupulous manner." [3]

Starting in August, 1954, abundant opportunities arose for the sign-ing of manifestos by officers who had what Castello called "functional authority." Early that month air force Major Rubens Vaz was assassi-nated, and a few days later it was discovered that the crime was the con-sequence of an order given by Gregório Fortunato, head of Vargas' per-sonal guard, to end the life of oppositionist politician and journalist Carlos Lacerda, who was wounded during the shooting. Amidst a popu-lar clamor that Vargas resign, Mascarenhas, with Castello at his side, presided gravely over meetings of irate military figures.

One of the earliest of these meetings took place at the marshal's resi-dence before dawn on August 12 to consider a groundless rumor that Vargas was considering either revising his cabinet or turning the govern-ment over to War Minister Zenóbio da Costa. Castello, consulted by Mascarenhas, said that a cabinet reform would be of no interest to the military leaders and that if Vargas resigned he should turn the govern-ment over to Vice-president Café Filho, as called for by the Constitution of 1946. After Mascarenhas said that he agreed with Castello, Juarez Távora expressed agreement with Mascarenhas. Then Zenóbio and Mas-carenhas each issued a press statement in favor of order, discipline, and the Constitution.[4]

Within the following days, as the corrupt practices of presidential guard Gregório Fortunato came to light, Mascarenhas was advised that army officers in the lower ranks felt that pressure should be exerted to get Vargas to resign. That officers in the higher ranks felt the same way

[3] HACB, "Os Meios Militares na Recuperação Moral do País," speech at the Escola Superior de Guerra, September 19, 1955 (copy in the collection of Castello Branco papers, Escola de Comando e Estado Maior [ECEME], Praia Vermelha, Rio de Janeiro).
[4] João Baptista Mascarenhas de Moraes, Memórias, II, 581, 582–583.

Mascarenhas learned at a meeting in his home on August 22. There the marshal, Castello, and other army officers were informed by Brigadeiro Eduardo Gomes and Admiral Salalino Coelho that most of the air force *brigadeiros* had signed a manifesto calling on Vargas to resign and that their position was backed by most of the admiralty. It was also backed by the Democratic Crusade generals who had asked to attend the meeting with Mascarenhas: Military Club officers Canrobert Pereira da Costa and Juarez Távora and Army Chief of Staff Álvaro Fiúza de Castro.

Mascarenhas reported this turn in events to Vargas and heard the president say that he would not resign, but only "leave here dead." The marshal renewed his pledge to discipline and the Constitution.

For Mascarenhas that pledge meant refraining from exerting pressure on the president, as he had an opportunity to make clear on the night of August 22 when he was approached by Major Plínio Pitaluga, who had headed the FEB's Reconnaissance Squadron in Italy. Pitaluga spoke of a manifesto that army generals were signing, calling on Vargas to resign. "The document," Mascarenhas said, "does not merit my attention, and I shall not sign it because it is contrary to discipline and to my point of view." [5]

On this point the marshal and Castello parted company. Castello agreed to support his Democratic Crusade friends, who were painting a gloomy picture of what Brazil would be like if Vargas continued in office; he added his signature to theirs on the manifesto. [6]

On August 23 Castello joined Mascarenhas' office chief, Lieutenant Colonel Édson de Figueiredo, in suggesting to the marshal that the gravity of the situation required a special meeting of the chiefs of staff of the armed services and the top men of Mascarenhas' group. The marshal agreed, and late on August 23 he presided at this new meeting. Noting the strong feeling that only a presidential resignation would settle the crisis, he could only hope that if such were the outcome it would be a voluntary act by Vargas and not the result of pressure. [7] He made his way to Catete Palace, arriving there at midnight, in plenty of time for the cabinet meeting that started about 2:00 A.M. on August 24.

---

[5] For information in this and the preceding paragraphs, see ibid., pp. 585–587.

[6] Carlos de Meira Mattos (interview, Washington, D.C., January 5, 1976) expressed the feeling that Castello Branco's signing of the manifesto of the army generals was "part of a collective position [*posição coletiva*]" rather than a personal position.

[7] Mascarenhas de Moraes, *Memórias*, II, 589–590.

When Vargas asked Mascarenhas to express his view to the cabinet, the marshal delivered some remarks about Vargas' lack of support in the air force, the navy, and the lower ranks of army officers. At the end of the cabinet meeting Mascarenhas heard Vargas offer to take a leave of absence "provided that order be maintained by the military ministers"; if it were not maintained, the president added, he would resist—at the cost of his life, if necessary. A patriotic statement, thought Mascarenhas, as he presided at 7:20 in the morning over yet another meeting at his residence—this one to reveal Vargas' decision to Castello and others, including Távora and the chiefs of staff of the military branches.[8]

The old marshal, exhausted from emotion, felt that Vargas' decision to withdraw gave him the opportunity and duty to resign from his own post. Learning at 10:00 A.M. of Vargas' dramatic suicide, Mascarenhas was more determined than ever to retire, and he rejected pleas by Távora, Canrobert, and Fiúza de Castro that his name be presented to the new president, Café Filho, as a possible war minister.[9]

Mascarenhas' retirement brought an end to Castello Branco's three months with the Staff of the Armed Forces (EMFA). Although Mascarenhas had not completely shared Castello's point of view during the crisis, the marshal had warm praise for the assistance of the officer who, he recalled, "had been a supreme factor" in the success of the planning and execution of operations in the Italian campaign, and who, at his invitation, had recently "left the elevated post of commander of the Tenth Military Region." Thanking Castello for his superb collaboration and "affectionate assistance" during the intranquillity that had characterized the marshal's "last mission," Mascarenhas regretted that his own separation from his post prevented him from availing himself longer of such a "useful, meritorious, and agreeable collaboration."[10]

2. Lott's Coup (November 11, 1955)

In the administration of Café Filho the top military posts went to officers who had called for the resignation of Vargas. The twenty-seven

8 Ibid., pp. 591–593.
9 Ibid., pp. 594–595.
10 "Folhas de Alterações," File G3, Estado Maior das Forças Armadas, period July 1 to September 14, 1954, CPDOC.

generals who had advocated that solution in the army manifesto included Juarez Távora, who became head of the new president's Casa Militar; Henrique Batista Duffles Teixeira Lott, who became war minister; and Military Club President Canrobert Pereira da Costa, who succeeded Mascarenhas as head of the EMFA.[1]

Early in September, 1954, Castello Branco, another signer of the army manifesto, was named commander of the army's Escola de Estado Maior. The appointment deeply gratified Castello, for the school, an organization made up of the army's intellectual elite, was considered to be a sort of "sanctuary" that lived apart from politics; its commanders were chosen for the professional reputation that they enjoyed among their peers.

As the new commander, Castello succeeded General Antônio José Coelho dos Reis on September 15, and when he spoke to the graduating class later in the year he paid a tribute to his old friend Toné as well as to the recently departed director of instruction, Colonel Orlando Geisel. He urged the graduating officers not to rely solely on tact in order to handle well the posts they were about to occupy, those of assistants to commanders. Stressing that they should avoid being mere conformists, or screens between superiors and subordinates, he told them to struggle against conservatism and to be open to new ideas in order to escape from formalism and routine.[2]

The new *regulamento* of the EEM, drawn up while Castello directed the instruction there (1945–1949), was put into effect with the opening of the school year on March 1, 1955, and it broadened the responsibilities of the commander by the inclusion of the duties formerly exercised by the director of instruction;[3] at the same time the school, which had long borne the title of its French equivalent, was renamed the Escola de Comando e Estado Maior do Exército (ECEME, Army Command and Staff School).

---

[1] The generals' "Manifesto to the Nation," dated August 22, 1954, bears twenty-seven signatures. The first two are those of Álvaro Fiúza de Castro and Canrobert Pereira da Costa. Juarez Távora's is the fourth signature, Alcides Etchegoyen's the fifth, and Castello Branco's the eleventh (immediately following that of Peri Constant Bevilaqua), Lott's is nineteenth. See Bento Munhoz da Rocha Netto, *Radiografia de Novembro*, 2d ed., pp. 118–119.

[2] HACB, *Discurso Pronunciado pelo Gen. Bda. Humberto de Alencar Castello Branco, Comandante da Escola de Estado Maior* [1954], File J, Part 1, p. 9v, CPDOC.

[3] "Folhas de Alterações," File G3, ECEME, first semester, 1955, CPDOC.

As had been expected by instructors and students, Castello's return to the halls at Praia Vermelha was followed by a renewed emphasis on his favorite teaching methods. "The classic situations," Murilo Gomes Ferreira says, "were replaced by the studies of Diverse Operations," in which the officers were faced with unexpected situations designed to develop analyses and rapid decision making.[4]

As on previous occasions, Castello stressed that the first duty of a good officer was to keep the army away from politics.[5] In one of his talks at the ECEME, Castello declared that "the adepts of the policy of intervention by the Armed Forces in the activities of the national political power want militarist pronouncements, by means of speeches or threatening sentences, and intimidating maneuvers of tanks, all on behalf of the seizure by themselves of the political power." With his eye on the political groups, Castello said that "everyone wants to grasp the sword and turn its sharp edge against his opponents." Legality, Castello went on to say, required that those who were in authority have respect for the missions and aims of the armed forces. He called for "a silence" that sprang from "a coherent attitude of discipline" and that was "not conformity, not the act of being an accomplice, nor a desertion of the professional life." He wanted "reciprocal loyalty, reciprocal purposes, all outside of, and above, partisanship."[6]

Prominent military leaders, however, showed an increasing tendency to play a role in politics. Full of worries, they presented Café Filho with a manifesto in January, 1955, after electioneering for the presidency had been started by Minas Gerais Governor Juscelino Kubitschek, whom they critically regarded as a representative of the Vargas political wing. This new manifesto, signed by Mascarenhas, Canrobert, and Távora as well as the military ministers and chiefs of staff, was regarded by many as the voice of the military against Kubitschek's candidacy. It called on Café Filho to avoid a "violent electoral campaign" by finding a candidate "of national unity."[7] The president tried and failed.

---

[4] Murilo Gomes Ferreira, "O General Castello Que Conheci," Part 4, "Escola de Comando: Estado Maior 1955" (transcript of tape prepared for interview), Rio de Janeiro, November 12, 1975.

[5] Jarbas Passarinho interview, Brasília, November 11, 1975.

[6] HACB lecture at the ECEME in the 1950's, reproduced in *Jornal do Brasil*, April 11, 1976.

[7] João Café Filho, *Do Sindicato ao Catete: Memórias Políticas e Confissões Humanas*, II, 485, 492.

Four candidates, including Kubitschek and Juarez Távora, campaigned for the presidency. The anti-Vargas military, horrified at Kubitschek's agreement to have former Labor Minister Goulart as his running mate, solemnly observed the first anniversary of the assassination of Major Vaz by hearing Military Club President Canrobert decry the "democratic falsehood" in which, he said, "Brazil insisted on living." War Minister Lott expressed preoccupation about Communist support for the Kubitschek-Goulart ticket.[8]

While some predicted a military coup in case the voting in October, 1955, favored Kubitschek and Goulart, Castello spoke against coups. He insisted that the democratic regime, which military officers had sworn to support, should be maintained and defended, regardless of the price. As Castello added that he would be glad to hear the opinions of his subordinates, he received a long communication from Major Jarbas G. Passarinho, a third-year ECEME student who wrote that he was speaking for his companions as well as himself. "I am," Passarinho wrote, "in full agreement that undemocratic regimes (regimes de exceção) do not merit our approval, particularly because, as Your Excellency also emphasized, they limit liberty. I am, like Your Excellency, against any coup, military or civilian. I am against the absence of a representative regime— against, in short, the mutilation of Democracy."[9]

In September, 1955, when ECEME commander Castello Branco criticized the "manifesto of the colonels" in a speech at the Escola Superior de Guerra, he also assailed dictatorships. Dictatorships, he declared, repressed "human liberty and the rights of citizens" and were detrimental to professionalism in the military. Besides, he added, they promoted corruption. Citing "painful lessons" provided by "recent times" (a reference that included the Vargas dictatorship), Castello said that during dictatorships "the so-called elite gained experience in despotism and in thievery."[10]

Presently Castello, opposed to coups, would decide to support a coup as the price of defending democracy. Among the events that led to this situation was the reporting of the October, 1955, election returns as

[8] *Correiro da Manhã*, August 6, 18, 1955.
[9] Jarbas G. Passarinho to HACB, Rio de Janeiro, August 15, 1955, File L1, CPDOC.
[10] HACB, "Os Meios Militares."

favorable to Kubitschek and Goulart, followed by pronouncements in which the ministers of the navy, the air force, and foreign relations found reasons, such as electoral fraud and Communist votes, for denying the inauguration of the apparent victors. Then Canrobert died, and Colonel Mamede, speaking in the rain during the burial, delivered a controversial funeral oration in which Colonel Golberi do Couto e Silva, principal author of the "manifesto of the colonels" of 1954, had had a hand.[11] According to Mamede's oration, given on behalf of the Military Club, the recent election confirmed Conrobert's remark about the "democratic falsehood" existing in Brazil.

War Minister Lott, approached by friends of Kubitschek, seemed to adhere to Castello's position of preserving democracy, regardless of the price. After discharging Coastal Artillery Inspector Alcides Etchegoyen for opposing the inauguration of Kubitschek and Goulart, the war minister set out to punish Mamede for his funeral oration. But in this he was blocked by Carlos Luz, who became interim president of Brazil when Café Filho fell ill and who decided to name a new war minister—Fiúza de Castro, the first signer of the generals' manifesto calling for Vargas' resignation. Fiúza de Castro turned to Ademar de Queiroz to be his right hand in the ministry,[12] and he asked Alcides Etchegoyen to take the place of Lott's friend Odílio Denys as head of the Eastern Military Zone (with headquarters in Rio).[13]

Early on November 11 Lott joined Odílio Denys in carrying out a successful army coup against interim President Luz and the opponents of the inauguration of Kubitschek and Goulart. Lott explained the step as necessary to preserve discipline in the army, Luz having prevented him from punishing Mamede.

But the coup was also regarded as a means of assuring the inauguration of those elected in October, and for this reason it appealed to Mascarenhas.[14] The marshal, accompanied by General Floriano de Lima Brayner and some of Lott's troops, went to Catete Palace to remove Fiúza de Castro and Etchegoyen, who remained there faithful to Luz.

[11] Herrera interview, December 16, 1975.

[12] Ibid. Heitor Herrera sent a radio message to Ademar de Queiroz inviting him to be *chefe de gabinete* of Fiúza de Castro.

[13] Floriano de Lima Brayner to JWFD, Rio de Janeiro, October 25, 1975.

[14] Mascarenhas de Moraes, *Memórias*, II, 597.

After a dramatic scene in which these two infuriated anti-Vargas generals were arrested, Etchegoyen, over-excited, had to be taken in an army ambulance to a hospital.[15]

Luz, who had been at the Navy Ministry, went aboard the *Tamandaré* with Mamede, Carlos Lacerda, and others who supported him. Then the cruiser, with its distinguished passengers, made its way slowly out into the ocean while artillery fire against it from Fort Copacabana, ordered by Lott, failed to sink it. Emotions ran high on November 11, 1955.

3. Lott Punishes the ECEME and Dismisses Castello

On the morning of November 11, ECEME commander Castello Branco called together his instructors and students, many of whom had tearfully watched, from Praia Vermelha, the shooting against the *Tamandaré*.[1] To restrain these hundreds of army officers from trying to play a role in defeating the coup led by Lott, Castello related the official version of the events that had been issued by Lott. The school commander added that anyone desiring further clarification could see him in his office. As almost the entire school disagreed with his position, a long line formed outside his office on the second floor of the school building. Deciding to receive the officers in groups of ten instead of individually, Castello assured them that no dictatorship would result from the military coup. Although Castello's efforts to justify Lott's action did not satisfy most of the officers, his handling of the matter prevented an immediate demonstration by instructors and students in opposition to Lott.[2]

On the evening of November 11, after Congress declared that Luz was in no position to continue as president, War Minister Lott—in the company of Mascarenhas, Zenóbio da Costa, Brayner, and others who had forced Luz from office—presided at ceremonies making Senate head Nereu Ramos the new acting president of Brazil. Nereu Ramos, favor-

[15] Brayner to JWFD, October 25, 1975.

[1] "O Caso Castelo Branco: Boletim Dedicado aos Cegos que Não Querem Ver," mimeographed circular regarding the letter of HACB to the directors of the Frente de Novembro, November, 1956, File L1, CPDOC.

[2] Ibid.; Ivan de Souza Mendes interview, Rio de Janeiro, July 26, 1976.

able to the inauguration of Kubitschek and Goulart, named Brayner to be head of his Casa Militar.[3]

By this time it was clear that Castello Branco had not been very convincing in his talks with the ECEME instructors and students; almost all of them signed a manifesto condemning the "treason of Lott." When Castello learned what was going on he let it be known, through one of his assistants, that he believed that the manifesto would serve no practical purpose and would only increase the confusion.[4] He hoped that it would not be issued.

Lott, receiving a report that officers at the ECEME were conspiring, called Castello to his office, only to hear Castello deny the charge. But a few days later, after the *Tamandaré* had returned from its short voyage in the ocean, Lott received a list of ECEME "conspirators," including one or two officer-students said to have been on the *Tamandaré*.[5] Ordering Castello to his office again, he argued that the "conspirators" should be transferred from the ECEME. Castello would not agree. Lott, irate, told Castello that as the ECEME commander he should have known about the conspiracy at the school and that he could not remain at his post as school commander. "You will be transferred to command in Pará," Lott told Castello, who, Lott observed, became very upset.[6]

After Castello departed from the War Ministry, Lott arranged to imprison, for several days, some of the ECEME students and instructors. Castello made sure that the families of the arrested men received assistance. In the meantime, at the school the officers responsible for the manifesto condemning the "treason of Lott" decided to respect the wishes of their chief by refraining from issuing it. They were impressed that Castello, although a supporter of Lott's coup, had resolutely sought to defend the school's instructors and officer-students against what they called "the furies of Lott." [7]

But there was little that Castello could do about the mood of his instructors and officer-students. When Lott appeared at the exercises closing the school year, he received a cold reception that contrasted with the

[3] Floriano de Lima Brayner, "Brochado da Rocha, um Grande Caráter," *Diário Carioca*, September 30, 1962.

[4] "O Caso Castelo Branco."

[5] Henrique Batista Duffles Teixeira Lott interview, Rio de Janeiro, October 13, 1975; "O Caso Castelo Branco."

[6] Lott interview, October 13, 1975.

[7] "O Caso Castelo Branco."

applause given Castello. And when Lott left the school, following the ceremonies, he was loudly booed by the families of the officers.[8]

The war minister, who had arrested Colonel Mamede and sent him to a recruitment post in the interior of the state of São Paulo, now set to work punishing the ECEME personnel by transfers, and he did this without consulting or even advising Castello. Murilo Gomes Ferreira, who graduated at this time at the ECEME, asserts that "a majority of the instructors and almost all of the members of our class . . . were transferred to different regional staffs, outside of Rio, without the right to vacation or to the regulation transfer period."[9]

Castello Branco submitted his resignation, "dictated by motives more compelling than my desire to remain in such an honorable post."[10] On January 2, 1956, after the resignation had been accepted, the instructors and administrators of the ECEME, although on vacation, held a special session to express their support and admiration for their departing commander. In his words of thanks, Castello said that during his lifetime he had had many emotional moments and that "this is one of the most emotional that I have ever had." After speaking highly of the spirit, character, and generosity of those who had honored him, Castello referred briefly to the role he had played in the post he was giving up: "I am now in the last phase of military life, in full command. Therefore I tried not to give you an example of incapacity, nor of omission or absence. At all times I sought to avoid being a cause of unrest, and to be loyal to superiors and subordinates, without ever making use of easy but dissociative demagoguery. . . ."[11]

To succeed Castello as ECEME commander, Lott named General Emílio Maurel Filho, who had participated with Mascarenhas and Brayner in the seizure of Generals Fiúza de Castro and Alcides Etchegoyen at Catete Palace. An anti-Lott circular commented: "For Lott, no independent person could remain in a key position."[12]

---

[8] Ibid.

[9] Ferreira, "O General Castello Que Conheci," Part 4, "Escola de Comando."

[10] Passage from speech of HACB turning over the ECEME command to Assistant Director of Instruction Antônio Henrique Almeida de Morais (who occupied it provisionally), given in *Boletim Escolar*, no. 2 (January 3, 1956). See File G1, CPDOC.

[11] HACB, "Discurso de Passagem de Comando," ECEME, January 2, 1956, File J, Part 2, p. 11, CPDOC.

[12] "O Caso Castelo Branco."

For Castello it was a disappointment to find that Toné (Antônio José Coehlo dos Reis) was serving Lott in the War Ministry.

4. Transfer to the Escola Superior de Guerra (April, 1956)

With the inauguration of President Kubitschek on January 31, 1956, it was not surprising that General Lott, now the "strong man" of Brazil, continued in his post of war minister.

Castello, who returned on January 3 to his former position of assistant chief of staff of the armed forces, might have been the new administration's president of Petrobrás (the government petroleum extraction monopoly) had he not insisted on remaining in the army. When Kubitschek, right after his election in October, had offered the Petrobrás post to Castello, several reasons for declining were given by the general, who was known to have remarked that "one day of absence from the Army might cloud one's devotion to the profession."[1] He had explained to the president-elect that he did not want to leave the army during a difficult moment, and he had also pointed out that he had voted for Juarez Távora for president and that a more suitable appointment would be a Kubitschek supporter.[2]

Early in April, 1956, Castello was transferred to the Escola Superior de Guerra (ESG). There he directed the instruction of the nine-month Armed Forces Staff and Command Course,[3] which was restricted to military officers of the three branches of the service; at the same time, during 1956 he attended the other principal course, the Curso Superior de Guerra, in which civilians and military men were enrolled, also for nine months.

National security was studied broadly in the classrooms and on the ESG trips. Students of the Curso Superior de Guerra, assigned problems to resolve, gave attention to foreign policy and to economic, political, and social development. It was this breadth that led Osvaldo Aranha, father of Corporal Aranha, to describe the ESG as "a Brazilian Sor-

---

[1] HACB quoted in Edmar Eudóxio Telesca, "Depoimento sôbre o General Humberto de Alencar Castello Branco," Rio de Janeiro, April 24, 1976, p. 4.

[2] Telesca, "Depoimento," p. 4.

[3] "Folhas de Alterações," File G3, CPDOC.

bonne"; the nickname stuck, and intellectual Colonel Golberi do Couto e Silva was sometimes referred to as "the Pope of the Sorbonne."[4]

Most of the ESG's approximately thirty instructors were civilians, and the civilian students, men of importance who were admitted upon the recommendation of the government's branches, made up a majority of the more than one hundred who were admitted to the ESG each year. Upon graduation they joined a well-knit body of alumni that kept in close touch with the ESG.

Writing about the civilians at the ESG, Luís Mendes da Silva states that Castello, "in his fellowship with the businessmen who were receiving training together with his uniformed colleagues, completed the long chain that he had been putting together all of his life. His name gained dimension in the world of private business. The respect that the Armed Forces bestowed on him overflowed beyond the military area and assumed a national scope."[5]

Influential civilians, having the opportunity to exchange opinions with Castello at the ESG, became acquainted with the personality of the man who, although inclined to be unassuming in his dealings with them, always commanded respect. Together with recollections of the logical approaches that he used in attacking problems, small but illuminating details about his unusual character would remain in their minds.[6] There was, for example, the experience of those who were picked up each morning by the ESG bus—a busload that included majors, lieutenant colonels, colonels, brigadier generals, and civilians, most of them engaging in horseplay, a throwback to their younger days that not infrequently affects the middle-aged who become involved in college again. They were not apt to forget Castello entering the bus with his cheerful "Good morning, gentlemen," because at that point the horseplay ended.[7] This is not to say that they regarded him as a killjoy; he had a keen sense of humor, was often jocular, and enjoyed his own jokes and the jokes that he heard. But after Castello entered the bus, dignity prevailed.

[4] Humberto de Melo and Knaack de Souza interview, November 30, 1967.

[5] Luís Mendes da Silva, "Testemunho," Part 5, "Na Escola Superior de Guerra."

[6] Ibid. Lincoln Gordon ("Recollections of President Castello Branco," typewritten, Washington, D.C., July 28, 1972, p. 12) describes Castello Branco, as president, attacking a problem: "Castello Branco set forth the alternatives in his own words, and then developed a chain of logical reasoning from each one, weighing the possible moves and countermoves at each branch in the chain like a master chess player."

[7] Manuel Pio Corrêa interview, Rio de Janeiro, December 23, 1974.

Civilians were impressed, too, when Castello emphasized the importance of the military remaining apart from politics and resisting the efforts of politicians to make use of the military for their own ends.[8] Word got around. San Tiago Dantas, who continued seeing Hélio Vianna and his circle, was much influenced by the reports of Castello's ideas about the role of the military. Citing these among his reasons, the influential corporation lawyer from Minas remarked that if it should ever seem advisable to have a military man in the Brazilian presidency, that man should be Castello Branco.[9]

Perhaps what most impressed those who came to know Castello at the Escola Superior de Guerra was his mental agility during discussions. His mind and learning allowed him to handle himself in debate in a more striking manner than when delivering a lecture,[10] and he had no fear of dueling verbally with the most prominent of the ESG's many guest speakers. Ambassador Osvaldo Aranha, talking about Soviet policy in Asia, is said to have been amazed at the clarity and knowledge revealed by Castello during questioning; after the diplomat severely criticized the policy of the West, the audience was highly amused when Castello concluded by remarking that "if what you say is true, then I think that I had better side with Khrushchev." Castello was at his best when one of the speakers insisted that police action should reign supreme in dealing with the Marxist philosophy. The general, who felt that in the combat against ideas it was necessary to have other and better ideas, is said to have devastated the speaker by the evidence he presented.[11]

Glycon de Paiva, who had headed the National Development Bank (BNDE) during Café Filho's administration, lectured at the ESG at the same time that Castello did. Although the Glycon de Paivas were neighbors of the Castello Brancos, the families did not exchange visits, but the engineer and the general conversed quite frequently in the street or local drugstore, occasionally about Napoleon, whose military feats Castello seemed to admire, and often about politics. Glycon de Paiva found Castello Branco a modest person who was an especially good listener, a man who could convince and be convinced. Castello, Glycon learned,

[8] See HACB, "Os Meios Militares."
[9] Renato Archer interview, Rio de Janeiro, September 30, 1975.
[10] Reynaldo Melo de Almeida interview, Rio de Janeiro, October 17, 1975.
[11] Telesca, "Depoimento," p. 3.

had had to turn to the army to get an education and had made the best of himself, relying heavily on the virtues learned in the home—virtues that had provided him with a solid character, marked by truthfulness and frankness, and a great fondness for meditation. Glycon decided that Castello was a very hard worker and that he had an unusual ability to evaluate people.[12]

5. Brazilian Military Doctrine (1957)

Military officers and civilians belonging to the ESG listened attentively when Castello Branco delivered a speech about Brazilian military doctrine, for Castello was not in the habit of wasting their time by reciting platitudes. As he said at the outset, he was going to be critical, not in order to condemn people, but in order best to discuss what concretely pertained to an important subject.[1]

Observing that the armed forces needed to have their objectives established by military doctrine, lest political or economic groups try to use the military for improper purposes, he turned early in his speech to the military doctrines of foreign countries. With the United States armed forces concentrating on matters of warfare in Europe and Asia and required to provide assistance at home only in the case of a public calamity, he saw no probability of internal operations by the army in the United States, where, he declared, public order was a matter for the police and only the police. In Russia, on the other hand, Castello saw a dual purpose of the armed forces: operations against the western powers and the internal defense of the activities of the Communist Party. Castello declared that the principal purpose of the Argentine armed forces was to overthrow and organize governments. In Bolivia, he said, the recent revolution had practically destroyed the armed forces, and they were being reorganized to provide a small amount of military instruction and to participate significantly in the national production.

Warfare, a purpose of the Brazilian armed forces, could tacitly be taken for granted to include warfare in South America, although this was not explicitly stated in documents. If, Castello, said, no clear definitions existed about the uses of the Brazilian armed forces in the cases of

---

[12] Glycon de Paiva interview, Rio de Janeiro, December 9, 1975.
[1] HACB, *A Doutrina Militar Brasileira*, p. 1.

a South American war or a conflict with Russia, it was a reflection of the lack of firmness and vision in national policy.

To these failings Castello added the "politicizing of elements" in the Brazilian armed forces, especially in the army. Furthermore, due to the effects of the Vargas dictatorship and the periodic threats of another dictatorship, Castello saw the army being drawn sometimes to the role of a political party militia and sometimes to the role of a praetorian guard. All of which, he pointed out, contributed to the disintegration of professional efficiency and made it difficult for the army to be in a condition necessary for fulfilling its purpose of carrying out warfare.

In thoughts not dissimilar to those expressed in 1933 by "Colonel Y," Castello commented unfavorably on the state police organizations and on the use of the armed forces for "secondary purposes." Some of the state police organizations, he told the ESG, were readying themselves for inclusion as participants in a foreign war, should one arise, and the result was that they no longer felt capable of carrying out police work.

The increasing interest in building up secondary purposes for the Brazilian armed forces, Castello said, was creating "serious difficulties" and was due to "the lack of knowledge of the purposes of the armed forces by politicians and the elite of all sectors. . . , together with the lack of a military mentality adequate for the national security on the part of many military officers." [2] While Castello was not yet willing to include among the "serious difficulties" the use of the navy and air force for transportation, and the use of army units for railroad and highway construction, he did feel that if this work were much expanded, it would be detrimental to the principal purposes of the armed forces and would result in reductions in the already scant resources intended for combat equipment.

A more serious matter, a "great difficulty" advocated in official documents, was the proposed employment of army troops for growing crops and raising cattle. Castello addressed himself to the arguments that military service of this sort would take "the Army from the apathy in which it lives" and would contribute "to solving the most grievous problem of the moment—the feeding of the Brazilian people." [3] Was the indolence and lack of spirit of a military unit to be corrected by having many of its members till the soil and raise cattle? Castello asked. In reply he

[2] Ibid., p. 46.
[3] Ibid., p. 47.

pointed out that such activities would require a large increase in the army's budget, and he predicted that the budget of the Agriculture Ministry would not decrease; the results, he said, would show neither military efficiency nor efficiency in the production of food, "and the Army, with one foot in military pursuits and the other in the area of the producing class, will continue to lose time and will spend the nation's money uselessly." [4]

Some of the civilians, Castello said, proposed turning the military to agricultural pursuits because they believed that it had a lot of extra time. Refuting this argument, he pointed out that the army had set up programs that occupied all of the time of its conscripts, only to have the government reduce that time for budgetary reasons. "When civilians observe that soldiers have a lot of leisure, it is not because they have too much time in the barracks; it is because some of the barracks are given over to idleness, the fault lying exclusively with their officers, principally the commanders." [5]

Castello called for a clear definition of the role of the armed forces. In the end, he said, the lack of a military doctrine, confusion about the doctrine, or the existence of an erroneous doctrine "all give about the same results." [6] His own position was clear. In the case of transport and road construction, the role of the military should be limited, with the emphasis placed on training for such work in warfare. As for secondary purposes that were beyond "the present structure of the armed forces," a "decisive definition" was needed. Either an organization should be set up "as projected by the present government of Bolivia," or else "we should, once and for all, eliminate such considerations" and have the military devote themselves exclusively to their "rational tasks." [7]

The uncertainty about the role of the armed forces prompted Castello to quote a statement made by Rui Barbosa concerning a military reorganization carried out in his time: "A work of rhapsody, confusion, and pomp, leading only to an increase of soldiers, an increase of barracks, an increase of expenses, an increase of confusion, and an increase of military inefficiency." "Today," Castello said, "Rui Barbosa would

[4] Ibid., p. 49.
[5] Ibid.
[6] Ibid., p. 65.
[7] Ibid., p. 57.

probably repeat, more opportunely and with more vigor, this vehement criticism." [8]

6. The Sword of Gold (November, 1956)

War Minister Lott shocked Castello Branco and others at the Escola Superior de Guerra; apparently taking steps to build up a political following, he showed no sign of wanting to disclaim the support of the Brazilian Communist Party (PCB). The PCB, having backed the candidacies of Kubitschek and Goulart, was delighted with the coup of November, 1955, and sometimes immodestly and unrealistically took credit for the outcome.[1] Communists supported the Frente de Novembro (November Front), which was launched to glorify Lott and the coup and to demand the formation of a "Popular and Nationalist force" to be made up of "workers and military people, bureaucrats, employees in commerce, and small proprietors." [2]

On November 8, 1956, Castello, addressed as "illustrious chief," learned from a communication from the Auxiliary Committee of the Federal District of the Frente de Novembro that the organization was "counting on" his presence at a "magnificent tribute" to be rendered on November 12 to General Lott, "eminent commander of the Army of November." On this occasion Vice-President Goulart was to present Lott with a sword of gold (*espada de ouro*).

The invitation advised Castello that the Auxiliary Committee considered as "decisive" his "public adherence to the gigantic popular demonstration in honor of the brave leader of the legitimate ideals of the emancipation of the national worker. . . . We hold it true that from the union of the workers and soldiers there will emerge the guarantee of victory in the struggle in which we are engaged against reactionary coups." [3]

---

[8] Ibid., p. 67.

[1] Osvaldo Peralva, *O Retrato*, pp. 140–148.

[2] HACB to Senhores Membros do Comitê Auxiliar do Distrito Federal da Frente de Novembro, Rio de Janeiro, November 8, 1956 (longhand draft and typed copy with signature), File L1, CPDOC (also in *O Globo*, November 10, 1956).

[3] Invitation to the Manifestação da Espada de Ouro, underlined by HACB, File L1, CPDOC.

Castello was so disturbed by the invitation that he felt it important to give publicity to his reply, and therefore he sent to Rio's leading afternoon newspaper, O Globo, a copy of his letter to the Auxiliary Committee. He listed some of the reasons that, he said, obliged him to be absent from "the projected political-party meeting."

Above all, Castello wrote, the regimentation of the military as a class, at the side of other classes, "aligned in a politically suspect manner," was subversive. He quoted that section of the manifesto of the Frente de Novembro which declared that the front wanted to "unify" the armed forces "by a process of democratization, whereby any differentiations within their ranks would be eliminated." Acknowledging that for political reasons differences did exist within the armed forces, Castello argued that the front's proposal to eliminate them showed that it planned to use "the odious process of purging" those who were opposed to it. This was, he added, a totalitarian approach, Communist or Nazi in character.[4]

Noting also that the front's manifesto called for "militarizing the national economy," Castello suggested that such a step would contribute to the destruction of the military capacity of the armed forces and would achieve neither economic nor military efficiency. "At a time when many worthy people honestly proclaim the need of avoiding the militarization of Brazilian democracy, in order to strengthen the civilian power and vitalize the military professionalism of the armed forces, there comes this manifesto, out-of-date and reactionary, threatening to militarize the government and national activities."

In conclusion, Castello pointed out that the army's regulations forbade the participation of its members, especially collectively, as the Auxiliary Committee wished, in "political meetings such as the one on the 12th, in which soldiers and workers are called upon to guarantee the victory of a type of political party."[5]

On November 10, 1956, two days before Lott was to receive his golden sword from Goulart, O Globo published Castello's letter under a headline calling attention to subversion and "a serious breach of military regulations." The newspaper said that Castello Branco, "one of the

---

[4] HACB to Senhores Membros do Comitê Auxiliar do Distrito Federal da Frente de Novembro, November 8, 1956, File L1, CPDOC.

[5] Ibid.

most brilliant and respected figures of the national Army," was at the moment acting commander of the Escola Superior de Guerra.[6]

In the legislative halls, members of the oppositionist UDN made speeches in support of Castello Branco's position. Daniel Krieger, a UDN senator from Rio Grande do Sul, had learned about Castello's letter before it was published, so he was able to use it when he attacked Lott on November 10 in the most carefully prepared senate speech that he had ever given. To this day Lott remembers the attacks by UDN Congressman Carlos Lacerda as being the most disconcerting of all those made about the *espada de ouro* matter.[7]

On the twelfth, the press was full of adherences to Castello Branco's position. General de Divisão Emílio Rodrigues Ribas Júnior, who had run in 1950 on the unsuccessful Military Club slate headed by Cordeiro de Farias, declared that he could not support a demonstration of a subversive character "such as is planned for today by the Frente de Novembro." Brigadier General Ademar de Queiroz, who had run on the same slate, expressed his complete agreement with the reasons enunciated "perfectly" by "his friend" Castello Branco, and he suggested that the "subversive" invitation could only have been sent to him "due to erroneous addressing."[8]

In agreeing with Castello Branco, General Floriano Peixoto Keller, chief of recruitment, mentioned the placards in front of the War Ministry that proclaimed Goulart the workers' guide and Lott their defender. General Tasso Tinoco, who had acted against Lott's coup a year earlier, expressed his opposition to "those demonstrations of a political-ideological character—subversive, or, rather, Communist." Other generals, quoted on the twelfth, described Castello Branco's words as "very opportune," "very good," and "very sensible."[9]

These generals, unlike thousands of workers, missed the celebration in front of the War Ministry in which Lott was eulogized in prose and verse by sixteen speakers. There the mayor of São Paulo declared that

[6] *O Globo*, November 10, 1956.

[7] Daniel Krieger interview, Brasília, October 21, 1975; Lott interview, October 13, 1975.

[8] "O Caso Castelo Branco."

[9] Ibid. Among the other generals whose pro–Castello Branco sentiments were published on November 12, 1956, were Nicanor Guimarães de Souza, a former Democratic Crusade candidate for the Military Club presidency, and Armando Vilanova Pereira de Vasconcellos, director of armament.

Lott was clearly the man to take the place left vacant by Vargas' suicide.

On the next day the press carried more pro–Castello Branco sentiments by generals, among them Peri Constant Bevilaqua, Garrastazu Teixeira, Ignácio José Veríssimo, Paulo Kruger da Cunha Cruz, Armando Vasconcelos, Eudoro Barcelos de Morais, Delso Mendes da Fonseca, and Artur da Costa e Silva.[10] Like Tinoco and some of the others, Costa e Silva, director of the army's motorized service in the Federal District, had received no invitation. "Had I received one," Costa e Silva wrote, "I would have acted exactly as General Castello Branco did."

Castello Branco received so many letters of support that he resorted to a form letter to send acknowledgments. Apologizing for his tardiness, he pointed out that "two Escola Superior de Guerra trips, the college's demanding year-end work, and the setting up of studies for the new year" did not allow him to send his thanks at once. "I am very grateful for the expressions in your congratulatory message, and I am proud that we have the same ideals."[11]

Friends of Castello Branco see the *espada de ouro* episode as important for being the first occasion on which he publicly took a personal stand in opposition to those in authority,[12] a stand against "aventurismo, comunismo, and peleguismo."[13] But, in the opinion of João Adyl de Oliveira, nothing of a "revolutionary" nature should be attributed to Castello; he simply "exploded within himself," so upset was he with the behavior of Lott, an officer long renowned for his careful observance of discipline.[14]

While Lott's choice of supporters could only have vexed the Grupo da Sorbonne, whose antipathy to Communism was shared by Castello, it is perhaps more important to note that Lott's use of the military for political ends was precisely what Humberto had been emphatically opposing in his public utterances.

[10] "O Caso Castelo Branco." Ignácio José Veríssimo, Paulo Kruger da Cunha Cruz, and Delso Mendes da Fonseca had signed the generals' manifesto of August 22, 1954, calling for the resignation of Vargas.

[11] HACB letter of thanks for support of his position (typed), Rio de Janeiro, January 22, 1957, File L1, CPDOC.

[12] Ademar de Queiroz interview, Rio de Janeiro, October 13, 1975.

[13] Meira Mattos interview, January 5, 1976. *Peleguismo* is a reference to labor leaders with close government connections.

[14] João Adyl de Oliveira interview, Rio de Janiero, October 18, 1975.

Castello, speaking in 1958 at the Instituto de Geografia e História Militar, turned to Brazilian history to drive home his point about the place of the military. He recalled that General Manuel Luís Osório, admonished by a cabinet minister of the empire for failing to support the conduct of the government, replied that if the army should have the right to approve government positions, it would have a corresponding right to disapprove. Declaring that "this lesson is still valid," Castello told his audience that no leader should say that the military backed this or that government policy; such backing, he said, would be the arrogation of "an illegal, supervising function" and would represent an extension of the military into the political realm, improper and especially to be condemned for "speaking in the name of subordinates who do not delegate to their superiors the right to express their political opinions."[15]

Lott's coup of 1955 was the subject of so much discussion that it was inevitable that Castello should often be asked about it. When he was in São Paulo to give a lecture in 1958, one of his listeners asked him to comment on the coup. Avoiding a reply, Castello said that questions should be related to the subject of the lecture. But the listener, insisting on an answer, explained that he had served in the FEB and knew the rules that applied to military figures—they were free to discuss matters unrelated to the subjects of lectures. Castello closed the incident (and the meeting) by remarking: "You were in the war; it is much more difficult to be a military man in times of peace."[16]

7. The Military Club Election of 1958

Lott could not count on much support from officers in the navy and air force; the killing of Major Vaz had contributed to the strong anti-Getulista feeling in the air force, and the artillery fire against the *Tamandaré*, ordered by Lott, was not to be forgotten in the navy. But Lott had support among army officers, as revealed by the victory in mid-1956

[15] HACB, address at the Instituto de Geografia e História Militar, 1958, in Castello Branco collection at the ECEME, Praia Vermelha, Rio de Janeiro (reproduced in part in "Os Archivos do Marechal Revelam um Militar Revolucionário e Liberal," *Veja*, April 5, 1972).
[16] César Tácito Lopes Costa interview, São Paulo, July 28, 1977.

of the "nationalist" wing over the Democratic Crusade in the Military Club election. However, the victory, which brought João de Segadas Viana to the club presidency, was by the narrowest of margins.

After that election, the incidents of November, 1956, increased the polarization in the army. Juarez Távora issued pronouncements attacking Lott one week after Lott received his golden sword; the *"tenente* with white hair" was therefore sentenced by Lott to forty-eight hours of house arrest for violating a recent order of the administration that prohibited retired as well as active military figures from making political statements—unless they happened to be ministers in the president's cabinet.[1]

For a somewhat less grievous sin General Ademar de Queiroz was among those who were subsequently disciplined. Ademar, in command of troops in Mato Grosso, failed to attend a lunch honoring the visiting Kubitschek. When Artur Hescket-Hall, commander of the Second Army (formerly Central Military Zone) punished him for this failure, Ademar appealed in vain to Lott for a reversal of the decision and then turned to Rio lawyer Justo de Morais to get the stain removed from his record.[2]

Castello Branco's pessimism is revealed in a letter he wrote to former Minister João Neves da Fontoura on February 21, 1957: "Today perhaps the Army commemorates the battle of Monte Castello, a victory over Nazism, over the regime of arms at the service of one man and one party. If the commemoration takes place, at the top echelon it will be an empty ceremony, merely formal, because the mentality defeated at Monte Castello is the one that prevails among those who wield the 'Sword of Gold.' "[3]

Castello, still at the Escola Superior de Guerra early in 1958, became the candidate of the Democratic Crusade for the Military Club presidency that year; his name, heading the list of thirteen candidates on the Democratic Crusade's Blue Slate, was followed by that of the first vice-presidential nominee, General João da Costa Braga Júnior, who had belonged to the same study group as Castello when they had taken the

[1] Juarez Távora interviews, Rio de Janeiro, October 5, 20, 1966; November 27, 1967.

[2] Queiroz interview, October 13, 1975; Prudente de Morais Neto interview, Rio de Janeiro, October 8, 1975.

[3] HACB to Fontoura, February 21, 1957, in Luís Viana Filho, *O Governo Castelo Branco*, p. 41.

course at the Escola de Estado Maior in 1929–1931. The pro-Lott Yellow Slate was headed by General Joaquim Justino Alves Bastos, whose close friend Odílio Denys commanded the First Army (formerly Eastern Military Zone).[4]

The interest in the Military Club election, scheduled for May 22, 1958, was so intense that campaigning began in January.[5] Alves Bastos made an issue of who was, and who was not, a friend of the war minister. When Colonel Malvino Reis, famed for fighting the 1935 Communist uprising in Recife, declared at a Military Club gathering that he would vote for the Blue Slate, Alves Bastos asked him: "Why are you going to do that, if you are a friend of General Lott?" The Yellow Slate candidate told the gathering that Malvino Reis should be regarded as no true friend of Lott.[6]

Castello Branco felt that the Blue Slate's program and the men who were on the ticket with him were far superior to anything that the Yellow Slate had to offer. He hoped that these factors, together with the "dedicated work" of the directorship of the Democratic Crusade and the support coming from "the best that there is in the armed forces and the Reserve," would bring victory to the Blue Slate.[7]

When leaders and supporters of the Democratic Crusade met at the Casa de Deodoro in March to go over financial accounts and develop campaign strategy, Castello Branco gave a speech in which he said that "pressure" had placed the Democratic Crusade in a situation that was "difficult and unequal." He also attacked the "untruthful propaganda" of the Yellow Slate: "They say that the candidate of the Crusade is a a *golpista* and a traitor, and that we want to control the directorship of the Military Club in order to carry out business deals." Amidst applause, he called on members of the Democratic Crusade to reply to "these accusations" by means of their "honorable and honest work." General Manoel Henrique Gomes, president of the Conselho of the Directório Central of the Democratic Crusade, told the gathering that despite all of the

[4] Schneider, *Political System of Brazil*, p. 370.

[5] HACB reply to communication of War Minister Lott, May 29, 1958, File L1, CPDOC.

[6] HACB to War Minister Lott, August 21, 1958, File L1, CPDOC. According to this letter, Joaquim Justino Alves Bastos said that Malvino Reis must be "amigo de fora do General Lott e não de coração" (not a "friend of the heart" of Lott).

[7] HACB to Paulo V. Castello Branco, Rio de Janeiro, May 25, 1958, File L1, CPDOC.

difficulties, including the lack of financial resources, obtained exclusively from voluntary contributions of Military Club members, the crusade was finding great support all over Brazil.[8]

The campaign brought Castello into daily contact with Colonel Golberi do Couto e Silva, coordinator of the effort of the Democratic Crusade.[9] To Golberi and Castello it became evident that the Yellow Slate was receiving the greater financial assistance. Humberto, writing to his son Paulo, said that Captain Janari Gentil Nunes, president of Petrobrás, supplied eight hundred thousand cruzeiros to the Yellow Slate, and that the São Paulo Federation of Industries also contributed handsomely. Plenty of money seemed to be available to cover the traveling expenses of the agents of the Yellows. Furthermore, Humberto complained, the positions of these officer-agents were such that their campaign work was detrimental to the proper functioning of the army; "our own agents," Humberto said, were "limited to the very young or the retired, in order that Army service not be neglected."[10]

But the principal concern of the Democratic Crusade was the pressure that it thought it saw exerted by officers who had been assigned important command posts by Lott. As the campaign entered its last days, Humberto was convinced that "the pressure, here in Rio, attained a depth and intensity that was unprecedented. Regimentation became an order, and threats were openly declared, . . . with Lott heading this activity and the pressure. . . . I never imagined that the pressure would be so strong. Corruption entered the military camp."[11]

The result of the election was not known until the votes came in from around the nation late in May. They showed 8,972 votes for the Yellow Slate and 7,697 votes for the Blue Slate.[12]

The result, Golberi do Couto e Silva says, was bitter for Castello.

[8] "Repele acusações o gal. Castelo Branco," *O Estado de S. Paulo*, March 21, 1958. A *golpista* is one who favors a coup.

[9] Golberi do Couto e Silva interview, Brasília, October 22, 1975.

[10] HACB to Paulo V. Castello Branco, May 25, 1958, File L1, CPDOC.

[11] Ibid. See also Viana Filho, *O Governo Castelo Branco*, p. 41.

[12] Newspaper clipping, File L1, CPDOC, about the visit of General Segadas Viana to advise War Minister Lott of the victory of the Yellow Slate. J. Justino Alves Bastos writes in *Encontro com o Tempo*, p. 307: "While strongly contested, the election was carried out in an exemplary manner. Over 7,000 members went to the urns, and our victory was by a margin in excess of 2,000 votes."

"It was not so bitter for us. We had lost often, and so we had developed thick skins," Golberi adds.[13]

Castello, exhausted and his thoughts "in turmoil from the recent events," attended briefly the Military Club session at which the Yellows were declared victorious. With distaste he watched while Justino Alves Bastos, "accompanied by his wife and several women in the main room, put on a 'veritable show,' amidst applause and picture taking." Castello refrained from congratulating the new club president, for he considered his "low behavior" responsible for personal attacks made during the campaign.[14]

8. A Reprimand from Lott (June, 1958)

Castello Branco, proud to feel that he and the other Democratic Crusaders had conducted themselves ethically during the campaign for election in the Military Club,[1] decided to protest against the "corruption" practiced by his opponents. Therefore he issued a note to the press in which he conceded "with melancholy" the success of a slate that had "used propaganda to become known, for illegitimate purposes, as the slate of General Lott."[2] To support his contention that many who had been prepared to vote for the Blue Slate had been "in danger of reprisals," Humberto quoted from an article that had appeared on May 22, the day of the election, in a newspaper that he described as being "intimate with the military power." According to this article, "many officers, serving in posts of confidence but favoring the Democratic Crusade, today are going to have to disclose their positions or else refrain from voting, for informers will not allow anyone to get by without an annotation."

Castello Branco's note to the press brought him a formal communica-

[13] Couto e Silva interview, October 22, 1975.

[14] HACB to Paulo V. Castello Branco, May 25, 1958, File L1, CPDOC.

[1] HACB to Paulo V. Castello Branco, Rio de Janeiro, May 25, 1958, File L1, CPDOC.

[2] "Declaração do candidato azul: Apesar da pressão aberta, 7697 oficiais discordaram da chapa do General Lott" (Despite the open pressure, 7,697 officers opposed the slate of General Lott), from *Jornal do Brasil*, clipping attached to War Minister Lott's communication 085-D2 to HACB, May 27, 1958, File L1, p. 19, CPDOC.

tion from War Minister Lott, dated May 27, 1958. Lott instructed Castello to advise whether or not he was responsible for the press release; in case of an affirmative answer, Castello was told to clarify what he meant by "reprisals," by "military power," and by "informers" who recorded voting preferences.[3]

Castello, acknowledging authorship of the note to the press, wrote Lott that an example of the "reprisals" had been the transfer of the commander of Fort São João simply because, during a debate, he had declared that he would vote for the Blue Slate. Castello said that he understood "military power" to mean, in the army sector, the War Ministry and the top echelons subordinated to it. He added that the newspaper that he had quoted boasted of such intimacy with the military power that its reporter on military matters claimed to be influential in bringing about promotions for those below the rank of lieutenant who were, "according to his expression, Lottistas." Castello admitted that he had "at the moment" no evidence to prove the use of "informers" to note voting preferences of Military Club members, but he defended his right to entertain the possibility of their having existed.[4]

Lott's decision on what to do about Castello Branco was made known in a long letter addressed to him on June 7, 1958. In it the War Minister explained that he had taken into consideration Castello's possible state of fatigue. He had therefore written on May 27 for information, thus giving Castello an opportunity to "make amends" for having expressed false statements to the press in a discourteous manner. But, Lott added, Castello had not appreciated, or availed himself of, this opportunity. Instead, he had mentioned the transfer of the Fort São João commander—a transfer that Lott said had been due to behavior which, while related to the election question, was unbecoming to the barracks. Besides Lott observed, even if Castello's allegation about the transfer had some basis, it was not logical to suppose that a single case, out of 7,697 votes, justified the generalization made by Castello.[5]

Criticizing Castello's transcription of "insinuations" from a newspaper, Lott concluded that Castello's public declaration fell short of the standards of discretion incorporated in the military rules. Besides, Lott

[3] Lott communication 085-D2 to HACB, May 27, 1958, File L1, p. 19, CPDOC.

[4] HACB reply to Lott, May 29, 1958, File L1, CPDOC.

[5] War Minister Lott communication 101-D2 to HACB, June 7, 1958, File L1, CPDOC.

wrote, it violated regulations by contributing to discord between comrades and by seeking to discredit superiors, equals, and subordinates.

Lott explained that he would not hesitate to classify Castello's "failure" as "serious" were it not for the consideration that he felt he should
give to Castello's notable contributions to the army and the nation during forty years of service in war and peace. As war minister, he said, he
had to "watch over the dignity" of "outstanding leaders" who would
soon be in the top commands. He therefore decided to classify Castello's
"transgression" as "moderate," thus allowing the punishment to be restricted to "the reprimand, which I now issue to you." [6]

In July Castello fell ill with what appeared to be jaundice and was
admitted to the army hospital. Therefore not until August 21 did he
send Lott a reply—one that he said he was not making public. In it he
called his reprimand unjust, and he accused Lott of having insulted him
by criticizing his "standards of discretion" and by alleging that he had
contributed to discord. "I conducted myself all during the campaign,"
Castello wrote, "in an elevated manner. . . . My commander and comrades at the Escola Superior de Guerra can testify that I did not control
a single vote, nor want to know (as I do not yet know) who did not
vote for the slate to which I belonged." On the other hand, Castello
wrote, the "condemnable practices" of the members of the Yellow Slate
were well known throughout the armed forces.[7]

For the good of the army, Castello advised Lott, it was best not to
bring up the "lamentable episodes" that had contributed to the climate
in which the Military Club election had taken place. "For me it is a
page turned over, a page left behind."

"But," Castello concluded, "the scar that remains with me is the
result of the judgment that Your Excellency made of my conduct and
of my person." He pointed out that if Lott felt it his duty, as he said,
to watch over Castello's dignity, he had not been guided by that feeling
when he had judged him responsible for creating discord in the army.
Castello denied that frivolity, or some hidden purpose, had led him to
give his note to the press late in May about the outcome of the Military
Club election.[8]

[6] Ibid.
[7] HACB to War Minister Lott, August 21, 1958, File L1, CPDOC.
[8] Ibid.

9. The Cancellation of a Dinner (December, 1958)

In the ordinary course of events, Castello was due to be promoted to *general de divisão* on August 25, 1958. However, as that date approached, rumors from the War Ministry indicated that Castello's name would be passed over.[1]

Castello's nervousness on the eve of the twenty-fifth was extreme, and it was shared by his friends, among them General Ademar de Queiroz, Colonel Waldetrudes Amarante, and Colonel Mendes da Silva, and by his devoted aide, Captain Edmar Eudóxio Telesca. Those who sought to comfort Castello told him that the denial of his promotion, besides being a thoroughly political act, would be such a dishonor to an authentic army leader that it would have enormous unfavorable repercussions.[2] Apparently these considerations prevailed, because on August 25 Castello's promotion was made known.

About the end of August Castello was back in the hospital, this time for a gall bladder operation to cure the trouble that he had been having. With the operation about to be performed, his friends learned that he was to be appointed military commander of Amazônia and of the Eighth Military Region, with headquarters in Belém, Pará. This fulfillment of Lott's statement of November, 1955, ("You will be transferred to command in Pará") was considered by some of Castello's friends as a sort of "exile" assigned to Castello, a vindictive act by Lott.[3] They decided to keep the news from Castello lest it upset him just before the operation. But when Castello was about to be wheeled into the operating room, a sergeant-nurse, who had learned of the Amazônia appointment and thought that it must be good news, gave the information to the patient.[4]

Castello, following the operation, went with Argentina to relax in São Lourenço, Minas Gerais. From there the sixty-one-year-old general wrote to Colonel João Carlos Gross to thank him for some papers. "Here I am in full recuperation and gathering strength to become commander

[1] Telesca, "Depoimento," p. 5.
[2] Ibid.
[3] João Carlos Gross and Osvaldo G. Aranha interview, Rio de Janeiro, October 2, 1975.
[4] Telesca, "Depoimento," p. 5.

of Amazônia," Castello said. He described Lott ("the person on the ninth floor" of the War Ministry) as having "the most unusual talents: if he was, before, dumb and of narrow vision (*bitolado*), now he has acquired an intellectual position and has demonstrated spiritual values. . . . Today he is known as the democratic savior of democracy." Castello observed that all of this would be more interesting if the war minister's new intellectual position had been brought about "by nature or conviction." Commenting also on Gross's having been passed over in what should have been his promotion to general, Castello said that the matter could only be understood by bureaucracy. "Although I do not understand why you are not given the position that you deserve, I continue to consider you very intelligent. . ."[5]

Escola Superior de Guerra commander Vasco Alves Secco, who had been Kubitschek's first air force minister, issued the customary formal praise of the departing assistant commander, mentioning his "solid general and professional education, on a par with his constant interest in the problems of national security."[6] More emotional were the farewell words of Colonel José Lindenberg, delivered on September 25, 1958, to a gathering in a conference room of the ESG. Lindenberg recalled the innumerable times that he and his colleagues had met "in this room" to receive Castello's orders, missions, and directives. He spoke of Castello's democratic way of analyzing missions with his associates and of his custom of always giving "each person a part of the responsibility and effort." After stressing that Castello had been ever vigilant in upholding dignity, character, and merit, the colonel touched on a contemporary concern: "moments disturbing to military discipline and to the cohesion of the armed forces." Castello, he concluded, had demonstrated the knowledge and authority necessary "to indicate the correct path to those who let themselves be led astray. In the fact of demagogic, discord-producing charges by suspect groups, he does not vacillate in the realm of ideas or in any other realm."[7]

Castello hoped to fly to Belém with Argentina before the end of September. But a return to confinement in the hospital postponed the

[5] HACB to Gross, São Lourenço, 1958.

[6] Folhas de Alterações," File G3, second semester, 1958, CPDOC.

[7] José Lindenberg, typed pages, Rio de Janeiro, September 25, 1958, File G1, CPDOC.

trip until December. The new confinement also caused the postponement until the evening of December 8 of a dinner at the Santos Dumont
Airport Restaurant planned in his honor by officers of the armed forces
and ESG instructors and alumni. Castello, reluctant at first to attend
such a dinner, agreed to do so when he became convinced of the "generous and elevated intentions that inspired its sponsors." [8]

Key administrators of the War Ministry (which now included Brayner as army chief of staff) appeared to be as worried as those of the
other miltiary ministries about the possible influence of important officers who were considered "discontented." [9] The offering of lunches or
dinners in honor of such personalities was not to be lightly regarded if
the chief authorities made their objections clear. Under such circumstances a luncheon given in 1957 to honor air force Colonel João Adyl
de Oliveira, investigator of the Major Vaz shooting, had had profound
political and military repercussions that included the fall of Kubitschek's
second air force minister, Henrique Fleiuss.

Word reached Castello Branco that the dinner scheduled to be given
in his honor was regarded by one of the military sectors as a "conspiracy." Therefore on December 2 he wrote the commission that had organized the dinner to advise that it should not take place. Lest his decision in the face of the "new development" be misunderstood, Castello
explained that it did not represent conformity on his part to the idea of
those who had misinterpreted the objective of the dinner. What most
concerned him, he told the commission, was a desire not to cause difficulties for any of his comrades. [10]

Without publicity, eight or ten close army friends of Castello, among
them Ademar de Queiroz and Antônio Carlos da Silva Murici, gave him
a farewell luncheon at a restaurant in Botafogo. [11]

---

[8] HACB to Dr. Ithamar Vasconcellos, Colonel Itiberê Gouveia do Amaral, Lieutenant Colonel Edmundo Neves, Comandante Berutti, and Major Arnizant Matos, Rio de
Janeiro, December 2, 1958, transcribed in "Homenagem ao General HACB—Cancelamento" (see File L1, p. 28, CPDOC).

[9] Brayner became army chief of staff in October, 1958 (Floriano de Lima Brayner
to JWFD, October 14, 1975).

[10] HACB to Dr. Ithamar Vasconcellos et al., December 2, 1958, transcribed in
"Homenagem ao General HACB—Cancelamento."

[11] Antônio Carlos da Silva Murici interview, Rio de Janeiro, November 18, 1975.

10. Depressing Days in Amazônia (1959)

On December 10, 1958, Humberto and Argentina reached Belém, the headquarters of an army command that was mostly to its west and that covered 52 percent of Brazil's territory.[1] During their first five months, Argentina said in a letter to Hélio and Edith Vianna, they awaited "the arrival of the heat, with the end of the great rains that go on until late May."[2]

Castello's letters made it clear that he was "by no means an exile" but was "fulfilling a completely regular role."[3] The role called for traveling—at least one long trip per month—to fourteen widely scattered garrisons such as those at Manaus (on the Amazon), Clevelândia (in Amapá Territory), Boa Vista (in Roraima Territory), and distant Tabatinga and Ipiranga. To reach the frontier troops at Tabatinga, adjacent to Peru and Colombia, or those at Ipiranga, near the border of Colombia, Castello had to make a trip that equaled the span between Belém and Rio de Janeiro.

The immense problems of commanding so extensive an area were reduced, Castello found, by the cooperation that he received from Fourth Naval District commander Ernesto de Melo Batista and First Air Zone commander Armando Serra de Menezes, who were also stationed in Belém and who provided "very pleasant companionship" as well as assistance. Air force planes regularly visited Castello's fourteen garrisons; the navy fleet, he wrote Colonel Waldetrudes Amarante, carried "tons and more tons for me to Oiapoque (Clevelândia), Manaus, Tabatinga, etc."[4]

A more serious problem was mentioned in this letter to Amarante: "Nobody wants to come to Amazônia, and the government (???) no longer has the authority to send anyone." Of the thirty-two officers assigned to his Belém headquarters, Castello wrote that twenty-four had gotten their assignments changed, five had not shown up, and, of the remaining three, two had left on account of illness! Almost all of his staff, Castello added, was "frantic to return" from Belém. "In the troops

---

[1] HACB to Waldetrudes Amarante, Belém, November 28, 1959, File L1, CPDOC.
[2] Argentina to Hélio and Edith Vianna, Belém, May 6, 1959, File D, CPDOC.
[3] HACB to Waldetrudes Amarante, November 28, 1959, File L1, CPDOC.
[4] Ibid.

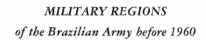

MILITARY REGIONS
of the Brazilian Army before 1960

First Army area includes 1st and 4th regions
Second Army area includes 2d and 9th regions
Third Army area includes 3rd and 5th regions
Fourth Army area includes 6th, 7th, and 10th regions

Map 4

the problem is also grievous. The companies do not have seconds-in-command, and some of them are under lieutenants in apprenticeship with the CPOR."[5] His fiscal agent, Castello complained, was a captain, called up from the reserve, who had two investigations on his back, the first resulting from an accusation of fraud and the second due to his having three wives.

Another problem was created by doctors in Manaus who sold exemptions from army duty as well as pajamas belonging to the hospital. Castello opened proceedings against them.[6]

For the army and for the nation the outlook seemed rather cheerless to Castello. "We are," he wrote Amarante, "in a crucial period for the Army. Everything is demoralized: a decrepit organization, and a roster of generals made up of some thick-skinned individuals and a number of good younger men who are very tired (tired for what reason?). They think that time waits for us. But events are moving faster than the thinking of this illustrious company." Pointing out that "a reorganization, a profound rebuilding," of the army was needed, Castello suggested that Amarante and other younger officers were the appropriate ones to bring it about, but he added a warning: "Do not forget that you and others will have to confront military corruption, generated by accommodation, incapacity, adulation, the enjoyment of immoral privileges, and fear—fear of opposing the predominance of power."[7]

Reflections on having entered his sixties brought reminiscences of the past and thoughts about old age. "Time marches steadfastly ahead," Humberto wrote his sister Beatriz, "and the worst is that we march in the same cadence." Making plans for the family to gather in Campo Maior at the end of June, 1960, to observe the one hundredth anniversary of their father's birth, Humberto recalled the "simplicity and modesty" of General Cândido Castello Branco. Especially Humberto felt a deep longing for his mother, "so full of spirit and affection for us . . . , always in poverty, resignedly helping Papai and heroically wanting to educate us. I cannot forget—37 years have passed—the 29th of June, 1922, the afternoon when I saw her for the last time in the house at Visconde de Itamarati Street, being cared for by you and Nina, with

[5] CPOR: Centro de Preparação de Oficiais da Reserva, roughly equivalent to the ROTC in the United States.
[6] HACB to Waldetrudes Amarante, November 28, 1959, File L1, CPDOC.
[7] Ibid.

such limited resources. Although much time has passed and I am already old, I still feel myself in the last embrace and kiss that we exchanged." [8]

Argentina, Humberto told his sister, was "a companion more priceless than ever before, in tough and difficult Amazônia." However, Humberto could not fail to observe that the hardship came as a shock to his sensitive wife. "I face the adversities," he told Amarante, "as though I were in combat. Argentina, I see, accepts them without complaining, enduring them discreetly. I trust in God that this effort which, with resolute spirit, my wife gives to support me in a moment that is not one of the best, will be crowned, for the two of us, by a happy situation, even if it be in the Reserve." [9]

Describing his future as "very uncertain," Humberto wrote Amarante that he was considering retiring to the army reserve. "I do not see the way open for a good final period of my military life. Probably until the end of 1960 I can examine possibilities before making a decision. I want to work, and work well to the last day of active service. But already I am thinking a good deal about avoiding an upsetting and puny final period." [10]

11. Accomplishments in Amazônia

Edmar Eudóxio Telesca, the only officer to accompany Castello from Rio to Amazônia, feels that the Amazônia mission was the most difficult undertaken by Castello after the one in the FEB. In his letter to Waldetrudes Amarante, Castello said that sometimes at the end of the day he would reach his residence with the feeling that he was going to flag. But, he added, although everything was difficult, it was his habit to return to the struggle "with his old vigor." [1]

Writing in a similar vein to Hélio Vianna, Castello said that the military life, and the decisions he was called on to make, were very hard. "Some days I have the impression that I am going to lose heart, espe-

[8] HACB to his sister Beatriz, Belém, June 30, 1959, File B, CPDOC.
[9] HACB to Waldetrudes Amarante, November 28, 1959, File L1, CPDOC.
[10] Ibid.
[1] Telesca, "Depoimento," p. 7; HACB to Waldetrudes Amarante, November 28, 1959, File L1, CPDOC.

cially when I encounter here the effects of the inflamed commotion in the War Ministry by the Marshal of the 'Sword of Gold,' and feel his desire to disparage me." But Humberto told his brother-in-law that he would relax momentarily and then plunge ahead.[2]

When a message from the War Ministry advised that Lott planned to visit Belém and stay at the official army residence used by the military commander of Amazônia, Castello, acknowledging receipt, let it be known that he would make use of a hotel at that time. A reply from the War Ministry said that the proposed visit was simply under study, and that if it were made, Lott would use a hotel.[3]

"Castello Branco," Navy Captain Euclides Quandt de Oliveira observes, "was a strict disciplinarian in Amazônia and never mentioned openly his unhappiness about the Brazilian situation or his feeling about Lott. His goal was to be a good commander of the region."[4] Quandt, an electronics expert who was director of the Merchant Marine Officer School in Belém, worked with Castello's staff in the latter part of 1959 to help Castello realize a dream: a joint maneuver of the army, navy, and air force in the Amazon area—the first one to be carried out there in ten years.[5] When the maneuver took place in November, 1959, Quandt commanded some of the ships.

The joint maneuver came about after Castello convinced Admiral Melo Batista and Brigadeiro Serra de Menezes of its value, and the result was a testimony to the good relations among the three commanders. Elsewhere admirals and *brigadeiros* were feuding over the control of the planes on the aircraft carrier *Minas Gerais*, and admirals were disdaining to work with generals, a situation reflected in the refusal of some navy officers to serve green olives, whose color reminded them of army uniforms. The success of the joint maneuver gave Humberto something on the positive side to report to Waldetrudes Amarante: "There were large movements in the rivers, operations in the jungle, etc."[6]

Together with the joint maneuver, Edmar Eudóxio Telesca lists other accomplishments that he witnessed. Instruction, he says, was "substantially improved." And so was the performance by the frontier units.

[2] HACB to Hélio Vianna, Belém, September 3, 1959, File L1, CPDOC
[3] Aurélio de Lyra Tavares interview, Rio de Janeiro, July 25, 1977.
[4] Euclides Quandt de Oliveira interview, Brasília, October 21, 1975.
[5] Telesca, "Depoimento," p. 7.
[6] HACB to Amarante, November 28, 1959, File L1, CPDOC.

These, previously pretty much restricted to the areas around their barracks, were sent out on patrol missions, maneuvers, and reconnaissance trips so that they gained considerable knowledge of the territory. Castello, always emphasizing that the soldier could play a useful role, regardless of isolation and a lack of funds, used boats and planes to be everywhere. Before he left his command in April, 1960, he spent about 530 hours in air travel in Amazônia.[7]

One of Castello's tasks was to receive a congressional commission that was investigating "the problem of the establishment of a United States industry in the Jari Valley."[8] In his office Castello listened to some of the congressmen, including Almino Afonso (PTB, Amazonas), expound on the evils of having foreign enterprise operate in the area. Castello asked if any of the congressioal investigators, who were present or not present, had ever sought to bring about a project of the sort that was being discussed. Upon receiving a negative response, Castello launched into what Edmar Eudóxio Telesca says was "one of the most complete sermons" that he ever heard. It ended with a statement: "You gentlemen prefer that poverty and misery continue to exist in the area and are reminded of them only when someone, with reasonable profits in mind, takes the initiative to do something." That remark quickly ended the meeting and the work of the commission in that region.[9]

12. Quadros Visits Belém (January, 1960)

Humberto found the government of Amazonas state deep in "ridiculous demagoguery."[1] Expecting that 1960, a presidential election year, would be "highly agitated," Castello did his best to prevent his subordinates from becoming involved in electoral incidents.

With Lott the PSD-PTB candidate for president, Castello advised Amarante that "the days ahead are going to be difficult because the War Ministry has become a large political party center, an open organ of electoral propaganda, and a perfidious checker of who is against and who is in favor." In a letter to Lieutenant Colonel Edmundo Neves, long

[7] Telesca, "Depoimento," p. 7.
[8] Ibid., p. 8.
[9] Ibid.
[1] HACB to Waldetrudes Amarante, Belém, November 28, 1959, File L1, CPDOC.

a close associate of Cordeiro de Farias, Castello said that never in his forty years of military life had he seen so much regimentation of this sort.[2]

For Humberto and Argentina it was a disappointment to find that San Tiago Dantas supported the slate of Lott for president and João ("Jango") Goulart for vice-president. "I understand San Tiago Dantas less and less," Argentina wrote Hélio Vianna. "Such an intelligent man should not bow, as he does, before a Jango. What a pity!" When Humberto wrote to Hélio Vianna, he had Lott on his mind: "The man who, according to our San Tiago, is going to command workers and soldiers, has given the Army a sad alternative: courtier or slave. I have never had the disposition to be a courtier, and this is especially true now that I am old and am certain that it is best not to be a lackey. Slave?"[3]

After reading that Bishop Hélder Câmara had conferred for two hours with Lott, Humberto asked his sister Beatriz whether "the saintly little man from Ceará" sought to expel the hound from the body of the "strong man" and bless him.[4] He added that the only way really to handle the "low behavior of the sword of gold" was to use the broom—the symbol employed by opposition presidential candidate Jânio Quadros, who offered to sweep out corruption.

Jânio Quadros, an authoritarian and apparently temperamental administrator, had served a successful, if somewhat turbulent, term as governor of São Paulo and then in 1958 had been elected federal congressman from Paraná on the PTB (Labor party) ticket. His dramatic campaigning attracted multitudes, and even before he was nominated for the presidency by a small political party in April, 1959, Carlos Lacerda urged that the UDN also nominate Quadros.

All over the republic Janistas were displaying miniature brooms in September, 1959, when Castello Branco reached Rio for his holidays. The general made the courtesy call on War Minister Lott that was expected of region commanders, but the visit did not turn out to be the usual hour devoted to exchanging impressions. It lasted for only fifty seconds and thus provoked considerable comment by those occupying the waiting room. Castello's aide, Edmar Eudóxio Telesca, was about to

2 Ibid.; HACB to Edmundo Neves, Belém, September 3, 1959.
3 Argentina to Hélio and Edith Vianna, Belém, May 6, 1959, File D, CPDOC; HACB to Hélio Vianna, Belém, September 3, 1959, File L1, CPDOC.
4 HACB to his sister Beatriz, Belém, June 30, 1959, File B, CPDOC.

pay his compliments to Lott's aide when he suddenly discovered that Castello was already out of Lott's door, having completed what he believes was "the most rapid presentation ever witnessed during my military life." But Telesca may not have been surprised, for already he had come to find that "even in matters that were of little importance—such as the designation of assistants, the request for an automobile, or the issuance of invitations"—Lott always "summarily" ruled against Castello.[5]

These matters of "little importance" were not really so little, for, as Henrique G. Müller, then a colonel, has pointed out, Lott's "doing everything to handicap Castello" added to the reasons why officers decided to decline assignments in Belém.[6] When Müller, who had studied under Castello at the ESG, surprisingly accepted a transfer to Belém from a mission in Washington, D.C., Castello and Argentina went out of their way to fix up a house for the Müllers and to organize a "reception committee."

Castello, his visit to Rio completed, was back at his command post in November, 1959, when Quadros, overcoming some opposition by Juraci Magalhães, received the UDN nomination for president. Having become the principal election opponent of Lott, Quadros undertook a strenuous campaign. Orating in Belém on January 14, 1960, he violently attacked the widespread corruption, the government of Pará, and the Bank of Amazônia. Petrobrás, Quadros added, was just "playing" at searching for petroleum in Amazônia. "How many drillings does it have in the immense area of 3,300,000 square kilometers?" he asked and then declared theatrically, "Six, only six!"[7]

Major Jarbas Passarinho, superintendent of Petrobrás in Amazônia, belonged to the Military Club sector that favored Quadros' candidacy, but he felt compelled to prepare a note correcting the candidate's gross factual errors and defending, as anything but playful, the work of his six thousand employees, some of whom had lost their lives in the search for petroleum. The note, taken to Quadros before the candidate's radio interview of the fifteenth, was apparently well received, but when Quadros went on the air he used emotional language to ridicule the "second-rate" superintendent of Petrobrás, who, he grandly asserted,

[5] Telesca, "Depoimento," Rio de Janeiro, April 24, 1976, p. 5.
[6] Henrique G. Müller interview, Rio de Janeiro, July 25, 1977.
[7] Jarbas Passarinho interview, Brasília, November 11, 1975.

might think he was dealing with a candidate but was really dealing with the president-elect. Passarinho then placed an open letter in the local press that included correct statistics, appropriate technical observations, and a reminder that Quadros' furious reaction to the note was reminiscent of Hitler's style. Mentioning his own background, Passarinho said that although he had opposed Lott's coup of 1955, Lott had never taken a step against him and had, in fact, asked him to help the War Ministry with his knowledge of Amazônia.[8]

Quadros, leaving Belém on the sixteenth, dashed off a note to Castello Branco in which he referred to the "uncalled for" incident "provoked" by Major Passarinho. "I do not understand," Quadros wrote, "how a man who is any good could write, with manifest political purposes, the letter that I read today in the press of Belém. It doesn't matter. Let us move ahead. Count on me, General, and count on my admiration."[9] Quadros thanked the "noble and courageous" general for the attentions shown him in Belém.

From his headquarters Castello phoned Passarinho about the open letter. There were, Castello said, only two organs that "do not carry out politics in Amazônia": the command headed by Castello and the organization headed by Passarinho. Castello expressed annoyance at the good things that Passarinho had written about Lott. He could not, he said, agree with them.[10]

13. Aragarças

Early in December, 1959, Castello's longtime friend Colonel Luís Mendes da Silva participated with a few air force officers in a small rebellion at Aragarças, near the border of Goiás and Mato Grosso states. The rebels declared that force and corruption, ruling the nation, had brought about an unparalleled state of disorder, and they looked to a military junta to replace "fictitious legality" and do away with "demogogic laws," the misuse of public funds, and Communist infiltration in

8 Jarbas Passarinho, "Carta Aberta ao candidato Jânio Quadros," *A Província do Pará*, January 16, 1960.
9 Jânio Quadros to HACB, Grande Hotel, Belém, January 16, 1960, File L1, p. 38, CPDOC.
10 Passarinho interview, November 11, 1975.

and out of government.[1] The outbreak led Quadros to declare that "even the greatest courage, even the purest ideals," could not justify insurrection.[2]

After the ineffectual revolt had been quelled quickly by forces loyal to Lott, Castello commented on it in a letter to Lieutenant Colonel Nilton Freixinho:

The episode of Aragarças is one more shove that we received down the inclined plane on which the armed forces are skidding. Idealism, possibly. But, besides being inept, it represents an error of vision—the mistaken belief that Brazil cannot improve within the constitutional regime. Only and only within the Constitution, I believe, as I have always believed. A revolution is made only within an ideology and when there is a strong current of public opinion to carry it forward. Brazil does not want a barrack uprising, nor a revolution, at least in the present period.

As a consequence of the rebellion of Luís Mendes da Silva and Haroldo Veloso, the worm-eaten backstage of the Palace of War and its press take me for a rebel. Only with infamies can they combat my person.[3]

At the end of January, 1960, Castello received an *ofício* from the War Ministry, signed by his Porto Alegre and Realengo classmate, General Estevão Taurino de Resende Neto, asking about his possible involvement in the Aragarças rebellion. General Taurino, delegated by Lott to investigate, made a weak case against Castello. He presented confused bits of information and misinformation received from a rebel air force major who had spoken with several men, one of whom, possibly a conspirator, claimed to have "ties" with Castello. According to the reports, Castello had been prepared to act against a coup by Lott, had planned an army–navy–air force maneuver in November, and had declined to be Quadros' running mate so as to remain at his military post.[4] The *ofício* also referred to a document, apparently sent to Rio conspira-

---

[1] Manifesto of the "Revolutionary Command," *Correio da Manhã*, December 4, 1959.

[2] *Correio da Manhã*, December 4, 1959.

[3] HACB to Nilton Freixinho, Belém, December 23, 1959, File L1, CPDOC. Air Force Lieutenant Colonel Haroldo Veloso had once received military school instruction from Luís Mendes da Silva.

[4] Estevão Taurino de Resende Neto, Ofício 18-IPM to HACB, War Ministry, Rio de Janeiro, January 22, 1960, File L1, p. 38v, CPDOC.

tors by some Belém air force officers, which estimated that a rebellion would be supported by 5 to 10 percent of the air force, whereas a reaction against a pro-Lott coup would be supported by 95 percent. This document said that if the first-mentioned alternative, that of rebellion, were undertaken, "we would have to arrest or detain General Castello Branco until he decides in our favor."

The *ofício*'s request for information provided Castello with a splendid opportunity to comment on the pro-Lott movement. In reply, Castello wrote that ever since 1956 he had heard officers of the three armed forces and civilians speak in favor of a movement for a "Lottist military dictatorship," it being clear that groups of "extreme Lottists" pressurized national politics, making of the official candidacy a military candidacy and thus acting in an "illegitimate manner."[5] Castello acknowledged that invariably he had made known his opposition to a movement for a Lott dictatorship and had said that he would participate in a military reaction against it.

Castello described the Amazônia military maneuver of 1959 as "highly professional and instructive," and he suggested that a "scurrilous distortion" had perhaps been given to the word "maneuver." Turning to the report that he had been invited to be Quadros' running mate, Castello called it "absurd" and "nothing but nonsense." Finally, Castello discussed the document apparently sent to Rio conspirators; it simply proved, he said, that he opposed not only a coup by extreme Lottists but also a coup by the other side—to such an extent that its supporters felt that he would have to be arrested.[6]

These statements of Castello Branco went without reply from the office of the war minister. Nor did the office waste time looking into Castello Branco's possible involvement in another, small, unsuccessful revolt that took place much closer to Castello Branco's headquarters at the same time as the Aragarças revolt. This "far leftist" movement, which occurred in Belém and elsewhere in the far north and momentarily controlled the important Santarém airport, clearly appeared to have no connections with Castello Branco. Its handful of sponsors called on laborers, peasants, and young military officers to use "the tac-

[5] HACB memorandum to Estevão Taurino de Resende Neto, January 28, 1960, File L1, CPDOC.
[6] Ibid.

tics of Fidel Castro" to overthrow "corrupt and traitorous Brazilians."
Castello Branco, after a thorough investigation, punished two army
captains.[7]

On February 16, 1960, when Castello completed his official report
about this strange revolt in the far north, Lott was no longer war minister. Preparing to campaign for the presidency, Lott had turned over
his cabinet post to First Army commander Odílio Denys, an admirer of
Castello.[8] Most of the Aragarças rebels, having by then found asylum in
Buenos Aires, were earning a living at menial chores, such as dishwash-
ing. Luís Mendes da Silva had become a stevedore.[9]

In April, 1960, Castello was transferred to the Army Staff as director of the instruction of cadets (*diretor do ensino de formação*). When
he and Argentina took their leave at the Belém airport on the sun-
drenched morning of April 23, they were surrounded by a large crowd
of affectionate well-wishers with whom they had lived and worked for
almost a year and a half.[10]

Captain Edmar Eudóxio Telesca, who was to continue serving as
Humberto's aide, brought with him to Rio memories of happiness experienced by Castello in the north. "At the parties and receptions, in life
at home, and on the platforms," he writes, "Dona Argentina was a
radiant figure, and the pleasure that this gave her husband was very
moving to see." Telesca liked to recall pleasant evenings that he and
his wife spent with the Castello Brancos in Belém: "General Castello
reading in a hammock, Dona Argentina sewing at his side, Lucia and I
conversing at a nearby table, with soft, lulling music around us."[11]

Due to Castello's transfer in April, 1960, he and Argentina flew
from Rio, rather than from Belém, when making the sentimental trip to
Piauí to observe the one hundredth anniversary of his father's birth on
June 30. With Humberto's brothers and sisters, Humberto and Argentina visited the simple house in Campo Maior where General Cândido

[7] *O Estado de S. Paulo,* July 6, 1961. See also statement of Colonel Hugo Delaite
given in testimony of José Chaves Lameirão (declaration at the Twenty-fourth Criminal
Court, Guanabara State, regarding Processo 9,899), May 8, 1961.

[8] Telesca, "Depoimento," p. 8.

[9] Haroldo Veloso interviews, Marietta, Georgia, January 6, 7, 1966.

[10] Telesca, "Depoimento," p. 8.

[11] Ibid., p. 11.

had been born, and they attended Mass in the little church where he used to go. The municipal chamber of Campo Maior held a ceremony at which Humberto was named honorary citizen of the town.[12]

[12] Piauí, Campo Maior Municipal Chamber, Act 605, formal session, June 30, 1960, File B, CPDOC.

VIII

The Cold Warrior
(1960-1963)

Mediocrity is dominant. We are a giant nation governed by dwarfs—and have been for a long time.

1. Director of Instruction in the Army Staff (1960–1962)

WHEN Castello Branco went to work for the Army Staff in April, 1960, the army chief of staff was Floriano de Lima Brayner. However, in his post of *diretor do ensino de formação*, which required traveling to visit the *colégios militares*, Castello reported for the most part to the general director of instruction. This chain of command may have suited him just as well, for in one of his last letters written from Italy to his wife he had expressed the hope that he would not have to serve in Brazil as an assistant to Brayner.[1]

At the end of January, 1961, Castello was among those who, at the invitation of War Minister Odílio Denys, went to Brasília, the new federal capital in the interior, to attend the inauguration of Jânio Quadros as president of Brazil and the inauguration of "Jango" Goulart to serve a second term as vice-president.[2] Early in this new administration Castello was moved a notch ahead, becoming general director of instruction, which put him in contact wth the more advanced and specialized schools of army instruction. At about the same time, Brayner left the Army Staff, for he was named by President Quadros to be a minister of the Superior Military Tribunal.[3]

[1] HACB to Argentina, Alessandria, June 13, 1945, File H2, p. 83, PVCB.

[2] "Folhas de Alterações," File G3, first semester, 1961, CPDOC. It was not necessary to vote for the presidential and vice-presidential candidates of the same political party. Quadros had been nominated for president by the UDN and some smaller parties. Goulart had been nominated for vice-president by the PSD and PTB, which had supported Lott for president.

[3] Floriano de Lima Brayner to JWFD, Rio de Janeiro, October 14, 1975.

Castello's high hopes for a good new presidential administration, with much use of the broom, were shattered in August, 1961. Quadros, on poor terms with Congress, provoked a heated public debate about his "independent" foreign policy, which promised to give Brazil closer relations with the Soviet Union and Cuba, and then he suddenly resigned the presidency with the remark that "confidence and tranquility, already broken but indispensable for exercising my authority, cannot be maintained."

If Quadros believed that a popular clamor in his favor, together with the military ministers' dislike of Vice-president Goulart, would trigger his immediate return to office, better able than before to bring about the reforms he wanted, he was mistaken. Although the military ministers vetoed the succession of Goulart in the presidency (with a warning that it would mean the transformation of the armed forces into "simple Communist militias"), most of the public clamor was raised on behalf of legalidade and the rights of the vice-president under the Constitution. Lott called for upholding the Constitution and was therefore locked up in a Rio fortress on the orders of the military ministers. Goulart's friends in organized labor also called for legalidade. And Goulart's brother-in-law, Rio Grande do Sul Governor Leonel Brizola, put his state on a war footing to fight for legalidade. After Third Army commander José Machado Lopes gave his backing to Brizola and legalidade, thus defying the military ministers, civil war seemed possible.

The crisis was settled early in September, 1961, when Congress amended the Constitution to give Brazil a parliamentary form of government in which the powers of the president were supposed to be much restricted. The military ministers then allowed Goulart to take office.

However, with the selection of the first Council of Ministers, worked out by Goulart and other politicians, it became evident that the influence of Goulart was considerable. The prime minister, Tancredo Neves, was the choice of Goulart and Kubitschek, who was eager to be elected president in 1965 and who therefore shared Goulart's hope that the parliamentary system would not be of long duration. The new military ministers, described as "men of Goulart," included War Minister João de Segadas Viana, an opponent of the recent military veto against Goulart. Goulart's close friend Amauri Kruel, chosen to head the presidential Casa Militar, had also opposed the veto.

While evidence accumulated that the parliamentary system, with a president unsympathetic to it, was ineffective, the rate of inflation continued to increase. Goulart, conferring much with labor leaders, seemed to his foes in the military to be intent on turning Brazil into a "*república sindicalista.*" In December, 1961, pro-Goulart labor leaders, the ones who favored cooperation with the Communists, won control of the National Confederation of Workers in Industry (CNTI), Brazil's largest labor confederation. At ceremonies installing the new CNTI officers, the president and the prime minister of Brazil shared the spotlight with Francisco Julião, Marxist leader of peasant leagues in the northeast. "Cuba, Cuba, Cuba" was the frenzied response to Goulart's well-received speech defending an "independent" foreign policy for Brazil.

These events plunged Castello Branco into renewed pessimism. During a vacation early in January, 1962, in Campos do Jordão, in São Paulo state, Castello expressed some of his feelings in a letter to João Henrique Gayoso e Almendra, whom he had taught at Realengo in the late 1920's and had commanded on subsequent occasions. "You say," Castello wrote, "that you are 'melancholic and apprehensive.' That is the psychological state of all patriots like yourself."[4] Castello told João Gayoso that the "parliamentary solution" (enacted by Congress in September, 1961) had been simply a step to deal with a momentary situation (the opposition of Quadros' military ministers to Goulart), and that the "grave" national crises, "the economic, financial, and military crises," continued. "Mediocrity is dominant," he wrote, "We are a giant nation governed by dwarfs—and have been for a long time." Noting João Gayoso's remark about "divisions" in the military, Castello promised to send him from Rio a copy of his recent speech given at the ECEME.[5]

In Rio, Castello decided to call on his old friend San Tiago Dantas, who had become the leading brain truster of the PTB and was now the foreign minister. As head of the Brazilian delegation at Punta del Este in January, 1962, San Tiago Dantas had criticized the anti-Castro position of the United States; his defense of Cuba was bringing him the hearty applause of Brazilian nationalists, Communists, and organized students and workers, but it worried Castello.

Because San Tiago Dantas was on a mission abroad, Castello was

[4] HACB to Gayoso e Almendra, Campos do Jordão, January 3, 1962, File L1, CPDOC.

[5] See section 3, "Military Duty," below, this chapter.

received instead by Acting Foreign Minister Renato Archer, a politician from Maranhão. He told Archer that he detested the idea of Castro's "popular tribunals" for judging people. Archer explained to the general that on the previous evening, when dining at home with Graham Greene, he had asked the visiting British author: "How can you, an Englishman, support Castro?" Greene had replied that he had known Cuba during Batista's rule, when there had been no justice whatsoever, and that Castro had brought about an improvement. Castello, not much mollified by this report, expressed again his distaste for Castro's "popular tribunals": "It revolts me to see people condemned with no recourse to normal judicial channels. People should be able to count on the hope which justice provides."[6]

2. Books in Castello's Library

Castello's reaction to the deteriorating political and economic situation was to analyze it with care in order to formulate for army men a policy that he hoped would be useful to Brazil. He was stimulated by his responsibilities as general director of instruction for the army and by his long interest in political matters and in the role of the military.

Castello brought to bear on the subject a background of ideas built up from a vast amount of reading. His shelves were filled with serious books, their pages often well underlined and their margins often replete with signs of approval or disapproval and with occasional question marks and comments. Only a very few of the books that he had marked were fiction: *Mississipi*, a posthumous novel about Ceará by Gustavo Barroso; *A Beata Maria do Egito*, a play about the northeast by his good friend Rachel de Queiroz; and *Luzia-Homen*, a novel (originally published in 1903) by another Cearense, Domingos Olímpio Braga Cavalcanti. José de Alencar's *Iracema* was usually kept within easy reach.

Many of the books, it is true, had no direct bearing on the pronouncement that Castello prepared as a guide to army officers worried about the ideological question late in 1961, for he had accumulated numerous specialized studies about military strategy, about Brazilian military history (including the FEB), and about the Brazilian northeast and

[6] Renato Archer interview, Rio de Janeiro, September 30, 1975.

its literature. But a large number of the general's books, written in Portuguese and French, were aimed at solving the great problems of society. In those that commented on recent Brazilian political history, such as *A Crise do Poder no Brasil*, by Guerreiro Ramos, Castello's marginal observations showed his dislike of the Vargas dictatorship and "the military candidacy'" of Lott. In books that were of a more general nature, Castello liked to underline bits of wisdom, such as Bernard Baruch's statements about liberty requiring self-discipline, Alceu Amoroso Lima's biblical quotation about man being born unto trouble (just as surely as sparks fly upward), and L. J. Lebret's admonition against taking a position before having full knowledge of the question.[1] Castello carefully noted the sentences in which Lebret wrote that "what the world most lacks today, in all areas, is the man who is able to grasp the totality of the problem. At times some such men appear, but they are not authentic. They did not begin with a detailed analysis. Either they lack the necessary training, or they forget the human element. All this is necessary at the same time."

In brief, Castello's pencil markings in his books revealed a thorough dislike for Communism and an almost equally harsh judgment of anti-Communist conservatives who put selfishness ahead of improving the lot of the common man.

Underlinings, check marks, and vertical margin lines called attention to Baruch's statement that "the Communist creed preaches openly that the people are not to be trusted to manage their own affairs," Lebret's observation that "Communism, not understanding man, is compelled to mistreat man," and Fulton J. Sheen's remarks about Communism (it "ignores the personal rights of man") and about totalitarianism (it "denies the value of a person").[2]

Castello read carefully an account of "the evolution of Communism in Brazil" in Padre Agnelo Rossi's *A Filosofia do Comunismo*, and he heavily marked a concluding statement (p. 122): "Fortunately there still exists in Brazil an Army, fully aware of its dignity, the vigilant guardian of the glorious traditions of the Nation. That Army knows the

[1] Bernard Baruch, *Uma Filosofia para o Nosso Tempo* (translation of *A Philosophy for Our Time*), p. 64; Alceu Amoroso Lima, *O Trabalho no Mundo Moderno*, p. 31; L. J. Lebret, *Princípios para a Ação*, tr. Carlos Pinto Alves, chap. 5.

[2] Baruch, *Uma Filosofia para o Nosso Tempo*, p. 65; Lebret, *Princípios para a Ação*, p. 26; Fulton J. Sheen, *O Problema da Liberdade*, chap. 7; Fulton J. Sheen, *Filosofias em Luta*, p. 32.

history of Communism in Brazil." In one of the works of Lenin in his library,[3] Castello wrote: "The Communist Party in Brazil is illegal, it lives clandestinely and it recommends a struggle for legality. It disparages the legitimacy of the government." Alongside a passage in which Nelson Werneck Sodré (*Introdução à Revolução Brasileira*) referred to isolationism of the USSR (p. 216), Castello jotted, "And 1935?" in reference to the year in which the Communists carried out their unsuccessful rebellion in Brazil.

Castello's check marks and vertical lines called attention to paragraphs, especially two of them, in Gustavo Corção's *Patriotismo e Nacionalismo*. One spoke of the grave danger of the world when "totalitarianism and its correlate, nationalism," take hold in a strong country and pointed also to the evils of a more limited "domestic nature," when "totalitarianism and its correlate, nationalism" are found in weak countries like Portugal and Brazil. The other paragraph concluded: "Before public opinion, the anti-Americanism motivated by socialist postulates comes dangerously close to the anti-Americanism stimulated by xenophobia and by collective resentment." In a sentence that Castello underlined, Corção wrote that "in the ideal of progressive socialism, there is a certain irresistible inclination toward totalitarianism."[4]

As for democracy, Castello used his pencil to call attention to Jacques Maritain's statement that "democracy in America is based on a solid and clearly recognized sentiment of the dignity of the common man." This dignity, according to passages underlined by Castello in other books, was not recognized by the conservative class and the capitalists. In one of these passages Lebret wrote that "capitalism . . . thinks that justice can only be on its side; having money, it believes that it can do anything." Perhaps Castello's heaviest use of the pencil stressed the arguments set forth by Fulton J. Sheen for giving workers a participation in company profits. Page after page of Sheen's reasoning, including a quotation from the encyclical *Rerum Novarum*, was underlined, check marked, and given added emphasis by double and triple vertical lines in the margins.[5]

[3] V. I. Lenin, *Le Socialisme et la Guerre*.

[4] Gustavo Corção, *Patriotismo e Nacionalismo*, pp. 27, 33, 37.

[5] Jacques Maritain, *Princípios de uma Política Humanista*, tr. Nelson de Melo e Souza, p. 49; Lebret, *Princípios para a Ação*, p. 26; Sheen, *O Problema da Liberdade*, pp. 112–120.

3. "Military Duty"

Ideas developed while reading were reflected in the speeches that Castello Branco gave at the advanced army schools during the closing exercises in December, 1961. The speech that he presented at the ECEME was issued for distribution in mimeographed form with the explanation that it would be impossible for the author to address all of the schools. Bearing the timely title of "Military Duty in the Face of the Ideological Struggle," it pointed out that the army continued "to suffer from the consequences of the recent political crisis" and that "contradictory ideas about legality, Communism, and the role of the Armed Forces abound."[1]

The opening paragraphs praised democracy for recognizing the dignity of man and condemned totalitarianism for suppressing fundamental rights. Democratic ideology, Castello said, sought to supply the greatest good to the greatest number and aspired to international peace. Communist ideology was pictured as creating a single class in order later to abolish it. "It seeks the existence of human beings absorbed by the state and permanently affiliated with the Soviet Union. It preaches the domination of the world" and "is an ideology not spread by propaganda alone. It is imposed by interventionist processes, by pressure, violence, terror, and revolutionary war."[2]

Castello warned that the Communist ideology was preached with stubbornness and energy, often by fanatics, and had penetrated university and intellectual circles. The democratic ideology, he said, had some devoted admirers along with timid and vacillating followers, and others who avoided the risks of struggle. Finding that the democratic ideology was often limited to an anti-Communist movement or was confused with a defense of capitalism, he argued that it should affirm its elevated human, philosophical, and political concepts. It should not "lose itself in the interests of capitalism" when those interests were disconnected from "the interests of the national community and the well-being of the people."

---

[1] HACB, "O Dever Militar em Face da Luta Ideológica: Palestra proferida a 15 de dezembro de 1961, na ECEME" (typewritten), p. 1. The speech, with slightly different wording, has been printed in HACB, *Marechal Castello Branco: Seu Pensamento Militar*, pp. 213–222.

[2] HACB, "O Dever Militar em Face da Luta Ideológica," p. 4.

Castello stated that the two antagonistic ideologies were in a global conflict, and he added that anyone failing to recognize this conflict lived in isolation from the world and neglected Brazil. Discussing "revolutionary war," a Communist tool for winning the conflict in non-Communist countries, Castello quoted Lenin's advice that a good way to prepare for such wars was to divide the armed forces.[3]

Turning to Brazil, Castello commented on the writings of Professor Guerreiro Ramos, who cited two opposing tendencies: the *entreguista* ideology and the "nationalist" ideology.[4] It was difficult, Castello said, to agree with those who called the democratic ideology *entreguista*, and the Communist ideology "nationalist," but, "In any case, the professor sees the Armed Forces as ideologically divided, and many civilians and some military men believe that he is right."

Castello asserted that he, personally, did not support this view, for while the army had some Communists in its ranks, they made up a small minority. But he admitted that it was impossible to avoid, in military circles, repercussions stemming from two occurrences: the ideological conflict among civilians, and the "distance" spreading between "personalistic capitalism" and the great areas of poverty in Brazil.[5]

This second occurrence, Castello said, caused a legitimate anxiety, "a conviction of the need of the advent of social justice—not a matter of electoral statements or demagoguery." Castello found a growing understanding that the Right was not solving "the Brazilian case," that the extreme Left would sink Brazil in chaos and servitude, and that the Center always wanted to temporize, leading to stagnation.

According to this growing understanding, Castello said, the solution to Brazil's acute problems could be found in the Left.[6] But, he emphasized, this state of affairs did not amount to an ideological struggle in the army: "It is a process of mental evolution, carried out peacefully, no doubt connected with the political and social evolution of Brazil, and is, really, a defense against the onslaughts of Communism in the military area."

What was needed, Castello said, was a clarification for officers, to-

[3] Ibid., p. 6.
[4] *Entreguista*: a Brazilian said to be working to turn Brazil or Brazil's assets over to foreigners.
[5] HACB, "O Dever Militar em Face da Luta Ideológica," p. 7.
[6] Ibid.

gether with a firm enunciation of the democratic ideology. But as such a clarification and enunciation had been lacking, political party struggles had spread to the military sphere, and the repercussions of the ideological conflict had gotten out of hand. Communists had turned these repercussions into "divisions" by "stimulating the appetites" of military officers who were courtiers of politicians.[7] Castello said that these politicians and the Communists were the only ones to derive advantages from a divided army, and he accused them of having insulted the army by picturing its officers as divided, first, between "nationalists" and *entreguistas*, and, most recently, between *legalistas* and *golpistas*.

Castello (who had been called a *golpista* during the 1958 Military Club election campaign) tried to throw some light on the so-called nationalism and legalism of the Brazilian Communist Party (PCB), always "under the control of Moscow." After the party had lost its legality, Castello said, it had offered votes to politicians in return for deals and compensation, the politicians becoming dependent on the Communists. It had affiliated itself with an anti–United States nationalism, so that "now, the part of the ideology of Brazil that ought to be concerned with our economic interests sees itself exploited and perturbed by the Soviet game in the international arena."[8] The PCB had declared itself "furiously legalistic," apparently suspending for a time the revolutionary option in order to infiltrate all sectors of Brazil and control armed forces posts and commands by masquerading as the defender of the legal regime. Discussing future Communist conduct, Castello said that it would never give up the struggle to achieve the Communist state, the advent of which, he added, would not result from a popular decision but from a coup or a revolutionary war.

Castello expressed a poor opinion of what he called "short-range anti-Communism," and he emphasized "the immense value of a vigorous and active ideology" in the struggle against Communism. Turning to the army, he discussed what the reactions should be to a whole "range of manifestations." He said that men who read and meditated on Communist ideology, as an educational pursuit, could be helpful to army commanders. They were, he said, making use of an elementary right, as were those who delivered commentaries after they read. But if the commentaries seemed "exaggerated" it was the duty of the command to

[7] Ibid., p. 8.
[8] Ibid., p. 9.

seek to "improve the position" of the subordinate. In turn, Castello dealt with more serious cases, in which it was imperative for the command to apply the military penal code.[9]

Castello said that in a democratic nation the acceptance of any idea constituted an "elementary right," and he further maintained that to participate in a revolution was "a legitimate recourse." However, he said, members of the military who put the preaching of Communism ahead of their commitment to defend the nation's institutions ought to abandon the armed forces. And if they did not, they should admit the "legality and legitimacy" of reactions against them and "even the nobility" of efforts made to change their way of thinking, because, Castello pointed out, lack of unity in the army opened the way for "the expansion of militialike or praetorian tendencies."[10]

In conclusion, Castello called on the highest army leaders to reestablish unity by reinvigorating the military spirit, by developing instruction, by acting with responsibilty and authority, and by clarifying the ideological struggle.

4. Nationalism (1962)

During 1962, while the annual inflation rate advanced to about 50 percent and while the prestige of the "parliamentary government" collapsed, Castello Branco made more speeches that touched on timely topics. The old warrior continued to lash out against Communism, whose influence seemed to be growing among the leaders of organized students and labor.

Castello is said to have been one of the first Brazilian army officers to denounce "revolutionary war" as a Communist weapon.[1] "Revolutionary war," he warned in 1962, "is a class struggle, fundamentally ideological, imperialistic, seeking the conquest of the world; it has a doctrine, the Marxist-Leninist doctrine." Explaining that "revolutionary war" was a threat to weak nations and a disturbance to all democratic regimes, Castello called it a weapon of the cold war.

[9] Ibid., p. 11.
[10] Ibid., pp. 12, 13.
[1] "Castello: Os Archivos do Marechal Revelam um Militar Revolucionário e Liberal," *Veja*, April 5, 1972, p. 44.

According to Castello, the cold war "was conceived by Lenin in order to advance . . . the world Soviet revolution." It was, he said, an undeclared global war carried out in accordance with a plan of conquest that sought to excite enthusiasm and fear. Listing the objectives of the Lenin-conceived cold war, he mentioned the division of national and international opinion, the creation of indecision, and, principally, the extinction of the capacity of nations to struggle.[2]

Castello, who considered himself devoted to "legality" and "nationalism," was displeased by the use made of these terms by the Brazilian Communists. Communist party Secretary General Luís Carlos Prestes, who in 1960 had called Lott "the natural candidate of the nationalists," extolled "nationalism" almost daily and above everything else. The Brazilian Communist leader, following Moscow policy, was seeking to organize a "nationalist united front" that would include the Brazilian bourgeoisie, capitalists, and large landowners to struggle against "North American imperialism" and its Brazilian "agents," the *entreguistas*.[3] Pleased with the formation of a Nationalist Parliamentary Front in the Brazilian Congress, Prestes praised the "nationalist and democratic" movement in Cuba, and in December, 1961, he cheerfully predicted that Brazil would follow the Cuban path.[4]

Castello Branco, visiting São Paulo in May, 1962, delivered a paper, "Nationalism in Underdeveloped Nations," in which he pointed out that nationalism was not a panacea for the ills of a nation and warned of its serious defects in underdeveloped countries. It was, he said, likely to be used entirely apart from a realistic appraisal of the circumstances and served at times as a "national and international instrument of Soviet Communism." Besides, he found it to be great banner for the ambitions of dictators and would-be dictators.[5]

These comments did not prevent Castello from praising what he considered authentic economic nationalism. "Development without na-

---

[2] Ibid.

[3] Luís Carlos Prestes quoted in *Correio Paulistano*, May 19, 1959, and in *Novos Rumos*, July 29–August 4, 1960. See also *Jornal do Brasil*, April 14, 1960, and article on the expulsion of Amazonas, Grabois, and others from the PCB, in *Novos Rumos*, December 29, 1961.

[4] Luís Carlos Prestes declarations to the press upon returning to Brazil early in December, 1961, following a trip to the Soviet Union and the People's Republic of China.

[5] "Castello," *Veja*, April 5, 1972, pp. 40, 45.

tionalism," he declared, was "perverted work, separated from the primacy of the national interest." Going on to discuss his ideas in some detail, he made it clear that he was no advocate of complete freedom for foreign investments. He argued that underdeveloped nations should discipline capital from abroad, establishing, in the case of each investment, conditions that would assure a suitable collaboration with the goals of the host country and regulating both profits and their remittance abroad. He mentioned also the advisability of establishing proper arrangements to govern the acceptance of foreign aid and the need to avoid "obstinate protectionism" for manufacturing plants in developing nations. He urged periodic corrections to tariffs lest excessive protection result in unreasonable prices and a lack of "honesty in national manufacture." [6]

Castello defended the establishment of state-run organizations for the purposes of fostering "pioneer undertakings" and directing enterprises that were closely related to the national security. Choosing petroleum as an example, he said that the industry, unless guarded by the state, would fall into the hands of the trusts before full production would be reached because private capital was hardly ever available without the prospect of immediate profits. He added that the trusts considered the time factor only from the point of view of their own interests and not as an "imperative of the development of an underdeveloped country." [7]

5. Life in Recife

On July 25, 1962, Castello Branco was promoted to the four-star rank, *general de exército*, and on September 13 he was named commander of the Fourth Army, with headquarters in Recife, replacing his Porto Alegre classmate Artur da Costa e Silva. Costa e Silva, a suave trooper who had become *general de exército* as early as November, 1961, was known for liking poker and disliking Leonel Brizola (Goulart's radical leftist brother-in-law), and his transfer from Recife to a Rio desk job, director of army personnel, was frequently attributed to his

6 HACB, "O Nacionalismo nos Paises Subdesenvolvidos," Castello Branco papers, Escola de Comando e Estado Maior, Praia Vermelha, Rio de Janeiro.
7 Ibid.; "Castello," *Veja*, April 5, 1972, p. 40.

dislike.[1] At about the time that this change in the Fourth Army occurred, another Porto Alegre classmate made the news: Amauri Kruel became war minister although his rank was only *general de divisão* (three stars).

A pleasant four-and-one-half-hour flight brought Humberto and Argentina to Recife on September 26, and on the next day Humberto took over the command from Costa e Silva.[2]

In Recife Humberto and Argentina found themselves in the midst of heated campaigning for the October 7 elections. While the whole country was about to choose federal congressmen, governorships were being contested in some states, among them Pernambuco. There, far leftist Miguel Arraes de Alencar was in a tight gubernatorial race against the UDN's João Cleófas. "Humberto," Argentina wrote her father on October 1, "will not lack work, because everyone is stirred up with the approach of the elections. Yesterday the electioneering ended, but still we sometimes see parades of students, who yell 'Arraes! Arraes!' It seems that the two principal candidates are very close, with a slight edge in favor of the victory of Cleófas. This year we shall not vote. The nation is going to lose good and conscientious votes."[3]

Castello, who had always voted the UDN ticket, wrote later in the month to Waldetrudes Amarante to tell of the defeat of the UDN at the hands of Arraes.[4] And in Guanabara state, the voting residence of Humberto and Argentina, the far Left won another important victory when Brizola received more votes than had ever before been cast in Brazil for a federal congressman.[5]

In her letter to her father, Argentina advised that she had brought her cook from Rio, "a perfect solution." She went on: "We have a very spacious house, with good verandas and large grounds. It is not the way

[1] Nelson Dimas Filho, *Costa e Silva: O Homen e o Líder*, pp. 53–54; João Adyl de Oliveira interview, Rio de Janeiro, December 20, 1965. In 1962 Leonel Brizola, governor of Rio Grande do Sul, was running for federal Congress from Guanabara, the geographically small state that replaced the former Federal District in 1960, when the federal capital was moved from Rio de Janeiro to Brasília.

[2] Argentina to Arthur Vianna, Recife, October 1, 1962, File D, Part 1, CPDOC.
[3] Ibid.
[4] HACB as president quoted by Oscar Dias Corrêa in interview, Rio de Janeiro, September 24, 1975; Aliomar Baleeiro, "Recordações do Presidente H. Castelo Branco" (typewritten), p. 17; HACB to Waldetrudes Amarante, Recife, October 19, 1962, File B, CPDOC.
[5] Thomas E. Skidmore, *Politics in Brazil*, p. 230.

I would like it, because it is located between the barracks and the schools of the university. Facing us is the Law School, right in the middle of May 13 Square."

Under Argentina's supervision the cook from Rio prepared dishes that featured local seafoods, and at Sunday lunches and on numerous evenings the dishes delighted the guests, who often included Castello's chief assistant, Major Gustavo Morais Rego Reis; Castello's aide, Captain Anysio Alves Negrão; and Arminda, Negrão's wife. Following the meal, during a period of relaxation with coffee on a veranda, Castello would serve a liqueur, and he might reminisce about thc Clevelândia frontier troops and incidents that occurred during his days in Amazônia. The general, likely also to comment on current events, one evening told his after-dinner guests that the Kennedy administration's decision to appoint Kubitschek coordinator of the Alliance for Progress was a "disastrous" one.[6] More than once on the veranda Castello praised the character and efficiency of Ademar de Queiroz, who was then in Rio commanding Coastal and Antiaircraft Artillery.

When asked about democracy, Castello said that it did not reflect, simply, the right to vote, but also had to do with a philosophy of life and the desire of every person to improve himself, finding his place in society. Recalling his own struggle up the ladder, Castello said that he had never mentioned to his commander or anyone the financial and other hardships experienced as a young Realengo instructor, and he added that young officers and soldiers no longer felt the same concern about resolving their problems themselves but considered them matters for the commander and even the army itself.[7]

When the guests gathered on a veranda of the Castello Brancos' Recife residence, the tendency was for the men and women to separate into two groups, but Castello, always enthusiastic and usually gallant in his talk with the women, would sometimes remark that he was staying with the ladies, finding them "more interesting." In his discussions with the men Castello revealed no great fondness for "yes-men," but rather an enjoyment of verbal dueling; with his irony he continued to make his friends laugh. His appearance had somehow improved with the weight that he had put on since middle age, and some observers saw an inspired

[6] Anysio Alves Negrão diary, November 17, December 2, 1962, File I, CPDOC.
[7] Ibid., February 5, March 6, 1963.

face, not an ugly one. Although he had never participated in sports, he had kept himself very fit and, unlike many older generals, had not developed a paunch. His bearing was very military.

Argentina never told her husband what to do. She simply helped him with her sensible, wise opinions and occasionally calmed him with her "HUM-berto." Sandra Cavalcanti, who saw much of Argentina and Humberto before they went to Recife, describes Argentina as "wonderful, sweet, knowing, and courageous." Another of Argentina's many admirers was Virgílio Távora, whose inauguration as governor of Ceará was attended by Humberto and Argentina in March, 1963. Távora feels that Argentina not only inspired her husband but had much to do with developing the polish that he showed in society.[8]

Like many a resident of Recife, Castello was fond of taking new arrivals for drives through scenic parts of the picturesque city and nearby Olinda while he commented on the history of the region. He enjoyed being present at gatherings of intellectuals at Pernambuco University, and there he became a great admirer of Gilberto Freyre. After one university meeting he remarked: "Each day a new facet of Recife and Pernambuco appears. Today I saw a monument of culture." [9]

Usually Argentina accompanied her husband on his inspection trips. In Natal, on such a trip, the couple dropped in one evening at the residence of Brigadier General Antônio Carlos Murici, infantry commander of the Seventh Infantry Division. Finding Murici disciplining his children, Argentina, joking, said that his manner was appropriate for a lieutenant or, at best, a captain. From that day on, Humberto, given to the playful use of nicknames, liked to refer to the general as "Capitão Murici." (Humberto had been calling Sra. Senna Campos the "*fazendeira*," or ranch owner, ever since he and Argentina learned one day in Rio that she was about to leave for her country place in Friburgo.)[10]

[8] Contributing to the thoughts expressed in this and the preceding paragraph were Virgílio Távora (interview, October 22, 1975), José Jerônimo Moscardo de Souza (interview, October 23, 1975), João Batista Barreto Leite Filho (interview, November 25, 1975), Sandra Cavalcanti (interview, November 18, 1975), and Antônio Carlos da Silva Murici (interview, November 18, 1975).

[9] Negrão diary, November 18, December 26, 1962; January 10, 1963, File I, CPDOC.

[10] Murici interview, November 18, 1975; Aguinaldo José Senna Campos interview, Rio de Janeiro, November 26, 1975.

On quiet evenings at the Recife residence Humberto read about the northeast and its military history or joined Argentina and a few friends to watch television—especially when he could see the program *Você Faz o Show*. But Humberto and Argentina were frequently out, calling on the families of Humberto's subordinates and accepting some of the invitations to lunches, teas, and dinners. Occasionally Humberto and Argentina, helping themselves to sweets, attended the cocktail parties given by Pernambuco officials.[11]

Like Admiral Arnaldo Toscano, commander of the Third Naval District, and Brigadeiro Silva Gomes, commander of the Second Air Zone, Castello Branco paid a courtesy call on outgoing Governor Cid Sampaio on the last day of 1962, and with him went "Capitão Murici" and Brigadier General Augusto César Moniz de Aragão, chief of staff of the Fourth Army. But Castello was careful not to attend functions that might be considered political. For this reason he declined, early in January, 1963, a lunch given in honor of anti-Goulart Congressman João Calmon, of the Chateaubriand newspaper chain.[12]

Castello decided that he would also rather not attend the inauguration, on January 31, of Governor Miguel Arraes. However, he had to change his mind because of a message from the presidential Casa Militar naming him Goulart's representative; so, after spending the whole morning worrying about the prospect, he struggled with multitudes to gain admittance to the legislative assembly and the Palácio das Princesas. More relaxed after it was over, Castello exchanged impressions with some of his officers about the "violent" inauguration speech of the new governor.[13] "He described the atmosphere that he had found," General Murici recalls. "He said that he was preoccupied with what he had seen."[14]

When Carnaval time arrived, in February, 1963, Humberto, Argentina, and their military friends sat in animated groups at the dances sponsored by the municipality of Recife and the Clube Caxangá, staying up one night until 4:00 A.M.[15] Occasionally, but not often, the commanding general danced with his still-beautiful wife.

[11] Negrão diary, December 11, 1962; January 27, 1963.
[12] Ibid., January 9, 1963.
[13] Ibid., January 31, 1963; Murici interview, November 18, 1975.
[14] Murici interview, November 18, 1975.
[15] Negrão diary, February 16, 23, 1963.

6. A Joint Maneuver against Guerrilla Warfare (November, 1962)

In his letter to Amarante, Castello said: "The Fourth Army is difficult and, at the same time, absorbing. I am going to employ all that remains of the strength that I gathered as a boy in Ceará, helped by my parents (how long ago!), nostalgic for the classroom of the blessed sisters of Pequeno Grande and for the fun of playing on the sidewalks ..., and in Messejana."[1]

It was a disappointment for Castello to find that in the year before his arrival in Recife, army maneuvers in the northeast had been cancelled by Costa e Silva, who had cited a shortage of funds. Despite the shortage, Castello planned maneuvers for the third week of November, 1962, in which the theme was to be "revolutionary war" and the emphasis placed on dealing with possible guerrilla movements. Together with this innovation, Castello produced something new for the area when, as in Belém, he persuaded the district commanders of the navy and air force to make it a joint maneuver. He went even further; he obtained the participation of the state police forces.[2]

João Carlos Palhares dos Santos, chief of staff of Third Naval District commander Toscano, was struck by the rather weak participation of the navy in comparison with that of the air force, which brought in reinforcements, and especially with that of the Fourth Army, whose large staff, headed by General Moniz de Aragão, was augmented by specialists sent from Rio. The navy, its admirals in Rio concentrating in an isolated manner on antisubmarine warfare, seemed to be neglecting large geographical areas as well as work against subversion, all of which, Palhares felt, must have made a poor impression on Castello.[3]

The army also provided Castello with some disappointments. As he liked to do, Castello introduced the unexpected in order to stimulate initiative; to units outside of Recife he sent officers bearing documents with make-believe situations for local commanders to handle as a part of the

[1] HACB to Waldetrudes Amarante, Recife, October 1, 1962, File B, CPDOC.

[2] João Carlos Palhares dos Santos, "Depoimento sôbre a Minha Convivência com o Presidente Humberto Castello Branco, Prestado ao Seu Historiador, Dr. Luiz Vianna Filho," São Paulo, December 1971, File R2, p. 21, CPDOC; Murici interview, November 18, 1975; Murilo Gomes Ferreira, "O General Castello Que Conheci," Part 6, "Comando do IVº Exército: Recife" (transcript of tape prepared for interview), Rio de Janeiro, November 12, 1975.

[3] Palhares dos Santos, "Depoimento sôbre Minha Convivência."

maneuvers, and the results often revealed more perplexity than mental preparedness.[4]

During the week of the maneuvers, Castello, accompanied by Morais Rego, Negrão, and others, flew to João Pessoa, Paraíba, and, as was his custom during such flights, he sat in front with the pilot in order to nap undisturbed. In João Pessoa, where he spent a few hours, he gave the colonel commanding the 15th RI a severe lecture. The general's words, Negrão wrote in his diary, were "really fearful, but were just."[5]

Officers of the various armed forces gathered in Recife on Friday afternoon, November 23, for a well-prepared concluding session devoted in part to evaluations. After Castello spoke with self-assurance, officers came away with the feeling that the points made for opposing guerrilla warfare were useful. Negrão's diary records the remarks of an air force officer, who was greatly taken by Castello's intelligence, and a navy captain, who expressed satisfaction with the "aggressive spirit" imposed on the maneuvers by the "famous General Castello Branco."[6]

At times during the months that followed, the "famous general" showed himself even more irritated than he had been on the João Pessoa visit. In Maceió, Alagoas, on an inspection of the instruction, he was furious at what he considered the lassitude of the soldiers, both in action and in speech. "They do not know their jobs," he charged, and when a major tried to justify the situation, Castello became more upset than ever. Castello could not stand indolence. Witnessing yet another example of it a few days after his visit to Maceió, he denounced a group of army officers and clerks for their "mental anarchy."[7]

7. Castello Speaks to the Sergeants (December, 1962)

Diarist Anysio Alves Negrão, seeking to explain Castello Branco's "grumpy" (*"irritadiço"*) behavior in December, 1962, wrote of "political-military events in Rio."[1] There the General Command of Workers (CGT), recently organized by Communists and pro-Communists, was

---

[4] Ibid.
[5] Negrão diary, November 21, 1963, File I, CPDOC.
[6] Ibid., November 23, 1963.
[7] Ibid., December 19, 21, 1963.
[1] Negrão diary, December 22, 1962, File I, CPDOC.

Birthplace of Humberto de Alencar Castello Branco—Rua Solon Pinheiro 38, Fortaleza, Ceará.

Left. Cândido Borges Castello Branco, father of Humberto. *Right*. Antonietta Alencar Castello Branco, mother of Humberto.

Left. Young Humberto with his mother, sisters, and brother in Fortaleza, Ceará, late April, 1902. Antonietta Alencar Castello Branco is shown at the left as she appeared before the birth of her youngest child, Lauro. To the right of Beatriz, whom she is holding, are Nina (center of picture), Candinho, and Maria de Lourdes (far right). Humberto is in front of Candinho. *Right.* Humberto at the time of his first communion. Fortaleza, November 1, 1907.

Left. Sister Inês, teacher of Humberto in Fortaleza, 1907–1908. *Right.* The Colégio Militar of Porto Alegre, Rio Grande do Sul, which Humberto Castello Branco attended from 1912 to 1917.

Cadets at the Colégio Militar, Porto Alegre. From left to right: Milton Cezimbra, Artur da Costa e Silva, Nestor Souto de Oliveira, Humberto Castello Branco, Almerindo Silva, Pedro Marques da Costa, Floriano de Azevedo Faria, Adir Guimarães, not identified, Geraldo, not identified, Sadi Ayres, not identified, Décio Palmeiro de Escobar.

Dormitory at the Colégio Militar, Porto Alegre.

Classroom at the Colégio Militar, Porto Alegre.

A group of students at the Colégio Militar, Porto Alegre. *Standing, left to right*: Gabriel Mena Barreto, Edgar Alvares Lopes, Carlos da Silva Paranhos, Amauri Kruel, Humberto Castello Branco, Riograndino Kruel, and Sérgio K. Pereira da Costa. *Kneeling, left to right*: Antônio Fernandes Barbosa, Celso Mena Barreto, and Jurandir Palma Cabral.

Directorship of the Sociedade Cívica e Literária of the Colégio Militar, Porto Alegre, elected on October 26, 1916. *Seated, left to right*: Gabriel B. F. Mena Barreto, president, and Riograndino Kruel, vice-president. *Standing, left to right*: Almerindo Silva, librarian; Milton Cezimbra, first secretary; Humberto Castello Branco, official orator; Décio Palmeiro de Escobar, second secretary; and Amauri Kruel, treasurer.

Humberto Castello Branco and Amauri Kruel as students at the Colégio Militar, Porto Alegre. April 12, 1917.

The Castello Branco family residence, Rua Visconde de Itamarati 158, in the Tijuca district of the city of Rio de Janeiro, at the time that Humberto attended the Escola Militar in Realengo, 1918–1921.

Cearenses at the Escola Militar of Realengo. The tallest person in the middle row is Juarez Távora. Next to him (to the right in the picture) is Humberto Castello Branco. Further to the right (at the end of the row) is João Batista Rangel.

Left. Argentina Vianna. *Right.* Humberto and Argentina Castello Branco with Lauro, Humberto's younger brother.

Argentina, Nieta, and Humberto Castello Branco, 1923.

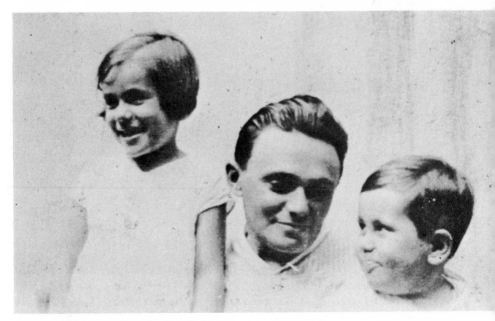

Nieta, Humberto, and Paulo Castello Branco.

The family of Arthur Vianna, Belo Horizonte, January, 1925. *Top row, left to right*: Arthur, Cherubina (Arthur's wife), Lourdes, Hélio, Argentina Castello Branco (holding her son Paulo), and Humberto Castello Branco. *On the first step*: João, Genuino, and Niso. *Bottom row*: Arthur Filho, Ivan, Eneida, Celina, Fábio, Nieta Castello Branco, and Lincoln.

Left. Humberto Castello Branco and João Hipólito da Costa. Hipólito da Costa was married to Humberto's sister Maria de Lourdes (Lourdinha), and it was at their home in Belo Horizonte that Humberto met Argentina Vianna in 1919. *Right*. Humberto Castello Branco, July 27, 1929, in his first year as a student at the Escola de Estado Maior do Exército (Army Staff School).

Humberto and Argentina Castello Branco.

Left. Castello Branco and Colonel Langlet of the French Military Mission to Brazil. *Right*. Captain Castello Branco in Curitiba, Paraná, 1935.

Humberto Castello Branco and his son Paulo aboard HMS *Arlanza* on the way to France in October, 1936.

Left. Aboard HMS *Arlanza*: Argentina Castello Branco with her maid, To-mázia, and her daughter, Nieta. *Right.* Fifty-five, avenue de Suffren, Paris, where the Castello Brancos occupied an apartment from 1936 to 1938.

Left. The Castello Brancos at the Vatican, 1937. *Right.* Infantry Captain Castello Branco and Artillery Major Nestor Penha Brasil at the Waterloo Monument, Belgium, 1938.

Argentina Castello Branco (left) and her children Nieta and Paulo in the Paris apartment, 1937.

Captain Castello Branco during a trip of maneuvers of the Ecole Supérieure de Guerre in France.

Argentina and Humberto Castello Branco in the outskirts of Paris, 1938. Their new 1938 Ford is in the background.

Teaching corps of the Escola Militar of Realengo, 1942. Major Castello Branco is at the bottom right.

Left. Castello Branco instructing at the Escola de Estado Maior do Exército (Army Staff School), 1939. *Right.* General João Batista Mascarenhas de Morais and his Brazilian Military Commission visit North Africa in December, 1943. Standing at the center is United States Army Captain Vernon Walters. Mascarenhas de Morais is seated the closest to Walters, and in the chair next to him is Medical Colonel Emanuel Marques Porto. Just above Mascarenhas de Morais is Lieutenant Colonel Ademar de Queiroz (under one of the overhead lights).

Brazilian troops departing for Italy from Rio de Janeiro, 1944.

On the high sea, July, 1944.

Above. Brazil's Day of the Soldier, August 25, 1944. Brazilian troops pass in review before, *left to right*, Generals Chadebec de Lavallade (former head of the French Military Mission to Brazil), Mark Clark (USA), and Mascarenhas de Morais (Brazil). *Below*, American Major Vernon Walters (tallest, in dark uniform), singing the Brazilian national anthem with Brazilian soldiers in Italy, 1944.

Generals Mark W. Clark (USA) and J. B. Mascarenhas de Morais (Brazil) in Italy, September, 1944.

Brazilian soldiers being greeted in Massarosa, the first Italian town they liberated, September 16, 1944.

General Mascarenhas de Morais (third from the left) and Colonel Floriano de Lima Brayner (sixth from the left) greeting some of the men who arrived in Italy with the Second and Third Detachments of the Brazilian Expeditionary Force, October, 1944. The new arrivals included General Osvaldo Cordeiro de Farias (second from the left), General Olímpio Falconière da Cunha (fourth from the left), and Lieutenant Colonel Ademar de Queiroz (fifth from the left). They are seen in one of the small landing craft (LCI's) that brought them to Livorno from Naples after the ocean crossing.

Encampment of the Second and Third Detachments of the FEB near Pisa, October, 1944.

Acting Chief of Staff Castello Branco, U.S. General Robinson Duff, and General Mascarenhas de Morais, January 15, 1945.

Castello Branco during the winter of 1944–1945 in the Apennines.

Left to right: Generals Euclides Zenóbio da Costa, João Batista Mascarenhas de Morais, and Osvaldo Cordeiro de Farias.

Brazilian mortar crew in action in Italy.

Left. The town of Montese, in northern Italy, taken by the Brazilians on April 14, 1945, in a display of great courage. *Right.* An armored car brings soldiers of the Brazilian Reconnaissance Squadron to a town where they are surrounded by Italians eager to hail their liberators.

Left. Lieutenant Colonel Castello Branco receiving the Bronze Star from U.S. General Lucian K. Truscott, Jr., while Major Vernon Walters (left) looks on. Alessandria, Italy, May 14, 1945. *Right.* Lieutenant General Willis D. Crittenberger, commander of the Fourth Corps. The photograph is inscribed for Castello Branco.

Castello Branco, in Italy in October, 1945, as a member of the Brazilian commission to visit the European theater of recent military operations, discusses tactics in the vicinity of Monte Castello.

Colonels Castello Branco, Penha Brasil (far right), and Bandeira de Melo (far left) with French officers in Europe in October, 1945.

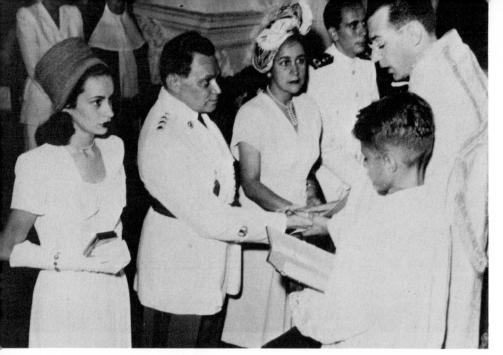

Humberto and Argentina observing their twenty-fifth wedding anniversary with their son and daughter, Rio de Janeiro, February 6, 1947.

At the Latin Quarter in New York, April, 1951. *Left to right*: Humberto and Argentina Castello Branco, Sra. and Colonel Potiguar, and Paulo V. Castello Branco.

Brigadier General Castello Branco, after taking command of the Tenth Military Region, visits with Raul Barbosa, governor of Ceará, in Fortaleza, November, 1952.

Left. Humberto and Argentina Castello Branco enjoy a visit to a ranch in Ceará, 1953. *Right.* The Castello Brancos at a dance in Ceará, 1953.

Brigadier General Castello Branco, commander of the Tenth Military Region, inspecting his troops.

Castello Branco presents a prize to an exhibitor of animals at a fair in Ceará in 1952. At the general's side (center, white suit) is State Agriculture Secretary Plácido Aderaldo Castelo.

Argentina and Brigadier General Castello Branco with a group of officers and their wives during the time he commanded the Escola de Estado Maior do Exército (Army Staff School), 1954–1955.

Left. War Minister Henrique Lott holds up the sheath of the sword of gold, while Vice-President João Goulart (smiling, at right) examines the sword itself. The small photographs on display are of Goulart. Rio de Janeiro, November 12, 1956. (Courtesy, *O Globo*) *Right*: Brigadier General Castello Branco delivering a lecture at the Escola Superior de Guerra (National War College), where he directed the Armed Forces Staff and Command Course, 1956–1958, and served as assistant commander and sometimes as acting commander.

Students and staff on a trip of the Escola Superior de Guerra. At the far left is Antônio Mendes Vianna, who in 1964 was named ambassador to France by President Castello Branco.

Reunion at the Nascimento Silva Street residence, Rio de Janeiro, in 1959. *On the step, left to right*: Maria Luiza Castello Branco (Paulo's wife, known as Nena), Carlos Humberto Diniz (oldest child of Salvador and Nieta Diniz), and Salvador Diniz. *Seated in chairs, left to right*: Argentina, Vernon Walters, Humberto, and Ivan Vianna.

General de Divisão Castello Branco while serving (1958–1960) as commander of Amazônia and the Eighth Military Region, with headquarters in Belém, Pará. Next to Argentina is Fourth Naval District Commander Ernesto de Melo Batista, who in 1964 was named navy minister by President Castello Branco.

Four alumni of the Realengo Escola Militar class of January, 1921. *Left to right*: Generals João de Almeida Freitas, Humberto Castello Branco, Ademar de Queiroz, and João Punaro Bley, about 1961.

General de Exército (four-star general) Castello Branco arriving in Recife with Argentina on September 26, 1962, to assume command of the Fourth Army. At his side is the preceding Fourth Army commander, Artur da Costa e Silva.

Castello Branco at ceremonies transferring Fourth Army command from Artur da Costa e Silva, September 27, 1962.

Fourth Army commander Castello Branco with his chief of staff, Brigadier General Augusto César de Castro Moniz de Aragão. A picture of Osvaldo Cordeiro de Farias, a former commander of the Fourth Army, hangs on the wall between Castello Branco and Moniz de Aragão.

Attending the Fourth National Congress of Philosophy at the University of Ceará, Fortaleza, November 10, 1962. At the far right is Castello Branco's older brother, Candinho. At the far left is Castello Branco's chief aide, Major Gustavo Morais Rego Reis.

The Fourth Army commander and his wife in Fortaleza.

Castello Branco with President João Goulart (center) and Pernambuco Governor Miguel Arraes (right) in Recife, July, 1963.

Castello Branco, chief of staff of the Brazilian army.

At Fort Copacabana late on the afternoon of April 1, 1964. *Left to right*: Castello Branco, General Hugo Panasco Alvim, General Ernesto Geisel, and Lieutenant Colonel Arídio Brasil, commander of the fort. (Courtesy, *Jornal do Brasil*)

Left. President-elect Castello Branco leaving his Rio de Janeiro residence on April 15, 1964, in order to be inaugurated in Brasília that afternoon. *Right.* Castello Branco after visiting Argentina's grave just before making the flight from Rio de Janeiro to Brasília on April 15, 1964.

calling strikes to obtain 80 percent wage increases and the payment of an extra month's wages (the "thirteenth month"). Also in Rio disgusted admirals were turning in their Naval Merit medals to protest the awarding of this decoration, by Navy Minister Pedro Paulo Araújo Suzano, to a political-minded group that included Lott's daughter Edna and Congressman Leonel Brizola. Castello also learned that in Rio, in the first part of December, First Army commander Osvino Ferreira Alves, friendly with sergeants and the CGT, had joined the navy and air force ministers in attending a meeting at which sergeants from various states expressed their grievance that members of their class, elected to legislative bodies, were constitutionally prohibited from being seated.[2] Brizola, who was touring the country preaching revolution and a Brazilian break in commercial relations with the United States, urged the sergeant to fight for political rights denied them by the Constitution.

December, 1962, stands out as the month when Fourth Army commander Castello Branco made his greatest effort to communicate with sergeants about their position. Early in the month, while visiting the 14th RI in nearby Socorro, he called the sergeants to meet with him in the regiment's movie theater, and there he stressed three "basic" points: (1) before the sergeants insisted on their rights, they should demonstrate their efficiency in fulfilling their duties; (2) a sergeant was not an intermediary between officers and corporals and soldiers, but was a direct assistant of the officers and commanders; and (3) petitions from sergeants should be addressed personally to him, as Fourth Army commander, through the chain of command, and he would not recognize requests made through politicians or through military men who were acting in situations not connected with their army functions.[3]

Later in the month Castello decided to speak to sergeants again lest they follow the "evil example" set by General Osvino and organize public meetings to debate the controversial constitutional matter.[4] Arriving in Fortaleza on December 27, he cut short the ceremonial and concentrated on his talk about the military function of officers and sergeants. The federal Supreme Court, he said, was preparing to issue a decision about the seating of sergeants in legislative bodies, and the necessary tranquility for this decision would only be impaired if sergeants held

[2] Ibid., December 11, 1962.
[3] Ibid., December 3, 1962.
[4] Ibid., December 26, 1962. The wording is Negrão's.

political meetings. While admitting the right of sergeants to work for their political goals, he argued that this should be done through the political parties to which they belonged and not through the army. After Castello had spoken, one of the sergeants, with a copy of the Constitution, sought to make a point to Castello. Castello, who knew the Constitution well, appeared "very angry" for a moment, but at the meeting's end the sergeant apologized for a gesture that he admitted might be misinterpreted and everything apparently ended well.[5]

On the next day, in São Luís, Maranhão, Castello gave another lecture to his men, this time deploring "the emergence of demagogic and exploiting politicians and military men who bring great harm to the Army and to Brazil." To those who clamored for a new era, favorable to the equality of all, Castello enunciated a somewhat different philosophy, at least as far as the military was concerned. The military democratic conscience, he said, did not reside in the "leveling" of men in their roles, but rather in "selection" according to merit.[6]

8. The Plebiscite of January 6, 1963

The federal government was making an intense effort to assure a large voter participation in the "popular referendum," or plebiscite, that Congress had authorized for January 6, 1963, to determine whether Brazil should abandon the parliamentary form of government. To guide army commanders, War Minister Kruel issued instructions on December 26, and they were transmitted at once by the Fourth Army to its military regions. They authorized the employment of vehicles and the assistance of civilian government workers to take voters to the polls, provided that they could be spared and that the local electoral tribunals so requested.[1]

On December 29 Hugo Faria, head of Goulart's Casa Civil (presidential office staff), visited Fortaleza to stimulate a large turnout for the plebiscite. He asked local federal agencies to provide vehicles; he set up

---

[5] Ibid., December 27, 1962.

[6] Ibid., December 28, 1962.

[1] Amauri Kruel instructions in radio message 361/D-2a of December 26, 1962, quoted in Section 5c of HACB, "Solução de Averiguação" (Solution of inquiry), Recife, January 19, 1963, File L2, CPDOC.

a "transport commission" and persuaded Tenth Military Region commander Nicolau Fico that the head of the commission should be the Tenth Region's chief of staff, Colonel Durval Coelho Macieira. Hugo Faria completed his work, as he explained to General Fico, by calling on the Federation of Industries of Ceará to provide the transport commission with the funds that it would require.[2]

At a Federation of Industries meeting on January 2, transport commission chairman Macieira, accompanied by a major, emphasized the need of funds, with the result that the federation voted 540,000 cruzeiros for the commission. But, after the army officers left, a federation member objected to military pressure, and the federation voted to hold up the funds. General Fico, learning of what had happened, resolved that Colonel Macieira should not receive the money and that it should be spent directly by the federation.[3]

Castello, who had not been informed of these developments, received a telegram on January 4 from an upset Cearanse complaining of the role of the Tenth Military Region staff officers in extracting money. Castello ordered Moniz de Aragão to investigate.

In Recife Castello granted the request for troops, made by the local electoral tribunal, to guarantee a peaceful plebiscite. The voting on January 6 went calmly, and Humberto and Argentina, after casting their ballots in a booth at the Law School, relaxed for Sunday lunch in their residence. To his guests Humberto mentioned that Pernambuco had 851,000 registered voters and Recife 244,000, and that it would be interesting to learn how many had participated in the plebiscite.[4]

On a national scale, only 62 percent of the registered voters participated,[5] but, as the outcome favored "presidentialism" by a five-to-one margin, Goulart felt well satisfied.

Castello was soon troubled by accusations, made in public, about the conduct of officers of the Tenth Military Region in connection with the plebiscite. But the charges went unanswered as far as the public was concerned because Castello, with reports from Moniz de Aragão and Fico, insisted on keeping the findings and his own conclusions confiden-

[2] HACB, "Solução de Averiguação."
[3] Ibid.
[4] Negrão diary, January 6, 1963, File I, CPDOC.
[5] Institute for the Comparative Study of Political Systems, Brazil: Election Factbook, no. 2 (September, 1965), p. 19.

tial. Although this policy was regarded by some officers and civilians as a sort of "retreat" by Castello, he wanted to protect the honor of General Fico.[6] Fico, he concluded in his report to the War Ministry, had erred in not keeping him informed but had acted in good faith when presented with a request that came from the head of the office staff of President Goulart.

No doubt a release of Castello's conclusions would have embarrassed the presidency most of all, for while Castello characterized the conduct of Colonel Macieira as "ill advised," he wrote that the "big culprit—and probably the only one" was Hugo Faria, who "used the authority of the President of the Republic" to tell military officers to act in a manner contrary to army regulations and Kruel's instructions. In Castello's judgment, the "abusive behavior" of Faria was responsible for all of the errors, including the ill will built up between the military and civilians and the accusations "that are hurled at the Army today."[7]

9. A Warning about Communist Penetration (January, 1963)

While Castello was clearing up the question of the Tenth Military Region's violation of Kruel's instructions, he became involved in a more serious matter with the war minister. It sprang from declarations made by Castello on January 16, 1963, during a visit to Bahia to observe the forty-third anniversary of the Nineteenth Infantry Battalion.

After being met at the Salvador airport by his friend Bahia Governor Juraci Magalhães, Castello delivered a speech at the battalion (in which he pointed out that "friendship is lasting only when it is born from work").[1] Then, exchanging impressions with a group that included journalists, Castello said: "I believe that Communist infiltration is facilitated by the placement of disseminators of Communism in posts of the administration, of teaching, and of government-controlled corporations."[2]

[6] Negrão diary, January 21, March 26, 1963, File I, CPDOC. Negrão says that HACB's failure to release the "Solução de Averiguação" was interpreted as a recúo (retreat or backing down).

[7] HACB, "Solução de Averiguação."

[1] Negrão diary, January 16, 1963, File I, CPDOC.

[2] HACB memorandum to War Minister Amauri Kruel, Recife, January 22, 1963, File L2, CPDOC.

This opinion and comments it elicited were quickly made public on radio and television programs and in the press. Two of Rio's most conservative dailies, *O Globo* and *Jornal do Commercio*, devoted long articles to Castello and his pronouncement.

O Globo described Castello as one of the most eminent figures in the army, highly intelligent and unusually well educated—an idealist convinced that the greatness of the armed forces rested on the rigorous fulfillment of their specific and constitutional duties. If such an officer, who did not belong to factions or give interviews, felt it imperative to speak out, it was, *O Globo* wrote, only because the situation was really serious and required that steps be taken to end the "Red penetration." Seeking to present evidence to confirm Castello's view, *O Globo* classified the new directors of the Institute of Advanced Brazilian Studies (ISEB), a dependency of the Education Ministry, as "all Communists." Explaining that this was one of dozens of examples, it spoke of Communist penetration in the army, "certainly due to the need of General Kruel, a well-known anti-Communist, to temporize during this uncertain period of a cabinet change."[3]

Jornal do Commercio, citing Castello's "lucid words," called attention to Pernambuco, where, it said, invasions of plantations, with assaults on human life and private property, left no one safe. This usually unsensational daily concluded that a deliberate and systematic plan of anarchy was being put into execution. "What we are witnessing is the occupation of the most important positions by people connected with subversive activities, which means that we are, with our own hands, turning the nation over to agents of destruction, who do not sleep."[4]

On January 21 Castello receive a coded radio message from Kruel asking for information about the statement attributed to him so that the war minister could deny the news that had been published about it.[5]

But Castello, in a memorandum to Kruel, advised that he had been quoted correctly. Although Castello said that some newspapers had falsely assumed that he was referring particularly to the Brazilian northeast, he gave Kruel no help for issuing a denial. He wrote that Com-

[3] "O Rebate que Faltava" (The Rebuttal that was lacking), *O Globo*, January 19, 1963.

[4] "Séria e Brava Advertência" (Serious and brave warning), *Jornal do Commercio*, January 19, 1963.

[5] Amauri Kruel radio message 03-LD to HACB, January 21, 1963, quoted in HACB memorandum to Kruel, January 22, 1963, File L2, CPDOC.

munist propaganda, once risky to impart, was now openly supported by those who found themselves in government posts—not as the result of elections but because they had been named in accordance with a policy that underestimated the Communist threat. Castello told Kruel that he had spoken out of a desire to collaborate with the government in the defense of democracy. He added that he had revealed no secrets, since it was well known that Communists were in the areas that he had mentioned.

What worried Castello was the impression given by Kruel's message that he should not have made his declaration. He therefore pointed out that generals and sergeants had used press interviews, telegrams, and speeches to make their views known on a wide range of subjects. Observing that all of these declarations had praised the government, Castello argued that to restrict pronouncements to favorable ones would be a "flagrant inequity," antidemocratic, and totalitarian. "If my declaration had been against the government—which was not the case because it can only be considered an unpretentious collaboration—I would doubtless be protected by a right already guaranteed to a number of military men." [6]

Two days after sending these thoughts to Kruel, Castello left Recife on a trip to Fortaleza and João Pessoa to attend the installations of the successors of Generals Nicolau Fico and José Lindenberg. Just before making his flight, Castello dashed off a note to Major Morais Rego, who was visiting relatives in Rio. With his note he sent a copy of his memorandum to Kruel, and he asked Morais Rego to show it (in an "absolutely confidential and secret" manner) to a few close army friends in Rio. Castello added: "Later, together with the letter that Paulo will give you, place the same information in the hands of General Ademar." [7]

10. The "Revolutionary" Northeast

Newspaper reports about the Brazilian northeast, one of the largest underdeveloped areas in Latin America, were gaining it a reputation throughout the world as an explosive region in which impoverished

---

[6] HACB memorandum to Kruel, January 22, 1963, File L2, CPDOC.
[7] HACB to Gustavo Morais Rego Reis, Recife, January 24, 1963, File L2, CPDOC.

peasants, stimulated perhaps by the speeches of radical politicians like Congressman Francisco Julião, might easily revolt. The region attracted official visitors who wanted first-hand knowledge, and many of them conferred with Castello Branco.

As Castello advised Kruel, the northeast was not particularly on his mind when he issued his warning about Communist penetration in the federal government. He did not feel that the northeast was ripe for Communism, and he took exception to the sensational newspaper reporting about the region. Finding much that interested him in Alceu Amoroso Lima's *Visão do Nordeste*, he marked well the passages which argued that northeasterners, due to "historical-social circumstances," were notable for their individualism and for their religious inclinations and therefore resisted Communist and fascist movements, which depended on molding individuals into homogeneous masses.[1]

Early in December, 1962, when Castello spoke in Recife to 105 visiting ECEME officer-students, he said that the ideals that led the northeasterners to expel the Dutch in the seventeenth-century—religious liberty, liberty for commerce, and national unity—still persisted, forming a guarantee against the "expected revolutionary war" in the region. Listeners told the heartily applauded general that his words were opportune, for further south it was beginning to be believed that the northeast was "already in revolution."[2]

The press seemed eager to publish columns about the "invasions" of properties in the northeast. In January, 1963, when officers of the Fourth Army undertook some reconnaissance work in preparation for troop exercises, newspapers in João Pessoa published reports that private landholdings were being invaded by army men. The reports, reprinted by the press in Rio, caused enough comment to require Castello to publish a clarifying note that included a denial by War Minister Kruel.[3]

Exaggerated newspaper stories about the "invasions of landholdings" by agricultural workers brought a Justice Ministry official to the northeast in February, 1963, to make an investigation. Castello, meeting with the official in João Pessoa, learned that the newspaper stories were so plentiful in Rio that "the impression existed that things were on a war

---

1 Alceu Amoroso Lima, *Visão do Nordeste*, pp. 33–37, 50.
2 Negrão diary, December 5, 1962, File I, CPDOC.
3 Ibid., January 19, 1963.

footing" in the northeast.[4] Indeed, the official hoped for military protection while he investigated.

Castello's disagreement with sensational reporting about the northeast did not mean that he ruled out the possibilities of disturbances there in the future. He mentioned these possibilities in a letter written in April, 1963, to his son-in-law, Salvador Diniz, who had a friend who was considering investing in industry in Pernambuco.

As Castello saw it, industry, its workers well paid by Pernambuco standards, was unlikely to be hurt by the program of Governor Arraes: "I have been here seven months and as yet no industrial strike has occurred. If one should take place it will be due to imposition on the part of the CGT [General Command of Workers] of Rio." Castello also explained that Arraes' program was not concerned with the backlands, in the interior, where large landowners raised cattle.[5]

The ambitious program of the new governor, Castello wrote, affected the area of small farmers, the city of Recife, and the sugar-raising zone. The first-mentioned, being injected with loans, was not on Castello's list of possible future trouble spots, but in Recife, where federal and foreign funds were used to construct popular housing, Castello could foresee trouble. There he saw the threat of a class struggle, "the poor and the miserable against those with money. . . . It could come about if hunger increases and if stimulated by party politics (of the state government, or of Jango); the chief target of this struggle will be the commercial class."

The other threat to the local peace, Castello wrote, was a possible "convulsion in the sugar-raising zone," where the governor, "full of contempt" for the owners of sugar mills and lands, sought to end the structure that had historically exploited the worker; an uprising, which might occur if nothing were done for the sugar workers, would be against the "individualist capitalism of sugar," and, if Julião's prestige were high enough, it might even oppose the state government itself, Castello noted.[6]

Castello had a good working relationship with Vice-governor Paulo Guerra. It began just after Castello arrived in Recife, when Guerra explained to him that his party, the PSD, not wanting to lose its political

[4] Ibid., February 21, 1963.
[5] HACB to Salvador Diniz, Recife, April 14, 1963, File L2, CPDOC.
[6] Ibid.

bases in the interior, felt it necessary to support Arraes, who was running for governor with the backing of leftist parties, including the Communist party. Later, when Arraes disappointed Paulo Guerra and surprised Castello by selecting Colonel Humberto Freire de Andrade to be state security secretary, Castello asked Guerra not to veto Freire de Andrade's name.[7] Freire de Andrade was just the man Arraes was seeking, because, while he was a prominent member of the army's "nationalist" wing (opposed to the Democratic Crusade), he had also worked closely with Castello, serving as office chief of the Army Staff's Directorship of Instruction when Castello was the director. "Could be worse," Castello told Guerra.[8]

The relationship between Arraes and Castello, both respecters of the Constitution, was formal but apparently not unsatisfactory. When Finance Minister San Tiago Dantas lunched with Arraes and Castello at the governor's palace on April 9, the governor made it clear that he regarded Castello as his friend.[9] But it was with Vice-governor Paulo Guerra that Castello discussed the political situation more frequently, due perhaps to the numerous absences of Arraes, who was giving speeches outside of Pernambuco in order to build up his candidacy for the presidency.

Paulo Guerra complained that Arraes had the habit of leaving Pernambuco just when strikes required the attention of the governor's office. During one of the first of these absences, when thousands of agricultural workers were striking in ten municipalities, Guerra asked that Castello use federal troops to help the state military police restore order. Castello, who disapproved of employing federal troops in this manner, said that such a step could not be undertaken without the approval of the war minister. But he added that he would be agreeable to having coffee with Guerra in the governor's palace, the news of which might be helpful to Guerra, and this was done.[10]

[7] Paulo Guerra interview, Brasília, November 11, 1975; Skidmore, *Politics in Brazil*, p. 231. HACB, in letter to Gustavo Morais Rego Reis (Recife, January 24, 1963, File L2, CPDOC), expressed the belief that Colonel Donato would be named state security secretary. Paulo Guerra, following a conversation with HACB, supported Colonel Donato. (Paulo Guerra interview, Brasília, November 11, 1975).

[8] Hélio Silva, *1964: Golpe ou Contragolpe?*, pp. 289–290; Guerra interview, November 11, 1975.

[9] Archer interview, September 30, 1975.

[10] Guerra interview, November 11, 1975.

When Goulart visited Rio Grande do Norte early in April, 1963, Castello, together with five state governors, was among the group of civilian and military authorities who met the president in the rain at the Natal airport.[11] After receiving the president, the greeters returned to their plane, which was to accompany the presidential plane on a short trip of commemorations, inaugurations, and banqueting. While the nonpresidential plane waited for Goulart and his party to take off, a captain entered it to bring the request that Castello travel in the president's plane. Goulart had much deference for Castello, and he was well impressed with views that the general offered about the northeast during the flight.[12]

On some of his occasional visits to Rio, Castello mentioned the northeast while conversing with Colonel Vernon Walters, who had returned to Brazil in October, 1962, as United States defense attaché. Castello criticized the "individualistic capitalism" of the sugar plant owners and told his old friend that he hated the idea of the "use of troops to protect the sugar plant owners." But, he added, one could not allow the disorder that would result if people simply took to seizing property. Castello, Walters decided, was a "centrist," to neither right or left.[13]

11. Called by Goulart to Rio (April, 1963)

At lunch at the Recife residence of the Fourth Army commander on Monday, April 15, 1963, Humberto discussed with Argentina and their guests, Major Morais Rego, the Negrãos, and a navy admiral, a cryptic order that he had received from the War Ministry and the presidential Casa Militar to go to Rio for a meeting at noon the next day.[1] A presidential plane, Castello learned, was being sent to take him to Rio.

Argentina was not feeling well although she had almost completely recovered from a painful furunculosis that had impaired her walking

[11] Negrão diary, April 2, 1963, File I, CPDOC.

[12] Gustavo Morais Rego Reis interview, Brasília, October 22, 1975; Negrão diary, April 2, 1963, File I, CPDOC.

[13] Vernon Walters interview, Arlington, Virginia, July 15, 1976.

[1] Negrão diary, April 15, 1963, File I, CPDOC.

earlier in the month.[2] The radio message to Humberto left her apprehensive.[3] It could well mean the loss of Castello's command post, perhaps at the instigation of the far Left forces that Goulart often courted. Brizola, seizing the leadership of those forces, was delivering violent speeches over a radio network of forty stations. He called on peasants to arm themselves to fight for their rights, and he called on his brother-in-law, Goulart, to make sweeping administrative changes acceptable to the far Left.

Despite her apprenhension, Argentina chose to be comforting while guesses were being made about the reason for Castello's summons to Rio. Goulart, she ventured, wanted to present a public demonstration of tranquility in the army before he made his visit to Chile.[4]

Morais Rego told Argentina that he was accompanying Castello on his trip and he asked her not to worry. But the whole thing seemed so strange that Castello decided to take his pistol with him, which was rather unusual.[5]

Castello and Morais Rego left Recife on the evening of the fifteenth. As Argentina continued in poor health, Negrão's wife Arminda spent the night with her. On the next morning a radio message from Humberto brought Argentina the news of the good health of the families of Nieta and Paulo.[6]

Argentina's guess about the purpose of Humberto's trip proved to be correct. The demonstration of harmony was felt to be necessary because of the poor relations that had developed between Kruel and First Army commander Osvino Ferreira Alves. After Osvino had offered army protection for a "monster meeting" to be held by organized workers and students to protest Governor Carlos Lacerda's prohibition of a pro-Cuba congress, Kruel had reprimanded the "people's general" and made him withdraw his offer. Later Osvino had accused Kruel of planning to incite the masses for political reasons.

Castello learned about the reason for the presidential summons after he and Morais Rego called at the War Ministry and were told by Kruel that Goulart wanted to speak with Castello. Going to Laranjeiras Palace,

[2] Ibid., April 6, 1963.

[3] Morais Rego Reis interview, October 22, 1975.

[4] Negrão diary, April 15, 1963, File I, CPDOC.

[5] Antonietta Castello Branco Diniz and Paulo V. Castello Branco interview, Rio de Janeiro, December 13, 1975.

[6] Negrão diary, April 16, 1963, File I, CPDOC.

they found the rooms there filled with people, many of them labor union leaders. The atmosphere seemed tense.[7]

Goulart, who was wearing no necktie, surprised Castello and Morais Rego by taking them to his bedroom, with the explanation that it was difficult to talk in a confidential way in the palace. "Please forgive the conditions," he said.[8] Then, sitting on his unmade bed, the president spoke of the "crisis" caused by the squabble between the war minister and the First Army commander. Finance Minister San Tiago Dantas had suggested that the president call all of the four-star generals to a lunch for a sort of smoking of the peace pipe. The news that the army generals were together was supposed to show that the rift between Kruel and Osvino had been mended.

Castello told Goulart that the problem that the president would face would come from the sergeants. He left the interview disappointed by its informal setting, for he had definite ideas about the dignity that should be associated with the office of president.[9]

On April 18 Castello returned to Recife, generally satisfied with his trip and full of information about the family and military friends in Rio. But the news in Recife, he learned, was not good. Argentina had been troubled on the night of the seventeenth by pressure in her chest.[10]

12. Days of Sorrow (April, 1963)

Throughout the night of April 19–20 Argentina was afflicted by nausea and a feeling of suffocation, but although Humberto wanted to call a doctor at once, she preferred to wait until morning. When doctors came on the twentieth, an electrocardiogram showed indications of a heart attack, and Argentina was put to bed on a strict diet and a nurse was engaged. During the night of April 20–21, the nurse, Humberto, and Arminda (Negrão's wife) took turns at Argentina's side; as on the previous night, Humberto got practically no sleep.[1]

On Sunday, April 21, another test showed that the attack had been

[7] Morais Rego Reis interview, October 22, 1975.
[8] Ibid.
[9] Diniz and Castello Branco interview, December 13, 1975; Walters interview, July 15, 1976.
[10] Negrão diary, April 18, 1963, File I, CPDOC.
[1] Negrão diary, April 20–21, 1963, File I, CPDOC.

severe. Humberto put the news in a letter for Paulo and Nieta, and it was taken by his brother Lauro, passing through Recife on his way from Fortaleza, to the Rio airport; there Waldetrudes and Justina Amarante picked it up, as Humberto had requested in a telegram to those friends. The Amarantes went to Paulo's home, but they found that he was out, attending the inauguration of the Major Vaz Tunnel, and so they called on Nieta, who was expecting the birth of her fourth child.[2]

Starting that night, Paulo kept in close touch with his father by telephone. Humberto, able to advise Paulo on the morning of the twenty-second that Argentina was no worse, and perhaps a bit better, prepared to spend about an hour at the army headquarters, but exhaustion and worry, he found, made work impossible. And so he was home when a second heart attack struck Argentina at noon. At the lunch table the general drummed the table with his fingers and ate practically nothing.[3]

On the night of April 22–23, while Arminda again helped take care of Argentina, Morais Rego slept in the guest room and Negrão in the general's study. But none of them got much sleep because at 2:30 A.M. a movement by the patient unfastened a needle that was bringing her serum, and her blood pressure plunged. Only at 5:00 A.M., after a doctor had been called, did Argentina fall asleep, this time with a peaceful smile on her face.[4] Later that morning she died.

Paulo reached Recife in an air force plane at 4:00 P.M., and two hours later the casket bearing Argentina's body was flown to Rio in the same plane, accompanied by Humberto, Paulo, and Morais Rego. The plane was met at Rio's Santos Dumont Airport by a sorrowing, silent crowd of about five hundred.[5] One witness has written that "the arrival of the plane at Santos Dumont bringing the casket of the deceased Argentina on the cold night of April 23–24, 1963, was one of the most sorrowful moments that I have witnessed in my life. In the deep silence there was only the echo of the curt and firm footsteps of those who were present to receive her. And General Castello, pale and sorrow-stricken, looked at everyone as though to ask, 'How could God permit this?' "[6]

[2] Waldetrudes and Justina Amarante interview, Rio de Janeiro, November 21, 1975.
[3] Negrão diary, April 22, 1963, File I, CPDOC.
[4] Ibid., April 23, 1963.
[5] Ibid.
[6] Edmar Eudóxio Telesca, "Depoimento sôbre o General Humberto de Alencar Castello Branco," Rio de Janeiro, April 24, 1976, p. 10.

The burial at São João Batista cemetery on the morning of April 24 was attended by a considerable multitude.[7] A few days later Castello took a train from Rio to Belo Horizonte to visit with his seventy-eight-year-old father-in-law and other members of the family.

When Castello returned to Recife on April 30, he had with him his daughter-in-law, Maria Luiza Castello Branco (known as Nena), and his sister, Lourdinha Hipolyto da Costa, "the great heart of the family, helpful and happy"[8]—the one who had brought Humberto and Argentina together in Belo Horizonte in 1919. Descending from the plane, the dejected general appeared to have aged and to have lost weight.[9] Receiving words of sympathy from some among the crowd that greeted him, he was obviously nervous and eager to get started to his residence.

Aide-de-camp Negrão found Lourdinha "a very likeable and happy person." But his account of the days that she and Nena spent in the Recife residence, which the general resolved to keep just as Argentina had arranged it, stresses deep sadness. On May 2, by which time more than five hundred messages of condolence had arrived, the general took Lourdinha and Nena on a sentimental drive to Olinda; he showed them all the places that Argentina had visited.[10] Nena left on May 5, and Lourdinha on May 7.

Castello, writing to his two children on May 5, said that everything had struck precipitously, bringing the unexpected, the grievous, and the irremediable, as though the world were suddenly spinning very quickly. "And in all of this, we lost Argentina without even time to be with her leisurely, in a less abrupt ending." The sorrowing father said that his professional work continued and that he planned to intensify it. But he deeply missed Argentina's spiritual, unique presence, "incomparable for me, full of enchantment and dignity, charming in sentiment."[11]

He wrote that Argentina, during their married life, had given the perfect example of being always at his side. "Calm and resolute, she came with me to the north and to the northeast. And in the battle which

[7] Negrão diary, April 24, 1963, File I, CPDOC.

[8] Ana (Nina) Castello Branco Santos Dias and Beatriz Castello Branco Gonçalves, "Depoimento sôbre o irmão Humberto de Alencar Castello Branco, 1973, File B, CPDOC.

[9] Negrão diary, April 30, 1963, CPDOC.

[10] Ibid., May 2, 1963.

[11] HACB to his son and daughter, Recife, May 5, 1963, File C, CPDOC.

I am waging in the Fourth Army, she was the first loss, the greatest loss. The contradictory happenings here, the surprises, the unrest, the uncertainties, the insecurity—all these things came to her eyes, her mind, and her feelings. But she did not abandon her place, and although she had misgivings, she was not touched by fear or the idea of getting away from the realities here. In this setting of struggle, in this atmosphere of adversity, she fell at her post, identified with her duty."

Argentina, Castello wrote, had become accustomed to Recife, finding beauty in the rivers; in the fountainheads of Olinda she had sought the gentleness of fresh evenings. "When she died, the northeast was giving her the pleasure of an agreeable climate. She did not want to leave Recife so soon."

Castello pointed out that they had never isolated themselves from their setting or the world, but had lived with the reality of the earth, its people, and its things. "It was the Full World, the world in which we integrated ourselves. But we also had our own world, very much our own, ours alone. And you two knew it and can therefore understand my sorrow."[12]

13. Brizola Insults Murici (May, 1963)

On May 5, when Castello Branco was writing to his children, United States Ambassador Lincoln Gordon was in Natal to speak about the Alliance for Progress at the invitation of the governor of Rio Grande do Norte. On the same day Congressman Brizola arrived in the same city and was grandly received by the mayor of Natal, an outspoken opponent of the "imperialistic" Alliance for Progress.[1] That evening, while the governor, accompanied by local army commander Murici and other authorities, dined with Gordon and his group at the American Foreign Service guesthouse, Brizola and the mayor, using a nationwide radio network, criticized the Alliance for Progress and the presence of Ambassador Gordon in the northeast. Brizola appealed to the soldiers to use their weapons on behalf of reforms. He called General Murici "a *golpista* and a gorilla" and criticized his anti-Goulart, anti-Brizola be-

[12] Ibid.
[1] Lincoln Gordon interview, Washington, D.C., June 11, 1975.

havior in Rio Grande do Sul immediately following Quadros' resignation in 1961.[2]

Murici, after dining with the Americans, had all that he could do at the Natal army barracks to restrain his officers and men as well as navy and air force officers who had joined them; they wanted to storm the residence where Brizola was staying, seize the congressman, and "debag" him—take off his trousers and march him up and down the main street.[3] Murici, appreciating that this action would create a serious situation, prohibited any violence. To prevent it, he put all of his troops on the alert.

After a sleepless night, Murici received at his barracks a manifestation of support by representatives of the local military units, including the state police. To the men who had gathered to back him, including some sergeants, Murici said that when "revolutionary war" failed to attract the armed forces, the technique of Communist leaders, from Lenin to Mao Tse-Tung, called for splitting the armed forces, stimulating indiscipline, and disparaging the military leaders, "to divide them and to throw officers against officers, sergeants against sergeants, and sergeants against officers." Explaining his position in 1961, Murici said that he could not back "legalidade" as it was presented at that time.[4]

On the afternoon of May 6, following these remarks, Murici flew to Recife to report to Castello. Castello observed, "This precipitates things too soon; it is too early for things to happen."[5] He asked Murici for a written report, and Murici, who returned at once to Natal, sent him one on May 8, together with a recording of Brizola's Natal speech.

Brizola, who had flown to Recife on the morning of May 6, told the press that Murici had been a *golpista* in 1961. On the seventh the congressman conferred with Arraes. Then, after lunching at the governor's palace, he left for Rio.[6]

Castello prepared a reply to Brizola in which he pointed out that the "insult" hurled at Murici in Natal appeared to be part of a plan to un-

[2] Silva, *1964: Golpe ou Contragolpe?*, pp. 268–269.

[3] Gordon interview, June 11, 1975.

[4] "Discurso do General Murici" in Silva, *1964: Golpe ou Contragolpe?*, pp. 455–456.

[5] Murici interview, November 18, 1975.

[6] *O Estado de S. Paulo*, May 8, 1963, quoted in Silva, *1964: Golpe ou Contragolpe?*, p. 270.

dermine Brazil's armed forces.[7] But, after thinking things over, Castello decided that the matter probably concerned the military institutions as a whole, not just the Fourth Army, and should be handled by the War Ministry. Therefore on May 7 he sent a memorandum to Kruel insisting that the charges made by Brizola were unfounded and that Murici was neither a reactionary nor a conspirator.

Castello suggested to Kruel that Brizola, in his speeches in the northeast, used the term *golpista* for military men who did not support his own coup, and the term *gorila* for those who did not participate in his effort to dominate the country, by hook or by crook. Brizola, Castello added, was well known for trying to divide the army into "Brizolistas" and "gorillas" and for turning to sergeants for support while disparaging generals and colonels. "Already one sees how this process of defamation and treachery is being adopted among students, in labor unions, and in the press—an affront to the military institutions at a very difficult time for the nation."[8]

Kruel, after receiving Castello's report, spoke with Goulart. The nation, Kruel warned Goulart, seemed headed for four stages: agitation by the labor unions, indiscipline by sergeants, disparagement of military leaders, and, finally, "the assault on the power." The war minister expressed doubt that the president would survive the fourth stage. Perhaps, as *Jornal do Commercio* suggested, Kruel hoped that Goulart would prevent Brizola from making further attacks on troop commanders, but Goulart seemed to be in no position to control Brizola's language. At any rate, Kruel was able to prevent the transfer of Murici. Castello learned that Murici would remain in the northeast as long as Castello headed the Fourth Army.[9]

The War Ministry received such an avalanche of messages from army officers supporting Murici that Hélio Fernandes, writing in *Tribuna da Imprensa*, said that Brizola was "a new Caxias, a true pacifier of the army, for the response that he evoked was so impressive and solid that it united the most divergent groups, putting generals, colonels,

[7] HACB memorandum to War Minister Kruel, Recife, May 7, 1963, File L2, CPDOC.

[8] Ibid.

[9] Amauri Kruel interviews, São Paulo, November 15, 1965, and Rio de Janeiro, October 21, 1967; *Jornal do Commercio*, Rio de Janeiro, May 8, 1963, quoted in Silva, *1964: Golpe ou Contragolpe?*, p. 272; Murici interview, November 18, 1975.

majors, captains, and lieutenants together in one trench."[10] But at the same time, in Brasília, federal Congressman Hércules Correia announced that he had been authorized by the General Command of Workers (CGT) to give its unrestricted support to the declarations of Brizola against Murici.[11]

14. Comments from Ademar de Queiroz (May, 1963)

When the UDN's Otávio Mangabeira, long a combative anti-Vargas conspirator from Bahia, lay dying in Rio's São Vicente Hospital in 1960, he told Bahia political leader Aliomar Baleeiro that if the Brazilian situation should deteriorate further, the man for him to see was General Ademar de Queiroz. Mangabeira also mentioned Castello Branco, but above all he urged that Baleeiro consult Ademar de Queiroz in case of an emergency endangering the country's democratic life. Baleeiro, who regarded the roles of Quadros and Goulart as calamitous for Brazil, met with Ademar de Queiroz in the early 1960's. He asked him to suggest the name of a general in a high command post who could inspire the confidence necessary to lead a defense of the institutions in case the president of Brazil violated the legal order but who would not abuse the leadership role to establish his own personal power. At once Ademar named Castello Branco, whose character and record he described to Baleeiro. Ademar mentioned General Murici as a second possibility and added that both Castello and Murici were, at the moment, in troop command posts in the north.[1]

It is not surprising that old Otávio Mangabeira referred Baleeiro to Ademar de Queiroz. Ademar, close to those who were responsible for the 1954 colonels' manifesto, had become known as a "fellow-conspirator" by military officers who were loath simply to sit back and watch developments unfold in a manner that greatly upset them. "Ademar de Queiroz," Morais Rego recalls, "was always conspiring."[2]

[10] Hélio Fernandes in *Tribuna da Imprensa*, May 10, 1963 (reprinted in *Diário de Pernambuco*, May 11, 1963), quoted in Silva, *1964: Golpe ou Contragolpe?*, pp. 273–274.

[11] Silva, *1964: Golpe ou Contragolpe?*, p. 272.

[1] Aliomar Baleeiro interview, Rio de Janeiro, September 19, 1975; Baleeiro, "Recordações," p. 3.

[2] Morais Rego Reis interview, October 22, 1975.

Civilians also turned to Ademar de Queiroz as they sought to organize, and gain adherents for, a movement that might effectively resist a trend that seemed to them to be taking Brazil to chaos and, probably, to a dictatorship to be implanted by the far Left. Daniel Krieger, who had spoken in the Senate in 1956 to defend Castello's *espada de ouro* position, claims to have been "conspiring with Ademar de Queiroz ever since 1937." Rio journalist Prudente de Morais Neto, associated with veteran anti-Vargas conspirator Júlio de Mesquita Filho (of *O Estado de S. Paulo*), maintained contacts with Ademar de Queiroz.[3]

Frederico Mendes de Morais, who was appointed aide of Ademar de Queiroz in March, 1962, found that the general had become "the point of convergence, the depository of the apprehensions of companions of various ranks who were dissatisfied with the planned, progressive, and violent deteriorization to which the national institutions were submitted. . . ."[4] That so many turned to Ademar de Queiroz was due, Mendes de Morais says, to the general's well-known leadership qualities.

Ademar de Queiroz was in Rio in May, 1963, still heading Coastal and Antiaircraft Artillery, when he learned of the Brizola-Murici affair and its sequel, a lively meeting of hundreds of sergeants held in a Rio auditorium on May 11 for the purpose of honoring General Osvino Ferreira Alves. During this meeting, Sergeant Gelci Rodrigues Correia read a manifesto that praised the CGT and that said, "We swear to defend order in this country, but not the one that presently exists, because it benefits only a few privileged people."[5] The arrest of Gelci Rodrigues Correia was quickly ordered by Kruel.

Ademar de Queiroz, writing to Castello Branco, said that Brizola, "the vulgar brother-in-law of the President," had shown "a lot of audacity to malign a military leader in the very city of his command! What a situation we have reached! Everything is due to impunity." "Without doubt," Ademar observed, "the episode here of the sergeants in the auditorium . . . was geared to the episode of Natal. They are all like integral pieces making up a system of disrespect for the military leaders

[3] Daniel Krieger interview, Brasília, October 21, 1975; Prudente de Morais Neto interview, Rio de Janeiro, October 8, 1975.

[4] Frederico Mendes de Moraes, "Depoimento de Frederico Mendes de Moraes a Pedido do Sr. John W. F. Dulles . . ." (typewritten), Rio de Janeiro, December 19, 1975, pp. 1–2.

[5] Mário Victor, *Cinco Anos que Abalaram o Brasil*, p. 449.

and disparagement of the armed forces, whose destruction is so much sought by those who want to bring chaos to the nation." [6]

Ademar wrote that the problem of the sergeants had become very serious. Explaining that the problem was created by a minority, as he said was also true among the "student" and "worker" classes, Ademar added that it was a minority directed "by criminals, as we know, for they act against the regime and Brazil itself." According to Ademar, the Communists had a well-defined objective while the democrats let their personal interests stand in the way of dealing with the problem. As for the generals, Ademar told Castello that they commonly united to support Kruel's position whenever grave "episodes" occurred, but "after the passing of the storm" they returned to their apathy, registering no protests when new errors were made by the administration. "What we have is a lack of confidence in the authorities."

Ademar felt that Goulart, although zigzagging, was committed to "the 'left,' " and he believed that Kruel, "without a background to recommend him, and without any well-defined pattern," was making so many mistakes that it might not be good to have Generals Alfredo Souto Malan and Carlos Flores de Paiva Chaves promoting manifestos of support for the war minister. "How many errors have been committed by the Ninth Floor?! . . . Why don't we speak frankly, insisting on a definition of attitude, a line of conduct? If that were done, those protestations of solidarity would no longer be necessary. It has to do with establishing a climate of confidence that does not exist and that cannot be imposed, considering the pasts of the people involved." [7] Commenting on a circular in which Kruel attacked "those who want to subvert the hierarchy and malign the military leaders," Ademar suggested to Castello that Kruel bore some responsibility for the situation; Kruel, Ademar added, had received, in his office in the War Ministry, sergeants dressed in civilian clothes. [8]

Ademar, who had been working on the draft of a future army promotion law, complained that mediocre professionals and men of dubious morals were being rewarded, while good men with backbone, such as Colonel Luís Mendes da Silva, Lieutenant Colonel Carlos de Meira Mattos, and Lieutenant Colonel Antônio Carlos de Andrada Serpa, were

[6] Ademar de Queiroz to HACB, Rio de Janeiro, May 27, 1963, File L2, CPDOC.
[7] Ibid.
[8] Ademar de Queiroz to HACB, Rio de Janeiro, May 30, 1963, File L2, CPDOC.

being "persecuted" by the deferment of promotions and the assignment
of unimportant commissions. "Are these men '*golpistas*?' Are they 'gorillas?' Are they 'americanists?' " Ademar asked. "No," he replied,
"they are good soldiers, and good Brazilians. They simply are not 'Communists,' 'nationalists,' 'Fidelistas,' 'traitors,' 'Brizolistas,' 'Osvinistas,'
and other such things." [9]

With pleasure Ademar wrote of the "failure" of Osvino's Copacabana lunch "to honor Goulart" (a ceremony at which neither Goulart
nor Kruel made an appearance) and of the defeat of Sergeant-"Congressman" Antônio Garcia Filho in the elections of the Clube dos Sub-
Tenentes e Sargentos. Describing the Navy Club election, Ademar said
that the admirals, supporting a slate headed by Admiral Augusto Hamann Rademaker Grünewald, lost to a slate backed by officers of lower
rank, and he wondered whether the "people's admirals," Pedro Paulo
de Araújo Suzano and Cândido Aragão, would seek to widen this breach
among navy officers.[10]

Ademar's letters, full of news, had high praise for Guanabara Governor Carlos Lacerda, "really a great pillar of democracy." About Guanabara Vice-governor Elói Dutra, a far leftist foe of Lacerda, Ademar
felt otherwise. He wrote Castello that Elói Dutra, on a radio-television
program had called Kruel "the big gorilla" who ought to be placed in
the Zoological Garden, where he could be a companion of Sophia, the
monkey.[11]

Kruel, as Ademar informed Castello, was also being rudely attacked
on the radio and television programs of Brizola, "who keeps repeating
that he is speaking in the name of the 'downtrodden majority' of the
Brazilian people." [12] Although Ademar had as yet no news about what
would occur in the military ministries as a result of the new cabinet revision that Goulart was planning late in May, 1963, such were the attacks of the far Left on Kruel that the appointment of another war
minister seemed likely.

Ademar was able to advise Castello of the forthcoming retirement

[9] Ademar de Queiroz to HACB, May 27, 1963, File L2, CPDOC. Luís Mendes da
Silva and other Aragarças rebels had returned to Brazil following the inauguration of
Quadros early in 1961.

[10] Ademar de Queiroz to HACB, May 30, 1963, in L2.

[11] Ademar de Queiroz to HACB, May 27, 31, 1963, File L2, CPDOC.

[12] Ademar de Queiroz to HACB, May 30, 1963, File L2, CPDOC.

of Justice Minister João Mangabeira, a Socialist party leader whom he described as "decrepit" and "unfortunately the brother of the beloved and never-to-be-forgotten Otávio Mangabeira." [13]

15. Trouble with the Spinal Column (May–June, 1963)

Following the death of Argentina, Castello Branco's spinal column, which had always been afflicted by a curvature, began to give him trouble. So severe was the pain on Saturday, May 25, that Castello cut short his plans to work in order to rest and consult a doctor. "The pain," Negrão wrote in his diary on May 29, "has been intense." [1]

Nonetheless, on May 30 Castello set forth on an inspection trip scheduled to take him to Teresina, Piauí, São Luís, Maranhão, and Fortaleza. But in Teresina, where members of the Joint Brazil–United States Military Mission were on a visit, Castello found that he could not move when he tried to get up from a chair to give a talk. Instead of continuing on to São Luís, he was flown back to Recife on June 1, was examined by an army doctor and a professor, and was put on a hard bed. Unable to fulfill his duties, he declared himself officially on vacation. [2]

FEB veteran Nestor Penha Brasil, who was in the northeast with the Joint Brazil–United States Military Mission, telephoned Paulo Castello Branco about the Teresina incident. And from Recife Paulo heard from Major Morais Rego, whose relationship with Castello, in the absence of Castello's family, was not unlike that of son and father. Paulo and Morais Rego agreed that it would be best to move the general to Rio, where his children lived and where outstanding medical specialists were to be found. [3] Paulo, thanks to the well-known Dr. Paulo Albuquerque, obtained the names of the three best specialists in Rio.

Castello, receiving visitors and sorting his papers on his hard bed, did not want to leave Recife. [4] But Paulo, who reached Recife on June 7, persuaded him to do so and made the arrangements for him to be flown on June 12, accompanied by Morais Rego. As the general could

[13] Ademar de Queiroz to HACB, May 30, 31, 1963, File L2, CPDOC.
[1] Negrão diary, May 25, 29, 1963, File I, CPDOC.
[2] Paulo V. Castello Branco interview, Rio de Janeiro, December 21, 1974; Negrão diary, June 5, 1963, File I, CPDOC.
[3] Morais Rego Reis interview, October 22, 1975.
[4] Ibid.; Negrão diary, June 5, 1963, File I, CPDOC.

not walk, he had to be carried to the airport car by soldiers. He re-marked that he never would have believed that Argentina was to leave their Recife residence in a casket and he "practically on a stretcher." [5]

From the Rio airport, where he was met by Ademar de Queiroz and Paulo, Castello was taken to the Strangers' Hospital (Hospital dos Es-trangeiros) and examined by one of the doctors who had been recom-mended to Paulo. After Castello refused to undergo a suggested opera-tion, the doctor designed a stiff corset for him to wear.[6]

Castello's stay in the Strangers' Hospital coincided with the revision of the Goulart cabinet that Ademar de Queiroz had mentioned when writing late in May. In the course of making changes in every cabinet post, the president gratified Brizola by dismissing War Minister Kruel and Finance Minister San Tiago Dantas. In Kruel's place he appointed Jair Dantas Ribeiro, a Realengo classmate of Kruel and Castello.

General Jair Dantas Ribeiro, generally regarded as "Brizola's candi-date to be War Minister," [7] had come to know Brizola when command-ing the Third Army in the south in 1962. In Porto Alegre in Septem-ber of that year Jair had created a sensation by sending telegrams to President Goulart, Prime Minister Brochado da Rocha, and War Min-ister Nelson de Melo to advise that in view of the "intransigence" of Congress and the resulting demonstrations in the territory occupied by the Third Army, he was not in a position to assure the maintenance of order unless Congress agreed that a plebiscite be held no later than Oc-tober 7, 1962, to determine the fate of the parliamentary system.[8] One result of these extraordinary telegrams was that General Ernesto Geisel, heading a garrison in Curitiba and therefore under Jair's command, an-nounced that he was having no trouble maintaining order.[9] Another re-sult was a message from War Minister Nelson de Melo telling Jair that his telegrams were conducive to indiscipline and should not have been sent.

[5] Negrão diary, June 12, 1963, File I, CPDOC.
[6] Castello Branco interview, December 21, 1974.
[7] Joaquim Justino Alves Bastos, *Encontro com o Tempo*, p. 323.
[8] Victor, *Cinco Anos que Abalaram o Brasil*, p. 442.
[9] Paulo V. Castello Branco interview, Rio de Janeiro, October 11, 1975.

IX

Trying Persuasion
(September, 1963–early 1964)

The Army Chief of Staff cannot play a mar-
ginal role in the decisive events of the life of
the Army.

1. Castello Defines His Role as Chief of Staff
(July–September, 1963)

CASTELLO BRANCO, released from the Rio hospital and disappointed not to find himself completely cured of his spinal trouble, went on July 5 to the War Ministry to see Jair Dantas Ribeiro, his acquaintance of forty-five years. The war minister, a quiet, bespectacled northeasterner who described himself as a man of the Center, had returned recently from Brasília, where he had told Goulart of his intention to change the commanders of the four armies—and of regiments as well. Speaking now in a friendly manner to Castello, Jair suggested that his old classmate become army chief of staff when that post became vacant.[1]

In dealing with General Osvino Ferreira Alves, the president and war minister were careful. The First Army commander, forced by age to retire since he had not been chosen war minister, said that he wished to see the continuation of a *dispositivo militar* capable of sustaining "the present national policy."[2] To satisfy this request, it was agreed that four Osvinista colonels would be promoted to generals and that one of them would become head of the presidential Casa Militar. From the list of four colonels, Goulart picked Colonel Argemiro de Assis Brasil, a Gaúcho, for the Casa Militar; when Assis Brasil, pleased to become a general, expressed a desire to continue as military attaché in Argentina, the

---

[1] *O Estado de S. Paulo*, June 16, 1963; Carlos Castello Branco, *Introdução à Revolução de 1964*, vol. 1, *Agonia do Poder Civil*, p. 199; HACB to Jair Dantas Ribeiro, Recife, July 30, 1963, File L2, CPDOC.

[2] Castello Branco, *Introdução à Revolução de 1964*, I, 211. *Dispositivo militar* means military setup or arrangement.

Osvinistas sought to persuade Goulart to appoint General de Brigada
Luís Tavares da Cunha Melo to head the Casa Militar in case they could
not convince Assis Brasil to take the post.[3]

Castello was back with the Fourth Army when the promotions of
the colonels to generalships were made known. He, Ademar de Queiroz,
and Waldetrudes Amarante were especially upset at what Castello called
the "sacrifice" of their friend Mário de Barros Cavalcanti, who had been
a colonel for ten years (to eight for Assis Brasil). Writing to Amarante,
Castello said that War Minister Jair had made commitments to the "ap-
palling patrimony of Osvino." What had been done, Castello added,
was a "grave injustice based on ravenous personalism. [Mário Caval-
canti] was sacrificed by *peleguismo militar.*"[4]

On July 28, when Humberto wrote this letter, Goulart was in the
northeast stirring up crowds to get backing for agrarian and other reforms. Speaking with Castello in Recife on July 29, the president extended the war minister's invitation that Castello become chief of staff
in the place of General José Machado Lopes, who was being appointed
a minister of the Superior Military Tribunal. Castello gave the president
his acceptance, which allowed the war minister, as the press had already
reported, to put the Fourth Army command in the hands of General Joaquim Justino Alves Bastos, who had defeated Castello for the Military
Club presidency in 1958.

On July 30 Castello wrote a long letter to the war minister, the
theme of which is contained in one sentence: "the Army Chief of Staff
cannot play a marginal role in the decisive events of the life of the
Army."[5] Castello, disclaiming any intentions of "presenting conditions"
for undertaking the new assignment, said that he was "reminding" the
war minister of the importance of the role of the Estado Maior solely
in order to collaborate with him. He made the point that the professional military situation "in all of its aspects, including its implications with
politics," had become a challenge to the war minister, and he added that
the challenge could only be met with the full integration of the Estado

[3] Ibid. Luís Tavares da Cunha Melo, an officer in Castello's Third Section in Italy,
served in 1963 as chief of staff of First Army commander Osvino Ferreira Alves.

[4] HACB to Waldetrudes Amarante, Recife, July 28, 1963, File L2, CPDOC.
Pelego was a term used to describe a labor union leader who supported, and was supported by, the government.

[5] HACB to Jair Dantas Ribeiro, Recife, July 30, 1963, File L2, CPDOC.

Maior "as a living body . . . backed by the government." In Rio on August 2 Castello discussed these thoughts with Jair, and he found the war minister in agreement with them.

Many of Castello's friends, learning of his new position, attributed his transfer from the command of troops, after only one year, to motives of the Goulart administration that they considered less than admirable. Most frequently the administration was pictured as appeasing Brizola and anti-Castello sergeants. But Morais Rego does not think that was the reason for Castello's transfer.[6] He believes that Jair, and perhaps also Goulart, invited Castello to the high post of army chief of staff because of respect for him and because it was important for the war minister to conciliate worried officers who shared Castello's anti-Osvino and anti-Brizola views.

Castello bade farewell to his friends in Recife. When he called to say good-bye to Third Naval District Chief of Staff Palhares dos Santos, the admiral's wife spoke of the friendship that she had enjoyed with Argentina and gave Humberto some newspaper clippings about her. Humberto's chin began to tremble, and he had to control himself to hold back tears.[7] He did not remain in Recife long enough to pass the command of the Fourth Army directly to General Justino Alves Bastos, but instead turned it over provisionally to General Murici.

Writing to Morais Rego from Rio on September 10, Castello said: "On entering the Sixth Floor I sense a trustful welcome by many people. I note, however, some misgivings. . . . For one thing, they tell me that the handling of personnel—promotions, transfers, and classifications—is unbridled in Brasília and here. . . . I am doing my best not to take office already upset. I am to assume my post next Friday, the 13th. A favorable or unfavorable augury?" A week later he wrote Morais Rego: "By no means am I yet installed, and, much less, holding the reins. The situation is very difficult, and the Sixth Floor is overwhelmed by a devastating lack of prestige. What to do, and how to do it?"[8]

Morais Rego has pointed out that Castello made it clear in his letter of July 30 to Jair that his new post was to be one of influence.[9] Castello

---

[6] Gustavo Morais Rego Reis interview, Brasília, October 22, 1975.

[7] João Carlos Palhares dos Santos interview, Rio de Janeiro, November 22, 1975.

[8] HACB to Gustavo Morais Rego Reis, September, 1963, in Luís Viana Filho, *O Governo Castelo Branco*, p. 5.

[9] Morais Rego Reis interview, October 22, 1975.

stressed this point again in the speech at his installation ceremony on September 14. With Jair among those present, Castello quoted army regulations to remind his listeners that the Estado Maior of the Army (EME) was supposed to handle "all basic questions of organization, training, mobilization, logistic support, and the employment of land forces, in peace and in war." [10] Working under the war minister and observing the orientation of the Armed Forces Staff (EMFA), the EME was described by Castello as pledged to uphold the structure and doctrine of the army.

In his speech Castello lashed out at "opportunistic reformers" who sought unpatriotically to replace the army structure with a so-called "Popular Army, an imitation of a militia, with an ambiguous ideology, designed to employ worn-out verbal pronouncements to agitate the nation, and to avail itself of subversion and riots to create public disturbances. . . . In their process of destruction, these opportunistic reformers seek to disparage professional standards, push aside those who care for the profession, belittle values, and use discrimination to bring about discord in military circles." These "opportunistic reformers," Castello said, had in mind no revolutionary structure, but merely an organization that was capable of taking over the power, for they were at the service of whoever would pay their expenses and back them.[11]

The speech disturbed the war minister. On September 17 Jair wrote Castello to say that while he agreed "in general lines" with Castello's thinking, he nevertheless found it necessary to remind Castello that he, as war minister, had the obligation to maintain the army united and disciplined and apart from political debates. Castello and other army leaders should therefore understand the need to refrain from making pronouncements "that might be exploited by currents of political parties." Jair added that with this in mind, he was going to issue a directive.[12]

[10] HACB speech upon becoming army chief of staff, "Discurso de Posse na Chefia do Estado Maior do Exército," Rio de Janeiro, September 14, 1963, File G1, CPDOC.
[11] Ibid.
[12] Jair Dantas Ribeiro to HACB, Rio de Janeiro, September 17, 1963, File L2, CPDOC.

2. The Request for a State of Siege (October, 1963)

War Minister Jair Dantas Ribeiro's prestige was high because of the failure of a "sergeants' revolt" that had broken out in Brasília before dawn on September 12 to protest a Supreme Court decision that sergeants could not hold legislative seats. For one thing, although more than one hundred sergeants led about five hundred enlisted men and corporals in rebellion, only two or three of the sergeants belonged to the army. For another thing, the revolt was put down with the help of army contingents that Jair had posted in Brasília soon after becoming war minister.

During the two weeks that followed the sergeants' revolt and Castello's assumption of his new duties, Jair dealt with problems that were serious for the army, but he did so in a way that made it seem likely that the army chief of staff could expect no more than "a marginal role in the decisive events of the Army." Late in September, after Governor Lacerda gave a sensational interview describing Brazil as being in the hands of Communists and others who sought to "stop the country," the war minister joined the navy and air force ministers in issuing a manifesto condemning Lacerda, "the bad citizen," and attacking also São Paulo Governor Ademar de Barros, who had warned against steps to socialize Brazil. Then on October 3, with the administration apparently worried about a possible coup by Lacerda and Ademar de Barros, Jair suggested to Goulart that the administration ask Congress to declare a state of siege, which would suspend numerous constitutional guarantees.

Castello learned about these acts of the war minister through newspapers, the radio, and television, and only late on October 4 was he advised that the military ministers were delivering a message to Congress requesting the state of siege.[1] In a letter written to Jair that evening, Castello pointed this out, mentioning also that the war minister on the third had spoken only vaguely to him about "the direction which events might take." "I do not think that the Chief of Staff is a person who should be left out in examining the situation or in reaching conclusions," Castello wrote.

Going on to give Jair his "point of view," he turned first to the message of the military ministers condemning Lacerda. He said that this

---

[1] HACB to Jair Dantas Ribeiro, Guanabara, October 4, 1963, File L2, CPDOC.

message, a response to "a violent interview by an oppositionist politician" had opened "the acute phase" of the crisis and was a warning that the armed forces would act decisively to defend the nation. But, he added, an obligation also existed to issue warnings about other matters, such as the "illegal and subversive" action of the General Command of Workers and the "insurrectional agitation" fostered by Brizola.

Castello pointed out that the army could handle the "crucial matter of the sergeants" without a state of siege and that the military leaders were already giving priority to internal security. He warned that a state of siege, obliging the army forces to devote themselves entirely to police action, which he considered unnecessary, would completely disrupt the normal life of the forces; it would, he said, undermine the army's efficiency and cohesion, urgently needed for "situations of domestic commotion." Furthermore, he said that police work by the army would provide ammunition to those who liked to call army men gorillas, reactionaries, *golpistas*, and blockheads.

"I am not," Castello concluded, "overstepping bounds in giving you my judgment. I am Army Chief of Staff and member of the High Command. . . . The members of the High Command were not consulted." [2]

Two days after this letter was written, it became clear that a state of siege was feared by organized labor as well as by Goulart's traditional foes and that Congress would not enact it. Goulart, his military ministers, and his justice minister therefore delivered new messages to Congress withdrawing the earlier requests for a state of siege. Following this humiliation for the administration, War Minister Jair turned to Castello's criticism.

Expressing pleasure that Castello had cited their forty-five years of friendship, Jair wrote: "As a simple man from the northeast, I pay little attention to flattering expressions, and yet I hold very dear the frank and loyal cooperation of a military leader of your experience and distinction. I could not expect any other behavior from a soldier of your virtues and am honored by your long-standing friendship. Moved by the same spirit and making use of the same frankness that you employed, I submit my reply." [3]

Jair reminded Castello that he had already made it clear that he was, as war minister, determined to keep the army out of political disputes

2 Ibid.
3 Jair Dantas Ribeiro to HACB, Rio de Janeiro, October 8, 1963, File L2, CPDOC.

and would be the only one to speak for the army on such matters. The prerogative of establishing the policy of the army with respect to the national situation belonged, he said, to the war minister, who, besides being commander of the army, was also a member of the president's cabinet, a political ministry. "Of course this must be done in harmony with the President," Jair added. As for the High Command, Jair said that the law of 1956 which created it did not define its functions, and whether it should be heard or not was a decision for the minister to make.[4]

Jair took exception to Castello's description of the military ministers' late September manifesto as one issued in response to "a violent interview by an oppositionist politician." One of its purposes, Jair said, was to hold back subversive activities by important governors. But what brought on the heaviest underlining by Castello were Jair's statements about the need to have the Brazilian army's role "in tune with" the "just, Christian, and democratic demands of the people." "This role," Jair wrote, "will convincingly allow the evolution of our society without the shedding of the generous blood of our people. The comprehension of this problem by our military leaders is fundamental for overcoming momentary difficulties."[5]

Two days after this letter was written, Jair could only have been vexed by the attention given to Castello's position in the leading editorial of O Estado de S. Paulo. According to the editorial, the war minister had been forced to withdraw his support of the state of siege because Castello, after conscientiously weighing events and the public clamor against the state of siege, had presented his opinion in a formal document for the war minister. O Estado de S. Paulo reported that "obviously the sensible gesture of the Army Chief of Staff reflected the sentiment of almost all of the commanding generals."[6]

---

[4] Law 2,851, August 25, 1956, about "the basic organization of the Army," established (in Article 6) that the "High Command, presided over by the War Minister, is made up of the Chief of Staff of the Army, the Chiefs of Staff of the Army Departments, and the Army Commanders." The army departments were: Department of General Supply, Department of Production and Works, and Department of Personnel. There were four armies. In his letter to HACB, Jair Dantas Ribeiro said that Article 6 of Law 2,851 had not yet been regulated and that he was inclined to take steps to regulate it.

[5] Dantas Ribeiro to HACB, Rio de Janeiro, October 8, 1963, File L2, CPDOC.

[6] O Estado de S. Paulo, October 10, 1963, editorial, p. 3.

3. Abstaining from Conspiracy (October, 1963)

Castello had about seventy army officers working for him on the fifth and sixth floors of the War Ministry building.[1] He had an able chief assistant in General de Divisão Emílio Maurel Filho, whose troubles in 1962 with Amauri Kruel and Osvino Ferreira Alves, when those two worked in harmony, had cost him his command of the First Military Region.[2]

Usually it was between 9:00 and 10:00 A.M. when Castello reached his office, a large sixth-floor room that looked out onto Avenida Getúlio Vargas and the statue of the Duque de Caxias. He would start his day by hearing his secretary, Lieutenant Colonel Murilo Gomes Ferreira, present the latest information. Gomes Ferreira recalls, "He listened attentively, agreed or disagreed, added information, and reflected on the direction that events were taking." Then, after Castello and Gomes Ferreira had attended to the correspondence and the preparation of documents, Castello would call in his section heads and assistant heads and distribute tasks. The chief of staff, his former secretary says, had words of affection and consideration for all who came to his office and was zealous about the observation of all forms of military discipline. "He was affectionate within the limits that he imposed and did not allow those limits to be exceeded."

We are told that Castello never required of his assistants more than was established by the regulations. But for himself it was a different matter. Trying to overcome his loneliness as a recent widower, he would carry work papers with him when he went home to the Nascimento Silva Street house (where the domestic chores were attended to by a devoted maid, Romana, who had been at the side of the dying Argentina).[3] Not infrequently he spent Saturday afternoons working with EME First Assistant Chief Aurélio de Lyra Tavares in the latter's apartment.[4]

[1] Leônidas Pires Gonçalves interview, Rio de Janeiro, October 17, 1975.

[2] Armando Falcão interview, Rio de Janeiro, November 30, 1966; Emílio Maurel Filho interview, Rio de Janeiro, October 11, 1965.

[3] Murilo Gomes Ferreira, "O General Castello Que Conheci," Part 7, "Estado Maior do Exército," transcript of tape prepared for interview, Rio de Janeiro, November 12, 1975, pp. 9–10; Murilo Gomes Ferreira, in Ferreira and Paulo V. Castello Barnco interview (untaped portion), November 12, 1975; Antonietta Castello Branco Diniz and Paulo V. Castello Branco interview, Rio de Janeiro, December 13, 1975.

[4] Aurélio de Lyra Tavares interview, Rio de Janeiro, July 18, 1977.

When he did not bury himself in work, Castello would visit with his children and their families or with close friends such as Waldetrudes and Justina Amarante and Vernon Walters. Rarely he might drop in on acquaintances of long standings, such as Brigadeiro and Sra. João Adyl de Oliviera, whose house was close by. All of them noted that the neckties worn by Castello following Argentina's death were invariably black, and they were aware of the numerous visits that he made to Argentina's grave.

Castello's most intimate friend was Ademar de Queiroz. One of the pleasures of working in the war ministry building, Castello found, was his proximity to Ademar, whose office was on the fifth floor. Each day, in the office of one or the other, they lunched together on sandwiches or light snacks that they sent an aide out to buy.[5] Ademar's jokes appealed to Castello.

On Castello's birthday, September 20, 1963, Ademar went to Castello's office. Not finding him there, Ademar wrote a note: "Castello: Here I leave my very friendly embrace on account of this day. I telephoned you around nine o'clock and did not find you at your house. Much health, peace, and happiness. The Army and Brazil need you very much and rely on you. May God be with you and help you."

Late in September their mutual friend General de Brigada Antônio Carlos Murici was installed on the ministry's fourth floor with the title of assistant head of the Diretoria da Reserva. An extrovert who was inclined to view the government as taking steps that merited its overthrow,[6] Murici came to Rio convinced that all was ready in army circles in the northeast for the overthrow of the government. He felt certain that Fourth Army commander Justino Alves Bastos, considered to be a friend of Goulart, was an expert at hiding his true feeling and was really as favorable to a movement against the administration as were most of the other Fourth Army officers. When Murici had met for the last time with Colonel João Dutra de Castilho of the 16th RI, the colonel had told him: "Murici, if you start things in Rio, I shall start things here in Socorro."[7]

Murici, who found his Rio job not very time-consuming, went to

[5] Frederico Mendes de Morais interview, Rio de Janeiro, December 20, 1975.

[6] Artur da Costa e Silva, "Costa e Silva Relata Episódios da Revolução" (speech at ECEME), April 1, 1965, in O Estado de S. Paulo, April 4, 1965, pp. 5–6.

[7] Antônio Carlos da Silva Murici interview, Rio de Janeiro, November 18, 1975.

work at once with the foremost conspirator, Osvaldo Cordeiro de Farias. Cordeiro, having been a four-star general much longer even than Costa e Silva or Castello, was ranked in the *Almanaque do Exército* at the top of the list of generals in active service, but ever since Goulart had become president he had held no army post and was active only in preparing for a movement against the government. Some of his work was done in São Paulo, where Lieutenant Colonel Rubens Resstel, a Second Army artillery officer who had served under him in Italy, was building up a group of conspiring officers below the rank of general.[8]

Resstel and his conspirators, joined in October, 1963, by Colonel Cid Osório, considered their work defensive: they hoped, with connections that they sought to develop elsewhere, to have a force strong enough to topple the administration if it should take the initiative in acting undemocratically (and many of them felt certain that this would happen). Brigadier generals in Rio, such as Murici, may have had the same objective in mind from the start, but for the first two months that Murici was in Rio they were apt to picture their work as nothing more serious than that of organizing support for top generals who wanted to persuade the administration to mend its ways.[9]

Not long after reaching Rio, Murici received an invitation to conspire from General de Brigada José Pinheiro de Ulhoa Cintra, who, as assistant head of army recruitment, was also on the ministry's fourth floor. Murici told Ulhoa Cintra that on his own he had already followed Ulhoa Cintra's example of joining with Cordeiro. For Murici it was a pleasure to discover Ulhoa Cintra conspiring for the first time in his life and doing so with zest.[10] Costa e Silva, head of the army's Department of Production and Works with offices on the ministry's seventh floor, came to consider Ulhoa Cintra "an irritable, desperate, and violent man, acting irresponsibly," but Colonel Edmundo Neves, working closely with Cordeiro, found Ulhoa Cintra courageous and decisive.[11]

---

[8] Luís Werneck, Flávio Galvão, Roberto Brandíni, Luís Maciel Filho, and Héber Perillo Fleury interview, São Paulo, November 24, 1965.

[9] Rui Mesquita interview, São Paulo, November 6, 1975; Antônio Carlos Muricy, *Os Motivos da Revolução Democrática Brasileira: Palestras Pronunciadas na Televisão Canal 2, nos Dias 19 e 25 de Maio de 1964*, p. 19.

[10] Murici interview, November 18, 1975.

[11] Costa e Silva, "Costa e Silva relata episódios da Revolução"; Edmundo Neves interview, Rio de Janeiro, July 20, 1976.

Murici learned that his Realengo classmate, General de Brigada Orlando Geisel, director of Engineering Equipment (Material de Engenharia), was working for the cause. So was Orlando's younger brother, General de Brigada Ernesto Geisel, who served for a while as commander of the artillery of the Fifth Infantry Division in Curitiba, Paraná, and who, after helping to prepare the ground there for a possible antiadministration movement, was transferred to a desk job, becoming assistant head of the army Department of Supply (Provisão Geral) on the fourth floor of the ministry. The Geisel brothers were prominent in army circles, Orlando having been chief of staff of the First Army and Ernesto having been a member of Café Filho's Casa Militar and the army's representative on the National Petroleum Council. Another brigadier general without troops who conspired with Murici in Rio was José Horácio da Cunha Garcia, a transfer from Rio Grande do Sul.[12]

These generals would sometimes come to the office of Castello, explain their disgust with the way things were going, and try to convince their old instructor to head the leaderless and confused conspiracy. But they got nowhere because of Castello's strong devotion to legality and because of his concept of his responsibilities as chief of staff.[13]

Castello's position was fully appreciated by General de Divisão Ademar de Queiroz. Nevertheless, the veteran conspirator, who was due to retire from the army on November 22 when he reached sixty-four, kept Castello informed of every step that he took.[14] These steps are described by his aide as a "tireless work of mobilization and unification of forces" (incansável trabalho de mobilização e aglutinação de forças).[15]

Aliomar Baleeiro, recently elected federal congressman from Guanabara, got in touch with Ademar de Queiroz in October after Argemiro de Assis Brasil had become head of the presidential Casa Militar. Baleeiro, having discovered that Assis Brasil was "generally considered to be a Communist,"[16] exchanged gloomy impressions with Ademar and

---

[12] Murici interview, November 18, 1975; Muricy, *Os Motivos da Revolução Democrática Brasileira*, p. 23.

[13] Ferreira interview (untaped portion), November 12, 1975.

[14] Ademar de Queiroz interview, Rio de Janeiro, October 13, 1975.

[15] Frederico Mendes de Moraes, "Depoimento de Frederico Mendes de Moraes a Pedido do Sr. John W. F. Dulles . . ." (typewritten), Rio de Janeiro, December 19, 1975, p. 3.

[16] Aliomar Baleeiro, "Recordações do Presidente H. Castelo Branco" (typewritten), p. 5.

then learned from the general that Castello Branco would receive him.

Castello suggested that they meet at night at his Nascimento Silva Street house and that Ademar come along, and he agreed with Baleeiro's request that his UDN colleague, Congressman Olavo Bilac Pinto, also be present. Bilac Pinto was preparing a series of antigovernment speeches for which he wanted UDN backing, but Baleeiro, not certain that the situation was exactly as Bilac Pinto described, felt the consultation with the generals would be helpful.[17]

When the meeting took place, Castello listened to the two congressmen speak about the situation, and he occasionally asked a question. He agreed that the outlook was grave, but said that the president of the republic headed the armed forces and should be upheld by, and obeyed by, the armed forces. This was like "a dose of cold water" to Baleeiro.[18] However, the lawmaker was given a bit of satisfaction because Castello added that Congress was also one of the powers that should be protected by the armed forces.

Bilac Pinto and Castello discussed the Communist technique of "revolutionary war." Following the meeting, Bilac Pinto used "revolutionary war" as the theme of his attacks against Goulart and Brizola made in Congress and in the press.[19]

4. A Prescription for Reviving Professionalism (October, 1963)

Castello Branco hoped to save legality in Brazil by persuading the war minister to take steps to cure the ills that professionals felt had developed in the army. Therefore on October 23 he submitted to Jair a lengthy memorandum, carefully divided and subdivided, entitled "The Political-Military Situation."[1] In it he said that the Army Staff agreed that the armed forces should be identified with Brazil's political-social evolution, but he also felt it imperative that the military be protected from groups contending for political power. The chief questions, he

---

[17] Olavo Bilac Pinto interview, Brasília, October 21, 1975.

[18] Aliomar Baleeiro interview, Rio de Janeiro, September 19, 1975.

[19] Baleeiro, "Recordações do Presidente H. Castelo Branco," p. 6. See Olavo Bilac Pinto, *Guerra Revolucionária.*

[1] HACB memorandum to War Minister Dantas Ribeiro, October 22, 1963, File L2, CPDOC (see also covering letter dated October 23).

added, were whether the armed forces would remain "in tune with" the will of the Brazilian people, who wanted them to guarantee elections, mandates, and the powers of government, and whether at the same time the armed forces would remain efficient, disciplined, and legal, so as to permit full development of Brazil's social and political evolution.

Before giving suggestions for bringing these things about, Castello's memorandum analyzed the situation for the war minister. Listing contending groups in Brazil, it mentioned one which favored a legal approach to immediate political-economic-social evolution and a second group, with "an ambiguous ideology," which wanted to seize power and which sometimes called for reforms and sometimes advocated the elimination of the forces opposing it. This group, Castello wrote, sought to make use of the first group and also of a third group, the Communists, who, in turn, infiltrated the first group and usually made use of the second group. In a fourth category Castello placed the antigovernment groups which supported the Constitution and struggled against the second and third groups.

While the first group sought the "guarantee" of the armed forces, and groups in the fourth category sought military support for their political activities, the second and third groups, Castello reported, were working, especially through sergeants allied with labor unions, to place the military "at their service." Castello pictured sergeants ("not yet in large numbers") as using sergeants' associations to back the forces that favored subversion, and he said that politicians had come to consider sergeants as outweighing commissioned officers in importance in the troops.

Within the military, Castello insisted, a cause of "the present crisis" was "without doubt" the deflation of professionalism. This problem he attributed in large part to insufficient funds, but he added two other causes: the use of the army for police work and the attention given to "personal-political" attitudes rather than to professional qualifications. "As a result, efficiency is the attribute that has become most neglected."

Adding to the difficulty for the armed forces, Castello said, was the "antimilitary" conduct of those officers ("still not a great many") who supported "pseudorevolutionary politicians" and who helped to exert pressure, compromising their commands and giving the impression that the army was becoming militialike or was participating in the first stage of the move of the so-called popular forces.

According to Castello, the so-called popular forces aggressively threatened the army's unity, its professional life, and its normal structure. While he classified the "illegal and subversive" CGT as the outstanding component of these "popular forces," he went on to provide what he called "one of the most authoritative definitions of 'popular forces'" by quoting PTB Congressman Almino Afonso, who had recently been Goulart's labor minister. According to Almino Afonso the "popular forces" consisted of the CGT, the National Student Union (UNE), the Nationalist Parliamentary Front (FPN), and the Brazilian Union of Secondary School Students (UBES) as well as "sergeants, corporals, soldiers, nationalist officers, political leaderships of the vanguard, peasant leagues, etc." Almino Afonso, Castello reminded the war minister, had recently declared that Brazil, "with Goulart's policy of conciliation," would experience a series of crises ending in a "*golpista* solution" or else in "the social revolution" made by the "popular forces." ("A gloomy forecast," Castello wrote, "either a *golpe*, or a revolution by subversive processes.")

Castello denied the existence of a military conspiracy, but he detected "collusion" among civilians "who seek to involve workers, members of the state police forces, and a few officers and sergeants of the armed forces in order to take full control of the government, close Congress, and establish an undemocratic regime."[2] Meanwhile the Brazilian people, as described by Castello, wanted legality, peace, and well-being and opposed military pressure and the constant strikes.

In the analysis presented to Jair, and in the conclusions as well, Castello expressed thoughts that he had often expressed in the past about the failings of the state police troops and about the distortion of the purposes of the armed forces. "With secondary purposes becoming the principal ones," he saw a neglect of professionalism and of the defense of the democratic institutions.

As in 1961, Castello considered the unity of the armed forces a guarantee against subversion of the civil and juridical order. However, he was more worried than before about the maintenance of that unity. He warned the war minister that it was in danger.

Castello had four suggestions: (1) the Army High Command should be vitalized and consulted; (2) troop commanders should be guided so

[2] HACB originally used the word *ditadura* but crossed it out and wrote *um regime extra-legal*.

that, in a unified manner, they would promote legality and guarantee the Constitution; (3) political and other illegal strikes should be "banished"; and (4) the state police forces, negligent in their jobs, should be instructed and reorganized—"with full respect for the autonomy of the states"—in order that they, rather than the army, perform all police duties.

The Army Staff would take what steps it could to remedy the situation. It would propose a directive for the war minister to use to "regulate completely" the role of the army in internal security. And it would itself issue a directive to make the instruction of sergeants and commissioned officers appropriate for the situation.

In a brief reply to Castello's long memorandum, Jair expressed his agreement "in principle," but he went on to say that he feared that the High Command, "whose attributes should be specifically military," would become essentially political if Castello's views prevailed; the war minister resolved once again to regulate the law of 1956 to define the attributes of the High Command. Jair also emphasized that Castello's document was filled with "implications that transcend the sphere of this Ministry, even interfering with the autonomy of the states and with the legislative and judicial powers."[3]

5. The Retirement of Ademar de Queiroz (November, 1963)

A few days after Castello submitted his memorandum to Jair, the General Command of Workers (CGT), some of whose most important leaders were Communists, started what it hoped would be a "general strike" in São Paulo and Santos to get 100 percent pay increases with living cost adjustments every three months. The state government of big, gruff Ademar de Barros denounced the impending strike as a scheme for creating chaotic conditions which would allow the federal government to intervene in São Paulo.

The srike paralyzed the port city of Santos, but it was only a partial success, since fewer than half of the seven hundred thousand workers associated with the eighty-odd striking unions heeded the strike call. After four days the strike ended, with the regional labor tribunal declar-

[3] Jair Dantas Ribeiro to HACB, Rio de Janeiro, October 30, 1963.

ing it illegal but ruling that in most of the industries the workers should receive 80 percent wage increases.

Contributing to the strike's lack of success was the action of the state police and Second Army troops in arresting strike leaders and protecting workers who stayed on their jobs. Goulart and Assis Brasil felt that Second Army commander Peri Constant Bevilaqua was falling under the influence of Governor Ademar de Barros and possibly also of conspirators. Therefore in November General Bevilaqua was removed from the command of troops by being appointed chief of staff of the armed forces, which had become largely a decorative position.

To succeed Bevilaqua in the Second Army, Goulart turned to Amauri Kruel, who was not on good terms with Ademar de Barros. It was no doubt comforting for Goulart to have so close a friend in the key São Paulo army command, and the appointment allowed the president, unhappy with the CGT's opposition to his recent state of siege request, to show that he could act independently of the wishes of the CGT. Kruel, who hoped to solve Brazil's problems by bringing Goulart to the anti-Communist side, was disliked by the CGT.[1]

With the promotions that went into effect on November 25, Amauri was advanced to *general de exército*, the appropriate rank for his new position, which meant that his obligatory retirement from the army would be at the age of sixty-six instead of sixty-four. But it was otherwise with General de Divisão Ademar de Queiroz, and late in November he left active service after more than forty-six years in the army. Upon entering the *reserva*, he was elevated to the rank of marshal because the regulations stipulated that retirees were to receive one advancement in rank for each of the following achievements: (1) service of over thirty-five years, (2) combat against the Communist uprising of 1935, and (3) participation in World War II. Castello, presiding at the retirement ceremony, praised Ademar's "aversion to sensationalism and rejection of demagoguery."[2]

Artillery Captain Frederico Mendes de Morais, Ademar's aide (*ajudante de ordens*), had impressed Castello so well that arrangements were made for him to become Castello's aide on the day after Ademar

[1] Riograndino Kruel interview, Rio de Janeiro, September 19, 1975; Luís Tenório de Lima interview, São Paulo, November 21, 1968; Dante Pelacani interview, São Paulo, November 24, 1968.

[2] HACB, "Despedida de Oficial General," November, 1963, File G1, CPDOC.

retired. Mendes de Morais writes that Ademar, after his retirement, continued to work at the *mobilização* and *aglutinação* of forces that were dismayed by acts of the administration.[3] The marshal conferred with his companions of the 1954 "colonels' manifesto," particularly Generals Ernesto Geisel and Golberi do Couto e Silva, and with General Cordeiro de Farias. Cordeiro and Ernesto Geisel, like Ademar, were artillerymen. Golberi, an infantry officer who had retired from the army after heading the intelligence work of the National Security Council under President Quadros, was now associated with the Instituto de Pesquisas e Estudos Sociais (IPES), which businessmen of Rio and São Paulo supported in the hope that it would create intellectual barriers against the spreading of Marxist ideas; Golberi ran an intelligence service for IPES.

At the moment the anti-Goulart army men were furious that in the promotions list of November 25 Orlando Geisel and Ulhoa Cintra had been bypassed.[4] If anything else were needed to clarify the determination of Goulart and Assis Brasil to make use of promotions and appointments to build up the presidential *dispositivo militar*, it was the promotion of Admiral Cândido Aragão, poorly educated and poorly regarded in the navy, and his appointment to be commander of the Marines. Equally irritating to the advocates of professionalism in the military was the belief that Goulart and Assis Brasil were establishing a *comando paralelo* whereby the Casa Militar was used to communicate with, and give orders to, officers in a manner that ignored the regular military chain of command.[5]

Despite the stimulus given to conspiratorial work by these and other developments, Marshal Ademar de Queiroz left no doubt in the mind of Frederico de Morais that a movement against the regime would fail without the participation of Castello. Mendes de Morais writes that "Ademar could visualize a successful action against the worsening state of affairs only if that action were directed by a chief with the qualities

[3] Mendes de Moraes, "Depoimento," Rio de Janeiro, December 19, 1975.

[4] See IPES intelligence reports (copies of which were supplied in 1965 and 1966 to Rollie E. Poppino and JWFD by Heitor Ferreira), report for December 5, 1963. Another general whose promotion was said to have been denied because of his lack of connections with the Goulart *dispositivo militar* was General de Divisão Otacílio Terra Ururaí.

[5] Carlos de Meira Mattos interview, Washington, D.C., January 5, 1975. See Carlos Castello Branco, *Introdução à Revolução de 1964*, vol. 2, *A Queda de João Goulart*, p. 105.

of leadership that he saw in his old comrade. To bring this about was his great objective, and for this he worked without stint." [6]

Ademar had a good point, for a majority of the officers remained committed to legality.[7] Morais Rego, in charge of troops of the armored division (*divisão blindada*) at Vila Militar, has pointed out that "we military men lived through an intensely dramatic conflict—a terrible conflict—about whether to participate in something not legal. For me it was a grave problem to decide what to order my soldiers to do." Morais Rego adds that the participation of Castello, the foremost exponent of legality, in an antiadministration movement would resolve this dissonance for most of the great number of officers who had learned from Castello, listened to him, and come to respect him over the years.[8] It would be the signal that the administration itself had become too much the violator of legality to be sustained.

If anything, Ademar in retirement felt freer to conspire than before. And while he appreciated that the chief of staff was not a man to take steps behind the backs of the men he was serving, he nevertheless saw the possibility of Castello eventually leading a movement to sustain democracy against an attack by Goulart and the far Left. As Murici has put it: "Ademar de Queiroz was always careful to preserve the image of Castello, so that at the opportune moment he would be in a condition to assume the leadership of the movement." [9]

Loyally, Castello persevered at trying to keep the war minister out of the quicksand of the influences surrounding Goulart, and in the meantime, a large number of army officers could not be budged from the reverence for legality that they shared with Castello. Augusto César Moniz de Aragão, who had been Castello's chief of staff in Recife, has written: "I did not conspire, nor did I confabulate, and much less did I associate with any group or assume any commitments." [10] When Júlio de Mesquita Filho, of *O Estado de S. Paulo*, tried to convince Costa e Silva that he should join an anti-Goulart conspiracy, the army's head of production and works stoutly rejected the idea.[11]

[6] Mendes de Moraes, "Depoimento," p. 2.
[7] Muricy, *Os Motivos da Revolução Democrática Brasileira*, p. 18.
[8] Morais Rego Reis interview, October 22, 1975.
[9] Murici interview, November 18, 1975.
[10] Augusto César Moniz de Aragão, "O Depoimento do General Moniz de Aragão," *O Globo*, March 30, 1975.
[11] Rui Mesquita interview, November 6, 1975.

6. Studies for Army Reorganization (December, 1963)

For Castello Branco the foremost appeal of being chief of staff lay in the possibility of providing Brazil with a complete army reorganization, the urgent need of which he had stressed when writing to Amarante from Belém in 1959.

During Castello's first two months as chief of staff, he and his team carried out studies that resulted in the formulation of seven documents that he considered basic for this work. In November and December, 1963, Castello drew up the first draft of the reorganization plan.[1] Its "imperative" need was explained in the opening remarks: (1) weapons and methods of war had changed, with repercussions on the organization and use of Brazilian forces; (2) world conditions required reconsideration of the "types and forms" of conflict in which Brazil might become engaged; and (3) army organization should be suited to the nation's political-social-economic evolution not only in order to establish a proper relation between the military and civilian structures, but also to correct, before it became too late, errors occasioned by "deviations and misconceptions" that the evolution had brought to the armed forces. As examples of the "deviations and misconceptions" Castello listed the collapse of professionalism, the tendency to ignore "selection" in the ranking of officers, and the attacks against standards that were basic for organization and discipline.

The December 5, 1963, typed draft of the plan of reform, as modified by many handwritten changes, sets forth Castello's conclusions. According to them, the organization of the land forces into army units was excellent because the armies constituted economical and simple means for handling of troops. Army corps, Castello argued, should be formed in wartime only, in order to coordinate the work of the divisions.

Infantry divisions were described as useful but handicapped by the existence of regiments, which Castello felt lacked flexibility and were difficult to handle logistically. The infantry battalion was praised as a truly satisfactory unit to use. And the organization of the artillery into groups was pronounced to have been the best feature of the army reorganization of 1943, as shown by subsequent experience in war and peace.

[1] HACB, "Reorganização do Exército" (typewritten draft, with the date December 5, 1963, crossed out and with handwritten changes), File J, Part 2, p. 14v., CPDOC.

Castello called for the extinction of the horse cavalry and the end of cavalry divisions, accompanied by the evolution of mechanized cavalry units. He had little esteem for armored divisions, for he found that they served only as decorations in parades and as "catalysts" at times when the public order was disturbed.

Turning to the expansion of "secondary purposes" of the army, Castello criticized the increased emphasis on construction engineering, a development harmful to combat engineering, and he also criticized the proliferation of *colégios militares*, describing them as expensive and as tying up many members of the fighting force in providing secondary education. Citing the ineptitude of the military police forces, he called for their reorganization with more control by the army (but without disrespecting the autonomy of the states).

After touching on the possible need to employ new techniques for future coastal defense (mines, missiles, and detection systems), Castello mentioned the consideration being given to naval and army aviation. As far as the army was concerned, he said that the creation of a new branch, aviation, would be costly, impractical, and logistically difficult and that, at least for a long time to come, the army should rely on the air force with the help of instruction common to both.

Castello, often known as a centralizer, preached decentralization when he dealt with the reform of military administration. The hypertrophy of the ministry, he said, made some organs innocuous and stifled the functioning of others. Citing the proliferation of organs directly dependent on the war minister, Castello asserted that rational and efficient operation had become lost. He added that the position of the Army General Staff (Estado Maior) would have to be reappraised, and he also suggested a revival of the importance of the roles of the army's departments.

Another matter that interested Castello was a revision of the retirement promotion system that was producing scores of marshals of the army in considerable contrast to the extremely restrictive use of that rank in France. "Perhaps those of us who retire as *generais de exército* are to become 'Popes,' " Castello joked to General de Divisão Lyra Tavares when reflecting on the three jumps beyond the top general rank. But Marshal Mascarenhas de Morais wanted the preservation of the advantage that the arrangement brought to those who had served in the FEB, and so no proposal was advanced for reforming a practice that Castello described as "absurd."[2]

7. Legality during Administrative Incompetence (late November, 1963)

While working on the Army Reorganization Plan, Castello Branco sat in at the sessions of a two-month course about "revolutionary war" given by the Army Staff under the direction of General Emílio Maurel Filho. In the closing speech for the course, written in November, 1963, Castello said that one of the most serious matters before the Army Staff was the formulation of the part of Brazilian military doctrine that concerned revolutionary war in Brazil.[1] Only the heedless, he added, would fail to see that the outbreaks of random riots and urban agitation were part of the relentless course of revolutionary war.

This speech, which Castello asked his listeners to regard as secret for the time being, contained a vehement attack on the manner in which democracy was practiced in Brazil. The worsening national situation, Castello declared, was helpful to Marxist-Leninist action but was more to be blamed on a lack of orderly evolution than on the ever-increasing Communist infiltration. Democracy, he said, was doing nothing about the standards of living for the people of all regions, while the leftists, associated with the Communists, worked frantically in support of the demands of workers in ports, transportation, and industry, causing a serious social disequilibrium. "While democracy is remiss, Communism carries on with its role."

Castello argued that a continuation of these conditions would help bring on the revolutionary war. "Should the democrats simply mark time by denouncing what the Communists want?" Anti-Communist vigilance, he pointed out, was all very well, but he added that in an under-

---

[2] Lyra Tavares interview, July 18, 1977.

[1] HACB, "Observações Finais," November, 1963 (handwritten speech closing Estado Maior do Exército course "Guerra Revolucionária"), File L2, CPDOC. Some thoughts from this speech are given in HACB, *Marechal Castello Branco: Seu Pensamento Militar*, pp. 223–227.

developed country an anti-Communism that did not also attend to national evolution was limiting itself to vigilance and doing nothing to combat Communism.

"Our democratic political system preserves outmoded standards and says, sometimes challengingly and sometimes humbly, that it is up to the armed forces to stop or destroy Communism. Well, that is not the proper way to handle Brazilian evolution and much less is it the way to combat Communism. Truly it reflects the political and administrative incapacity of our democracy."

Although in the months ahead Castello would continue to urge adherence to legality, much as he had in the past, he admitted in this speech that circumstances were such as to prevent legality from saving the situation. For one thing, he noted that legality provided Communism with "large and small opportunities to infiltrate." For another thing, he felt that legality was handicapped by the prevalent political practices and by capitalism, both harmful to true democracy. "One can understand legality's inadequacy to promote the political, economic, and social evolution of Brazil."

8. A Report of Plans for a Coup (December, 1963)

From time to time Castello Branco joined Costa e Silva in paying calls on army men who were closer than they to the president. These two *generais de exército*, at the top of the hierarchy of the Army High Command, were backed by their subordinates when they pleaded with the war minister that steps be taken to prevent Goulart from falling under Communist control.[1] They took their message also to First Army commander Armando de Morais Âncora, a Realengo classmate who had served in the FEB and had become known as a Vargas supporter.

Early in December Castello was told by Murici that Goulart had a plan to carry out a coup to dominate Brazil. Murici, after explaining that his report was based on sources linked to Laranjeiras Palace, put his informant in touch with Castello and others, including Ulhoa Cintra and former President Dutra. From all that Castello could learn from his

---

[1] Muricy, *Os Motivos da Revolução Democrática Brasileira*, p. 19.

own intelligence men and from Golberi, it appeared that Murici's information was accurate.[2]

Castello and Costa e Silva called again on Jair Dantas Ribeiro, whose prestige had recently been dimmed because his recommendation of the promotion of Ulhoa Cintra had been overruled by the president's office.[3] Speaking aggressively, Costa e Silva said that a coup was being planned by the administration and that he was going to fight against it. Jair declared that despite the evidence brought by Castello, he did not believe the report about Goulart's plan for a coup.

"But, Jair," Castello asked, "supposing it is true?"

"I am a democrat," the minister replied, "and I shall oppose a coup by the president."

"Good!" Castello exclaimed, "Now we have a leader."[4]

The need for a leader in the work to prevent a possible coup was illustrated by an incident in the northeast. Murici, upon hearing the story about Goulart's plan, sent an emissary to alert Hélio Ibiapina and other colonels in the Fourth Army. But the colonels in Recife were puzzled, because at the same time they received another emissary, Colonel Jaime Portela, who worked closely with Cordeiro de Farias, to inquire about the possibility of an uprising. Neither emissary had known what the other was doing.[5]

Castello's remark, "Now we have a leader," got around. But it was not what the conspirators wanted. They felt that Jair was too ambitious politically to do much else but go along with Goulart. "We did not believe," Murici explains, "that Jair would change his ways. We wanted Castello Branco or Costa e Silva, who were working together; most of all we wanted Castello."[6]

The story about Goulart's intentions persuaded the conspirators in Rio that it was futile to rely on the hope that Goulart could be converted to their way of thinking, and they resolved "to prepare the counter-revolution, to act in order to face up to the coup."[7] At about the same

---

[2] Ibid., pp. 19–20.

[3] IPES intelligence report for December 5, 1963.

[4] Muricy, *Os Motivos da Revolução Democrática Brasileira*, p. 20.

[5] Ibid., p. 21.

[6] Murici interview, November 18, 1975.

[7] Muricy, *Os Motivos da Revolução Democrática Brasileira*, p. 21.

time, the plotting in São Paulo military circles, which had been organized
by Lieutenant Colonel Rubens Resstel, gained great strength as a result
of the late October "general strike" by the CGT. Now sixty or seventy
young anti-Goulart officers would attend the Friday night meetings
where earlier only five or six had gathered.[8]

9. The Army and Agrarian Reform (January, 1964)

"Popular forces," such as those listed by Almino Afonso, had
formed the Frente de Mobilização Popular to push for a "popular" program, including the suspension of payments on foreign debts, the prohibition of the remission of profits abroad, agrarian reform, voting rights
for illiterates, and political rights for noncommissioned officers. Men
associated with the *frente*, such as Brizola, labor leaders, and PCB leaders, often squabbled, but they agreed that Goulart was "vacillating,"
and therefore they all denounced the president.

Early in January, 1964, following more than two months of attacks
from the far Left, Goulart brought his "vacillations" to an end. Heed-
ing Assis Brasil and other close advisers,[1] the president intervened in
support of the Communists in the election of the huge National Confederation of Workers in Industry (CNTI), thus assuring Communist
domination of organized labor. While this significant Communist victory would make it increasingly difficult for the president to reject the
demands of the Communists and their allies, it gained for him some
ostensive "popular" backing as he sought to exert pressure on a balky
Congress on behalf of reforms. Chiefly, Goulart called for a constitutional amendment to advance agrarian reform by allowing that bonds,
instead of cash, be used for indemnifications when large landholdings
were expropriated for redistribution.

The Frente de Mobilização Popular, after consulting Brizola and
Governor Arraes, issued a manifesto on January 18 to point out that the
president had full authority to handle numerous matters himself regardless of Congress. He could, the *frente* insisted, carry out at once a limited agrarian reform program under which the Superintendency of
Agarian Reform Planning (SUPRA) would make cash payments for

[8] Eldino Brancante interview, São Paulo, November 24, 1965.
[1] Gilberto Crockatt de Sá interview, Rio de Janeiro, October 9, 1967.

expropriations of land adjoining federal highways, railroads, and hydraulic projects. And, the *frente* added, he could expropriate the country's largest privately owned petroleum refinery so that would come under the management of Petrobrás.

This second demand should not be taken to mean that the Petrobrás management was universally admired. Besides being corrupt, it was noted, as General Bevilaqua pointed out, for its partiality to Communists. Glycon de Paiva, who considered Petrobrás "the most important Communist bastion in America, after Cuba," calculated that the government petroleum extraction monopoly had twenty-nine key posts, of which twenty-one were in the hands of "militants of the Russian line" and one in the hands of a follower of the Chinese line.[2]

For the time being Goulart concentrated on plans to expropriate landholdings near federal highways, railroads, and hydraulic projects. The military ministers, meeting with Goulart and SUPRA officials, agreed to help with this program.

Castello Branco learned about the war minister's commitment to SUPRA on January 27 when he received a copy of the agreement from the director of the Army Geographic Service. The document revealed that the Army Geographic Service, a section that reported to the Army Staff, was to carry out aerial photography; undertake studies of soil, climate, forestry, and geoeconomics; and join with SUPRA in indicating what areas should be surveyed.[3]

Immediately Castello discussed with the director of the Geographic Service the feasibility of complying with Jair's commitment. Then he wrote an "urgent" memorandum to the war minister. Pointing out that the Army Staff had been given no opportunity to offer an opinion about the participation of an organ subordinated to it, Castello advised that the Geographic Service lacked the knowledge and equipment necessary to participate in studies of soil, climate, forestry, and geoeconomics. Castello stated that the indication of areas for agrarian reform should be made by SUPRA, with the Army Geographic Service limiting itself to comments on the practicability of surveying them.[4]

---

[2] Glycon de Paiva, "Petrobrás como Banco da Subversão Nacional e Escola Prática de Corrupção," *Jornal do Brasil*, February 16, 1964.

[3] HACB memorandum (Ofício 6-64-S/5-1) to War Minister Dantas Ribeiro, Rio de Janeiro, January 27, 1964, File L2, CPDOC.

[4] Ibid.

Castello, who disliked the idea of the army doing this sort of work at any time, appreciated that the subject was fraught with emotion at the moment. While Brizola and others urged farm workers to use arms to seize landholdings, property owners were organizing to resist invasions, and some of them were prepared to defy the terms of any SUPRA decree that the president might sign. Castello reminded the war minister that as a result of his new agreement with SUPRA and "in view of the tendencies of the agrarian policy," the army might well be called on to participate in other aspects of the contemplated reform—"for example, the employment of troops, specialized or not, in the areas being considered. This could involve the Army in questions that are outside of its competency and give it a position that does not correspond to its functions."

The press reported that Castello, backed by "a large number of top-ranking officers," was describing the military agreement with SUPRA as something designed simply to "give an air of respectability to the plan for the progressive communization of the nation." It also reported that Castello was about to be dismissed from his post and replaced by the commander of the First or Fourth Army. Hastily Jair issued a denial of any intention to make changes in the "high Army commands."[5]

[5] *O Estado de S. Paulo*, February 19, 21, 22, 1964.

Preparing to Prevent a Coup
(early 1964)

The only signs I saw were hammers and sickles.

1. "We Have a Chief and a Leader" (January–February, 1964)

DURING December, 1963, and January, 1964, Castello Branco, a man who detested inaction, became convinced of the need to plan resolutely to prevent the much discussed coup. Ademar de Queiroz therefore felt that the time had come to bring Castello, the foremost legalist, together with Cordeiro de Farias, the foremost conspirator, for the relations between the two had been strictly formal. Castello, Ademar appreciated, would be a more acceptable leader for the anti-Goulart movement not only because of the esteem in which he was held by the legalists, but also because Cordeiro had some liabilities. Cordeiro had become regarded as a "military-politico" during a long and prominent career that had brought him into the disfavor of some sectors; other sectors had been disenchanted with his performance during the crisis of August–September, 1961, when, after being appointed head of the Third Army, he had been unable to deal with the situation in the south.

The key meeting of the three FEB veterans, Cordeiro, Castello, and Ademar, took place one night late in January, 1964, at Ademar's home and lasted for many hours. Early the next morning Murilo Gomes Ferreira was told by Ademar, "Now we have a chief and a leader." [1]

From these few words Gomes Ferreira knew that Cordeiro was placing in Castello's hands the important organization that Cordeiro had been helping to build up for a long time. A reaction of the Cordeiro men is contained in the remark of Colonel Sebastião Ferreira Chaves

---

[1] Murilo Gomes Ferreira, "O General Castella Que Conheci" (transcript of tape prepared for interview), Rio de Janeiro, November 12, 1975, p. 11.

when he learned of the new situation from a colonel working with Castello: "We are the ones who have been in this for over two years! And
you fellows are coming in now."[2]

Castello was not only "coming in now." He was making sure that
the future work of those who had been conspiring for an armed overthrow of the Goulart regime would have a strictly legalist interpreta-
tion. The result can be seen in the final text of a confidential communication, "Lealdade ao Exército" (Loyalty to the Army), that had been
originally prepared by Ulhoa Cintra, with some help from Cordeiro, for
distribution to "fully trustworthy" officers in command posts in the different army regions.[3]

Late in January Castello went over the wording of Ulhoa Cintra and
Cordeiro, making observations and suggestions in his handwriting and
deciding on the omission of one section.[4] It has been said that the document—which became known, for short, as Le-Ex—sought to harmonize
the views of the legalists and those of the longtime proponents of an
armed overthrow of the Goulart regime.[5] But the final document was
thoroughly legalist, and if its thoughts appeared too legalist for some of
the veteran conspirators, they were accepted to satisfy Castello and because the conspirators were confident that Goulart would violate the
law.[6]

The opening sentence of Le-Ex, Murici points out, was intended to
let it be known that Castello was "in the movement." It read: "A large
number of officers of the Armed Forces, consisting of military men of
rigorously democratic background and convictions, free of any political
party connections, equidistant from rightist and leftist radicalism, entirely dedicated to professional tasks, and of proven experience, some of
them in high posts of the hierarchy, have resolved, in view of the grave
situation in which the nation is struggling, to coordinate the goals and
efforts that have been observed in vast areas of the Armed Forces."[7]

The document went on to say that the officers mentioned in the first

[2] José Stacchini, *Março 64: Mobilização da Audácia*, p. 80.

[3] Antônio Carlos da Silva Murici interview, Rio de Janeiro, November 18, 1975;
Osvaldo Cordeiro de Farias interview, Rio de Janeiro, December 16, 1974.

[4] Murici interview, November 18, 1975.

[5] Stacchini, *Março 64*, p. 80.

[6] Vernon Walters interview, Arlington, Virginia, July 15, 1976.

[7] "Documento Leex (Lealdade ao Exército)," in Hélio Silva, *1964: Golpe ou Contragolpe?*, pp. 466–471.

sentence were determined to save Brazil's Christian traditions and democratic institutions and wanted the Goulart administration to complete its term and turn the government over to those scheduled to be elected in 1965 to succeed it. To bring this transition about, Le-Ex warned, it was necessary to avoid partial and isolated actions and manifestations that could only favor "the energetic and brash minority" that looked for an opportunity to implant a Communist regime.

The document declared that "false nationalism" did not conceal the Marxist-Leninist convictions of the agitators, and it went on to express the "justified fear" that certain governmental sectors, "through a fraudulent and shrewd use of their prerogatives," would destroy the social order and representative democracy. It lamented the control that Communists had gained over Petrobrás.

Commenting on the military, Le-Ex denounced the efforts to malign the armed forces and to use them to carry out "illegal and criminal missions." It decried the subversion of professional and moral values, "most evident in military promotions and assignments." The armed forces, Le-Ex said, would not submit to "the game" of sowing discord among their components, undermining discipline, destroying efficiency, and, in the end, replacing the armed forces by an imitation of a Red Army or a Cuban militia.

This first part of Le-Ex, which Ulhoa Cintra had prepared for the guidance of "trustworthy" officers, was followed by a second part which he intended to use as a survey by having the Le-Ex recipients submit a list of questions to subordinates. The questions were drawn up to reveal the officers' reactions to the Brazilian situation and their ideas as to precisely what antidemocratic steps by the administration would be sufficient to lead them to feel that the "exact moment" had come to start an antiadministration military uprising. A further question in the second part asked whether the decision about the "exact moment" should rest with "a military leader of outstanding reputation, nonpolitical, who is highly regarded in military circles."

It was this second part, with its questions, that Castello eliminated. The first part was distributed in the northeast and, more extensively, in Rio Grande do Sul—where it made a favorable impression on, among others, Major Leo Etchegoyen, son of General Alcides Etchegoyen.[8]

---

[8] Murici interview, November 18, 1975. Alcides Etchegoyen had been arrested by Lott's supporters on November 11, 1955.

2. The Leading Interpreter of Army Thinking (February, 1964)

Some of Castello's thoughts at the beginning of February were expressed in a letter that he sent to Recife for Lieutenant Colonel Hélio Ibiapina, whom he had instructed as a third-year cadet late in 1940 and recently come to know well in the Fourth Army. It was an affectionate letter in which Castello expressed regret that he would not be stopping in Recife on his forthcoming trip to Ceará. "I hope that your children have a good time during Carnaval. How I remember them, happy and enjoying themselves during the festivities at the Casino of the Fourteenth RI! Argentina didn't take her eyes off them, following with pleasure the warm smile of each."

Turning to military matters, Castello wrote: "The conviction grows that it is necessary to react vigorously, with initiative, in the case of the always coveted coup d'etat. There is, in fact, an open work going on that has nothing to do with conspiracy but seeks to demonstrate to comrades the need to act offensively on behalf of legality." Castello added that in this work, and considering the situation in Brazil, legality should be defined as assuring the operation of Congress, together with the executive and the judiciary branches, and guaranteeing the electoral process, the elections, and the inauguration of January 31, 1966. "There you have the military position."

Foreseeing the possible need to employ the armed forces, Castello also told Ibiapina: "In the legalist reaction, the Fourth Army is essential. It will be enough that it remain in action for about 48 hours. It will not stand alone."[1]

"The need to act offensively on behalf of legality" was an idea that Castello incorporated in the speech that he was preparing to give at the opening of the new school year at the Escola de Aperfeiçoamento de Oficiais. Defense, he wrote in longhand on one of the large, unlined white sheets that he used, was an attitude of waiting and was admissible only on a temporary basis and only if employed to strengthen a counterattack. An offensive attitude, the tactician added, would bring decisive results.[2]

[1] HACB to Hélio Ibiapina, Rio de Janeiro, February 2, 1964, File L2, CPDOC.
[2] HACB, "A EsAO na Atualidade Militar," File L2, CPDOC. Twelve hundred copies of this speech were printed by Estabelecimento General Gustavo Cordeiro de Farias, an organ of the army, in February, 1964.

Castello delivered his Escola de Aperfeiçoamento speech, in the presence of Jair, to about four hundred army captains on February 20. Before getting to the heart of his message, the sixty-six-year-old army chief of staff opened by saying that at his stage of life it was difficult to summon the vigor and strength necessary for instructing young officers. But he remarked that his post made it fitting for him to address them, and he went on to discuss some of their concerns, not omtting the effect of the great inflation on their lives.

Acknowledging that one concern was the shortage of funds available for modern army esuipment, Castello pointed out that it was due in part to the "undeniable need" of the government to devote an increased percentage of its resources to the well-being of the Brazilian people. In spite of this need, he said, the War Ministry had a program for modernizing the army's weapons, and he added that the military accord with the United States could be expected soon to result in the reequipment of some units. He mentioned the modernization of the army structure and administration, to be provided by the reorganization plan devised by the Army Staff, and he stressed the importance of a forward-looking mentality, opposed to anachronisms, on the part of officers.

Turning to another matter that, he said, quite rightly concerned his listeners, Castello spoke of national and internal security. In this connection he declared that the relentless conflict between democracy and Communism presented the world with the greatest ideological struggle of the entire twentieth century.[3] Brazilians who did not recognize this struggle were guilty of "neglecting" their homeland.

While Castello counseled against being dominated by "any sort of anti-Communist complex, any obsession that the Red wave has already soiled Brazil," he pointed out that one had only to read the propaganda of the Communists to appreciate that they constituted a danger to the Brazilian institutions and were determined to "subvert the Brazilian armed forces." He went on: "If the Marxist-Leninist Revolutionary War enslaves the nation, who is going to defend the democratic institutions?"

Repeating admonitions expressed in past speeches, Castello said that in the case of party politics, every military officer should reveal no position, lending no support to the government party or to the opposition. He should hover above political struggles because the methods used in

[3] Ibid.

them were incompatible with military duty, and he should insist that party politics be kept apart from the professional military setting. But this did not mean that officers should foresake the "sacred right" of voting.

The army leaders, Castello declared, had grave responsibilities in these matters. Reminding themselves that they were the leaders of a permanent national army and not of militias or praetorian guards, they should set perfect examples. They were also to "anticipate events in order to clarify, guide, and lead."

On the next day, February 21, Castello spoke at a lunch given by the Clube dos Veteranos da 2ª Guerra Mundial (Club of Veterans of World War II) to observe the nineteenth anniversary of the victory at Monte Castello. Recalling Nazi subversion in Brazil early in the war, Castello asserted that Brazil, "now as then," was not insulated from world struggle.[4]

On the same day Castello went to the commemorations held at the monument to those who fell in World War II. He was the only general there, for most of the generals were attending another lunch to observe the fall of Monte Castello, this one in honor of Goulart at Vila Militar—an occasion that was considered a show of military backing for the president.[5] Goulart, with Jair at his side, gave an unprepared talk advocating the enactment of "basic reforms."

The president's effort to use the occasion to promote reforms drew a rebuke the next morning in an editorial of O Estado de S. Paulo, which described him as "preaching subversion." The influential daily said that the president was not the one to interpret the ideas of the top officers of the armed forces. The man to do this, the newspaper suggested, was Army Chief of Staff Castello Branco.[6]

Already, three days earlier, when Castello's dismissal was rumored, a long lead editorial in O Estado de S. Paulo had described Castello as the army's top leader: "Due to his exceptional personal merit he fulfills the role that none of his colleagues disputes as the interpreter of the general thinking within the Army." Explaining that Castello had gained this prestige by his extremely brilliant conduct "as Chief of Staff of the FEB," O Estado de S. Paulo added that "from then on his renown only

[4] O Estado de S. Paulo, February 22, 23, 1964.

[5] Hernani D'Aguiar, A Revolução por Dentro, p. 113.

[6] O Estado de S. Paulo, February 23, 1964 (editorial).

increased, and, reaching beyond the limits of his professional field, spread to all the other sectors of Brazilian social life."

"General Castello Branco," the editorial declared, "is one of those figures who mark an era and is a testimony to the permanence of our national virtues. A soldier above everything else, he always sought to maintain himself rigorously within the strictest discipline, but he never abdicated his civic sentiments." [7]

3. Chatting with Politicians (February, 1964)

One evening Castello dropped in alone to see his old friend Francisco Negrão de Lima, who was back in Rio after having served as ambassador to Portugal. Negrão, who had just been named head of a committee organized to work for Kubitschek's reelection, was rather careful to avoid discussing politics, and he found this a subject about which Castello was also reserved.

Negrão, however, could not refrain from asking the big question of the day: "Humberto, do you think that Goulart is in a position to carry out a coup?" Castello replied that if Goulart were able to carry out a coup very suddenly, it would be because all matters necessary for its success had already been taken care of. But Castello added: "If he needs twenty minutes to carry it out, he will not succeed."

As the hour grew late, Castello ended the evening in his playful manner. "Negrão," he remarked, "we military men, like you diplomats, have nothing to do. But there is a difference. You diplomats get up late and we military men get up early." [1]

UDN Congressmen Bilac Pinto and Aliomar Baleeiro found that Castello had become less cautious about discussing politics than he had been when they had first visited with him in October. Their second visit to the Nascimento Silva Street house, again in the company of Ademar de Queiroz and again at night, took place in February. By then Osvino Ferreira Alves, "the people's marshal," had been named president of Petrobrás, and Goulart was calling for the legalization of the Brazilian Communist Party (PCB).

[7] Ibid., February 20, 1964 (editorial).
[1] Francisco Negrão de Lima interview, Rio de Janeiro, December 10, 1975.

As Castello discussed the Brazilian situation with the two congressmen, they noted a confidence that he had lacked in October. With assurance he declared: "The Armed Forces will not support any movement that favors giving personal or dictatorial power to Jango, but at the same time they will not condone assaults against his rights, as long as they are constitutional rights."

Much of the discussion concerned Goulart. Castello appeared to agree with Bilac's thesis that the president would adhere more and more to the technique of Communist revolutionary war, and he acknowledged that Jango wanted to use sergeants, workers, and Communists for an objective that as yet was not perfectly clear. When Baleeiro suggested that Jango might have in mind crushing the Brazilian Community party after using it, Castello agreed that Jango, interested only in gaining dictatorial powers, might shift to carrying out a rightist coup. He regarded Jango as a "cynic."[2]

The congressmen learned that Castello, asked by Goulart why the generals didn't "converse with the sergeants," had given the president a reply that alluded to the failure of the top authorities to "converse with the generals." Castello explained to the congressmen that the president never listened to the High Command.

When the congressmen asked Castello whether the United States might take any step that would significantly affect the Brazilian picture, he replied in the negative. His advice to Bilac and Baleeiro was to have Congress persevere in its constitutional work, thus helping to close "the iron circle" that was to contain illegal ambitions of Goulart.[3]

Besides appealing to congressmen, Castello appealed to leaders of the press to warn the public against a coup by Goulart and to help build up opinion favorable to a possible legalist reaction by the military. To *O Globo* President Roberto Marinho, with whom he spoke from time to time at the Nascimento Silva Street house, Castello explained that the Brazilian armed forces would act only if moved by public opinion.[4]

---

[2] Aliomar Baleeiro, "Recordações do Presidente H. Castelo Branco" (typewritten), p. 7.

[3] Ibid.

[4] Roberto Marinho interview, Rio de Janeiro, August 11, 1977.

4. Organizing the "Estado Maior Informal" (late February, 1964)

Early in March Castello addressed the sessions that opened the academic years at the ESG and the ECEME. Speaking on behalf of legality to the ECEME students on March 2, he decried the excessive and injudicious employment of the army for police work. Such use, he said, was not helpful to the police forces and contributed both to a decline of professionalism in the army and to a corrosion of the status of the army in the eyes of the people.[1]

Speaking of the ESG, Castello said that whereas in some countries the army was forced to support dictatorial regimes, that was not true in Brazil, "where the regime is backed principally by the people and where the Army can, without difficulties, place itself on the side of legality."[2]

While Castello prepared these messages for advanced students, he and Ademar de Queiroz completed plans for the military defense of legality. The most important step was taken by Ademar de Queiroz, who, at the suggestion of Castello, organized the "informal staff" (*estado maior informal*) consisting of four men: Castello, Ademar de Queiroz, Ernesto Geisel, and Golberi do Couto e Silva.[3]

Thus Ademar de Queiroz, who had recently been instrumental in the understanding reached between Cordeiro and Castello, now brought about a union between Castello and the group known as the "colonels of the 1954 manifesto" or the "*turma do memorial*." The group included, as well as Ernesto Geisel and Golberi, General de Brigada Jurandir de Bizarria Mamede, commander of the ECEME, and retired General Heitor A. Herrera, who worked in IPES with his fellow Gaúcho, Golberi. These men, once associated with the late General Canrobert Pereira da Costa, had resolutely resisted Lott's coup in 1955. Now Ademar de Queiroz argued with them that Castello was probably less hurt by their 1954 manifesto than they thought he was. "He likes you people," Ademar said, "and you should invite him in."[4]

[1] HACB, "Destinação Constitucional e Finalidades do Exército" (address at ECEME, March 2, 1964), in Castello Branco papers, Escola de Comando e Estado Maior. See also excerpt given in Stacchini, *Março 64*, p. 69.

[2] HACB, address at the Escola Superior de Guerra, excerpt given in newspaper clipping, "Como É Facil Ser Legal," File L2, CPDOC.

[3] Golberi do Couto e Silva interview, Brasília, October 22, 1975; Ademar de Queiroz interview, Rio de Janeiro, October 13, 1975.

[4] Heitor A. Herrera interview, Rio de Janeiro, December 16, 1975.

Aside from Castello's reputation, his position as chief of staff was important in the eyes of the longtime conspirators. In the opinion of Heitor Herrera, their movement gained all of Castello's *autoridade moral* when he went in as the leader. "It was our good luck," he says, "that *the* chief became *our* chief." As Golberi has expressed it, "the presence of Castello Branco in the movement meant that it was not an *aventura*." [5]

Emygdio Miranda might feel that Castello persisted in his custom of "associating with reactionaries," but he is quick to point out that Castello, in his new role, was the brains of the planning and "centralized everything." [6] Castello's role is reflected in the summation of the *estado maior informal* given by Murilo Gomes Ferreira, Reynaldo Melo de Almeida, and others. The informal staff "of General Castello," they say, was made up of General Ernesto Geisel, Marshal Ademar de Queiroz, and General Golberi, with cooperation from Generals Mamede, Ulhoa Cintra, and Murici. The *estado maior informal* was also served by many devoted colonels. The meetings, held at night two or three times a week, sometimes at Castello's home and sometimes at Ademar's, were often presided over by Ernesto Geisel and were sometimes attended by officers from posts located in various parts of the country. [7]

The purpose of the *estado maior informal* was the organization of a network in army circles throughout Brazil—the "iron circle" that Castello had mentioned to Bilac and Baleeiro. The informal staff was also to serve as a coordinating body that would assure rapid simultaneous action, if action were needed, and avoid what Le-Ex called "partial and isolated actions and manifestations" that could be easily crushed and thus assist the implantation of a dictatorship.

5. A Military Plan

The *estado maior informal* of Castello Branco inherited a military plan that had been occupying the attention of some of the anti-Goulart conspirators for months.

---

[5] Couto e Silva interview, October 22, 1975. *Aventura*: hazardous enterprise or escapade.

[6] Emygdio da Costa Miranda interview, Rio de Janeiro, December 1, 1975.

[7] Ferreira, "O General Castello Que Conheci," p. 12; Reynaldo Melo de Almeida interview, Rio de Janeiro, October 17, 1975. Early in 1964 Reynaldo Melo de Almeida,

As originally conceived by Ulhoa Cintra in 1963, the plan called for anti-Goulart troops in São Paulo and Minas Gerais to march on Rio, where the top commanders were loyal to Goulart. At certain points in the Rio area these troops were to be greeted fraternally by the Rio troops. To Ulhoa Cintra's annoyance, this idea was modified, still in 1963, by officers who felt that his notion of *fraternidade militar* was a bit exotic. As a result of the study carried out by these officers, among them Francisco Deschamps, Carlos de Meira Mattos, and Murilo Gomes Ferreira, the areas of *fraternidade militar* were designated as areas where "serious decisions" would be reached and where, it was hoped by the conspirators, the officers of lower rank would prevent any engagement against the approaching troops.[1] In the latter part of 1963 Colonel Jaime Portela, working with Cordeiro, showed the plan to General Olímpio Mourão Filho, who was conspiring in Juiz de Fora, Minas Gerais; at about the same time, the plan was taken to São Paulo conspirators by Meira Mattos, who had been transferred from Rio to Mato Grosso because of an attitude considered unfriendly by the administration. Speaking in São Paulo with Ademar de Barros, Meira Mattos found the governor a bold conspirator. "You can," Ademar de Barros told him, "use São Paulo as a bulwark for the revolution."[2]

Castello's *estado maior informal* gave considerable attention to São Paulo. Especially it wanted a pledge from Second Army commander Amauri Kruel to cooperate in an active movement if one became necessary. For although the Fourth Army was felt to be reliable, its location would not allow it to make any rapid contribution in the Rio area.[3]

At the beginning of March, Orlando Geisel discussed with Amauri's brother, retired General Riograndino Kruel, the plans that were being made. Riograndino asked who was to lead the forthcoming pro-legality "revolution." Orlando explained diplomatically that although "the indicated chief" was Amauri Kruel, the plans were being worked out by Castello because he was the chief of staff. Riograndino, immensely surprised to learn that "the famed legalist" was "conspiring," expressed

---

a colonel, was in Curitiba, Paraná, where he had been on the staff of General Ernesto Geisel.

[1] Carlos de Meira Mattos interviews, Washington, D.C., November 18, 1975; August 2, 1976.

[2] Meira Mattos interview, August 2, 1976.

[3] Antônio Carlos Muricy, *Os Motivos da Revolução Democrática Brasileira*, p. 26.

confidence that Amauri would "come to our side." When Riograndino spoke of discussing the situation with Castello, Orlando said, "Speak with great care; Castello does not like to talk about this." [4]

Indeed, Castello, described as *fechado* (closed) under ordinary circumstances, was particularly *fechado* about this matter, as has been made clear by Padre Antônio Godinho, then serving as UDN congressman from São Paulo, and by Adalberto Pereira dos Santos.[5] When General Adalberto, on a visit to Rio, came to the office of the chief of staff to tell Castello about the situation in the far south, he noted that Castello changed the subject quickly when the door opened and an officer entered.

Castello never mentioned the *estado maior informal* and its work when he spoke with Waldetrudes Amarante. Certainly he did not mention it to Guanabara Social Services Secretary Sandra Cavalcanti despite her conspiratorial work at the side of Cordeiro and despite the affectionate relationship that Sandra had enjoyed, ever since her school days in Belo Horizonte, with Argentina and Humberto. It was from Cordeiro that Sandra learned that "Castello heads the conspiracy." [6]

United States Defense Attaché Vernon Walters dropped in frequently at the Nascimento Silva Street house, but while the two friends exchanged impressions about Brazilian events that upset them, Humberto furnished no information about his role with the "conspirators," and Walters was always careful not to take advantage of his friendship by inquiring into areas about which Humberto was reserved. However, at the end of February or early in March the American colonel learned from Colonel Édson de Figueiredo, who had served in the artillery in Italy, that Humberto was involved in a military plan.[7]

Castello limited himself to providing a brief message to oppositionist federal legislators who were determined to press ahead aggressively for the defense of Congress and the Constitution when Congress reconvened in mid-March. Without mentioning any details, he let it be known that the "military plan" had been "worked out." Senator Daniel Krie-

[4] Riograndino Kruel interview, Rio de Janeiro, September 21, 1975.

[5] Antônio de Oliveira Godinho interview, São Paulo, November 7, 1975; Adalberto Pereira dos Santos interview, Brasília, July 23, 1976.

[6] Waldetrudes and Justina Amarante interview, Rio de Janeiro, November 21, 1975; Sandra Cavalcanti interview, Rio de Janeiro, November 18, 1975.

[7] Vernon Walters interviews, McLean, Virginia, June 12, 1975, and Arlington, Virginia, July 15, 1976.

ger, always in touch with Ademar de Queiroz, received such a message from Castello through Irineu Bornhausen (UDN senator from Santa Catarina).[8] This message allowed Krieger, as soon as he had the opportunity, to deliver a Senate speech that could have been regarded as a warning to the administration. The senator declared that "the army of Caxias, the Air Force of Eduardo Gomes, and the Navy of Tamandaré will not associate with the sinister work of the destruction of constitutional order."[9]

6. The Rally of March 13, 1964

With Congress scheduled to reconvene on March 16, the General Command of Workers (CGT) and the Goulart administration spent the second week of March organizing a pro-reform mass meeting to be held in front of the War Ministry building in Rio on March 13. Arrangements were made to have troop protection and a large turnout of organized workers for speechmaking by prominent far leftists such as Brizola, Arraes, Elói Dutra, and student and union leaders, as well as by the president of the republic.

Castello appreciated that the administration wanted the military ministers to attend its "show of strength," but he believed that the war minister's presence would appear to commit the army to a possible undemocratic coup. A majority of the generals felt the same way. Like the army chief of staff, Costa e Silva, Ademar de Queiroz, and others debated the matter with Jair and finally obtained from him a promise that he would not participate in the rally.[1]

From his office in the War Ministry Castello watched the gathering of the crowd for the rally,[2] which was attended by about 120,000. He

8 Daniel Krieger interview, Brasília, October 21, 1975.

9 *O Estado de S. Paulo*, March 18, 1964.

1 Ferreira, "O General Castello Que Conheci," p. 12; Artur da Costa e Silva, "Costa e Silva Relata Episódios da Revolução" (speech at ECEME), April 1, 1965, in *O Estado de S. Paulo*, April 4, 1965, pp. 5–6; Silva, *1964: Golpe ou Contragolpe?*, p. 306.

2 Vernon Walters interview with Phyllis Parker, McLean, Virginia, January 20, 1976, reported in Phyllis Parker, "Separate . . . but Equal? U.S. Policy toward Brazil, 1961–1964," Independent Research Project, Lyndon B. Johnson School of Public Affairs, Austin, Texas, May, 1976, p. 78.

saw a sea of placards bearing Communist slogans, attacks on "gorillas," and calls for reforms, including the legalization of the Brazilian Communist Party (whose "rights" were declared to be "sacred"). Then he went home to follow the speeches on television.

During the aggressive opening speeches by fifteen orators, Brizola "guaranteed" that if a plebiscite were held the Brazilian people would vote for overthrowing the existing Congress and installing a constitutional assembly "with a view to creating a popular Congress, made up of laborers, peasants, sergeants, and nationalist officers, and authentic men of the people." [3]

Before Goulart appeared, the justice minister and the military ministers, among them Jair Dantas Ribeiro, mounted the platform and were greeted by ovations, of which the loudest was that for Jair. Then Goulart delivered a fighting speech in which he announced that he had just signed two decrees, one expropriating all privately owned petroleum refineries and another allowing the expropriation of land adjacent to federal highways, railroads, and hydraulic works. He called for a more radical agrarian reform than this SUPRA decree would allow, and he attacked "so-called democrats" who, he said, condemned popular rallies and wanted the kind of "democracy" that was a thing of privileges and intolerance. At the president's side, sometimes prompting him, was the leader of the stevedores, Osvaldo Pacheco, a member of the Central Committee of the Brazilian Communist Party.

When Vernon Walters dropped in at the Nascimento Silva Street house on the night of the thirteenth, Castello asked him, "Did you see the rally on TV?" Walters said that he had. Castello remarked, "The only signs I saw were hammers and sickles." [4]

Waldetrudes Amarante also spoke with Castello shortly after the rally, and he found the army chief of staff greatly disturbed by what he had witnessed. When Castello wrote on March 14 about the rally to Paulo, who had left for an advanced course given by the United States Navy, he told his son of "the large military apparatus (whatever for?), combat vehicles, marines, troops and more troops," and he reported that "the government spent more than two hundred million cruzeiros!" Mentioning the "threatening speeches," he said that "Brizola wants to take us over the cliff." "I believe," he added, "that there will be reper-

[3] *Correio da Manhã*, March 14, 1964
[4] Walters interview with Phyllis Parker, January 20, 1976.

cussions: invasions of landholdings, general strikes, and the involvement of the Army in all of this."[5]

Ademar de Queiroz concluded that the war minister had become "associated with the subversion."[6] Castello did his duty; calling on Jair, he recited principles about the role of the army that he had been expressing at the advanced military schools, and he added that he was going to issue a circular with advice for his subordinates about the situation.[7] Jair agreed with what Castello said, but by this time Castello had little or no remaining confidence in Jair.[8]

Costa e Silva, asking Jair what had happened, was told that Navy Minister Sílvio Mota, Air Force Minister Anísio Botelho, and Generals Amauri Kruel and Otacílio Terra Ururaí had come to his office and convinced him that his absence from the rally would be a blow to the president. "I am sorry you had to go," Costa e Silva said, "because now there is no way out for you." After Costa e Silva argued that he had done everything possible to help the minister, Jair said: "Costinha, you are right, but what can I do? I am a government minister." Gruffly, Costa e Silva replied that the "Army is more important than the government."[9]

Costa e Silva's interest in military plans to prevent a coup followed this conversation. He spoke with Jaime Portela on the afternoon of March 16 to tell the colonel that he knew that he had been conspiring. Portela admitted to having done some "planning for a revolt." "We are only waiting for a leader," Portela said to Costa e Silva. "Well, you have him," the general said. "I assume command of the Revolution." As Costa e Silva remarked later, he did not then know "who else was involved in the conspiracy."[10]

Like Costa e Silva, citizens throughout Brazil organized to act against

[5] Waldetrudes Amarante, in Amarante interview, November 21, 1975; HACB to Paulo V. Castello Branco, Rio de Janeiro, March 14, 1964, File L2, CPDOC.

[6] Ademar de Queiroz, deposition, July, 1974, quoted in Silva, *1964: Golpe ou Contragolpe?*, p. 306.

[7] HACB to Jair Dantas Ribeiro, Rio de Janeiro, March 23, 1964, File L2, CPDOC.

[8] Ademar de Queiroz, deposition, July, 1974, in Silva, *1964: Golpe ou Contragolpe?*, p. 306.

[9] Costa e Silva, "Costa e Silva Relata Episódios da Revolução." See also Baleeiro, "Recordações do Presidente H. Castelo Branco," p. 11, in which Baleeiro says that he learned from Castello that Costa e Silva, giving a warning to Jair Dantas Ribeiro in a frank and gruff manner, received a promise from the war minister "to take no more imprudent steps."

[10] Costa e Silva, "Costa e Silva Relata Episódios da Revolução."

aims that they attributed to the speechmakers of March 13. In the meantime the CGT spoke of calling a general strike if the president's reform program were not enacted, and Luís Carlos Prestes, secretary general of the Communist party, gave a speech in which he claimed credit for the idea of the recent rally. Word was received that the president would hold similar rallies in other important cities.

At the home of Ademar de Queiroz on Leopoldo Miguez Street, Aliomar Baleeiro explained to Castello and Ademar that at the suggestion of his congressional colleagues, among them Pedro Aleixo and Adauto Lúcio Cardoso, he was planning to introduce a bill of impeachment against Goulart; arrangements had already been made to have the final document prepared by Heráclito Fontoura Sobral Pinto, the famed lawyer who had been representing Governor Lacerda in his conflicts with the federal government.[11]

Castello was cautious. After Baleeiro showed him and Ademar a draft of an impeachment bill, he told Baleeiro that impeachment proceedings were "inopportune" and might provoke a general strike as a protest.

Baleeiro argued that Jango should be liquidated before he liquidated the institutions, "including the armed forces." Then he told Castello and Ademar that while Chamber of Deputies President Ranieri Mazzilli would be the next in line to succeed Jango, his own feeling and that of Bilac Pinto was that conditions required Congress to choose a suitable military man to take over the presidency for a limited number of years. Mentioning the qualities needed for that office, Baleeiro rapidly fired a question at Castello: "Do you know who appears to me to have all of these attributes and qualities?" When Castello shook his head, Baleeiro said, "From everything I have heard, sir, it is you." Castello remained silent, gazing at a corner of the rug.[12]

7. Examining the Military Situation (March, 1964)

As a result of the rally of March 13, Murilo Gomes Ferreira tells us, the *estado maior informal* of Castello Branco sped up its work of

---

[11] Heráclito Fontoura Sobral Pinto interview, Rio de Janeiro, December 9, 1975; Baleeiro, "Recordações do Presidente H. Castelo Branco," p. 10.

[12] Baleeiro, "Recordações do Presidente H. Castelo Branco," p. 12.

reaching understandings with important command posts outside of Rio.[1] Murici recalls that "the conspiracy, after March 13, entered into a phase of overt activity, almost—let us say—free. I do not know how they did not see that in front of the house of General Castello on Nascimento Silva Street, a quiet street, traffic was becoming jammed; at night, at Eugênio Jardim Square, the location of the apartment of General Cordeiro de Farias, it became almost impossible to pass. I was busy, in touch with Ademar de Queiroz, Golberi, the Geisel brothers, Cintra, José Horácio, and [Moniz de] Aragão, informing General Castello and General Costa e Silva, trying to unite our companions, including those in lower echelons."[2]

Reviewing the military situation, Castello's *estado maior informal* felt that it could count on the Fourth Army, the smallest of Brazil's four armies.[3] Colonel Fernando Menescal Vilar and Lieutenant Colonel José Costa Cavalcanti (a UDN federal congressman from Pernambuco) brought encouraging reports from the northeast, where General Justino Alves Bastos was becoming disgusted with the Goulart administration and where Colonels Hélio Ibiapina, João Dutra de Castilho, Antônio Bandeira, and Ednardo d'Ávila Melo, Lieutenant Colonel Ivan Ruy Andrade de Oliveira, and Major Manoel Moreira Paes were preparing for "the legalistic reaction" that Castello had mentioned in his letter to Ibiapina.[4] The northeastern forces, considered a well-united "bloc," included army units in Bahia, where General de Brigada Manoel Mendes Pereira and Colonel Humberto de Souza Melo were associated with the "military plan."

Like the Fourth Army, the Third, in the far south, was a long way from the nation's political center. It was a large army in which, Murilo Gomes Ferreira says, "the situation was difficult and initially we could count on the commander of the Sixth Infantry Division, General Adalberto Pereira dos Santos."[5] In Porto Alegre, headquarters of both the Third Army and the Sixth Infantry, General Adalberto condemned the March 13 rally in a memorandum to Third Army commander Benjamin Rodrigues Galhardo. "There is no doubt," Adalberto told Galhardo,

---

[1] Ferreira, "O General Castello Que Conheci," p. 12.
[2] Muricy, *Os Motivos da Revolução Democrática Brasileira*, p. 23.
[3] Ferreira, "O General Castello Que Conheci," p. 12.
[4] Muricy, *Os Motivos da Revolução Democrática Brasileira*, p. 26; Murici interview, November 18, 1975; Sizeno Sarmento interview, São Paulo, November 21, 1967.
[5] Ferreira, "O General Castello Que Conheci," p. 12.

"that the rally, in which one of the speakers exhorted the dissolution of the legislative power, was an attack against the Constitution." [6]

Ernesto Geisel was optimistic about the Fifth Military Region, which embraced Paraná and Santa Catarina and was under the jurisdiction of the Third Army. Work for the "military plan" in that area was being carried out by General de Brigada Dario Coelho, Colonel Reynaldo Melo de Almeida, and Lieutenant Colonels Milton Pedro, Florimar Campello, and Francisco Boaventura Cavalcanti Júnior (who had been disciplined by the Goulart administration after he refused to act against Lacerda). A couple of generals, Murici felt, might give trouble in the Fifth Military Region but would be unable to prevent action. [7]

The "great question mark" was the Rio area, where First Army commander Armando de Morais Âncora and most of his top subordinates, such as First Region commander Ladário Pereira Teles, were unswervingly loyal to Goulart. [8] Although this area, with its superior weapons, was considered "very difficult" by Murici, no one doubted the anti-Goulart sentiments of the leading generals in Minas Gerais who organizationally formed a part of the First Army. Fourth Military Region commander Olímpio Mourão Filho, with headquarters in Juiz de Fora, had already prepared in Rio Grande do Sul and São Paulo for an uprising against Goulart, and now he organized well in Minas, where his sentiments were shared by General Carlos Luís Guedes in Belo Horizonte.

Mourão, who had started his career with Castello as an *aspirante* in Belo Horizonte, was a determined little pipe smoker known as "Popeye." Although sometimes his plans to revolt were not taken seriously by his listeners, he argued for them ceaselessly during visits to Rio and Petrópolis. In Rio in December, 1963, he invited Murici to command his troops when they acted. At meetings in Petrópolis he exchanged im-

[6] Adalberto Pereira dos Santos, Ofício 19-E2 to Commander of Third Army, Porto Alegre, March 17, 1964, File L2, CPDOC. (See also Silva, *1964: Golpe ou Contragolpe?*, pp. 310–311.)

[7] Murici interview, November 18, 1975 (for list of officers). Muricy, *Os Motivos da Revolução Democrática Brasileira*, p. 27. See Carlos Castello Branco, *A Queda de João Goulart*, pp. 129–133, and Thomas E. Skidmore, *Politics in Brazil*, p. 263, for the problems that Boaventura Cavalcanti, brother of José Costa Cavalcanti, had with the Goulart administration.

[8] Ferreira, "O General Castello Que Conheci," p. 12.

pressions with retired Marshal Odílio Denys, with civilian conspirator Antônio Neder, and with discontented admirals such as Sílvio Heck, Augusto Hamann Rademaker Grünewald, and Ernesto de Melo Batista.[9]

As in Minas, the military conspirators in São Paulo were assisted by spirited anti-Communist popular demonstrations, of which the largest was the Sao Paulo "march" of March 19, which attracted several hundred thousand. Cordeiro de Farias and a fellow-conspirator, recently retired General Nelson de Melo, felt that in São Paulo they could count on the antiadministration sentiments of most of the army officers, but Amauri Kruel remained another question mark. At least three of Amauri's key subordinates were loyal to the president, and he himself had a very close relationship with Goulart. Some felt that his connection with the presidency might have been helpful to him when he secured a Bank of Brazil loan for his agricultural pursuits in Espírito Santo state.

At the Plaza Hotel in Rio, Castello, Cordeiro, Ademar de Queiroz, Costa e Silva, and Ururaí paid a call on Riograndino Kruel.[10] Castello showed Riograndino some messages that he had received from Justino Alves Bastos and Adalberto Pereira dos Santos indicating their agreement with the military plan of the *estado maior informal* but saying that they wanted to know about Amauri's attitude. "Show these messages to Amauri," Cordeiro said to Riograndino.

Riograndino concluded that Castello was doing all of the work for the military plan to save Brazil from the Communists around Goulart. Costa e Silva, he felt, was doing absolutely nothing.[11] Already Costa e Silva had disappointed the Kruel brothers by returning from a vacation in Rio Grande do Sul without giving them information they had asked him to supply about the situation in the far south.

Costa e Silva, however, believed that he had made a contribution to the cause because, before making his trip south, he had persuaded Amauri to bury his differences with Ademar de Barros, the anti-Communist governor of São Paulo.[12] Ademar de Barros and Amauri Kruel started seeing each other late in February, 1964. Soon after the rally of

[9] Murici interview, November 18, 1975; Stacchini, *Março 64*, p. 91.
[10] Riograndino Kruel interview, Rio de Janeiro, September 19, 1975.
[11] Ibid.
[12] Costa e Silva, "Costa e Silva Relata Episódios da Revolução."

the "hammers and sickles" on March 13, the governor sent Castello and Ademar de Queiroz a message via Aliomar Baleeiro that was optimistic about the path that Amauri would take.[13]

Following this message, Riograndino reported that Amauri agreed with the positions taken by Generals Justino Alves Bastos and Adalberto Pereira dos Santos. However, with Amauri still primarily interested in persuading Goulart to break with the Communists, the uncertainty about Amauri continued.

8. Castello's Circular of March 20, 1964

As he told the war minister he would, Castello set down his comments about the March 13 rally in a restricted circular for officers of the Army Staff and of the organizations reporting to it. While releasing the first copies of his circular, dated March 20, he was shown a copy of a speech in which Justice Minister Jurema had recently heaped ecstatic praises on the March 13 rally. Jurema, addressing what was described as the largest meeting yet held for the expression of grievances by soldiers and corporals, agreed with his cheering listeners that they were "workers in uniform." He said that the political awakening of soldiers and corporals was a sign of democracy becoming strong, and he added that the large size of his audience, present to make demands, "should serve as a warning to those who do not listen to the people."[1]

In Castello's circular, which had the merit of being much briefer than Jurema's flowery remarks, the army chief of staff expressed his understanding of the "intranquility" prevailing in the armed forces following the March 13 rally, and he noted two "threats": the advent of a constitutional assembly for obtaining basic reforms, and increased agitation by "the illegal power of the CGT."[2]

The armed forces, Castello wrote, were not to let themselves be used to serve the privileges of the rich or to support fascist or Communist–labor union dictatorships. They were to uphold the constituted powers

[13] Baleeiro, "Recordações do Presidente H. Castelo Branco," p. 11.

[1] Abelardo Jurema, "Discurso do Ministro Abelardo Jurema—4º Aniversário da Associação dos Cabos e Soldados da Polícia Militar do Estado de Guanabara," (typed), File L2, CPDOC.

[2] HACB, "Circular do Chefe do Estado Maior do Exército," in *Marechal Castello Branco: Seu Pensamento Militar*, pp. 303–306.

and the laws, but that was not to say that they should defend specific government programs; much less should they defend government propaganda.

Castello saw the achievement of the proposed constitutional assembly as requiring revolutionary violence, the closing of the existing Congress, and the institution of a dictatorship. While declaring it legitimate for people to turn to insurrection, he expressed the feeling that the Brazilian people were not at the moment asking for a constitutional assembly or a civilian or military dictatorship.

The armed forces, he said, would be acting against the people and the nation if they were to help the "pseudosyndical group whose leaders live on subversive agitation, which is daily becoming more costly to the public coffers" and which might "submit the nation to Moscow Communism." Noting that the CGT had announced plans to paralyze the nation, he declared that the armed forces should not remain idle but should guarantee the application of the law that prohibited such "a public calamity."

In conclusion, Castello wrote that the war minister had given assurances that he would respect Congress, the elections, and the inauguration of those who won at the polls.

Before issuing the document on March 20, Castello sought to show it to Jair Dantas Ribeiro. But he learned from General Genaro Bontempo, who was handling matters in the minister's office, that he could see Jair neither then nor on the following days because ill health kept Jair from his office. Castello's decision to issue the circular without discussing it with the war minister was not considered advisable by all of his leading subordinates, but it was backed by most of them. Generals Francisco Damasceno Ferreira Portugal and Rafael de Sousa Aguiar came to Castello's office on the afternoon of March 20 to urge its issuance, and for this reason at a later date Castello described their support as "the final drop of water that made the pitcher overflow, creating a current."[3]

Among those who expressed caution was General Aurélio de Lyra Tavares, first assistant chief of the EME.[4] Expanding his thoughts in a

[3] Rafael de Sousa Aguiar interview, Rio de Janeiro, August 8, 1977. See HACB handwritten note dated August 19, 1966, on p. 17 of Sousa Aguiar's copy of Humberto de Alencar Castello Branco et al., *A Revolução de 31 de Março: 2º Aniversário*.

[4] Sousa Aguiar interview, August 8, 1977.

letter to Castello dated March 21, Lyra Tavares said that he continued
to feel that the circular should first be discussed with Jair because of the
"great risk in seeing the authority of the Minister weakened, above all
in the present circumstances, it being a thousand times preferrable to
give him advice and backing, in order not to compromise the greater
and common objective of protecting the Army from . . . pernicious influences. . . ." Lyra Tavares, while expressing admiration for the circular's description of the situation, felt that his own recommendation
might help preserve unity in the army, "never more needed than now."
Besides, Lyra Tavares wrote, Castello's circular might well be picked up
by the press, "and we all must admit the ills that could result from this,
in the atmosphere of passion in which we live, with press freedom that
is complete and often used irresponsibly." [5]

On March 23 Castello wrote Jair a letter in which he explained that
the purpose of the circular had not been to create confusion, seek personal backing, or start a polemic; it was simply to enlighten subordinates
and demonstrate "the seriousness attending military conduct." [6]

9. Effects of the March 20 Circular

As soon as Castello Branco's March 20 circular was issued, the
officers of the Army Staff were called together on the War Ministry's
sixth floor to hear it read aloud. [1] Others who quickly became acquainted
with it were the four hundred officers who made up the student body
and teaching staff of the ECEME. ECEME commander Mamede, following a visit by Castello, arranged to have the circular read aloud in the
school's auditorium, and there it was praised for its "incisiveness and
vigor." [2]

Castello showed copies of the circular to Salvador and Nieta Diniz
and to a nephew, Air Force Colonel Roberto Hipólito da Costa. Ademar
de Queiroz and the other members of the *estado maior informal* were
familiar with it. Cordeiro, very enthusiastic, felt that the circular should
have a fairly wide distribution. Others agreed with Cordeiro, for it

[5] Aurélio de Lyra Tavares to HACB, Rio de Janeiro, March 21, 1964, PVCB.
[6] HACB to Jair Dantas Ribeiro, Rio de Janeiro, March 23, 1964, File L2, CPDOC.
[1] Paulo de Tarso Saraiva interview, Washington, D.C., March 18, 1977.
[2] D'Aguiar, *A Revolução por Dentro*, p. 120.

could be expected to exert a decisive influence over officers who were undecided.[3]

Castello's secretary, Murilo Gomes Ferreira, noted that the list of recipients kept growing.[4] To be delivered confidentially to key officers of the "military plan," copies were taken to Minas by Lieutenant Colonel Luís Gonzaga de Andrada Serpa,[5] to Rio Grande do Sul by Major Jaime Ehlers, and to the northeast by Colonel Fernando Menescal Vilar and Lieutenant Colonels Sebastião Ferreira Chaves and José Costa Cavalcanti.

As early as March 23 Justino Alves Bastos addressed a confidential reply to "My friend General Castello" which was brought from Recife to Rio by Sebastião Ferreira Chaves.[6] "I am," Alves Bastos wrote, "in full agreement" with the document. "Without any doubt," he added, "the responsibility of the High Command of the Army is at this moment immense and extraordinary, and principally in the case of those members who are in the Ministry and at the center of the grave events that we are witnessing. Permit me to go further and say that the responsibility of the Chief of Staff is superlative—superlative because of the importance of the post and because of the professional and moral attributes of the man in the post." Alves Bastos asked to be kept informed of developments and said that the Fourth Army, united and characterized by the traditional bravery of the northeasterners, "ardently" desired to serve "the great causes of Brazil and of the Law." Murilo Gomes Ferreira felt certain from this "positive and firm" reply that Alves Bastos "would be at the side of General Castello Branco."[7]

In Porto Alegre a copy of Castello's circular reached Governor Ildo Meneghetti, who remarked, "Now we have a leader." The "personal and secret" reply that was addressed to Castello by General Adalberto Pereira dos Santos was brought from Porto Alegre to Rio by Lieutenant Colonel Ângelo Irulegui Cunha. In it Adalberto said that he had shown

[3] Sebastião Ferreira Chaves interview, São Paulo, November 22, 1967; D'Aguiar, *A Revolução por Dentro*, p. 120.

[4] Murilo Gomes Ferreira, in Ferreira and Paulo V. Castello Branco interview, Rio de Janeiro, November 12, 1975.

[5] Luís Gonzaga de Andrade Serpa to HACB, Paris, France, November 24, 1965, File N1, CPDOC.

[6] Chaves interview, November 22, 1967; Stacchini, *Março 64*, p. 85.

[7] Joaquim Justino Alves Bastos to HACB, Recife, March 23, 1964, File L2, CPDOC; Ferreira, "O General Castello Que Conheci," p. 12.

Castello's circular to Third Army commander Benjamin Rodrigues Galhardo, who had remarked that it was "very opportune" and reflected his own opinion.[8]

When Castello showed a copy of his circular to Riograndino Kruel in Riograndino's room in the Plaza Hotel in Rio, Riograndino suggested that the anti-Goulart "revolution" be carried out at once because the circular would result in Castello's imprisonment. Castello pointed out that the circular was written in such a way that he could not be dismissed for it. But Riograndino worried about what would happen to the "revolution" if Castello and Amauri should lose their posts. He said to Castello: "You two are separated. But in the revolution you need to work together." To bring this about, Riograndino offered to give a lunch for Amauri and Humberto. Humberto accepted the invitation, and Riograndino accepted Humberto's suggestion that Costa e Silva be included.[9]

In the circles of President Goulart the reaction to Castello's circular was about as Riograndino expected. Goulart expressed his opinion on the evening of March 24 at a meeting in his Copacabana apartment that was attended by Assis Brasil, Oromar Osório, Ladário Pereira Teles, Luís Tavares da Cunha Melo, and other leaders of the presidential *dispositivo militar*. After Castello's circular was read to the gathering, Goulart told these army friends that he planned to dismiss Castello, for no longer meriting his confidence, as well as Sixth Infantry Division commander Adalberto Pereira dos Santos, who was known to be conspiring.[10] To strengthen the president's position in Rio Grande do Sul, Ladário Pereira Teles was to take over the Third Army from Galhardo, whose position the president's office considered dubious. Galhardo would be named army chief of staff.

The president's office had had access to Castello's circular through Dulcídio do Espírito Santo Cardoso, commander of the Colégio Militar of Rio de Janeiro, who had received a copy from Army Director of Instruction Rafael de Sousa Aguiar.[11] On March 24, after Dulcídio sent a copy to the president's office, the pro-Goulart daily, *Última Hora*, car-

---

[8] Silva, *1964: Golpe ou Contragolpe?*, p. 312; Adalberto Pereira dos Santos to HACB, Porto Alegre, March 26, 1964, File L2, CPDOC.

[9] Riograndino Kruel interview, September 21, 1975.

[10] Silva, *1964: Golpe ou Contragolpe?*, pp. 353–354 (based on deposition of Ladário Pereira Teles).

[11] Rafael de Sousa Aguiar, declarations in *O Globo*, April 20, 1964.

ried a story saying that Dulcídio had denounced the circular for being a political document. Castello dashed off a note to Genaro Bontempo, of the war minister's office, explaining that the circular had been confidential and that General Dulcídio had been indiscreet.[12] Soon after that Justice Minister Abelardo Jurema cited Castello's "confidential manifesto" on a radio and television program.

Tired of inexact public remarks about his circular, Castello decided no longer to try to keep it confidential. He released a statement in which he said that "as the press has made erroneous references about a document issued by the army chief of staff, and as Minister Jurema has called it a confidential manifesto, when it is only a note to subordinates, General Humberto Castello Branco has resolved to declassify it." He asked the press to publish it.[13]

Already the circular had had a formidable repercussion because of the esteem in which its signer was held and because it was forceful and remarkably timely. Acclaimed as the most important document that Castello had ever written, and described as "a document for posterity," it was the signal that conscientious legalists, such as Morais Rego at Vila Militar, were awaiting. Despite its careful wording, it was, Murilo Gomes Ferreira says, "practically the Preparatory Order for the reaction, and the clear affirmation of Castello Branco's leadership."[14]

10. United States Embassy Impressions

United States Ambassador Lincoln Gordon writes that he received a copy of Castello's circular as early as March 23, when it was handed to him by Walters at an embassy staff meeting. The ambassador adds that "contrary to many published statements, however, neither Colonel Walters nor I was familiar with the planning for possible military action against Goulart."[1]

It is true that Walters found Castello reserved and Murici unwilling

---

12 HACB to Genaro Bontempo, March 24, 1964, File L2, CPDOC.

13 HACB handwritten note, File L2, CPDOC.

14 D'Aguiar, *A Revolução por Dentro*, p. 120; Ferreira, "O General Castello Que Conheci," p. 12.

1 Lincoln Gordon, "Recollection of President Castello Branco," (typed manuscript, Washington, D.C., July 28, 1972), p. 2.

to answer his questions.[2] But from others he soon picked up some pretty good ideas about what was going on. Most helpful of all to Walters was Ulhoa Cintra, who, Walters noted, was "in the thick of the revolutionary conspiring."[3] At Ulhoa Cintra's home, which Walters found "well stocked with arms and often filled with conspirators," Walter spent some memorable moments in the middle of Holy Week (*Semana Santa*, which began on March 22). Following a phone call that warned of an impending police raid on Ulhoa Cintra's home, Walters remained there at the general's request. Only after half an hour passed without a raid did Ulhoa Cintra and Walters conclude that they had been worried by a false alarm.

From all of the information that the United States Embassy put together, much of it provided by Walters,[4] Ambassador Gordon reported to Washington on March 27 that Castello Branco preferred to make a coup after some obvious unconstitutional move by Goulart but that Goulart might consciously avoid unconstitutional acts "while continuing to move toward an irreversible . . . assumption of power." Gordon said that Castello was "therefore preparing for a possible move sparked by a Communist-led general strike call, another sergeants' rebellion, a plebiscite opposed by Congress, or even a major government countermove against the democratic military or civilian leadership." The embassy concluded that if Castello moved against Goulart on an issue which was not clearly unconstitutional, he would want political coverage from the governors and/or Congress.[5]

In this message to Washington Gordon expressed the fear that if Goulart succeeded in seizing dictatorial powers, Brazil would fall under Communist control. Although it was felt in the United States Embassy that an anti-Goulart coup of resistance by Castello Branco would probably quickly dominate most of the country, it was also felt that a civil war might take place in some parts of Brazil. Therefore, while the embassy agreed with Walters' recommendation against any show of United

---

[2] Murici interview, November 18, 1975. Murici said: "I did not talk with Walters about the revolution. Walters would ask me."

[3] Walters interviews, McLean, Virginia, June 12, 1975, and Arlington, Virginia, July 15, 1976.

[4] Parker, "Separate . . . but Equal?," p. 86.

[5] Lincoln Gordon to Rusk et al., March 27, 1964, quoted in Parker, "Separate . . . but Equal?," p. 86. For this, Phyllis Parker consulted National Security Files (Country File: Brazil) at the Lyndon B. Johnson Presidential Library, Austin, Texas.

States leadership in an anti-Goulart coup or the sending of United States troops to Brazil, nevertheless two contingency plans were developed by an embassy task force. Researcher Phyllis Parker, reporting recently on these plans, writes that it was believed that they "could be used to tip the balance in favor of the side friendly to the U.S. (the anti-Goulart conspirators)." As described by Phyllis Parker, the first plan dealt with petroleum supplies for the insurgents, and the second contemplated sending a United States carrier force to Brazil as a "flag showing" gesture (to "assist in maintaining stability") and for the evacuation of United States citizens if necessary.[6]

11. The Sailors' Mutiny (March 25–27, 1964)

Castello Branco's daughter, Nieta Diniz, going frequently from Leblon to supervise the work of the maid Romana at the Nascimento Silva Street house, observed that with the issuance of her father's circular on March 20, the house became more frequently crowded with army officers. Each day seemed to bring new developments for Castello and his associates to evaluate. There was Marshal Dutra's appeal to all democrats to save the constitutional regime "while time still allows."[1] And there was a manifesto by seventy-two retired army generals, including Luís Mendes da Silva, condemning "subversion by progressive acts, culminating in the rally of March 13." According to word from the war minister's office, all the signers who were still in the reserve could expect to be punished by thirty days of arrest.[2]

Nieta, speaking of her father's house, says that the downstairs reception hall, living room, and study became so full of generals that the younger officers had to be content with space in the pantry. "Ademar de Queiroz," she recalls, "came at peculiar hours. Among the others who came were Golberi, Ernesto Geisel, Mamede, and Cordeiro. Also Colonels Carlos de Meira Mattos, José Nogueira Paes, and Walter de Menezes Paes."[3] And there were some younger, radical army men, to

---

[6] Parker, "Separate . . . but Equal?," p. 88, based on interviews with Lincoln Gordon and Vernon Walters, January 19, 20, 1976.

[1] *O Estado de S. Paulo*, March 20, 1964.

[2] Ibid., March 22, 24, 1964.

[3] Antonietta Castello Branco Diniz, in Diniz and Paulo V. Castello Branco interview, Rio de Janeiro, December 13, 1975.

whom Castello's advice was apt to be: "Take it easy." Castello's secretary, Lieutenant Colonel Murilo Gomes Ferreira, and his aide, Captain Frederico Mendes de Morais, were ever present.

One who did not come, Nieta says, was Gustavo Morais Rego Reis, "because he was at Vila Militar." And another who she says did not come was Vernon Walters. The American defense attaché usually limited himself now to driving past the house that he loved so much, finding it a center of activity; on rare occasions, late at night, when he found Castello alone he might drop in, but he learned nothing about the work of the *estado maior informal.*

A visitor who might have come was Admiral Augusto Hamann Rademaker Grünewald, but he simply failed to show up. With the CGT and its allies gaining considerable support among the sailors, Admiral Ernesto de Melo Batista, who had been so helpful to Castello in Amazônia, suggested that Castello drop in for a discussion at Rademaker's home. Castello, who wore four stars to Rademaker's three, countered by asking Melo Batista to bring Rademaker to the Nascimento Silva Street house. But Rademaker did not come.

Castello had concluded, largely from his observations in Recife in 1962, that the local navy commands would have no initiative in an emergency. But despite this impression of the navy—which Castello, using English, referred to as "the old Navy"—he could hardly have expected the stunning humiliation of the navy that began on March 25; nearly one thousand sailors, with the blessing of the CGT, used the Guanabara Metalworkers' Union building to hold a tumultuous meeting during which Navy Minister Sílvio Mota was described as "infantile" and "subversive" for having taken some disciplinary steps. After the mutinying sailors refused to leave the building, Sílvio Mota sought help from the army. As Jair Dantas Ribeiro was undergoing a kidney operation, the navy minister spoke with Genaro Bontempo.

Castello, who normally should have been named acting war minister during Jair's illness, sought assistance for the navy during conversations that he had with Bontempo and officers of the First Army. While newspaper reporters wrote that Castello was assuming command of the War Ministry,[4] twelve army tanks and five hundred soldiers were sent to the streets outside the union building. But these troops could do nothing

---

[4] Murilo Gomes Ferreira and Paulo V. Castello Branco interview, Rio de Janeiro, November 12, 1975.

because the president's office was determined to avoid a conflict in the union building. The sailors left the building only on Good Friday, March 27, after labor leaders Osvaldo Pacheco and Dante Pelacani, sent by Goulart to negotiate, agreed on amnesty for the rebelling sailors and the installation of a new navy minister acceptable to the rebelling sailors and the CGT.[5]

The settlement terms, a clear rebuke to the sober words of Castello's circular of March 20, shocked most military officers. Equally shocking to them and to much of Brazil were the newspaper accounts of the victory celebration of the recent mutineers in downtown Rio on Good Friday evening. Photographs showed Marine commander Cândido Aragão and another "people's admiral" (the newly designated navy chief of staff) being carried on the shoulders of rejoicing sailors.

Despite his concern, Castello did not forget that March 28 was the birthday of Justina Amarante. It was a special occasion for him because Argentina had promised to bring Justina a bible on that day. Dropping in at the Amarantes' apartment, he gave her an affectionate *abraço* (embrace)—a gesture that was rare for Castello, particularly after he had taken to wearing his corset. With him he brought a large bible that he had appropriately inscribed, as Argentina would have wished.[6]

12. A Visitor from Pernambuco (March 25, 1964)

On March 25, when the sailors' mutiny began, Castello conversed with Colonel José Costa Cavalcanti. As a federal congressman from Pernambuco, Costa Cavalcanti had helped Bilac Pinto prepare his sensational antiadministration speeches, and now he was studying the large pay increase that Goulart had recently proposed for the military.[1]

Castello, learning that Costa Cavalcanti planned a trip to Recife on the next day, asked him to speak with General Joaquim Justino Alves Bastos and the younger army officers in the northeast who wanted to act offensively on behalf of legality. After urging the colonel to bring these men up-to-date on the developments in Rio, Castello said, "Jango thinks that Joaquim will help with the government's scheme, but he is mis-

[5] Dante Pelacani interview, São Paulo, November 24, 1968.
[6] Amarante interview, November 21, 1975.
[1] José Costa Cavalcanti interview, Brasília, October 15, 1965.

taken, because the Fourth Army continues at our side, opposed to chaos, indiscipline, and disrespect for the military hierarchy. . . ."[2]

Castello pointed out that Alves Bastos' reply to his March 20 circular, together with the activities of the Fourth Army staff and unit commanders, were positive signs that "a favorable attitude" prevailed in the army in the northeast. "But talk to all of them, and speak also in the name of Costa e Silva. Go see Admiral Augusto Dias Fernandes and the commander of the Air Force Zone, get their reactions and carefully explain the sentiment existing here, where many have lost all patience. It is likely that the armed movement will begin shortly, but nothing should be started precipitously. Murici has become practically impossible to hold back."

Castello added that Costa Cavalcanti should tell Justino Alves Bastos that "we do not intend to close down the state legislatures or tribunals," and he added that Miguel Arraes was the only governor in the northeast who would be deposed. In conclusion, Castello advised Costa Cavalcanti to speak with Costa e Silva before he left. "Like me, he once commanded the Fourth Army; besides, he is closer to the present commander than I am."

Together with messages and instructions from Castello and Costa e Silva, Costa Cavalcanti took to Recife suggestions for Colonel Ibiapina that came from Generals Murici and Ulhoa Cintra. During his talk with Alves Bastos on March 26, Costa Cavalcanti learned that the Fourth Army was "ready to act" and even agreeable to sending men overland to Rio de Janeiro, if necessary. "As for not closing the assemblies and tribunals," Alves Bastos said, "I am in agreement, as I am about the decision regarding Miguel Arraes. But tell Castello and Costa e Silva that there is another northeastern governor who is going to be thrown out: Seixas Dória, because of his behavior as a Communist and agitator." (João de Seixas Dória, governor of Sergipe, had given a speech at the March 13 rally of "the hammers and sickles.")

Before Costa Cavalcanti returned to Rio, the sailors' mutiny had ended in the Good Friday victory celebration of the sailors and the "people's admirals." Therefore, during his last conversations in Recife,

---

[2] José Costa Cavalcanti, "Revolução no Nordeste: Uma Missão Recebida" (typewritten statement), October, 1976.

Costa Cavalcanti found the military officers "more indignant than ever about the situation, which was on the verge of chaos."[3]

13. Visitors from Minas (March 25, 1964)

Among the others who called on Castello Branco on the day of the outbreak of the sailors' mutiny were three representatives of Minas Gerais Governor José de Magalhães Pinto: two Minas state cabinet members and a nephew of the governor. The emissaries, having been advised that Castello was "the general coordinator of the military groups in conspiracy,"[1] went to the Nascimento Silva Street house to explain that Magalhães Pinto planned to assume the civilian leadership of the anti-Goulart movement, to be started by state and federal troops in Minas, and would issue a manifesto. The governor's representatives told Castello that they had just come from discussing these matters with Dutra and Ulhoa Cintra and had learned from Dutra that it was urgent to move quickly against Goulart but that Minas should not do so before being assured of the backing of Amauri Kruel.

Castello agreed that it was indispensable to have the adherence of São Paulo, and he added that while he had no definite knowledge that Kruel would back an uprising, the reports about Kruel were generally favorable. Castello told his visitors that an uprising carried out with the support of São Paulo would constitute a "calculated risk." He went on: "In the *estado maior* a calculated risk is acceptable, whereas an *aventura* never is. Without the adherence of São Paulo everything would be an *aventura pura e simples*." Rash action (*temeridade*), he added, was "inadmissible."[2]

For the governor's representatives Castello outlined the situation in the army. No difficulties were to be expected in the Fourth Army, where Justino Alves Bastos was considered to be "one hundred percent" in agreement with the plans. The situation appeared good in the interior of Rio Grande do Sul but unfavorable in Porto Alegre. Castello saw

[3] Ibid.
[1] Pedro Gomes, "Minas: Do Diálogo ao 'Front,'" in Alberto Dines et al., *Os Idos de Março e a Queda em Abril*, p. 93.
[2] Ibid.; Silva, *1964: Golpe ou Contragolpe?*, p. 348.

"serious problems" with the First Army in Guanabara, where, he said, the strength of Jango's *dispositivo militar* was concentrated.[3]

From Castello's home, Magalhães Pinto's representatives went to confer with Marshal Odílio Denys, who also stressed the need to have the participation of the Second Army.[4] Then the two Minas state cabinet officers flew to São Paulo (despite the bad weather) to seek a commitment from Amauri Kruel.

The Second Army commander, awakened in his residence at 2:00 A.M. by the callers, was surprised that Magalhães Pinto would send men whom he had never met before. He stressed the close personal ties that prevented him from turning against Goulart. Agreeing that the president was taking the country to chaos, the general promised to try to get him to rectify his conduct. Although Kruel would not give the Mineiros the commitment they sought, he assured them that he would not allow Brazil to become a "trade union republic" or a "Communist republic."[5]

In Rio Marshal Denys followed up the Mineiros' visit by seeking a meeting with Magalhães Pinto. It took place at the Juiz de Fora airport on March 28 in the company of Generals Olímpio Mourão Filho and Carlos Luís Guedes and the commander of the Minas state troops. After Denys said that the time had come to act, Magalhães Pinto offered to save time by issuing a manifesto alone instead of participating in a joint governors' manifesto. Mourão said that the manifesto would have to include a clear call for Goulart's overthrow, and he further insisted on controlling the time of its release so that his troops would have the element of surprise in marching on Rio. But he found that the governor and General Guedes opposed his idea of making such a march; they spoke of "fencing in Minas and then negotiating," a strategy that Mourão was certain would fail.[6]

[3] Gomes, "Minas: Do Diálogo ao 'Front,' " p. 93.

[4] Ibid., p. 94.

[5] Amauri Kruel interview, Rio de Janeiro, October 21, 1967; José Monteiro de Castro deposition in Silva, *1964: Golpe ou Contragolpe?*, pp. 359–360.

[6] Olímpio Mourão Filho deposition in Silva, *1964: Golpe ou Contragolpe?*, pp. 349–352.

14. "Dutra Would Take This Country on the Correct Path" (March 28, 1964)

Commenting on "the disintegration of the Navy," Murilo Gomes Ferreira says, "The fuse was lit." He adds that Castello's *estado maior informal* resolved that the moment had come to dispatch emissaries with instructions for "the final coordination of the action." [1]

Early in March the *estado maior informal* had estimated that it could count on at least 70 percent of the army. Making its plans during the weekend after the sailors' mutiny, it considered that São Paulo and Minas would be "solid blocs" in which the people, the state governments, and the troops were prepared to act, and with Governors Ademar de Barros and José de Magalhães Pinto ready to issue an appropriate proclamation.[2] In the Rio area the events in the navy had had the most profound effect. According to Sizeno Sarmento, these events, and the work of Castello Branco, Costa e Silva, Denys, and Cordeiro, made groups of key officers at Vila Militar willing to defy the Vila commander, Oromar Osório, who could be expected to be loyal to Goulart. Sarmento and Murici have pointed out that the fear of a Communist takeover had become so strong among the younger army officers in the Rio area that a problem was the prevention of some premature isolated "barrack uprising." [3]

The military plan continued to adhere to the general concept formulated in 1963 by Ulhoa Cintra. The march on Rio of troops from Minas was to be the signal for an almost simultaneous march on Rio by the Second Army (where colonels and majors in the Paraíba Valley were eager to lead their men against Goulart). While these movements were underway, outbreaks were to occur in the northeast and in Rio Grande do Sul. As for the "neutralization and fall of Guanabara," Murilo Gomes Ferreira writes that "General Castello Branco was certain" that once the Minas and Second Army forces "faced the troops quartered in Rio, understandings would be reached, with the Rio troops adhering quickly to our side." [4]

[1] Ferreira, "O General Castello Que Conheci," p. 13.

[2] Muricy, *Os Motivos da Revolução Democrática Brasileira*, pp. 36, 37.

[3] Sarmento interview, November 21, 1967. The names are listed in the order given by Sizeno Sarmento. Muricy, *Os Motivos da Revolução Democrática Brasileira*, p. 36.

[4] For the plan, see D'Aguiar, *A Revolução por Dentro*, p. 129. See also Ferreira,

Castello's *estado maior informal* hoped to complete all understandings in time for the movements on Guanabara State to start on April 2,[5] but it was appreciated that this might take a little longer, running to sometime in the period between April 2 and April 10, for the objective was a movement with as little violent conflict as possible. The *estado maior informal* felt that it still faced a serious problem in Rio Grande do Sul, home state of Goulart and Brizola, where, according to the most optimistic conspirators, no more than 50 or 60 percent of the army could be expected to adhere to an anti-Goulart movement.[6]

Castello was aware that the sailors' mutiny and its settlement had so upset the military that there was no predicting what might occur before April. In a conversation with Meira Mattos on Saturday, March 28, he learned that the colonel planned to conclude his Holy Week vacation in Rio by returning on Monday to Mato Grosso, where he and others, including Generals Hugo Panasco Alvim and Sizeno Sarmento, had been planning for revolution. "Monday," Castello said to Meira Mattos, "might be too late. Leave tomorrow, Sunday."[7]

On March 28 José Costa Cavalcanti reported at Nascimento Silva Street about his trip to Recife. From everything that he learned from Castello he concluded that the Goulart government could be considered as good as deposed—"maybe today, maybe tomorrow, maybe in a week, maybe in a few months."[8] It seemed to the colonel-congressman from Pernambuco that the coordinating work had been completed and that the armed movement was ready to commence. Therefore, he asked Castello, "How soon, General, do you think we will take charge of this government?"

"Murici expects a struggle of from thirty to sixty days," Castello replied.

"General, to whom do you think we should turn over the administration of this country after the fall of the Goulart government?"

"O General Castello Que Conheci," p. 13, which speaks of "a simultaneous movement" from Minas and the Paraíba Valley.

[5] Ferreira, "O General Castello Que Conheci," p. 13.

[6] Muricy, *Os Motivos da Revolução Democrática Brasileira*, p. 37. Hernani D'Aguiar mentions (*A Revolução por Dentro*, p. 129) April 2 to April 5.

[7] Meira Mattos interview, August 2, 1976.

[8] José Costa Cavalcanti, "Depoimento do Ministro Costa Cavalcanti sobre a escolha do Presidente Castello Branco para a Presidência da República" (transcript of tape), October 22, 1976, p. 1.

Castello calmly answered: "To Marshal Eurico Gaspar Dutra. Marshal Dutra is a man of greatest integrity, most highly respected in political circles and in military circles, and I believe that he would take this country on the correct path."

"May I tell Governor Carlos Lacerda everything that you have told me?"

"You may; there is no reason not to."

"Should I speak in my name, General, or in yours?"

"You may speak in my name, although I do not know Governor Carlos Lacerda."[9]

15. More Appeals to Kruel (March 28, 1964)

José Costa Cavalcanti went from Castello Branco's home to find Costa e Silva and Lacerda. But before he took his leave of Castello, he noted the departure, from the Nascimento Silva Street house, of an emissary bound for São Paulo to speak with Amauri Kruel.[1]

Also on March 28 Amauri Kruel received two separate appeals directly from Minas to cooperate with action there. The first was made when emissaries of Governor Magalhães Pinto vised him again, but they found that his response to the settlement of the sailors' mutiny was to resolve once more to give strong advice to the president. This Kruel did promptly; in a telephone call to Brasília he told Goulart to pacify the army by dismissing the new navy minister and Marine commander Cândido Aragão and by personally handling the problem in the navy. Although the president angrily cut off the connection, he returned the call a few hours later in order to say that he had resolved to go to Rio to direct the solution of the navy matter.[2] After this, an agent of General Olímpio Mourão Filho arrived in São Paulo to appeal to Kruel to join forces with Mourão for "saving the nation from Communism." In declining, the Second Army commander told of Goulart's promise to order an investigation of the sailor's mutiny. He told Mourão's agent

[9] Ibid.

[1] Cavalcanti, "Depoimento," p. 1. Carlos de Meira Mattos advised (interview, Washington, D.C., March 18, 1977) that the emissary was Lieutenant Colonel Antônio Lepiane.

[2] Amauri Kruel interview, October 21, 1967.

that he felt that he should await one more illegal act by the federal government, an act that he said "will certainly appear, because each day the federal government commits new illegal acts."[3] In conclusion Kruel warned Mourâo against carrying out "an isolated movement."

Riograndino Kruel, in touch with Mourão through Antônio Neder, a judge (desembargador) in Petrópolis, also warned that Mourão should not start things alone, and he added that the "revolution" was "in the hands of Castello in Rio."[4] Although Riograndino was still unable to bring about the lunch that he had mentioned to Castello, he continued hopeful of getting a clear commitment from Amauri that would fit in with the plan of the estado maior informal. And in the meantime rumors about Amauri were plentiful. It was even being suggested that he would have to take an anti-Goulart position lest subordinates arrest him and replace him with conspirator Nelson de Melo, a Porto Alegre classmate of Amauri and Castello who had headed the Second Army in 1962 before becoming war minister in the parliamentary government.

UDN Congressman Herbert Levy, phoning Aliomar Baleeiro from São Paulo on Sunday, March 29 (and speaking in English), said that Kruel would lead an uprising that very night. When Ademar de Queiroz, his home full of army officers, received this inaccurate information from Baleeiro, he told the congressman from Guanabara to advise his São Paulo friends that they were three days ahead of schedule and were not to be precipitous.[5]

16. New Missions for Murici and Ulhoa Cintra (March 28, 1964)

During the weekend of March 28–29 most of the newspapers in Brazil denounced the settlement of the sailors' mutiny and carried angry manifestos of civilian and military organizations, including the Military Club. Every important conspiring group in Brazil was approached by individuals who felt it their duty to offer to undertake "missions." General de Brigada Sizeno Sarmento, who had come from his command

3 Olímpio Mourão Filho in Brazil, Army, First Army, General Headquarters, Juiz de Fora, Relatório da Revolução Democrática Iniciada pela 4ª RM e 4ª DI em 31 de Março de 1964, Boletim Especial, May 9, 1964; Olímpio Mourão Filho interview, Rio de Janeiro, October 9, 1965.

4 Riograndino Kruel interview, September 21, 1975.

5 Baleeiro, "Recordações do Presidente H. Castelo Branco," p. 12.

post in Mato Grosso to take the ESG course, now joined the "secret revolutionary staff" of his old friend and former sports companion, Costa
e Silva; thus Sizeno Sarmento, having prepared troops in Mato Grosso
to participate in an anti-Communist movement, teamed up with José
Horácio da Cunha Garcia, Jaime Portela, and others.[1]

On March 26 Castello had received an offer to "fulfill a mission"
when he had been visited at his war ministry office by Augusto César
Moniz de Aragão, the Democratic Crusade candidate for the Military
Club presidency who had previously refused to conspire. Although Castello had had no suggestion then, it was otherwise when Moniz de Aragão repeated the offer during a visit with Castello at the Nascimento
Silva Street house before dawn on Sunday, March 29. Castello suggested
that the former Fourth Army chief of staff get instructions from Cordeiro, but Moniz de Aragão decided to act on his own, and he set up a
"command post" with three companions in Marechal Hermes in order
to convert more Vila Militar and Realengo troops to the "reaction
against the subversive government."[2]

When Murici and Ulhoa Cintra spoke with Castello and Ademar de
Queiroz late at night on March 28, it was to report that Olímpio Mourão Filho, using intermediaries who included a son and a son-in-law of
Denys, was calling the two brigadier generals to Juiz de Fora to command troops in the forthcoming action against Goulart.[3] Castello and
Ademar de Queiroz told Murici that they thought that Mourão was
"crazy," but they urged that Murici and Ulhoa Cintra accept Mourão's
request because they wanted men of their own with Mourão.[4] Bearing
in mind the April 2 date, Murici and Ulhoa Cintra did not hurry to Juiz
de Fora. Murici, who regarded his new assignment as a "filet mignon"
that he could not resist, invited two of his officers to make the trip with
him from Rio.

[1] Sarmento interview, November 21, 1967; Muricy, *Os Motivos da Revolução Democrática Brasileira*, p. 40.

[2] Augusto César Moniz de Aragão, "O Depoimento do General Moniz de Aragão,"
O Globo, March 30, 1975.

[3] Muricy, *Os Motivos da Revolução Democrática Brasileira*, p. 36.

[4] Murici interview, November 18, 1975.

17. Sergeants at the Automobile Club (March 30, 1964)

Information reaching the *estado maior informal* on March 29 led it to expect that Castello would be placed under arrest.[1] Nor was a raid of the Nascimento Silva Street house by Cândido Aragão's Marines out of the question. Therefore a new meeting place was chosen—the apartment in Leblon that was left unoccupied when Paulo Castello Branco, accompanied by his family, went to take the navy course in the United States. While the meetings in this apartment lasted until early morning hours, Murilo Gomes Ferreira "gave coverage" to Castello by staying at the Nascimento Silva Street house; answering phone calls, he sought to allay suspicions by saying that the general was expected to return home soon.[2]

Castello spent the night of March 29–30 at Paulo's apartment.[3] When he and Murilo Gomes Ferreira reached the War Ministry on Monday morning, March 30, they found it a beehive, alive with irate officers eager to give advice and learn about developments. Many of Castello's anti-Goulart followers congregated in Castello's change room,[4] a room of medium size that adjoined the office of the chief of staff and was used by him for getting into and out of his uniform. There they discussed the sailors' mutiny, the new list of promotions that was due to be released at any moment by the presidency,[5] and the reports of impending changes in high command posts; all weekend army circles had buzzed with speculation that First Infantry Division commander Oromar Osório would replace the ailing war minister. The plans of the president's office for putting Ladário Pereira Teles in charge of the Third Army and naming Galhardo army chief of staff became known.

Despite some talk about how Castello might be shifted to the headship of the EMFA, his arrest seemed more likely, for even if officers

---

[1] Muricy, *Os Motivos da Revolução Democrática Brasileira*, p. 40.

[2] Ferreira interview, November 12, 1975.

[3] Antonietta Diniz, in Diniz and Castello Branco interview, December 13, 1975.

[4] Murici interview, November 18, 1975.

[5] In this new promotion list Orlando Geisel received his overdue advancement to *general de divisão*. (See *O Estado de S. Paulo*, March 31, 1964.) Goulart advised Orlando Geisel of his promotion and added that he expected to be able to count on his cooperation. Geisel told the president that it sounded as though the president were trying to make a deal, and that he, a military man who would continue to fulfill his duty, was not a man who made deals. (See Muricy, *Os Motivos da Revolução Democrática Brasileira*, pp. 28–29.)

loyal to Goulart were unfamiliar with all of the details of what he was doing, the broad outline had become common knowledge in army circles.[6] Therefore on the fifth and sixth floors of the ministry the officers of the Estado Maior kept their pistols handy and organized to fight off any attempt to place Castello under arrest.[7]

Like Castello, Costa e Silva was visited by officers who argued that the time had come to overthrow the "Communist-dominated" regime. "Well, old friend," asked General Otacílio Terra Ururaí, "does this country have to stay at the mercy of these people?" "No," replied the director of Army Production and Works, and he added: "Don't worry, we are working on it."[8]

On the seventh floor the staff of Costa e Silva distributed copies of his unrestricted circular addressed to his subordinates. In that message Costa e Silva expressed "complete agreement" with Castello's March 20 circular and recommended that it be read with care.[9] He pointed out that Castello's warning about "increased agitation by the illegal power of the CGT" had been fulfilled sooner than might have been expected because the sailors' mutiny had been "prepared, stimulated, and unleashed by Communists and active members of the so-called CGT, who, in the end, had a decisive influence in the lamentable solution of the crisis."

Noting that similar occurrences could be expected soon in other branches of the armed services, Costa e Silva said that they would mean the total collapse of the armed forces by "the violent demolition" of their structural principles: "hierarchy and discipline, as defined in the Constitution of the Republic (Article 176)." He concluded by quoting Castello Branco: "The Armed Forces cannot be traitors to Brazil."[10]

On the second floor of the War Ministry building, First Army commander Morais Âncora met to "review the situation" with his chief sub-

---

[6] The public was given some idea of what had been transpiring when *O Estado de S. Paulo*, in its editorial on the morning of March 31, wrote that "the understandings" being reached between the army "high command" and the leaders of the Second, Third, and Fourth armies would block any movement by the president "against the institutions."

[7] Muricy, *Os Motivos da Revolução Democrática Brasileira*, p. 40.

[8] Costa e Silva, "Costa e Silva Relata Episódios da Revolução."

[9] Artur da Costa e Silva, "Aos Exmos. Snrs. Generais e demais militares subordinados ao DPO," circular, March 30, 1964, File L2, CPDOC.

[10] Ibid.

ordinates, such as Ladário Pereira Teles (who was about to leave for the south), Oromar Osório, and Luís Tavares de Cunha Melo (commander of the garrison of the state of Rio de Janeiro).[11] Genaro Bontempo, the representative of Jair Dantas Ribeiro at the meeting, said that the war minister's health was much improved, and he denied reports that Jair would step aside.

A topic discussed in army circles on March 30 was the commemoration of the fortieth anniversary of the Benevolent Association of Military Police Sergeants to be held that evening at the Automobile Club. Goulart, after arriving in Rio from Brasília on Sunday evening, had been quickly persuaded by Assis Brasil to ignore Kruel's advice, and now he was determined to attend the sergeants' meeting together with his cabinet (with Bontempo representing Jair). As the president wanted a large turnout of sergeants from all branches of the armed forces, Assis Brasil phoned Oromar Osório to make sure that sergeants from Vila Militar would go to the Automobile Club.[12]

Castello was back at Paulo's apartment, with the *estado maior informal* and its associates, when the speechmaking began at the Automobile Club. As Paulo's apartment had no television set, Nieta phoned to suggest that they all watch the commemoration of the sergeants' organization on the set at the Nascimento Silva Street house, and the suggestion was accepted.

Like radio listeners and television viewers throughout Brazil, Castello and his group heard the frenzied acclaim that greeted the president and Corporal José Anselmo (leader of the recent sailors' mutiny). They listened to speeches that were aggressive and optimistic. In the words of one speaker, a sergeant, the struggle was against the "narrow-minded mentality of those who make of military discipline an accursed whip to enslave the Brazilian people."[13] Jango, jostled by sergeants, gave a strong improvised speech in which he vowed not to allow any disorder to be carried out in the name of order. Speaking of those who had opposed his inauguration as president in 1961, Goulart said that "in the crisis of 1961 these same hypocrites, who today show a false zeal for the Constitution, wanted to tear it up and bury it in the cold grave of Fascist dictatorship."

[11] *O Estado de S. Paulo*, March 31, 1964.
[12] Silva, *1964: Golpe ou Contragolpe?*, p. 363.
[13] Mário Victor, *Cinco Anos que Abalaram o Brasil*, p. 506.

"Who is speaking about discipline today? Who is trying to stir up trouble for the President in the name of discipline? They are the same ones who in 1961, under the name of false discipline, arrested dozens of officers and Brazilian sergeants."[14]

With these words ringing in their ears, and with the scenes at the Automobile Club fresh in their memories, Castello and the officers with him returned late at night to Paulo's apartment.

[14] *Correio da Manhã*, March 31, 1964.

In the Revolution of March 31, 1964

Mourão has acted ahead of time; we have the choice of supporting him or of letting him be crushed.

1. "You Are Being Precipitous" (March 31, 1964)

LISTENING in Juiz de Fora to a radio broadcast of Goulart's address to the sergeants, General de Divisão Olímpio Mourão Filho became so incensed that he resolved to lead his men against Rio on the next morning, March 31, in an attack on the government and to issue his own incisive manifesto at the appropriate moment. He was disappointed in Governor Magalhães Pinto for issuing a proclamation on March 30 without consulting him, but he deemed it an insipid statement and not a clear summons to arms which would rule out a surprise attack on Rio. Mourão, who would reach retirement age on May 9, was tired of being told by Rio generals without troops that it was necessary to keep postponing action, and he had come to feel that if he did not start the revolution no one would. Although he had only fourteen hundred men in Juiz de Fora, he could expect General de Brigada Carlos Luís Guedes, in Belo Horizonte, to furnish additional troops for his march, and he believed it possible that the younger officers in Rio would not allow his men to be attacked.[1]

At about 5:00 A.M. on March 31, Mourão revealed his decision in telephone calls to General Guedes and to a few conspirators in Rio and São Paulo. In his calls to Rio he asked Colonel Jaime Portela to tell Murici and Ulhoa Cintra to come at once to Juiz de Fora, and he asked Armando Falcão, federal congressman from Ceará, to advise former Navy Minister Sílvio Heck, an active worker against Goulart.[2]

[1] Olímpio Mourão Filho interview, Rio de Janeiro, October 9, 1965.
[2] Olímpio Mourão Filho, in Brazil, Army, First Army, General Headquarters, *Re-*

Mourão's telephone calls generated many more calls. Portela notified Costa e Silva and urged him to leave his home for a friend's house, which the general did.[3] Falcão notified Governor Lacerda and General Castello Branco, whom he had met in Ceará in 1952 and subsequently seen from time to time in Rio. When Castello thus learned of Mourão's decision, he could not believe it, and he asked Falcão to confirm the information. Falcão phoned Mourão and then phoned Castello again with the verification.[4]

Before the verification was received from Falcão, Riograndino Kruel, having learned of Mourão's plans in a telephone call made from Petrópolis by Antônio Neder, called Castello from São Paulo. Castello spoke of the "rumors" and said that he would check. Presently he called Riograndino with the confirmation.[5]

Castello also took steps to prevent Mourão from marching, for, as he had just explained to Riograndino, the coordinating work had not been completed, and an isolated movement might be crushed with disastrous results. He expressed his concern in a telephone call to José Luís de Magalhães Lins, Magalhães Pinto's nephew in Rio who had visited with him six days earlier. But Magalhães Lins, after phoning the Minas governor, reported to Castello that nothing could hold back the movement already started. Castello, turning to the officers who were with him, said, "Mourão has acted ahead of time; we have the choice of supporting him or of letting him be crushed." [6]

Murici, who first received the news of Mourão's decision in a call from Antônio Neder, rushed to the home of Ademar de Queiroz. Ademar's reaction was the same as that of Castello: "It is not possible." After a phone call from Ademar's house brought a confirmation from

---

latório da Revolução Democrática Iniciada pela 4ª RM e 4ª DI em 31 de Março de 1964, Boletim Especial, Juiz de Fora, May 9, 1964.

[3] Artur da Costa e Silva, "Costa e Silva Relata Episódios da Revolução" (speech at ECEME), April 1, 1965, in O Estado de S. Paulo, April 4, 1965, pp. 5–6; Nelson Dimas Filho, Costa e Silva: O Homem e o Líder, p. 65.

[4] Armando Falcão interviews, Rio de Janeiro, November 30, 1966; October 10, 1975.

[5] Riograndino Kruel interview, Rio de Janeiro, September 21, 1975.

[6] Pedro Gomes, "Minas: Diálogo ao 'Front,'" in Alberto Dines et al., Os Idos de Março e a Queda em Abril, p. 106; Vernon Walters interview, Rio de Janeiro, December 19, 1966.

Juiz de Fora, Murici prepared to leave to gather his officers and join Mourão. "May God be with you," Ademar said to Murici.[7]

The concern of Ademar de Queiroz and Castello reflected a feeling that was widespread at that moment. José Stacchini, a careful researcher of the military movement of March 31, reports that "it can be asserted, without fear of error, that many of the most dedicated conspirators, even after Corporal Anselmo led the sailors in mutiny, would have replied, 'it is not convenient,' if they had been consulted ahead of time about the decision to march from Minas Gerais."[8]

Castello had not finished trying to stop the *temeridade* or *aventura*. At 9:00 A.M. he phoned Governor Magalhães Pinto and General Guedes in Belo Horizonte. He insisted that the governor have the troops in Minas return to their barracks. But the governor told Castello that they were "already approaching the Paraibuna River," one section of which separates the states of Minas Gerais and Rio de Janeiro.[9]

Speaking with Guedes, Castello asked, "What is happening in Belo Horizonte?"

"We have already left," Guedes replied, "One battalion of the 12th RI is rolling along to Juiz de Fora. One battalion of the Polícia Militar of Minas Gerais is on its way to Três Marias."

"Don't be precipitous. You are being precipitous."

"We have already left, but there is no risk. We are going only as far as the Paraibuna."

"Careful, careful," Castello said, and then, after a slight pause, he added, "I am going out to advise my men."[10] In advising his men, Castello gave to Mourão's uprising the backing of all of the organizational work done by the *estado maior informal* since its inception. Furthermore, Mourão's march now received the help of fresh arguments in its favor given to officers who would be called on to crush it. Ademar de Queiroz, after consulting with Castello, sped to Vila Militar.[11]

To bolster the cause in the south, Castello wrote a note for Lieutenant Colonel Confuncio Pamplona to take to General Adalberto Pereira

[7] Antônio Carlos Muricy, *Os Motivos da Revolução Democrática Brasileira*, pp. 40–41.
[8] José Stacchini, *Março 64: Mobilização da Audácia*, p. 78.
[9] Oswaldo Pieruccetti to JWFD, January 18, 1968, p. 5.
[10] Stacchini, *Março 64*, p. 75.
[11] Golberi do Couto e Silva interview, Brasília, October 22, 1975.

dos Santos, who had not yet lost his post in Rio Grande do Sul. The note, a succinct listing of the purposes of the uprising, reveals what was uppermost in Castello's mind. It said:

To restore legality:
The reestablishment of the Federation;
Eliminate development of plan for communism to take over power;
Defend the military institutions that are beginning to be destroyed;
Establish order for the advent of legal reforms.[12]

UDN legislators were quick to get in touch with Castello when the news about Mourão began circulating. Daniel Krieger and Adauto Lúcio Cardoso were told by Castello that a precipitous outbreak had occurred but that it would be well backed in the army.[13]

President Goulart learned on the morning of March 31 about Mourão's plans from Kubitschek (who had been advised from Belo Horizonte by politician José Maria Alkmin). Like many others, President Goulart at first appeared incredulous. Later that morning he met at Laranjeiras Palace with the navy and air force ministers, Casa Militar chief Assis Brasil, and the commanders of the First Army and of Vila Militar. Informed that the center of the conspiracy in the War Ministry was the office of the army chief of staff, he ordered First Army commander Morais Âncora to arrest Castello.[14] The dismissals of Mourão and Guedes were agreed upon. General Luís Tavares da Cunha Melo was named to replace Guedes and was assigned the task of directing the operation of a large force against the Minas rebels.

[12] HACB copy of handwritten note to Adalberto Pereira dos Santos, March 31, 1964, File L2, CPDOC.

[13] Daniel Krieger interview, Brasília, October 21, 1975.

[14] Hélio Silva, *1964: Golpe ou Contragolpe?*, pp. 394–395, 397; Muricy, *Os Motivos da Revolução Democrática Brasileira*, p. 40. At about this time, Phyllis Parker reports, U.S. authorities in Washington considered and approved "a military contingency plan that went beyond the embassy's two suggestions that petroleum and a carrier fleet be sent to Brazil. This third plan involved arrangements for actual arms and ammunition to be sent to Brazil as contingency support for the conspirators" (Parker, "Separate . . . but Equal? U.S. Policy toward Brazil, 1961-1964," Independent Research Project, Lyndon B. Johnson School of Public Affairs, Austin, Texas, May, 1976, pp. 95–97).

2. The Chief of Staff at His Place of Work (March 31, 1964)

In the days before Mourão unexpectedly started his march against Goulart, Castello (like Marshal Dutra) had indicated his interest in accepting an invitation given by Magalhães Pinto's emissaries to participate in military operations in Minas, and he had also considered accompanying Cordeiro de Farias, who flew south. But on the morning of March 31 Castello remarked that his Army Staff office was where he belonged because it was "his place of work."[1] Rejecting the advice of those who said he should not go to the War Ministry, he left for his office at about 10:15 A.M. When Costa e Silva learned what Castello had done, he was surprised, for he had understood that Castello would go to Minas; now, Costa e Silva thought to himself, Castello Branco has walked straight into "the wolf's mouth."[2]

At the War Ministry Castello received a touching surprise. To help protect him against arrest there, fifty officer-students came from the ECEME, whose commander, General Jurandir de Bizarria Mamede, had attended many of the meetings of the *estado maior informal*. The fifty ECEME officers-students, bearing their arms and wearing their uniforms, were assigned to the Army Staff conference room on the War Ministry's sixth floor and were integrated into the defense already organized by officers of the Army Staff.[3] Among the leaders of the defense was Lieutenant Colonel Leônidas Pires Gonçalves, member of the Third Section of the Army Staff.

In his office Castello received further confirmation of the Minas uprising and warnings that he would be arrested. Although he could hardly have known that Morais Âncora was in no hurry to carry out Goulart's arrest order, he went ahead with his normal duties. As presiding officer of the Army Promotions Commission, he opened its meeting at 2:00 P.M.; due to the absence of some of the members, however, he had

[1] Gomes, "Minas: Do Diálogo ao 'Front,' " in Dines et al., *Os Idos de Março*, p. 93; Osvaldo Cordeiro de Farias interview, Rio de Janeiro, December 26, 1974; Antonietta Castello Branco Diniz and Paulo V. Castello Branco interview, Rio de Janeiro, December 13, 1975.

[2] Dimas Filho, *Costa e Silva*, pp. 63, 66; Costa e Silva, "Costa e Silva Relata Episódios da Revolução."

[3] Murilo Gomes Ferreira, "O General Castello Que Conheci" (transcript of tape prepared for interview), Rio de Janeiro, November 12, 1975, p. 14.

to adjourn the meeting.[4] In his office he discussed the military situation with Emílio Maurel Filho, Ernesto Geisel, and Colonel Ariel Pacca de Fonseca, who had served under Cordeiro in Italy and was now office chief of the army's Directorship of Instruction.[5] As he had done earlier in the day, Castello spoke by phone with Brasília. Reaching the UDN leadership on the twentieth floor of the congressional office building, he urged Paulo Sarazate (Ceará), Bilac Pinto (Minas Gerais), Ernâni Sátiro (Paraíba), and others to carry on with the speechmaking that he still considered an important part of the "iron circle" for defending legality.[6]

During the afternoon Castello received a visit from Costa e Silva, who urged him to get out of the War Ministry and told him about the secret command post that Costa e Silva was setting up at the home of a civilian in the Botafogo district. Another secret command post being organized in the Copacabana district by the Castello Branco estado maior informal gave the prospect of two such posts, an unplanned development that had security advantages but that promised some confusion. Castello and Costa e Silva, who had been working in harmony, agreed to keep in close touch. A division of the areas of activity was suggested by Castello, with his own post giving attention to national matters and with Costa e Silva's getting in touch with local pro-revolutionary commanders and sending officers to take charge of nearby units. This idea was accepted by Costa e Silva, for although he headed the hierarchy of generals in active service, he recognized that he had joined the movement much more recently than Castello.[7]

From a window in the War Ministry building Castello calmly watched a contingent of the Mechanized Reconnaissance Regiment (Regimento de Reconhecimento Mecanizado) surround the building. Then he was approached by Augusto César Moniz de Aragão and other gen-

[4] Ibid.

[5] Ibid.; O Jornal, April 1, 1964. Ariel Pacca da Fonseca, an artillery captain in the FEB, was chefe de gabinete of the Diretoria de Ensino e Formação.

[6] Ernâni Sátiro interview, Rio de Janeiro, December 17, 1975.

[7] This account of a proposed division of activities is based on information received in Rio de Janeiro on July 22, 1976, from Murilo Gomes Ferreira. Discussing the same subject, Nelson Dimas Filho writes (Costa e Silva, p. 66) that "Castello would be in charge of the political part of the revolution. Costa e Silva would assume command of the military operations."

erals who agreed with Costa e Silva that it would be best for all of them to leave the building if they could.

Costa e Silva left the ministry with Generals Moniz de Aragão, José Horácio da Cunha Garcia, Estevão Taurino de Resende, and Rafael de Sousa Aguiar, and at the command post in Botafogo they were greeted by Sizeno Sarmento, Jaime Portela, and others.[8] While on their way, Moniz de Aragão telephoned the War Ministry to advise those remaining with Castello that no difficulty had been experienced in getting out of the ministry.[9]

At 5:00 P.M., before Moniz de Aragão made his phone call, radios in the War Ministry brought the voice of Olímpio Mourão Filho, being carried via a telephone connection from Juiz de Fora to Rádio Globo in Rio.[10] Now that his force of twenty-five hundred men, known as the Tiradentes Column and led by Murici, had reached the Paraibuna River, Mourão delivered his manifesto to the nation and the armed forces. He spoke of "spurious organizations of political syndicalism, manipulated by enemies of Brazil, confessedly Communist" and "particularly audacious" because of the "support and stimulation" provided by President Goulart. The government, Mourão declared, allowed these organizations to name and dismiss cabinet ministers, generals, and high officials in order to destroy the democratic institutions. Mourão referred to the work of demoralizing and humiliating the navy "in the most depraved and shameless outrage against its discipline and hierarchy."

"The people, state governors, and armed forces, impelled by fervent patriotic sentiment, oppose this process of degradation of the vital forces of the nation, so well conceived and capriciously carried out by the President of the Republic." Calling on all Brazilians to restore the authority of the Constitution, Mourão accused Goulart of turning himself into the chief of a Communist government. He should, Mourão concluded, be thrown out of the position of power he was abusing.

Castello, after hearing the proclamation, completed his last day of work as the army chief of staff in a government that had refused to listen to him. When his decision to leave the building became known at

[8] Costa e Silva, "Costa e Silva Relata Episódios da Revolução."
[9] Ferreira, "O General Castello Que Conheci," p. 14. According to this deposition, Moniz de Aragão left the ministry at about 5:00 P.M.
[10] Mourão Filho, in First Army, *Relatório da Revolução Democrática.*

5:30 P.M., five ECEME officer-students sprang into action. Together with Murilo Gomes Ferreira, they stepped with Castello into the elevator reserved for generals. So quickly was this done that Castello remarked, "It seems that I am being kidnapped."[11]

Castello and Gomes Ferreira, leaving the building in an official car, were escorted by another car filled with armed ECEME officer-students. From that moment on, Castello said, he would be playing a directive role in the military movement begun that morning and would therefore be using civilian clothes. He made the change at the Nascimento Silva Street house and then was driven to the Copacabana apartment of a nephew of Cordeiro that had been selected as the secret command post of Castello's *estado maior informal*: Apartment 101 at Avenida Atlântica 3916 (the Igrejinha Building).

Together with Castello at this command post on the rainy night of March 31 were Ademar de Queiroz, Ernesto Geisel, and Golberi do Couto e Silva. Younger officers, each "attached to" one of these four, often came and went, as "missions" demanded. Among them were Lieutenant Colonels Murilo Gomes Ferreira, Leônidas Pires Gonçalves, and Ivan de Sousa Mendes, a friend of Ernesto Geisel who had reached Rio on March 13 after being transferred from Mato Grosso to a bureaucratic function.[12]

3. Telephone Calls at Night (March 31–April 1, 1964)

Murilo Gomes Ferreira records some of the telephone calls made from the Avenida Atlântica apartment by Castello's *estado maior informal* on the night of March 31: "Telephone contacts with the command post of General Costa e Silva, with General Mamede, commander of the ECEME. Information about the progress of the troops of Minas Gerais. Command post of the War Ministry, Army Staff, via Colonel Darci Lázaro of the Second Section."[1]

This is but a partial list. So much telephoning was done from the command posts of Castello and Costa e Silva that it is remarkable that

[11] Ferreira, "O General Castello Que Conheci," p. 14.

[12] Ibid., p. 15; Leônidas Pires Gonçalves interview, Rio de Janeiro, July 20, 1976; Ivan de Sousa Mendes interview, Rio de Janeiro, July 26, 1976.

[1] Ferreira, "O General Castello Que Conheci," p. 15.

they were able to make telephone contact with each other. Costa e Silva's civilian friend in Botafogo, the general records, "had two telephone lines" that came in very handy. According to Costa e Silva's recollection, by 11:00 P.M., which was still rather early, "we had already participated in some hundred calls." [2] This was a superlative achievement, for in Rio in 1964 it was often difficult to get a dial tone in good weather and more difficult yet during rainy weather. However, the revolutionaries had the cooperation of retired General Landri Sales Gonçalves, a high official of Companhia Telefônica Brasileira.[3]

Some of the telephoning between the two principal secret command posts concerned a manifesto that was drawn up during the evening by Golberi do Couto e Silva to point out to army men that the position of the army's top command in the revolutionary movement had been dictated by the stern duty to shield the Constitution against illegal acts of Goulart.[4] It was decided that the manifesto should be issued by "members of the High Command," and this decision brought a phone call from Ademar de Queiroz to the home of four-star General Décio Palmeiro de Escobar, Castello's brilliant fellow-officer of the Sociedade Cívica in Porto Alegre in 1916; Décio Escobar, who now headed the army's Department of General Provision, asked to have the document read to him and then agreed to add his signature, the last of three that were arranged in order of hierarchical status: Costa e Silva, Castello, and Décio Escobar.[5] To assure broadcasts of the manifesto, telephone calls were made to São Paulo and Minas, for the radio stations in the Rio area had been seized by Goulart's supporters.

The strain on the telephones and the fear that conversations might be monitored led to a considerable use of "messengers"—army officers with cars at their disposal. This method of communication was particularly used between the Castello and Costa e Silva command posts. But neither telephoning nor messengers achieved the fulfillment of the policy according to which, as Costa e Silva recalled a year later, "Castello Branco was in charge of making external connections and maintaining understandings in the civilian area," while Costa e Silva "was concerned

[2] Costa e Silva, "Costa e Silva Relata Episódios da Revolução."
[3] Sousa Mendes interview, July 26, 1976; Hernani D'Aguiar interview, Rio de Janeiro, July 29, 1976.
[4] Luís Viana Filho, O Governo Castelo Branco, pp. 26–27.
[5] Décio Palmeiro de Escobar interview, Rio de Janeiro, July 25, 1977.

with internal connections."[6] From each command post, for example, calls went out to friends at Vila Militar, regardless of policy. Leônidas Pires Gonçalves, phoning a colonel about the possible adherence of a regiment, was told that "the revolutionary movement" seemed to be "in great confusion." The lieutenant colonel replied, "Well, the courses given at the ECEME do not include one on how to make a revolution."[7]

At 7:00 P.M. Costa e Silva sought to explain what was happening in Brazil when he had a telephone conversation with General Emílio Garrastazu Médici, commander of the military academy at Resende, between Rio and São Paulo. "It is," he said to Médici, "a revolutionary movement of which I, your friend, am the leader, that is, I and Castello Branco." Costa e Silva assigned Médici the mission of helping to form a vanguard for the troops from São Paulo "in case they should come."[8]

From Castello's post Ademar de Queiroz telephoned Governor Carlos Lacerda, who was working with the state police and hundreds of retired officers and enthusiastic volunteers to defend Guanabara Palace against an attack expected from Admiral Cândido Aragão's Marines. As the defense appeared to be no match for Aragão's heavy guns, Ademar suggested that Lacerda leave the palace and not try to resist there. Castello called to tell Lacerda that martyrs were not what the cause needed. But Lacerda told Castello that he had consulted his wife, Marshal Dutra, and Eduardo Gomes, and all of them disagreed with the advice of Castello and Ademar de Queiroz.[9]

A phone call from Castello brought ECEME commander Mamede to the Avenida Atlântica post, and there Castello ordered him to coordinate all of the revolutionary activity in the Praia Vermelha–Urca area of military schools, including the Escola Superior de Guerra (ESG). Mamede returned to the area, going first to the ECEME, which soon be-

[6] Costa e Silva, "Costa e Silva Relata Episódios da Revolução."

[7] Pires Gonçalves interview, July 20, 1976.

[8] Costa e Silva, "Costa e Silva Relata Episódios da Revolução." This telephone call to the military academy (which had been moved from Realengo to Resende in 1945) is mentioned in Dimas Filho, *Costa e Silva*, p. 70. It is discussed fully by Emílio Garrastazu Médici in a handwritten memorandum to Rafael de Sousa Aguiar (Brasília, July 23, 1971). Médici points out that Sousa Aguiar, speaking from Rio, opened the telephone conversation by mentioning a mutually known episode, thus identifying himself, and then gave two numbers at which Médici could reach Costa e Silva. When Médici phoned Costa e Silva, the latter advised that he headed a revolution that had broken out. "Issue your order, chief," Médici said, "the military academy is yours."

[9] Carlos Lacerda interview, Rio de Janeiro, October 11, 1967.

came known as the "nerve center" of the revolution, an "ostensive general barracks" that became the gathering place of officers who were neither students nor instructors but who wanted to carry out missions. After giving instructions to ECEME *subcomandante* João Bina Machado, Mamede proceeded to the ESG, where he found the officers, among them Colonel Mário David Andreazza, ready to act against the government.[10] When a call to the ESG from Castello's command post advised that Castello himself proposed visiting the ESG, officers at the ESG succeeded in discouraging the idea by pointing out that Castello would have to pass the Tupi television station and that it had been taken over by Marines of Cândido Aragão who were eager to capture Castello.[11]

During the night Ivan de Sousa Mendes, of Castello's command post, drove Colonel Reynaldo Melo de Almeida to the airport to catch a commercial flight to Curitiba. From Costa e Silva's command post General Sousa Aguiar was sent to Vila Militar "to assume command of the First Infantry Division,"[12] José Horácio da Cunha Garcia was sent to install a command post at the First Battalion of Combat Vehicles, and Moniz de Aragão was sent to command the paratroopers at Vila Militar. Costa e Silva told his Realengo classmate Estevão Taurino de Resende (who was "very irritable and impulsive") that he needed him at his side.[13]

4. Kruel Adheres (March 31, 1964)

Much of the telephoning from Rio was for Amauri Kruel in São Paulo. It began earlier in the day with the series of three or four calls between Goulart and Kruel, during which the president repeatedly rejected Kruel's advice that he leave the people who surrounded him lest he "sink with them." This series ended at 6:00 P.M., when Kruel said, "We are separated."[1]

[10] Hernani D'Aguiar, *A Revolução por Dentro*, pp. 147–149.

[11] Luís Vieira Duque interview, Brasília, July 23, 1976.

[12] Dimas Filho, *Costa e Silva*, p. 67. Rafael de Sousa Aguiar, in his declarations in *O Globo*, April 20, 1964, says, "we received a mission to be accomplished in the pre-dawn hours in Vila Militar."

[13] Costa e Silva, "Costa e Silva Relata Episódios da Revolução."

[1] Amauri Kruel interviews, São Paulo, November 16, 1965; Rio de Janeiro, October 21, 1967.

Later in the evening Costa e Silva, who was considering going by sea to São Paulo, called Kruel from the Rio Yacht Club.[2] He used this phone connection to help Kruel convince two of his subordinate generals that they should adhere to the revolution, and then he returned to the Botafogo post.

Kruel was refusing to answer phone calls from Justice Minister Jurema or further calls from Goulart. But he did answer when Castello called. Except for a few perfunctory remarks when Kruel was war minister, this was the first time in over nineteen years that the two had conversed.

"How are things going?" Castello asked.

"My troops are leaving the barracks," Amauri Kruel replied.[3]

Castello took a nap. When he awoke at around 11:00 P.M. some younger officers told him that they were worried about Kruel's position, but they found Castello unconcerned and certain that all was well in São Paulo.[4] Meanwhile, at the Botafogo post Costa e Silva phoned Kruel again, this time to get the latest news, and he learned that Kruel's Second Army Troops were nearing Resende. Kruel told Costa e Silva that the last words of his manifesto were being typed.[5] Costa e Silva, a more demonstrative man than Castello, shouted with joy at his command post: "Long live Brazil!"[6]

Kruel's manifesto, released soon after 11:00 P.M., stated that the fight of the Second Army "will be against the Communists, and its objective will be to break the circle of Communism which now compromises the authority of the government." The broadcast of these words, the first adherence by an important troop commander to Mourão's position, caused a sensation and brought its signer messages from Magalhães Pinto, Justino Alves Bastos, and Emílio Garrastazu Médici, asking if the manifesto was authentic.[7]

In Rio, Kruel's old FEB friend, Floriano Brayner, found himself in the dark after he heard the broadcast in his apartment, for the electricity, undependable in a rainstorm, went off in a part of Copacabana. "A colonel wants to see you," Brayner was told. Opening the door to the

[2] Ibid.; Costa e Silva, "Costa e Silva Relata Episódios da Revolução."

[3] Amauri Kruel interview, Rio de Janeiro, December 11, 1975.

[4] Sousa Mendes interview, July 26, 1976.

[5] Amauri Kruel interview, October 21, 1967.

[6] Costa e Silva, "Costa e Silva Relata Episódios da Revolução."

[7] Amauri Kruel interview, October 21, 1967.

service entrance, Brayner found the colonel. The candle in the visitor's hand lit up the face of Vernon Walters, who said that he was calling to get information about the situation to transmit to Ambassador Gordon. "Kruel has issued his manifesto," Brayner told him. "*Graças a Deus!*" Walters exclaimed.[8]

Kruel's affirmative reply to Justino Alves Bastos' radio inquiry about the manifesto's authenticity almost coincided with the postmidnight telephone call in which Goulart asked the Fourth Army commander about his position. Justino Alves Bastos comforted the president with the news that the Fourth Army was on "rigorous alert." Then at 3:00 A.M. Justino Alves Bastos' agent in Rio, in touch with the Castello and Costa e Silva command posts, sent a radio message to Recife to say that the Fourth Army could "start its work."[9] The Fourth Army had been prepared, in part by Castello in 1962 and 1963, to deal with subversive guerrilla warfare; now it found no such warfare to deal with, and it spent its time energetically rounding up those suspected of being Communists or allies of the Communists.

The news from the Paraibuna River was all that the command posts of Castello and Costa e Silva could have wished. Before midnight most of the men of the First Infantry Battalion, sent from Petrópolis to oppose Mourão, adhered to the anti-Goulart movement.

At the vanguard of the well-armed troops sent by the government from Vila Militar was the 1st RI, the Sampaio Regiment of FEB fame. At about 3:00 A.M., when it was approaching the Paraibuna River, its commander, Colonel Raimundo Ferreira de Souza, received a telephone call from his longtime friend Marshal Denys, who had been with Mourão since noon on March 31. "Are you going to fight for the Communists?" the laconic marshal tersely asked the colonel.[10] Colonel Raimundo and his renowned regiment adhered to the anti-Goulart movement.

The telephone calls between Goulart and Kruel had had important consequences, despite the planning of some of Kruel's officers to put

[8] Floriano de Lima Brayner interview, Rio de Janeiro, October 6, 1975. (*Graças a Deus!*: Thank God!)

[9] Joaquim Justino Alves Bastos, *Encontro com o Tempo*, pp. 354, 358–359. For Goulart's impression of his conversation with Justino Alves Bastos, see Seixas Dória, *Eu, Réu Sem Crime*, p. 48.

[10] Odílio Denys interview, Rio de Janeiro, December 14, 1965. The role of Marshal Denys is told in "Denys Conta Todo," *Fatos & Fotos*, May 2, 1964.

Nelson de Melo in his place if he did not adhere to the anti-Communist movement. But of all the telephone conversations on the night of March 31–April 1, Mourão would give the greatest importance to the brief one between Denys and Colonel Raimundo. The revolution, Mourão has said, was victorious when it was joined by the Sampaio Regiment.[11] General Cunha Melo, charged with overpowering Mourão, saw his army disintegrate.

Ulhoa Cintra, long delayed in reaching Juiz de Fora because of a traffic jam, was at Mourão's side. But, Mourão has written, Ulhoa Cintra received no mission "due to the swiftness of the victory."[12]

5. Revolutionaries Seize the Coastal Artillery Barracks (April 1, 1964)

Castello Branco spent all night at the Copacabana command post, and in the meantime Murilo Gomes Ferreira and another lieutenant colonel slept in the Nascimento Silva Street house.[1]

When they awoke on the morning of April 1, the situation was unclear in many parts of the country, such as Rio Grande do Sul, Brasília, and Guanabara. In the city of Rio, Admiral Cândido Aragão's Marines, protecting CGT leaders and invading anti-Goulart newspapers, were still thought to be preparing to assault Guanabara Palace.

Cariocas, their radios tuned in to broadcasts from São Paulo and Minas, heard the manifesto for the army that bore the signatures of Costa e Silva, Castello, and Décio Palmeiro de Escobar. It advised that Goulart, in a conspiracy "with notorious Communists" to undermine democratic and Christian traditions, had violated state sovereignties and exerted "illegitimate pressures," some through labor unions, on Congress. The manifesto pictured the nation as being on the verge of chaos, and it denounced the "systematic effort" to overthrow the democratic regime through the destruction of the military institutions, with the president himself fostering indiscipline. It declared that as the armed forces were required to guarantee "the constitutional powers, law, and

[11] Mourão Filho interview, October 9, 1965.

[12] Muricy, *Os Motivos da Revolução Democrática Brasileira*, p. 36; Mourão Filho, in First Army, *Relatório da Revolução Democrática*.

[1] Antonietta Diniz, in Diniz and Castello Branco interview, December 13, 1975.

order," all the military should work together to avoid the "fratricidal struggle, irresponsibly and criminally prepared by the President and his Communist allies."[2]

From the Guanabara State Security Department and other sources Castello learned that his command post had become known to the pro-Goulart people; therefore, as Costa e Silva had already done several times, Castello moved his organization to a new post. There, an apartment on Avenida Rui Barbosa in the Flamengo district, the telephone connections were found to have been cut, necessitating still another move. Lieutenant Colonel Ivan de Sousa Mendes suggested that since he had only recently come to Rio and was not generally known to be there, the use of his apartment might be prudent; although he had but one telephone, arrangements could be made to use the telephone of a neighbor.[3] The suggestion was accepted, and the men were driven, several at a time, to this third post: 307 Belfort Roxo Street, Apartment 602, in Copacabana. The group, fully installed in its new location by noon, included Colonel Ariel Pacca da Fonseca, of the army's Directorship of Instruction, and cavalry Lieutenant Colonel Túlio Chagas Nogueira, who had joined Castello during the night.

Soon after this final installation of Castello's secret command post, the Goulart administration suffered a well-publicized setback in Rio. It resulted from the resolve of two officers of the Coastal Artillery directorship, Colonel César Montagna de Sousa and Lieutenant Colonel Oscar Couto de Souza, to seize the pro-Goulart Coastal Artillery barracks, thus eliminating what they called the "impasse" between the barracks and nearby Fort Copacabana, which had adhered to the revolution during the night.

Although Castello was known to oppose any clash in the Rio area, the two artillery officers received the permission they wanted when they spoke with Orlando Geisel, who had gone to the ECEME. Then, thanks to the cooperation of Lieutenant Colonel João Batista Figueiredo of the ECEME command, they set forth with Major Dickson Melges Grael and nineteen of the major's ECEME first-year classmates.[4] The Coastal Artil-

[2] *Jornal do Brasil*, April 2, 1964.

[3] Ferreira, "O General Castello Que Conheci," p. 15; Sousa Mendes interview, July 26, 1976.

[4] César Montagna de Sousa interview, Brasília, July 23, 1976; D'Aguiar, *A Revolução por Dentro*, pp. 157–161.

lery barracks fell at about 12:30 P.M. after a skirmish in which two men were wounded. The pro-Goulart commanding general had been absent from the barracks, and when he returned he was arrested and replaced by General Hugo Panasco Alvim, sent by the ECEME. Reports of the fall of the barracks, witnessed by many, spread quickly through Rio and distressed the members of the Goulart administration who were in the city.

6. Victory in Rio (April 1, 1964)

Already on the morning of April 1 War Minister Jair Dantas Ribeiro, in the Hospital for Public Servants, had submitted his resignation, with the result that Goulart had appointed First Army commander Morais Âncora to be acting war minister and had placed Oromar Osório in charge of the First Army. The president, after asking Morais Âncora to confer with Amauri Kruel, flew to Brasília at 1:00 P.M. to the disappointment of his supporters in Rio. Before leaving Rio he remarked to Justice Minister Jurema: "Our military plan has inexplicably failed. I can only count on the Third Army, and that is not enough."[1]

At about 1:45 P.M. Costa e Silva phoned his old friend, Morais Âncora, at the War Ministry. Speaking from his most recent secret command post, Costa e Silva said, "Âncora, haven't you noticed that you are all alone in that enormous mansion?" The acting war minister acknowledged that he felt "a little abandoned."

"You will notice," Costa e Silva said, "that this revolution hasn't just sprouted up by itself, like weeds. It had to be cultivated and prepared."

Morais Âncora, referring to his intention to confer with Kruel at the military academy in Resende, told Costa e Silva, "I realize that I am lost but I was given a mission by the President and I have to carry it out."[2]

After Goulart's departure from Rio, the tanks that had been guarding Laranjeiras Palace were taken over by the men of the ECEME. Three

[1] *O Estado de S. Paulo*, April 2, 1964. This statement was confirmed by Abelardo Jurema (interview, Rio de Janeiro, July 27, 1976).
[2] Costa e Silva, "Costa e Silva Relata Episódios da Revolução."

of the tanks headed for Guanabara Palace to assist with its defense. But the defense proved unnecessary, for by then it was all over for the pro-Goulart forces in Rio. Radio and television transmissions, freed from the control of Goulart supporters, brought declarations of Governor Lacerda and Social Services Secretary Sandra Cavalcanti from Guanabara Palace. Lacerda praised Castello Branco and described him as "the chief of the forces of national liberation." [3]

Cariocas began to celebrate the turn in events, and the anti-Goulart military, with the ECEME officer-students much in evidence, started to round up "subversives." From the ECEME, officer-students were sent by assistant commander João Bina Machado to arrest Abelardo Jurema, reportedly about to take a flight from Santos Dumont. The arrest group received the cooperation of the air base chief of staff after it explained that it was acting "in the name of General Castello Branco." Jurema, seized at the military airport and conducted to the ECEME, was treated well by Mamede, who had supper with him after Bina Machado and João Batista Figueiredo "declined the honor." [4]

Jurema was impressed by what he saw at the ECEME, where he was held against his will. He concluded that the school had produced the leader of the revolution, Castello Branco, together with the plans of action and the "philosophy of the revolutionary movement." [5]

7. Costa e Silva, Commander in Chief

During the afternoon of April 1, while Morais Âncora was driven to Resende to negotiate with Kruel, Costa e Silva told the officers at his command post that as he headed the hierarchy in the High Command, he had decided "to take over the War Ministry." [1] He sent out orders for the army officers in Guanabara to report in uniform to the ministry. While younger members at the Belfort Roxo Street post therefore went to fetch uniforms, Castello's *estado maior informal* concluded its work by issuing a bulletin for the public: "General Castello Branco advises

[3] *O Jornal*, April 2, 1964.
[4] D'Aguiar, *A Revolução por Dentro*, pp. 164–167.
[5] Ibid., p. 143; Jurema interview, July 27, 1976.
[1] Dimas Filho, *Costa e Silva*, p. 71.

that the commander of the First Army has resolved to terminate military operations in the territory of his command and is taking the steps necessary to achieve this end."[2] According to the information that reached *O Estado de S. Paulo*, Castello Branco, the builder of "the national military organization of the revolution," had full control of Rio de Janeiro and the surrounding areas.

When Castello and his group left their post to be driven away in three official cars at about 5:45 P.M., Castello was applauded in the street.[3] Before setting out for the War Ministry, the cars made their way to the Coastal Artillery barracks and Fort Copacabana, because Castello wanted to congratulate Colonel Montagna de Sousa and the officers who had acted with him.[4]

Castello, the victorious commander, was believed by officers of Fort Copacabana to be the new war minister, and he was honored there by a salvo of shots from some old Schneider cannons; although twenty-four shots were planned, the noise caused such panic among civilians in the neighborhood that the ceremony was ended after the fifth shot.[5] At the fort Castello declared that "the only purpose of the movement against Goulart was the restoration of legality and the defense of the patriotism of the National Army."

In the drive downtown to the ministry, an effort was made to avoid the most congested streets, but even so, rejoicing throngs frequently forced the cars to stop, and one of the three cars became lost in the congestion. Occasionally, when the cars were at a standstill, people recognized Castello and offered him their congratulations. Before reaching the ministry Castello's car passed the headquarters of the UNE (National Students' Union), and therefore Castello witnessed the burning of leftist banners and placards of the UNE, together with some of its furniture and papers, carried out by anti-Communists in front of the building.[6]

Castello was in his office shortly after 8:00 P.M. While the rooms of the Army Staff filled with officers, news was received about the pro-

[2] Ferreira, "O General Castello Que Conheci," p. 15.

[3] Sousa Mendes interview, July 26, 1976.

[4] Ferreira, "O General Castello Que Conheci," pp. 15–16.

[5] *Jornal do Brasil*, April 2, 1964, p. 6; Montagna de Sousa interview, July 23, 1976; Duque interview, July 23, 1976.

[6] Celso dos Santos Meyer interview, Washington, D.C., July 15, 1976.

gress of the revolution, and decisions were made for the consolidation of the successes so far achieved.

The officers learned that at about 6:00 P.M. Morais Âncora, nervous and suffering from emphysema, had explained to Kruel in Resende that his "mission" on Goulart's behalf had ended. Reports told of a movement of troops to the far south, set in motion by Kruel, and of forces advancing on Brasília, including a column from distant Mato Grosso led by Colonel Meira Mattos. Shortly after 10:00 P.M. the officers at the War Ministry learned that Goulart had flown from Brasília, and it was believed that he would go to Rio Grande do Sul.

Costa e Silva, who arrived at the ministry shortly after Castello, assumed with ease and vigor the role of commanding general of the operating forces. Sizeno Sarmento, chief of staff of the commanding general, ordered Rafael de Sousa Aguiar to go from Vila Militar to Brasília to take over the army forces there and protect Congress.[7] Lieutenant Colonel Celso Meyer, who had come to the ministry from the Coastal Artillery barracks with Castello's group, was asked by Sizeno Sarmento to use the ministry's radio to obtain news of General Orlando Ramagem in the far north and General Adalberto Pereira dos Santos in the far south.

Meyer's messages to the far south went by teletype to the fifth-floor communications room of the Third Army headquarters in Porto Alegre, where they were received by Major Álcio Costa e Silva, Artur's son. Although the major's task was complicated by the presence of Brizola, who had been sending radio messages from the same room to Goulart, Celso Meyer in Rio was able to learn that Adalberto had gone to the interior of Rio Grande do Sul with the governor.[8] Then General Costa e Silva phoned Cordeiro in Curitiba to order the long-time conspirator not to go on south. "Kruel," the new commanding general told Cordeiro, "has an old personal matter he wants to settle with Brizola. Leave Rio Grande do Sul for Amauri to handle." [9]

Costa e Silva had the final word about the army appointments that were to place units in the hands of the victors of the revolution. He named Terra Ururaí commander of the First Army, explaining to the

[7] Sousa Aguiar, declarations in *O Globo*, April 20, 1964.

[8] Meyer interview, July 15, 1976. Yolanda and Álcio Costa e Silva interview, Rio de Janeiro, July 15, 1977.

[9] Stacchini, *Março 64*, p. 99.

hierarchy-conscious army men that Ururaí had the greatest length of service as a *general de divisão*.[10] General de Divisão Estevão Taurino de Resende became commander of the First Military Region, General de Divisão Orlando Geisel became commander of the First Infantry Division (at Vila Militar), General de Brigada Augusto César Moniz de Aragão became head of the System of Army Advanced Training Units (Grupamento de Unidades Escola), and General de Brigada José Horácio da Cunha Garcia became commander of the First Armored Division (Primeira Divisão Blindada).[11]

After midnight the generals gathered in Castello's office for their first meeting. Castello presided, sitting at the head of the well-filled table with Costa e Silva at his right. Many of the generals had to stand.

Castello declared that his mission had ended. Observing that it was urgent to put the affairs of the War Ministry in order, he suggested that Costa e Silva head the War Ministry because of his top place in the hierarchy. Turning to Costa e Silva, he said, "I ask you to leave me here on the sixth floor, as Army Chief of Staff, for there is much that I still have to do."[12]

The meeting was adjourned at the suggestion of Costa e Silva, who went upstairs with the generals to assume his post formally at a new meeting on the ninth floor. Before announcing appointments and assigning missions, he declared himself commander in chief of the army—a position customarily held by the president of the republic. As it was presumed that Brazil had no president, this was the title agreed upon by Castello and Costa e Silva,[13] and it was the title mentioned in the official note released later that night by the Army Staff to inform the public about the ninth-floor "ceremony" and the new army appointments.

It was felt that the control of Vila Militar was critical for the success of the revolution, and therefore Orlando Geisel lost no time in organizing a staff to help him carry out his new command. Among those who accompanied him to Vila Militar were officers who had served in Castello's command post: Colonel Ariel Pacca da Fonseca and Lieutenant Colonels Leônidas Pires Gonçalves and Ivan de Sousa Mendes. At Vila

---

[10] First Army, *Relatório da Revolução Democrática*.
[11] Estado Maior do Exército, official note in *O Jornal*, April 2, 1964.
[12] Ferreira, "O General Castello Que Conheci," p. 17.
[13] Meyer interview, July 15, 1976.

Militar, which they reached shortly after 2:00 A.M., they found few troops.[14]

In the War Ministry Castello learned, during a telephone conversation with Mamede, that Abelardo Jurema's only wish was to return to his home state, Paraíba, and retire from politics. Castello authorized Mamede to set the prisoner free, and so Goulart's justice minister departed from the ECEME at 3:00 A.M.[15]

At about the same hour Castello was driven to the Nascimento Silva Street house to sleep there for the first time since Goulart had addressed the sergeants. Officers who accompanied him to his home asked whether he wished to have a guard on duty. It would not be necessary, Castello said. "If they try to find me, this will be the last place they will look."[16]

[14] Gonçalves interview, July 20, 1976; Ariel Pacca da Fonseca interview, Brasília, July 23, 1976; Sousa Mendes interview, July 26, 1976.

[15] D'Aguiar, *A Revolução por Dentro*, p. 168.

[16] Meyer interview, July 15, 1976.

XII

The Road to the Presidency
(April, 1964)

I accept.

1. Organizing for Operação Limpeza (April 2, 1964)

WHEN Cariocas awoke on the morning of April 2, they learned that during the night Congress had installed Chamber of Deputies President Ranieri Mazzilli (PSD, São Paulo) as acting president of Brazil. Goulart, in Rio Grande do Sul, was known to be seeking asylum in Uruguay. Three governors were reported to have been deposed and arrested: Miguel Arraes (Pernambuco), Seixas Dória (Sergipe), and Badger Silveira (Rio de Janeiro).

For more than a week the anti-Communists in Rio de Janeiro had been looking forward to April 2; that afternoon had been set aside for their "March of the Family with God for Liberty" to protest, as the Paulistas had done on March 19, the influence of the far Left in the Goulart administration. Amélia Molina Bastos, the determined organizer of the march of the Cariocas, was arranging to turn the demonstration into a mammoth victory celebration when reports reached her that Castello Branco favored its postponement so that full attention could be given to Operação Limpeza, the business of cleaning up the country. "Tell Castello Branco not to interfere with my march," she declared.[1]

While Cariocas prepared for an afternoon of celebrating, Costa e Silva took steps that would allow him to direct Operação Limpeza. The new commander in chief of the army organized a Revolutionary Command of three, to be made up of the leader of each branch of the armed forces. A phone call brought the acceptance of Brigadeiro Francisco de

[1] Amélia Molina Bastos interview, Rio de Janeiro, December 13, 1965.

Assis Correia de Melo, the anti-Communist air force chief of staff, high in the air force hierarchy.[2]

Vice Admiral Augusto Rademaker Grünewald, who had taken over the Navy Ministry with the help of other vice admirals (including Levi Aarão Reis and Melo Batista), dropped in at the War Ministry to advise that he controlled the navy. Costa e Silva and Castello, he believed, had no choice but to accept him as navy minister and Revolutionary Command member despite the fact that he was outranked in the hierarchy by four fleet admirals and five vice admirals. He felt that Castello Branco and Costa e Silva were surprised to find the navy under an officer who was not the *mais antigo*. "It is easy," he has observed, "to understand this point of view of Castello Branco and Costa e Silva, because those two played no part in the revolution."[3]

Rademaker's ideas for carrying out Operação Limpeza were more radical than those of Costa e Silva and Castello. Because the two generals did not wish to close Congress, he considered that they wanted only half a revolution, not a real revolution. Rademaker's program included the dismissal of three Supreme Court justices, the elimination of all aldermen, and the "cleansing" of the state assemblies, the military sectors, the Bank of Brazil, and the Caixa Econômica. The purge would take, he felt, at least one month.[4]

Costa e Silva agreed that Operação Limpeza could not be accomplished in less time, and therefore he decided that Mazzilli should serve as acting president for no fewer than the thirty days which the Constitution stipulated were to pass before Congress could choose another chief executive. He planned to work in harmony with Mazzilli (an idea that did not appeal to Rademaker), and therefore he asked Mazzilli to fly from Brasília to Rio on April 3 to discuss with the Revolutionary Command the coming month of penance and the cabinet. Costa e Silva invited his São Paulo friend Professor Luís Antônio da Gama e Silva to be justice minister and took other steps to have a cabinet list ready for Mazzilli.

Costa e Silva was working on these matters when he received a visit from Ambassador Gordon and Vernon Walters. In response to the am-

---

[2] Augusto Hamann Rademaker Grünewald interview, Rio de Janeiro, December 15, 1965.

[3] Ibid.

[4] Ibid.

bassador's plea for the preservation of legality, the commander in chief stressed that Brazil had come close to dissolving in chaos.

Walters did not leave the War Ministry with Gordon in the embassy limousine. Instead, he stopped on the sixth floor to speak with Castello. "What are you going to do with Ademar de Queiroz?" was one of the questions he asked. The marshal, Walters learned, would take over Petrobrás, where his administrative talents and ability at handling people were expected to be effective in cleaning up the widespread corruption and subversion.[5]

Early in the afternoon, throngs were already on Rio Branco Avenue, and by the time the Marcha da Família was scheduled to begin, the avenue was a river of anti-Communist placards and rejoicing humanity. Concluding a passionate speech to the enormous crowd, estimated at over eight hundred thousand, Amélia Molina Bastos exclaimed, "We extol, we bless, we glorify God and the Brazilian soldier."[6]

A stupendous acclaim greeted seventy-eight-year-old former President Eurico Gaspar Dutra, who was regarded by many politicians as an appropriate figure to be selected by Congress, after thirty days, to complete the remaining twenty-two months of the presidential term. Cariocas recalled that the marshal, a quiet, virtuous man of simple tastes, had given Brazil a constructive and "very civilian" presidency (1946–1951) in which his own party, the PSD, had cooperated well with the UDN and in which strong measures had been adopted against Communism. Although UDN Congressman Costa Cavalcanti had not transmitted Castello's suggestion about Dutra to Carlos Lacerda, the Guanabara governor had reached the same conclusion independently and had even given Marshal Dutra to understand that he would back his candidacy.[7]

While the Marcha da Família was underway, the presidential succession was much discussed. Businessmen in the Rio office of IPES, pleased with the cheers in the streets below and highly satisfied with the result of their anti-Communist work, spoke with General Heitor Herrera about the qualifications that they wanted to see in the next president of Brazil.[8] They decided that he should be a man not associ-

[5] Vernon Walters interview, Arlington, Virginia, July 15, 1976.

[6] O Jornal, April 3, 1964, p. 7.

[7] Sigefredo Pacheco interview, Brasília, October 16, 1965.

[8] Gilberto Huber and Heitor A. Herrera interview, Rio de Janeiro, November 29, 1965.

ated with any of the three leading governors, Lacerda, Magalhães Pinto, and Ademar de Barros, because the three were competitors, along with Kubitschek, in the general presidential election to be held in 1965. The businessmen showed some concern about Dutra's PSD connections, and they recalled the qualities that Castello had revealed while with the Escola Superior de Guerra.

Despite her shyness, Nieta Diniz participated in the Marcha da Família (where someone gave her a flag to wave), and then she dropped in at the Nascimento Silva Street house to see her father. She found him alone, reading a book in a rocking chair.[9] Only later that night, while watching a television program at her own home in Leblon, did she learn that her father was among those being considered for the presidency. News broadcasts mentioned Dutra, Castello Branco, Magalhães Pinto, and Amauri Kruel. Occasionally the name of Mourão Filho was included.

2. A Ground Swell for Castello (April 3, 1964)

On the morning of April 3 Castello Branco joined the three members of the Revolutionary Command to welcome Acting President Mazzilli at the military airport of Santos Dumont. At the War Ministry, however, Castello remained on the sixth floor.[1] Thus he did not participate in the discussions that resulted in Mazzilli's announcement of administrative appointments: Gama e Silva as justice minister, Vasco Leitão da Cunha as foreign minister, Otávio Gouveia de Bulhões as finance minister, Arnaldo Sussekind as labor minister, and Ademar de Queiroz as Petrobrás president. The new cabinet ministers, including the three military ministers (Revolutionary Command members), would be assigned to handle the unfilled cabinet posts, Mazzilli told the press.

While Costa e Silva thus arranged for a start of the thirty days of Operação Limpeza, anti-Goulart politicians swarmed to Rio from Brasília and the states. Many of them went to Guanabara Palace to exchange views with Carlos Lacerda, the probable UDN standard-bearer in 1965.

Although most of those who spoke with the governor agreed with

[9] Antonietta Castello Branco Diniz, in Diniz and Paulo V. Castello Branco interview, Rio de Janeiro, December 13, 1975.

[1] Olavo Bilac Pinto interview, Brasília, October 21, 1975.

him that the immediate presidential succession should not be postponed for thirty days, few agreed with his choice of Dutra. Augusto Frederico Schmidt, the prominent Kubitschek adviser and industrialist who had known Castello when Castello was at the Escola Superior de Guerra (ESG), took the trouble to phone Lacerda from Europe to tell him that he had learned of his support for Dutra and that it was a great mistake. "Castello Branco," Schmidt said, "is a brilliant man, a brilliant military man. It is a miracle that at a critical moment like this we have such a moral man, such a patriot." [2]

Lacerda heard more or less the same story from others. Brigadeiro Eduardo Gomes, he learned, was strongly opposed to Dutra. Dutra's age was against him, and, as Lacerda was inclined to agree, so were his PSD connections, which might prove helpful to Kubitschek's ambitions. When Lacerda called on Dutra, he found the marshal's house full of old-time politicians. The revolution, Lacerda decided, had not been fought to bring these people to power.[3]

Lacerda sent Rafael de Almeida Magalhães, a young, intelligent, and popular member of the Guanabara state cabinet, to the War Ministry to ask Castello whether he thought that the thirty days for Mazzilli were necessary. Castello, presenting a written legal opinion, said that they were. Castello urged that the next president not be himself; nor was he certain about his eligibility, for the Constitution stated that in the case of an election for president, the army chief of staff was ineligible unless he had resigned three months before it was held. Castello suggested to Rafael de Almeida Magalhães that the presidential succession be discussed at a meeting of all of the civilian leaders of the revolution— governors and congressmen.[4]

Within the army the overwhelming opinion of officers favored Castello, the respected instructor who had given many of them training that they would not forget, the chief who had gained a superb reputation in Italy and Brazil. "You must always remember," Ulhoa Cintra said somewhat later to Carlos Lacerda, "that for at least two generations

[2] Rafael de Almeida Magalhães interview, Rio de Janeiro, November 19, 1975.
[3] Carlos Lacerda interview, Rio de Janeiro, October 11, 1967. Among those who accompanied Lacerda on this call to Dutra was journalist Hélio Fernandes, who feels that Goulart sought to establish a dictatorship (Hélio Fernandes interview, Rio de Janeiro, July 6, 1977).
[4] Almeida Magalhães interview, November 19, 1975.

military men have learned three things: topography, riding without stirrups, and Castello Branco." When Lacerda asked, "Why Castello Branco?" Ulhoa Cintra replied, "Because from captaincy on up he was the instructor of all of us, and we respect him as the most intellectual, and as the man in the army who is most committed to juridical order." [5]

In the Navy Club Rademaker's reservations about Castello found little support. There a navy commander received an ovation when he declared: "I have taken up arms for the third time in my life, but now, my companions, I shall turn to arms again only if they do not want to place Humberto de Alencar Castello Branco in the presidency of the Republic." [6]

Castello's confidential circular of March 20, published by the press just as Goulart was overthrown, made a favorable impression in civilian as well as military circles. It strengthened the image of Castello as the brains behind the revolution and as a leader who would see to it that legality was sternly respected. Women's groups that had been close to IPES in Rio and São Paulo pointed out that Castello's connections with the ESG, the Grupo da Sorbonne, gave him a familiarity with studies about what needed to be done together with a broad point of view and civilian intellectual connections that Costa e Silva and Kruel were said not to have.

At a time when the consensus of the victors favored the completion of the presidential term by a military man unconnected with political parties, Kruel's ties to Goulart's PTB were remembered. The Campanha da Mulher pela Democracia (CAMDE), Rio's influential anti-Communist women's organization, called for "a non-party leadership, firm and forceful." CAMDE's manifesto, signed by Amélia Molina Bastos, declared that the women wanted "General Humberto Castello Branco in the presidency of the Republic." [7]

The swell of support for Castello was already strong on the afternoon of April 3 when Olavo Bilac Pinto, who had arrived in Rio with Mazzilli, called on Castello in the War Ministry. The UDN president warned that if the situation were not quickly "defined," the nation would find itself under a dictatorship. Bilac proposed that constitutional lawyer

[5] Carlos Lacerda interview, Tucson, Arizona, February 17, 1976; Carlos Lacerda, "As Confissões de Lacerda," *Jornal da Tarde*, June 8, 1977.

[6] *O Jornal*, April 4, 1964, quoting Commander Nelson Brum.

[7] *O Globo*, April 4, 1964. CAMDE: Women's Campaign for Democracy.

Carlos Medeiros Silva, whom he had known in law school in Minas, draw up a *"minuta"* for dealing with the situation and that it be submitted to Castello. Castello agreed.[8]

Lacerda, taking steps to implement at least a part of Castello's suggestion to Rafael de Almeida Magalhães, had phoned Mauro Borges, the PSD governor of Goiás, and asked him to come to discuss the presidential succession with him and other governors who were on their way to Rio.[9] Mauro Borges, although he governed with a state administration in which Communists were influential, had broken with Goulart.

Before the day was over, Lacerda held a preliminary meeting with Mauro Borges, Governor Nei Braga of Paraná, and José Monteiro de Castro, the representative of Magalhães Pinto. *O Jornal's* front-page report of that meeting, appearing on the morning of April 4, said that Lacerda had expressed his support for Castello.

3. Costa e Silva Opposes a Military President (April 4, 1964)

The reluctance being shown by Castello about having his name considered for the presidency, as revealed in conversations with Rafael de Almeida Magalhães and others, worried Ademar de Queiroz. The new president of Petrobrás therefore called on Cordeiro de Farias, who had just returned from Paraná, and asked him whether he was agreeable to having Castello serve as president. "Ademar de Queiroz already knew my answer," Cordeiro said years later.[1]

Ademar de Queiroz and Cordeiro called on Castello in the War Ministry. Their discussion with him took place in the chief of staff's change room next to his office. After hearing the arguments of these long-time friends, Castello told them that he would accept the presidency.[2]

The question of Castello's eligibility, like that of the timing of an election by Congress, was debated in public. Former Justice Minister Vicente Rao declared that the constitutional provision about the ineligi-

---

[8] Bilac Pinto interview, October 21, 1975.

[9] Mauro Borges, *O Golpe em Goiás: História de uma Grande Traição,* p. 109.

[1] Osvaldo Cordeiro de Farias interview, Rio de Janeiro, December 16, 1974.

[2] Osvaldo Cordeiro de Farias conversation with Paulo V. Castello Branco, Rio de Janeiro, December, 1975.

bility of chiefs of staff in office applied only to regular, popular elections, and constitutional lawyer Pontes de Miranda maintained that an election was required within, not after, thirty days of the vacancy caused by Goulart's fall. On the other hand, *Correio da Manhã*, bitterly anti-Lacerda and fearful of threats to legality and democracy, quoted the Constitution to show that Castello was ineligible and that no speedy election could be held.[3] Carlos Medeiros Silva, receiving a telephone call from Bilac Pinto on April 4, turned to the solution of these and other juridical problems by drafting articles for an "Ato Adicional," a set of emergency rules that some of Bilac's colleagues felt might be enacted by Congress.

In the meantime more governors reached Rio with the purpose of making their contributions to a "definition of the situation" at the meeting scheduled to be held at Guanabara Palace on the evening of April 4. They spent the day attending political discussions and issuing declarations to the press about the revolution and usually about the need for the immediate selection of a new president. Lacerda warned that a "thirty-day hiatus" would impede the formation of a good government, and, in a reference to the Dutra candidacy, he said, "We do not want Sr. Juscelino Kubitschek to become a Brazilian Frondizi and rob us of this revolution, as he has robbed the country."[4]

Governor Nei Braga, a former ECEME student of Castello, was well prepared for the evening meeting. Before leaving Paraná he had sounded out the politicians and military men of the revolution in his state, not overlooking the labor sector. He brought to Rio a unanimous expression of backing for Castello Branco. Among those he had consulted were a few who recalled the Castello Brancos' year in Curitiba and more who had heard about it; others were familiar with General Castello Branco's pronouncements. Many in Paraná, some of them now in labor unions, had served as volunteers in Italy and were, Nei Braga learned, enthusiastic about Castello's qualifications as a leader.[5]

---

[3] *Correio da Manhã*, April 5, 1964. See also "Terrorismo, Não," *Correio da Manhã*, April 3, 1964. According to Article 79, Paragraph 2, of the Constitution of 1946, if the vacancies (president and vice-president) "occur in the second half of the presidential term, the election for both posts shall be held by the National Congress 30 days after the last vacancy." The opinion of Pontes de Miranda is given in *O Globo*, April 4, 1964.

[4] *Jornal do Brasil*, April 5, 1964.

[5] Nei Braga interview, Brasília, October 23, 1975.

Early on the afternoon of April 4 Nei Braga spoke with Congressman Colonel José Costa Cavalcanti, who had arrived from Brasília the previous evening. The two men agreed on the need to have Castello Branco in the presidency—an opinion that was shared by that day's front-page editorial in *O Globo*. They therefore called on the chief of staff in his office. "We feel," Costa Cavalcanti told Castello, "that you must accept the difficult task for the good of Brazil." [6] Was Castello in agreement, the UDN congressman asked, and could they work in military and political circles for his election?

Castello replied that he was in agreement and that they could work on behalf of his election, but he added that they were to avoid saying anything that might make it appear that he himself was seeking to be elected. Before Castello's visitors left, Costa Cavalcanti advised him that they would discuss the matter with Costa e Silva.

Costa e Silva received Costa Cavalcanti and Nei Braga promptly on the ninth floor and was expansive and frank in his comments on Costa Cavalcanti's report about incidents in Brasília. As the visitors started to discuss what was on their minds, they were joined by Juarez Távora. The renowned marshal, a federal congressman from Guanabara, entered the office in time to hear Costa Cavalcanti stress the importance of launching the presidential candidacy of "a highly respected military figure."

Now the commander in chief became vehement. It was too early, he said, to consider the presidential succession, and no thought should be given to placing a military man in the office. Mazzilli was to continue in his role while the Revolutionary Command continued to clean up Brazil, "purging the roughnecks and Communists" who had taken the nation to chaos. Launching into a dissertation about how the selection of a military man would foment divisions in the armed forces, Costa e Silva spoke about the early days of the Republic.

Juarez Távora came to the support of the Paraná governor and the Pernambuco congressman when they argued that a speedy "definition" was required to face up to the growing list of candidates, many civilian and some military. Names were examined by the visitors on the ninth floor, but when they mentioned Costa e Silva's name, the commander

6 José Costa Cavalcanti, "Depoimento do Ministro Costa Cavalcanti sobre a Escolha do Presidente Castello Branco para a Presidência da República" (typewritten transcript of tape), October, 1976, pp. 3–4.

in chief was emphatic in declaring that he should not, at the moment, be considered; he wished to remain "Military Commander." Although he had praise for Castello Branco's ability, which he described as "superior to that possessed by any of us," he deemed it "inopportune" to place Castello in the presidency. It was too soon to consider the matter. Operação Limpeza lay ahead.[7]

Governor Magalhães Pinto, who had made an appointment, was in the waiting room, and so the discussion ended, but not without Costa e Silva's agreement to continue with it that night. "Phone Sizeno," the commander in chief suggested.

4. Governors in Agreement (April 4, 1964)

General Augusto César Moniz de Aragão, Democratic Crusade candidate for the Military Club presidency, had already heard Costa e Silva expound his ideas, but he remained unconvinced; he opposed the postponement of the election by Congress for thirty days while Costa e Silva headed a *"junta militar."*[1] Sympathetic to the wave of sentiment in the army in favor of the immediate election of Castello Branco, Moniz de Aragão resolved to speed from Vila Militar to Rio at the appropriate moment in order to "intervene" among the politicians. He therefore arranged to have Colonel Gustavo Borges, Guanabara state secretary of security, keep him informed about the schedule of the governors. After Colonel Borges phoned Vila Militar on Saturday evening, April 4, to say that the governors would gather at Guanabara Palace at 9:00 P.M., Moniz de Aragão started on his way.

Seven governors attended the meeting: Lacerda (Guanabara), Ademar de Barros (São Paulo), Magalhães Pinto (Minas), Ildo Meneghetti (Rio Grande do Sul), Nei Braga (Paraná), Fernando Correia da Costa (Mato Grosso), and Mauro Borges (Goiás). All favored an immediate election by Congress. When the governors undertook to decide whether their candidate should be a military man or a civilian, Ademar de Barros argued for a civilian. Most of the governors felt that any civilian at the moment would find himself "practically a puppet of the

---

[7] Ibid., pp. 5–7.
[1] Augusto César Moniz de Aragão, "O Depoimento do General Moniz de Aragão," *O Globo*, March 30, 1975.

Revolutionary Command," [2] and they further appreciated that with three of the governors planning to run for president in 1965, it would be difficult to agree on a name of a civilian. Finding himself alone, the São Paulo governor admitted defeat in a manner that did nothing to disrupt the harmony. As he put it later, "Jango left such a devil of a mess that a military man was considered necessary." [3]

When the governors were asked to submit names of possible candidates, Nei Braga, Magalhães Pinto, and Mauro Borges had only one to suggest, each putting forth the name of Castello Branco. Some of the governors had two or more names, Lacerda mentioning Castello Branco and Dutra, and Ademar de Barros supplied five suggestions, including Kruel and Castello Branco. Not one mention was made of Costa e Silva. Lacerda, who presided, noted that Castello Branco's name was on the list of each governor, and he recommended that they all agree on Castello Branco. [4]

While this discussion took place, Moniz de Aragão arrived at Guanabara Palace. Greeted by Colonel Gustavo Borges, the general was conducted to the *salão nobre*, a large room filled with congressmen and other politicians. He launched into a passionate speech in which he spoke of the role of the armed forces in the revolution and of their "inalienable duty" to carry forward the work of achieving the aspirations of the nation. He was almost tearful when he exclaimed, "Faithful to the sentiment of the great majority, or, quite possibly, of all of those in the Army, and faithful also to my own conviction, I indicate to the representatives of the people, gathered here, General Humberto de Alencar Castello Branco for the presidency of the Republic!" [5]

The reaction to the general's words was enthusiastic. In a speech of reply, Congressman Afrânio de Oliveira (UDN, São Paulo) declared that Congress, faced by "a national imposition" made by the people and the armed forces, would elect Castello Branco within a few days: "If

---

[2] Borges, *O Golpe em Goiás*, p. 110.

[3] Ademar de Barros interview, São Paulo, December 1, 1965.

[4] José de Magalhães Pinto interview, Brasília, October 24, 1975; Braga interview, Brasília, October 23, 1975; Carlos Lacerda interview, Rio de Janeiro, September 23, 1975; Lacerda, "As Confissões de Lacerda."

[5] Moniz de Aragão, "O Depoimento do General Moniz de Aragão." See also Augusto César Moniz de Aragão, "O Seu Castigo É Decompor-se Vivo," *O Globo*, August 29, 1967.

Congress does not perform its duty at this historic moment, I shall be the first to ask, in Congress itself, that the Parliament be closed." [6]

The applause given to the general and the congressman brought Carlos Lacerda to the door of the room, and presently he escorted Moniz de Aragão to the meeting of the governors. There, Moniz de Aragão vouched for the admiration that the army officers felt for Castello Branco, and he repeated the sentiments he had just expressed in the *salão nobre*. "General," Lacerda said, "You are trying to crash through an open door. Everyone here favors the same solution." [7] The governors unanimously named Castello Branco their candidate for president. They resolved to present his name to Costa e Silva and, after obtaining the agreement of the Revolutionary Command, to speak with Castello and the party leaders.

Television cameras and newspaper reporters recorded Lacerda's announcement of the governors' choice and of their insistence on an election before the middle of the following week. Ademar de Barros, remarking that it was not a time for disunity, expressed satisfaction with the decision. Nei Braga told reporters that the agreement on one name represented a unanimity rare in Brazilian political history.

Lacerda made his announcement while Castello Branco was watching television at the Nascimento Silva Street house with Vernon Walters. "When the general heard the announcement," Walters recalls, "his expression was masklike; he had no comments." [8]

5. The Governors Call on Costa e Silva
(April 4, 1964, late at night)

Starting at about 11:00 P.M. on April 4, the governors, together with Congressmen Juarez Távora and Costa Cavalcanti, waited on the ninth floor of the War Ministry to see Costa e Silva about the presidential succession. The commander in chief was busy dealing with reports from Porto Alegre; an attempt had been made on the life of Brigadeiro Lavanère-Wanderley, recently appointed head of the Fifth Air Zone, and the assailant had been killed.

[6] Quoted in Moniz de Aragão, "O Depoimento do General Moniz de Aragão."
[7] *O Jornal*, April 5, 1964; Lacerda, "As Confissões de Lacerda."
[8] Walters interview, July 15, 1976.

At about midnight the governors and the two congressmen were escorted by Sizeno Sarmento to a spacious seventh-floor office, and there they were joined by Costa e Silva, who seated himself at the head of a long table. "You people," Costa e Silva said, "think that the revolution is over, but it is not."[1] He told of the incident in Porto Alegre.

Lacerda, speaking on behalf of the governors, started to reveal their decision, but at the outset Costa e Silva interrupted to say that he should be addressed not as war minister but as commander in chief of the revolutionary forces.[2] Nor was Lacerda able to elaborate after explaining the governors' wish for an immediate election, with a military man as the candidate of the revolution. The commander in chief was quick to cut in with the assertion that a military candidate might disrupt the unity of the army's revolutionary forces. He himself, Costa e Silva said, had no wish to be a candidate but would continue heading the Revolutionary Command. He added that an election should not be held until Mazzilli had been in office for the thirty days required by the Constitution, and that during that time the nation should suffer penance and be purged of subversion and corruption. The new "revolutionary" administration, whose executive was to be chosen by Congress, should be spared that disagreeable work. Mazzilli was cooperating and doing what was requested of him.

Lacerda declared that the revolutionary ideals did not include having a puppet in the presidency. Besides, with the passage of a little time, "Mazzilli and the PSD might roll you up," Lacerda added, using the word *enrolar*. The general affirmed that no one was going to roll him up. Lacerda suggested that he could use another word for a PSD maneuver if the commander in chief preferred, and he informed him of press reports that Mazzilli had named Israel Pinheiro, a Kubitschek man, to head the Casa Civil. "If Mazzilli appointed him," Costa e Silva retorted, "he is going to unappoint him!"[3]

Costa e Silva was hardly cordial to Magalhães Pinto, who Mauro Borges recalls, "spoke in a parochial tone, trying to carry on with thoughts Lacerda had originally sought to express." Costa e Silva, the Goiás governor writes, "referred to the separatist character of the move-

[1] Lacerda interview, September 23, 1975.
[2] Borges, *O Golpe em Goiás*, p. 112.
[3] Lacerda interviews, October 11, 1967; September 23, 1975; Lacerda, "As Confissões de Lacerda."

ment started by the Minas governor and warned that he would not tolerate any whim in that sense."⁴

When Magalhães Pinto asked what had become of Seixas Dória, the commander in chief replied, "Seixas Dória is in prison," and in a loud voice he added that "many others will be put in prison." An inquiry by the Minas governor about the banking holiday, which was affecting the states, brought a cutting comment from the commander in chief (who was aware of the governor's banking interests): "You are just the right person to be asking about the banking situation."⁵

Magalhães Pinto decided that the meeting was fruitless and spoke of his need to return to his state. "Your return there," Costa e Silva said, "represents no danger to the armed forces, because my forces are much stronger than yours. We have a *dispositivo* that can take care of whatever comes up. What we need to do is keep that *dispositivo* united. I fear that a military candidate at this time could divide us."⁶

Like Magalhães Pinto, Governors Mauro Borges, Ademar de Barros, and Nei Braga mentioned the urgent need of returning to their states. But Juarez Távora, at the far end of the table from Costa e Silva, interrupted this talk to ask that Lacerda be heard. Thus the Guanabara governor, who had been sullenly doodling, hotly defended his position. Costa e Silva reverted to his theme about the need to maintain unity in the military, and he embellished it by references to events that had transpired during the first years of the Republic.⁷

Lacerda accused the general of wanting to be a dictator. Defending his right to be heard without asking the general's permission, he exclaimed: "I don't know where you were in 1945. I don't know where you were in 1954. But I know where you were on November 11; you were at the side of General Lott."⁸ Then, when Lacerda sought to emphasize a point by raising his hand and pointing his finger, Costa e Silva imitated the gesture and declared that he could summon stronger forces and arguments than the governor.⁹

But Távora did not agree with the arguments of the commander in

⁴ Borges, *O Golpe em Goiás*, p. 113.

⁵ Lacerda interview, September 23, 1975.

⁶ Cavalcanti, "Depoimento do Ministro Costa Cavalcanti," p. 11.

⁷ Borges, *O Golpe em Goiás*, pp. 113–114.

⁸ Braga interview, October 23, 1975; Lacerda interview, September 23, 1975; Lacerda, "As Confissões de Lacerda."

⁹ Cavalcanti, "Depoimento do Ministro Costa Cavalcanti," p. 11.

chief. Banging the table for emphasis, Távora said, "I do not believe that in thirty days—or in sixty or ninety—the Military Command of the Revolution will be able to exterminate the germs of subversion and corruption from Brazil or even from its governmental machinery."[10] Távora also felt that, with the passage of a month, the group commanding the revolution would lose the unity necessary for easily arranging to have Congress elect a good president.[11] If governors of different political parties had been able to reach agreement, he did not see why the army generals could not do so.

Costa e Silva smiled. "We are hearing the same idealistic and unwary *tenente* of 1930," he said.

"No, Costa e Silva," Távora answered, "it is not so. In 1930 we exercised restraint in not wanting to assume the government directly. We thought of putting the civilians in front and handling them from nearby. What an illusion, ours! Within a short time we were pushed back, . . . unable to do any of the things we had planned."[12]

As it was approaching 4:00 A.M., and most of the participants at the meeting were exhausted, Sizeno Sarmento suggested that they adjourn and continue the discussion at a time to be set by Costa e Silva. While the men were leaving the room, Lacerda sought to have a word with Costa e Silva, but the commander in chief turned his back on the governor.[13]

Upon returning to his apartment, Lacerda discussed the situation with some of his UDN colleagues until sunrise. Then, putting his thoughts in a letter to Costa e Silva, Lacerda wrote that the governors, hoping to find in Costa e Silva the liberator, had found, instead, the usurper. Lacerda added that he was therefore resigning the governorship and retiring from political life.[14]

After Danilo Nunes, UDN leader in the Guanabara state assembly, delivered the letter to the War Ministry, Sizeno Sarmento telephoned

<hr>

[10] Juarez Távora, "Esclarecimentos Prestados pelo Marechal Juarez Távora à Margem da Escolha do Marechal Castelo Branco para a Presidência da República em Abril de 1964." See Leoncio Basbaum, *História Sincera da República*, vol. IV, *De Jânio Quadros a Costa e Silva (1961–1967)*, pp. 135–137.

[11] Juarez Távora, *Missão Cumprida: Relatório sôbre Atividades do extinto Ministério de Viação e Obras Públicas, no Triênio Abril, 1964–Março, 1967*.

[12] Borges, *O Golpe em Goiás*, p. 114.

[13] Ibid.

[14] Ibid., p. 115; Braga interview, October 23, 1975.

friends of Lacerda to suggest that they try to persuade the governor to withdraw it before it reached Costa e Silva.[15] The telephone calls may have been unnecessary because a group that gathered with Lacerda later in the morning argued that the letter had been a mistake. Nei Braga and Costa Cavalcanti rushed to the War Ministry to make sure that the letter would not reach Costa e Silva. Juraci Magalhães, who shared their concern, arranged to get the letter from Sizeno Sarmento. But the UDN politician from Bahia never returned it to Lacerda.[16]

6. Sandra Cavalcanti's Rally (April 5, 1964)

Castello Branco spent a large part of Sunday, April 5, receiving pleas that he be a candidate for president. The pressure began at 6:00 A.M., when Augusto Frederico Schmidt, who had reached Brazil on Saturday, came to the veranda at the Nascimento Silva Street house.[1] "Someone dropped in at 6:00 A.M.; how do you like that?" Castello asked his daughter on the phone after Schmidt left to speak to the press about Castello Branco.

Castello's modesty, Schmidt told reporters, could be compared "only with his understanding of authority and his love of justice." "He was," Schmidt added, "the leader of the overthrow of Communism in Brazil. He has every attribute to be the leader in the reconstruction of democracy in Brazil."[2]

Messages arriving from all over the country urged that Castello occupy the presidency.[3] Politicians swarmed to his residence. To help him take care of them, Salvador and Nieta Diniz, Murilo Gomes Ferreira, and Frederico Mendes de Morais came to the house. They mingled with the crowd downstairs while the general received callers individually and in groups upstairs, where he had turned Nieta's former bedroom into a study.

[15] Sizeno Sarmento interview, São Paulo, November 21, 1967.
[16] Juraci Magalhães, "Juraci Acha que Lacerda É Ciclotímico," *Jornal do Brasil*, November 23, 1966.
[1] Antonietta Diniz, in Diniz and Castello Branco interview, December 13, 1975.
[2] *O Globo*, April 6, 1964.
[3] Ibid.

In front of the house on Sunday afternoon a demonstration was staged by Professor Sandra Cavalcanti, an effective oragnizer of rallies and a believer in the importance of radio and television coverage. Together with the trucks of a television chain and Rádio Globo, she brought several speakers and more than one thousand women, who, like herself, were worried that Castello might not agree to be a candidate.

Castello was in his upstairs study, reminiscing with a relative and thinking about Argentina, when he was surprised by the shouts of "Castello, Castello" from the street.[4] Upon reaching the ground floor, which was rather crowded, he was accosted by Congressman Jorge Curi, who mistook him for a servant. "Where is the man of the house, where is Castello?" the congressman demanded to know.[5]

Soon Castello was approached by Sandra Cavalcanti.

"You have been reluctant," Sandra told him, and added happily: "People are at the door; it is a *comício* (rally)."

"*Não diga*! (You don't say!)"

"A rally to launch your candidacy," she explained.[6]

From the veranda, Castello and his family and visitors could see that men and women filled the street for more than three blocks. Murilo Gomes Ferreira and others held hands to form a blockade to keep order while César de Alencar, a well known radio personality, mounted a table set up on the sidewalk in order to act as the master of ceremonies. Castello, obviously much moved, had Marshal Mascarenhas de Morais at his side.[7] Vernon Walters, who had also hoped to see something of Castello on Sunday, drove off without stopping when he saw the throng.

The preliminary speakers included two women, one a representative of CAMDE, as well as an admiral, an industrialist, and a sailor (who complained that for two years he and his companions had been "persecuted by Communists"). They were followed by Sandra Cavalcanti, who described General Castello Branco as "a professor of democracy at the Escola Superior de Guerra." She declared that the revolution, "essentially a movement of the middle class," had to go forward. "It is urgent that Brazil have a government of authority, capable of carrying out a

---

[4] Antonietta Diniz, in Diniz and Castello Branco interview, December 13, 1975.

[5] Antônio de Oliveira Godinho interview, São Paulo, November 7, 1975.

[6] Sandra Cavalcanti interview, November 18, 1975.

[7] *O Globo*, April 6, 1964.

program of action, to bring peace through courageous steps that can only be taken by a man of the ability, the honesty, and the moral stature of General Castello Branco." [8]

Augusto Frederico Schmidt, who watched the rally on television, admired the manner in which Castello responded to the speakers. Castello's closing remarks, Schmidt wrote in *O Globo*, were in contrast to the "understandable vehemence" of the orators. "In the place of threats, loud outcries, and blasts of hatred, he gave a dignified, serene, and faultless talk, and, above all, he revealed the modest attitude of one who does not let himself be deluded by events that have placed him in an exceptional position in Brazilian life. He made it clear that he possesses the qualities of a statesman of the highest caliber." [9]

In the talk that impressed Schmidt so well, Castello declared that the words and applause he had heard placed him far above his merits. The revolution, he said, was not made by any one man, by any one team, but by many people. The applause of the crowd belonged to comrades in the armed forces, to fearless governors, to men who had opposed the "intolerant government," and to the Brazilian women, who had revealed their hearts as well as their combativity.

Forecasting an even greater struggle in the days ahead, Castello spoke of the need to eliminate factors of disunity and destruction so that Brazil could renew its march on the road to social justice, economic plenty, and international independence.[10]

During the ensuing applause Castello went into the house. On the upstairs porch he relaxed with his daughter and one of his granddaughters before being driven to the War Ministry. Although it was Sunday, he and Costa e Silva had business to take up at the ministry.

7. A More Amiable Costa e Silva (April 5, 1964)

Costa e Silva took a much needed nap after the governors left him at 4:00 A.M. on Sunday morning. During the afternoon his callers, including high army officers, supported opinions that he had been opposing, and they stressed the advisability of choosing Brazil's next president

---

[8] Ibid.

[9] Augusto Frederico Schmidt, "Castelo Branco," *O Globo*, April 7, 1964.

[10] *Jornal do Brasil*, April 7, 1964.

at once.[1] The Sunday newspapers were full of pronouncements in favor of a quick election, and all of the Rio press gave front-page coverage to what *O Jornal* called the unanimous choice of Castello Branco by "the seven governors who commanded the revolution of April 1."

The commander in chief called for a new meeting with the governors, to be held at 7:00 that evening. Lacerda asked Juraci Magalhães, a former UDN president, to represent him. Magalhães Pinto, also deciding not to appear at the War Ministry, named José Maria Alkmin to be his representative. Alkmin, although a PSD politician, had been included in the state cabinet of UDN governor Magalhães Pinto, shortly before the revolution, to help give the Minas cabinet a wider political horizon.

In contrast to the earlier meeting, the new one was held not around a seventh-floor table, but in armchairs on the ninth floor. There, Juraci Magalhães explained that Lacerda felt it best to be absent, hoping in that way to contribute to the existence of an atmosphere less "brutal" than the one that had prevailed at the earlier meeting. Upon hearing the word *brutal*, Costa e Silva thought that it was being used to describe the commander in chief.[2]

Despite this unpromising start of the new meeting, the five governors, the two governors' representatives, and Costa Cavalcanti found that Costa e Silva had become more amiable. They heard him say that he had given much thought to the matters already discussed and had reached the conclusion that it would be best, after all, to make the presidential selection quickly and to decide on a military officer.

"Neither do I want to be a candidate, nor should I be one," Costa e Silva explained. "My mission is quite different; it is to continue directing, maintaining the army united, and performing the necessary preliminary work in a nation that was on the verge of real chaos. But I would be pleased if you would give me the name of a military figure who you believe is capable of being president."[3]

After a silence Nei Braga stated that they all believed that the ablest man for the post was General Castello Branco.

Costa e Silva, agreeing with this choice, praised Castello, his Porto

[1] Cavalcanti, "Depoimento do Ministro Costa Cavalcanti," p. 14. See also Luís Viana Filho, *O Governo Castelo Branco*, p. 52.
[2] Cavalcanti, "Depoimento do Ministro Costa Cavalcanti," October, 1976, p. 19.
[3] Ibid., p. 14.

Alegre classmate, and he suggested that they extend the invitation to him at once. "He is here. . . . Before you all arrived, Castello was in my office to discuss some other matters." The commander in chief instructed Sizeno Sarmento, who was also present, to send for him.

Sizeno Sarmento found that Castello had left the War Ministry. When he gave this information to the group, Costa Cavalcanti, who knew Castello well, thought to himself that Castello had probably gone home, not wanting the candidacy to be offered to him in the office of the minister of war.[4] Costa e Silva had his own explanation, and he expressed it aloud: "You see, gentlemen, General Castello Branco is such a soldier that he does not want to deal with political matters in a barracks, which the War Ministry is."[5]

As the group left to go to Nascimento Silva 394, the commander in chief cordially wished all a good night. But, Mauro Borges noted, he wore an expression of sadness.[6]

8. "I Accept" (April 5, 1964, late at night)

At Nascimento Silva 394, the five governors, along with Juraci Magalhães, José Maria Alkmin, and José Costa Cavalcanti, were received by Colonel Darci Lázaro, Lieutenant Colonel Murilo Gomes Ferreira, and Captain Frederico Mendes de Morais. Castello, wearing a dark suit, greeted his guests in the living room. When Costa Cavalcanti lit up a cigarette, Castello said playfully: "That congressman, whenever he comes here, dirties my ashtrays with all the cigarettes he smokes."[1]

As the oldest of the governors, Ademar de Barros had been delegated to deliver their message. Although the room was small, the São Paulo politician orated in a loud voice, as though he were in a vast and well-filled auditorium.[2] He assailed Goulart, praised the revolution, and spoke of the universal desire to see Brazil follow the right path. After mentioning the meetings of the governors with Costa e Silva, Ademar

---

[4] Ibid., p. 15.

[5] Borges, O Golpe em Goiás, p. 116.

[6] Ibid.

[1] Borges, O Golpe em Goiás, p. 116; Cavalcanti, "Depoimento do Ministro Costa Cavalcanti," pp. 15–16.

[2] Cavalcanti, "Depoimento do Ministro Costa Cavalcanti," p. 16.

de Barros asked whether Castello would accept the candidacy for the presidency.

To describe the "completeness" of the silence that followed this question, Costa Cavalcanti has observed that if any flies had been in the room, the noise made by them would have seemed to be a roar. It was a short silence, but for the visitors the suspense was so great that a long time seemed to elapse before Castello replied calmly with two words: "I accept." [3]

Then the governor of São Paulo, resuming with pomp his role of spokesman, asked Castello some questions. Did he believe that his candidacy would divide the army?

"In reply to that question, let me ask you a question. Does the war minister think that I would divide the army?"

After the governors, almost in a chorus, replied in the negative, Castello said that he felt able to say that he would not divide the army. "And in saying this I rely on the word of companions who came here earlier to suggest my candidacy."

The governor of São Paulo continued: "If you assume the presidency, will you preside impartially over the elections scheduled for 1965?"

Castello, with a slight show of irritation, replied that his past was the best guarantee that he could give.[4]

Ademar de Barros next spoke of the concern that many felt about the government's invasion of the sphere of the private sector. "It would be reassuring to hear your support of private initiative. Further, to show your appreciation of the business classes, we would like you to promise, here and now, to annul the recent decree that expropriated private petroleum refineries."

Mauro Borges strenuously objected to Ademar de Barros' request. The governor of Goiás, launching into a defense of Petrobrás, was interrupted by Juraci Magalhães, who pointed out that it was not the time to become involved in such a debate.[5]

Breaking the silence that followed, Costa Cavalcanti suggested that the press be informed of the invitation that had been extended to Castello by the "governors of the revolution" and of his acceptance.

[3] Ibid.

[4] *O Estado de S. Paulo*, April 7, 1964. See also "Como o General Castelo Deu o Sim," *Jornal do Brasil*, April 7, 1964.

[5] Borges, *O Golpe em Goiás*, p. 117.

First, Alkmin suggested, the political parties should be consulted. Thereupon Juraci Magalhães said that, as the representative of the UDN, he could vouch for its full agreement with Castello's candidacy. Nei Braga, speaking for the Christian Democratic Party (PDC), and Ademar de Barros, speaking for the Social Progressive Party (PSP), said that their parties likewise backed Castello's candidacy.

The governors named members of their group to advise the parties and Acting President Mazzilli of their decision to work for Castello's election. Alkmin said that he would go directly to the Copacabana Palace Hotel, where he expected to find Senate President Auro de Moura Andrade (PSD), and perhaps also PSD President Ernâni do Amaral Peixoto, who was playing an active role despite his poor health.[6]

The meeting at the Nascimento Silva Street house was about to break up when UDN Congressmen Bilac Pinto and Pedro Aleixo arrived with Carlos Medeiros Silva and his draft of an Ato Adicional—or Ato Institucional, as it came to be called. It provided for a speedy presidential election by Congress and the elimination of ineligibilities such as the debated one about the chiefs of staff, and it would allow the Revolutionary Command to cancel, for five years, the political rights of citizens who were considered to have played important roles in making revolution necessary.

After the draft, read aloud by José Maria Alkmin, had been approved by the men in Castello's home, Castello arranged to have a copy delivered at once to Costa e Silva.[7]

9. Meeting with PSD Leaders (April 6, 1964, at night)

Walls of buildings in Rio, still bearing slogans painted during past campaigns, offered something new on April 6: "Castello for President."

A strong movement to place Castello in the presidency was evident. His name was favored at assemblies that gathered on April 6 at the Military and Navy clubs.[1] Peracchi Barcelos, PSD congressman from

---

[6] Cavalcanti, "Depoimento do Ministro Costa Cavalcanti," pp. 17–18. Ernâni do Amaral Peixoto was recovering from a circulatory ailment that had afflicted him shortly before the fall of Goulart.

[7] Carlos Medeiros Silva interviews, Rio de Janeiro, November 12, December 18, 1975; Viana Filho, O Governo Castelo Branco, p. 56.

[1] Jornal do Brasil, April 7, 1964.

Rio Grande do Sul, told the press that Castello could almost be said to be "already elected" due to the large support for him "in the UDN, the PSD, and even the PTB." Civilians of all social classes, Peracchi said, wanted Castello.[2]

In his War Ministry office Castello received a stream of delegations and distinguished visitors, among them Congressman Paulo Sarazate, who brought a telegram from Governor Virgílio Távora expressing the satisfaction of the people of his state at the prospect of a Cearense in the presidential palace.[3] When the general went to Ipanema he was greeted by a crowd in the street and by callers at his home.

One of the callers, Francisco Negrão de Lima, was worried. The co-ordinator of Kubitschek's campaign for the 1965 election asked, "What are the military going to do?"

"They are not going to establish a dictatorship," Castello assured his old friend. Adding that he wanted his own election by Congress to be carried out "in the proper way," he received Negrão's offer to secure some PSD votes. The general, who adhered to a rule never to ask for help of this sort, accepted the offer.[4]

The PSD, to which Negrão de Lima belonged, was the largest party. Its leaders, in the first hours after the fall of Goulart, had been under the impression that a civilian would complete, in a normal way, the five-year presidential term that had begun in January, 1961.[5] It took little time, however, to convince them that the movement of March 31 was more profound than they had originally thought. Immediately after Castello gave his acceptance to the governors, the party leaders held a series of meetings in Rio under the presidency of Ernâni do Amaral Peixoto, who had met Castello before while drafting an administrative reform for the Goulart government. The party leaders heard Mauro Borges and Alkmin, and they received reports from some of the PSD state organizations. They agreed unanimously that Castello should be their candidate, and they committed the party "more or less" to support

[2] *Correio da Manhã*, April 7, 1964.
[3] *Jornal do Brasil*, April 7, 1964.
[4] Francisco Negrão de Lima interview, Rio de Janeiro, December 10, 1975.
[5] Ernâni do Amaral Peixoto interview, Rio de Janeiro, December 20, 1975. One of the civilians occasionally mentioned as a presidential possibility was Carlos Alberto Carvalho Pinto, a former governor of São Paulo. This suggestion prompted Carlos Lacerda to remark sarcastically that Carvalho Pinto "has all the qualifications, including that of having been a cabinet minister of João Goulart."

him, but they felt that it would be best to meet with him before taking a definite position about the election by Congress. By this time, as Castello had recently remarked to Negrão de Lima, he had received from Costa e Silva the "green light" to discuss his candidacy with politicians.[6]

The arrangements for a meeting were worked out by Martins Rodrigues, PSD leader in the Chamber of Deputies, and the UDN's Paulo Sarazate, both from Ceará.[7] In order to avoid any suggestion that either Castello or the PSD sought favors from the other, the meeting was held not at the home of PSD President Amaral Peixoto, but in "neutral territory," the apartment of Congressman Joaquim Ramos (PSD, Santa Catarina). There, at 9:00 P.M. on April 6, Castello met with Amaral Peixoto, Alkmin, Martins Rodrigues, and Ramos.

The PSD, Amaral Peixoto told Castello, did not insist on having any cabinet ministries and only wished that the Constitution be respected. Castello replied that he had always been a legalist and felt that most of the officers in the armed forces held the same view. He emphasized that he had no political commitments. If he served as president, he said, the 1965 election would be held as scheduled and would be followed by the inauguration of those elected.

Amaral Peixoto pointed out that the PSD already had a candidate for the 1965 presidential election, Kubitschek having been nominated in March, 1964, and that it would be well if Castello, "in our presence," would speak with him. Castello readily agreed, and therefore a new meeting in the Ramos apartment was set up for the following evening, April 7. The objective, a conversation between Kubitschek and Castello, had for days been advocated by Negrão de Lima and Augusto Frederico Schmidt.[8]

---

[6] Amaral Peixoto interview, December 20, 1975. According to Hélio Fernandes (*Recordações de um Desterrado em Fernando de Noronha*, p. 38), "On the eve of the revolution . . . it was decided that former President Dutra should replace Goulart," and the generals made an agreement that none of them should present himself as a candidate to be Goulart's successor. "In forty-eight hours," he adds, "things took another turn. . . ." Ademar de Queiroz, Osvaldo Cordeiro de Farias, Juraci Magalhães, and José Eduardo Prado Kelly (former UDN leader and close friend of Eduardo Gomes) were asked by Aliomar Baleeiro on July 18, 1977, whether Castello Branco and other top generals had made an agreement not to be candidates for the presidency. They reported knowing of no such agreement (Aliomar Baleeiro conversation, July 18, 1977, and memorandum of approximately the same date).

[7] Amaral Peixoto interview, December 20, 1975.

[8] Ibid.; Juscelino Kubitschek de Oliveira, "Comentários de Juscelino Kubitschek

10. Meeting with Kubitschek (April 7, 1964, at night)

On April 7 *Jornal do Brasil* published an editorial in support of Castello, who, it said, would provide much needed confidence and authority.

That morning *Jornal do Brasil* also carried some excerpts from Jânio Quadros' long letter of April 6 to Castello. In it the former president, who had resigned from office, asked Castello to accept the candidacy and, once elected, bring an end to the "violations and brutalities" that Quadros saw being practiced all over Brazil. Describing himself as a life-long detester of dictatorship, Quadros opposed the formulation of lists of citizens who were to be deprived of their political rights. In his letter he praised his own past democratic conduct, his "sacrifice," and his "martyrdom," and he made it clear that he had a large following, particularly among the proletariat.[1] Castello showed the letter to Costa e Silva, whose past experience with Quadros in São Paulo had not been to his liking.[2] "Look here," Costa e Silva said to Castello, "that man sees how things are changing, and now he wants to worm his way into our favor, but he is a dangerous person, and I am going to put him on the list. This is a responsibility that I shall assume."[3]

In São Paulo, where Quadros wrote his letter, PTB congressmen advanced the presidential candidacy of Amauri Kruel. The head of the Second Army declared that the "military high command" was taking no position about the candidacies because to do so "would be an improper intervention into matters belonging exclusively to the federal legislature."[4] But Kruel's support in the federal legislature, San Tiago Dantas told the press, was "flabby" and lacked "depth." The influential PTB congressman who had served in Goulart's cabinets recalled his long acquaintance with Castello and described him as a man of "extraordinary professional competence, probity, and intelligence."[5]

The São Paulo PSD federal congressmen, meeting on April 7 under

---

de Oliveira sobre a Indicação do General Castelo Branco pelo PSD em Abril de 1964," May 21, 1975, p. 1.

[1] Jânio Quadros to HACB, São Paulo, April 6, 1964, File L2, CPDOC.

[2] Lacerda interview, October 11, 1967.

[3] Viana Filho, *O Governo Castelo Branco*, p. 55.

[4] *Jornal do Brasil*, April 7, 1964.

[5] *O Estado de S. Paulo*, April 8, 1964; *Jornal do Brasil*, April 8, 1964.

the leadership of Antônio Sílvio Cunha Bueno, decided unanimously to vote for Castello Branco in the election which by this time Congress had arranged to have carried out in the near future. The *bancada paulista* of PSD federal congressmen dispatched telegrams to the candidate and to the PSD national directorship to advise of its resolution.[6]

By the time that Castello set out for his second evening at the Ramos apartment, he had abundant messages of support; one advised that the governors of almost all of the Brazilian states, eighteen of them, would work for his candidacy. Paulo Guerra, who found himself in the Pernambuco governorship after the "impeachment" and imprisonment of Miguel Arraes, telegraphed Kubitschek and Amaral Peixoto to say that he would leave the PSD if the party would not vote for Castello.[7]

Despite the overwhelming political movement for Castello—a movement that left the Dutra and Kruel candidacies with hardly a mention—Kubitschek believed that Castello's election depended on whether or not Kubitschek and his friends decided to work for it. Besides, upon being invited to meet with Castello, Kubitschek believed that the general was seeking his support. Castello, in accepting the invitation given him in Ramos' apartment on April 6, had no such idea.[8]

If Kubitschek was a little late to the meeting, or if he was nervous, it can be ascribed, Renato Archer feels, to an anti-Kubitschek demonstration held in front of the Kubitschek apartment on Ipanema Beach.[9] Kubitschek, arriving at the Ramos apartment with Negrão de Lima and a colonel of the Minas state forces, was greeted by the host and by Castello, Amaral Peixoto, Alkmin, and Ladislau de Abreu, a friend of Amaral Peixoto and Kubitschek. Martins Rodrigues, present at the earlier meeting, had gone to Brasília.

When Castello wrote his recollections of the meeting, he pictured Kubitschek as "very fidgety, with the demeanor of a person who wants, at every possible opportunity, to bring an end to the encounter, and even running his comb through his hair." Kubitschek, in a more lengthy report, has described the men as seated at "a sort of round table," where

[6] *O Estado de S. Paulo*, April 8, 1964.
[7] Ibid.
[8] Juscelino Kubitschek de Oliveira interview, Rio de Janeiro, September 29, 1975; HACB quoted in Viana Filho, *O Governo Castelo Branco*, p. 54.
[9] Renato Archer interview, Rio de Janeiro, September 30, 1975.

Amaral Peixoto, in his introductory remarks, said that the PSD, unlike other parties, had a candidate for the 1965 election.[10]

The candidate for that election was rather short with the candidate for the immediate election, but he did praise Castello's well-known democratic principles as demonstrated by the backing given to Lott on November 11, 1955. Then Kubitschek mentioned some of the names being considered for completing the term begun by Quadros and Goulart: Dutra, Castello, Kruel, and Mourão Filho. "Members of the PSD and of our ally, the PTB," Kubitschek said, "have been backing first one, then another, and what we need is an articulation for directing members who are still hesitant."[11]

Therefore, the former president said, the PSD needed information on two essential questions: (1) Would the candidates for the immediate election fully respect "the constitutional commandment" calling for the October 1965 election? and (2) Were they willing to turn over the office to the winner of that election, "respecting this sacred democratic precept"?[12]

Castello gave strong assurances, spoke of his own "democratic tradition," and pointed out that a purpose of the revolution had been the defense of the Constitution and Congress.[13] He said that he was not committed to any party and was not inclined toward any of the candidates for the 1965 election; if he served as president, all the candidates would have guarantees. During the questioning by the congressmen, who showed more interest than did Kubitschek in the interview, Castello declared that he had never belonged to the Grupo da Sorbonne.[14]

The general's democratic and legalist assurances, Kubitschek said, would enable the party leaders to present his name for the consideration of the PSD National Directorship and would reduce to a minimum any reasons for opposing his name. It would now be up to Party President Amaral Peixoto, using information furnished during the dialogue, to

[10] HACB, quoted in Viana Filho, *O Governo Castelo Branco*, p. 54; Kubitschek de Oliveira, "Comentários," p. 2.

[11] Ibid.

[12] Ibid.

[13] Testimony of Joaquim Ramos in "Depoimentos sôbre Encontro Castelo-Juscelino Provocam um Novo Tumulto," *Jornal do Brasil*, January 21, 1967, p. 4.

[14] Ernâni do Amaral Peixoto (interview, December 20, 1975) recalled this remark of HACB about the Grupo da Sorbonne.

proceed with the matter.[15] Amaral Peixoto promised to get in touch with PSD state organizations.

Kubitschek, according to notes that he wrote years later, asked a last question, prompted by friends who could not forget episodes that had created "serious difficulties to the normal constitutional process" in 1955. Castello's reply, Kubitschek has written, made it clear that Castello, as president, would not permit "military sectors" to work with the government to prevent the continuation of the Kubitschek campaign or impede his inauguration in 1966 in case of his election. In 1967, when congressmen sought testimony about the meeting in the Ramos apartment, a spokesman for Castello told them that the general had merely promised to respect the Constitution of 1946 "and also the Ato Institucional, then being elaborated."[16]

Whatever was said, Kubitschek had soon heard enough; eager to be on his way, he asked permission to leave. The men, who rose to say goodbye to him, kept on conversing after he departed.

"Let's sit," Ramos suggested.

"I set this evening aside for the PSD," Castello said, apparently not well impressed by Kubitschek's early departure, "I am at your disposal."[17]

The conversation that followed was merely a repetition of much that had been said before. Asked again to respect the Constitution, Castello promised to do so. The PSD repeated that it was not interested in having posts in the cabinet.

Kubitschek, who held a federal senate seat from Goiás, flew to Brasília soon after his talk with Castello. Upon arriving in the federal capital, he spoke well of Castello and revealed that he had recently been with him. He prepared to issue a declaration in favor of the general's candidacy, "reiterating," as *O Estado de S. Paulo* put it, "the position already assumed by the majority of his party."[18]

However, Kubitschek decided to delay issuing his declaration after a strongly anti-Kubitschek manifesto appeared in Rio on April 8, this one signed by nearly one thousand military officers. The former president was led to believe that the Ato Institucional, much desired by Costa

[15] Kubitschek de Oliveira, "Comentários," p. 4.

[16] Testimony of Luís Viana Filho in "Depoimentos sôbre Encontro Castelo-Juscelino Provocam um Novo Tumulto," *Jornal do Brasil*, January 21, 1967.

[17] Amaral Peixoto interview, December 20, 1975.

[18] *O Estado de S. Paulo*, April 8, 9, 1964.

e Silva, might be promulgated by the Revolutionary Command and that it might contain, in its preamble, disparaging remarks about Kubitschek. He would wait and see whether he had cause to review his position.[19]

11. The Ato Institucional (April 9, 1964)

Throughout the discussions about the presidency voices were raised to express the need to clean up Brazil by punishing those considered responsible for subversion. Olímpio Mourão Filho, giving an interview following the fall of Goulart, said that if Operação Limpeza were not carried out, starting in the armed forces and Congress, "we shall have won the battles and lost the victory."[1]

After Cardinal Jaime de Barros Câmara declared that "to punish those who err is an act of mercy," Ademar de Barros pointed an accusing finger at the Nationalist Parliamentary Front and called the cancellation of mandates a *sine qua non* for the achievement of the objectives of the Revolution.[2] Businessmen joined the campaign. A spokesman for the National Confederation of Producers agreed with the São Paulo governor that the liberation of Abelardo Jurema was "a crime," and he added that those who had "ceased to be Brazilians by hiring out to a foreign power" should lose their political rights. The president of the Federation of Industries of Guanabara urged the cancellation of the political rights of all who were "responsible for the chaos." A Rio Commercial Association director said, "The greatest obstacle to freeing the country from Communism is Juscelino Kubitschek."[3]

Fourteen ECEME officers, asked by Mamede for suggestions, submitted a memorandum on April 4 that advocated the cancellation of the mandates and political rights of Communist congressmen, "extreme nationalists," professional agitators, and all important officials of the Goulart regime who had committed acts "considered criminal."[4] The ECEME officers also called for a law that would allow the immediate

---

[19] Ibid., April 9, 10, 1964; Carlos Castello Branco, "Coluna do Castello," *Jornal do Brasil*, April 10, 1964.

[1] *O Jornal*, April 3, 1964.

[2] Ibid., April 4, 1964; *Jornal do Brasil*, April 5, 1964.

[3] *O Jornal*, April 3, 4, 5, 1964.

[4] ECEME memorandum, File L2, CPDOC.

expulsion from the armed forces and labor organizations of "Communo-agitators" and all who, by acts or omissions, had become "threats" to those organizations.

The ECEME officers recommended "the solution of these vital problems" before the inauguration of the next president. However, with the decision to have a speedy election, the prospect of a preinaugural "solution" became problematical, especially as it was to Congress that the Revolutionary Command turned to get needed legislation.

The text of Carlos Medeiros Silva's draft of an Ato Adicional, sent by Castello to Costa e Silva on the night of April 5, was taken at once to Brasília by Senator Auro de Moura Andrade, president of Congress. In Brasília Mazzilli and Justice Minister Gama e Silva met with congressional leaders to examine the possibilities of the passage of Medeiros' act or something similar, perhaps an act that would give Congress itself the authority to cancel mandates.[5] Not unexpectedly, some of the congressmen issued passionate statements against the idea.

Mazzilli, back in Rio on April 7, discussed the matter with congressional leaders late into the night at Laranjeiras Palace. At best, one of the congressmen maintained, the passage of legislation would take about a week. Bilac Pinto pointed out that "tenseness in the military area" required more speedy action.

When congressional leaders in Brasília expressed hope for the passage there of an Ato Institucional, Castello was asked for his opinion. He replied that he was simply following the developments and at no time had played any role in elaborating an Ato Institucional.[6]

On Wednesday, April 8, Bilac Pinto, again in Brasília, phoned Carlos Medeiros Silva to suggest that he show his draft to Francisco Campos, author of the 1937 constitution that had ushered in Vargas' autocratic Estado Novo. Thus Francisco Campos, whom Medeiros had once served as secretary, was discussing the draft with Medeiros on the afternoon of the eighth when the two constitutional lawyers were summoned to the War Ministry. There, Francisco Campos told the members of the Revolutionary Command that they had the option of submitting the act to Congress or decreeing it outright, for the existence of Congress and the Mazzilli administration were dependent on the Revolutionary Com-

---

[5] Bilac Pinto interview, October 21, 1975.

[6] "Congresso Concorda em Aprovar Ato Institucional," *Jornal do Brasil*, April 9, 1964.

mand, which held the real power as the result of revolution.[7] Medeiros agreed.

At the invitation of Costa e Silva, the two constitutional lawyers spent the evening of April 8 at the War Ministry. Francisco Campos rolled up his sleeves and turned Medeiros' conventional preamble into a ringing prologue, a message to the nation proclaiming the right and the responsibility of the victorious revolution, represented by the commanders in chief of the three branches of the armed forces, to issue the Ato Institucional. A government that had "deliberately sought to bolshevize the country" had been toppled by the revolution, which now alone had the authority to dictate rules that would give the new government the power necessary for acting on behalf of the nation.

The suspension of the political rights of individuals for five years, as originally proposed by Medeiros, was considered too short a period by Gama e Silva and Rademaker (who wanted fifteen years), and it was altered to ten years, an interval considered appropriate by Costa e Silva, who remarked that Goulart and Quadros were relatively young.[8] The members of the Revolutionary Command, the act declared, could suspend these rights and legislative mandates "in the interest of peace and the national honor." When the new president took office, these powers were to be transferred to him to use in accordance with recommendations of the National Security Council. However, after the passage of sixty days no new names were to be added to the list of those who would lose their political rights or mandates.

The Ato Institucional ruled that within two days of its promulgation Congress should elect a president and vice-president in an election in which no one was ineligible. Important for the incoming president were the provisions affecting congressional procedure. Legislative projects submitted by the president were to become law if not acted on within thirty days. Budgets submitted by the president were not to be increased by Congress. These provisions, together with one permitting presidentially sponsored constitutional amendments to be enacted by a majority vote, were to expire, together with the *ato*, on January 31,

---

[7] Medeiros da Silva interview, November 12, 1975; Francisco Campos interview, Rio de Janeiro, December 14, 1965.

[8] Medeiros da Silva interview, November 12, 1975; Rademaker Grünewald interview, December 15, 1965; Luís Antônio da Gama e Silva interview, São Paulo, November 18, 1966.

1966. This was the date when a new administration was to take office, and, despite the fact that the 1966 transfer of power was spelled out in the Constitution, it was repeated in the Ato Institucional at the special request of Castello Branco.[9]

In a ceremony held at the War Ministry on the afternoon of April 9, Costa e Silva, Rademaker, and Correia de Melo signed the Ato Institucional. Castello Branco, who had been kept informed of changes made to Medeiros' original draft, was present at the occasion, along with top military commanders. When reporters asked him to comment, he had nothing to say.[10]

The Revolutionary Command made it known at once that it was suspending for ten years the political rights of Goulart, Quadros, and Luís Carlos Prestes. On the next day, April 10, it issued a list of one hundred persons thus affected, including forty federal legislators, many of them leaders of the Nationalist Parliamentary Front. On April 11, in accordance with authority given by the Ato Institucional, the Revolutionary Command transferred 122 military officers to the reserve.

12. Dutra and Kruel Withdraw (April 9–10, 1964)

On April 8, one day before the Ato Institucional was promulgated, Kruel and Dutra became definite candidates in the presidential election to be held by Congress at a date not yet established. "KRUEL '64" appeared in enormous letters on walls in Brasília.

The movement for Kruel, which had been initiated by São Paulo PTB federal congressmen such as Hugo Borghi and William Salém, culminated in the announcement of his candidacy by Senators José Ermírio de Morais (PTB, Pernambuco) and Juvenal Lino de Mattos (PTN, São Paulo). Lino de Mattos stated that Kruel's name could not divide the armed forces because the armed forces had refrained from declaring themselves in favor of any candidate. In Rio, Congressman Cunha Bueno, of the São Paulo PSD *bancada*, assured Castello that the movement in favor of Kruel was being poorly received in the more influential political circles.[1]

[9] *O Estado de S. Paulo*, April 14, 1964, p. 3.
[10] *Correio da Manhã*, April 10, 1964.
[1] *Jornal do Brasil*, April 9, 1964.

Dutra's decision ("after much hesitation I have decided to accept") caused surprise, because he was considered to have no chance to win. Dutra's party, the PSD, was known to be preparing an announcement in favor of Castello, and the pages of the newspapers were filled with excerpts from pro-Castello manifestos, some bearing thousands of signatures, that were sent to Congress and the armed forces by university groups and organizations of women, businessmen, and professional men. On April 9 *O Estado de S. Paulo* declared on its front page that "the entire nation supports Castello Branco."

Mascarenhas de Morais recalled qualities (bravery, serenity, level-headedness, and activity) that Castello had displayed in Italy. General Carlos Luís Guedes told reporters that Castello was "already elected" and that Dutra, who had served the nation well during an important hour, was now too old.[2]

But the marshal was reported to be insisting that he would remain a candidate "*até para zero votos*" (even if he received no votes). Commentators suggested that his obstinacy sprang from resentment at the behavior of some who had earlier advanced his name.[3]

The commentators were right. Dutra recalled that Magalhães Pinto had used a flowery expression in connection with his candidacy immediately after the revolution and that Amaral Peixoto, with his eye on the military, had asked him about the strength that he would enjoy in the army in case he were elected. While these remarks had not been serious expressions of support, Dutra had no doubt that Lacerda's early pronouncement had been serious, and the switch that Lacerda appeared to have made caused him deep bitterness. When Senator Sigefredo Pacheco (PSD, Piauí), a close friend of Dutra's, pleaded with the marshal to withdraw from a hopeless contest, Dutra replied that he had been asked to be a candidate and would remain one despite Lacerda's "betrayal."[4] Others, who also felt great affection for Dutra, made the same appeal, but with no more success than Pacheco.

Supporters of Kruel approached the marshal to suggest that if no candidate received the necessary absolute majority on the first ballot, then Dutra or Kruel, whoever had the fewer votes, should transfer his support to the other in an effort to defeat Castello. With puritanical vir-

2 Ibid., April 9, 10, 1964.
3 *O Estado de S. Paulo*, April 10, 1964.
4 Pacheco interview, October 16, 1965.

tue, and a remark about his unwillingness to participate in "secret under-standings," Dutra rejected the proposal, but he maintained his candidacy.[5]

Senator Pacheco telephoned Castello at 2:00 A.M. on April 9 after it was reported that Dutra was unhappy that Castello, his *comandado* (one he had commanded in the past), had never advised him of his plans to be a candidate. Dutra, Pacheco told Castello, was in a difficult position. The senator from Piauí recommended a letter from Castello explaining to Dutra the circumstances under which the Castello candidacy had arisen and suggesting that he would accept the candidacy provided that Dutra agreed.

Castello followed Pacheco's advice, and late on April 9 Dutra withdrew his candidacy. When Castello wrote him again, on the tenth, in response to the withdrawal, Dutra replied at once, sending congratulations on an election that he considered assured. "In this connection," Dutra wrote, "I must tell you that I made no comment to anyone about the fact that my comrade and old friend failed to seek my approval of his candidacy."[6]

Kubitschek in Brasília, like Dutra in Rio, was approached by Kruel's backers. They argued on April 8 and 9 that if Kubitschek did not now help Kruel and the PTB, he could expect the PTB to be cool toward his own candidacy in 1965.[7] But Kubitschek stuck to his position, ready to issue a statement favorable to Castello.

In Brasília on the evening of April 9, after the Ato Institucional had been signed by the Revolutionary Command, Amaral Peixoto presided over a meeting of the PSD national directorship. By a vote of 135 to 26 the directorship resolved to recommend to PSD legislators that they vote for Castello Branco. Then, to wrap everything up, the Chamber of Deputies floor leaders of nine political parties (PSD, UDN, PSP, PDC, PR, PL, PTN, PRP, and MTR) "reaffirmed, in perfect harmony," the proposal of their parties to elect Castello Branco to the presidency by means of the votes of their congressmen.[8]

Late that night Kubitschek released his declaration. He said that he

[5] Ibid.; *O Estado de S. Paulo*, April 10, 1964.
[6] Pacheco interview, October 16, 1965; Eurico Gaspar Dutra to HACB, April 10, 1964, File L2, CPDOC.
[7] *O Estado de S. Paulo*, April 10, 1964.
[8] Ibid.; *Jornal do Brasil*, April 10, 1964.

was going along with his party and giving "his agreement to the nomination of Castello Branco, in the certainty that the deportment and the career of this illustrious military figure ensure full adherence to the democratic processes . . . and respect for the will of the people to be expressed in the ballot boxes in October, 1965." Kubitschek, with the Ato Institucional in mind, included a warning against "any radicalization," and he counseled prudence in the face of the "grave" Brazilian situation.

On the next day, April 10, Amauri Kruel sent a telegram from São Paulo to Senator Lino de Mattos, withdrawing from the race. The Second Army commander, who could expect to receive about 50 votes out of a total of 475 to be cast by congressmen and senators,[9] explained that he had reached his decision in order to "preserve the climate of confidence and good will that ought to prevail in the military family." [10]

In Brasília Congressman Armando Falcão (PSD, Ceará) received a message for the lawmakers from the sole remaining candidate. It allowed Falcão to announce that Castello, if elected, would make a disclosure of his property holdings when he assumed office and again when he relinquished the presidency.[11]

As Castello's election on April 11 had become assured, Minas Gerais women belonging to the Liga da Mulher Democrática offered to provide him with a new presidential sash. This, they said, would allow him to avoid using the traditional one that had "become defiled by the bad Presidents who preceded him." [12]

The assurance of Castello's election prompted the United States Embassy to inform the White House and interested agencies in Washington about his background and character. It dispatched a confidential telegram, drafted by Walters, giving a resumé of Castello's career together with other observations:

Personal appearance: short, stocky. Very short neck and large head gives him appearance of being hunchbacked.

Attitude toward U.S.: Admires U.S. and appreciates role U.S. has played since World War II as defender of freedom.

[9] *Jornal do Brasil*, April 10, 1964.
[10] *O Estado de S. Paulo*, April 11, 1964.
[11] Ibid., April 12, 1964.
[12] Ibid., April 11, 1964. Liga da Mulher Democrática (LIMDE): League of Democratic Women.

Other: Considered an intellectual, Castello Branco is a man of high ideals and unquestionable ethics. Widely respected within and without armed forces. Basically apolitical, he sees Brazilian armed forces as guardians of democracy. Has participated in two efforts to remove threat of dictatorship: 1) was one of signers of 1954 manifesto against Getulio Vargas, and, 2) was leading military personality of revolution which deposed Goulart.

ARMA [army attaché] who has been intimate friend of Castello Branco since 1944, included following in recently-completed bio report: Castello Branco "is one of the most intelligent men I have known and has an integrity of character rarely found in anyone. He is a deeply and genuinely religious man of Catholic faith, and attends early morning Mass on Sundays and sometimes on week days. He has a mordant wit that has made him enemies. He is a brilliant intellectual and will not put up with mediocrity. He has a sense of dignity that keeps undue familiarity at a distance. He is somewhat formal and reserved with those he does not know well and does not make friends easily. When provoked, he can administer a tongue-lashing not readily forgotten by the recipient. He is not susceptible to flattery and views those who try to ingratiate themselves with him with a certain reserve. Mention of his wife can bring tears to his eyes.

"General Castello Branco has always expressed himself as a liberal progressive individual who believes in a considerable amount of state direction for economic planning, yet feels private initiative is essential to the development of Brazil. He is a patriot in that he places the interest of Brazil above all else but is not a narrow nationalist or xenophobe." [13]

13. Election to the Presidency (April 11, 1964)

As he had on April 10, Castello spent most of Saturday morning, April 11, receiving visits by governors, military figures, and leaders of the professions. He interrupted this program only to spend time at the grave of Argentina.

At Guanabara Palace early in the afternoon, Olímpio Mourão Filho was spotted by reporters after conferring with Lacerda. The military leader of the Minas uprising declared that "today Brazil is going to get the best President in its history. Now we are calm and confident. Gen-

[13] Telegram, signed Gordon, April 11, 1964, copy in Lyndon B. Johnson Presidential Library, Austin, Texas.

eral Castello Branco is a diamond without a flaw, and he will reconstruct this nation."[1]

By 4:00 P.M., when the senators and congressmen gathered for their joint session in Brasília, the television set at Nascimento Silva 394 was surrounded by friends and relatives of Castello. In addition to Ademar de Queiroz, who spent the day with him, the dozens of callers included Mascarenhas de Morais, Ernesto Geisel, and Antônio Carlos Murici.

At 5:00 P.M., with the voting about to commence, Castello made his way through the crowd in front of his home with the help of Murilo Gomes Ferreira. To follow the election results, he went to the residence of his sister Nina, who was recovering from a cataract operation.[2]

In the balloting for president the results were as expected. Castello received 361 votes (123 from the PSD, 105 from the UDN, and 53 from the PTB), while Juarez Távora was given three votes and Dutra two. Seventy-two abstained (due in large part to the PTB), and 37 absences were recorded (on account of the delay in getting alternates to replace congressmen who had lost their mandates).

Senator Kubitschek cast his vote for Castello to the accompaniment of a demonstration in the gallery. Mingled with the applause given the former president were the jeers of Rio and São Paulo women's groups that had traveled to Brasília for the historic occasion.[3]

Kubitschek Finance Minister José Maria Alkmin, already picked by the PSD leadership to be its candidate for vice-president, was being good-humoredly referred to by Castello as "Corporal José Maria," his nickname as a recruit serving under Lieutenant Castello Branco in the early 1920's in the 12th RI.[4] Although this astute politician from Minas had taken a firm anti-Goulart position before the revolution, he was not in a position to obtain a majority of votes as easily as Castello had. For one thing, his principal opponent, Congress President Auro de Moura Andrade, had considerable support among the representatives of his home state of São Paulo; besides, many of the electors, such as Senator João Agripino and Congressman Aliomar Baleeiro, both of the UDN, condemned Alkmin's past public record as incompatible with the aims of the revolution. Just before the election, O Globo reprinted Correio da

[1] O Estado de S. Paulo, April 12, 1964.
[2] Diniz, in Diniz and Castello Branco interview, December 13, 1975.
[3] O Estado de S. Paulo, April 12, 1964, p. 4, col. 6.
[4] Viana Filho, O Governo Castelo Branco, p. 59.

Manhã's editorial accusing the "infamous" Alkmin, "the former director of the Penitenciária das Neves," as having been the "grand master of budgetary anarchy."[5]

After the first ballot gave Moura Andrade 150 votes to 203 for Alkmin, Moura Andrade withdrew and Alkmin won the vice-presidency with 256 votes on the second ballot. Moura Andrade then called on Congress to reconvene at 3:00 P.M. on April 15 for the ceremony at which Castello and Alkmin would take the oaths of office.

The vice-presidential contest had yet to be settled when Castello, already president-elect, returned home. He found that the crowd in front of his house not only had grown but also had become so excited that some people were in tears when they greeted him. Led by the women of CAMDE, the crowd sang the national anthem with elation.

Speaking to the press, Castello said that he would go to Brasília on Wednesday, the fifteenth, to assume his new post. "Brazil needs to work, and work hard," he told interviewers for a United States television program.

The house, Nieta recalls, was "invaded" by callers. When Negrão de Lima came to pay his respects, he was booed in the street by participants in the growing campaign to discredit Kubitschek. "Take that man from this house," demonstrators yelled after the former Kubitschek foreign minister entered the door. But Negrão stayed for twenty minutes, and then Castello, in the face of demonstrators unfriendly to his visitor, made a point of escorting him beyond the house to the street.[6]

In the living room Castello addressed the nation briefly on a radio-television broadcast that had been arranged by Agência Nacional. His election, he said, represented a heavy burden of responsibilities that he had appreciated when he had accepted the appeal of influential political forces led by state governors. His resolve to undertake the responsibilities, he added, had been stimulated by "the warm response of public opinion revealed in authentic popular manifestations."

"Now I hope that God will let me live up to the hopes felt by my fellow-citizens in this decisive hour of Brazil's destiny, so that I might fulfill completely the great objectives of the victorious movement of April, in which all the people and the armed forces joined together in

[5] *Correio da Manhã*, April 8, 1964; *O Globo*, April 10, 1964.
[6] Diniz, in Diniz and Castello Branco interview, December 13, 1975.

aspiring to the restoration of legality, the reanimation of democracy, the reestablishment of peace, and the stimulation of progress and social justice."

Castello expressed the further hope that the collaboration of all Brazilians and their understanding of the gravity of the hour would allow him in January, 1966, to turn over to his successor—legitimately elected by the people in a free election—a unified nation, more confident in its future and no longer beset by "fears and distressing problems." [7]

14. Selecting Members of the Team

Castello Branco was president-elect for a little less than four days. Even considering that his election seemed probable several days before it occurred, he was not provided an interval that he considered adequate to select a cabinet of the revolution, let alone to familiarize himself with the problems faced by a nation in economic distress. As he pointed out to Ambassador Lincoln Gordon not long after taking office, he was confronted by a situation that differed from that enjoyed in 1961 by John Kennedy, who came to the United States presidency after analyzing the issues for several years while he sought the office and who had the advice of dozens of task forces while he was president-elect.[1]

Just before Castello became president-elect, he discussed one of his cabinet choices while lunching at *O Globo* with Roberto Marinho, Augusto Frederico Schmidt, and Armando Falcão. He said that he wanted Milton Campos, a strict legalist and former UDN governor of Minas Gerais, to be his justice minister. Castello explained that in making this appointment he hoped to leave no doubt that the armed forces were responding to the wishes of the Brazilian people, who had asked the military to intervene for the purpose of saving the nation from the Communist subversion. Brazil, he pointed out, did not have military *caudilhos* who wanted to perpetuate themselves in power, but it did have military leaders who were willing to make the sacrifices necessary to fulfill missions when these were needed by the nation. The appointment

[7] HACB, "Saudação ao Povo Brasileiro," File L2, CPDOC.
[1] Lincoln Gordon, "Recollections of President Castello Branco" (notes prepared for Luís Viana Filho), Washington, D.C., July 28, 1972, p. 13.

of Milton Campos would make it clear that the nation was not going to abandon juridical rules.[2]

Another name favored early by Castello was that of Juarez Távora. On April 4, when Távora, Nei Braga, and José Costa Cavalcanti had urged Castello to be a candidate, he had said to Távora: "If I become President, are you willing to help me?" Távora had replied that if Castello and Costa e Silva took Brazil to a dictatorship his reply was "no," whereas if they were interested in carrying out "the revolutionary changes that Brazil needs, in a reasonably democratic setting, you can count on my help even if I am assigned a job of carrying rocks."[3] On April 12 Távora was called to Castello's residence and asked to choose either the Ministry of Mines and Energy or the Ministry of Transport and Public Works. He asked for two days to decide, somewhat complicating Castello's pressing task.

While Távora made up his mind, Castello received countless suggestions from governors and other politicians. Ademar de Queiroz, Ernesto Geisel, and Golberi do Couto e Silva, Nieta recalls, were at Castello's residence every day. Her father, she adds, was invariably calm in appearance, and at the end of a day's work he would sit and chat with her and her husband before the couple went home to Leblon.[4]

Castello Branco could pick his cabinet ministers without concern about the payment of political debts. Rachel de Queiroz points out that his election was unusual in that he owed nothing to anyone, and for this reason she concludes that probably no man ever reached the Brazilian presidency with greater power than he.[5] Even the largest political party, the PSD, announced soon after the election that it was seeking no posts in the new administration in order to leave Castello Branco in complete freedom to make his choices.

Castello let it be known that the appointments would be based on merit. But this did not rule out considering the views of political leaders of the revolution and the sensitivities of important states. In reply to a question submitted by *Correio da Manhã*, Castello said that he would do his best to attend to the "expectations of the different regions," and he emphasized the need for administrative efficiency and teamwork in his

[2] Roberto Marinho interview, Rio de Janeiro, August 11, 1977.

[3] Távora, *Missão Cumprida*, p. 16.

[4] Diniz, in Diniz and Castello Branco interview, December 13, 1975.

[5] Rachel de Queiroz, *O Jornal*, July 14, 1968.

cabinet. Answering another of *Correio da Manhã*'s questions, he said that Brazil needed reforms and would get them, "but not in an emotional climate."[6]

Magalhães Pinto and Lacerda, keen on offering advice, found themselves with less influence than they wanted. Luís Viana Filho, Castello's biographer, writes that the governor of Minas considered himself more adept at politics than the general and disagreed completely with his ideas about the cabinet. The governor of Guanabara, according to São Paulo UDN leader Roberto de Abreu Sodré, expressed a "violent verbal reaction against the future President" when he found it difficult to get in touch with him.[7] Finally, after Congressman Armando Falcão arranged for a meeting at the home of Juraci Magalhães, Lacerda conversed for the first time with Castello. The governor, remarking that he was "physically drained, emotionally exhausted, and in bad financial shape," expressed his wish for a temporary mission abroad that would allow him to have foreign specialists attend to his wife's hearing problem. Lacerda recommended that Juraci be included in the cabinet and that Bahia banker Clemente Mariani be considered for finance minister, a position Mariani had held under Quadros.[8] To these suggestions by a politician he had long admired, Castello's response was silence.

Castello, seeking a competent team, learned about men he did not know from men he trusted. The work brought surprises to appointees who had not known Castello, as in the case of Luís Viana Filho, scholar and congressman from Bahia, who found himself invited to head the Casa Civil of the presidency. Furthermore, the work in some cases required that Castello make convincing appeals to overcome hesitancy. Milton Campos, it turned out, did not wish to serve in a "revolutionary government" and came close to refusing the justice ministry when it was offered to him during a telephone call made by Magalhães Pinto on behalf of Castello. But Castello took the phone from Magalhães Pinto to urge that the illustrious lawyer help "reimplant juridical order in Brazil."[9] Milton Campos accepted, somewhat to the regret of those who felt that he was "too legalistic" for "revolutionary times."

[6] Viana Filho, *O Governo Castelo Branco*, p. 63; *Correio da Manhã*, April 14, 1964.

[7] Viana Filho, *O Governo Castelo Branco*, p. 65; Roberto de Abreu Sodré to Luís Viana Filho, São Paulo, September 28, 1971, p. 5.

[8] Viana Filho, *O Governo Castelo Branco*, pp. 63–64.

[9] Ibid., p. 65; Almeida Magalhães interview, November 19, 1975.

Another whom Castello had to convince was Guanabara state Congressman Raimundo de Brito, who was serving as Lacerda's secretary of health. Selected by Castello from a list of three possibilities for the federal Health Ministry, this dynamic physician and administrator explained to Castello that he was afraid of air travel.[10] Only on the eve of flying to Brasília was the president-elect able to talk Raimundo de Brito into accepting the federal post.

Sociologist Gilberto Freyre, whom Castello had come to know in Recife, was less amenable to serving in the cabinet, and after he declined to be education minister, Ceará federal Congressman Paulo Sarazate suggested the name of Flávio Suplicy de Lacerda, *reitor* of the University of Paraná.[11] The *reitor*'s past work had also impressed General Ernesto Geisel, who was to become head of the presidential Casa Militar. When Castello asked Nei Braga if he would "indicate" the name of Flávio Suplicy de Lacerda, the governor of Paraná agreed to do so although he could hardly be regarded as responsible for this nomination. A nomination for which Nei Braga was responsible a little later was that of Leônidas Bório, who became head of the Brazilian Coffee Institute.

Before Castello flew to Brasília early on April 15, the incomplete cabinet list included representatives from São Paulo (agronomist Oscar Thompson Filho to be minister of agriculture) and from Rio Grande do Sul (PSD Congressman Daniel Faraco to be minister of industry and commerce). Távora had accepted leadership of the Ministry of Transport and Public Works, which he felt would best permit him to help the north and northeast, and his decision allowed Castello to turn to the PSD of Minas, which had supported the revolution, for an engineer to be minister of mines and energy.

After Amaral Peixoto furnished suggestions for this ministry, Castello decided on one of them: Mauro Thibau, a respected engineer and longtime board member of Companhia de Energia Eléctrica de Minas Gerais (CEMIG).[12] The selection was made so close to the time of the inauguration that it was not known to the press before the new cabinet was sworn in.

More nominations remained, particularly as Castello wanted to make

---

[10] Raimundo de Moura Brito interview, Rio de Janeiro, December 22, 1974.

[11] Braga interview, October 23, 1975. *Reitor*: university president.

[12] Viana Filho, *O Governo Castelo Branco*, p. 65; Mauro Thibau interviews, Rio de Janeiro, June 5, 6, 1972.

changes in at least some of the military ministries. But these changes were left pending until after the inauguration, along with decisions about retaining Foreign Minister Leitão da Cunha, Finance Minister Gouveia de Bulhões, and Labor Minister Sussekind.

Apparently the decisions already made by Castello were not viewed with much satisfaction by Lacerda, for he remarked to Abreu Sodré: "I shall not attend the inauguration of a government whose cabinet is made up of conservatives and *entreguistas*." Besides, Lacerda's wife was not well. The governor named Sandra Cavalcanti and others to attend the inauguration on his behalf.[13]

15. Retirement from the Army (April 13, 1964)

The president-elect conferred at his home with Moura Andrade and at Laranjeiras Palace with Mazzilli about the details of the transfer of power. As he had promised before his election, he drew up a list of his possessions, and it was delivered to Moura Andrade on April 14. It revealed that he owned an apartment in Rio, paid for in part by Argentina's inheritance from her mother and in part by monthly installments made between 1936 and 1946. Castello also listed 3,045 shares of Cia Siderúrgica Belgo-Mineira, 345 shares of Mineração Trindade, 1,657 shares of the Banco do Comércio e Indústria de Minas Gerais, and 1,830 shares of the Banco Nacional de Minas Gerais.

Other assets were a 1961 Aero Willys automobile and a plot in the São João Batista cemetery. His Nascimento Silva Street residence, he declared, had been paid for over a fifteen-year period and had become the property of his children following the death of Argentina.[1]

Of all the steps that Castello had to take as president-elect, the most momentous from his personal point of view was that of retiring from the army. The ceremony at which he did this, turning over his position of army chief of staff to Emílio Maurel Filho, was held at the War Ministry on April 13 in a crowded room on the sixth floor. Sprinkled among the many uniforms were the civilian attires of congressmen, judges, and intellectuals (including Brazilian Academy of Letters President Austregésilo de Athayde).

[13] Roberto de Abreu Sodré to Luís Viana Filho, September 28, 1971, p. 6.
[1] *O Globo*, April 15, 1964.

The ceremony was attended by the military ministers, the head of the EMFA, and former army chiefs of staff such as Brayner and José Machado Lopes. Also present were Osvaldo Cordeiro de Farias, Ademar de Queiroz, Juarez Távora, Amauri Kruel, Orlando Geisel, Estevão Taurino de Resende, Aurélio de Lyra Tavares, Olímpio Falconière da Cunha, Otacílio Terra Ururaí, Benjamin Rodrigues Galhardo, and Décio Escobar (who was being considered for the post of army chief of staff, which Maurel was filling provisionally). As Castello wanted, and as Costa e Silva had instructed, the ritual, despite Castello's position as president-elect, was strictly that of the transfer of an army post from one general to another.[2]

In his opening remarks Castello mentioned the work of the Army Staff during the past seven months and praised his subordinates. It was, he added, a great comfort to know that the officers of the EME had unanimously chosen to defend the military and political institutions when they were threatened by "ideological and opportunistic subversion." Turning to his own departure from active army service, Castello said that it was a great honor for him to be taking that step in the EME, "the supreme organ of our professional structure in the Army."

Castello became nostalgic. Reviewing his past, he mentioned his father, "a modest and old soldier," and he recalled his enrollment, at an early age, in the Colégio Militar of Porto Alegre, "where I gathered the fruits of a civic education and the thrill of patriotism that flourished there." He had next attended the Escola Militar of Realengo, he said, "in a setting devoted entirely to professional activity and in the warmth of the purest enthusiasm for a military career." "Unremitting toil" at the other military schools, as student and instructor, had enabled him to carry out the tasks in the posts he had occupied in his long military life:

Nor did I lack the unparalleled opportunity of participating in operations of war in the ranks of the glorious Força Expedicionária Brasileira.

If in the school rooms I found myself hammering out a military ideal, in all the other echelons I was never without stimulating examples of devotion and of the greatest dedication.

Based on this long and arduous experience, I would like to transmit here to my last subordinates, among whom I see old comrades, a final message—

<hr/>

[2] Emílio Maurel Filho quoted in *O Estado de S. Paulo*, April 14, 1964.

one affirming that the standards of military life require some indefectible constants in order that missions be carried out with the highest efficiency: professional capacity, pride in fulfilling any function, the maximum diligence in creating a wholesome climate of comradeship, indestructible loyalty in every sense, respect for authority within the law, and initiative guided by a conscious intellectual discipline—these are the principles that should guide soldiers in service. This is the way it is and this is the way it must be on any occasion, in peace and in war, and, above all, in difficult moments.

In closing, Castello referred to himself as "the old soldier" who, on leaving professional life, was turning his thoughts to the national army. Never in his career, he said, had he strayed from the army to serve in any civilian post, but had remained for forty-six years fulfilling only functions appropriate to the military profession itself. "To the Army I owe everything, my education, the formation of my character, and the qualifications that I was given the opportunity to acquire. It is therefore with a feeling of profound gratitude that I express the wish that the Army, instructed, disciplined, united, and efficient, always be in a position to realize its constitutional charge, the guarantee of a strong, progressive, and sovereign Brazil." [3]

Maurel Filho, in his response, told Castello and the audience that the sadness brought about by the loss of the chief was mixed with the elation caused by his elevation to the presidency

by those who, like Shelley, believe that "happiness of the soul lies in action." Your excellency achieved the supreme award of your superb career by knowing how to apply, throughout all of it, one unmistakable constant—the courage to act. And this steadfast characteristic, which describes accurately your eminent personality, was practiced, precisely and providentially, in the present hour, in perfect harmony with the supreme desires of the nation, so cruelly attacked, up to a few days ago, by the ruthless agents of disorder and corruption.

May God protect and guide you, Mr. President of all Brazilians. [4]

[3] HACB quoted in ibid.
[4] Emílio Maurel Filho quoted in ibid.

Glossary, Sources of Material, and Index

GLOSSARY

Ação Integralista Brasileira: National political party founded in São Paulo in 1932 to promote nationalism. Green-shirted Integralistas, marching on behalf of "God, Country, and Family," were strongly opposed to Communism.

Agência Nacional: Brazilian government information agency.

aglutinação: unification.

Aliança Liberal (Liberal Alliance): Oppositionist political party in the 1930 elections. Backed by the political machines of three Brazilian states, it supported Getúlio Vargas for president of Brazil in those elections.

Alvorada Palace: Presidential residence in Brasília, the capital of Brazil since April, 1960.

Aperfeiçoamento de Oficiais: Advanced Training of Officers.

aspirante a oficial: officer-candidate.

Associação dos Ex-Combatentes do Brasil: Association of Brazilian Combat Veterans.

Ato Adicional: Draft of an act developed early in April, 1964, for the purpose of amending the political legislation.

Ato Institucional: Act issued on April 9, 1964, by the three leaders of the Revolutionary Command, amending the political legislation.

aventura: hazardous enterprise; risky venture.

bancada: representation of a state in the federal legislature.

Banco Nacional do Desenvolvimento Econômico (BNDE): National Economic Development Bank.

batalhão de caçadores: infantry battalion.

BC: batalhão de caçadores (infantry battalion).

Blue Slate: Slate of officers put up by the Democratic Crusade in the Military Club election of 1958.

BNDE: Banco Nacional do Desenvolvimento Econômico (National Economic Development Bank).

boletim: bulletin.

Botafogo: District in the heart of the city of Rio de Janeiro. It lies north of Copacabana and south of Laranjeiras and Flamengo.

brigadeiro: brigadier. An officer of general rank in the Brazilian air force.

Brizolista: Pertaining to or connected with Leonel Brizola, politician from Rio Grande do Sul.

cabo: corporal.

Caixa Econômica: Savings institution run by the government.

caju: cashew.

Câmara dos Deputados: Chamber of Deputies (House of Representatives).

CAMDE: Campanha da Mulher pela Democracia (Women's Campaign for Democracy). Anti-Communist organization in Rio de Janeiro.

Carioca: Pertaining to, or native of, the city of Rio de Janeiro.

carnauba: Brazilian wax palm.

Casa Civil: Civilian staff of the presidential office.

Casa Militar: Military household; military staff of the presidential office.

caudilho: chief.

Cearense: Pertaining to, or native of, the state of Ceará.

Central do Brasil: Railroad running out of the city of Rio de Janeiro.

centralizador: centralizer.

Centro de Preparação de Oficiais da Reserva (CPOR): Reserve Officer Preparation Center (roughly equivalent to the ROTC in the United States).

CGT: *See* Comando Geral dos Trabalhadores.

chefe da turma: group leader.

cidade maravilhosa: wonderful city. A term referring to the city of Rio de Janeiro.

Clube Militar: Military Club. Elections of officers have been held every two years.

CNTI: *See* Confederação Nacional dos Trabalhadores na Indústria.

colégio: school.

colégio militar: preparatory school with military training.

Comando Geral dos Trabalhadores (CGT): General Command of Workers. An unofficial labor organization of considerable influence, 1962–1964.

comando paralelo: term used to describe the understandings and arrangements between the presidential administration of João Goulart and military officers which circumvented the regular military chain of command.

Confederação Nacional dos Trabalhadores na Indústria (CNTI): National Confederation of Workers in Industry. A large official labor confederation.

conselho nacional: national board of directors.

continuísmo: continuation in office.

conto: unit of currency equal to one thousand mil-réis (1:000$000). The mil-réis (1$000) in 1942 became known as the cruzeiro, with a value at that time of about 5.5 cents U.S. currency. *See* cruzeiro.

Copacabana: District in the city of Rio de Janeiro, south of the Botafogo district. Fort Copacabana is at the southwest end of Copacabana Beach.

CPOR: *See* Centro de Preparação de Oficiais da Reserva.

cruzeiro: Brazilian unit of currency instituted in 1942 to replace the mil-réis. Worth about 5.5 cents U.S. currency during World War II, the cruzeiro declined in value so that by the end of March, 1964, it took 1,840 cruzeiros to purchase one dollar.

curso de adaptação: preliminary course.

depoimento: deposition, testimony, statement, declaration.

Democratic Crusade (Cruzada Democrática). An anti-Communist wing in the Military Club. Starting in 1952, it regularly put up a slate of officers in the club's biennial elections.

Diário Oficial: Official daily gazette covering legislative activities.

dispositivo: arrangement, layout.

dispositivo militar: military arrangement or setup.

divisão: division (army).

divisão blindada: armored division.

doce de manga: sweet made from mango.

ECEME: *See* Escola de Comando e Estado Maior do Exército.

Ecole Supérieure de Guerre: Advanced War College of the French army (Paris, France).

EEM: *See* Escola de Estado Maior.

EME: Estado Maior do Exército (Army Staff).

EMFA: Estado Maior das Forças Armadas (Staff of the Armed Forces)

entreguista: term used to speak of a Brazilian said to be working to turn Brazil or Brazil's assets over to foreigners.

escola: school or college.

Escola de Aperfeiçoamento de Oficiais (EsAO): School for Advanced Training of Officers.

Escola de Comando e Estado Maior do Exército (ECEME): Army Staff and Command School. Name given to Escola de Estado Maior (EEM) in 1955.

Escola de Estado Maior (EEM). Army Staff School, renamed Escola de Comando e Estado Maior do Exército (ECEME) in 1955.

Escola Militar: Military Academy, transferred from Realengo to Resende in 1945.

Escola Superior de Guerra (ESG): National War College, established in

1949 for the study of national security by civilians and advanced officers of the three branches of the armed services.

ESG: *See* Escola Superior de Guerra.

espada de ouro: sword of gold.

estado maior: staff.

Estado Maior do Exército (EME): Army Staff.

Estado Maior das Forças Armadas (EMFA): Staff of the Armed Forces (all three branches).

estado maior informal: informal staff.

Estado Novo: New State; the autocratic federal government headed by Getúlio Vargas, 1937–1945.

exército: army.

FEB: *See* Força Expedicionária Brasileira.

feijão: black beans.

Fidelista: Pertaining to or connected with Fidel Castro.

filha: literally, daughter, but used here in a broader sense to refer affectionately to the wife. *minha filha*: my dear girl or my dear wife.

Flamengo: District in the heart of the city of Rio de Janeiro, north of Botafogo.

Folhas de Alterações: Pages of the official records of the careers of army officers.

Força Expedicionária Brasileira (FEB): Brazilian Expeditionary Force, consisting of one army division (about twenty-five thousand men), which fought in northern Italy during World War II.

FPN: *See* Nationalist Parliamentary Front.

Frente de Novembro: Front of November, organized in 1956 to honor the army coup of 1955 headed by General Henrique Lott.

Gaúcho: Pertaining to, or native of, Rio Grande do Sul (southernmost state).

general de brigada: brigadier general, lowest rank of generalship.

general de divisão: divisionary general (three stars). One rank above *general de brigada*. Through 1945 this was the highest rank of generalship in the Brazilian army.

general de exército: army general (four stars). One rank above *general de divisão*. This rank, created in 1946, is the highest rank of generalship in the Brazilian army.

golpista: one who favors a coup (*golpe*).

Graf Zeppelin: German dirigible that made Atlantic Ocean crossings.

Grupo da Sorbonne: Term applied to an influential group of instructors at the Escola Superior de Guerra (ESG).

Instituto de Pesquisas e Estudos Sociais (IPES): Institute of Social Research and Studies. Anti-Communist organization established by businessmen in the early 1960's.

Integralistas: *See* Ação Integralista Brasileira.

Ipanema: Residential district in the city of Rio de Janeiro, west of Copacabana.

IPES: *See* Instituto de Pesquisas e Estudos Sociais.

ISEB: Instituto Superior de Estudos Brasileiros (Higher Institute of Brazilian Studies). Nationalistic, government-supported organization established during the presidency of João Café Filho (1954–1955); it was rather influential during the following administrations until the fall of President João Goulart in 1964.

Janguista: Pertaining to or connected with President João ("Jango") Goulart.

jeca: rustic Brazilian.

Laranjeiras Palace: Presidential palace in the city of Rio de Janeiro, used by the presidency before and after the transfer of the federal capital to Brasília in April, 1960.

Leblon: Residential district in the city of Rio de Janeiro, west of Ipanema.

Le-Ex: Abbreviated form of reference to "Lealdade ao Exército" (Loyalty to the Army), a communication drawn up by army officers distrustful of President João Goulart and circulated confidentially among army officers in command posts who were considered to be "fully trustworthy."

legalidade: legality.

liceu: secondary school.

mais antigo: officer with seniority (holding for the longest time any given military rank).

maracujá: passionflower or passionfruit.

Marcha da Família com Deus pela Liberdade: March of the Family with God for Liberty. Anti-Communist demonstration carried out in São Paulo on March 19, 1964, and repeated in other cities during the remainder of the month. The mammoth Marcha da Família in Rio de Janeiro took place on April 2, 1964.

memorial: memorandum or manifesto.

Memorial dos Coroneis: Manifesto of the Colonels (of 1954).

Military regions: Brazilian army areas into which each of the four Brazilian army zones is divided.

mil-réis: unit of currency used until 1942, when one mil-réis (1$000) was renamed one cruzeiro. *See also* cruzeiro.

Mineiro: Pertaining to, or native of, the state of Minas Gerais.

minha filha: *See* filha.

MTR: Movimento Trabalhista Renovador (Renovating Labor Movement), a small political party established in 1961 when a PTB leader broke with Goulart.

National Security Council: Important body for studying matters related to the national defense, described by the 1946 Constitution as made up of "the cabinet ministers and the chiefs of staff as determined by the law" (Article 179). The head of the Casa Militar usually served as secretary. When Castello Branco became president of Brazil he resolved to make regular use of the council, and he established clearly its membership: the cabinet ministers, the heads of the Casa Militar and Casa Civil, the chief of the EMFA, and the chief of staff of each branch of the military.

Nationalist Parliamentary Front: Frente Parlamentar Nacionalista (FPN). A nationalist group of federal legislators.

NCO's: noncommissioned officers.

Ninth Floor: Term often used to refer to the minister of war, whose offices were on the ninth floor of the ministry building in Rio de Janeiro.

ofício: official written communication on government business.

Operação Limpeza: Operation Cleanup. A program launched by the victors of the 1964 revolution with the intention of ridding Brazil of corruption and subversion.

Operation Aggressive Defense: Phase of the military operation of the Allied forces in northern Italy that lasted from November 5 to December 12, 1944. It was followed by Operation Stabilization, which lasted until February 18, 1945.

Operation Encore: Phase of the military operation of the Allied forces in northern Italy that lasted from February 18, 1945, until the first part of April, 1945. It was followed by the phase known as Spring Offensive.

orderly: A noncommissioned officer or soldier who attends a superior officer to carry out his orders.

Osvinista: Pertaining to or connected with General Osvino Ferreira Alves.

padrinho: sponsor, usher, best man (at a wedding).

Palácio da Luz: Governor's palace in Fortaleza, Ceará, until 1973, when the Palácio da Abolição was inaugurated.

papai: papa, daddy.

Partido Federalista: Political party in Rio Grande do Sul in the 1920's and earlier. It was the traditional enemy of the dominant state party, the Partido Republicano Riograndense.

Partido Republicano Riograndense: Dominant political party in Rio Grande do Sul at the time when Humberto Castello Branco was at school there.

partigiani: Italian antifascist guerrilla fighters.

Paulista: Pertaining to, or native of, São Paulo.

PCB: Until 1961, the Partido Comunista do Brasil (Communist Party of

Brazil). After 1961, the Partido Comunista Brasileiro (Brazilian Communist Party). Headed by Luís Carlos Prestes and affiliated with Moscow.

PDC: Partido Democrata Cristão (Christian Democratic Party).

pelego: term used to describe a labor union leader who supported, and was supported by, the government.

peleguismo: term used to describe the practices or characteristics of a *pelego*.

penitenciária: penitentiary.

PL: Partido Libertador (Liberator Party), a small political party.

Planalto Palace: Presidential office building in Brasília, the capital of Brazil since April, 1960.

polícia militar: military police.

portadores: messengers, porters. Term used for officers who, while making trips between Italy and Brazil in 1944 and 1945 for the purposes of the armed services, carried packages and letters on behalf of other officers and their families.

posto de tratamento: medical treatment post.

PR: Partido Republicano (Republican Party), a small political party.

pracinhas: Brazilian soldiers.

Praia Vermelha: District in the city of Rio de Janeiro, east of Botafogo and Copacabana and adjoining the Urca district. The Escola de Comando e Estado Maior do Exército (ECEME) is in the Praia Vermelha district.

PRP: Partido de Representação Popular (Party of Popular Representation), a small political party.

PSD: Partido Social Democrático (Social Democratic Party), founded in 1945 by Vargas supporters.

PSP: Partido Social Progressista (Social Progressive Party), in which Ademar de Barros, of São Paulo, was influential.

PTB: Partido Trabalhista Brasileiro (Brazilian Labor Party), founded in 1945 by Vargas supporters in the labor movement.

PTN: Partido Trabalhista Nacional (National Labor Party), a small political party.

quartel: barracks.

quartel general: barracks occupied by a general and his staff.

Queremistas: Supporters of Getúlio Vargas, largely within the working class, in 1945. The term was derived from one of their slogans, "Queremos Getúlio." (We want Getúlio).

Rádio Globo: Radio station associated with the popular daily afternoon newspaper, *O Globo*.

regulamento: set of regulations.

réis: Plural of *real*, a unit of currency used until 1942, when the cruzeiro replaced the mil-réis (one thousand réis), the standard unit of currency, then worth about 5.5 cents U.S. currency.

reitor: university president.

república sindicalista: syndicalist republic. Said to be a republic run by labor unions.

Revolutionary Command: Comando Revolucionário. Organization set up by high-ranking military victors of the 1964 revolution to handle national problems; it was made up of one leader from each of the three branches of the military. Occasionally called the Revolutionary High Command.

RI: *regimento de infantaria* (infantry regiment), commanded by a colonel.

salão nobre: large, formal room or hall; sometimes used to refer to an auditorium.

sítio: country place.

Sociedade Cívica e Literária: Civic and Literary Society. Organization founded by students at the Colégio Militar of Porto Alegre, who were concerned with political matters, oratory, and literature.

Spring Offensive: Phase of the military operation of the Allied forces in northern Italy that began in the first part of April, 1945, and ended with the German surrender less than one month later.

subcomandante: assistant commander.

subtenentes: noncommissioned officers.

SUPRA: Superintendência de Planejamento da Reforma Agrária (Superintendency of Agrarian Reform Planning). Office established by the government of President João Goulart.

tenente: lieutenant. As a term, the word is often used to denote a military officer who participated in the movements that resulted in the revolutions of 1922, 1924–1927, and 1930.

testemunho: testimony.

Tijuca: District in the northern part of the city of Rio de Janeiro. It lies northwest of Botafogo and Flamengo and north of Leblon.

Turma do Memorial: Group of army officers who played a role in issuing in 1954 the *Memorial dos Coronéis* (Manifesto of the Colonels).

UBES: União Brasileira dos Estudantes Secundários (Brazilian Union of Secondary School Students). Secondary school students' organization that was official in 1964 and earlier years.

UDN: União Democrática Nacional (National Democratic Union). Political party organized in 1945 to oppose Getúlio Vargas.

UNE: União Nacional dos Estudantes (National Students' Union). Organization of university students that was official until it was dissolved by a judicial body in January, 1966.

Urca: District in the city of Rio de Janeiro. It adjoins Praia Vermelha, lying to the east of Botafogo. The Escola Superior de Guerra (ESG) and Fort São João are in the Urca district.

Vila Militar: Army barracks about thirty-five kilometers west of downtown Rio de Janeiro.

Yellow Slate: Slate of officers put up by the supporters of War Minister Lott to oppose the Blue Slate in the Military Club election of 1958.

SOURCES OF MATERIAL

WHEN there is more than one item to list under one name, the order has been guided principally by chronological considerations, and the interviews with JWFD have been placed at the end. The references to CPDOC are to the Centro de Pesquisa e Documentação de História Contemporânea do Brasil in the Instituto de Direito Público e Ciência Política, Fundação Getúlio Vargas, Rio de Janeiro.

Academia Cearense de Letras. *A Antologia Cearense.* Fortaleza: Imprensa Oficial, 1957.

Aguiar, Rafael de Sousa. Declarations in *O Globo*, April 20, 1964.

———. Interview, Rio de Janeiro, August 8, 1977.

Albuquerque, Theódulo de. Speech in Congress. Typewritten manuscript. N.d. [probably 1967].

Alencar, Edgard Antunes de. Interviews, Fortaleza, Ceará, December 27, 28, 1975.

Almeida, Reynaldo Melo de. Interview, Rio de Janeiro, October 17, 1975.

Amarante, Waldetrudes, and Justina Amarante. Interview, Rio de Janeiro, November 21, 1975.

Âncora Filho, Armando de Morais. Interview, Bethesda, Maryland, March 18, 1977.

Andrade, Delmiro Pereira de. *O 11º R.I. na 2ª Guerra Mundial.* Rio de Janeiro: Biblioteca do Exército, 1950.

Aragão, Augusto César Moniz de. "O Seu Castigo É Decompor-se Vivo." *O Globo*, August 29, 1967.

———. "O Depoimento do General Moniz de Aragão." *O Globo*, March 30, 1975.

Aragão, Renato Moniz de. Interview, Rio de Janeiro, November 22, 1975.

Aranha, Oswaldo Gudolle. Typewritten memorandum about the Associação dos Ex-Combatentes do Rio prepared for Luís Viana Filho but not delivered to him.

———. Interview, Rio de Janeiro, September 25, 1975.

————. *See also* Gross, João Carlos.

Archer, Renato. Interview, Rio de Janeiro, September 30, 1975.

Baleeiro, Aliomar. "Recordações do Presidente H. Castelo Branco." Typewritten manuscript in possession of JWFD.

————. Memorandum (replying to questions), Rio de Janeiro, July, 1977.

————. Conversations, Rio de Janeiro, July 11, 18, 1977.

————. Interviews, Rio de Janeiro, September 19, December 26, 1975.

Barbosa, Raul. Interview, Washington, D.C., June 13, 1975.

Barros, Ademar de. Interview, São Paulo, December 1, 1965.

Baruch, Bernard. *Uma Filosofia para o Nosso Tempo.* Rio de Janeiro: Editôra Civilização Brasileira, S.A., 1955.

Basbaum, Leoncio. *História Sincera da República,* vol. IV, *De Jânio Quadros a Costa e Silva (1961–1967).* São Paulo: Editôra Fulgor, 1968.

Bastos, Amélia Molina. Interview, Rio de Janeiro, December 13, 1965.

Bastos, Joaquim Justino Alves. *Encontro com o Tempo.* Pôrto Alegre: Editôra Globo, 1966.

————. Interview, Rio de Janeiro, August 10, 1977.

Bertelle, Luiz Gonzaga. *Castello Branco, o 1º Presidente da Revolução.* N.p., n.d. [In File HP8, Castello Branco Collection, CPDOC.]

Bley, João Punaro. "Depoimento do Companheiro João Punaro Bley," Rio de Janeiro, July 25, 1974, in File G1, Castello Branco Collection, CPDOC.

————. Note in File G2, Castello Branco Collection, CPDOC.

Borges, Mauro. *O Golpe em Goiás: História de uma Grande Traição.* Rio de Janeiro: Editôra Civilização Brasileira, 1965.

Braga, Nei. Interviews, Rio de Janeiro, December 21, 1965; Brasília, October 23, 1975.

Braga, Rubem. *Com a F.E.B. na Itália: Crônicas.* Rio de Janeiro: Livraria Editora Zelio Valverde, 1945.

Brancante, Eldino. Interview, São Paulo, November 24, 1965.

Branco, Argentina Vianna Castello. Letters in the Castello Branco Collections, CPDOC and in possession of Paulo V. Castello Branco.

Branco, Cândido Borges Castello. Resumé of career in File B, Part 2, Castello Branco Collection, CPDOC.

Branco, Carlos Castello. *Introdução à Revolução de 1964.* 2 vols. Rio de Janeiro: Editora Artenova S.A., 1975.

————. Interview, Brasília, October 24, 1975.

Branco, Humberto de Alencar Castello. Papers in the Castello Branco Collections, CPDOC and in possession of Paulo V. Castello Branco.

————. Papers in the Castello Branco Collection at the Escola de Comando e

Estado Maior do Exército (ECEME), Praia Vermelha, Rio de Janeiro.

———— ["Coronel Y"]. Articles in *Gazeta do Rio,* November, December, 1933.

————. "Promoção e Despedida." Speech to the Ecole Supérieure de Guerre, Paris, France, 1938, in File G1, Castello Branco Collection, CPDOC.

————. *O Alto Comando Aliado na Guerra entre a Tríplice Aliança e o Paraguai.* Rio de Janeiro: Curso de Alto Comando, 1940.

————. "Viagem à Libya, Egito, e Palestina, Mês de Março." Handwritten diary, 1945, in File H2, Castello Branco Collection, in possession of Paulo V. Castello Branco.

————. "A Doutrina de Guerra e a Guerra Moderna." Speech at the Escola de Estado Maior (EEM), 1946, in File J, Castello Branco Collection, CPDOC.

————. *Discurso Pronunciado pelo Gen. Bda. Humberto de Alencar Castello Branco, Comandante da Escola de Estado Maior.* N.p., n.d. [1954]. [In File J, Castello Branco Collection, CPDOC.]

————. "Os Meios Militares na Recuperação Moral do País." Speech at the Escola de Comando e Estado Maior do Exército, September 19, 1955, in the Castello Branco collection of papers at the ECEME, Praia Vermelha, Rio de Janeiro.

————. *A Doutrina Militar Brasileira.* Rio de Janeiro: Escola Superior de Guerra, 1957.

————. "O Dever Militar em Face da Luta Ideológica: Palestra Proferida a 15 de Dezembro de 1961, na ECEME." Typewritten manuscript received by JWFD from Paulo V. Castello Branco.

————. "Discurso de Posse na Chefia do Estado Maior do Exército," September 14, 1963, in File G1, Castello Branco Collection, CPDOC.

————. "Observações Finais." Handwritten speech closing the EME course "Guerra Revolucionária," November, 1963, in File L2, Castello Branco Collection, CPDOC.

————. "Reorganização do Exército." Typewritten draft with handwritten changes, December, 1963, in File J, Castello Branco Collection, CPDOC.

————. "A EsAO na Atualidade Militar." Speech at the Escola de Aperfeiçoamento de Oficiais, February, 1964, in File L2, Castello Branco Collection, CPDOC.

————. "Destinação Constitucional e Finalidades do Exército." Speech to the Escola de Comando e Estado Maior do Exército, March 2, 1964, in the Castello Branco collection of papers at the ECEME, Praia Vermelha, Rio de Janeiro.

————. "Oração Proferida pelo Excelentíssimo Senhor General Humberto de Alencar Castello Branco ao Deixar a Chefia do Estado Maior do Exército." *O Estado de S. Paulo*, April 14, 1964. [Also in File G1, Castello Branco Collection, CPDOC.]

———. *Discursos, 1964*. Secretaria de Imprensa, n.d.

———. "Sugestões para a Lourdinha (sugestões dadas a sua irmã que ia ao Ceará visitar o filho)" [ca. 1964]. Letter in File B, Castello Branco Collection, CPDOC.

———. "Discurso na Saída de Osvaldo Cordeiro de Farias." Brasília, June 15, 1966, in File M, Castello Branco Collection, CPDOC.

———. *Marechal Castello Branco, Seu Pensamento Militar*. Introduction by Reynaldo Mello de Almeida. Rio de Janeiro: Imprensa do Exército, 1968.

———, et al. *A Revolução de 31 de Março: 2º Aniversário*. Rio de Janeiro: Biblioteca do Exército, 1966.

Branco, Manoel Thomaz Castello. *O Brasil na II Grande Guerra*. Rio de Janeiro: Biblioteca do Exército, 1960.

Branco, Paulo V. Castello. "Um Liberal, um Revolucionário, e um Democrata." *Jornal da Tarde*, July 13, 1972.

———. Statements in "Castello Branco, Meu Pai." *Manchete*, March, 1973. [In File HP7, Castello Branco Collection, CPDOC.]

———. Interviews, letters, and memoranda, Rio de Janeiro, 1974–1977.

———. *See also* Diniz, Antonietta Castello Branco; Ferreira, Murilo Gomes.

Brandíni, Roberto. *See* Werneck, Luís.

Brayner, Floriano de Lima. Documento Interno, Gabinete do Ministro da Guerra, Rio de Janeiro, approved May 15, 1936, in File G1, Castello Branco Collection, CPDOC.

———. "Brochado da Rocha, um Grande Caráter." *Diário Carioca*, September 30, 1962.

———. *A Verdade sôbre a FEB: Memórias de um Chefe de Estado-Maior na Campanha da Itáliá, 1943–1945*. Rio de Janeiro: Editôra Civilização Brasileira S.A., 1968.

———. "Comentando um Livro de Memórias." Typewritten manuscript about J. B. Mascarenhas de Moraes' *Memórias*. Copy in possession of JWFD.

———. *Luzes sôbre Memórias*. Rio de Janeiro: Livraria São José, 1973.

———. Letters to JWFD, Rio de Janeiro, September 11, October 14, 25; December 3, 1975.

———. Letter in *Jornal do Brasil*, January 25, 1976.

———. *Recordando os Bravos; Eu Convivi com Eles; Campanha da Itália*. Rio de Janeiro: Civilização Brasileira, 1977.

———. Interviews, Rio de Janeiro, October 6, November 25, 1975.

Brazil, Army. *Boletim Escolar.* [Copies in Castello Branco Collection, CPDOC.]

———, ———, Força Expedicionária Brasileira (FEB). *Depoimento de Oficiais da Reserva sôbre a F.E.B.* 3rd ed. Rio de Janeiro: Publicações Cobraci, n.d.

———, ———, Military Attaché, Montevideo. Oficial No. 96, February 3, 1941, in File G1, Castello Branco Collection, CPDOC.

———, ———, First Army, General Headquarters. *Relatório da Revolução Democrática Iniciada pela 4ª RM e 4ª DI em 31 de Março de 1964.* Boletim Especial, Juiz de Fora, May 9, 1964.

———, ———, Twelfth Infantry Regiment. "Boletim do 12º RI," February 28, 1921, in File G1, Castello Branco Collection, CPDOC.

———, Ministry of the Army. *Almanaque do Exército.* Rio de Janeiro: Estabelecimento General Gustavo Cordeiro de Farias, 1970.

———, ———, Army Staff. *História do Exército Brasileiro: Perfil Militar de um Povo.* Vol. 3. Brasília and Rio de Janeiro: Edição do Estado-Maior do Exército, 1972.

———, ———, Colegio Militar de Porto Alegre. Memorandum, September 13, 1973, in File G2, Part 1, Castello Branco Collection, CPDOC.

———, ———, Public Relations Center. *This is the Brazilian Army.* N.p., n.d.

———, Ministry of War. *Almanaque do Exército.* Rio de Janeiro, 1948, 1963.

———, ———, Colegio Militar de Porto Alegre. Letter, January 22, 1914, in File G1, Castello Branco Collection, CPDOC.

———, ———, ———. *Boletins.* 1917. [In File G2, Castello Branco Collection, CPDOC.]

Brintnall, Clarke. Conversations, Rio de Janeiro, July, 1976.

Brito, Raimundo de Moura. Interview, Rio de Janeiro, December 22, 1974.

Cabral, Jurandir Palma. *See* Caminha, Heitor Lopes.

"Caderneta de Oficial" and "Folhas de Alterações," 1918–1964, in Files G2 and G3, Castello Branco Collection, CPDOC.

Café Filho, João. *Do Sindicato ao Catete.* 2 vols. Rio de Janeiro: Livraria José Olympio, 1966.

Caminha, Heitor Lopes, and Jurandir Palma Cabral. "Humberto de Alencar Castello Branco, O Cearense: Colégio Militar de Porto Alegre, Período de 1912–1917," in File G1, Castello Branco Collection, CPDOC.

Campos, Aguinaldo José Senna. *Com a FEB na Itália: Páginas do Meu Diário.* Rio de Janeiro: Imprensa do Exército, 1970.

———. *A Conquista de Monte Castelo, pela FEB: Conferência Proferida no*

Auditório do Clube Militar em 20 de Fevereiro de 1975. Rio de Janeiro: Clube Militar, Departamento Cultural, 1975.

―――. Interview, Rio de Janeiro, November 26, 1975.

Campos, Francisco. Interview, Rio de Janeiro, December 14, 1965.

Carvalho, Ferdinando de. Interview, Rio de Janeiro, October 30, 1975.

Carvalho, Nelson Rodrigues de. *Do Terço Velho ao Sampaio da F.E.B.* Rio de Janeiro: Biblioteca do Exército, [ca. 1952].

"O Caso Castelo Branco: Boletim Dedicado aos Cegos que Nao Querem Ver." Mimeographed circular, November, 1956, in File L1, Castello Branco Collection, CPDOC.

"Castello: Os Arquivos do Marechal Revelam um Militar Revolucionário e Liberal." *Veja*, April 5, 1972.

Castelo, Plácido Aderaldo. Material supplied to JWFD, January, 1976.

"Castelo Nasceu em Fortaleza. . . ." *Gazeta de Notícias* [Fortaleza], June 21, 1964.

Cavalcanti, José Costa. "Revolução no Nordeste: Uma Missão Recebida." Typewritten statement, October, 1976, received by JWFD from Paulo V. Castello Branco.

―――. "Depoimento do Ministro Costa Cavalcanti sôbre a Escolha do Presidente Castello Branco para a Presidência da República." Typewritten transcript of tape, October 22, 1976, received by JWFD from Paulo V. Castello Branco.

Cavalcanti, Sandra. Interview, Rio de Janeiro, November 18, 1975.

Chandler, Billy Jaynes. "The Role of Negroes in the Ethnic Formation of Ceará: The Need for a Reappraisal," *Revista de Ciências Sociais* 4, no. 1 (1st Semester, 1973): 31–43.

Chaves, Sebastião Ferreira. Interview, São Paulo, November 22, 1967.

Clark, Mark W. *Calculated Risk*. New York: Harper & Bros., 1950.

Colégio Militar de Porto Alegre. Letter, January 22, 1914, in File G1, Castello Branco Collection, CPDOC.

―――. *Boletins*. 1917. [In File G2, Castello Branco Collection, CPDOC.]

―――. Memorandum, September 13, 1973, in File G2, Part 1, Castello Branco Collection, CPDOC.

Corção, Gustavo. *Patriotismo e Nacionalismo*. Editôra Nacional de Direito Ltda., 1957.

Corrêa, Manuel Pio. Interview, Rio de Janeiro, December 23, 1974.

Corrêa, Oscar Dias. Interview, Rio de Janeiro, September 24, 1975.

Correio da Manhã. [Rio de Janeiro newspaper.] Issues of 1955–1964.

Costa, César Tácito Lopes. Interview, São Paulo, July 28, 1977.

Costa, Euclides Zenóbio da. Statement about Humberto de Alencar Castello

Branco, October 12, 1944, in "Campanha da Itália," File G1, Castello Branco Collection, CPDOC.

Costa, Joffre Gomes da. *Marechal Henrique Lott.* Rio de Janeiro, 1960.

Costa, Lena Ferreira. "Uma Família na História," in File A, Part 3, Castello Branco Collection, CPDOC.

Cunha, Mário da. Interview, Tucson, Arizona, April 14, 1976.

D'Aguiar, Hernani. *A Revolução por Dentro.* Rio de Janeiro: Editora Artenova S.A., 1976.

———. Interview, Rio de Janeiro, July 29, 1976.

Denys, Odílio. "Denys Conta Tudo." *Fatos & Fotos,* May 2, 1964. [Also published as a brochure.]

———. Interviews, Rio de Janeiro, December 14, 1965; November 29, 1966.

"Depoimentos sobre Encontro Castelo-Juscelino Provocam um Novo Tumulto." *Jornal do Brasil,* January 21, 1967.

Dias, Ana (Nina) Castello Branco Santos, and Beatriz Castello Branco Gonçalves. "Depoimento sôbre o irmão Humberto de Alencar Castello Branco," 1973, in File B, Castello Branco Collection, CPDOC.

Dimas Filho, Nelson. *Costa e Silva: O Homem e o Líder.* Rio de Janeiro: Edições *O Cruzeiro,* 1966.

Dines, Alberto, et al. *Os Idos de Março e a Queda em Abril.* 2d ed. Rio de Janeiro: José Alvaro, 1964.

Diniz, Antonietta Castello Branco. Statements in "Castello Branco, Meu Pai." *Manchete,* March, 1973. [In File HP7, Castello Branco Collection, CPDOC.]

———, and Paulo V. Castello Branco. Interview, Rio de Janeiro, December 13, 1975.

Dória, Seixas. *Eu, Réu sem Crime.* 3rd ed. Rio de Janeiro: Editôra Equador Ltda, n.d.

Duque, Luís Vieira. Interview, Brasília, July 23, 1976.

Escobar, Décio Palmeiro de. Memorandum, Rio de Janeiro, January 15, 1974, in File G1, Castello Branco Collection, CPDOC.

———. Interview, Rio de Janeiro, July 25, 1977.

Estado de S. Paulo, O. [São Paulo newspaper.] Issues of 1958–1964.

Ex-Combatente 1, no. 11 (November, 1947). [Also in File H3, Part 3, HACB papers in possession of Paulo V. Castello Branco.]

Falcão, Armando. Interviews, Rio de Janeiro, November 30, 1966; October 10, 1975.

"Família Alencar." Manuscript in File A3, Castello Branco Collection, CPDOC.

"Família Castello Branco." Manuscript in File A, Castello Branco Collection, CPDOC.

Farias, Osvaldo Cordeiro de. Interviews, Rio de Janeiro, December 16, 26, 1974.

———. Conversation with Paulo V. Castello Branco, Rio de Janeiro, December, 1975.

Fernandes, Hélio. *Recordações de um Desterrado em Fernando de Noronha.* Rio de Janeiro: Editôra Tribuna da Impresa, 1967.

———. Interview, Rio de Janeiro, July 6, 1977.

Ferreira, Murilo Gomes. "O General Castello Que Conheci." Transcript of tape prepared for interview, Rio de Janeiro, November 12, 1975.

———. Replies to questions, received in Rio de Janeiro, July 22, 1976.

———, and Paulo V. Castello Branco. Interview, Rio de Janeiro, November 12, 1975.

Fleury, Héber Perillo. *See* Werneck, Luís.

"Folhas de Alterações." *See* "Caderneta de Oficial"

Fonseca, Ariel Pacca da. Interview, Brasília, July 23, 1976.

———, Antônio Ferreira Marques, and Ismael da Rocha Teixeira. Interview, São Paulo, November 6, 1975.

France, Army, Ecole Supérieure de Guerre. Letters from seconds in command, Paris, 1937, 1938, in File G1, Castello Branco Collection. CPDOC.

Galvão, Flávio. *See* Werneck, Luís.

Gilberto, Joaquim, "Duas Épocas." *Jornal de Luziânia* [Goiás], May 30, 1977.

Girão, Raimundo. *Palestina, uma Agulha e as Saudades.* Fortaleza, Ceará, 1972.

Globo, O. [Rio de Janeiro newspaper.] Issues of 1956–1964.

Godinho, Antônio de Oliveira. Interview, São Paulo, November 7, 1975.

Gonçalves, Beatriz Castello Branco. *See* Dias, Ana (Nina) Castello Branco Santos

Gonçalves, Leônidas Pires. Interviews, Rio de Janeiro, October 17, 1975; July 20, 30, 1976.

Gordon, Lincoln. Telegram to Washington officials, April 11, 1964. Copy in Lyndon B. Johnson Library, Austin, Texas.

———. "Recollections of President Castello Branco." Typewritten manuscript prepared at the request of Luís Viana Filho, Washington, D.C., July 28, 1972. Copy in possession of JWFD.

———. Interview, Washington, D.C., June 11, 1975.

Grandes Acontecimentos da História, November, 1973. [In File HP7, Castello Branco Collection, CPDOC.]

Gross, João Carlos, and Oswaldo Gudolle Aranha. Interview, Rio de Janeiro, October 2, 1975.

Grünewald, Augusto Hamann Rademaker. Interview, Rio de Janeiro, December 15, 1965.

Guerra, Paulo. Interview, Brasília, November 11, 1975.

Hastings, Andrew D., Jr. Letter to JWFD, October 6, 1976.

Herrera, Heitor A. Interviews, Rio de Janeiro, December 7, 1965; December 16, 1975.

————. See also Huber, Gilberto.

Huber, Gilberto, and Heitor A. Herrera. Interview, Rio de Janeiro, November 29, 1965.

Institute for the Comparative Study of Political Systems. *Brazil: Election Factbook*, no .2. Washington, D.C., September, 1965.

Instituto de Pesquisas e Estudos Sociais (IPES). Typewritten intelligence reports, 1963. Copies in possession of JWFD.

"Jânios Quadros em Hora e Meia de Debate no 'Encontro Marcado.'" *A Provincia do Pará*, January 16, 1960.

Jornal, O. [Rio de Janeiro newspaper.] Issues 1958–1964.

Jornal do Brasil. [Rio de Janiero newspaper.] Issues 1958–1964.

Jornal do Commercio. [Rio de Janeiro newspaper.] Issues of 1955 and 1963.

Jurema, Abelardo. *Sexta-Feira, 13: Os Últimos Dias do Govêrno João Goulart.* 2d ed. Rio de Janeiro: Edições O Cruzeiro, 1964.

————. "Discurso do Ministro Abelardo Jurema—4º Aniversário da Associação dos Cabos e Soldados da Polícia Militar do Estado da Guanabara," March, 1964, in File L2, Castello Branco Collection, CPDOC.

————. Interview, Rio de Janeiro, July 27, 1976.

Krieger, Daniel. Interview, Brasília, October 21, 1975.

Kruel, Amauri. Interviews, São Paulo, November 16, 30, 1965; Rio de Janeiro, October 21, 1967; December 11, 1975; July 6, 1977.

Kruel, Riograndino. Interview, Rio de Janeiro, September 21, 1975.

Lacerda, Carlos. "As Confissões de Lacerda," chap. 11. *Jornal da Tarde*, June 8, 1977.

————. Interviews, Rio de Janeiro, October 11, 1967; September 23, 1975; Tucson, Arizona, February 17, 1976.

Lacombe, Américo. Interview, Rio de Janeiro, November 3, 1975.

Lavanère-Wanderley, Nelson Freire. *A Aeronáutica Militar Brasileira.* N.p., n.d.

————. Interviews, Rio de Janeiro, December 10, 1974; August 12, 1977.

Leal, João de Deus Pessoa. "Minhas Recordações de Humberto de Alencar Castello Branco," Rio de Janeiro, July 13, 1974, in File G1, Castello Branco Collection, CPDOC.

Lebret, L. J. *Princípios para a Ação*. 4th ed. São Paulo: Livraria Duas Cidades, 1961.

Lee, Ulysses. *The Employment of Negro Troops*. Washington, D.C.: Office of the Chief of Military History, United States Army, 1966.

Leite Filho, João Batista Barreto. "Atrocidades Alemãs." *O Jornal*, September 26, 1944.

―――. Interview, Rio de Janeiro, November 25, 1975.

Lenin, V. I. *Le Socialisme et la Guerre*. Paris: Editions Sociales, 1952.

Lima, Alceu Amoroso. *O Trabalho no Mundo Moderno*. Rio de Janeiro: Livraria Agir Editora, 1959.

―――. *Visão do Nordeste*. 2d ed. Rio de Janeiro: Livraria Agir Editora, 1962.

Lima, Francisco Negrão de. Handwritten observations to JWFD about HACB, Rio de Janeiro, December, 1975.

―――. Interview, Rio de Janeiro, December 10, 1975.

Lima, Luís Tenório de. Interview, São Paulo, November 21, 1968.

Lindenberg, José. Remarks at ceremony marking HACB's promotion to *general de divisão*. Typewritten. Rio de Janeiro, September 25, 1958. In File G1, Castello Branco Collection, CPDOC.

Linhares, João de Machado. Letter to Paulo V. Castello Branco, Porto Alegre, April 5, 1976.

Lins, Maria de Lourdes Ferreira. *A Força Expedicionária Brasileira: Uma Tentativa de Interpretação*. São Paulo: Editoras Unidas Ltda., 1975.

Lott, Henrique Batista Duffles Teixeira. Interviews, Rio de Janeiro, August 27, 1963; October 13, 1975.

Macaulay, Neill. *The Prestes Column: Revolution in Brazil*. New York: New Viewpoints, 1974.

Maciel Filho, Luís. *See* Werneck, Luís.

Magalhães, Juraci. "Juraci Acha que Lacerda É Ciclotímico." *Jornal do Brasil*, November 23, 1966.

―――. Interview, Rio de Janeiro, December 3, 1974.

Magalhães, Rafael de Almeida. Interview, Rio de Janeiro, November 19, 1975.

Magalhães Júnior, Raymundo. Suggestions for improving manuscript, 1977.

Marinho, Roberto. Interview, Rio de Janeiro, August 11, 1977.

Maritain, Jacques. *Princípios de uma Política Humanista*. Rio de Janeiro: Livraria Agir Editôra, 1946.

―――. *O Homen e o Estado*. 2d ed. Rio de Janeiro: Livraria Agir Editôra, 1956.

Marques, Antônio Ferreira. *See* Fonseca, Ariel Pacca da

Mattos, Carlos de Meira. Interviews, Washington, D.C., January 5, August 2, 1976; March 18, 1977.

Maurel Filho, Emílio. Interview, Rio de Janeiro, October 11, 1965.

McCann, Frank D., Jr. *The Brazilian-American Alliance, 1937–1945.* Princeton: Princeton University Press, 1973.

———. Suggestions for improving manuscript in letter to JWFD, Brasília, February 25, 1977.

Médici, Emílio Garrastazu. Handwritten memorandum for Rafael de Sousa Aguiar, Brasília, July 23, 1971.

Mello, Newton C. de Andrade. *Meu Diário da Guerra na Itália: De 30-VI-1944 a 18-VII-1945.* Rio de Janeiro: Imprensa Nacional, 1947.

———. *A Epopéia de Montese: Conferência Proferida no Dia 14 de Abril de 1954, por Ocasião das Comemorações do 9° Aniversário da Conquista de Montese Realizadas na "Casa do Expedicionário" de Curitiba.* Curitiba: Secretaria do Interior e Justiça, Imprensa Oficial do Estado, 1954.

———. *O Brasil na II Grande Guerra.* Curitiba, 1955.

———. Interview, Rio de Janeiro, November 1, 1975.

Melo, Humberto de, and Geraldo Knaack de Souza. Interview, Rio de Janeiro, November 30, 1967.

Melo, Luís Tavares da Cunha. Interview, Rio de Janeiro, November 17, 1975.

Mendes, Ivan de Souza. Interview, Rio de Janeiro, July 26, 1976.

Mesquita, Rui. Interviews, São Paulo, December 2, 1965; November 6, 1975.

Meyer, Celso dos Santos. Interview, Washington, D.C., July 15, 1975.

———. Letter to JWFD, Washington, D.C., August 26, 1977.

Miranda, Emygdio da Costa. Interview, Rio de Janeiro, December 1, 1975.

Moraes, Frederico Mendes de. "Depoimento de Frederico Mendes de Moraes, a pedido do Sr. John W. F. Dulles e do Sr. Paulo Vianna Castello Branco, sobre o General Humberto de Alencar Castello Branco, abrangendo o período que antecedeu a vitória da Revolução de Março de 1964 até o dia de sua posse na Presidência da República." Typewritten manuscript, Rio de Janeiro, December 19, 1975.

———. Interview, December 20, 1975.

Moraes, João Baptista Mascarenhas de. Official statements issued 1944–1945 praising Humberto de Alencar Castello Branco. In File G1, Castello Branco Collection, CPDOC.

———. *A F.E.B. pelo Seu Comandante.* 2d ed. São Paulo: Instituto Progresso Editorial S.A., 1947.

———. *Memórias.* 2 vols. Rio de Janeiro: Livraria José Olympio Editôra, 1969.

Morais Neto, Prudente de. Interview, Rio de Janeiro, October 8, 1975.

Moura, Arthur Santos. Interviews, Rio de Janeiro, December 11, 1974; July 19, 1976.

Mourão Filho, Olímpio. Interviews, Rio de Janeiro, October 9, 1965; November 29, 1966.

Müller, Henrique G. Interview, Rio de Janeiro, July 15, 1977.

Muricy, Antônio Carlos. *Os Motivos da Revolução Democrática Brasileira: Palestras Pronunciadas no Televisão Canal 2, nos Dias 19 e 25 de Maio de 1964.* Recife: Imprensa Oficial, n.d.

——. Interview, Rio de Janeiro, November 18, 1975.

Negrão, Anysio Alves. Diary, Recife, 1962–1963, in File I, Castello Branco Collection, CPDOC.

Neves, Edmundo. Interview, Rio de Janeiro, July 20, 1976.

Notes on the back of a photograph of officers of the Sociedade Cívica e Literária, Porto Alegre, November, 1916, in File G1, Castello Branco Collection, CPDOC.

Novos Rumos. [Rio de Janeiro Communist weekly newspaper.] Issues of 1960 and 1961.

Oliveira, Euclides Quandt de. Interview, Brasília, October 21, 1975.

Oliveira, João Adyl de. Interviews, Rio de Janeiro, December 20, 1965; October 18, 1975.

Oliveira, Juscelino Kubitschek de. "Comentários de Juscelino Kubitschek de Oliveira sobre a Indicação do General Castelo Branco pelo PSD em Abril de 1964." Typewritten manuscript, May 21, 1975. [Furnished to JWFD by Kubitschek.]

——. Interview, Rio de Janeiro, September 29, 1975.

Pacheco, Sigefredo. Interview, Brasília, October 16, 1965.

Paiva, Glycon de. "Petrobrás como Banco da Subversão Nacional e Escola Prática de Corrupção." *Jornal do Brasil,* February 16, 1964.

——. Interview, Rio de Janeiro, December 9, 1975.

Palhares, Gentil. *De São João del-Rei ao Vale do Pó (Ou a Epopéia do 11º R.I. na 2ª Guerra Mundial): Documentário Histórico do 11º, 6º e 1º R.I.* São João del-Rei: Gráfica Diário do Comércio, 1951.

Parker, Phyllis. "Separate . . . but Equal? U.S. Policy toward Brazil, 1961–1964." Independent Research Project, Lyndon B. Johnson School of Public Affairs, Austin, Texas, May, 1976.

Passarinho, Jarbas. "Carta Aberta ao Candidato Jânio Quadros." *A Província do Pará,* January 16, 1960.

——. Interview, Brasília, November 11, 1975.

Peixoto, Ernâni do Amaral. Interview, Rio de Janeiro, December 20, 1975.

Peixoto, Gilberto. *A Campanha da Itália.* Rio de Janeiro: Departamento de Imprensa Nacional, 1949.

Pelacani, Dante. Interview, São Paulo, November 24, 1968.

Peralva, Osvaldo. *O Retrato*. Rio de Janeiro, Porto Alegre, São Paulo: Editôra Globo, 1962.

Pessoa, Júlio Sérgio Vidal. Interview, Rio de Janeiro, December 16, 1975.

Pieruccetti, Oswaldo. Letter to JWFD, January 18, 1968.

Pinheiro, Raimundo Teles. Interview, Fortaleza, Ceará, December 28, 1975.

Pinto, Heráclito Fontoura Sobral. Interview, Rio de Janeiro, December 9, 1975.

Pinto, José de Magalhães. Interview, Brasília, October 24, 1975.

Pinto, Olavo Bilac. *Guerra Revolucionária*. Rio de Janeiro: Editôra Forense, 1964.

———. Interview, Brasília, October 21, 1975.

Poppino, Rollie F. Collection of material about Humberto Castello Branco supplied to JWFD, December, 1975.

Queiroz, Ademar de. Interview, Rio de Janeiro, October 13, 1975.

Queiroz, Rachel de. "Terra," "Última Página" column in *O Cruzeiro*, mid-1960's. In File B, Castello Branco Collection, CPDOC.

———. Article in *O Jornal*, July 14, 1968.

———. Interviews, Rio de Janeiro, November 15, 1974; July 25, 1976.

Ramos, Guerreiro. *A Crise do Poder no Brasil*. Rio de Janeiro: Zahar Editores, 1961.

Ramos, José de Oliveira. *A Epopéa dos Apeninos*. Rio de Janeiro: Gráfica Laemmert, Ltda., n.d.

Reis, Antônio José Coelho. Letter to Humberto de Alencar Castello Branco, Rio de Janeiro, January 1, 1937, in File E, Castello Branco Collection, CPDOC.

Reis, Artur César Ferreira. Interview, Rio de Janeiro, September 29, 1975.

Reis, Gustavo Morais Rego. Interviews, Brasília, October 22, 23, 1975.

Rocha Netto, Bento Munhoz da. *Radiografia de Novembro*. 2d ed. Rio de Janeiro: Editôra Civilização Brasileira, 1961.

Rossi, Agnelo. *A Filosofia do Comunismo*. Petrópolis: Editôra Vozes Ltda., 1947.

Sá, Gilberto Crockatt de. Interview, Rio de Janeiro, October 9, 1967.

Santos, Adalberto Pereira dos. Interview, Brasília, July 23, 1976.

Santos, Ademar Vilela dos. "Depoimento: Humberto de Alencar Castello Branco no 12º RI," Rio de Janeiro, March, 1974, in File G1, Castello Branco Collection, CPDOC.

Santos, João Carlos Palhares dos. "Depoimento sôbre a Minha Convivência com o Presidente Humberto Castello Branco, prestado ao Seu Historiador, Dr. Luiz Vianna Filho," São Paulo, December, 1971, in File R2, Castello Branco Collection, CPDOC.

————. Interview, Rio de Janeiro, November 22, 1975.
Saraiva, Paulo de Tarso. Interview, Washington, D.C., March 18, 1977.
Sarmento, Sizeno. Interview, São Paulo, November 21, 1967.
Schmidt, Augusto Frederico. "Castelo Branco." *O Globo*, April 7, 1964.
Schneider, Ronald M. *The Political System of Brazil: Emergence of a "Modernizing" Authoritarian Regime, 1964–1970.* New York and London: Columbia University Press, 1971.
Sheen, Fulton J. *O Problema da Liberdade.* 4th ed. Rio de Janeiro: Livraria Agir, Editôra, 1954.
————. *Filosofias em Luta.* 3rd ed. Rio de Janeiro: Livraria Agir Editôra, 1957.
Silva, Álcio Barbosa da Costa e. Interview, Rio de Janeiro, July 15, 1977.
Silva, Artur da Costa e. "Costa e Silva Relata Episódios da Revolução." Speech at the ECEME, April 1, 1965, in *O Estado de S. Paulo*, April 4, 1965.
Silva, Carlos Medeiros. Interviews, Rio de Janeiro, November 12, December 18, 1975.
Silva, Golberi do Cuoto e. Interviews, Rio de Janeiro, December 8, 1965; October 4, 1966; Brasília, October 22, 1975.
Silva, Hélio. *1944: O Brasil na Guerra.* Rio de Janeiro: Editôra Civilização Brasileira S.A., 1974.
————. *1964: Golpe ou Contragolpe?* Rio de Janeiro: Editôra Civilização Brasileira S.A., 1975.
Silva, Luís Antônio da Gama e. Interviews, São Paulo, November 18, 1966; November 5, 1975.
Silva, Luís Mendes da. "Testemunho." Typewritten manuscript received from Paulo V. Castello Branco in 1974.
Silva, Riograndino Costa e. Interview by telephone call from Rio de Janeiro to Porto Alegre, November 28, 1975.
Silva, Yolanda Costa e. Interview, Rio de Janeiro, July 15, 1977.
Silveira, Joel: *Histórias de Pracinha.* 2d ed. Rio de Janeiro: Cia. Editôra Leitura, 1945.
————. Interview, Rio de Janeiro, December 25, 1975.
Simões, Raul Mattos A. *A Presença do Brasil na 2ª Guerra Mundial: Uma Antologia.* Rio de Janerio: Biblioteca do Exército, 1967.
Skidmore, Thomas E. *Politics in Brazil: An Experiment in Democracy.* New York: Oxford University Press, 1967.
Sodré, Nelson Werneck. *Introdução à Revolução Brasileira.* Rio de Janeiro: José Olympio, 1958.
Sodré, Roberto de Abreu. Letter to Luís Viana Filho, São Paulo, September 28, 1971.
Sousa, César Montagna de. Interview, Brasília, July 23, 1976.

Souza, Geraldo Knaack de. *See* Melo, Humberto de

Souza, José Jerônimo Moscardo de. Interviews, Brasília, October 23, 27, 1975.

Spinelli, Mário. "A Marcha da Coluna Meira Matos." One-sheet publication "no Aniversário da Cidade de Cuiabá." [Copy received by JWFD from Vernon Walters.]

Stacchini, José. *Março 64: Mobilização da Audácia.* São Paulo: Companhia Editora Nacional, 1965.

Tavares, Aurélio de Lyra. Letter to HACB, Rio de Janeiro, March 21, 1964, in possession of Paulo V. Castello Branco.

———. Interview, Rio de Janeiro, July 18, 1977.

Távora, Juarez. "Esclarecimento Prestado pelo Marechal Juarez Távora, à Margem da Escolha do Marechal Castelo Branco para a Presidência da República em Abril de 1964." Typewritten manuscript. Rio de Janeiro, October 12, 1966. [Prepared for JWFD. Full text also given in Basbaum, *História Sincera da República,* IV, 135–137.]

———. *Missão Cumprida: Relatório sôbre Atividades do extinto Ministério da Viação e Obras Públicas, no Triênio, Abril, 1964–Março, 1967.* Rio de Janeiro, 1969.

———. Interviews, Rio de Janeiro, October 5, 1966; October 20, November 27, 1967.

Távora, Virgílio de Moraes Fernandes. Interviews, Brasília, October 22, 25, 1975.

Teixeira, Ismael da Rocha. *See* Fonseca, Ariel Pacca da

Telesca, Edmar Eudóxio. "Depoimento sôbre o General Humberto de Alencar Castello Branco." Typewritten manuscript, Rio de Janeiro, April 24, 1976. Copy in possession of JWFD.

Thibau, Mauro. Interviews, Rio de Janeiro, June 5, 6, 1972.

Trigueiro, Osvaldo. "Humberto Castelo Branco." Typewritten manuscript. Copy in possession of JWFD.

———. Interview, Brasília, October 23, 1975.

U.S., Army, Forces South Atlantic (USAFSA), Historical Section. "History of United States Army Forces South Atlantic." Typewritten manuscript, Historical Manuscript File, Office of the Chief of Military History, Washington, D.C.

———, ———, Fourth Corps. "The North Apennines Campaign, 10 September 1944 to 4 April 1945." Typewritten manuscript, Historical Manuscript File, Office of the Chief of Military History, Washington, D.C.

———, ———, ———. *The Final Campaign across Northwest Italy, 14 April–2 May 1945.* Milan: Pizzi and Pizio, 1945.

Veloso, Haroldo. Interviews, Marietta, Georgia, January 6, 7, 1966.

Viana Filho, Luís. *O Governo Castelo Branco*. Rio de Janeiro: Livraria José Olympio Editôra, 1975.

———. Letter to Paulo V. Castello Branco, Bahia, April 12, 1976.

Vianna, Hélio. "Humberto." *Jornal do Commercio*, July 18, 1968. [Also in File HP4, Castello Branco Collection, CPDOC.]

Vianna, Ivan Martins. "O Estadista Castello Branco." *Forum Econômica*, no. 87 (1977).

Vianna, Maria de Lourdes. "Humberto e Argentina." Typewritten manuscript, Belo Horizonte, September 14, 1974. Copy in possession of JWFD.

Victor, Mário. *Cinco Anos que Abalaram o Brasil (de Jânio Quadros ao Marechal Castelo Branco)*. Rio de Janeiro: Editôra Civilização Brasileira S.A., 1965.

Walters, Vernon. Letter to JWFD, Washington, D.C., July 11, 1975.

———. Interview with Phyllis Parker, McLean, Virginia, January 20. 1976. [Reported in Parker, "Separate . . . but Equal? U.S. Policy toward Brazil, 1961–1964."]

———. "Humberto de Alencar Castello Branco." Typewritten manuscript. Copy in possession of JWFD.

———. Interviews, McLean, Virginia, June 12, 1975; Arlington, Virginia, July 15, 1976.

Werneck, Luís, Flavio Galvão, Roberto Brandíni, Luís Maciel Filho, and Héber Perillo Fleury. Interview, São Paulo, November 24, 1965.

Wondolowski, Peter S. "History of the IV Corps, 1941–1945." Typewritten manuscript, Historical Manuscript File, Office of the Chief of Military History, Washington, D.C

Index